ROANOKE COUNTY PUB
HEADQUARTERS / 419
3131 ELECTRIC ROAD SW
ROANOKE, VA 24018

W9-BWZ-671

NO LONGER PROPERTY OF ROANOKE COUNTY PUBLIC LIBRARY

NO LONGER PROPERTY OF ROANOKE COUNTY PUBLIC LIBRARY

STEVE McQUEEN

THE LIFE AND LEGEND OF A HOLLYWOOD ICON

0 1197 0611687 6

STEVE McQUEEN

THE LIFE AND LEGEND OF A HOLLYWOOD ICON

Marshall Terrill

TRIUMPH
BOOKS

To Zoe,
who always gives more than she takes

Copyright © 2010 by Marshall Terrill

No part of this publication may be reproduced, stored in a retrieval system, or transmitted in any form by any means, electronic, mechanical, photocopying, or otherwise, without the prior written permission of the publisher, Triumph Books, 542 South Dearborn Street, Suite 750, Chicago, Illinois 60605.

Triumph Books and colophon are registered trademarks of Random House, Inc.

Library of Congress Cataloging-in-Publication Data

Terrill, Marshall.
    Steve McQueen : the life and legacy of a Hollywood icon / by Marshall
Terrill ; foreword by Peter O. Whitmer.
        p. cm.
    Includes bibliographical references and index.
    Includes filmography.
    ISBN 978-1-60078-388-3
1. McQueen, Steve, 1930-1980. 2. Motion picture actors and actresses—United
States—Biography. I. Title.
    PN2287.M547T48 2010
    791.4302'8092—dc22
    [B]   2010023340

This book is available in quantity at special discounts for your group or organization. For further information, contact:

Triumph Books
542 South Dearborn Street
Suite 750
Chicago, Illinois 60605
(312) 939-3330
Fax (312) 663-3557
www.triumphbooks.com

Printed in U.S.A.
ISBN: 978-1-60078-388-3
Designed by Sue Knopf
Title page photo courtesy of Getty Images

CONTENTS

FOREWORD

"History does not happen until it is recorded on paper. What we are about to do will not be recorded, therefore it never happened."

—*Richard Crenna's orders from* The Sand Pebbles *as Captain of the* USS San Pablo *to the crew as it breaks rank and heads up river to save American missionaries.*

CULTURAL HISTORY, IN THE 21ST CENTURY, is recorded on paper and on film. Steve McQueen recorded his personal history cinematically; it became cultural history because of his ability to portray a certain dimension of every individual, constantly struggling, fighting, hammering against conformity from the inside out, a one-man war against the mainstream of tradition. This universal theme of behavior made him an international star, an icon, and a myth that lasts 30 years after his death.

Marshall Terrill works with paper and has documented the life—both on and off film—of Steve McQueen. In this paper realm, there exist biographers and psychological biographers. This book offers an amalgam of both, something without precedent. The role of a clinical psychologist as used here is to find the connective tissue that created the man and then bound him tightly to his movies and explains rather than describes how this came about.

Fans and students of Steve McQueen now have the opportunity to go one orbit above both paper and film and in the process gain a better understanding of the "why" of the man; the source of his motivations to compete and to excel; the reasons underlying his truly American form of iconoclasm; how he harnessed his inner demons into a form of creativity that allowed him to carve a shelf into world consciousness and, when the same demons slipped their leashes, to destroy meaningful personal relationships and—ultimately, at one point—his career and his very self. What follows is the best possible effort at making Steve McQueen, his movies, and his enduring star quality make perfect sense.

The use of psychology as a tool to gain a better understanding of important figures is both time-honored and fraught with problems, pitfalls, misinterpretations, and straightforward skepticism as to its most base value added.

Numerous well-known public figures have gone to extraordinary means to either destroy their own works or impose legal injunctions to ward off what they perceive as bone-sucking grave-robbers, all to little avail. A brief list of some of these individuals is intriguing for the diversity that share the same sentiment of becoming a human fly caught in cultural amber: Ken Kesey, T.S. Eliot, J.D. Salinger, George Orwell, and Joe DiMaggio. At the other extreme, the reason that Richard Nixon installed his now-famous Oval Office tape recorder was that contemporaneous legislation had banned public officials from selling their notes to libraries. A tape recording fell into a loophole in the law. And Richard Nixon was, after all, an attorney.

Steve McQueen could not do the same thing as either J.D. Salinger or Joe DiMaggio—his life was already permanently captured on film. This similarity between Steve McQueen the person and Steve McQueen the character is as eerie as it is wonderful. There does not appear to be another cinema star whose real-life story is so perfectly paralleled by his film life. In short, from *Somebody Up There Likes Me* through *The Great Escape*, from *The Getaway* to *The Hunter*, we can sit and watch Steve McQueen's autobiography. And now, with Marshall Terrill's new book, we can understand it.

When I was a student at the University of California at Berkeley during the 1960s, there were no doctoral programs in biography. The most logical area was clinical psychology. What better training to unscrew the inscrutable of the human condition? And so here are my offerings on Steve McQueen, after having written, or assisted in writing, five books that approach biography from this perspective and using some of the tools of a clinical psychologist.

Steve McQueen's childhood, adolescence, and early adulthood could easily pose as an American copy of a Charles Dickens story: Oliver Twist meets Martin Chuzzlewit. As is more often than not the case, his angry and erratic path through life began before he was born, at least with his parents.

By the time Steve McQueen was a toddler, he had been completely abandoned by a father that he never knew; he had moved with his mother several times to at least three different places; he had been left by his mother with his grandparents who subsequently moved in with his great-uncle; and he later roamed the streets of Los Angeles because he was continually abused by his stepfather. Clearly, this was a childhood blatantly lacking in controls, concerns, and care.

This was Steve McQueen's landscape of life by age 11. There are a small number of universal psychological factors, identified, defined, and measurable, that appear from this pattern. When one is born into a world of constant flux and chaos and unhappiness, there exist predictable outcomes. Steve's "family" and his developmental disruption was the sum total of repeated change both of caregivers and caregiving—his father, his mother, his mother's number of unknown husbands and lovers, his grandparents (especially his mentally ill grandmother Lillian), his great-uncle and his young wife, and then his mother and her other husbands whom Steve did not know. The past was forgettable; the future was a bleak, pinched horizon; and the present was fighting the battle of survival with no rules other than his own. Welcome to puberty. Who really is your daddy? This is the stuff that is called "psychological homelessness."

In clinical psychology, the result of this bitch's brew of existence is labeled "313.89 Reactive Attachment Disorder of Infancy or Early Childhood." The DSM-IV states, "...the essential feature of Reactive Attachment Disorder is markedly disturbed and developmentally inappropriate social relatedness in most contexts that begins before age 5 years and is associated with grossly pathogenic care." Pathogenic care is defined as including at least one of the following: (1) persistent disregard of the child's basic emotional needs for comfort, stimulation, and affection; (2) persistent disregard of the child's basic physical needs; (3) repeated changes of the primary caregiver that prevents formation of stable attachments (e.g., frequent changes in foster care).

Grossly pathogenic care is a defining feature of Reactive Attachment Disorder. However, unless firsthand observations of the child's behavior before age five are available and valid, this diagnosis cannot be used. Instead, the more general term "Attachment Disorder" is used. There is considerable overlap between the two, both in what they look like in children and in the adult personality. There are five main dimensions of behavior that earmark individuals who have, from their earliest years, experienced similar disruptive and developmentally damaging life events, as Steve McQueen did, and then crawled out of that traumatic crucible of early Attachment Disorder and into adulthood, still freighted with a heavy load of unresolved psychological issues. As mentioned before, these are maladaptive variants—*extremes* of normal personality traits. In the following biography, one will find the life experiences that first caused these five themes of personality and then in later years shaped the life that was Steve McQueen.

From a very early age, Steve McQueen created his own rules of interpersonal behavior as a protective callous to shield his human sensitivities. This worked on the screen like no one could have imagined. However, in his personal life it worked—like no one could have imagined—undermining and destroying his most significant human relationships. His core of defensive emotional posturing even extended beyond his life, as we shall see, and wreaked posthumous havoc with his family and loved ones.

Steve McQueen's inner demons would never go away. Regardless of their negative effects on his life and on others, the fact that he could hold them in such tight rein and direct them in such a creative manner, speaks clearly of his single-mindedness and his burning desire to achieve.

Without these fires burning within him, he never would have gotten to Hollywood, let alone around the world, to begin with.

—Peter O. Whitmer, Ph.D., is a writer, author, clinical psychologist, and the first drummer for the Turtles. He divides his time between Montserrat, the British West Indies, and Massachusetts.

AUTHOR'S NOTE: WELCOME ALL AGAIN

WHEN JOHN LENNON STATED in the December 1980 edition of *Playboy* that if given the opportunity, he'd rerecord every Beatles song in their musical catalog, I thought it was the craziest statement I'd ever heard. After all, how do you improve upon perfection?

As I got older, I came to understand Lennon's thinking. No matter how good or talented you are, there's always room for improvement. The same might be said for the book you hold in your hands. In 1993, I wrote *Steve McQueen: Portrait of an American Rebel.* The book was an instant best seller. It received international and national reviews, went through several printings, and has been hailed by many fans and critics as the definitive biography on McQueen. Despite the accolades and the book's success, John Lennon's statement has kept echoing through my head over the past few years. If I had a chance to rewrite the actor's story, would I do it again?

The answer is yes and for several reasons. On a basic level there is no denying that a great story is worth telling again and again, and what better story to revisit than the life of Steve McQueen? Furthermore, in the years since *Portrait*, McQueen's legend has grown, and his popularity has reached new heights. He remains one of the few true Hollywood icons with a wide fan base, including diehards not even born during his life who look up to him. He resonates with younger fans today, as relevant as ever. McQueen's story has evolved as new information has come to light, and his story demands retelling, if only for them.

However, my ultimate motivation for writing this book is personal. When I started researching and writing *Portrait*, I was 25 and a recent college graduate (I was on the seven-year plan). Other than the occasional term paper or book report, I had never written anything of great depth or length. The research on *Portrait* was exhaustive, over the top, and extraordinarily detailed because of my enthusiasm for the subject. This was in the "prehistoric days" before the Internet was launched, and finding information required more sweat than the stroke of a key, especially at the massive Library of Congress, where I did most of the research for my 463-page biography.

Today I have written more than a dozen books, and I am almost the same age that McQueen was when he died. I'd like to think I've matured and grown wiser. I have a better perspective on things and now possess some understanding about the complexities of life, including a healthy dose of cynicism and a healthier dose of humility from which true compassion and understanding springs.

As a rookie scribe, I fell prey to the "McQueen Mystique," which was easy to do. Information back then didn't flow as easily as it does now, and McQueen, not unlike a good PR man, carefully cultivated his image to appeal to the masses. Many journalists of his time simply accepted what McQueen passed on as the truth because he was the main storyteller—a movie star concealing a past that hurt him and a man who took to heart the words, "When the legend becomes fact, print the legend," from *The Man Who Shot Liberty Valance.*

McQueen was able to succeed in getting "the legend" printed because of the era of journalism in which he started. It was a time when reporters turned their backs on the indiscretions of presidents, royalty, diplomats, and movie stars because they needed to toe the line with their sources if they wanted to keep their jobs. Access to public records was a minefield of red tape and a daunting task at best. Taking a man at his word was something one simply did. The press of his era demanded heroes, and McQueen wanted to be seen as one, not unlike the stars of any generation. In the new era of "gotcha" journalism, paparazzi ambushes, and social media, there simply are no more secrets or privacy. Factor in that public documents do not lie. Although the information may sometimes be wrong, the intent is to document the truth. With access to public records now more readily available, it's easier to discern fact from fiction today than when McQueen was alive. These public records also give a more truthful glimpse into his painful history and produce a more objective look into his life.

Though he could be candid at times, McQueen was a master embellisher and gifted at creating his own mythology, which still continues three decades after his death. As an example, McQueen once told a reporter that he and a few buddies had taken their motorcycles on a ferry from Key West, Florida, and headed to Cuba in the fall of 1956. He played up that Hurricane Audrey, one of history's worst recorded natural disasters, was in full bloom when they made their journey. Shaken and stirred, the men got off the ferry after reaching their destination safely, McQueen said. Although it is true the men visited Cuba (a telegram from Steve's first wife Neile asking her for bail money verifies the trip occurred), Hurricane Audrey's rampage actually took place in June 1957. Why did McQueen feel the need to add Hurricane Audrey to the anecdote? Because Steve's story built his reputation as a fearless daredevil, battling the elements as well as nature itself, and he knew it made for great copy. You can even imagine McQueen, age 49, telling the same story again outside his aircraft hangar in Santa Paula, holding court with his tall tales.

Ten years after I started research on *Portrait*, I began my apprenticeship as a journalist. During that time I was instructed to view the world differently than I had done in the past. As a civilian and first-time author, I took everything at face value and didn't really question beyond what I was told, nor did I always apply logic to a situation or time line. But as a reporter, I was forced to question motives, thoroughly research the issues, and predict outcomes by employing a little logic and a lot of common sense.

My decade-long tenure as a journalist gave me an incredible life education and a skill I could apply to my future literary endeavors. It also caused me to look back and question how I could have written and researched *Portrait* differently. In *Portrait*, I focused mainly on McQueen's years in Hollywood, the making of his films, the public persona versus his private life, and his frantic search for a cure to his cancer while in Mexico.

In this offering I wanted to take a deeper examination of his childhood in Beech Grove, Indianapolis; and Slater, Missouri; as well as the alcoholic, dysfunctional parents who emotionally and physically abandoned him. I wanted to learn more about his life-altering stay at the Boys Republic in Chino, California; his three-year stint in the Marines; and his early acting career in New York. I also wanted to generally dispel a lot of the myths that McQueen created during his Hollywood career to pump up his legend.

Just as McQueen himself rewrote his own history, so must his story be told again. This is not simply just a retelling of the same story. It is an expansion, a development, a deeper and more personal account of Steve that can now be told.

I hope I have succeeded.

1

A MOST INCONVENIENT BIRTH

STEVE MCQUEEN ONCE SAID, "When I believe in something, I fight like hell for it." Given his start in life, it is not hard to see where he acquired this determination. He had to fight from the moment he came out of the womb.

Terrence Steven McQueen's birth was unplanned, the timing ill-conceived, and the infant almost certainly unwanted, as reflected in the fact that both parents were absent for the majority of Steve's childhood. His conception was most likely the product of a courtship fueled in a bar and sustained by alcohol that ended in heartbreak. Steve's parental environment would have an indelible impact upon him and profoundly influence the type of person he would become, defining his behavior and attitudes. This was most notable in the way he treated women and his relationships with his children, friends, and colleagues.

His mother was not maternal. She had little time for Steve, and she often exposed him to relationships with men who had no interest in him. His father, who inauspiciously named his kid after a one-armed bookie, did little else for him. He deserted the family when Steve was six months old. This instilled in Steve a deep mistrust of people that affected him throughout his life. He only allowed a select inner circle to see the real Steve at any one point. This child, who was to become one of the greatest cinematic figures of the 20th century, was emotionally left to fend for himself.

Fighting seemed to be in the McQueen blood. According to his family genealogy, Steve was probably more suited for a career in the military than the silver screen. On his father's side this can be traced all the way back to Dugal McQueen of Corrybrough, Scotland, who was the first McQueen to touch American soil after his capture and imprisonment at the Battle of Preston by the English on November 14, 1715. Dugal and the Highlanders believed that James of the Royal House of Stuart should be the King of Great Britain and was one of the main instigators of the Jacobite Rebellion of 1715. Dugal was convicted and sentenced to transportation to the United States. He arrived in Baltimore, Maryland, on August 20, 1716, on the *Friendship of Belfast,* commanded by Michael Mankin. Dugal was sold into seven years of indentured servitude to William Holland, Esq. While in servitude, Dugal married Grace Brown and fathered five children: William, Ruth, Sarah, Thomas, and Francis.

For six generations, the McQueens fought in the Revolutionary, Civil, and Spanish-American Wars, clashed with frontier Indians, and homesteaded on unforgiving soil amid freezing temperatures. The McQueens fanned out into states as diverse as Pennsylvania, Kentucky, Ohio, Missouri, and Indiana, where Louis Dugal McQueen[1], Steve's grandfather, was born on October 1, 1869. Louis married fellow Hoosier Caroline Culbertson on November 16, 1902. The couple had one son, William Terrence, who was born on March 15, 1907, in Nashville, Tennessee. William fathered his own son just 23 years later, known to the world as Steve McQueen.

Steve's mother, Julia Ann Crawford, was also of Scottish descent, and her maternal bloodline, the Thomsons, possessed the same fighting spirit as the McQueens. The Thomson saga in Colonial America begins with Samuel Thomson of Virginia, who was believed to have emigrated from Ayrshire, Scotland, in 1717. Samuel is thought to have been married three times, resulting in at least 11 known children. Nearly a century later, Captain John William Thomson traveled by boat from Hempstead, Kentucky, to Saline County, Missouri, in the early 1800s with his wife Nancy. Their first son, Pike M. Thomson, was born on August 20, 1819.

When Pike was 24, he married Elizabeth Eleanora Goodwin of Fayette, Kentucky, on October 15, 1843. Three years later they moved to Saline County, Missouri, with enough money to purchase about 1,700 acres of farmland. Like many generations of farmers, helping hands were needed to work and nurture the land, which usually came in the form of children. Pike and Elizabeth had seven children: John W., Lloyd G., Lucian M., Pike M., Ruth, Laura, and Polly Jane.

Pike was in his forties when he answered Governor Claiborne F. Jackson's call in 1861 for men to fight for the Confederate Army. He "enlisted" in the Missouri State Guard during the Civil War under the staff of George K. Dills, Parsons' 6th Division. Loren Thomson, who is a distant relative of both Pike Thomson and Steve McQueen, said Pike's service wasn't exactly done on a voluntary basis.

---

1   Louis D. McQueen, as listed on his 1898 military service card, is described as 5'7½", dark brown hair, and blue eyes.

"My dad said that Pike hated the military because the Confederates came through town, took his horse, and told him he was going to fight for them," Thomson said. "It didn't sound to me like he had much of a choice in the matter."[2]

Later Pike served as a captain under command of General Sterling Price. He fought in the battles of Dry Wood and Lexington, Kentucky, before his capture by Union soldiers. Pike was set for execution until a compassionate Yankee captain interceded. Serendipity seems to have run in Steve's bloodline. The war ended soon after Pike's sentence, and he and his family were able to reestablish their lives.

Pike's natural leadership abilities boded well for him in the private sector, and he served as the president of the Slater (Missouri) Bank. He was a member of the Cumberland Presbyterian Church and also, according to his obituary, one of the oldest and most highly respected citizens of Saline County, remaining remarkably strong and vigorous to the age of 83. On April 2, 1902, Pike traveled by horse to Slater from his home outside of town but was thrown out of his buggy and sustained injuries from which he never recovered. He died shortly after the accident.

Pike's son, John William Thomson, followed in his father's footsteps and joined the Confederate Army as a member of Company E, Gordon's Regiment, in Shelby's Brigade. After engagements at Independence, Westport, Little Blue, and Fayetteville, Arkansas, Thomson's company was cut down and surrendered at Shreveport, Louisiana, on June 21, 1865.

Four years later, John married Julia Franklin Graves on October 15, 1869. According to his obituary, John was a staunch supporter of the Socialist Party, a lifelong member of the Rehoboth Baptist Church, and an expert stock breeder. "He was honest, straight-forward, square in all of his dealings and could always be relied upon," stated *The Slater Rustler*, the town's first newspaper.

John and Julia (who was baptized in the Methodist faith) also raised excellent stock when it came to most of their children, including Claude William (Steve's great-uncle), Emmett, Emma, Lillian, and Polly, who unfortunately died when she was just 16 months.

---

2   Not all of the Thomson men went into war kicking and screaming. Steve's fourth great-grandfather, Asa Thomson, who was born in 1764, tried to enlist as a soldier in Virginia during the American Revolution. He was rebuffed and told he was too young. He was an impatient sort and traveled to North Carolina where he was readily admitted into the militia. Captain John W. Thomson, Steve's third great-grandfather, commanded a Missouri militia and was shot by a sentinel at an encampment in Richmond, Missouri, in 1822. And the actor's fourth great-grand-uncle, David Thomson, served as a Kentucky state senator from 1811 to 1820 and as a general in the War of 1812.

The town of Slater, named after John Fox Slater, a prominent railroad tycoon of the Chicago and Alton Railroad, was first incorporated in January 1878. Lillian, who was Steve's maternal grandmother, was born in January 1879, a year later. The area's fertile soil made it some of the finest farmland in the country. This gave rise to Claude Thomson's specialty—hog farming.

Claude, who inherited his father's 320-acre farm, was no country bumpkin—he was shrewd and clever, working every angle to increase his wealth. These traits will no doubt be familiar to any fan of Steve McQueen. Slater resident C.H. Hines recalled that Claude often came by his stepfather's farm to buy coal, but it wasn't to stoke his furnace or to burn fuel.

"We lived out there in the country in Orearville, about five miles from Slater. I lived about two miles east of the Thomson home in what was called 'The Blackberry Patch.' In other words, we were country hicks," Hines said. "Claude owned a large GMC flatbed truck that weighed close to about a ton, and he'd buy coal from my stepdad. We eventually found out he was feeding the coal to his hogs right before taking them into town to sell them because he got paid by the pound."

Stock farmers weren't the only people who fell victim to Claude—he was strangely the only sibling of four to inhabit his father's Orearville farm. "I never knew Claude, the man who practically raised Steve, but from what I gather, he was a shrewd and acquisitive businessman," said Loren Thomson. "A prosperous hog farmer, he eventually squeezed out all of his relatives from gaining a foothold on the family farm."

Claude was hard but fair on Steve when he took him under his wing. Claude certainly passed on his business acumen and desire to outdo everyone else. The adult Steve fought producers for top billing, made demands on scripts, and even got a slightly bigger horse or gun than his costars. On film sets, as the highest-paid actor in the world, Steve was not shy to make extravagant demands for everyday items from the producers. Jeans, shirts, toiletries, even teakettles, were all demanded. If Steve thought he could get more, he would ask and was rarely denied.

Claude's life itself could no doubt merit its own biography. Early Thomson, who was a constable in Slater and often dressed in black, was liberal in his intake of whiskey and in the use of his firearm. According to the *Slater Rustler*, Early emptied the contents of his .45 pistol in Claude's direction when the two met in the road south of town in December 1921. Claude was heading into Slater on a horse while Early was going home in his buggy. While the newspaper claimed the dispute "probably grew out of an old grudge and an altercation over some hogs," some of the locals said that story was pure hogwash.

"I'm almost positive it had to do with the affections of a woman," said Harold Eddy, who was raised on a farm next door to the Thomsons. "I've been a hog farmer all my life, and I've never heard of anyone getting shot over one."

The *Slater Rustler* reporter wrote that Claude rode to the home of his sister, Ruth Bush, where doctors Caldwell and Duggins were summoned. They found one bullet had penetrated the abdomen, one had struck his arm, and another had hit him in the hip. His wounds were first thought to be serious enough that a judge was sent for to write his will. The physicians thought Claude would not live through the night, but he rallied later on and was taken by train to Kansas City, where he received treatment at a hospital.

Early took legal counsel immediately afterward and set after Claude again. Persistence is clearly in Steve's genetics. Helen Kettler, whose family owned a farm next to the Thomsons for several generations, recalled, "Early didn't have much use for Claude. He burned his first house to the ground, but Claude built himself a nicer home. It was probably his way of getting back at Early."

The two men took this feud to the grave—quite literally, in fact, as both men were buried in different Slater cemeteries.

The only sibling who seemed to stick around and fight for what was rightfully hers was Lillian, who was four years younger than Claude. The brother and sister were polar opposites and, like Claude and Early, they didn't get along. Lillian was refined, artistic, and well-read. She spoke with excellent diction and was a woman of staunch faith, whereas Claude was gruff, profane, and prone to imbibing after a hard day from a homemade distillery he kept in the barn. Claude was also fond of the ladies despite the fact that he was married and had a child (a trait that his great-nephew Steve later picked up on and emulated). Claude's faith was in himself and the Thomson farm.

Lillian was adamant that her father, John William, will to her one-third of the farm, specifically the center section. For years she insisted that one-third of the profits Claude made belonged in her pocket even though there is no evidence that she had worked the land. Claude certainly wasn't the only shrewd negotiator in the family. However, with Claude's increasing controlling stake in the family farm, Lillian left in 1904 with her new husband, Victor Crawford, for St. Louis to make a life for herself. By 1916, when John William Thomson died, Claude was able to wrangle the land away from his siblings and he alone "inherited" the family farm.

Lillian was 31 and Victor was 43 when their daughter, Julia Ann Crawford, was born on April 10, 1910, in Missouri. As an only child, "Julian" had a charmed life. She was pampered by her parents, who did everything to please their blonde-haired, blue-eyed daughter. Lillian stitched her fine dresses, saved up money for a private education[3], and saw to it that she had "the right friends." Julian developed a reputation as being spoiled and a bit on the wild side, an opinion shared by Loren Thomson.

"My dad was a contemporary of Julian's and knew her, and I could tell he didn't like her even though he never said why," Thomson said. "I suspect it was because she was spoiled." Even after she eventually had her son, it would seem as though Julian would be unprepared to give up her self-possessed ways.

Numerous biographies and documentaries over the years (including this author's 1993 biography) have labeled Julian as an "alcoholic teenage runaway" who hungered for the bright lights of the big city. That depiction is partially true—Julian was indeed an alcoholic, just like many others of her generation. But was she a teenage runaway? Not according to Will Smither, a career librarian raised in Beech Grove who has been tracking McQueen's history in the city for two decades. Smither said that, according to the city directories for the years 1927–29, when Julian was 17 to 19, she was living with Lillian and Victor Crawford at 336 S. Flemming Street in Indianapolis, Indiana. The 1930–34 Indianapolis city directory shows that Julian continued living with her parents when they moved from the Flemming Street residence to 1311 N. Drexel Avenue.[4] That is also verified by the 1930 United States Federal Census, which states that Terrence Steven McQueen, born on March 24, 1930, lived at the same address.

This leads back to Beech Grove, Indiana—the birthplace of Steve McQueen. What is the connection, and why was he born there? It was simply a matter of convenience, according to Will Smither, who said the Crawfords lived in a cozy Indianapolis suburb called Little Flower, which was about a five-minute drive to Beech Grove.

"Beech Grove was a sleepy little town of about 15,000 people when I grew up there, and it was certainly less populated when Steve McQueen was born," Smither said. "I have to laugh when I read in all the McQueen biographies and

---

3 Julian attended St. Elizabeth Academy in Indianapolis, Indiana.

4 The 1930–1935 Indianapolis city directory lists "Julian McQueen" but with William McQueen's name absent except for the 1933 entry.

periodicals that Beech Grove is a grimy, blue-collar, industrial, hard-nosed, two-fisted drinking town. It's more like Mayberry RFD."

Although Steve McQueen's Marion County birth certificate does not list the hospital where he was delivered (although it does list Julian and William as his parents), he was most likely born at St. Francis Hospital at 1600 Albany Street in Beech Grove. However, that can't be confirmed, because the hospital purges its medical records over time and relies on the county to record its births and deaths.

Built by the Sisters of St. Francis of Perpetual Order in 1914, the 75-bed hospital was founded on the belief that human needs should be met in a holistic manner, which means Steve's birth must have been physically grueling for Julian. It may sometimes be difficult for fans of McQueen to see a sympathetic side to Julian, but she endured her share of hardships in her own way, too.

Julian was a woman who worked many menial jobs, and it stands to reason that the Order of the Sisters of Saint Francis picked up the cost of Steve's delivery. Charity and "helping thy neighbor" were cornerstones of the Catholic Church.

Although Steve's conception can be targeted, how Julian Crawford and William Terrence McQueen met may forever remain a mystery. "Dashing and romantic" is how Julian later described William McQueen, who either told her he was a barnstorming pilot, or she simply made up the tale.[5] There is no documentation to prove he was a barnstorming pilot[6]—he was a reservist in the U.S. Marines and held mostly low-level jobs on cruise ships and in the Merchant Marine for most of his life.

"A good majority of the barnstorming pilots were World War I veterans," said Mike Dewey, who is an aviation expert and stunt pilot who befriended Steve McQueen at the end of his life. "William McQueen would have had to be seven years old at the start of the war. I've never met a seven-year-old pilot and I'm pretty sure our country, no matter how bad things would ever get in wartime, would ever let a kid of that age fly a fighter plane into a combat situation."

What can be stated as fact is that William Terrence McQueen was born in Nashville, Tennessee, to Louis D. McQueen and Caroline (Culbertson) McQueen

---

5 William McQueen is listed the 1933 Indianapolis city directory as "McQueen, Wm (Julian) aviator."

6 William McQueen's U.S. Marine Corp file was most likely burned in a July 12, 1973, fire that destroyed approximately 16–18 million official military personnel files. If flight training was a part of William McQueen's military experience, that information is forever lost. There is also a family legend that William flew a biplane underneath San Francisco's Golden Gate Bridge in the late '30s, but no news item has been found to substantiate such a claim.

on March 15, 1907, where Louis was an agent for the MetLife Company.[7] A year later the family moved to Los Angeles, California, and rented a home at 207 N. Bunker Hill in the affluent Bunker Hill area. The neighborhood was filled with beautiful Victorian-style mansions and the famous incline railway Angels Flight of Los Angeles. According to the 1909–1918 Los Angeles city directory, Caroline was a milliner (hat shop owner)[8], and Louis was a barber and part-time insurance agent, vocations that furnished the family with a comfortable middle-class existence.

Perpetual motion appears to be a McQueen family trait inherited by Steve. As the money class and upper crust migrated west of downtown Los Angeles, so too did the McQueens. They moved six times within a 12-year period (1908–20) and finally settled at 1317 W. 23rd, which was sandwiched between Wilshire Boulevard and the West Adams district. These were wealthy neighborhoods where moneyed East Coast families and early Hollywood stars made their homes. However, tragedy struck the family when Louis suddenly died of a brain hemorrhage in 1919. He was just 51 years old. As a veteran of the Spanish-American War (Co. D, 3 Nebraska Infantry), Louis was buried at the Los Angeles National Cemetery for his distinguished service.[9]

In the 1920 census, recorded on January 14, Caroline was listed as a "widow," and under "occupation" it stated she was a sales clerk in a department store. Caroline and William stayed in the home at 1317 W. 23rd until 1922 when she moved back to her hometown of Indianapolis,[10] a fact verified by the city directory, which lists her residence at 516 E. St. Clair. The 1922 and 1923 directories also indicate that Caroline switched occupations and was a nurse. She most likely trained at the Methodist Hospital School of Nursing less than two miles away, a profession very much in demand during the height of Prohibition. The devastation of Louis' death and his mother's sadness combined with a serious social downgrade must have been a crushing blow to William. He was 13 when he lost his father, and he was most likely forced to drop his formal education to work full-time and help out his mother.

---

7 This is attributed to the 1907 Nashville, Tennessee, city directory.

8 Caroline's mother, Martha A. (Bridgeland) Culbertson, was also a milliner. Her father, Daniel T. Culbertson, was a farmer-turned-county commissioner according to the 1909–18 Los Angeles city directory.

9 Almost 80 years later, Terry McQueen, Steve's daughter, would be buried less than a mile away from her great-grandfather at Westwood Memorial Park, after she died of respiratory failure after a liver transplant in 1998.

10 By 1923 most of Louis D. McQueen's siblings had migrated to Indianapolis.

Psychologist Peter O. Whitmer, who has extensively studied the life of Steve McQueen and his family lineage, said Louis' death was a major blow to William. "The reaction to the death of anyone's father has a dimension of ambivalence, especially if there existed some clean and palpable deficits in this relationship. For William McQueen, the death of his father would have been fraught with ambivalence," Whitmer said. "Regardless, his formal education and going to work at age 13 caused a sense of being 'parentified'—taking over the adult's role of the provider and protector before one is old enough and emotionally matured enough to really understand this role. One normal reaction of individuals in such situations would be to take leave, to remove oneself, in order to live one's own life."

The paper trail on William picks up again on December 13, 1927, where he is listed as a private in the U.S. Marines, attached to Company F, Ninth Regiment, Central Reserve, Chicago, Illinois. He served from Kansas City and Joplin, Missouri, until 1929. When William returned to Indianapolis, he crossed paths with a blonde-haired, blue-eyed looker named Julian Crawford in the summer of that year. Almost nine months later, they produced a son, Terrence Steven McQueen,[11] who was born on March 24, 1930.

Steve's birth certificate lists William as his father and Julian as his mother. However, no official document in Marion County (Indianapolis, Indiana) or Saline County (Slater, Missouri) exists to prove that the two were ever married. However, Julian is listed as married in the 1930 U.S. Census and is presented as Julian McQueen in the 1930–34 Indianapolis city directories.[12]

The couple was a product of the roaring '20s. Buoyed by the decade's prosperity, young people threw raucous parties, drank illegal liquor, and danced the Tango, the Shimmy, and the Charleston. These were dances that involved physical contact between partners with swaying, hugging, and grinding. There was also the introduction of the ubiquitous drug marijuana, which filled the air of jazz clubs and speakeasies. Everything was an escape from the horrors of war and an opportunity to release pent-up emotions created by the social restrictions and morals of the time. Most likely it was at one of these speakeasies where William and Julian met. Julian, who was raised in a very strict Catholic household, with a stringent upbringing and charmed life, was ready to toast to the good times.

---

11 A noncertified copy of McQueen's birth certificate shows the spelling of his first and middle name as Terrance Stephen.

12 Veronica Valdez, the chief researcher of this book, believes Julian and William had a "shotgun wedding." Said Valdez, "You don't grow up Catholic, go to Catholic school, live with religious parents, and have a child out of wedlock."

Before long, alcohol had her in its addictive grip. Obsession and addiction were genes that she and William unfortunately passed on to their son.

Steve McQueen's birth was ill-timed. He entered this world five months after the Great Depression financially devastated the United States and shook the world economy. It was a most inconvenient birth, and the child's fate—born into an unstable relationship to a very young, fun-seeking mother and a father who was unable and unwilling to support them—seemed predestined. His start in life was about as far as possible from the brass ring that Steve would dream of and aspire to in his adult life. Emotionally and financially, Julian and William simply weren't equipped to bring a child into this world. Julian was weeks shy of her 20th birthday when she gave birth; William had just turned 23.

Domesticity wasn't in William's nature; he simply walked out of their lives. Steve was now left with just his mother, who was, in fairness, unfit for the role. It would often seem that a bottle of booze and the next man in line always took precedence over Steve.

But where did William go? Why did he leave? And was he still alive? These were questions his son continually asked growing up, even into adulthood. How could a man just up and leave his son and the mother of his child? How was he able to disappear without a trace for almost three decades, until Steve McQueen, with the help of a private detective, was just three months away from discovering where his father had been living?

Sadly, there would be no resolution for Steve—no reunion, no explanation for rejecting him as a baby, and no chance to reclaim the father he never knew. Abandoned for more than a quarter of a century but separated forever by mere days, William died before Steve had a chance to meet him. One can only speculate on the impact a reunion of the two men would have had on Steve's life and the complex yet contradictory person he had become.

William McQueen's death shut a door to the past—a Pandora's box that Steve did not want to open. Throughout his life there were times when this tremendously guarded man would strike up a strong bond with various father figures, perhaps in an attempt to negotiate his own undeveloped feelings for the father he never knew. Steve McQueen simply rewrote his own history, blocking and reinventing, turning his private fantasy into part of his public persona. McQueen, as reporters say, made for "good copy" and never failed to get excellent placement in magazines and newspapers. He was never one to let the facts get in the way of a good story.

"Did my husband embellish stories?" said Barbara McQueen, the actor's third wife and widow. "Of course he did. He was an actor, darling."

2

A MIDWESTERN BOY ON HIS OWN

From the start, confusion and ambiguity were the only constants in Steve McQueen's life. Where was his father? Were Lillian and Victor Crawford his parents? Where did Julian fit in? Was he a McQueen or a Crawford? Was he Steven Terrance or Terrence Steven? Various court documents and his birth certificate list him as "Terrance," but he spelled his name both ways throughout his life.[1]

McQueen could only dream of a conventional family and upbringing that would always be denied to him. A childhood spent not knowing who he was and how he got there would starve him of a sense of balance for the rest of his life.

According to many studies, Steve McQueen should have either been chemically dependent, in a mental institution, or in prison by the time he reached 18. To be fair, by all accounts he came dangerously close. McQueen later admitted to a reporter, "If I didn't find acting, I would have wound up a hood."

The National Institute on Alcohol Abuse and Alcoholism say children whose parents are alcoholics display numerous dysfunctional characteristics. They include having difficulty understanding balance; taking themselves very seriously; suffering from depression; judging themselves without mercy; having difficulty with intimate relationships; overreacting to changes; being hypersensitive to criticism; constantly seeking approval and affirmation; and tending to feel they are different from other people. They also show higher tendencies to lie, steal, and fight, and they are overactive and impulsive. Anyone with even just a passing knowledge of Steve McQueen will recognize these traits and could tick them off one by one on roll call. These are all characteristics that Steve displayed in both childhood and throughout most of his adult life. His first wife, Neile, once said,

---

1 Psychologist Peter O. Whitmer believes the different spellings also underscore McQueen's extreme dyslexia and hearing problems.

"Well, he was just wild to handle, and you just never knew what would trigger him off. He was the most maddening and the sweetest—I mean he was just everything. He was crazy!"

Most people affected by the disease of alcoholism never really grow up and fail to learn a healthy way of thinking, feeling, or reacting. As long as things go their way, the "adult-child" is fine. But when they experience conflict, controversy, or crisis, they tend to respond with less-than-adultlike reactions. No wonder Steve, in his late forties, started to collect vintage toys and other things that had been denied to him during his childhood. He resorted to regression as a method of coping.

The fact that Steve came from a fatherless home further complicated his life. It is widely accepted that children raised without fathers are more likely to show signs of psychological maladjustment. They are more susceptible to difficulties at school and often drop out altogether. They are more likely to be represented in the statistics on delinquency and unconventional social behavior, and they seem to have difficulty establishing and maintaining intimate relationships once they move into adulthood.

Whitmer believes McQueen suffered from "grossly pathogenic care," and his formative years were marked with the scars of early Attachment Disorder. "There are five main dimensions of behavior that earmark individuals who have experienced similar disruptive and developmental damaging life events as Steve McQueen did," Whitmer said. "The first theme deals with [people's] ability to regulate their emotions. Their emotional life can be seen as someone trying to water a garden with a hose that, out of their control, is being tramped on, twisted, and the pressure constantly changed. Great blasts of emotion are dumped on those around them. This might be followed by no reaction at all. Everything might flow evenly for some time, and then control is lost and all hell breaks loose; too much, too little, all perfectly unpredictable.

"It seems important to note that regardless of McQueen's deficit in his ability to properly and appropriately regulate his emotions, he was a highly energized person. There exists an entire bell-shaped curve of energy levels in different individuals in the general population. Steve McQueen was way out to the right; a very consistently highly energized individual, thus making the inherent difficulty in emotional regulation seen in the Attachment Disorder individual even more obvious—and problematical—in Steve McQueen.

"Artifice: support, structure, and control from outside of one's self—this is the base of substance abuse. As a means of self-medication, for the person who feels psychic pain and knows that emotional control has slipped from his hands, it is the default recourse to resort to alcohol, marijuana, and cocaine. For the individual with a poor ability to regulate one's emotions, the substance that is abused will act to either ease the pressure or to increase the peak of emotional high. The adult Attachment Disorder individual does not know what 'normal' is. Consequently they err to either side, wanting their highs to be even higher and their lows lower. It appears this defined Steve McQueen's life."

Despite this tremendous disadvantage, somehow McQueen beat the odds. But achieving success and worldwide fame wasn't easy. Adolescence and his journey into adulthood would prove eventful and remarkable as well as traumatic.

• • •

The Great Depression had far-reaching effects in virtually every nation, rich or poor. Families during this crushing economic fallout rallied around each other, and the Thomson clan was no different. Victor and Lillian Crawford lost whatever fortune they had and, like millions of other Americans, were tossed into financial despair. They moved back to Slater[2], the place where Steve spent a majority of his childhood. Today a billboard at the city limits proudly boasts, "Welcome to Slater: The Childhood Home of Steve McQueen."

"My brother Harry moved a 10-by-20 railroad 'cook shack' down from Slater for them," said Marion Fizer, who lived near the Thomson farm. The cook shack was situated on the property of Herbert and Helen Kettler, facing Lillian's brother Claude Thomson's large property. Lillian cooked for the Kettlers in exchange for the use of the land, but it was a serious downgrade from their cozy Beech Grove home. The cook shack was nothing more than a shell. It was spartan, to say the least, with no running water, electricity, or toilet facilities. But it was a roof over their heads. This would no doubt prepare a young adult Steve for his move to the bright lights where he would once again live in bare conditions in a cramped cold-water flat while trying to break into acting.

Fortune seemed to smile on Claude, even though he was hit hard by the Great Depression. But thanks to a loan from local businessman Henry Walker Gilliam, Claude's hog-farming and crop businesses survived and later thrived in the ensuing years.

"As long as you had food, you were okay during the Depression," said Slater resident Elizabeth Simmermon, who endured the horrors of those lean

---

2 Victor and Lillian Crawford are listed in the Indianapolis city directory from 1927–1934 and 1936–39. The only year they are not listed is 1935. Did the family all head to Slater in 1935 and then return to Indianapolis in 1936 and stay until 1939? Or was it just Lillian and Steve who lived in Slater, and Victor remained in Indianapolis to earn an income? These are all likely scenarios.

times. "Everything was rationed—gas, food, shoes, tires, coffee, and sugar. There were times when we practically existed on navy beans and bought them in 100-pound bags."

Although Steve was living in virtual poverty, he had a roof over his head and some form of security. With Steve safe with his grandparents, it is said that Julian took off[3] while Lillian, 54, and Victor, 66, raised her child. If that is true, it was to Julian's credit that she left Steve with her parents because she knew that financially and emotionally she was unable to provide a suitable life for her son. Besides, Julian's questionable go-go lifestyle and alcohol addiction were dominating forces in her life. Some of Steve's family and friends have intimated that Julian was a prostitute, while others claim she was just a "good-time gal" who ran off with anyone who possessed a little charisma and a fifth of whiskey. McQueen's first wife, Neile, said Julian was just too young to have a child and was making up for lost time. "She was too young. She wanted to party. She wanted to live," Neile said. "She wanted to do all the things that she hadn't been able to do when she was younger."

Julian was an especially scandalous figure in Slater, according to neighbor Harold Eddy. "There was a lot of scuttlebutt that went through the neighborhoods whenever she came to town," Eddy said. "Sure got a lot of tongues wagging."

The main source of tongue-wagging stemmed from Julian's succession of men. Steve had once complained, but after a while, he simply lost count. Whatever the case may be, Julian rarely visited Steve during the period her son lived in Slater. Although in reality this was probably a blessing in disguise. Steve continually pinned his hopes on the day his mother would come back for him. However, the fairy-tale reunion between mother and son was far off, and her abandonment of Steve left behind huge emotional scars that would never heal properly.

Claude took pity on Lillian, Victor, and Steve and eventually moved them into his farmhouse. This was definitely a move in the right direction for them in terms of stability. Today the farmhouse is owned by Harold Eddy, who grew up next to the Thomsons on an adjacent farm. He believes Claude purchased his home through Sears in 1919 for about $6,000.

"Some of it was modified, and Claude put in a lot of upgrades," Eddy said. "It was built here on-site and finished in 1920."

---

3   No evidence was found that Julian headed to New York as so many other biographies have claimed. It is the belief of this author and researcher Veronica Valdez that Julian actually headed to California to meet up with William McQueen, based on statements made by various family members and friends.

The Thomson home was also the site of a lot of well-talked-about parties, producing stories that have trickled down for generations in Slater. It was a great house for entertaining, and Claude held some famously wild shindigs at the Thomson home. After dinner, the libations always flowed, while musicians took their places at the bay window in the living room and played country and western music, and the guests drank and danced the night away. This was the Depression era after all, and escapism was in great demand.

Drinking, hell-raising, and partying were the constants in Claude Thomson's life, but he was by no means unstable. He worked as hard as he played. He rose before dawn to do the chores that a farm requires for its upkeep. He was thrifty with a dollar and invested wisely. Often stern and profane, he could be generous if the situation was warranted. His word was good as gold. Steve once said of Great-Uncle Claude, "He was a very good man. Very strong. Very fair. I learned a lot from him." For the first time Steve had principles to follow, structure in his life, and a real male role model.

Lillian was outright jealous of Claude because life had dealt him a much better hand. After all, it was she who attended church faithfully every week, performed volunteer work, and led an exemplary life. Yet it was Claude who was successful, and he ruled his roost with an iron fist. Whatever he said was the law.

Claude grew to love Steve like a son, filling the role of surrogate father in the absence of the real thing. Not a physically demonstrative type, Claude developed an emotional bond with "the boy." Steve became his companion when the two rode into town together, letting him sit in the front seat with wide-eyed wonder. When Steve became old enough, Claude enlisted his help around the farm. "He had no use for slackers," Steve said of his great-uncle. Steve learned through Claude that sleeping in past sunrise was a luxury and a rare occurrence on the Thomson farm. Claude could be counted on to get Steve up on cold, dark Missouri mornings for various chores. "I milked cows, worked the cornfield, cut wood for the winter.... There was always plenty to do. I came to love and understand animals and to feel that in a few ways they are superior to human beings," Steve said. Anyone who has seen how McQueen handles his horse in *Tom Horn* will know how much he learned. It is no wonder that in his final years he sought the simple pleasures of ranch life in Santa Paula, California.

On those rare mornings when Steve was not so eager to earn his keep, Claude didn't hesitate to use discipline. "When I'd get lazy and duck my chores, Claude would warm my backside with a hickory switch. I learned a simple fact: you work for what you get," Steve said.

Joe Giger confirms that his step-grandfather was formidable. "[Claude] was just a rough old dude. He wasn't like people you see today. He always wore a Stetson and was a real shit-kicker, always on the move, always doing something," Giger said. "He was one of those old boys who came through the Great Depression as a real survivor. Claude was a big farmer back in the day and had a lot of responsibilities. It wasn't easy back then, because the labor was a lot harder than it is today. Claude did farming the old-fashioned way, and it was not an easy life."

Claude was not always tough on Steve; he had a soft spot for the boy. He bought him small gifts and awarded him his own room (located upstairs with a view of the farmland), which was a luxury for a kid his age. Claude also treated Steve to Saturday matinees at the Kiva Theater[4] on Main Street in downtown Slater. "Westerns were my favorite," Steve said. "I used to bring my cap pistol and fire at the villains."

The Kiva was a typical movie house in America at that time—for 10 cents (25 cents for adults), kids could enjoy a serial (*Tom Mix, Captain Marvel, Zorro, Tarzan, The Lone Ranger,* or *Rin Tin-Tin*) and a double feature. The 250-seat single-screen theater also exposed McQueen to his first taste of segregation (whites on the floor, blacks in the balcony). It must have made an impression, because years later McQueen quietly lobbied for blacks to play key parts in his films.

McQueen's taste in cinema was shaped by Hollywood's golden age (1930–39) when the advent of sound, movie star glamour, epics, and blockbuster musicals changed film history. Many full-length films were produced during the decade in order to keep people's minds occupied and off their financial woes. The era produced a rich harvest of movies such as *Gone With the Wind, The Wizard of Oz, Snow White and the Seven Dwarfs, Frankenstein, King Kong, The Adventures of Robin Hood,* and *Duck Soup.*

The actors whom McQueen identified with were James Cagney, John Wayne, Spencer Tracy, Gary Cooper, and Humphrey Bogart. McQueen later proclaimed "Bogie" was it for him. "I first saw Bogart on the screen when I was a kid. He nailed me pronto, and I've admired him ever since. He was the master and always will be."[5] Early in his career, McQueen would forge a tough-guy persona of his own. He would develop this and add a sense of vulnerability to it that would firmly establish him as the biggest star of his time and rival, if not eclipse, the fame of his own boyhood big-screen idols.

---

4   The Kiva closed in 1960 and later reopened as Kiva Bowl, an eight-lane bowling alley. The building burned to the ground in the mid-1990s and has remained a vacant parcel of land ever since.

5   Incidentally, Julian McQueen and Humphrey Bogart are buried in the same Forest Lawn Cemetery in Glendale, California.

• • •

Physicality is a hallmark of McQueen's movies, and it was not by mere accident. He was often described by friends and associates as a hyperactive kid who was in perpetual motion. Claude perhaps recognized that his grandnephew needed something to help him burn off his excess energy, and bought Steve a red tricycle for his fourth birthday. McQueen credits the gift for triggering his racing fever. "There was a dirt bluff behind the farm, and I'd challenge the other kids in the area. We'd race for gumdrops. I usually reached the top first. Got some skinned knees, but I sure won a lot of gumdrops!" From there he would one day challenge bona-fide professional racers such as Stirling Moss and Mario Andretti to the glory of the checkered flag.

McQueen also won accolades from Slater resident William Kiso, whose first vision of McQueen was of him dancing the jig in a flatbed truck.

"Claude called on me to help with the threshing of the wheat because he and his oldest son, Mac, didn't get along so well," Kiso said. "I acted as their go-between. Steve was our entertainment. When he came out into the field and danced that jig in the flatbed wagon, he sure made his shoes talk."

Naturally, the bumps and bruises acquired in childhood can parlay into broken limbs, and McQueen pushed his luck falling out of a tree when he was six. Claude knew practically all the major players in Slater, including Alexander McBurney, a country doctor who moved to Slater in February 1936 and kept meticulous records. X-rays revealed that Steve's right arm was broken. McBurney set the limb back in place and put Steve in a cast. Six weeks later, it was removed.

When it came time for Claude to herd hogs along what is now known as Thomson Lane into the railroad pens at the main depot near the town's core, Steve rode shotgun in Claude's half-ton truck and fantasized he was a cowboy, handling the hogs into the pens. Farm life, for the most part, suited Steve well, and he would remember those days fondly. It was also the start of his lifelong love affair with the great outdoors.

Some positivity was now finally entering Steve's life, and these years sound almost like a story William Faulkner would have written—full of bumps, scrapes, misdeeds, and adventures. However, things were far from idyllic. McQueen continually thought about his mother Julian, wondering where she was and what she was doing. He hoped that one day she would come back with his father and that they could be a family. Julian's rare visits back home did nothing to alleviate the boy's inner turmoil and only served to disrupt his home life, though Claude was in no position to tell Steve he could not see his mother. Each brief visit must have brought him a new wave of false hope for a normal family that could never be. Nor could Claude tell Julian to start acting like a mother. Most likely Julian suffered from what substance counselors call "disassociation"—the act of cutting yourself off from others as well as your own feelings. The theory states that the alcoholic stops developing emotionally at the age she suffered a serious trauma or when she started drinking. The end result is that she has difficulty with relationships and uses alcohol to regulate her emotions. The alcoholic unknowingly looks for a solution to the problem but actually sets the stage for addiction, keeping her at the emotional level she was when she started abusing.

Most of Steve's early learning came from watchful observation. Nature was his first teacher. When he wasn't tending to the animals, fishing and hunting were two things that held his interest. "When I was eight, Uncle Claude would let me use the family rifle to shoot game in the woods. But he never gave me more than one shell. I either hit something first shot, or I came back empty-handed. Well, one day I came back carrying two dead pigeons. I said that I'd waited in the woods for them to line up, just right, side by side, and that I'd calculated things like the wind angle and muzzle velocity and that I'd killed 'em both with a single shot. Claude was amazed. Bragged about me to all his huntin' cronies back in town. I never did tell him the truth, which was that I'd gone into a neighbor's silo and shot at some nesting pigeons. The bullet hit one, went right through him, glanced off the side of the silo, and hit another. To his dyin' day, Uncle Claude remained convinced I was a miracle marksman with a rifle."[6]

McQueen's time on the farm would be one of the few positive experiences in his upbringing, so much so that he once famously declared, "I'm out of the Midwest. It was a good place to come from. It gives you a sense of right or wrong and fairness, which is lacking in our society." It wasn't exactly a Huck Finn or an idyllic existence, but Steve did have security, as well as a sense of family and placement in Slater. He had benefited from nurturing grandparents and a stern great-uncle who had given him more than just a roof over his head. "Uncle Claude was one of two important people in Steve McQueen's youth who provided him with the bedrock of stability, consistency, and predictability—and even encouraged him to utilize all of the talents that they saw within him," said psychologist Peter O. Whitmer. "A demanding task master, [Claude] was also the rudder that steered young Steve in a straight line—for a number of consecutive years. Uncle Claude was a spongy base of resilience, a buffer between the harsh and unforgiving times with his mother and her husbands, and the possibilities of

---

6   A few years later McQueen was declared a sharpshooter by the Marines.

another forward-looking life. In this relationship, Steve developed the awareness that the future was embedded in the present, and that the present was a natural continuation of the past."

Steve's eventual removal from the farm resulted in a period of pain that would lead him down a path in life that changed him forever. With such a history, it is little surprise that Steve once told his own son, "Well, Chad, another burn, another scar. That's what the world is all about, son."

Stability and anything approaching normalcy could not last. Julian re-entered the picture and turned Steve's world upside down again. This time around she introduced Steve to a dysfunctional environment where he got his first taste of verbal, emotional, and physical abuse. There would not be the "harsh but fair" discipline of Claude but rather exposure to random maltreatment and a complete disregard for his well-being. This period would threaten to unravel all the development he had recently achieved. Steve would be back with his mother, but it would not be the way he had hoped. Instead of a father figure, he would get several, and each would seem worse than the last.

3

BROKEN DREAMS, EMPTY PROMISES

WHATEVER INNOCENCE STEVE MCQUEEN HAD LEFT was shattered before he reached puberty. That's when his mother Julian came calling for her son with the promise of a reunion and a stable and fulfilling family life. However, Steve learned that his mother's promises always turned out to be empty.

Wherever Julian had run off to, she eventually made her way back to Slater, Missouri, sometime in the late '30s. This time she was taking Steve to Los Angeles. Claude didn't put up a fight, for he instinctively knew that it would be wrong to deny a boy his mother, even though he also knew deep down she was irresponsible and rarely acted in the best interests of her son. When Julian was ready to leave, Claude called Steve aside for a private moment when he gave the boy a gold pocket watch and said, "Here, I want you to have this to remember me by." Steve undoubtedly must have been touched deeply by the inscription. It read, "To Steve—who has been like a son to me."

Confused, fatherless, and dyslexic with an alcoholic for a mother and now uprooted from the only stable home he knew, Steve was tormented. Worst of all, he was forced to endure a succession of Julian's boyfriends, lovers, barflies, and drinking companions. They would range the full spectrum from completely apathetic toward Steve to simply abusive. Being pulled away from the fatherly care of Claude and dropped among these men would push the fragile child to the edge.

Considering how hard Steve had things, it will come as little surprise that he sought escapism and a release for his frustrations. His escape was the streets, where gangs not only ruled but were a way of life. He spent his days and nights on the streets, skipping school, breaking into shops, and participating in rumbles and fights. He claims he mastered two art forms during this period—stealing hubcaps and shooting pool. In gang life he would find a way to release the anger he felt at the world.

Quick to shed his "hick farm boy" handle, McQueen doubled his lawless street activities to enhance his reputation as the "baddest ass" of them all. If he were asked by a gang leader to steal 10 hubcaps, McQueen would bring back 20; if he was asked to break into a store and steal 5 bottles of wine, McQueen would return with 10. His tenacity catapulted his status from follower to leader, but he was clearly headed to reform school. A man named Hal Berri, whom Steve famously referred to as "a prime son of a bitch," gave him a good push in that direction.

Hal Berri was Julian McQueen's second husband, but who was he really? His birth name was Harold Teale Berry, and he was born in 1902 in Connecticut, the only child of British immigrants Ernest and Agnes Teale Berry. The couple moved to Los Angeles in 1910, leaving the overcrowded East Coast and many of their fellow immigrants to join a large national migration that headed west. The Berrys lived a middle-class life in the Silver Lake area of Los Angeles. Ernest was employed as a fireman for L.A. Gas and Electric Corporation, which afforded Hal the opportunity to study mechanical engineering at the University of California at Berkeley. After three years of rigorous academic study, Hal dropped out of college in 1923.[1] Both he and his mother, Agnes, who had followed her son to Northern California, returned to Los Angeles where Hal earned a living as a commercial artist. On December 26, 1924, Hal married fellow artist Tedi Halliwell-Strashum in San Bernadino, California. It was a tumultuous marriage that lasted 13 years.

How Julian met Hal Berry is unclear, but court documents show they married in 1937 in Monterey, California. Steve was informed he was about to get a new "daddy," and all three of them lived in Los Angeles where Julian landed a job as an estimator for a company called Smith Warren in Los Angeles.

Hal was also an estimator with a different company, Smith Martin, and was eight years older than Julian. Hal had divorced his first wife, Tedi, in March 1937 and quickly married Julian that same year. Tedi was an accomplished individual; she was a wholesale apparel designer, custom designer instructor, and published author. Tedi and Hal officially changed the spelling of Berry to "Berri" in 1928 midway through their marriage as documented in the 1928 Voter Registration

---

1   The Berkeley Blue and Gold Student Directory shows that Hal Berry had to repeat his sophomore
     year in 1922.

Index. Although no marriage license for Hal Berri and Julian Crawford can be located, she kept his last name for the remainder of her life.

After a succession of failed relationships, Julian was ready for a taste of domestic bliss. Hal, or Berri as Steve would refer to him later in life, had a steady job and a good income. Lowell Boardman, who was Berri's nephew by marriage, said, "He was a bit of a character, and people liked him. He was a favorite person of mine as a small child. I was told that he collected reptiles, and he was famous for stashing his snakes in his car and not letting passengers know. He had a peculiar sense of humor."

The Berris took up residence at 1810 Ewing Street in the Echo Park neighborhood. Julian soon discovered in short order that Hal was a man-child, always within arm's reach of his mother. According to Steve, he was also a wife beater[2], an alcoholic, and a bully. There is no denying that Julian had poor judgment in men.

Berri and Julian moved twice in the span of two years, eventually settling in a three-bedroom home at 1966 Preston Avenue, also in the Echo Park neighborhood. It was in this split-level home where McQueen said he suffered the physical beatings, emotional abuse, and verbal taunts that became a daily ritual. "He apparently beat me for the sheer sadistic pleasure it gave him—which included the joy he obviously derived from my pain," McQueen recounted to a reporter. "I was young. I even thought of bearing the beatings, vowing simply to hold on until I was old enough to run away. But I just couldn't. It wasn't in me. I just started fighting back."

It is at this point that Steve's unmistakable spirit and determination clearly emerged as he literally fought against the odds. Steve's build was slight and his fists were small, but he was insane with desperation. He was no match for his larger counterpart, but he must have felt relief when he felt his knuckles go hard against his stepfather's torso as he hoped to exact a little pain or, better yet, draw blood. "I would have borne any punishment—anything just for the pleasure of knowing that I had given back even a little of the pain he had inflicted on me. God, how I wanted that," Steve said years later.

After the inevitable beat-down, Steve claimed that Berri added to the humiliation by tossing him into a dark room without food or water for hours. Berri would bait Steve just to provoke a reaction; it gave him an excuse to beat the

---

2   According to divorce documents, Berri's first wife, Tedi, claimed her husband was intoxicated a good amount of their marriage. He also threw "wild parties" with other women and disappeared for days at a time; he was obsessively jealous and inflicted bodily harm on her many times.

boy and hurl verbal taunts. Like most abused children, Steve became unusually wary of physical contact with adults. He was afraid to go home, and he openly rebelled against authority. He was also withdrawn, uncommunicative, aggressive, and disruptive. He did poorly in his schoolwork and found an outlet for all of his frustrations and hostilities by stealing cars and thumbing his nose at law enforcement. "Steve's relationship with Berri solidified all the questions he held from an early age, when painful memories of abandonment and neglect are registered symbolically," noted psychologist Peter O. Whitmer. "Now they were confirmed in a real and physically painful way, and he could put word handles on them. Starting at such an early age, these emotions create so primitive and punitive a dynamic as to forever lock in the most virulent and potent aggression and hostility. This would be seen vented [especially, yet not exclusively] against authority figures or anyone exerting controls, going against 'Steve's rules of life.' However strong the walls behind which this explosiveness is locked away, there exist triggers within one's environment that can cause an unexpected and uncontrolled eruption."

Ted Petersen, who befriended "Buddy,"[3] recalled an incident that showed an angry side of a youth who was simmering with frustration and clearly headed for trouble.

Petersen, a former Navy pilot who died in 1992, recalled walking home from a movie in Hollywood with Buddy when he snapped. Steve's eyes grew wide when he spotted a police motorcycle parked outside of a local restaurant. The officer was inside eating and had left his helmet and gloves on the seat, which Buddy quickly tossed on the ground. Steve then threw his right leg over the seat and hopped up on the bike, placing both hands on the throttle and arching his body forward. "Vrooooom! Vrooooom! Vrooooom!" Steve said, putting the fear of God in Petersen, who felt that any moment they were going to get arrested. Steve soon hopped off the bike but not before breaking off the motorcycle's antenna. "He must have been angry about something because back then, that lack of respect toward law enforcement was quite uncommon," Petersen said. Psychologist Peter O. Whitmer believes the incident is a classic example of the capriciousness and volatility of a seeming random stimuli igniting inner anger.

McQueen had every reason to be angry. His home life was chaotic, hostile, and often violent. As a result, he was combative and resentful. Julian found herself once again the codependent "spouse" of an alcoholic, but she didn't want to give up what she deemed a comfortable lifestyle. Most likely she was fearful of

---

3   On his Social Security card application, Steve also used the name "Buddy Steven McQueen."

starting all over again. Julian's only coping mechanism, it seemed, was to reach for the bottle. Steve turned to the streets for his salvation.

But Berri had enough of the unruly teenager, and Steve had to go. With the beatings, phone calls from truant officers, and warnings from judges, Julian knew the situation was getting out of hand. In desperation, Julian wrote to Claude, informing him of Steve's lawless activities. She added that with no real alternatives, she was going to have to send her son to reform school. Claude interceded for Steve and told Julian to send the boy back to Slater. He'd set him on the right track. Once more, the young man was sent away from his mother—another rejection, another mental scar, another disappointment.

When Steve arrived back in Slater sometime in the early '40s, many changes had taken place in the small agricultural town since he was there last. Lillian and Victor Crawford, who raised Steve in his formative years, had virtually disappeared. While the two should have been living out their golden years in quiet contemplation and financial comfort, the couple had fallen on hard times. Seventy-six-year-old Victor developed and finally succumbed to chronic myositis, a rare disease in which the immune system chronically inflames the body's own healthy muscle tissue. Victor's death on June 20, 1943, sent Lillian into an emotional tailspin and triggered the beginning stages of what was later diagnosed as paranoid schizophrenia.

Lillian had retreated deeper and deeper into her own little world, her emotional pendulum swinging back and forth from despair, extreme piety, and mania. Neighbors eyed her walking up and down Thomson Lane, praying and muttering incoherently. As Lillian's legal guardian, Claude had her committed to Fulton State Hospital, located approximately 90 miles east of Slater. Lillian was declared indigent, and the state picked up the tab for her care. While Lillian was there, James Quisenberry, a psychiatric social worker who was assigned to Lillian, told writer Penina Spiegel that Lillian once confessed to him that she tried to murder her daughter, Julian, and then tried to kill herself. Her condition, Quisenberry added, was progressive and worsened over the years.

Lillian languished for another two decades in the sanitarium until she was admitted to St. Joseph's Home for the Aged, a Catholic nursing home in nearby Jefferson City, Missouri. Neither Julian nor Claude ever visited, and save for neighbor Helen Kettler, Lillian had no contact with the outside world. Lillian died quietly on July 26, 1964, at the age of 86, while her internationally famous grandson was more than 1,500 miles away, nestled in a gated Brentwood estate he dubbed "The Castle" and had purchased thanks to an infusion of cash from *The Great Escape*.

The Slater "family life" as Steve had once known it, had been fractured, and Lillian's positive influence was absent through no fault of her own. While Lillian and Victor faded from view, Claude had flourished. The spry farmer married his housekeeper, Eva Mae Stewart, a former St. Louis Follies dancer with a mane of red hair, long legs, a profane tongue, and a taste for the good life. They seemed like a perfect match despite one fact—he was approximately 70, while she was 33.

"[Eva] was a ring-tail tooter, I can tell you that," said Joe Giger, Eva's grandson. "She was a beer-drinking, card-playing ol' gal who did whatever she wanted."

Eva was a hard-luck story whose fortunes changed when she met Claude Thomson, who was a prime catch for the ex-burlesque dancer. She arrived in Slater with a husband, George Anderson, who ran a local trucking business. When Anderson's company went under, Claude hired the couple as his housekeeper and handyman. Anderson didn't stick around for long and left Eva high and dry. Sharp as ever, Claude didn't allow Anderson to have second thoughts and immediately asked for Eva's hand in marriage despite the huge age gap.

To keep Eva happy, Claude bathed her in furs, diamonds, exotic trips, and a brand new Cadillac every year. "Eva had a lot of personality and flash," said Mike Barnhill, a longtime Slater resident. "I remember the gravel and dust flying when she rode that pink Cadillac of hers into town, where she usually frequented a local beer joint. Eva was talkative, vivacious, and never knew a stranger. Let's just say that she stood out in a town like Slater."

Claude knew that Eva had a past. Hell, he had one, too. Eva brought to the marriage an out-of-wedlock teenaged daughter named Jacqueline Lee Stewart, otherwise known as Jackie. However, Jackie was introduced as Eva's niece, if nosy neighbors asked. She was just about the same age as her new housemate—Steve McQueen.

"He was a quiet boy," Jackie recalled. "You never knew what he was thinking. He had real fine hair, like cotton or down, and the same expression he had later. You'd know him right away."

Steve arrived on Claude's doorstep dirty, starving, and virtually empty-handed. Eva took in the troubled teen and immediately fed him, then made him take a bath. When his belly was full and he was clean, Claude laid down the law. "If you get into trouble, I'm going to send you back to your mother," Claude said. Steve knew that ultimately meant reform school, and more important, Steve knew Claude would keep to his promise. This was precisely the stern but fair discipline that Steve needed and could abide.

Claude kept Steve busy with chores and sent him to school. He was enrolled in the eighth grade as Steve Berri at the Orearville School. Schoolteacher Janice

Sutton, who was then Janice Jones, recalled that McQueen was not hard to miss because he was the only blond-haired, blue-eyed boy in class. He wore a red baseball cap and was "a bit of a smart aleck."

"He was kind of feisty, but I didn't have any real problems with him," Sutton said. "He acted up sometimes."

McQueen later admitted, "To most of the home folks, I must have seemed like a kook from Kooksville. In school, I was a dreamer like on cloud nine. When the teacher told me to do something, I was the one who had to ask why. I wasn't too clever in any academic way. School wasn't a big thing for me; I didn't click too well in it. I tried."

Neighbor Bob Holt recalled that McQueen might have tried, but it sure didn't show. "I can say with confidence that Steve wasn't a great student," Holt said. "It wasn't that he wasn't smart—it was just hard to get him to go to school, period. We'd often walk the old dirt road to the Orearville School, and many times he'd walk past it and go right on into Slater. He loved playing hooky."

Schoolmate Sam Jones also attests to the fact, several decades later, that McQueen wasn't in school that often. "I remember Steve playing outside of the school—he was a good baseball player and a terror on the teeter-totter. He'd get the girls on one side and then buck them off. Totally bounce them off the other end," Jones said. "But I have no recollection of him in the classroom. I don't think he attended school more than two weeks to a month for the entire year I was in school with him. I don't think there were any repercussions for him because he moved around so much. Steve was one of those kids who unfortunately slipped through the cracks."

Steve and school did not exactly go hand in hand for several reasons—the fact that he was hard of hearing played a part in this. The hearing loss was brought on by a mastoid infection, an inflammation of the temporal bone behind his right ear. Antibiotics could have cured the infection, but they were not yet available. Steve was also dyslexic, although he was not diagnosed until many years later, and it was painfully embarrassing to the youngster that he couldn't comprehend the written page. Regardless of McQueen's difficulty with reading and writing, psychologist Peter O. Whitmer said the young man's intellect was deceiving. "Looking at his scores on the Marine aptitude test when he was age 17, his intellectual assessment placed him near the top 20 percent," Whitmer said. "Added to this his intuitive sensitivity and his being a 'quick read'—street savvy—and there lies a sense of anger when his vocabulary, or intellect, or education was challenged."

To understand Steve as an adult, it is necessary to realize that during most of his life before the Marine Corps, he was really fighting against all odds: parental abandonment and alcoholism, physical and mental abuse, learning disabilities, and faithless households. However, these experiences made him a survivor, honed his instinct for self-preservation, and made him who he was. Nothing came easy to him.

There was also the social aspect of school—Steve was guarded about his private life and inevitably had to field questions from curious classmates about his parents and why they were not around. The playground can be a cruel place at times, and children often prey upon other's anxieties. Accordingly, Steve had to keep his guard up at all times. Life had thus far not proved to him otherwise. Even into adulthood, he told people that his father was a pilot with the Flying Tigers in China, under General Chennault, and was shot down by Japanese planes in 1939. (Steve's math was off by a few years—The Flying Tigers didn't actually form until 1940, and the first combat against the Japanese wasn't until late 1941.) Steve was becoming an expert storyteller, inventing an alternate family background as a coping mechanism for his real one. "In all likelihood, the stories McQueen invented about his father were comic book–like embellishments of stories he had been told of his father being an aviator," said Whitmer. "They both satisfied—briefly—his own need to create a parent; they also would work well to explain away the reasons for other peers to look down at him as a bastard, to taunt him, and to take out their own adolescent aggressions in a typical bullying way. Regardless, the more this charade worked to protect Steve, the more confused and curious he became about the reality of his father.

"From new material, it seems that his father was in the 1933 city directory of Indianapolis, living with Steve's grandparents, and listed as an aviator. Rather than a real aviator, perhaps his father simply worked briefly as a common laborer at a nearby airfield," Whitmer continued.

Although he never developed a taste for school or textbooks, Steve would nevertheless get an education—as a gambler, hustler, and dead-eye pool player. Steve frequented the local pool hall, Slater Recreation, owned by entrepreneur Eddie Simmermon. The pool hall was simply a front for a gambling joint upstairs, which, not unlike a speakeasy, featured a bolted metal door and peephole. Simmermon hosted several high-stakes craps and poker games in that room. No doubt Steve was able to draw on this experience for his role as *The Cincinnati Kid* more than 20 years later.

Despite its declaration that it was a God-fearing town, Slater was bustling with activity—both of the legal and the illegal sort. In the 1930s and 1940s, Slater was a boom town thanks to the connection of the Alton Railroad line. Slater also developed a reputation as a place where people worked and played hard. "Whenever I'd venture out to another city, everyone knew about Slater," Simmermon said. "They'd all go, 'Oh, Slater, that's a rough little railroad town.' We sorta had that reputation, and it was well-earned. People would go a little crazy on payday or howl at the moon on weekends, but they always went to work come Monday morning."

Lifelong resident Fran Rupert Donnelly said Slater was a town at odds with itself. "Sometimes in the middle of town you could hear a cow or a chicken. It was so innocent and sweet back then. There were lots of crops and the land was so fertile, like the Nile Valley. But frankly, that little town had a nest of alcoholism," Donnelly said.

Most farmers, including Claude, had a distillery in their barns to help make ends meet during the hard times. Steve was known to dip into Claude's supply every now and then. The affect alcohol had on his mother and her relationship with her son was no deterrent. "I can remember Jackie Stewart talking about how when Steve was a teen he would get wild and out of control because of his drinking," Donnelly said. "She said that when Steve got potted, they'd just lock him up until he sobered up." Psychologist Peter O. Whitmer believes that alcohol lit a fuse within McQueen. "The fact that alcohol melted away the barriers of his walled-up anger so that [Steve] had to be 'locked up' by a family member until sober is proof positive of the depth of the feelings, and quite possibly predictive of his future abuse of substance."

At the time, Jackie Stewart was perhaps the closest person to Steve, who had firmly established himself as a loner. It was she who often accompanied him on hunting trips in the woods or played tag. And when they didn't get along, Claude would put them to work with household chores. "We'd cut corn with a corn knife. He was always pretty good about his chores," she said. The discipline and work ethic drummed into Steve by Claude was a positive influence that Steve would often draw upon for the rest of his life.

According to Jackie Stewart's son, Joe Giger, his mother was feisty and mercurial, and she knew how to keep Steve in line. "Steve was giving [Jackie] lip one morning in the kitchen, and she pulled a frying pan from the stove and smashed him in the face," Giger said. "Steve was standing at the top of the stairs, which led to the basement, [and he] bounced down every stair until he was splayed out on the cement. It scared her because she thought she really hurt him. My mom had a bit of a temper."

It seemed like a typical Midwestern upbringing until McQueen revealed years later to a reporter there was a simmering frustration with life on the Thomson farm. "I worked from sunrises to sunsets. I must have been growing up, because

I began to feel a need for people my own age and I couldn't stand the desolation of the ranch," Steve said.

Loren Thomson, Steve's distant cousin, said raising hogs is a hard, dirty, 24-hour-a-day business. "The stock has to be fed, moved, and watered, and we haven't even mentioned birth assistance or castration," Thomson said. "Hogs are not clean animals, and they are usually infested with fleas if kept in the open."

Slater resident Charles "C.H." Hines, who befriended McQueen, said that Claude was a slave driver and often allowed Steve to miss school to work on the farm. "When you have a farm, hard work is the name of the game," Hines said. "Steve worked from sunup to sundown, and I am certain Claude would have continued working Steve harder if he had stuck around. Steve knew there was a bigger world out there, and it extended way beyond that farm on Thomson Lane." The hardworking simple life was never going to last. Steve had too much passion and curiosity for the wider world to remain just a farmer.

Steve's departure from Slater was marked by two coinciding events. It started when Steve and a couple of local kids shot out the windows and lights of a Slater restaurant with a BB gun. When word reached Claude, he was furious. He threatened to send Steve to an all-boys school. Steve was quick-witted and was not going to wait around for the inevitable punishment. Life had taught him to expect the worst and to take opportunities while he could. When a traveling carnival made its way to Slater, Steve grabbed his chance. This would start a long, often dubious, and sometimes dangerous list of exciting jobs.

William Kiso, who threshed wheat at Claude's farm on a semiannual basis, ran into Steve at the carnival. Kiso recalled the carnival featured a big Ferris wheel, rides, tents, and a boxing ring off to the side of the street. "Steve hollered out to me and walked over, telling me that he had taken a job with the carnival as he shook my hand," Kiso said. "I watched him duck under the boxing ring canvas and disappear. I never saw him again."

Neither did anyone else in Slater. Claude searched for days on end to find Steve, but he finally gave up. He was heartbroken. Joe Giger said his mother, Jackie, never heard from Steve ever again.[4] "She often wondered why, because she never did anything to him," Giger said. "They were close as two people could be, and though she never said anything about it, I could tell it hurt her."

This episode seems sad not least because the family in Slater had given Steve so much. It had provided a roof over his head, love, and discipline, even if the latter was not always effective. Claude had treated Steve like a son. However,

---

4   Jackie Giger died in the early 1990s. Her funeral was one of the largest attended in the history of Slater.

life had taught Steve that your family always deserts you. He just did not know any better. Steve had suffered and probably figured he deserved his chance at a clean break. It must have been liberating for him to be the one leaving everyone else for a change.

"I hated the farm life and didn't get along with small-town people," McQueen said almost a dozen years later. "I guess they were just as glad to see me go as I was to get out of there."

Steve had Claude's sense of opportunism coursing through him, and this spirit would take him far from Slater and onto many adventures. He was now master of his own destiny.

4

NOTHING WITHOUT LABOR

STEVE'S STAY WITH THE CARNIVAL WAS SHORT-LIVED, and he eventually meandered back to Los Angeles after months of hitchhiking, sneaking on freight trains, eating around campfires, and leading the life of a young hobo. It was exciting at first, McQueen said. "I was 14 then. Ran into some pretty cool broads," Steve said. "But I spent most of my time goofing off to watch the car races the carnival ran. Man, you should've seen those smashers get knocked dingy on the track. We were peddling these ballpoint pens, and man, they were like 16 cents apiece, but we was hustling them for a buck. My boss was scamming from the public, and I was scamming from him. The boss caught me, so I was canned."

Julian and Berri regretfully took him back, but Steve picked up right where he left off—running afoul of the law and locking horns with his stepfather. Steve was back in the hell that he knew as home.

Steve's relationship with Berri had lost none of its hostility, and Steve bore the brunt of his stepfather's angry vitriol and sadistic beatings. When Steve was caught stealing hubcaps from a Cadillac, Berri again went berserk, no doubt giving Steve yet another beating. When Steve appeared in court, the judge took note of Steve's past offenses and issued a decree from the bench: "Next time you appear before me, you will do some time in jail, young man." When Steve got home later that afternoon, Berri was waiting for him.

Per Steve's recollection, he came home to a standard beating following his altercation with the law. But this beating would be different because it would be the last. "In that instant, I made up my mind that man would never hit me again," Steve said. "It didn't matter whether I lived or died anymore. The only thing that did matter was that I would never ever bear the pain of his fists again."

Steve finally hit back, but he didn't have to worry about Berri much longer. By 1943, the relationship between Hal and Julian had seriously deteriorated. Their divorce complaint shows the two separated on May 22, 1943, and were living apart. No longer living the life of the dutiful housewife, Julian rejoined the labor force and found work as a draftsperson. Realizing that as a single working mother she would not be able pay the rent on their new home at 3266½ Descanso Drive and feed a growing boy, Julian made Steve apply for a Social Security Number[1]. At the age of 13, Steve was the new man of the house and was expected to work and contribute money toward the family expenses.

There is no proof that Steve ever held a job in Los Angeles during this time, but one thing is for sure: his delinquent activity continued. "What was I supposed to do? I had lost control of Steve, I had a very hostile husband, and I had to work," Julian confided to Steve's first wife, Neile, a few years before her death. "I had no other recourse other than to sign that court order that sent him to Boys Republic." The court order stated that Steve was incorrigible, and Julian had him shipped off to Chino.[2] Although this was not meant as a kind gesture, it was perhaps the best thing Julian ever did for Steve. "I was looking for a little love, and there wasn't much around. I guess I was difficult. I ran around with a bad crowd and I hated school—the regimentation and everything," McQueen offered. "I was suspicious of every person I met. I felt everyone was out to get me, no matter what I did, no matter how I behaved. That's why I've been a loner most of my life." Steve did not simply have a chip on his shoulder; it was a hard shell. He genuinely had more than enough reasons for why he developed into such a mistrusting and guarded person. After all, nearly everyone had let him down. But attending Boys Republic would be a turning point in Steve's life.

The Boys Republic has no documentation, file, or transcript that Steve McQueen ever attended there, save for an old team baseball photo taken in the mid-1940s.[3] But there is no question that McQueen is the school's most famous alumnus and over the years has become its patron saint. McQueen often credited

---

1   Steve's Social Security application is dated July 8, 1943, less than two months after Hal Berri and his mother separated.

2   Julian Crawford and Hal Berri's divorce complaint sheds a curious light on the subject. The complaint states the two separated on May 22, 1943, which is 17 months before McQueen was sent to Boys Republic. Julian and Steve both claim that that Hal Berri forced her to sign the court order. New documented evidence of Julian's marriage timeline to Hal Berri does not seem to support this previous claim.

3   The school has no records of McQueen's stay at Boys Republic other than his entrance and exit dates, according to executive director Max Scott, which listed him as Steve Berri.

his stint at Boys Republic for changing the direction of his wayward existence, and he supported the school throughout his life. It still continues three decades after his death. Although there are no official records, there is now an impressive plaque bearing McQueen's name that sits proudly on the school grounds.

The story of how Boys Republic came about is a story of will and determination. It was founded in 1907 with the counsel and assistance of William Rueben George, a social worker who had established a pilot program in upstate New York a dozen years before. George and wife Esther Brewster wanted to provide a means of training disadvantaged and troubled youths whose energies were misdirected. The couple, along with approximately 150 teens, mostly orphans, survivors of abuse, child neglect, and abandonment, took over an inhabitable farm in Freeville, New York, and transformed it into a place where they could start anew.

George, with his labor force of ragtag youth, constructed and renovated the farm buildings. Local residents interested in the curious venture supplied their brave new neighbors with food, clothing, and tents. The following summer, approximately 200 youths of both sexes came back to what was known as George Junior Republic, affectionately named after their beloved leader.

Using the larger society as a blueprint, the George Junior Republic community consisted of a farm, bakery, laundry, hotel, carpentry, blacksmith shops, and even a jail. To make his adolescent citizens understand how to properly function in society, George's students were responsible for running their own government through meaningful participation. They prosecuted crimes, imposed penalties, and enacted their own laws. They also produced much of their own food, printed their own newspapers and periodicals, repaired their own machinery, constructed buildings, and minted their own money. It was an honor-based reform school that inspired confidence and respect for the rights of others, and it instilled a sense of self-worth and sufficiency to those who had lacked proper guidance in the early part of their lives.

With great fanfare from the community and the media, California's George Junior Republic was dedicated on March 19, 1908, at the historic Old Boom Hotel in the San Fernando Valley. Two years later, thanks to the benevolent support of philanthropist Margaret Brewer Fowler, the colony relocated to a 211-acre parcel of farming land in Chino Valley, where it has remained ever since. "Nothing without Labor" was its motto, a message Steve would eventually adopt himself. As Steve said near the end of his life, "If you work hard, you get the goodies."

Steve arrived at Boys Republic on February 6, 1945;[4] the school had a capacity of about 100 students at the time. He could reel off his assigned number, 3188, years after his stay. In later life, Steve looked back on this experience fondly. When he moved to Santa Paula, California, in his late forties, he had the number MCQ3188 proudly displayed on the license plates of all his everyday vehicles. It was a reminder of his journey and how far he had come.

Getting Steve to adopt the school's methods and practices, as progressive as they were, was a daunting task for then-principal Frank Graves. After all, Graves was the arch authority figure, and Steve never took kindly to authority. Graves remembered Steve as "a quiet kid who stood pretty much on his own two feet. He was active and energetic—you knew he was around, all right—but he was not very articulate." Nor was he cooperative or popular with his contemporaries at the beginning of his stay.

Steve was assigned to live in the John Brewer dormitory cottage (built in 1912) with several other young boys age 14 to 18. Each cottage contained a living room or common area for the use of all boys, and it was supplied with magazines, games, and record players. A housemother was assigned to each cottage. She planned games and activities, read aloud, mended clothes, darned socks, and served as overall guide, philosopher, and friend, keeping a motherly eye on the young men.

The site also provided a hospital, post office, town meeting hall, memorial building for assemblies and religious services, a gymnasium, a 30-by-60-foot swimming pool, and a multiuse ball field for football, track, and baseball. The residents of Boys Republic were undoubtedly well provided for and given access to facilities of which they would otherwise have been deprived.

Life at Boys Republic was highly regimented and meant to keep its membership busy and productive with schooling, training, activities, and labor. Students were awakened around 5:30 AM to perform a battery of chores, including milking cows, before eating breakfast at 7:30 AM. About 50 boys attended school in the morning from 8:00 to 11:30 AM and broke for noon lunch, while the second shift of 50 attended school from 1:00 to 4:30 PM. Dinner was served to everyone at 6:00 PM. All meals consisted of meat, vegetables, baked goods, and plenty of milk, all of which was grown and produced on-site.

Because of his loner stance and refusal to participate on any level, Steve was shown the error of his ways with the fists and fury of his peers. Steve explained to writer Malachy McCoy, "Say the boys had a chance once a month to load in a

---

4   Julian McQueen paid $25 per month for Steve's room and board at Boys Republic.

bus and go into town and see a movie, and they lost out because one guy in the bungalow didn't get his work done right. Well, you can pretty much guess they're gonna have something to say about that. Yeah, I paid my dues with the other fellows quite a few times. I got my lumps, no doubt about it. The other guys in the bungalow had ways of paying you back for interfering with their well-being."

Former roommate Robert McNamara recalled McQueen's face as hardened, possessed with the aura of a wounded animal, and he exuded a "don't mess with me" body language that spoke volumes. "[Steve] was cut off emotionally and he was guarded, just like me. If I asked him a question, most likely I wasn't going to get an answer, so I didn't ask. Steve was the one who did the approaching if he wanted something. Reflecting back, he was emotionally in pain, and when I later saw him on screen, his independence and pain were real. There was always anger under the surface, and you can see the tragedy of his life in his films, which made him so compelling." McNamara said over time that they accepted each other and sneaked off to share cigarettes underneath the bridge at the school's entrance, where they plotted to run away. McNamara took off with a couple of buddies and wound up in Long Beach about 40 miles away. McQueen went solo, ever the loner, and did not make it very far, ending up caught underneath the entrance bridge.

"We were both the recipients of a spanking from [principal] Frank Graves, who used a 20-inch-long wood paddle filled with little holes to express his frustration with us," McNamara said. "After Mr. Graves finished with us, we both walked a little funny for a few days." Graves also turned over the two boys to the Boys Council, where punishment was meted out by a group of peers. "The Boys court was held every Monday night, and it [was] comprised of a judge and jury of kids, as well as a prosecuting and defense attorney," recalled Arden Miller, a Boys Republic alumnus who attended school with Steve. "Whenever there was an infraction, you'd go before the court. Once Steve committed an infraction and was given a penalty, and he promised one in return."

According to Miller, Steve was assigned to a series of punitive, laborious, and dirty jobs, which included uprooting tree stumps, digging ditches, mixing cement, and cleaning out the urinals in each of the school's five cottages. He didn't take the news well, according to Miller. "He warned the entire council, 'I'll get back at ya.' That was Steve, and he made good on his promise. He found a way to get back at the judge, jury, and the two attorneys. He'd ransack your room, turn over your bed, put shaving cream in your shoes. He dealt in street justice, which meant he could strike at anytime, anywhere."

Steve had learned to fight back. If someone hit him, he hit back harder. That was all part of his psychological makeup, said Peter O. Whitmer. "McQueen viewed himself as the downtrodden, benighted, and battered kid who defined himself as he grew up facing adversity and fighting back with no one else beside him," Whitmer said. "Inevitably, this primitive kind of interpersonal tension seems at the core of relationships that Steve had with authority, women, and his own professional persona. If an individual has an emotional peak experience, or an emotional peak period of time, at a relatively young chronological age, it can be very difficult for him ever to be socialized."

McQueen's education at the Chino Vocational School included both classroom and field work. Students either studied agriculture and dairying or industrial training, depending on their interest or whether or not they were being punished. Unsurprisingly, guess who fell into the latter category? McQueen was assigned to agriculture and dairying, otherwise known as "farm duty." McNamara said in the case of McQueen, it was by design from administrators. "Being put on farm training or milking cows meant you were on someone's shit list," McNamara said. "Steve was on farm duty as long as I knew him." McQueen's courses included:

Farm projects, farm mechanics	2 units; 20 hours per week
Farm English	½ unit; 2 recitations per week
Farm applications of science	½ unit; 2 recitations per week
Farm applications of mathematics	½ unit; 2 recitations per week
Hygiene	¼ unit; 1 recitation per week
Citizenship and its duties	¼ unit; 1 recitation per week
Physical training	6 periods per week

No doubt Uncle Claude would have approved of all this farm work, but Steve certainly didn't. He had only just left Slater, and here he was again—chin deep in mud.

Both McNamara and Miller confirmed that Boys Republic supplied an excellent and quality education to students, but life at the school could get confining at times. Miller recalls sneaking off to Pomona sometimes, which was an eight-mile trek and quite risky if caught. "Steve made that walk several times, mostly on Saturday nights," Miller said. "He took me with him a few times, and we had a lot of fun. At the time, it was worth the risk because we were young and got cabin fever."

Steve didn't leave the campus save for his discreet jaunts into Pomona. Although most other students received visitors or had a chance to return home during the holidays, that wasn't the case for Steve. Every holiday provided a numbing reminder that he had no home to return to. Julian had scheduled only one visit during Steve's entire stay, and Steve was looking forward to their reunion. Max Scott, who has been the Boys Republic executive director since 1976, said Steve once told him of a sorrowful tale regarding his mother. "Steve got up early in the morning and had his bag packed and was sitting out on the front porch waiting for her," Scott said. "All day long he waited, and she didn't show up. He finally gave up at ten o'clock at night and went back inside and burst into tears. He cried very, very hard. He was destroyed by this." This was Steve's level of commitment and determination. Despite the constant letdowns, he still hoped. Julian's no-show was an act Steve took years to forgive, and it drove another wedge into their already complicated relationship.

Taking pity on McQueen was guidance counselor Lloyd Panter, who saw a broken, confused young man in need of some fatherly advice. McQueen was planning another breakout when his case was brought to the attention of Panter, whom Steve fondly remembered, "He reminded me of my Uncle Claude—stern but just." Panter immediately perceived Steve as someone trying to find himself, and the two began spending evenings together, talking things out. "He was sayin' some straight things—and I began to listen, to soak in what he was tryin' to get across." Panter also told Steve that he saw something in him that was special. "Give life an honest shot," Panter told the teen. "You could be somebody special someday." Steve said years later, "No one in authority ever talked to me like that. No one seemed to give a damn about my future life as an adult—but he did, and it meant a lot to me."

Steve embraced Panter's advice, which eventually yielded results. Again, Steve revealed that when he was given some much-needed affection and understanding, he could show his better side and that he could develop into much more. He was a young man strongly in need of guidance, and he benefited greatly from Panter's sympathetic ear. McQueen explained, "Understanding is the magic word. That's something more important than love. And it ought to be easier to give. You don't have to beat your heart out to give someone understanding. Mr. Panter helped change my life. He didn't give me love, but he did give me understanding. It was enough."[5]

Psychologist Peter O. Whitmer said Panter's role in McQueen's life, though brief, held equal weight to Uncle Claude. "Mr. Panter spoke with Steve as a

---

5   In a June 1960 interview with *Silver Screen* magazine, McQueen credits Panter for introducing him to literature, which included the works of William Shakespeare. "In that way he laid the foundation for my later interest in the theater," McQueen said.

human being rather than a juvenile delinquent," Whitmer said. "Panter was the first and perhaps the only authority figure who said to him, 'You could be special someday.' These two father-like figures entered Steve's life briefly and at different times, yet with similar themes, and both provided him with the resiliency and self-confidence to raise himself above the snarling, nagging psychological issues of abandonment, anger, and interpersonal skepticism that had permanently resided within him since birth."

Before long Steve became a role model for others and was elected to the coveted Boys Council, which enforced the rules and standards for others. He also finished his ninth-grade courses before his release. This was a complete turnaround. His newfound self-confidence and his ability to function within a community were rays of hope. In return, Steve gave back tenfold to Boys Republic during his lifetime. "It's damn good for boys," he said of the program. "You know, those years 12 to 18 are pretty crucial in a boy's life. I mean, he really shapes up in that time, or he doesn't. I think it's a good idea for the boys to run the boys. After all, adults are deadly enemies to the young, especially to kids who have been in some kind of trouble. Believe me, a boy learns to toe the line when he's got the force of 20 other boys seeing to it that he behaves."

When Steve later became an international superstar, he would often go back to Boys Republic to dip into his spiritual reservoir for sit-down chats with the kids. The facility had given him so much that he was happy to return the favor, though often this side of Steve was overlooked[6]. Psychologist Peter O. Whitmer said McQueen's stint at Boys Republic was key in his development as he was about to enter adulthood and later Hollywood. "The lessons he learned at Boys Republic allowed him to operate at a fringe of social acceptability [which was all he was capable of doing for any length of time], while at the same time gave him the ineffable stage presence that galvanized others working with him, made the public adore him, created 'issues' with his women, all by projecting onto the screen a previously unseen form of drama.

"In their behavior control paradigm, if one individual kid screwed up, the monkey wrench in the machine, consequences were shouldered by the entire group. He noted how it took him a bit of time to learn this reality of one individual's actions resulting in consequences for the whole group.

---

6   Throughout his movie career Steve McQueen made outrageous demands on the set, asking for extra clothes and other items. Unbeknown to the studios, these items usually ended up at Boys Republic.

"Steve saw at Boys Republic the power of this tool [of] behavior control, or behavior change in creating conformity and a positive group effort. But he could also turn that upside down. He knew both what it took to operate as part of a conforming group and what the power of running solo, counter to the group, could do for him. And he was both savvy and emotionally calloused enough to pull it off.

"That was really the core, the parsimony, the uniqueness of Steve. This kind of creating tension, almost pugilistic interpersonal behavior, where he could have impact on the entire group and come out at the top of the heap, gave a target for his own 'controlling' motivation, created a public intrigue through the tabloids, and allowed him to become the straw that stirred his costars' and coworkers' drinks. He used this to his advantage on *The Magnificent Seven*, *Hell Is for Heroes*, *The Great Escape*, and *The Towering Inferno* in particular.

"Boys Republic was also a significant period for creating [Steve's] future in film. It was a psychological catalyst; it crystallized his free-floating anger at the world into a tool of both personal utility and professional gain."

Steve was nearing the end of his 14-month term at Boys Republic in 1946. Julian had been separated from Hal Berri for nearly three years; there was no reconciliation between the two. Berri's mother, Agnes, had passed away in 1944, which might have given him reason to pause[7]. Did he want to continue living a tumultuous life with Julian and her troublesome stepson? The answer would be no. Hal continued divorce proceedings, which became final in 1945. He relocated to the art community of Ojai, California, approximately 45 miles north of Los Angeles. On March 18, 1945, Hal Berri married his third wife, dancer and artist Billie Houghton.[8] Hal and Billie were active members of the community, and they opened a dance school and a retail shop that sold Hal's art along with other local artists' work and antiques, according to Billie Berri's nephew Lowell Boardman. Both were also involved with the Ojai Arts Center theater productions as actors and board members. In his writing *The Dunes*, fellow artist Elwood Decker recalls

---

7   Agnes Teale Berry is buried in an unmarked grave in the Eventide section of Forest Lawn Memorial Park in Glendale, California, where she would be joined for eternity in 1965 by her ex-daughter-in-law Julian Crawford McQueen Berri. Steve was most likely not aware, but it is interesting to note that not only are the two buried in the same cemetery but in the same area, with Julian's resting place high upon the hilltop from Agnes T. Berry.

8   Hal Berri died of a cerebral hemorrhage on January 2, 1950, in Ojai, California, the result of a head injury sustained in an accident in front of Union Station in downtown Los Angeles just a day earlier. Coincidentally, the car Hal and Billie occupied was struck by a drunk driver on New Year's Day, 1950.

seeing "Hal Berri…play the part of an alcoholic with thoroughly convincing accuracy. And no wonder. All of them were alcoholics in what we called real life."

While Berri was living a new and more peaceful life in Ojai, California, Julian was left to fend for herself, and she gravitated to a strange crowd, according to McQueen's Boys Republic roommate McNamara. "Steve rarely spoke of his mother, but I suspected even as a kid that something wasn't right. I don't know for sure if [Julian] was a hooker, but I do know that the four men she was living with weren't the only guys she was making it with. Steve really didn't tell me in so many words, but it didn't take a genius to figure out what was going on."[9]

As soon as she had enough money saved, Julian bolted for New York City, where she found shelter in Manhattan's Greenwich Village in the apartment of artist Victor Lukens. It was from his 240 Sullivan Street apartment where she wrote Steve, telling him of her plan for a mother-child reunion. She managed his release on April 1, 1946, and Steve was ready for a change of scenery.

Boys Republic student Arden Miller said Steve was euphoric on the eve of his release, and the two spoke excitedly of their futures. "I told Steve that I was going into the Marines, and he said, 'Well, I'm going into the Marines, too!' and we just laughed and smiled. It was the happiest and most expressive I'd ever seen him." Steve had his life ahead of him, and only he could control it. He'd be calling the shots from now on.

For the first time in Steve McQueen's life, he was a man with a plan.

---

9   Julian Berri is listed as the only tenant at the 3266½ Descanso Drive address in the 1944 California Voter Registration. In 1946, with Steve sentenced to Boys Republic, Julian Berri took in her Iowa neighbors Isaac and Haya Epstein and their daughter, UCLA college student Pauline Epstein, as boarders to defray the cost of rent, a fact documented in the 1946 California Voter Registration and confirmed by Pauline Epstein's 91-year-old brother, Ben Epstein of Berkeley, California.

5

LEATHERNECK

LIKE MANY ROLLING STONES, Julian McQueen came to a stop in New York's
Greenwich Village, a longtime haven for progressive avant-garde artists, bohe-
mians, eccentrics, radicals, and intellectuals. The largely residential area on the
West Side of Lower Manhattan became the new mecca of the art world, displacing
Paris as the cultural capital of the world. The Village was a hotbed of live and
experimental theaters, oddball art galleries, hip boutiques, lively coffeehouses,
and nightclubs. It was the birthplace of the Beat Movement; the folk music scene;
and new movements in abstract, avant-garde, and performance art. It provided
whatever one was looking for, in abundance.

Julian had taken up with another man—artist, filmmaker, and photographer
Victor Lukens, who was perhaps the great love of Julian's life and an important
figure in Steve McQueen's life and career. Julian, who worked in a Greenwich
Village bookstore and was about five years his senior, caught Victor's eye. "Victor
said Julian was the 'Golden Girl,' because she had gold hair and skin, and she
just had a glow about her," said his widow, Linda Lukens. "He said she was an
incredibly sexy and dynamic woman and that every head in the room would turn
when she made an entrance."

Steve's entrance to the Big Apple was nowhere near as grand. He recalled the
cross-country bus trip from Los Angeles to New York as an eye-opening experience. "My mother was going to get married again, so she sent me the bread and
I went across country. I got off the bus feeling like Li'l Abner. There I was in my
big high shoes, Levi's and Levi's jacket, a California tan, and a square-cut haircut.
I remember standing on 34th Street, and that was a bad crowd I was seeing."

Once again, the mother-child reunion between Julian and Steve hadn't
worked out as well as Steve had hoped. Julian was nervous when she picked
up Steve from the bus station, and it was obvious to him that she had been

drinking. However, Victor proved to be a salve in Julian and Steve's fractured relationship, and Victor took on a paternal role in Steve's life, according to Lukens' widow. "Victor told me that he was the one who insisted that Julian take him out of that school [Boys Republic] and that Steve was just a mixed-up kid in need of love and support," Linda Lukens said. "As it was told to me by Victor, he said Julian really didn't want Steve around. If it hadn't been for Victor, Steve still would have been in reform school. Victor did that for a lot of people—he raised their kids."

Julian had rented a room for Steve in a three-bedroom apartment down the street from an actor she knew and who happened to be gay. She foolhardily forgot to tell her son, who came home one night to find his landlord and another man in an embrace on the living room couch. He raged at his mother for her lack of concern and spent as much time as possible away from home. He often spent many nights in the arms of the young women who took pity on him, and he mostly lived on guile, grit, and survival skills for the next year.

After sharing drinks in a bar with two friendly sailors who relayed their tales of high adventures on the seas in the Merchant Marine, Steve boarded the SS *Alpha*, a ship based in Yonkers and headed toward the West Indies. It sounded adventurous to a 16-year-old in need of employment and excitement. Psychologist Peter O. Whitmer believes Steve hopping a ship was simply in his DNA. "While there exists the possibility that Steve had heard from someone that his father had Merchant Marine experience, one never knows," Whitmer said. "The Merchant Marines are a magnet for men with a high degree of wanderlust, curiosity about the world, a minimal tolerance of strict rules, a need for breaking out of boredom or avoiding people, places, and times in a fantasy life of travel. This seems to have applied to both father and son.

"His joining was also a brazen and understandably obscene gesture to the one woman whose lifestyle had been to let him down at every opportunity. He floated off—physically if not psychologically."

Steve's status as an able-bodied seaman was kept off the books, which adds to the mystery of it all. As soon as the *Alpha* headed out to sea, the embellished brochure version of ocean life delivered in the bar didn't exactly match with the reality of the situation.

"The Merchant Marines was bad duty all the way around," said Slater native William Kiso, who joined in the '40s.[1] "The ocean waves got up to 50 feet high,

---

1   Joining the Merchant Marine was just one of several parallels William and Steve McQueen would share in life.

and the ship would bob up and down. It was that way night and day all across the Atlantic. I was just in a year and a half and was seasick for a year and a half."

Promptly handed a mop and pail, Steve swabbed the decks of the *Alpha* under a blazing sun and unrelenting heat. That thankless task was followed by garbage and urinal duty. "I smelled so bad that nobody in the crew would come within a hundred feet of me," McQueen said. No matter where Steve ended up, whether it was his uncle's farm, reform school, or the Marines, hard work would surely follow.

The *Alpha* was scheduled to pick up a cargo of molasses in the West Indies, according to McQueen, and the ship sailed about as quickly as the cargo it was sent to retrieve. The *Alpha*, McQueen said, was in no condition to go that far and didn't anticipate a return. "That ol' tub was in really bad shape. It caught fire not long out of the harbor and damn near sank." But the *Alpha* did recover and docked at Santo Domingo in the Dominican Republic. Steve figured because he was underage, nothing would happen to him if he jumped ship. "Taking orders still bugged me," Steve said of his rebellious streak. "I decided to become a beachcomber and live the free life." Steve gave the free life a two-month trial run, where he enjoyed tropical weather, white-sand beaches, lush vegetation, strolls down cobblestone streets, and flirting with the island beauties. All of his nocturnal fantasies were realized when he snared a job as a towel boy in a brothel. It didn't pay very well, but it came with some superb fringe benefits. With a shortage of blond-haired, blue-eyed boys on the island, the prostitutes found McQueen attractive. "Got to sample some of the wares. Those ladies treated me real, real fine," Steve often told reporters with a wink and his trademark half-grin.

Half-starved, Steve found another ship back to New Orleans and drifted from job to job and state to state. McQueen eventually ran out of money and slept on a park bench in Cedar Rapids, Iowa, before a carnival took pity on him and hired him as a pitchman. "I ended up as a huckster, selling pens to anyone with the price," McQueen told reporter Jack Lewis. "I ate my first good meal in many days in Cedar Rapids and had a chance to sleep in a tent instead of the park."

"Somehow, that park bench held some meaning all its own for me. It's a feeling I can't put into words, but it's there. And sometimes, when I start to figure I've got the world by the tail, I think back to the bench and remember that it could've ended up a lot differently."

At the conclusion of the interview, Lewis asked McQueen whether he could still find that park bench in Cedar Rapids. McQueen nodded quietly.

"I could still find it," he solemnly answered.

Flanked by snake charmers, fat ladies, midgets, dancing girls, legless wonders, and sword swallowers, McQueen traveled the country and found himself moving in a world within a world. "Carnival people are clannish," he noted. Being shackled with them for 24 hours a day gave McQueen a keen insight into how to read people, tell them what they wanted to hear, and cajole them to his way of thinking. On some humble level of the entertainment world, the experience gave him his first glimpse of show business. This period would give him his analytical ability to read other people and their emotions. He would later use this ability as an actor, choosing to react to those opposite him on the screen, leveraging off their emotions to devastating effect.

Psychologist Peter O. Whitmer said "role reversal" is the art form of the Attachment Disorder, a secret language that allows access to others' thoughts and feelings in an almost magical manner. "Of all the psychological dimensions among Attachment Disorder individuals, role reversal can be the most baffling and clearly the fascinating feature to try and understand. It refers to the ability of these individuals to use an almost preternatural skill to 'reading' the behaviors of those around them. This is especially true of other's potentially hostile and angry and damaging behaviors. These individuals are highly adept at picking up on others' verbal and nonverbal communications—to the uninitiated observer, it can look like mind reading or some variant of ESP.

"Usually this skill is developed as a form of protective human radar, a distant early warning system. The evolving person, always on the receiving end of others' hostility and negativity, gradually—and less than fully consciously—learns to observe subtle cues that tell them danger lurks. Moreover, they create coping schemes, or protective manipulations intended to defuse the ever-present ticking human time bomb that is their 'pathogenic caregiver.'

"Role reversal, where the trauma recipient now controls his caregiver, can often become a bent tool, such that others' weaknesses and chinks in their armor become handholds that allow the traumatized to use others in a self-serving and egocentric manner. These skills grow from merely reading others into using others, exploiting them, squeezing dry the human orange, then tossing away the useless rind."

When the carnival moved north into Canada, McQueen heard that lumberjacks earned an excellent wage, so he joined a work camp in Ottawa. But McQueen's well-documented fear of heights or perhaps love for his native country brought him back to the United States. He eventually drifted to the Deep South, which, known for its down-home hospitality, had a unique welcome wagon in store for him. McQueen was quickly picked up as a vagrant and sentenced to

30 days with a chain gang, summoning shades of Paul Newman in *Cool Hand Luke*. If Steve thought he had worked hard before, then this really would be hard labor. He never did seem to find the easy option, even though he often looked for it. He eventually washed up on the shores of Myrtle Beach, South Carolina, to check out the Southern Belles. It didn't take long for McQueen to find what he was looking for. "Her name was Sue Ann. She had big green eyes." Steve celebrated his 17th birthday with Sue Ann and her family. Poignantly reflecting back on that particular birthday, McQueen wistfully noted, "I was an old man by the time I was 17."

Though he thoroughly enjoyed his time in Myrtle Beach, McQueen was a restless soul who was in perpetual motion—either running away from something or running to a new opportunity. He had no interest in a static life or one he perceived that might slow him down. He had no idea where he was running to, but it was always at full speed. His departure broke Sue Ann's heart, but he made good on his promise that one day he would return. He had plenty of firsthand experience of abandonment himself.

From Myrtle Beach, Steve worked his way back north to New York City, where he found employment as a checker in a department store and later loaded trucks at the docks. He was certainly becoming a jack-of-all-trades. Steve hadn't seen his mother in more than a year, and he sought out Julian in April 1947 to get her blessing to join the Marines. McQueen never really gave a reason for wanting to join other than it offered a new challenge. "It was in the unsettled days just after World War II had ended, and why I picked the Marine Corps I still don't know. I suppose I had heard enough of the stories about how tough the Corps was that I considered it somewhat of a challenge."[2] Steve had unknowingly followed in his father's footsteps once again, and it was also a McQueen family tradition to serve his country. It also made sense from a psychological standpoint, according to Peter O. Whitmer. "One could argue that the Marine Corps replicated all that had come before," Whitmer said. "All the tensions and mixed messages that created his first 17 years were there for him once again for the next three.

"First, the need to conform was there. He had to wear a uniform. He had to be part of a team effort. There was constant flux in his life, regardless of uniformity. It was always changing to whom he reported; he always changed his physical place and changed his duty, as well. These three years were 'déjà vu all

---

2   Military service seemed a part of McQueen's DNA, as his father William T. McQueen served in the U.S. Marine Corps from 1927–1929.

over again.' It reinforced what he already knew so well and set the blueprint for what was to come."

The law required that anyone under the age of 18 have a signed consent waiver by a parent. McQueen's United States Marine Corps Enlistment Contract shows that Julian received 75 percent of Steve's pay, an act that showed he deeply cared for his mother's financial well-being. The document also shows that McQueen falsified information on his application by answering "No" to the following question: "Have you ever been in jail, a reform school, or industrial school or penitentiary?" To ensure that there was no reference to his stay at the Boys Republic, McQueen listed Hudson, New York, as the last place where he received both his grammar and high school education.[3] His mother's New York City address aided in the cover-up.

"The Marines were a little bit more lenient back then and weren't as picky as they are today," said Bobby Joe Harris, a decorated Vietnam veteran, former drill instructor, and Marine historian. "Back then the Marines took in a lot of troubled youth and turned them into real men, and McQueen is the perfect example of this."

On April 28, 1947—almost a year to the day he left the Boys Republic— Steve McQueen walked into the United States Marine Corps Northeastern Recruiting Division District Headquarters at 90 Church Street in New York City to enlist. After he scored a 78 on his competency test, McQueen signed a three-year contract with USMC recruiter Captain Coburn Marston. A physical examination that day showed McQueen to be a healthy and robust 17-year-old, standing at 5'6½"[4] and weighing 135 pounds. (When he exited three years later, he stood 5'9½" and tipped the scales at 162 pounds.) The examination also revealed that McQueen had no noticeable hearing problems.[5] (He could hear up to 15 feet in both the right and left ears.) He had 20/20 vision and was diagnosed with second-degree flat feet. McQueen's pulse was 76 beats per minute, and his blood pressure was 126 (systolic) over 70 (diastolic). Declared fit for duty, McQueen was given his military number—649015.

Along with recruits Michael Thomas Devlin, John Leonard Hanlon, Seymour Maron, and Vincent Raymond Plower, McQueen raised his right hand and

---

3   McQueen's formal education ended in ninth grade at the Boys Republic.

4   Steve McQueen's height is often disputed and widely debated. Some parties reported him to be as tall as 5'11", others as short as 5'6". Most family and friends believe it was around 5'10" to 5'11".

5   A major oversight, given that McQueen once swore, "It would take an act of Congress to get me to wear an ear harness."

took the Marine oath to protect and uphold his country. When he was finished, McQueen became the property of the U.S. Marines for the next 36 months.

Travel orders for the five recruits show they took a ferry and no fewer than three connecting trains to reach their final destination—the Marine Corps Recruiting Depot in Parris Island, South Carolina. The 800-mile trek took almost a day and a half of travel, and the men arrived exhausted, disoriented, and emotionally spent, which was entirely by design, according to Bobby Joe Harris, a former marine drill instructor. "Recruits are screamed at immediately and are told how to stand, with their heels together, feet at a 45-degree angle, thumbs along the seams of the trousers with palms in, eyes forward, shoulders squared, chest out, and chin in. They are informed that if they eyeball one of their drill instructors, they'll never see again. That's when they start asking themselves, 'Lord, what have I gotten myself into?'" Harris said. "Once all their heads are shaved, their clothes are taken away, boxed and shipped back home. They are issued trousers, boxer shorts, tennis shoes, boots, T-shirts, and a cover. The Marines want to dehumanize the recruit so that there is no room for individuality. You want to scare the piss out of them to ensure they obey your every order. It has to be that way with recruits so that when the time comes in combat, they can take anything coming their way. If you tell them to do something, you don't want them questioning your authority. You start instilling discipline from the second they get there." Steve had enlisted in the most authoritarian regime he could have found, and given his long track record of animosity toward any form of authority, he must have surely wanted to give himself a challenge.

McQueen was fond of telling reporters that his stint in the service turned out to be less than perfect and gave it his own special spin. "I was busted back down to private about seven times. The only way I could have made corporal was if all the other privates in the Marines dropped dead," he joked. But that was not entirely true. McQueen's service records show no such demotion ever took place. Most likely that statement was made to enhance his rebel status and maintain his everyman reputation, but it was false. According to Bobby Joe Harris, McQueen ascended in rank rather quickly despite serving in the Marines during nonwartime, proving once again that he could excel if he applied himself. However, that wasn't to say McQueen didn't have a few chicken tracks in his military file.

All recruits are required to pass the Marines' boot camp, which is a grueling exercise designed among other things to instill discipline and to test a recruit's mental and physical toughness. From sunup to sundown, recruits must endure 12 weeks of drill instruction, physical training (which includes swims, hikes, jogs, and a timed obstacle course), qualification with an M-1 rifle, and familiarization with a Colt .45 1911 semiautomatic pistol. McQueen qualified as a sharpshooter in boot camp with the M-1 rifle and later attained sharpshooter status with the Colt. 45 while in advanced training. Handling firearms was a skill that Steve would take onto the screen to profound effect. The way he handles his rifle in *The Sand Pebbles* and *Tom Horn* or brandishes the pump action shotgun in *The Getaway* is deeply impressive. He made it seem as though he used those weapons his whole life; he made them become more than just props, and these weapons would become natural extensions of his body and exponents of the lengths his characters were prepared to go to.

In addition to weapons training, recruits are taught Marine Corps history, basic procedure, how to address officers, how to pack their gear, make their bunks, properly hang and fold their clothes, shine their shoes and belt buckles, as well as assemble and disassemble their weapons.

After completing boot camp, McQueen was assigned on August 7, 1947, to the 1st Battalion, 4th Marines at Camp Lejeune, North Carolina, for infantry training. Five weeks later he was transferred to the Second Amphibian Tractor Battalion, Second Marine Division, Fleet Marine Force for Military Occupational Specialty Training and advanced training.

A natural aptitude for engines landed Steve a job as a tank crewman/driver. He learned the ins and outs and subtleties of the M4 Sherman tank—its height (9'), length (19'2"), width (8'), operational range (120 miles), and speed (38.5 mph). However, he learned one simple truth: "I'd often wondered if a tank could be speed converted. We figured on havin' the fastest tank in the division. What we got was plenty of skinned knuckles. I found out you can't soup up a tank."

His military career was on the fast track when McQueen was promoted from private to private first class on September 18, 1947, a mere five months after his enlistment, which was considered exceptional for that era, according to Harris. McQueen's promotion coincided with his assignment to the Amphibious Tractor Company in Quantico, Virginia, approximately 35 miles south of Washington, D.C., where he received his military operational specialty training. Upon his arrival in September 1947, McQueen was given a medical examination by a doctor at the Navy Yard Dispensary, who noticed a 5-centimeter laceration on the inside of his lower lip. McQueen told the doctor he sustained the laceration as a result of being struck in the mouth with a Coca-Cola bottle in a gang fight; the laceration was sutured, but a small mass had formed. A year later, McQueen sustained another laceration on the same location as a result of a fall off a tank. The mass grew and caused McQueen considerable difficulty in eating and talking. Plastic surgery was scheduled for McQueen, where the mass was excised, and he was able to report for duty a few days later. McQueen once told a reporter the laceration caused him to mumble and made certain letters and words hard to pronounce, which is why he preferred monosyllabic dialogue.

It was in Quantico where McQueen distinguished himself as a charismatic individual, a stylish dresser, and a real ladies' man, according to former Sergeant Cliff Anderson. However, he was not someone who was going to have a long career as a Leatherneck. "He was very typical of a large percentage of the men in the Marines, but a good Marine? From a first sergeant's standpoint? A company commander's standpoint? Hell no!" Anderson said. "There was a term they used back then and it's a term they probably use now, and that is that Steve was a 'fuckup.' He was always fucking up."

The two lived on the second floor of the Brownfield barracks and were billeted within yards of each other, but Anderson had a couple of stripes on McQueen. In short order, the pair discovered they hailed from the same state. "We got talking about Slater and North Kansas City, where I'm from, because we were two guys from Missouri. Back then a lot of guys did that—you became buddies with someone from your home state. You were always looking for some-body close to home," Anderson said.

Anderson nicknamed him "Tough Shit McQueen" because of the first two initials on McQueen's uniform. "It read 'T.S. McQueen' and so I called him 'Tough Shit,' partly because he was pugnacious and partly because back then, you gave your buddies a nickname." Anderson learned quickly his new buddy was one shrewd customer. Shortly after he got settled in, McQueen approached Anderson to request latrine duty. Anderson was taken aback because it was a job that didn't solicit many volunteers. It took a while, but Anderson later discovered why. "He worked like hell those first few days and he'd get that floor shined good, real spic and span. After he got it in good shape, he'd go into the latrine, lock the door, bundle up his jacket and then sleep on the floor for another 45 minutes. He got a little extra sleep that way, but I really didn't care as long as he took care of business."

Steve's penchant for sleep earned him his first disciplinary action when he was caught taking a nap while on duty. For that infraction, McQueen was put on restrictive duty for a week, which meant he could not leave the base during that period. He never responded well to being caged in, as recalled by Cliff Anderson, who said McQueen usually headed to Baltimore, Maryland, where he had been making time with a young lady. "That was back when women wore lipstick and the two would be smooching all night and McQueen came back with rosy lips. Steve usually hitchhiked to and from Baltimore, and he'd come back late at night or early morning. Let's just say there was more than one time when I covered for him when we were at roll call and I'd wait a few extra minutes for McQueen so I wouldn't have to report him."

McQueen was still unable to conform. Anderson said McQueen dressed like a "Los Angeles pachuco" (peg pants, gold chains, and a comb in his back pocket) and sported a ducktail haircut when he wasn't in uniform. His individuality and code of dress sparked a lot of fistfights, said Anderson, who witnessed a superior dressing down McQueen in front of the troops. "The sergeant major on duty yelled out, 'McQueen, goddamnit, you're not getting any liberty until you get a haircut!' He made McQueen fall out right then and there. He said, 'McQueen, get that ducktail cut off. I want that barber to cut that son of a bitch off like it was back in boot camp!' And McQueen still didn't do it. I don't know if he got office hours for it or not, but he was proud of that ducktail. I wished I would have taken some pictures of him back then because he was a real piece of work."

Anderson had all but forgotten about his marine buddy until a decade later when Anderson was leafing through a copy of *TV Guide* in the letters section where a fan had asked about McQueen. Then it finally hit Anderson: *Holy cow, that's Tough Shit McQueen! The son of a bitch is famous!*

From Quantico, Virginia, McQueen was transferred to the United States Naval Gun Factory in Washington, D.C., on December 31, 1948, where he served in the 1st Guard Company. McQueen served as a guard at the site for five months and received his final assignment as a tanker at Camp Lejeune, North Carolina, in May 1949. The assignment brought McQueen much closer to Sue Ann in Myrtle Beach, which was approximately a two-hour drive. Their proximity eventually led to trouble for McQueen. According to his service record, McQueen received a deck court citation for going Absent Without Leave (AWOL) from July 11, 1949, to July 15, 1949. For the infraction, McQueen was docked $40 for a period of one month, confined to the base for 10 days, and placed on six months of probation.

The punishment didn't dissuade the unrepentant marine from pulling the same stunt almost five months later, when McQueen stretched his Thanksgiving holiday. He went AWOL again on November 28, 1949, and didn't return until December 6, 1949. "Marines going AWOL happens more than you think," said Bobby Joe Harris. "I can pretty much guess how the conversation went down. 'Hey, honey, can't you stay a little longer?' 'Yeah, it'll cost me some liberty, but you're worth it!' It happens all the time."

McQueen knew he was up for serious reprimand, which is why he got into a scuffle with Patrolman Floyd Denton of the Raleigh, North Carolina, Police

Department. The Marines had issued a "straggler" report on McQueen, who was apprehended and confined to the Wake County Jail.

While in jail, Denton took the following statement from McQueen on December 6, 1949:

> Statement Of Private First Class Terrance Steven McQueen (649015), USMC, Straggler
>
> I hereby certify that on 28 November, 1949, I was attached to and serving with "A" Co., 2d Amp Trac Bn, 2dMarDiv, FMF, Camp Lejeune, N.C.
>
> There are no criminal charges pending against me.
>
> I was apprehended by civil authorities on 6 December, 1949, while absent from "A" Co., 2d Amph Trac Bn, 2dMarDiv, FMF, Camp Lejeune, N.C., and delivered to DHRS, Raleigh, N.C.
>
> I did not register for the selective service. My Marine Corps serial number is 649015.
>
> I do not desire to make any further statement at this time.
>
> Terrance Steven McQueen

McQueen was transported back to Camp Lejeune the following day to face court martial, where they would "impress seriousness disobedience orders," according to a military document. On December 15, 1949, McQueen was given a summary court martial for going AWOL and fighting with authorities. He was sentenced to confinement for a period of 41 days and docked $30 per month for the next 90 days. McQueen had landed himself in the brig. "You think boot camp was bad? The brig was bad. Let's just say if you have an attitude coming in, you don't have one coming out," said Bobby Joe Harris. "Marines are put through endless drills and harsh punishment, and in some cases, they're asked to make little rocks out of big rocks."

In McQueen's case, he was placed on a work detail in the hold of a ship, cleaning and renovating the engine room. This would provide excellent experience for him to use in his numerous engine-room scenes that are so important to his character in The Sand Pebbles, such as, "Hello Engine, I'm Jake Holman," followed by a friendly pat to the machinery. A portion of the work included ripping out ceilings and pipes, both of which were lined with asbestos. McQueen later recalled to director John Sturges, "The air was so thick with asbestos particles that the men could hardly breathe." McQueen's court martial, intentioned to straighten him out, in all likelihood became a death sentence. Nearly 30 years later, he was dead from a rare form of cancer. The cause was asbestos inhalation.

• • •

McQueen admitted to a writer that his 41-day session (December 20, 1949, to January 29, 1950) in the brig didn't tame him much, but he got one message loud and clear: "When you're in the Marines, Uncle Sam calls the shots. What you *don't* do is go running off to see your chick."

Save for one final infraction for sleeping in late (he served 10 hours of KP duty), McQueen vowed to make time serve him instead of him serving time. He focused his energies on improving himself and staying out of trouble for the rest of his time in the military. He later acknowledged, "The Marines gave me discipline I could live with. By the time I got out, I was able to cope with things on a more realistic level. All in all, despite my problems, I liked being in the Marines."

Several curious rumors and oft-told sea stories have followed McQueen for more than five decades regarding his time in the service.

Rumor No. 1: McQueen rescued a crew of tankers during an exercise in the Labrador Sea near Newfoundland. That rumor emanated from an "as told to" story by McQueen to writer Jack Lewis (a lieutenant colonel in the USMC) for a story titled "Cast-Iron Coffin." The account appeared in the November 1961 issue of *Battle Station* and was later reprinted by *Leatherneck* in June 2009. The story went beyond fabrication; it was pure fantasy. Either McQueen had an overactive imagination or Lewis' prose went into overdrive, giving the story a *Soldier of Fortune* slant:

> The forest green amphibious tractor was pitching in the heavy seas like an unbroken bronc poisoned on loco weed, its several tons of metal riding cork-like on the incoming tide. Even as I tried, half-frozen, to shout instructions to the three men clinging desperately to the top of the foundered tank, I knew they couldn't hear me over the pounding surf and the sounds of my craft's engine.
>
> A giant wave—a wall of water at least a dozen feet high—crashed down upon the tracked amphib where I clung like a crab avoiding the boiling pot. It was like being hit by a fast freight. The force of the water and the frigid temperature drew the breath out of me, the shock making it impossible to move. And in that moment, I knew fear—the feeling of fighting something that's insurmountable.

It was drama on the high seas, with McQueen and his crew volunteering to save three tankers. That is, until McQueen tied a rope between the two tanks and hauled the crew back to safety. The account ended with the hero (McQueen) sitting on the sandy beach, his body heaving with exhaustion, sharing a bottle of medical brandy with the three men, or in one report five, whose lives he just saved. This is undoubtedly a story fit for any McQueen film. But was it true?

McQueen's service record shows the exercise, called *Operation Normax*, embarked at Little Creek, Virginia, and disembarked at Onlsow Beach, North Carolina. The landing ship tank was nowhere near Newfoundland, and McQueen's heroic actions would have surely garnered a commendation or medal for bravery. None exist in his service record; neither is this incident ever mentioned. However, the exercise was not without adventure. McQueen's service file indicates that he was hospitalized when his amphibious tank caught on fire. Though not burned, McQueen ingested a large amount of smoke, which resulted in gagging and violent coughing. Fifteen hours after the mishap, McQueen complained of a burning sensation in his chest and lungs. Perhaps this was the real reason why he embellished the story to Lewis—it was certainly nowhere near as exciting as the one that ended up in print.

Rumor No. 2: McQueen got hopped up on liquor, hijacked a tank, painted it pink, and went for a spin in the downtown area of a nearby municipality outside of Marine Corps Base Camp Pendleton in San Diego County, California. The story takes on epic proportions when McQueen smashes several cars in his path with MPs and local police in hot pursuit. The fact that McQueen was never stationed at Camp Pendleton should have immediately dismissed this rumor. A crime of that nature would have surely garnered news coverage, not to mention hard time in Fort Leavenworth prison. Still, the urban legend continues to be rehashed and told by civilians and exservicemen alike. McQueen himself probably fostered this daredevil tale himself to further his mystique.

Rumor No. 3: McQueen's highest honor in the Marines was serving as part of the Honor Guard who protected President Harry Truman's yacht, the historic *Sequoia*. That detail is not mentioned in McQueen's military file, and fellow soldier Cliff Anderson said even if it was true, it wasn't the *Sequoia* that McQueen guarded, nor was the duty much of an honor. "Harry Truman's first yacht was the *USS Potomac*, which was really in decline after he inherited it from President Roosevelt. Truman might have used the *Potomac* three times. It was so rarely used that a tree grew through the bottom of it, and [it] ended up on a sand bar. So by the time it gets out that you guarded Truman's ship, it sounds real good. The reality was you couldn't have a lower form of duty because nobody was going to screw with the boat."

Rumor No. 4: McQueen's tank unit was "wiped out" in the Korean crisis three weeks after his discharge. This statement first appeared in Neile McQueen's book, *My Husband, My Friend* in 1986, and it has often been repeated. There is no documented proof by the military this ever happened to the 2nd Assault Amphibious Battalion, which was deactivated on October 16, 1949, as a result of the costs associated with the program. The battalion was reactivated on August 10, 1950, and placed in Korea. A year later it was reassigned to Force Troops, Fleet Marine Force. This story is most likely an embellishment McQueen told his first wife to spice up his time in the military.

What cannot be disputed is that Private First Class Steve McQueen received an honorable discharge on April 27, 1950, at Camp Lejeune under the expiration of his three-year enlistment agreement. He received a muster-out pay of $40 and a set of valuable tools that stayed with him for the rest of his life. "[The Marines] made a man out of me," McQueen later admitted. "I learned how to get along with others, and I had a platform to jump off of." There is no denying McQueen got so many of his trademark nuances and experiences from his time in the Marines. He finally had some discipline that he could almost abide by, and he managed to establish relationships with others. Perhaps the most appealing aspect for McQueen was that he was able to play with firearms and anything with an engine to his heart's content, consolidating his lifelong passion with both.

McQueen was certainly able to jump off, as he put it, and he landed in the most unlikely of places—acting.

6
THE ACTOR'S LIFE

Steve McQueen celebrated his April 1950 discharge from the service with a group of college students in Myrtle Beach where he was greeted with sunshine, bikinis, the beach, and the waiting arms of a Southern Belle.

Armed with his muster-out pay, McQueen resumed his relationship with 19-year-old Sue Ann, who gave him a glimpse of a conventional life and an antebellum world that outsiders rarely experienced. "I'd been going with a girl there, so I stayed at the beach and ran around with her crowd, 18, 19 years old—college kids, you know," McQueen recounted to a reporter. "And I thought this was wonderful, going over to people's houses for dinner and getting dressed up, going to dances, and everybody liked you, and you were saying 'hello' to people. I mean, I never had this before." The relationship intensified to the point where a job offer was made to Steve by Sue Ann's affluent father, who was ready to set up Steve for the rest of his life if he married his daughter. The move backfired, and Steve reacted like a spooked horse; he left town abruptly that night. He never saw Sue Ann again. Life had already taught him to be wary of relationships and that people were hard to trust.

Steve made his way north to Washington, D.C., where he landed a job as a taxi mechanic and drove a cab part time, adding to his already eclectic résumé. To him, though, nothing was happening in the nation's capitol. He was still a wanderer, trying to find his place in the world. "New York seemed to be where the real action was, and that's where I headed."

• • •

New York City in the '50s was the place to be. As many of the world's great cities lay in ruin after World War II, Gotham emerged as the new world headquarters for commerce, finance, culture, fashion, media, and entertainment. Within its 12 miles of concrete, glass, and overcrowding arose a new openness that changed the way people expressed their creativity, with the embrace of psychoanalysis, marijuana, sexual expression, and the stirring of the women's movement redefining the times. It was the golden era of the white male in America, and it was the perfect place for Steve McQueen to reinvent himself.

Steve and Julian eventually patched things up, and upon her recommendation, he moved in with photographer and aspiring playwright Gene Lesser. "I knew Julian through her boyfriend Victor Lukens. She was a lovely looking woman and had a great sense of humor," Lesser said in 2010. "One day we were sitting at the bar and drinking a beer and she said, 'My kid's coming here and needs a place to stay. Can you put him up?' I said, 'Sure,' and that's how I was introduced to Steve."

Lesser rented a $19 per month cold-water flat in Greenwich Village, which included two beds, a shared community bathroom, and not much else. It didn't take Lesser long to discover his new roommate was different. "Steve was a complex guy, even back then. He made friends pretty easily, and yet he was a loner," Lesser said. "He was very careful about who he befriended and never discussed with me or anyone else his personal life. He was a brooder, and there were times when he shut down completely. There were certain touchstones, like the Boys Republic, that he never talked about. I learned very early on not to get into his face during those times. It was very easy to tell when he needed his space."

Greenwich Village offered plenty of refuge for a young man on the go. At its epicenter was Washington Square Park, a bohemian playpen where the freewheeling street-theater scene was in full bloom, where folk musicians wrote radical essays in song form, and where the Beat poets toked on their French cigarettes for creative inspiration. It was in this setting where McQueen forged an identity of his own. He immediately succeeded on one level: he naturally drew attention to himself with members of the opposite sex. McQueen developed a reputation for cruising around the park on a motorcycle, often with his shirt off. "Things happened in the Village," Steve said. "Good things. Bad things. People expected you to be a little off-center when you lived there. The chicks were wilder and the pace was faster. I dug it."

Lesser said McQueen's relationships with women were complex, with a mix of pleasure and frustration. "I remember one time we were at a party and there was this cute little blonde who gravitated toward him. He went to get a drink, and I ended up talking with this gal," Lesser said. "When Steve came back, he was pissed that I bothered to talk to her. He was furious and stomped off. Later that night I asked him what he was so hot about, and he said he thought I was trying to put the make on his girl. Women adored him, but there was a streak of insecurity within him. He never thought of himself in those days as a good-looking guy."

Lesser's apartment was within walking distance of Julian, who lived as a boarder at 117 MacDougal Street. By 1950 the relationship between Julian and Victor Lukens had cooled and the two were in a transitional phase.[1] Victor found her a room in a flat owned by friends Harold[2] and Felicia Anton. "My father was a starving artist and rented a room to Julian for about six months to help pay the bills," recalled professor Anatole Anton, who was around 10 at the time. "It was a heavy drinking scene, and Dad's drinking put a burden on the women and the children, but Julian added some lightness to our lives. Her presence helped alleviate a lot of tension in our household." As for Victor, Anton said he remembers an affable and generous man who would announce his presence by yelling, "Geronimo!" when he entered the apartment.[3]

Anton said Steve, who was not famous at the time, occasionally visited his mother at the flat. He did not witness a hostile relationship or a pair at odds with each other. "She was very sweet and loving with Steve, and watching them was touching," Anton recalled.

McQueen rarely displayed his tender side and showed a different face in public, often exuding an intensity behind the reserved cool. He liked the fact that he didn't spend many nights in his flat, somehow always managing to find shelter in a young woman's apartment. The arms of a beautiful young woman were more appealing than a cramped cold-water flat. Susan Oliver, an actress who dated McQueen when he lived in the Village, said he was hard to miss. "Steve had a casual, cool, don't-give-a-damn attitude that a lot of women found attractive. I rode with him on the back of his cycle. One thing I remember is how hungry he always was. He'd eat with a slab of pie in one hand and a sandwich in the other, as if each meal were the last. Intense. That's what Steve was—very intense. Even in the Village, people noticed him. And I think he liked the attention," Oliver said. She soon gave McQueen the heave-ho after floating him loans for gas, coffee, or meals. Oliver kindly suggested to McQueen that he find a girlfriend who had extra money and didn't mind footing the bill for him.

---

1   Linda Lukens said her late husband claimed he and Julian had a tumultuous relationship that included several breakups and reconciliations over a period of years.

2   Harold Anton was an abstract artist who shared a Sullivan Street art studio in Greenwich Village in the 1930s with abstract expressionist Arshile Gorky.

3   Victor Lukens was not only an artist but a great supporter and patron of the arts. He made art supply purchases for Harold Anton and helped him launch art exhibits of his work at commercial galleries.

Steve's lack of formal education didn't prevent him from finding employment, but it confined him to menial and mind-numbing jobs. For someone with
his energy and spirit, none of these would last. He handcrafted sandals, lugged
radiators out of condemned buildings, loaded bags in the post office, ran errands
for a local bookie, recapped tires in a garage, sold encyclopedias door-to-door,
made artificial flowers in a musty 3rd Avenue basement, and repaired television
sets. "I worked for a friend who had a TV repair shop. But I told a friend of mine
he was being taken by the shop owner because he'd tape on old burned-out tubes
when he returned the set and claim he'd taken them out of the set and put in
new ones when he hadn't," McQueen said. "He'd get any old beat-up tubes from
radios and stick them on top the repaired sets going back. So he found out what
I said, and I was out of a job. We got into a little hassle—he threw a lawn mower
at me. The cops came." McQueen also tried his hand at boxing. "After getting
knocked flat on my duff, I gave it a quick pass."

He even contemplated becoming a jazz musician after his exposure to one
of America's most original art forms in many of the Village's clubs. He loved the
music, the musicians' upside-down hours, and daily intake of marijuana (a habit
that stuck with McQueen for many decades). McQueen tried blowing alto sax
for a while, but he realized that making music wasn't for him. "If you want to be
a musician, you've got to devote all your time to it," Steve said. "Besides, it's a
rotten life. You don't eat steady."

McQueen fell back on the skills he had learned on the streets when he was
a gang member, resorting to lifting food from grocery stores, stealing tips from
bars and tables in coffeehouses, and giving impromptu tours of the Village to
unsuspecting tourists in exchange for a hearty meal. "Starving, I used to latch
on to some beautiful girl and offer her a guided tour of Greenwich Village. She'd
usually buy me lunch, and I'd really load up," Steve said.

He also developed a scam in which he walked into Hanson's, a Village drugstore, picked up a shower nozzle from the shelves, and then asked the clerk for
a refund on it. McQueen was promptly handed $5.30 and ate for two days on
that giveaway, and he used it many times later when scrounging for cash. His first
wife, Neile, would later recall that Steve often pulled this trick again many years
later, as a firmly established megastar, just to see if he still had the gift. He did.
Their home was also littered with nicked items from various hotels around the
world, which included paintings, ashtrays, and knick-knacks.

For all the excitement of living in New York, McQueen was living a hand-to-
mouth existence and was haunted by a vision that someday he would be standing
on the street corner at age 50, begging for spare change. He began to take stock

of himself. "I asked myself the bitter question: *Man, where are you going? When are you gonna get with it?* And I had no answer. Talk about beat! I was it!"

Many theories abound as to how Steve McQueen discovered acting, and he often perpetuated the notion that it was through "a little bird I knew, who was a part-time actress." McQueen was referring to Donna Barton, an entertainer from England, whom he spotted inside Hanson's Drugstore in the Village. Barton was a dancer at the world famous Copacabana nightclub, and she had recently divorced Sid Bulkin, a New York–based jazz drummer who played for Glenn Miller, Ella Fitzgerald, Frank Sinatra, and Nat King Cole. Barton was definitely McQueen's type: a buxom blonde with long legs, a taut body, and wholesome looks.

Barton later recalled to writer Tim Satchell, "He was small and gorgeous. Those blue eyes and a fantastic body, like a Greek god. He was very fit and very athletic. His face was perfect." The two met for their first date at the San Remo, an Italian restaurant at the corner of Bleecker and MacDougal Streets in Greenwich Village. Barton paid the bill, and the two went home together. McQueen moved into her place the next day. He was not ashamed to freeload and let the lady pick up the bill. If he was ever given an inch, McQueen would do his best to take a mile.

Barton was taking lessons at The Neighborhood Playhouse, a two-year drama school in Manhattan, when she suggested Steve should give acting a shot. "I got this crazy notion about going to Spain, where there's a lot of tile, and studyin' over there—but this chick I was with, who was tryin' to break into show business, had an idea that sounded even crazier. She told me I should become an actor," Steve told one reporter.

McQueen had firm encouragement about getting into acting from other quarters, too. Most likely it was Victor Lukens, Julian's on-again off-again boyfriend who gave Steve his first glimpse of the thespian's life. Lukens, a beatnik who hailed from the Lukens Steel family in Pittsburgh, was the director of cinematography for Audio Productions Inc., and he specialized in documentaries and industrial films. He was a member of the Directors Guild of America, as well as an architect, inventor, pilot, artist, furniture maker (his work has been featured in *Time, Life,* and *Vogue*), and racer (Lukens formed a team called Racemasters and competed in the Grand Prix, 12 Hours of Sebring, and Le Mans).

Widow Linda Lukens said her late husband is the person most responsible for McQueen choosing the actor's life, and Victor Lukens also introduced McQueen to professional racing. "Steve created this myth about his life and his childhood, and Victor has sadly been partially erased from his history," Linda Lukens said. "It would have taken away from the myth to credit Victor as the man who helped him become an actor. Steve was in all likelihood going to be a mechanic had Victor not interceded and introduced [Steve] to the legendary Sanford Meisner. It made for a much better story to say he fell into acting through a girlfriend."

Canadian television producer Henry Less, who was a protégé of Lukens, said McQueen was definitely championed by Lukens. "Victor told me he brought Steve to a couple of his sets to witness the behind the scenes of what went on during a shoot," Less said. "I don't know how [McQueen] eventually transitioned into acting, but I do know that Victor was the first person to plant the seed."

Linda Lukens and Henry Less certainly make a strong case for Lukens because McQueen used Lukens' 19 Barrow Street address. He also listed Lukens as a professional reference on his application to the Neighborhood Playhouse. Steve's application was dated June 25, 1951. Lukens also footed McQueen's bill for his application fee and first year of lessons. McQueen cited several industrial films he made with Lukens on his professional résumé, including one film called *Family Affair*, which was sponsored by Bell Telephone and cast McQueen as a sailor. This 26-minute film somehow survived through the years and is McQueen's earliest known celluloid appearance.[4] "Victor was in the film business and was friends with acting teacher Sanford Meisner. Victor called Meisner when he needed someone to appear in his films," Linda Lukens said. "Victor and Sanford both knew Steve was naturally talented, and they took a big interest in him."

Linda Lukens said her late husband also encouraged Steve to keep his name-sake. "Victor said Steve wanted to use 'Berri' as his last name," Lukens said. "Steve had been abandoned as a child and he was very ashamed of using his father's last name—McQueen. Victor insisted that Steve McQueen was a great name, so he kept it."

He had more than just a name. McQueen possessed an aura and presence that spells magic for an actor. Sanford Meisner, a sophisticated former actor and classical musician who ran the Neighborhood Playhouse for nearly a half-century, said of McQueen, "He was original—both tough and childlike like Marilyn Monroe, as if he'd been through everything but had preserved a certain basic innocence. I accepted him at once," Meisner said. McQueen was chosen, along with 71 other young men and women, from approximately 3,000 applicants. He joined the ranks of Playhouse alumni such as Gregory Peck, Robert Duvall, Eli Wallach, James Caan, Suzanne Pleshette, Mark Rydell, Diane Keaton, Leslie Nielsen, and Peggy Feury, who in time became an invaluable acting resource for

---

4   By this author's estimate, it appears to have been filmed in 1951 or 1952.

McQueen. Although the Neighborhood Playhouse's list of luminaries is long and prestigious, no one ever reached the heights that McQueen scaled.

Friend Mark Rydell, who would direct Steve in *The Reivers* in the late '60s, knew McQueen when he was debating his future as a tile setter. Steve asked Rydell, "What do you think? Do you think I ought to make bathrooms, or do you think I ought to go to the Neighborhood Playhouse?" Rydell said McQueen chose acting simply because he didn't want to bust his ass. Other friends say it was a great way for McQueen to meet women. Both statements, some say, were right on the money. "Steve and I spent most of our time trying to get laid and nothing else," said Richard Martin, who met McQueen at Louis' Tavern, a well-known Greenwich Village hangout at 196 West 4th Street. "We both knew quite a few actors at Louis' Tavern and eventually decided to try acting. When asked what we did for a living, we answered we were actors," Martin said. "It was a good excuse for not having to work a 9-to-5 job, which in our minds was not an option." Louis' Tavern also appealed to McQueen on another level—it offered a house special of spaghetti and meatballs with a lettuce and tomato salad for 65 cents. McQueen befriended a cook named Sal and told him he was an actor who was flat broke. But McQueen proposed that he'd pay Sal back upon his first job. The two men shook hands and Sal served up a scrumptious meal. With each job McQueen landed, he would pay back faithfully. "Trust is different when you're broke," McQueen explained. "You're on the other end then, and the common commodity is sharing with other guys. We all shared a lot in the old days in New York."

The two things McQueen and Martin certainly shared was an appreciation for fast cars and the opposite sex. When Martin let McQueen take a spin in his MG sports car, their friendship was solidified. It was inside Louis' Tavern where the two young men scored lots of beautiful women, though Martin said that wasn't much of a stretch. "Louis' had girls, girls, girls. If you couldn't get laid in there, you had something seriously wrong with you." One of the women they frequently ran into was Steve's mother Julian, whom Martin said was usually drunk and trying to pick up men. "Steve pretended not to know her, and she would do the same," Martin recalled. "It was painful to watch and a very sad thing for Steve to have to witness."

In August 1951, McQueen received a formal acceptance letter from the Neighborhood Playhouse and was directed to report to the drama school in September at 340 East 54th Street in Manhattan. The letter included a laundry list of items to bring to class: shorts, T-shirt, a dance belt, white cotton socks, leotards, and ballet slippers. The list unnerved him. Steve always felt deep down underneath there was something unmanly about acting. "Candy-ass" was a favorite term of his when describing the art form. He didn't find the company of actors very exciting, either. "Actors, they bore me. They're mostly cornballs."

Martha Graham, the high priestess of modern dance, was McQueen's dance instructor. Graham had a fearless reputation and unsurprisingly butted heads with McQueen many times, who often complained about having to wear leotards. "She walked over to me one day and grabbed me by the groin and lifted me off the floor," said Harold G. Baldridge, who has been the Neighborhood Playhouse's executive director since 1983. "She said, 'There, now you'll know how to stand up straight!'" McQueen, who had never taken a ballet dance class in his life, showed his inexperience to Graham when he was told to "go and warm up" the first day of instruction. Rather than head to the stretching bar to limber up, he headed over to the corner of the room and placed his backside on the radiator!

In another unscripted moment, McQueen slugged fellow student Susan Shawn when she slapped him in the face during a reading. "I forgot we were acting. I let her have a short one. She hit the deck and I was scared to death, so scared I stayed away briefly from class," McQueen said.

Baldridge said Meisner was the ideal instructor for someone like McQueen. "Mr. Meisner was gentle but demanding in his own way. He had his days where he could be tough and pushed, but you always knew he was rooting for you." Meisner sensed McQueen's natural and unflagging sensitivities combined with searing pain, a young man who was a jumble of emotions. McQueen said Meisner's patience and sensitivity toward him finally paid off. "Until [Meisner] got after me, I understood nothing," McQueen said. "Raw talent must be channeled carefully or it can be ruined. Meisner knew just how to bring out the best in me, and he made me look deep into myself and face up to my potentials as well as my limitations. And let me tell you, I was no prized package for any teacher. I used to sit at the back of the class and talk to nobody. Meisner gradually weaned me out of that shell."

Wynn Handman, Meisner's assistant, likened McQueen to a ball of clay that was transformed into a granite bust with the help of Meisner and fellow teachers Louis Horst, Carol Veazie, and Martha Graham. "Meisner preferred what he called 'untutored' students so that he could train them from the start to avoid bad habits. Steve didn't have any bad habits that I recall, but it did take some effort to reach him on a personal level," Handman said. McQueen was hardened—a tough street kid who was wary of almost everyone, plus he had a nonconformist attitude in the classroom, according to Handman. However, over time, Steve literally became part of the Neighborhood Playhouse family. "My wife Bobby and I lived one door away from the Neighborhood Playhouse. When our baby daughter

Laura was born, she was known as the 'Neighborhood Playhouse Baby' because many of the students took turns babysitting for us. Steve pitched in occasionally. I understand he became a very good parent when he had children. I'm glad to have given him the experience," Handman said laughing.

On the first day of instruction, Meisner always began the first course with this statement: "The foundation of acting is the reality of doing nothing." It also became McQueen's calling card as an actor. It took years to perfect, but McQueen worked on stripping away the layers of his characters to their core essence to where he was most impressive standing still and saying absolutely nothing. Later, on the set of *Papillon*, he would advise Dustin Hoffman on his less-is-more approach. "Less, Dusty. Do less…"

To many of his classmates, McQueen was a mass of contradictions. He was known as a talented actor, but he appeared lazy, undisciplined, and uncommitted. "His whole attitude was, 'Well, show me,'" recalled Carol Veazie, his voice teacher at the Neighborhood Playhouse. "He was awfully short-tempered. He'd cut classes as often as he dared, and even when he did show up, he'd sleep. Yet when he gave himself to a scene, he could be unbelievably compelling. I kept thinking, 'This boy is different,' and asking myself, 'Why is he doing this to himself?' One day I made him listen to his voice on tape. He must have realized how bad he really was, because from that day on he started trying."

As usual with McQueen, this was not a straightforward case of laziness. There was an underlying reason. McQueen later blamed his poor attitude on lack of self-confidence, which was induced by his lack of education. Roommate Gene Lesser said he remembers the day McQueen walked into their flat with a William Shakespeare book under his arm, and McQueen barely understood the text. "He walked in and said casually, 'You've got to cue me.' I said, 'What are you talking about?' He told me he had signed up for the Neighborhood Playhouse and he was going to become an actor. I said, 'Okay, great.' So I cued him and he didn't even know what half the words in the book meant, nor could anybody else in those days.

"He was stilted when he first started, but he worked at it. Before each class I would cue him, and that's how he was able to cut it. Little by little he became an actor."

McQueen discovered that by letting himself go in improvisation ("turning myself in tight"), he was electrifying. And his real-world experience served him in a manner that his more formally educated peers could not comprehend. When he began to sense his own abilities, his confidence grew and he applied himself to his studies with great intensity. When the class assignment was to bring in five improvisations, McQueen brought in 10.

Handman said the worst play he ever directed at the playhouse was Noel Coward's *Still Life*. Despite this dubious honor, McQueen was still sensational. "That really says it all about McQueen in many ways—no matter how bad the movie or play or project was, McQueen was always good in whatever role you gave him," Handman said.

That wasn't the case with McQueen's first paying job in a Jewish play at the Molly Picon Theater at 12th Street and Second Avenue in Manhattan's Lower East Side. The role paid McQueen $40 a week and called for the Midwestern native to appear on stage, looking grim, and mutter, "Nothing will help," in Yiddish. He was dismissed after his fourth performance. McQueen quipped years later, when he was pulling down close to a million dollars a picture, "I guess it was my lousy Yiddish."

Classmate David Hedison (then known as Al Hedison) said he didn't detect an ounce of insecurity in McQueen—only a young man brimming with confidence. "Steve's big strength was his belief in himself. You couldn't call him a character actor. He was himself, which makes someone a star. All movie stars essentially play a variation of themselves on screen, and Steve fit into that mold," Hedison said. McQueen would eventually go on to refine his screen persona, developing his very own niche.

At the end of his first year at the Neighborhood Playhouse, McQueen rewarded himself with a trip to Miami. He and a buddy hitchhiked to the Sunshine State, where they found jobs as beach boys at a large resort. McQueen said he hustled drinks and cigarettes for "the old daddies while I took a shot at their chicks. I learned a lot about aggressive women in Miami."

It was on that same trip where McQueen punctured his left eardrum while scuba diving, the very same ear in which he had suffered a mastoid infection as a child. McQueen dove too deep and didn't acclimate correctly, and the resulting air pressure permanently damaged his hearing. He saved up enough money to work his way back to New York, where he found employment as an assistant tile setter and as a bartender.

He may have objected to acting as a "candy-ass" profession, but McQueen certainly enjoyed the lifestyle and benefits it brought, especially the female variety. New York City was a fertile proving ground for actors, writers, and directors. And with his immense drive to succeed, McQueen was determined to take a bite of the Big Apple. "We would meet almost every day at Café Figaro on Bleecker Street, an espresso bar and restaurant," said Richard Martin. "We would hang out there, smoke some marijuana, then later in the day we would go to midtown Manhattan and have a juice at the Salad Bowl, a health food restaurant that just so happened to be a good place to meet women." It was also the site of great live theater according to Martin, who watched future actor-writer-director Paul Mazursky flip burgers as a short-order cook and *Route 66* actor George Maharis wait tables. "Steve and I got a big kick out of Maharis, because he threw down the knife and fork at people instead of laying it down like you would if you're waiting on tables. We got a lot of laughs watching him work."

Other days, Martin and McQueen walked to the third floor of the NBC Building on 6th Avenue, where actors took a breather and sat down to compare notes after making the casting rounds (where McQueen befriended writer and gadfly Dominick Dunne, who was the stage manager for NBC's *Robert Montgomery Presents*). The two usually ended their evenings at the Actor's Service on West 58th Street, a telephone switchboard service where actors could pick up their messages for casting calls or jobs, or they could just hang out in the lounge and play poker. Martin recalled a day in the lounge when someone took an informal poll about which actor would become the next big star. McQueen came in last and just let it go. McQueen, of course, had the last laugh. "What surprised me most, and probably hurt my ego, was when we started making rounds, the casting directors were fascinated with Steve but not very interested in me," Martin said. "I shrugged it off reasoning that the Marlon Brando types were in and the leading-men types were temporarily out of vogue. If you had asked me then if I thought Steve McQueen had a real chance to be a movie star, I would have answered no—which goes to show how much I knew."

In the Neighborhood Playhouse's year-end showcase, a production of *Truckline Café*, McQueen played the Marlon Brando role and was mesmerizing, according to agent Peter Witt, who was always on the watch for new talent. When the play was over, Witt was spellbound by McQueen, who looked like the all-American actor. After the performance, Witt gave McQueen his business card and asked if he needed an agent. "Not yet. I'm still a student," McQueen said cautiously. Witt eventually landed McQueen a few jobs and became his first agent of record.

Despite his trepidation with Witt at the time, McQueen was convinced that stardom was just around the corner for both him and his *Truckline Café* costar Al Hedison. "We both gave excellent performances that night. Afterward, Steve came up to me, put his arm around my shoulder and said, 'Al, you and I are going to be stars!'" The statement stuck with Hedison because not only did it strike him as funny, but also because McQueen was so sure of himself. McQueen's prediction of stardom was starting to come to fruition by the fall of 1958 when Hedison was cruising down Sunset Boulevard past the Oriental Theater. The double feature on the marquee almost floored him. Hedison couldn't believe his eyes. It read, "Steve McQueen—*The Blob* and Al Hedison—*The Fly.*" Hedison laughed aloud and shook his head in disbelief with McQueen's words from years before still ringing in his head.

7

THE YOUNG LIONS

WHEN STEVE MCQUEEN graduated from the Neighborhood Playhouse in 1952, he was once again at a crossroads in his life. He was living in a cold-water flat, driving a truck for the post office, and getting into all sorts of mischief, including a few run-ins with New York's finest. McQueen said he was on a first-name basis with a lot of the beat cops in Greenwich Village.

"Before, I could never find a level with society. I came from poor people used to having to make a living to stay alive," McQueen said. "I got into situations I wasn't bright about. I didn't have any conception of what I was like—so I existed in it—so I got into trouble."

Actor John Gilmore[1] and his girlfriend, Dianne Rico, were having a drink in Louis' Tavern when they heard the roar of a motorcycle engine, then a collision. Reflexively they snatched their drinks off their small table as McQueen and his bike plummeted down the steps into the barroom. According to Gilmore, McQueen plowed through a glass door and landed face down on the floor—that is until a couple of large gun-toting wiseguys carried McQueen out of the bar and deposited the struggling actor and his bike back on the sidewalk.

McQueen told columnist Hedda Hopper that he was so lost during this period that he became despondent for weeks at a time, and he even contemplated a singing career. "I went to three teachers and they gave me my money back. They said, 'We can do you no good, pal.' You know how long it took me to go up and down the scale? Four visits! We'd sit around and drink tea and I finally sang up and down the scale. The teacher finally stood up and said, 'I am sending you your money back. In all honesty, I must tell you to stick to acting.'" This was typical

---

1 Gilmore is one of America's most revered noir writers, and his 1997 memoir, *Laid Bare*, is one of the best books ever on Hollywood.

of McQueen and his mercurial nature. He would put a tremendous amount of energy into something, but if it did not pay back immediately, his enthusiasm would dwindle.

It was strictly fate when McQueen was introduced to Herbert Berghof and Uta Hagen by way of friend Richard Martin. Shortly thereafter, McQueen enrolled (he claims he won a scholarship) in their drama school, which was a fourth-floor loft at 23rd Street and Sixth Avenue in the Chelsea section of Manhattan.

German-born Hagen was a Broadway veteran of more than 20 major plays, and Berghof was a Viennese actor-turned-director and a refugee from Adolf Hitler's Europe. The couple conceived the studio as a workplace, an artist's home, and an outlet for practice and growth for both theater and footloose professionals. It was a crude space that was literally falling apart at the seams. Chairs collapsed, bureau drawers fell on the actors' feet, or curtains landed on their heads. Whoever happened to be around for a few hours was the office secretary and took charge of collecting the $3 fee per student; sometimes students studied for months without payment. This modest setting produced and nurtured incredible talent. McQueen's esteemed classmates included Jack Lemmon, Jason Robards, Harvey Korman, Frank Langella, Hal Holbrook, and Charles Nelson Reilly, who fondly recalled in 2006, "We all had three things in common. We wanted to be on stage, we had no money, and we couldn't act for shit."

It didn't take long for McQueen to grate on Hagen's nerves. McQueen often rehearsed with his shirt off and bedded many of Hagen's female pupils, then he bragged about this in class. Those comments eventually filtered back to Hagen, who saw through McQueen's macho swagger, boyish charm, devil-may-care attitude, and his all-consuming need to be famous. Her critiques were swift, cutting, and sometimes soul-crushing, especially to someone as sensitive as McQueen. Years later, Hagen told writer Penina Spiegel that her critiques were warranted. "Steve had so little technique I questioned whether he had been trained at all," Hagen said. "He was badly educated, defensive, hostile. Like Marilyn Monroe, Steve too wanted to be an intellectual while being unwilling to devote the preparation time."

Edward Morehouse affirmed Hagen's assertions that McQueen was not serious about learning his craft. "Uta didn't care much for actors who became famous, made millions, and never gave back. She turned out actors who wanted to be artists, not celebrities," Morehouse said. "[McQueen] didn't take class that seriously. I don't think he was very disciplined. I was amazed that he became a star because he was lazy in class."

After McQueen left school, Morehouse didn't see or hear from his former classmate for years. But then Morehouse caught a glimpse of him in *The Thomas Crown Affair* in a dark New York theater, and he was thunderstruck by the metamorphosis.

By God, he's made it, Morehouse said to himself.

Morehouse, who has been teaching at the school since the '50s, said McQueen broke all the rules, and Morehouse is still amazed that McQueen became a major movie star. "All the things we were taught to do, he didn't seem to want to do. We were told to work on this or that, and we did; and Steve didn't, and he was the one who became successful, the actor working more than anyone else. He really became a big star." This was one of McQueen's great skills—he could make the impossible work on the screen. After all, he had to scrape by and push hard for everything in his life, forcing something to fit. And if it didn't, he'd either try harder or toss it aside. Acting was no different for him; it would succeed on his terms, or it would not work out at all.

Despite what Hagen thought of McQueen, the young man was starting to catch fire thanks to agent Peter Witt, who snared him a minor role as an English squire starring opposite Margaret O'Brien in a summer stock play called *Peg O' My Heart* at the Playhouse in East Rochester, New York.

Actress Cloris Leachman remembered in her 2009 memoir, *My Autobiography*, that the original male lead fell ill six days before the start of the play, and McQueen was a last-minute find by her husband, producer and director George Englund. McQueen took the next train to Rochester and was whisked to the Playhouse. Leachman recalls McQueen was a "country boy" who was eager to please. He also brought along his squirrel rifle, hoping to take in a little hunting in his downtime. "At the beginning he was shy and awkward, but even on that first day, I saw he had a magnetic quality, an insouciance, which not too many years later would make him a star in television and films," Leachman wrote.

But the Steve McQueen of 1952 was a novice at best, and he was not comfortable with the stage. Leachman said McQueen was a mumbler and didn't know simple stage nomenclature such as upstage, downstage, stage right, and stage left. She and her husband rolled up their sleeves and went to work on McQueen. Leachman said she took on the responsibility of getting McQueen used to his costume while Englund taught him how to get around the stage. However, once again, Steve would prove that when he applied himself and was committed to something that he could impress. Within a week, McQueen improved to the point where he didn't embarrass himself. "On opening night, Steve didn't wholly resemble a country squire, but that alluring quality was there, and the audience felt it. They liked him, and we had a big, fat success on our hands," Leachman recalled.

McQueen often recalled that experience in upstate New York as one of the turning points in his career.

A few months later he appeared with the Rochester Stock Company in *Member of the Wedding*, which starred Ethel Waters. McQueen said watching Waters go to work was an education unto itself. "She knew how to reach an audience, make them care about what she was doing up there every minute on that stage. And I just soaked it in."

For his next acting gig, McQueen switched from live theater to the silver screen with an inauspicious film debut in *Girl on the Run*. The burlesque thriller and murder mystery, directed by Arthur J. Beckhard, features lots of "Girls and Guns," according to the film's poster. McQueen appears in two scenes as an uncredited extra, and he was given no dialogue. The actor never commented on the picture, and his appearance was first discovered nearly four decades later by filmmaker Mimi Freedman when researching the 2005 documentary *The Essence of Cool*. Not much else is known about the B-movie other than it was released in December 1953.

McQueen soaked up another movie production in early 1954—the classic *On the Waterfront*, thanks to an invite by friend Richard Martin, who worked as an extra in the film. The all-star cast featured Marlon Brando, the Method actor who forever changed the face of acting. "He was mesmerizing, and we knew we were watching something special," Martin said. "Everybody in New York at the time either wanted to be Marlon Brando or James Dean."

McQueen was infatuated with both actors, according to Dianne Rico, an exotic dark-eyed dancer and actress who lived with McQueen after his romance with Donna Barton had fizzled out. Rico said that McQueen stared at photos of Dean and Brando for hours, trying to ape and emulate their expressions and gestures in the mirror. Other times he'd work himself into a frenzy, burning with insane ambition and telling the reflection in the mirror, "I've *got* to make it. You're going to make it! You have to make it, man!"

When Dean died, McQueen did not mourn, according to actor-turned-writer John Gilmore, who dated Rico after she broke it off with McQueen. Rico pushed for a friendship between the two men, and a meeting was arranged outside of Gilmore's flat on 14th Street and Avenue C. Gilmore recalled that McQueen was straddling a British motorcycle, which was backed up against the stoop of his apartment complex overlooking an alley. It was the first conversation McQueen had with Rico after their breakup; it was a no-hard-feelings sort of chat despite the fact that she had found him in bed with another woman. She introduced the two men and casually informed McQueen that Gilmore had befriended Dean. Interpreting this as a personal attack on his pride, as if to suggest she was moving up in the world as she got closer to an established star like Dean, McQueen fought back with, "I'm glad Dean's dead—it makes more room for me." Gilmore felt honor bound to defend Dean, but he also didn't want to get into a pissing match with McQueen, either. "I told him, 'If I were superstitious, I'd say you might buy a curse from the gods with a statement about Dean's dying.' I sort of laughed to let him know I thought he was joking, when I knew he wasn't. His excitement over Jimmy's death making more room for him was a reflection of McQueen's bedrock, almost absolute self-absorption," Gilmore said.

A few days later, McQueen dropped by Gilmore's apartment in a ratty black raincoat to compare the size of their pads. McQueen was still reeling from the fact that Rico had dumped him, and he wanted to know more about the man who was taking his place. He surveyed the books that jammed every crevice of wall space of Gilmore's flat. "What is all this crap? You some kind of poet or something?" McQueen asked, using a veil of nonchalance to disguise the fact that these signs of intellectualism threatened him. Gilmore told him he was an actor by trade but an avid reader in his spare time. Gilmore said that McQueen eyed him with suspicion, mentally deducing the two would most likely be competing for the same parts.[2] After a period of uncomfortable silence, McQueen finally spoke. He met Gilmore's gaze and said that he didn't like any "goddamned" actors and heard that Dean was a "fairy." He said he preferred the company of dockworkers and blue-collar types. McQueen's mistrust of others and the defensiveness that had become intrinsic to his character manifested itself. Yet at the same time, his drive and determination to be a success would ultimately spur him on to fulfill his own bold proclamations.

"Then perhaps you're in the wrong business, Steve," Gilmore coolly replied. McQueen made a hasty exit and Gilmore was added to McQueen's persona non grata list. It was rare for someone to have the last word with McQueen.

"I knew he continued to carry a hatred for me, though I'd never crossed him in any way other than to continue working as a blond, blue-eyed, good-looking Method-type actor," Gilmore said.

McQueen carried no hatred for Brando, but Dean was another story. The two were born almost a year apart and hailed from the same Midwestern state

---

2   Gilmore said he did take a television part away from McQueen on television's *Lamp Unto My Feet* and forever endured the McQueen wrath.

about 80 miles from each other. They had a similar look and slender builds with common interests—motorcycles and fast cars. The two even dated the same woman—Broadway dancer/actress Selma Marcus. Actor Martin Landau, who knew both men, said of the two, "They were both complicated characters. Steve's complex personality emerged from a difficult childhood. Many things rise to the surface when you come from nothing and become a movie star. To build a life, you start with your childhood, and if there's a lot of stuff put on top of that foundation, it's going to feel like a great weight. The same applied to Jimmy," Landau said.

Landau said a chance meeting between the two took place at a Manhattan garage shortly before Dean's untimely death. Landau, who was on the back of Dean's motorcycle when it started sputtering, said Dean pulled into the nearest garage, where McQueen happened to be the mechanic on duty. "It was like a scene out of a movie," Landau recalled. "McQueen, who was working to pay the rent, was the one who examined [Dean's] bike. McQueen didn't pay any attention to me, but he sure was paying a lot of attention to Jimmy because Jimmy was taking parts away from him. I knew Steve was an actor, but I don't know if Jimmy knew or not. I think I told Jimmy afterward." Ever the pugilist, McQueen must have thought to himself, *This guy's got what I want, what I deserve*. He could never abide someone getting an edge on him and must have struggled knowing that Dean was finding superstardom while McQueen was in oil-stained overalls.

When he wasn't losing parts to Dean, McQueen was striking out all on his own. Theodore Mann was artistic director of the Circle In The Square Theater, located next door to Louis' Tavern. Mann remembers McQueen trying out for the production of the Tennessee Williams play *Summer and Smoke*. He said that McQueen simply wasn't right for the part nor did he have the passion for live theater. Mann maintained a casual friendship with McQueen by allowing him to use the theater's facilities when Louis' Tavern was jammed. "Louis' was a favorite watering hole for Broadway actors, musicians, and the Beat poets. It was also a place where James Dean, Jason Robards, Bob Dylan, and Jack Kerouac all hung out," Mann said. "Steve usually arrived every night around 10:00 PM on his motorcycle and parked it outside. It was a rather sensational entrance, even for an actor." Mann said when Louis' was packed, McQueen always seemed to find a stage. He was the guy in the middle of a circle, always the center of attention. "He'd hold court with a bottle of beer in one hand and a ham and cheese on rye in the other hand, telling stories all night."

But McQueen came up short when he failed to impress Karl Malden, who was casting *Tea and Sympathy* for director Elia Kazan. The play, written by Robert Anderson (who penned *The Sand Pebbles* screenplay), was about an unconventional lad tormented by his classmates at an all-boys school in New England. McQueen auditioned for the part of a school bully (eventually played by Lew Gallo) and found the rejection hard to swallow. Malden recalled that McQueen simply wasn't right for the part and said McQueen held a decade-long grudge toward him. Twelve years later, McQueen would have another shot at Malden, this time playing the lead with Malden in support in *The Cincinnati Kid*. The tables would be abruptly turned.

McQueen did have the right stuff when he auditioned for producer and director Shepard Traube in a national touring production of *Time Out for Ginger*. The Broadway comedy starring Melvyn Douglas had a yearlong run at the Lyceum Theater, and Traube was taking the show out on the road in the fall of 1953. McQueen replaced Conrad Janis as Eddie Davis, the captain of the football team.

It was McQueen's first real paying job, which yielded a paycheck of $175 per week. Acting prodigy Nancy Malone, who was in the Broadway production, was a teen when the road production of *Time Out for Ginger* opened in New Haven, Connecticut. She remembers McQueen adopted a brotherly attitude toward her on the tour. "For me, going out on the road was scary and lonely because I was the youngest member of the cast and it was my first time away from home," Malone said. "Steve acted in many instances like an older brother and worried about me. He would check in on me when he could and made sure I got home from the theater to the hotel at night. He was my caretaker and a very, very sweet and a dear fellow." McQueen would treat women as lovers, people to be mistrusted, or on rare occasions, as girls he could watch over like a brother.

Malone said McQueen was right there by her side when she purchased her first car, a new 1953 MG. "I was a grown-up, or so I thought, and felt it was time to drive a car," Malone remembered. "Steve had an MG and wanted me to have one just like his. So he took me to a place in Chicago called Arnolt, a place that sold MGs and Triumphs. I didn't know much about cars and I didn't have a checking account, so I just brought cash. I put $2,500 on the desk and said, 'Now, do I get driving lessons with it?' Steve, of course, doubled over with laughter and said he would give me driving lessons."

Unfortunately, McQueen never got a chance to follow through on his promise. If Malone had followed in his footsteps, she would probably have had as many speeding tickets. Chicago's Harris Theater was the last stop on the tour for McQueen, who could not find the right chemistry with the play's star. "Melvyn Douglas found it difficult to work with Steve because of his lack of discipline. Timing is everything in comedy, and Steve did not adhere to the form," Malone said. "Steve would say the line differently or walk to the wrong spot, and comedy has a certain rhythm and beat. Steve never gave Mel what he needed in order to get his laughs, and after all, it was a comedy."

Douglas called for McQueen's dismissal, which was especially damning since it was his first real paying job. Peter Witt pleaded with the play's producer and director Shepard Traube to allow McQueen to resign and preserve his reputation. McQueen turned in the letter of resignation in late March 1954 and headed back to Greenwich Village with his tail between his legs. When Nancy Malone returned to New York six months later, she inquired about McQueen to Peter Witt, who was also her agent. "I was preparing for another play when I asked Peter about Steve. Peter said, 'Don't worry about Steve. He's going to be a major personality in this business.' I said, 'My Steve?' Peter nodded his head yes. I was thrilled for Steve [and] even more so when he made it big."

To his credit, McQueen never gave up acting. He supported himself with various odd jobs, which included racing on weekends, poker nights, and various blue-collar jobs during the day. He even posed for pulp magazines such as *Crime Detective* and *Homicide Detective* to keep his foot in the door and his face in circulation. He also insisted that New York City photographer Roy Schatt, who immortalized James Dean and Marilyn Monroe, take his picture.

McQueen almost ended his dry spell when he was nearly cast in the role of Artie West in the gritty MGM classic *Blackboard Jungle*. McQueen was interviewed and screen-tested by casting director Al Altman. An interoffice communication from producer Pandro Berman to director Richard Brooks, dated August 4, 1954, showed that McQueen was the frontrunner for the role. "There is a boy named Steve McQueen whom Altman is anxious to test for the part of West. He is blond, 5'11", 170 pounds, about 24, has been playing boys in the 18 to 22-year-old range. Seems by all odds to be the best actor that has been discovered for the part according to Altman, having been a professional actor for four years," Berman wrote.

Unfortunately for McQueen, in correspondence dated October 21, 1954, Altman later deemed the actor "on the conventional side but his good looks might point to other slum types." Altman ultimately awarded the role to Vic Morrow.

With nothing going for him in New York, McQueen took off with actor Richard Martin on a cross-country trip to Los Angeles, where the two searched for prospective employment. Magician John Calvert, whom Martin knew, tendered an offer that would keep them in clover for the next two years. "[Calvert] was looking for actors to travel around the world with him on his yacht, the *Sea Fox*. When he told us the tour would take two years, we got cold feet," Martin said. Ever the commitmentphobe, McQueen turned it down.

Martin said McQueen made both a figurative and literal splash in Tinseltown. He recalled sharing a brew with McQueen in Barney's Beanery, a famous watering hole on Santa Monica Boulevard. Steve got the patrons buzzing when he ordered his beer on tap with ice. The two also sent shockwaves throughout the acting community when they skinny-dipped with two actresses at the Chateau Marmont. "We were busted by the hotel staff and kicked out, but it was worth it," Martin said with a smile. "Somehow our exploits reached the East Coast, and we were the talk of the acting world for the next month."

Live television was at its zenith in the mid-'50s and ultimately proved to be McQueen's salvation. The exposure he received would eventually lead to recognition and opportunities. He won critical acclaim for his role in a Studio One production of *Goodyear Television Playhouse*: "The Chivington Raid," which aired on March 27, 1955. It was McQueen's national television debut.

He also made a little-known appearance on *The Goldbergs*, television's first Jewish sitcom, which featured Gertrude Berg, the show's creator, writer, and star. McQueen got a walk-on part after Berg decided he was the right man for the job. "I was dating Arlene McQuade, who played Rosalie on the show. I was cast as an actor she falls for in school," said actor Robert Heller. "After three auditions, it was decided that I was not WASP-y enough to please Gertrude Berg, so a very gentile Steve got the part."

With some career momentum starting to build up behind him, McQueen heard about a new play called *Two Fingers of Pride*, an original work written by lawyer Jim Longhi and directed by Jack Garfein. The play, which highlighted corruption on the New York City docks, premiered at the Ogunquit Playhouse in Maine on August 8, 1955, with hopes of eventually taking it to Broadway that fall. Garfein remembers the first time he spotted McQueen. "I called the Neighborhood Playhouse and asked them to send over some of their graduate students. Steve walked in with a group of about 8 to 10 students and I spotted him immediately. I had a track record at the time of discovering new talent," said Garfein, who had a hand in nurturing the careers of James Dean, George Peppard, and Sydney Pollack.

McQueen interviewed for the role of Nino, a 22-year-old Italian American. It was the second lead in the play and a role that required substantial dramatic ability. Garfein was immediately drawn to McQueen and detected a spark and rawness in him. "I asked Steve if I could work with him for a few days to prepare him for a reading. McQueen immediately said yes. He never tried to convince me he was ready for the part. He was reticent but worked diligently. He could hardly believe it when he got the part, but I was very excited about the future of this young actor."

A tricky situation arose when McQueen informed Garfein and Longhi that he didn't have an Actors Equity card. Garfein asked him how he thought he could work without one. "Well, if you lend me the money, I can get one," Steve said. Garfein and Longhi looked at each other and shook their heads. This kid was a piece of work, but they had to admire his guts. They both chipped in $17.50 apiece to buy him his card, and a few days later, they informed McQueen that he had the part. Fifteen minutes later, McQueen called back almost frantic. Garfein remembered, "[Steve] said, 'Jack, I don't have an agent. I have no one. Please, can you help me?' I told Steve that I was the director and that this was highly irregular, and I was on the other end of it. Steve replied, 'No, Jack! You're not on the other end of it. You're on my end of it!' How could I say no to him? He was so charming and yet so innocent at the same time." Garfein called in a favor with MCA agent John Foreman, who agreed to take on McQueen so that he could get his Actor's Equity card and remain in the play. Foreman, who represented Paul Newman at the time, didn't give much thought to McQueen after the play and dropped him as a client.

The play featured a high-caliber cast of theater veterans—Gary Merrill, Sam Jaffe, John F. Hamilton, Peggy Feury, Olga Bellin, and McQueen, who was the only unproven actor, which plagued him with insecurities. He admitted to Garfein he was scared and auditioned only because he didn't think he'd get the part. Garfein carefully assuaged his fears, baby-stepping McQueen through the process.

The two men developed a deep bond, according to Garfein, who was a Holocaust survivor from Czechoslovakia. "The one big thing we had in common is that we were really both alone in this world," Garfein said. "After the war, I came to New York and had no one. Steve was emotionally in the same place as I was, and we had a very deep, deep connection." Garfein survived both Auschwitz and Bergen-Belsen concentration camps, where prisoners kept their spirits up by playing music, hosting lectures, and staging plays. He was an especially moving performer and was singled out by a member of the American council who arranged for his immigration to America at age 15. Garfein was almost three months younger than McQueen, but Garfein was light years ahead in sophistication and knowledge of the acting world.

The first order of business for Garfein was teaching McQueen how to properly prepare for a role, which meant McQueen was going to learn how to think, act, and behave like a dockworker. "Steve was living the life of a bohemian actor, and he needed to understand the life of a longshoreman and how they faced a life of futility. He worked very hard and later told me that was one of the most important experiences in his life," Garfein said.

The young actor leaned heavily on Garfein for professional advice; he helped mold and shape McQueen's early career. McQueen publicly acknowledged Garfein years later when he and costar Natalie Wood dropped into the Russian Tea Room after the New York premiere of *Love with the Proper Stranger* with a dozen photographers hot on their trail. Amid the chaos, McQueen spotted Garfein in the corner of the room. Hollywood's brightest new star calmly walked over to Garfein, and the two men embraced. McQueen placed his arm around the director and loudly announced to the room, "Pardon me for being corny, but I owe this man a lot."

Writer Jim Longhi called in a favor with Anthony Scotto, who was the president of the International Longshoreman's Association and son-in-law of mafia capo Albert Anastasia. He lorded over South Brooklyn and the borough's lucrative docks in Red Hook, where McQueen was put to work stacking wooden crates in the hold of a ship for a few weeks. As streetwise and tough as McQueen was, he found himself in another element. Police once famously tried to make a raid on the Long Pier at the foot of Columbia Street using the mounted patrol. Anastasia's crew was tipped off and placed long nails at the entrance to the pier to injure and stop the horses. McQueen told Garfein the foreman confused *reel* life with *real* life. "Steve called me and said, 'Jack, sometimes these guys don't realize I'm an actor and they're working me pretty hard. Please make sure I'm okay.' I had to assure him that he was going to be okay and was fully protected."

When McQueen returned from the docks, he was ready to tackle the role. Garfein taught McQueen that acting was mainly internal, natural, and unforced. He instructed his cast members to talk softly to one another to avoid "creating drama." The audience was smart and didn't need signals or to be telegraphed that a big dramatic or funny moment was coming their way. Garfein taught that the power of anyone's performance lay in its quiet simplicity. It became the hallmark of McQueen's acting style.

John Lane, who owned the Ogunquit Playhouse in Maine for almost half a century, agreed to host *Two Fingers of Pride* through his friendship with Gary Merrill and his wife, actress Bette Davis (who was present during the weeklong run). Lane remembered McQueen roaring up the playhouse driveway on a motorcycle with a girlfriend clinging to him for dear life. Lane was most impressed by the fact that McQueen braved the 300-mile trek through the pouring rain.

Two Fingers of Pride was a close-knit company. It was mostly a family affair, but the good vibes were interrupted one day during rehearsals when two federal agents showed up. Sam Jaffe, who had won an Academy Award for *The Asphalt Jungle* in 1950, had been blacklisted by the House Un-American Activities Committee a year later at the height of the McCarthy era. The film roles dried up after he was labeled a communist sympathizer, and Jaffe was reduced to teaching high school math and moving in with relatives. When the FBI learned Jaffe was making a return to the stage, Garfein was pulled aside by the G-Men. They specifically wanted to know why Garfein was employing a man who was a possible danger to the country, a country that was particularly good to Garfein in the aftermath of the Holocaust. "I am well aware that this country has been good to me, and I am quite appreciative," Garfein replied. "And now I'm going to do the most American thing I can think of, and that's to go back to work." Jaffe offered to resign, which drew the ire of Garfein. "Sam was in his seventies at the time and I in my early twenties, and I was a little fresh with him. I said, 'Sam, just do your fucking job and I'll do mine.' Steve piped in, 'Hey, if you can't work, Mr. Jaffe, neither can I. I stand behind Mr. Jack Garfein, so let's get to the fuckin' rehearsal!' That's how close we all were," Garfein proudly boasts today.

Some members of the cast were closer than others. He may have been the novice on the stage, but McQueen was an old pro when it came to romance. He conducted simultaneous affairs with two members of the cast—Olga Bellin and Peggy Feury. Garfein said today both women served different needs in McQueen. "Olga Bellin was in love with him. She sensed that he needed consolation. There were unspoken things within him," Garfein said. "I may be wrong about this, but when I look back, I realize that Steve did not know about love. He knew about sex and the confidence he got from it. Peggy Feury was attracted to him but mainly sensed the talent he had and the potential of becoming a star."

Feury was a slight, blonde-haired, blue-eyed natural beauty who radiated sex and was an obvious choice for McQueen. Bellin, a shy, soft-spoken, bob-haired brunette, was a surprise. Bellin claims she was near-virginal when she met McQueen, who was unlike any other men she had ever encountered. She fell prey to the bad-boy allure and McQueen's cocksure nature. "Steve had floods of women," Bellin told writer Penina Spiegel. "He was always looking for the next pleasure, the next conquest. He was as self-centered as a kid on Christmas morning, yet he had such vitality. He was so much fun to be with, I found myself drawn in." Some women would fall for McQueen's charm, others for his attitude, and still others wanted to protect that little boy inside of him, the one who had it so hard growing up.

Bellin depicted McQueen as tough and tender, sometimes cruel and bullish but generous in the bedroom. She was one of the few women he let penetrate his veneer; she sensed in him a frightened individual who showed a rough exterior to hide his fear but inside clamored for love. Many times she witnessed several emerging personalities—the bad boy biker, the sensitive lover, the country boy who charmed everyone in the room, and the hostile and defensive loner who didn't feel worthy. In time their relationship would run its course and Bellin would have filled that protecting, sensitive, almost maternal gap in McQueen's life, at least for a while.

Feury was a successful Broadway and television actress and later a highly successful acting coach.[3] Steve McQueen was, for all intents and purposes, her first unofficial student. "Steve was terribly needy, with a raw, helpless kind of need. All he wanted to do was to be able to look at himself and say, 'That's somebody,'" Feury said of McQueen before her death on November 20, 1985.

Under the tutelage of Garfein and with heavy support from Feury, McQueen was sensational in his role and was singled out by *The Village Voice* as one of the play's bright spots: "Steve McQueen gives a truly excellent performance during the first scene, after which he too seems to have been forgotten by the author."

The Village Voice gave the play a lukewarm review and came short of calling it a poor man's *On The Waterfront*. Garfein said the classic film prevented *Two Fingers of Pride* from reaching The Great White Way. "*On the Waterfront* had come out and made financing very hard for us. They didn't think it would be successful on Broadway," Garfein said.

Two Fingers of Pride folded after a week but it was by no means a failure—at least not for McQueen. He had come a long way from being a jack of all trades who moved from job to job to slowly gaining the respect and attention of his peers and the industry. The play bore him much fruit: friends, lovers, stage redemption, plus a mentor in Jack Garfein, who helped McQueen gain entree into the most influential acting institution in America—the Actors Studio. The seeds of McQueen becoming a full-fledged actor had been sown, and from here on in they would develop and blossom.

---

3   Her roster of famous alumni includes Lily Tomlin, Anjelica Huston, Sean Penn, Michelle Pfeiffer, Melissa Gilbert, Meg Tilly, and Eric Stoltz.

8

THE GREAT WHITE WAY AND THE SILVER SCREEN

STEVE MCQUEEN WAS LUCKY enough to take up acting in one of the most important periods in the profession. He was part of an era that led to performances and films that have left an indelible impression on cinema. The origins of this era can be traced back to Konstantin Stanislavski, who was enjoying a renaissance of his life's work in the New York theatrical scene in the late 1940s, almost a decade after his death. The Russian actor and cofounder of the Moscow Art Theater challenged the traditional stage approach and developed his own system of training actors to access their personal experiences to identify with and portray the emotional lives of their characters. He organized his realistic techniques into a coherent and usable system he called "Spiritual Realism." In America, it was known simply as "The Method."

Stanislavski's system found traction in Europe and later in America, where it was disseminated, dissected, and preached by master teachers, including Lee Strasberg, Stella Adler, Sanford Meisner, Michael Chekov, Herbert Berghof, and Uta Hagen, who developed their own technique over time but faithfully credited Stanislavski as their source. Their protégés included some of the most inspired and enduring actors, directors, and writers of their time: Marlon Brando, James Dean, Marilyn Monroe, Geraldine Page, Warren Beatty, Eli Wallach, Paul Newman, Gregory Peck, Sidney Poitier, Rod Steiger, Elia Kazan, George C. Scott, Robert Duvall, and, of course, Steve McQueen.

Theirs was an acting style of previously unseen raw emotion, sensitivity, and repressed individual expression that articulated an extreme dissatisfaction with the American dream; these were the young lions, the storytellers and interpreters of their generation, and they had taken the theater and film world by storm.

Founded in 1947 in New York by Elia Kazan, Cheryl Crawford, and Robert Lewis (Strasberg joined their ranks a year later), the Actors Studio is perhaps the most influential acting institution in America. For six decades it has produced a who's who of the theater and film world. It is not a school but a membership organization for professional actors, directors, and playwrights. Members must be invited after passing a series of auditions and, once accepted, they are members for life.

Strasberg was known as a scholar of the theater but also as a totalitarian who ruled with an iron fist; his poker face and brazen critiques instilled terror in his talented students, who slavishly sought a kind word, a nodding approval, or a verbal pat on the back. Strasberg's role often required him to act alternatively as a coach, parental figure, psychiatrist, and devil's advocate. Jack Garfein said Strasberg instilled the fear of God in most students, especially McQueen. "I think Steve was terrified by Strasberg," Garfein said. "He knew the teacher could destroy him by a comment. He kept giving Strasberg flattering looks of admiration to deflect attention away from him."

Ultimately McQueen could not dodge Strasberg and had to get his stamp of approval to gain entry. It helped to have Garfein in his corner, who carried a lot of clout at the Studio at the time. McQueen performed two auditions for his selectors, with his final in front of a heavy-duty panel: Kazan, Strasberg, Crawford, and John Dudley, the Actors Studio attorney. Garfein, who was present for the final audition, said McQueen was simply electrifying in a scene titled "The Park," from Clifford Odets' *Golden Boy*. "Kazan and Strasberg were immediately excited by his potential, and he was accepted into the Studio on his first attempt," Garfein recalled.

It was not only a huge personal triumph but also a monumental feat. Of the 2,000 performers that auditioned for the Actors Studio in 1955, only McQueen and Martin Landau were accepted that year. Landau eventually won an Academy Award, and Steve McQueen went on to become a movie legend. McQueen had the looks, the hunger, and the determination to win, and now the final piece of the jigsaw was falling into place—he was refining his talent, and he had the approval of those who counted. He had finally arrived.

"The electricity at the Actors Studio in those days was palpable," said Robert Loggia, who became a member in the '50s. "The actors worked together to develop their skills in an experimental environment where they could take risks as performers without the pressure of commercial roles. People did weird things to find themselves. Women pretended to put their diaphragms into their vaginas, all to show that anything was fair game. Those were the days of Stanislavski, and I imagine they don't do those things anymore. McQueen certainly didn't put himself out there emotionally. He was very shy and diffident. His style was more sitting back and taking it all in." McQueen would react rather than simply respond, leveraging off his counterpart's lines and magnifying the intensity of a scene. McQueen defended his style when he became popular a few years later. "I remember seein' real bad guys and how they say, 'If you step out, I'll kill you,' McQueen said. "Most actors play it up. I'll do it monotone. It's all there. You accept it, or you don't. It comes out of reality, out of people I've associated with."

McQueen wasn't as confident in his approach early on, and he couldn't or wouldn't project in terms of doing a scene under the scrutiny of fellow actors, directors, and playwrights. He knew he was still raw as far as his acting technique was concerned. Yet there was something about him that was rugged, tormented, and unhappy—all tools that an actor can use if reined in tightly. He had a natural aptitude for inventing colorful detail to replace stiff dialogue. "Lee Strasberg responded favorably to Steve [he loved his eccentricities] in sessions," said Bob Heller, who has been an Actors Studio member since the '50s. "Lee was kind and helpful even though Steve was being contrary and disrespectful to him."

Actor Martin Landau said Strasberg made exceptions for certain individuals, based on the results of how Strasberg treated James Dean in one session. "I remember one day Lee Strasberg beat the shit out of Jimmy, just devastated Jimmy in one of his critiques. Jimmy never came back to do scenes, although he still attended class," Landau said. "I think Strasberg learned from that, deciding that there were some people who could take it and others who couldn't. He often criticized me, which I always felt made me stronger; but he was over-gentle with Steve, who took advantage of the fact. Steve tested Lee, too."

From 1956 to 1969, Strasberg recorded various exercises, improvisations, monologues, lectures, and scenes, which are housed today at the Wisconsin Historical Society. On May 29, 1956, the Actors Studio recorded McQueen and actress Patricia Roe (*One Life to Live* and *Guiding Light*) performing a reading from a play titled *And All That Jazz*. The audio gives great insight as to how raw his acting technique was at the time. McQueen is so painfully quiet and his speech is so indecipherable that he left Strasberg frustrated when the scene was over.

"Where did you study?" Strasberg asked.

"At the Neighborhood Playhouse," McQueen replied. "For three years."

"They didn't work on your speech?" Strasberg asked incredulously. "I'll give you some exercises."

The exchange prompted Strasberg to lecture on projection, concentration, and vocal energy. However, Strasberg brought the point of the exercise back to McQueen and what he needed to do in order to improve. "From the audience point of view, Steve, a great deal of what you do would be lost," Strasberg said.

"But the actual work is coming well—the handling of the girl was very sound. It had a natural, believable quality; it was never forced. There was definitely progress in relation to what we've seen so far." Strasberg had correctly deduced that using a softer, more balanced approach toward McQueen would be most productive. Letting him know unequivocally what his flaws were was essential, but letting him know he was doing other things correctly was crucial. This approach would encourage rather than deter the combative young actor and would ultimately pay dividends.

McQueen certainly didn't need any lessons as far as his love life was concerned. In addition to a bevy of actresses, dancers, models, and one-night stands, Steve was juggling Peggy Feury, Olga Bellin, Aneta Corsaut, Selma Marcus, and Janet Conway, a 17-year-old dancer. Conway was a student at the American Academy of Dramatic Arts where McQueen was employed as a drama teacher under the direction of Viola Essen, who ran a dance studio inside of Carnegie Hall. "Steve probably wasn't qualified to teach drama at that point, but Viola liked having young men around," Conway said. "Marlon Brando came to many of our classes and played the conga drum while we did our routines. After class, Marlon and Viola usually headed up to her office where they locked the door behind them. We never knew for sure what went on, but we had our suspicions."

Conway had been touring in a musical called *The Amazing Adele*, which had opened in Philadelphia and a few weeks later closed in Boston. When she got back to Essen's dance class, McQueen was suddenly a fixture. "He was intense, attractive, and typical of that era. He kind of mumbled, had affectations that were charming, and had the most gorgeous blue eyes I had ever seen. I don't know how or when, but we became an item," Conway recalled.

Part of Conway's attraction to McQueen was that he was dead broke but absolutely driven. He lived in a small, run-down, cold-water flat with a stop sign weighted down by a cement post that he used as a barbell. When the two went out to dinner, Conway usually paid the tab, something she wasn't used to doing. But life with McQueen was never dull; he picked up Conway on his motorcycle, and they tore up the streets of Greenwich Village or hung out with friends who were artists. "One time, Steve took a detour and drove on a street that wasn't paved. All of the sewer lids were exposed, and Steve's front wheel sank into one of the holes, causing my head to hit his," Conway recalled. "I was cut above my left eye, and we ended up going to a nearby emergency room where I received a few stitches. At the time, Steve didn't have a license, so we told the doctor that I had fallen. The doctor sewed me up and gave me an eye patch to wear. I had an artist friend draw an eyeball for me. It was lovely."

Their romance coincided with the making of *Somebody Up There Likes Me*, a biographical drama on the life of boxer Rocky Graziano. The part was originally written for James Dean, but a few weeks before filming, on September 30, 1955, Dean died in a tragic car accident. McQueen had once nonchalantly declared that Dean's departure would make more room for him, but there would be another actor who had managed to get in the queue ahead of McQueen. Dean's death created a vacancy for Paul Newman, McQueen's contemporary at the Actors Studio. Somehow, McQueen felt the Graziano part belonged to him. After all, McQueen certainly had more in common with the real-life boxer than Newman. Like Graziano, the two endured abusive and poverty-ridden childhoods, shunned formal education, committed petty crimes, spent time in reform schools, and even went AWOL in the military. Graziano used boxing as an outlet for his violent behavior; McQueen chose acting.

McQueen excelled when he had focus, and nothing focused him more than picking someone who he could compete with and then do his absolute best to beat. Newman fit that bill perfectly, because he was tasting the success that McQueen thirsted for. Though Newman was five years older than McQueen and a more seasoned actor at the time, McQueen didn't feel Newman earned his real-life lumps in the same manner as he had. Newman hailed from Shaker Heights, Ohio, one of the wealthiest and most well-educated suburbs in America; McQueen had a ninth-grade education from a reform school. While Newman was away at college taking exams and swilling beer at frat parties, McQueen was stealing hubcaps, getting his melon smashed with Coke bottles, and earning his education on the streets. It didn't matter that Newman had already racked up almost two dozen television performances and starred in a feature film (*The Silver Chalice*); McQueen felt extremely competitive with Newman, according to his longtime publicist David Foster. "[McQueen] used to tell me, 'It was freezing, shitty weather, and I was a nobody.' The day players had one room they'd huddle in to keep warm and Newman had a limo with a heater, and a production assistant or somebody—it wasn't Paul—wouldn't let [McQueen] sit in it. He never forgot that. It was one of the small things that drove him to become a star. He associated [the incident] with Paul, though Paul had nothing to do with it."

Psychologist Peter O. Whitmer said Foster is correct. McQueen's attitude had nothing to do with Newman. "McQueen felt most fully integrated, most psychologically functional, in the heat of the battle," Whitmer said. "This behavior replicates the emotional high that he got early on when: (1) fighting with his stepfather; (2) gang involvement in Los Angeles; (3) the first part of his stay at Boys Republic; (4) his stint in the Marines when he was AWOL and running counter to their regimentation; (5) behaving badly in acting school as well as in his first professional roles; (6) on to Hollywood.

"Steve's angst and emotional craziness stemmed from the fact that he felt he intuitively knew that role better than Paul Newman. On another, less conscious, level, it was a weird 'professional sibling rivalry'—Steve acting out, against his projections onto Newman, of all of what Steve knew to be his own 'bad' traits. He had never had a brother with whom to go through this rite of adolescent passage, and Newman fit the bill."

Throughout his career, McQueen used Newman as a measuring stick for his success and vowed that one day he would catch up to Newman. Steve's fierce competitiveness would drive him ever onward. It was a footrace that took 18 long years to complete. Along the way McQueen would end up turning down *Butch Cassidy and the Sundance Kid* on the basis that he would not be billed over Newman, and being billed equally wasn't enough for the ever-ambitious McQueen. Steve would eventually emerge the victor of this battle that culminated in 1974's *The Towering Inferno*. McQueen demanded the character of his choosing, the script to be enhanced so he had exactly the same number of lines as Newman's character (a telling sign because he normally always requested less dialogue), and best of all, top billing over Newman.

However, the journey to attaining that level of power started right at the bottom. Director Robert Wise recalled that McQueen made quite a first impression when auditioning for the role of Fido, a part that paid $19 a day. "He came in, in a sport jacket, kind of gangly and loose, and he had a little cap, a little bill around the top of his head," Wise said. "I guess it was the cocky manner somehow—not fresh but just nice and cocky and a bit full of himself that just caught my eye, and I cast him in this small part. It was the part of some kid on a rooftop fighting back in New York." Nearly a decade later, Wise cast McQueen in his only Oscar-nominated role in *The Sand Pebbles*. McQueen was more than bemused when Wise drove to his large Brentwood estate to tender him the role along with a six-figure offer. No doubt McQueen relished the reversal of fortunes. By then the days of scrappy small parts and supporting roles would be long gone.

Conway remembered that McQueen trained for his part in *Somebody Up There Likes Me* with the intensity of an Olympic athlete, but his tool would not be a javelin or a discus—he would be using a knife. "It was a very small role for Steve, but he took it very seriously. He had a prop on the dresser—the knife that was used in the scene—and I remember him working very hard at trying to be comfortable with the knife and make the scene look very real. He had a lot of talent, and nothing was going to stop him," Conway said. Steve may have needed to work on several aspects of his acting craft, but no one could fault his determination and certainly not his uncanny ability with props.

Michael Dante, who played Shorty the Greek in the picture, said McQueen's first day on the job was almost his last. At the time Dante was a contract player for MGM studios, and he was waiting under the canopy of the Warwick Hotel for a limousine to take him to the set where he was to report at 8:00 A.M. "It was raining like hell, and it was so bad that you could barely see outside. I'm standing there waiting for my limo when this guy comes roaring up on this motorcycle, and he was soaking wet. Not a dry stitch of clothing on him. He pulls up to me and in this very hip, beatnik way, asks me, 'Hey man, can you tell me where the MGM company is filming today?' I told him I did and if he waited five minutes, he could follow the limo to the set."

McQueen followed the limo on his bike for about a half hour while the rain never let up. The two arrived safely to the set and were assigned by an assistant director to the same portable dressing room. Dante recalled that McQueen stripped down to his underwear and was standing in a pool of water as he changed into his wardrobe. "Now that's a pretty rough start in this business," Dante said. It was about to get worse.

One scene called for Paul Newman to stop a fur-coat truck and occupy the driver while a group of thugs (played by McQueen, Dante, and Sal Mineo) rummage in the back and raid the loot. When Robert Wise motioned for action, the scene went according to plan until the truck lost its brakes and careened out of control. "The master cylinder on the brakes went kaput, and Paul Newman got out of the way just in time," Dante said. "The truck plowed right into a 2-by-6 plank overlay, and the camera operator went straight up in the air like a Cape Canaveral rocket. Steve was quite frankly paying too much attention to these hundreds of pigeons by this huge wall and said, 'Have you ever seen so many birds in all of your life?' I finally had to push him out of the way. The truck narrowly missed him and hit the curb and lamppost instead."

McQueen thanked Dante for getting him out of a rough spot, but he failed to repay the favor more than a dozen years later. Dante, whose star was on the rise in the late '60s, said he was given a verbal agreement by *Bullitt* producer Phillip D'Antoni to costar with McQueen as his cop partner, a role ultimately awarded to Don Gordon. Dante, D'Antoni, director Peter Yates, executive producer Robert Relyea, and McQueen all met at a Beverly Hills restaurant for lunch. The meeting went well, but Dante made one crucial error—he was the first to stand up. "I had forgotten about McQueen's complex regarding height, and it was well known in the industry that he didn't work with actors who were taller than he was," Dante said. "He looked up at me and said, 'Hey, whoa, man, what did you do? Get taller?' I knew when I heard Steve say that I was out of the picture." A few hours later, Dante received a phone call from D'Antoni informing him of Steve's decision. This would be a harsh reminder of how ruthless and unstoppable McQueen could be to succeed and guard his status.

Dante said McQueen's actions stung for a very long time. "I was flying at the time, going from one project to another. But this picture [*Bullitt*] would have really put me on another level," Dante said. "I could have sued the studio because I had a verbal agreement from the producer, but then I would have never worked again in Hollywood. I liked Steve, thought he was a good guy and a terrific actor, but that one really hurt."

Somebody Up There Likes Me catapulted Newman to stardom and was one of those rare films that kick-started several other acting careers, including McQueen, Sal Mineo, Robert Loggia, Dean Jones, and Robert Duvall. The stardust that fell from the picture gave McQueen the confidence to audition for the lead role in *A Hatful of Rain*. He beat out some of the biggest names on Broadway, including John Cassavetes and George Peppard. "I'd go to an audition and find that they'd put me on stage right away because so many other actors had talked about me," McQueen said.

A Hatful of Rain, written by Michael V. Gazzo, was already a Broadway success when McQueen replaced Ben Gazzara in the lead role of Johnny Pope. The play was a rarity for its time in its startling depiction of drug addiction, which was a taboo subject in the Eisenhower '50s. Pope is a soldier who returns from the Korean War where a stay in a military hospital has left him secretly addicted to morphine.

McQueen was already familiar with the play, as were most Actors Studio members, who performed bits and pieces of the material to a stone-faced Lee Strasberg. Gazzo later fleshed out the material over a period of six weeks and transformed Johnny Pope from an alcoholic to a junkie, and the story explored substance abuse and its destructive effect on personal relationships. Despite a soft opening and a lukewarm reception in Philadelphia, by the time *Hatful* reached Broadway's Lyceum Theater in November 1955, it had a renewed vitality. That was in large part to its exciting cast, which included Ben Gazzara, Shelley Winters, Tony Franciosa, Henry Silva, and Harry Guardino, who worked out many of the play's kinks while on the road. *Hatful* was a huge critical and financial success, and it became the talk of the Great White Way.

Six months later, contracts for the cast had expired. *Hatful's* trio of stars— Gazzara, Franciosa, and Winters—used the play as a launching pad for their careers and left for greener pastures. The stage was set. A mere five years after his first acting lesson, McQueen's name was going to be in neon lights on Broadway.

• • •

Steve McQueen's life was a mixture of searing frustration and staggering accomplishment with rarely any middle ground. While he was finally starting to taste some success and gain recognition for his hard work, a cold reminder would always be there of how much was at stake and why he needed to succeed—his mother.

Julian was still in New York, living in the same area and still in the same mess. Her depression and addiction to alcohol were the root causes for Steve's inner turmoil, and yet at the same time, Julian was the driving force behind Steve's need to succeed. Julian's failed relationship with Victor Lukens, who was the most stable man in her life, signaled her slow descent into alcoholic madness.[1] Over time, the booze had taken its toll. Julian had aged considerably and packed on more than just a few pounds. Her youthful appearance gave way to a more haggard look, that of a person who no longer cared about life or how she appeared. Many times she'd track down Steve and wait on the stoop of his apartment complex or lie unconscious in the hallway, blocking his entrance. Steve often ran away or headed in the other direction, hoping that after a few days she'd find somewhere else to wait. Sometimes there was simply no avoiding her.

John Gilmore remembers Julian as a fixture at Louis' Tavern, often begging Steve's friends to buy her a drink with the promise that she'd show them a good time. "Once I saw her pass out and drop from a stool to the sawdust floor while Steve made a fast exit up the stairs. Stewed to the gills, she would press against some guy drinking with Steve and make a play for drinks," Gilmore said. "Another time when Ben Gazzara was there, she came on to him. He bought her a drink, just being friendly, but she took it as though it were a come-on and started touching him. Once or twice she passed out, fell to the floor." Girlfriend Dianne Rico said McQueen once confessed to her that he wished Julian were dead or that she would just simply vanish from his life and "quit hounding" him once and for all.

Julian's alcoholism often took her to the depths of depravity. Steve was sometimes forced to fetch her from Bellevue Hospital's detoxification center, which left scarring effects—her scars were physical, while his were emotional. As an adult he expected women to meet his desperate need to be mothered in a way he never was

---

1   Lukens and McQueen had a falling out over Julian's funeral, according to widow Linda Lukens. "Steve invited him to the funeral and wanted him to be there, but Victor was one of those individuals who didn't believe in funerals," Lukens said. "Steve never spoke to Victor again, and it broke his heart." Victor Lukens died on May 22, 1975.

as a child. As a result, he was left bitter toward them, mixed with fears that a member of the opposite sex could annihilate him emotionally. His easy-come, easy-go attitude was most likely a cover-up for his tremendous anxiety about women. The effects are clear in his treatment of them. In rare cases, women were to be protected like a younger sister, while at other times women were kept at an extreme distance for emotional safety. As was most often the case, however, women were there to be his next conquest and emotional crutch. Deep inside he had harbored a hidden belief that if he fell in love, that woman would have the power to hurt him, to engulf him and abandon him, just like Julian did to him so many times throughout his life.

Olga Bellin and Peggy Feury, whose relationships with Steve commenced around the same time, also ended together. Bellin's shy nature and lack of spunk failed to keep McQueen's interest, while Feury committed the ultimate sin— she kept another lover. Steve was certainly a mass of contradictions and was not adverse to having his own double standards. Steve showed up extra early one morning and found another man exiting Feury's apartment. The idea that Feury could possibly be involved with someone else infuriated McQueen, and Feury was the recipient of a vitriol-laced explosion of rage. Their friendship was destroyed, and Steve never spoke to her again.

His breakup with Janet Conway was not a big deal or a knock-down, drag-out fight. The two were getting ready to leave Carnegie Hall when Conway saw another actor who she thought was cute. McQueen picked up on the vibe and told Conway that he was heading to the Village and for her to hop on his bike. She politely declined.

"Either come now or forget it," Steve said, who was quick to issue an ultimatum.

"Then forget it," Conway said defiantly. McQueen kick-started his motorcycle and zoomed away and out of her life. This would do little but reaffirm his inherent mistrust of women. He'd had enough of being the one who was abandoned and preferred to do the ditching. However, Conway's departure would open up a new avenue in McQueen's life, one that would allow the entrance of a positive female presence of crucial importance whom he could depend upon and flourish alongside—the woman who eventually became his first wife, the mother of his children, and the seminal relationship in his life.

Her name was Neile Adams.

9

MR. ADAMS

HE DIDN'T WANT TO "FALL IN LOVE WITH SOME BROAD," and she had never been exposed to "that kind of man" before. He was a star on the rise, while she was Broadway's darling. He was a product of the Midwest. She was dark and exotic. He was surly and temperamental. She was easygoing and accommodating. On the surface the two seemed an odd pairing, but the attraction was instant and undeniable. Their fates seemed destined even though they were born half a world away from each other.

Steve McQueen met dancer Neile Adams for the first time in May 1956 when he was in rehearsal to replace Ben Gazzara in *A Hatful of Rain*, and she had just replaced Carol Channing in *The Pajama Game* and was having a radiant moment as Broadway's brightest emerging star. They knew of one another but caught each other's eye at Jim Downey's Steakhouse, an "in" spot for actors on 44th Street and Eighth Avenue. He was spooling a forkful of spaghetti when Neile strutted in wearing tight-fitting toreador pants and a tighter sweater. Half the pasta on Steve's fork dropped in his lap when Neile walked past his table, flashing him a megawatt smile. This was a reversal he was not used to. Normally he would be the one to make the grand entrance, usually holding court and piercing the air with a rev of his motorcycle. He was impressed.

"Hey—good one, kid," Neile said without breaking stride. Knowing that Neile had caught him openly staring, he could do nothing but laugh at himself. His reaction only endeared him to her. Throughout the meal Neile's friends noticed the starry-eyed looks the two gave each other. Neile got a quick debriefing from a friend. McQueen was a so-so actor who fucked anything that moved. It was suggested that she take a pass.

A few nights later at Downey's, the scene almost repeated itself. McQueen was eating with Ben Gazzara, director Frank Corsaro, and playwright Mike Gazzo, when Neile, who was flanked by date Mark Rydell, flashed Steve her most dazzling smile and said hello to no one in particular. Steve knew that smile was meant for him. When Neile excused herself from the table, McQueen walked over to Rydell, who was a classmate at the Neighborhood Playhouse, and laid his cards on the table—he was going to make a move on Neile. "Hey man, all's fair in love and war," McQueen proclaimed as he patted Rydell on the back. Steve then seized the moment and openly flirted with Neile but stopped short of asking her out. "He was strange-looking actually, in his T-shirt and jeans. And the way he talked! I'd never run across anyone like him. Here I was, a sweet, convent-bred girl from a Greenwich, Connecticut, boarding school, very conventional, and here was this unconventional individual." Neile recalled. At the end of his visit, Steve promised to stop by the theater to check out her show. When he did, they made a date for the following Sunday. She got decked out in her daintiest, frilliest dress, hoping he'd take her on a romantic stroll through Central Park or perhaps a movie. Those notions were quickly squashed when he zoomed up on a motorcycle wearing blue jeans and a black leather jacket.

"Hop on," he instructed.

"Hop on—in a dress?"

"You can ride sidesaddle. Nothing to it."

Gunning the bike at full throttle, McQueen zoomed along the city streets past cars, trucks, pedestrians, cops, and bicycles, weaving in and out of traffic while Neile clung tight with one arm and held down her crinoline skirt with the other. Their destination was Greenwich Village, where Steve exposed Neile to his part of the world. They visited friends, stopped at coffee shops, and talked about their lives. The two were uninhibited with their feelings and spoke of their childhoods, their mothers, and their fathers, and they realized that they had much in common. This openness and trust was something McQueen would rarely give even glimpses of, let alone fully confide in someone. The signs were good. "We went to the Village and started talking and talking and talking. Out of this marathon conversation we found that we had so many similarities in our backgrounds, and we knew that, somehow, from that moment on, we had only each other," Neile said.

They saw each other every night for the next week, taking rides on Steve's motorcycle, enjoying picnics in New Jersey, and shooting rifles in the country. Steve even tried to get Neile to join the Actors Studio. They watched George Peppard and Geraldine Page perform a scene and later Lee Strasberg dissecting their work, almost ripping them to shreds. Neile was horrified. The two walked outside for a breather, where Steve asked her what she thought. Neile pointed to a marquee on a theater and said, "Look there. See that theater over there? My name is up in lights there. What do I need them for?" McQueen never brought up the subject again.

A week into their courtship they moved in with each other. Four months later they were married.

Neile Adams was born Maria Rudy Neilan Adams Acostra y Salvador in Manila, Philippines, on June 10, 1933. Her parents divorced when she was an infant, and like Steve, she never met her father. Her mother, Carmen Salvador, was of Spanish and German descent. Carmen was a singer-dancer known as "Miami, Pearl of the Orient." Neile spent her formative years in a convent school in Hong Kong and was raised mostly by relatives while her mother traveled around the world, entertaining in nightclubs and theaters. Like Julian McQueen, Carmen's wants and needs often came before her own daughter's, who felt that she was an afterthought in her mother's life. "I was not close to my mother," Neile said in 2007.

Carmen entertained a long string of men, including General Douglas MacArthur, whom Neile recalled as a man who strutted like a proud peacock and smoked a funny-looking pipe. Whenever MacArthur's chauffeur-driven car appeared in their driveway, she was instructed by Carmen to go outside and play.

Weeks after the bombing of Pearl Harbor, Japanese troops invaded the Philippines in January 1942 and took control of the country. Carmen, who worked for the Allied underground, and nine-year-old Neile were incarcerated at a Japanese prison camp at the University of Santo Tomas for three years until they were rescued by American forces. Her time at the camp was as brutal as one would expect—even more brutal for a young and attractive girl.

Carmen partnered with Victor Rodgers, a wealthy New York City attorney, in an import-export business (selling postwar surplus commodities) that reaped tremendous profits. In 1948, Carmen sent her daughter to Rosemary Hall, a convent school in Wallingford, Connecticut, and then to Marjorie Webster Junior College in Washington, D.C., where she majored in dramatics. Neile went to New York to study with the American Theater Wing and discovered her real talent was dancing. She was good enough to earn a scholarship with instructor Katherine Dunham and worked as a Wall Street secretary to support herself. In July 1953, Neile was selected as one of three royal dancers in the Broadway version of *Kismet*, which had almost a two-year run. When the production was over, Neile signed a six-month contract at The Versailles, a famous New York City nightclub. A four-page spread in *Life* magazine commenced with her appearance in *The Pajama Game*. Stardom, it appeared, was just around the corner.

While Neile was kicking up her heels, her boyfriend was trying to fill the shoes of Ben Gazzara, who had garnered a Tony nomination in 1956 for his portrayal of Johnny Pope. It was a daunting task for McQueen because his stage experience was limited and his characters were often one-dimensional. Besides, he didn't have an ethnic bone in his body—his character called for someone of Latin descent—which prompted the cast and crew to nickname him "Cornflakes."

As he did before on *Two Fingers of Pride*, McQueen took deep-rooted steps to prepare for his role in *A Hatful of Rain*. In addition to dyeing his hair brown, he ventured to gritty Hell's Kitchen where he observed junkies courtesy of playwright Gazzo, who arranged for McQueen to get an up-close glimpse into their lives. He said McQueen melded into their world without making himself stand out.

However, McQueen lacked the inner techniques to make the role his own and was unable to deal with *Hatful*'s drug aspects. John Gilmore recalled that McQueen's projection and presence was not well suited for the stage. Gilmore saw the play with on-again, off-again girlfriend Dianne Rico after McQueen sent her two complimentary tickets, probably as a gesture to let her know exactly how far he had come since their split and to show Gilmore that he could have an intellectual edge, too. "We had choice seats but could barely hear his lines—a few rows from the footlights and he *still* wasn't audible," Gilmore said. "He gave a stiff, cardboard performance, and his movements seemed to blueprint the blocking and staging as if he were walking through a rehearsal. Harry Guardino, standing in for Tony Franciosa, gave a stunning, brilliant performance that rendered McQueen invisible."

The Broadway buzz was that McQueen had become progressively worse in the role. Actor Robert Culp remembers a couple of actors badmouthing McQueen's performance in front of the Lyceum Theater one night during his six-week stint. Culp felt immediately protective toward McQueen. "You guys are dead wrong! Sure, he's wrong for the part, but he's going to be a big, big star. You just wait and see."[1]

McQueen's performance wasn't the only reason he was floundering. He also did things to alienate himself from the company and crew, opting out of poker games and late-night bull sessions. He never felt part of the show. Actress Shelley Winters, who was later replaced by Vivian Blaine, remembers that McQueen, even at the start of his understudy, was not very serious. "He was supposed to watch the show, and instead he would make funny faces. He would be cross-eyed, and

---

1   Culp not only made this prophetic statement but also gave McQueen a helping hand a few years later with a guest-starring role in *Trackdown*, the television pilot for *Wanted: Dead or Alive*.

he would break us up. I thought it was some sort of a lark, that he must have been a rich kid who was just fooling around," Winters said.

Gilmore said he stumbled upon director Frank Corsaro admonishing his star one night in Downey's shortly before McQueen was given the axe. Gilmore recalled, "McQueen was complaining about his throat and that he didn't want to go on that night, while Corsaro insisted that he had to go on. No matter how Corsaro tried to convince him that 'the show must go on,' McQueen balked."

The next day McQueen was replaced by actor Peter Mark Richman.

The sting and rejection of *A Hatful of Rain* took years for McQueen to get over. Steve told a reporter, "I didn't have Ben's [Gazzara] technical facility—like the scene where the character goes delirious. Man, that threw me. Just depressed me." Privately, McQueen gave Richard Martin another reason why he was ousted. "The director of the play [Corsaro] kept coming onto him. Steve said no, and they canned him," Martin said.

Whatever the truth was, Steve was faced with one reality—Broadway was a closed avenue. And some say so was the Actors Studio. John Gilmore said McQueen's presence was disruptive to many in the Actors Studio and that Strasberg eventually had to cut him loose. "The consensus was that McQueen was a self-centered manipulator and a wholly insincere user who'd drop anything or anyone if a better offer came along," Gilmore said. "Strasberg made an announcement during class that 'certain individuals' could no longer feel welcome as members of the studio's close-knit family. Lee said, 'They prefer the empty glitter to dedicating themselves to the hard work committed here. A rattlesnake cannot be aligned with the heart of the family.' Though Lee never identified Steve, everybody knew who he was talking about."

Jack Garfein also confirmed that McQueen had a falling out with the Actors Studio but would not offer up a reason. "That's just something I don't want to discuss," Garfein said in 2010.

Gilmore's claims are disputed by Bob Heller, who said that McQueen was never kicked out of the Actors Studio. "Once you are a member, you are a member for life," Heller said. "It didn't happen. I would know, because I was there."

Whatever may be the truth, McQueen only publicly recognized Sanford Meisner, not Lee Strasberg, as the man who nurtured his talent.[2] McQueen also went on the record several times to dismiss The Method. "I used to be a Method School cowboy, and I think a lot of Stanislavski is so much Bullovslavski,"

---

2 Though McQueen used the Actors Studio on his résumé, he never commented on his work there nor talked publicly about Lee Strasberg.

McQueen said in 1964. "So as far as I'm concerned, acting for the movies is mainly intuition."

A few weeks after his Broadway fiasco, Steve felt that a spontaneous trip to Cuba would clear his head, and he offered to take Neile on a trek across the country. She took a pass, so McQueen, along with a poet plus a friend whom he later described as "just plain nuts," took a ferry that departed from Key West, Florida, and arrived in Cuba sometime in late September 1956. The three rented motorcycles and made the 967-kilometer trip from Havana to Santiago but encountered a military coup. Fidel Castro and his band of rebels were attempting a takeover of the government, headed by Fulgencio Batista, in Sierra Maestra.

"Seems Castro and Batista were shootin' at each other in Sierra Maestra, and things were kinda crazy over there." The three men made it back to Havana, where McQueen unsurprisingly got into some last-minute trouble.

"I got busted for selling contraband—which was actually a pack of American cigarettes—and was tossed in the local cooler," McQueen said. What McQueen didn't know was that Cuban cigars accounted for a good portion of the country's annual income and was its biggest export. American cigarettes, though highly desirable, cut into Cuba's Gross National Profit and were considered contraband. The fine was $100, money neither McQueen nor his equally broke buddies had in their pockets. The cooler wasn't so bad, according to McQueen. Besides, it probably gave him experience to draw from years later in his confinement scenes in *The Great Escape*. Except, in this instance, he didn't even contemplate a breakout.

"The guard was a friendly dude, and he'd let me come out of the cell so we could have lunch together—cheese and onions and wine and that hot sun with the smell of the Manzanita and the sewers," McQueen recalled.

McQueen reached Neile on October 3, 1956, and requested she wire him the money for the fine. Neile was in California for a period of 10 days to do a screen test for MGM's *This Could Be The Night*, a Robert Wise film. She received the following cable:

I LOVE YOU HONEY. SEND ME MONEY. LET ME KNOW WHAT'S HAPPENING. IN CARE OF WESTERN UNION CON AMOR. ESTEBAN

The cable also read that the sender was waiting for an immediate reply. McQueen never got one. Previous girlfriends and lovers had always relented and given in to lending him money, paying a bill, or bailing him out. This was different. He ended up having to sell his motorcycle helmet to get out of jail. He also resorted to pawning several of his personal belongings, bit by bit, to get back to New York. Neile returned from Hollywood four days before Steve's Cuban sojourn was over, and she was nervous that he'd be furious with her nonresponse to his cable. When Neile opened the apartment door, Steve was slouched in a living room chair, caked in dirt. She blurted out quickly, "I'm sorry I didn't send you the money." Steve, never one to forgive so easily, did an about-face that day and smiled.

"It's all right, baby. I admire your spunk," he said. "I love you, baby. It sure is nice to be home." Neile learned something about Steve that only a few people ever would—standing up to him and meeting him on his own terms would sometimes earn his respect.

Marriage seemed to be the natural order of things in terms of where Steve and Neile's relationship was headed, especially with Neile prodding him with not-so-subtle hints every now and then about his intentions. Her screen test for MGM went well, and Robert Wise sent for her once again. Neile pleaded with Steve to go with her, but his ego smarted by the fact that it appeared he was going to be the second banana when it came to their relationship. He had no money and no prospects at the time. She was making $50,000 a year compared to his $6,000, though he had no problems when it came to spending her money. Steve balked and told her to go to California without him. Upset and hurt, she left for the West Coast thinking she'd never see Steve again. He stewed in their apartment for a few days before he called Neile and proclaimed that he was going to "make an honest woman out of her." When McQueen told Richard Martin about the impending engagement, Martin suspected his buddy might have a hard time with monogamy, so he asked McQueen why he was marrying Neile. Steve replied, "Because I dig her, and she's making good bread out there."

Steve pawned his gold pocket watch that his Uncle Claude had given him and paid for a one-way flight to Los Angeles. "They don't make watches like this anymore," noted the pawnbroker, who examined the old-fashioned pocket watch in its burnished gold case.

"They don't make men like the man who gave it to me," Steve replied.

When Steve caught up with Neile on the MGM soundstage, he swept her off the floor and gave her a romantic kiss. He followed the gesture by proffering up a ring (he had put down a $25 deposit and let Neile pay off the balance over the next two years). Although she feigned happiness, Neile was thoroughly confused. A few weeks earlier, Steve wanted no part of the institution of marriage. Now he wanted to get hitched as soon as possible. Unpredictability and duality were aspects of Steve's character that she would have to quickly unravel and decide if she could accept.

Neile's smile was a temporary ruse to placate Steve. She quietly sneaked away to her dressing room, shut the door, and called her manager, Hilliard Elkins, in desperation. She was looking for a graceful way to say no to marriage yet still keep Steve. Elkins knew there was no middle ground in the situation and didn't mince words. "He's marrying you for your money. Don't be a schmuck," he warned. As Elkins saw it, McQueen was wrong for her. She was warm, friendly, wonderful, and very talented. McQueen was a spoiler, a very hardened, tough opportunist. Not only was he competitive with other actors, he was competitive with Neile. "It was that kind of passionate desire to succeed, to get out of the situation he was in, that was a thread that ran through his life, because he realized that if he didn't take care of No. 1, nobody else would," Elkins said.

Three days after his arrival, Neile realized she could no longer fend off Steve; she simply had to marry him. They rented a Ford Thunderbird and headed to the Mission San Juan Capistrano, long considered the jewel of California missions. McQueen picked the Mission because he and Neile had been raised as Catholics and because he had learned of the cliff swallow, a migratory bird that spends its winters in Goya, Argentina, but makes the annual 6,000-mile trek north to take refuge at the Mission. Romantic intentions notwithstanding, McQueen failed to realize that the birds migrated in the spring and not the winter. Making arrangements from a roadside telephone booth, McQueen learned from a nun that the Mission married only members of their parish.

"If you don't marry us, we are going to live in sin for the rest of our lives," he threatened, but to no avail. Neile was silently relieved, but Steve was not a man easily dissuaded. They made a run for the Mexican border but Steve was pulled over for speeding in San Clemente around 11:30 PM. "I explained to the cop that we wanted very much to get married this weekend, so he called up the pastor of the Lutheran Church in San Clemente and they took us to the church—they had lighted candles. The two state troopers came in and acted as witnesses. And here I'd been fighting cops my whole life."

On November 2, 1956, Steve and Neile were officially man and wife. Their quickie marriage was part of McQueen's signature thrill-seeking, risk-taking behavior, according to psychologist Peter O. Whitmer. "Impulsivity is a constant theme throughout Steve McQueen's life, and his marriage to Neile demonstrates the yin and the yang of his behavior," Whitmer said. "On one side he had a real longing for parsimony, simplicity, and order. On the other side, creating tension to that, were the factors of chaos and tumult.

"After Steve made a cross-country trip to jam a ring on her finger, where do they go get married? San Juan Capistrano. For what is San Juan best known? First off, it's a beautiful chapel near the ocean; religion and tranquility; a sanctuary. But most important, it is known because it is the place where the swallows return once a year on the exact same day. It is a symbol of natural order. These were two things that Steve never had in his life, yet on a less-than-conscious level, he knew that they were the anchors he needed.

"And so what happened when they found out they could not be married at this site of predictability and consistency and repetitiveness—like a grandfather clock ticking away? They zoomed away, got pulled over by the California Highway Patrol for speeding, ended up talking the cops into pulling a pastor from his home and marrying them, with those 'authority figure' police as witnesses.

"What a crazed, chaotic, tumultuous, wonderful scene! It puts the yin and yang—the higher-order tensions in his life—right out in front where everyone can see it."

After a short weekend honeymoon in Ensenada, Mexico, Neile immediately went back to work on *This Could Be the Night*, while Steve settled into her room at the Aloha Motel in Hollywood, just across the street from MGM. His foul mood returned, and his ego would simply not let him tolerate being second-best to anyone; he wanted the limelight and the fame all to himself. McQueen told a reporter he had a life-changing moment in the MGM commissary during the filming of the picture. "You know when I decided I'd better be successful? Right after Neile and I got married. She was making a movie in Hollywood. I was an out-of-work actor, and she was supporting me. In the studio commissary, all the guys were crowding around Neile, giving me the elbow, calling me 'Mr. Adams.' I was all uptight and pushed out of shape. I knew right then and there I'd better get ready to be somebody."

With nothing but free time on his hands, McQueen quickly went through Neile's money. He gambled, treated himself to a new Corvette, and bought himself anything he desired. He also became obsessed with finding his father again. Steve learned through Julian that the last time she had heard of his whereabouts, he was living in California. Steve dragged Neile around during her spare time, which was little if any, to search for leads to his father's whereabouts. Steve had picked up William's trail and was making progress. Neile remembers her husband's behavior as bordering on obsessive. "Steve had a very low patience quotient. He would throw himself into a project with an enormously concentrated effort, but when that effort proved fruitless, he would lose interest and drop the project abruptly, almost as if to recharge himself for the time to come when a sudden renewed interest would again spark the flame and he would resume with the same fury that had consumed him in the first place," Neile wrote in her 1986 memoir, *My Husband, My Friend.*

Steve had other aberrations—affairs and sexual liaisons—even before he was hitched. John Gilmore, who had later married Dianne Rico, said McQueen was still bedding her in his and Neile's West 55th Street apartment. "[Diana] had been married once before, the year she took up with McQueen. She claimed that she loved me, as Neile now loved Steve. But what neither of us knew was that McQueen and Diana were getting together in Neile's apartment while Neile was still doing the musical on Broadway and while I thought Diana was working with a new dance company." Neile simply put up with Steve's extracurricular activities because of her upbringing and because of a bit of advice her mother Carmen gave her—better the devil you know than the one you don't. "I told him as long as you don't flaunt it, I can handle it. I came from an Oriental and Spanish background, and in that family the man reigns supreme. Both of those cultures were so embedded in me that it was something I accepted, plus I was brought up in an area where really there were no married families around. Men could do what they wanted and it was cool," Neile said.

Not only did Neile work and pay the bills, Steve expected her to cook, clean, and cater to his whims. He expected her to simply conform to a traditional and antiquated role of the woman as housewife—an obsession that would later manifest itself with his second wife, Ali MacGraw. Neile was often tired after filming and didn't always have the energy to cook or put up with Steve's frenetic energy. One night she thought she could trick her husband into believing she had cooked him a homemade meal by heating up a TV dinner. She tried to disguise its appearance by unloading the contents from the tin tray onto a plate. With a nervous smile she presented it to Steve, who took one whiff and erupted. He picked up the dish and smashed it against the hotel wall. That prompted a phone call to her manager, Hilly Elkins.

"Hilly, you've got to do something about Steve," Neile pleaded. "He's driving me nuts." Elkins agreed to have lunch with McQueen, but he wasn't converted. He called Neile afterward and suggested she dump him. "He's rude, crude, and obnoxious," Elkins started off. "Besides, there are too many blond-haired, blue-eyed boys in Hollywood. I can't handle him."

Elkins' opinion soon changed when he caught a glimpse of McQueen on *The Defender*, a two-part television series shot at CBS's Studio 61 and presented on February 25 and March 4, 1957, as part of the *Studio One* series. "I saw one minute of *The Defender*, and he just broke through the screen," Elkins recalled. "Those eyes just lit up the fuckin' screen and came out at you." After the show was over, Elkins promptly called Neile, apologized, and signed Steve to a managerial contract. Once again, McQueen had thrown his weight around, made his unreasonable demands, and got his way. He forced fortune to smile upon him when he was wearing a frown.

The Defender follows a father and son legal team (Ralph Bellamy and William Shatner) as they take on a case to defend Joseph Gordon (McQueen), a notorious juvenile delinquent, who has been accused of murder. Shatner recalled in his 2008 autobiography *Up Till Now*, "I remember watching McQueen and thinking, 'Wow, he doesn't do anything.' He was inarticulate, he mumbled, and only later did I understand how beautifully he did nothing. It was so internalized that the camera picked it up as would a pair of inquisitive eyes. Out of seemingly nothing he was creating a unique form of reality." The camera would prove to be the perfect medium for his craft, far better than the stage ever would. There was no need to worry about mumbling when the microphone can pick it up and people could see his sparkling blue eyes crystal clear, beaming from the screen.

The role was Steve McQueen's first real attempt at creating his own on-screen persona instead of emulating Marlon Brando or James Dean. Neile instinctively knew her husband's personality wasn't showing in his performance and suggested Steve add some nuance to his character. "Smile a little bit. I know it's a tough thing to do because you're playing a killer, but when you're talking to your mother or something, you've got to be able to show something of you. So he did and for the first time he got fan mail, and he said, 'Yeah, yeah, that's good.' And for the first time he realized that I was on his team," Neile said.

His performance garnered solid critical praise within the industry. *Billboard* wrote, "The large cast performed excellently with special nods to Ralph Bellamy, Vivian Blaine, and Steve McQueen," while *Variety* exclaimed, "Steve McQueen as the defendant was powerful in his inscrutability and repulsiveness." Perhaps the highest praise came from CBS executive and Emmy Award–winner Herbert Brodkin, who lauded McQueen in a March 5, 1957, letter:

> *Dear Steve:*
>
> *Just a line to thank you for the work you did in "The Defender." We have already had many fine reports, both within the industry and without, and they convince me that, despite the skepticism of some of our reviewers, the show was a hit and had an enthusiastic audience.*
>
> *And, incidentally, it would appear you've had quite an audience of your own—we've had a couple of calls from "fans of Steven McQueen."*
>
> *All best wishes and again, my thanks.*
>
> *Sincerely yours,*
>
> *Herbert Brodkin*

The fan letters had started, and once the tap was turned, the trickle would one day become a flood. At his peak, McQueen would have so many fan letters that he would be able to read only a fraction, signing replies and photos with a rubber stamp—not bad for the "lazy actor" sacked from *A Hatful of Rain*. More important than the kudos and critical praise was that *The Defender* recharged McQueen's lethargic career with a spate of television and film opportunities. McQueen had a mercurial character, and his enthusiasm would ebb and flow, peak and subside, depending on how encouraged or determined he felt. Cracking film and television was no easy feat. All his life, McQueen had to be the one motivating himself to push forward and to succeed, all of which took tremendous energy and self-belief, even if he often wavered. But now he had Neile on his side and could taste triumph edging ever closer. This gave him renewed strength, and he was ready to build on this opportunity. McQueen would do it any way he could, and whether it was through hard work or pure ruthlessness, he would make it.

10

LOW BUDGET

In January 1957, Steve introduced his bride to his humble beginnings while attempting to bid farewell to his past. His future with Neile and the opportunities before him must have filled Steve with a sense of excitement and desire. However, to fully embrace the new life he was starting, he would have to confront the ghosts and traumas of his childhood.

Neile had been signed to a six-month revue contract in Las Vegas, but before she started, McQueen had other plans. The two drove from New York, making a pit stop in Slater, Missouri. It was Steve's way of peeling back a layer of his life for Neile and also to pay homage to his Uncle Claude, who was in his early eighties. For such a tremendously closed person like Steve, this was a milestone in his personal development and a rare moment of opening up. He was trusting someone with an insight into the elements that made him who he was. Steve wanted Claude to know that he had finally "got it together." Claude was happy to see Steve and held out his hand to shake.

"How ya doing, boy?"

"Fine, just fine," Steve replied. It was the first time Claude had seen Steve as a grown man, and the glint in his eye let everyone present know he was proud. Claude had been the first real disciplinary and guiding force in Steve's life, providing encouragement and punishment in fair and equal measure. Gaining Uncle Claude's approval validated to Steve that his struggles had started to pay off. Despite usually giving off an air of indestructible self-confidence and self-belief, approval was important for McQueen. He had been through trouble all his life, so reassurance and approval told him he had succeeded.

Neile recalled, "We went back to that farm in Missouri to the old wood house with his tiny room up under the leaves, and there was his grand-uncle and his grand-aunt, and it was like 'American Gothic.' You knew where Steve came from and where some of his principles came from."

Their visit had overtones of *Green Acres* and *City Slickers,* judging by Steve's description. "My uncle told Neile that when a cow drops a calf in the pasture, you have to go out and get the calf or the sows will eat it alive. He told her how I saved a calf once. I was going out to get milk at about 4:30 in the morning—I saw a cow who was trying to protect her newly born calf and throwing the sows around. I ran in and picked up her calf to take it to the barn, and the sows would make passes at me. I kicked them in the snout, and just as I got back to the barn one tackled me and I made a flying leap over the fence just at the last moment. So Neile suddenly got frightened of all pigs. Well, she walked around the corner of the barn and met a sow who was at least a hundred years old—the sow gave a surprised 'oink,' Neile screamed, and they both ran in the opposite direction."

Their visit was well-timed; Claude died on November 28, 1957. He was 83. Steve didn't attend his funeral, nor did he ever step foot in Slater again. It was a closed chapter and one that he intended never to reopen.

Neile was due to start her new contract for $1,500 a week at the Tropicana Hotel in Las Vegas, at the bottom of a bill featuring Vivian Blaine and comedian Dick Shawn. Before the start of the six-month stint, while Neile commenced her one-woman show, Steve was a man on a mission, looking to build his fame and gild his image as a superstar. While Neile was getting her name plastered on marquees, Steve was getting his name in films. He headed west to Los Angeles to test for the role of a young Jewish lawyer in Allied Artists' *Never Love a Stranger.* Based on a Harold Robbins' best-selling novel, McQueen's third screen assignment was his meatiest role to date. Days after he tested for the part, he was cast opposite John Drew Barrymore.

Despite its low budget ($800,000) and poverty-row location, the book's success (more than three million copies sold), which leaned heavily on shocking frankness concerning sex, was whitewashed in the film. McQueen hadn't yet learned how to transfer to the screen the ultra-cool, loner, tough-guy persona he would perfect within just a couple of years, an observation made by costar Richard Bright. "It was just his whole demeanor. He was wimpy. He didn't seem to be a knock-around kind of guy," Bright said. "I guess that ruggedness came later with the bikes. I didn't see any spark at all." Neither did *Variety,* who savaged the film: "It is so ineptly and unprofessionally done, especially in its handling of such volatile subjects as race and religion, that it has nothing else to recommend it except a vague topicality." Looking at the film retrospectively, it is clear that this movie was just a stepping stone. The character McQueen played, the good guy, the easygoing stand-up gentleman, was not the sort of character he would forge for himself in his later hit films. This was the complete opposite of his future on-screen persona. Soon he would turn this around and redefine the term *rebel* for a whole new generation.

McQueen couldn't find anything positive to say about *Never Love a Stranger*, either. He told writer William F. Nolan, "That turkey wasn't released for two years, and the only notice I got was from a critic who said my face looked like a Botticelli angel that had been crossed with a chimp." However, just because he was wholesome on the screen and the model citizen did not mean that in real life the leopard had changed its spots. It was the same old Steve, always finding an interesting angle—this time, unsurprisingly, of the female variety. McQueen said to fellow actor Richard Martin the best part of the film was sleeping with costar Lita Milan, who was "wild in the sack." The exotic brunette was the first in a long line of meaningless flings he conducted with his leading ladies. McQueen didn't just want fame; he wanted stardom and power with all the "benefits" that came with it.

What McQueen did in the dark did have consequences. He never failed to confess his transgressions to Neile, who was naturally hurt. "He had the need to tell me. The guilt would be released, you know—see, because he'd feel so guilty, he had to tell me, like the confessor. 'Bless me, father, for I have sinned. Now you know. Now I feel all right.' He can do it all over again. He had a lot of demons," Neile said. This demonstrates the insensitive and perhaps selfish side of McQueen. His confessions made him feel better, and that's what counted, even though he hurt those around him. But there was also another reason, according to psychologist Peter O. Whitmer. "Although it seems quite odd and perhaps totally incredulous for a husband to come home from work and tell his wife that he has just had a 'fling' with a colleague, in Steve McQueen's case, it was actually a calculated test of the strength of his marriage," Whitmer said. "In all his interpersonal relationships, there was a 'McQueen hallmark' of testing the limits, seeing how another would react to his aggressive behavior. And when it came to 'marriage'—the ultimate interpersonal relationship—McQueen was, at the core, both totally ambivalent about and lacking adequate trust. Thus he required near-constant confirmation that his spouse would always stand by her man.

"No profession, no community allowed greater opportunity for a 'working man' to have presented to him and to seize the opportunity for an extramarital 'fling,' than Hollywood. Neile knew it; it was in the air. Steve knew it; it was at his beck and call.

"The difference between Steve McQueen and others working inside a virtual harem was that flaunting these behaviors was a necessity to preserve his marriage. And given his lifelong dire skepticism of others, this was a handy tool to use for straight-arming that particular fear—that the person he had allowed to become the closest to him of anyone might possibly abandon him. Because for that, there was ample precedent."

Never Love a Stranger did nothing to advance McQueen's flagging career, who was better known in the press and public as Neile Adams' husband. A May 15, 1957, news item from famed New York City columnist Walter Winchell clearly underscored the point: "Neile Adams and bridegroom back from the Coast strolling along 6th Avenue in their Beverly Hills sweater-and-slax get-up." While Neile was swimming in film, television, and Broadway opportunities, Steve was treading water. He tried in earnest to negotiate a leading role in *Be Still My Heart*, a novel by crime writer turned screenwriter Steve Fisher. Fisher was a key figure in the development of film noir as a Hollywood genre, and he was one of the most important and influential screenwriters[1] of the 1940s. The deal eventually collapsed, but a more interesting offer came in the form of a quickie horror flick about a meteor that lands on Earth and morphs into a red ball of goo that feeds off humans. It was called *The Blob*.

While *The Blob* was in preproduction, McQueen joined the straw-hat circuit for *A Hatful of Rain*. The summer tour took place throughout June and July 1957 and was mostly an East Coast affair. It was packaged by a company who had nothing to do with the original Broadway production, and they were clueless about McQueen's prior sacking, which is why they offered him the role of Johnny Pope once more. Steve took the job but quite reluctantly, according to Howie Fishlove, who met McQueen backstage at the Playhouse-in-the-Park in Philadelphia a few weeks before *The Blob* commenced. "He wasn't very happy with what he had to do in the production," Fishlove said. "He said, 'I can't wait to get out of here. I'm yelling and screaming and I just can't stand it anymore.'" The role still haunted him.

The Blob, originally titled *The Molten Meteor* and later *The Glob*, was the brainchild of distributor-turned-producer Jack H. Harris and was based on an idea that came as a result of heated exchange with one of Harris' clients in a board meeting. "One of our suppliers called for a meeting in Chicago, and everybody there was imbued with food and booze and extolled the merits of the company that was supplying us with all of these films, which were just awful. I just sat there and the head of the company said, 'What do you have to say, Jack?' Well, I was the only one there who was sober and said, 'I have to say your program stinks, and I'm going to talk to another supplier about getting some other movies.' He

---

1   Fisher wrote the screenplays for *I Wake up Screaming*, *Lady in the Lake*, *Dead Reckoning*, and *Song of the Thin Man*.

said, 'Oh, and what do you suggest?' Just off the top of my head I said, 'A monster movie that's never been done before. Instead of black and white, it should be shot in color with a story that makes sense.' He said, 'Well, look, if you think so much about it, why don't you go ahead and do it?' A couple of years later, I did do it."

The $130,000 production was one of the few 1950s science-fiction films shot in color, and it gave Steve McQueen his first star-billing role, though at this point he was known as *Steven* McQueen as opposed to Steve.

Harris enlisted the help of director Irvin Shortess "Shorty" Yeaworth, a self-taught director who made films for the Christian marketplace. His company, Good News Productions, produced more than 400 missionary, motivational, and entertainment films. Yeaworth took on *The Blob* to see if he could communicate to a secular audience and earn some quick capital for his company.

How McQueen was hired will eternally remain a tug of war between two memories—Jack Harris and Russell Doughten, the film's production manager. Harris claims he insisted on casting McQueen after his scene-stealing turn on *The Defender*. "He electrified me. I was sitting in my chair half asleep and I woke up and couldn't get over how Steve McQueen looked and acted over the tube."

However, Doughten contends that Harris' claim is "pure horseshit," and McQueen chased down the part with full gusto. "Shorty and I met McQueen about six months before we started shooting the picture. He left quite an indelible impression on me," Doughten recalled. "I was standing on the steps of the administration building of Good News Productions, when I heard this strange sound out of the boondocks—it was the revving of the engine. I listened to it for about five minutes when Steve pulled up in a tiny MG. After he turned off the ignition, he jumped out of the car to ask if an actress [Neile] he had dated was around. I said she was but was in a studio across the street. He wasn't much on conversation but had plenty of charisma."

As it turned out, Neile had worked on a three-day shoot for one of Yeaworth's religious films, and McQueen had worn out his welcome in no time. He was highly opinionated, profane, and demanding despite the fact he had nothing to do with the production. Yeaworth was the first to say good riddance. Six months later, Doughten said he and Yeaworth were in New York City to cast the lead character and bumped into McQueen near Central Park while walking his dog, Thor. "McQueen recognized us and asked what we were doing in the Big Apple. When we told him we were there to find actors for our movie, he became a little friendlier."

McQueen asked if there was a part for him. Yeaworth politely told him all of the main parts were for older teenagers and that he was simply too old. McQueen, who had turned 27 that year, promised he could act much younger if given the chance, something he proved later in his career when he played the teenage title character in *Nevada Smith*. McQueen offered the two men an opportunity to kick up their heels in his apartment in between appointments while he read the manuscript and gave them a quick reading. "Let me try a line or two and see what you think," Steve said. "I can play young." He tried it, they liked it, and McQueen had the part. Doughten said today, "If anything, Steve got that role himself. He didn't really audition. And he was happy as a clam to get the part."

Produced in August 1957 in and around the Philadelphia suburbs (Chester Springs, Phoenixville, Downingtown, Valley Forge), the small cast and crew had a six-week shooting schedule, taking off only Sundays so that Good News employees could attend church.

McQueen came to the set with a heavy-duty reputation, and he literally started his employment on *The Blob* with a bang—by tossing firecrackers at the cast and crew. "My first impression, and excuse my language, was that McQueen was a real asshole," said Howie Fishlove, who was the head grip on the picture. "He was annoying. He drove around on his motorcycle and kept throwing firecrackers at all of us. I thought, 'What in the hell is the matter with this guy?'"

Fishlove wasn't alone in his assessment of McQueen, who insisted on a bigger dressing room, brought his dog to the set, raced his sports car and motorcycle in between takes, and upstaged costar Aneta Corsaut whenever he had the opportunity. He would become notorious for his obstinacy throughout his career. Harris was the recipient of several phone calls from Yeaworth, who prefaced most conversations with, "Well, your star's acting up again." The "blob" itself may have been featured on the posters and retained the title of the film, but this was the "McQueen show" as far as Steve was concerned. He was the star of this picture, not some special effect.

His behavior came to a head a few days into the shoot when McQueen was arrested in a neighboring town for reckless driving in his MG Sports Roadster. Harris bailed him out with the proviso that McQueen had to clean up his act. "I'd run out to the set, sit down with Steve, and try to figure out what was wrong. Steve's spiel, 'I'm going to call my agent, I'm going to call my manager, I'm going to call my lawyer,' eventually ran out of steam." Anyone who even had a remote understanding of McQueen's complexity of character may have sensed this was not simply a case of him being a spoiled brat. It stemmed from his need to be told he was doing well, that he was succeeding. Harris correctly realized that, "In the end, we came to terms. He wanted approval. What he was looking for was somebody to be Daddy and say, 'You're a nice guy and I like you.'"

Although McQueen and Harris had an understanding, the feisty star continually bumped heads with Yeaworth, who had a policy of not allowing his actors to view dailies. Harris was forced to play peacemaker and came up with a compromise. He ordered Yeaworth to invite McQueen to screenings every third day of filming. Harris noted that McQueen was a no-show to about half of the screenings, and when he did attend, he remained silent. Typical McQueen—he always got his way, one way or another. However, antics like this were not just passing fancies or whims; they were his way of laying down his marker and establishing his importance and place at the summit of the films he was in and the characters he created.

Over time, McQueen used his street smarts and finesse in tense situations, according to costar Robert Fields. McQueen even showed that he could occasionally give as well as take. "Steve was a good decade older than me when we worked together on the movie. I had just started my tenure at the Neighborhood Playhouse that summer. Steve took me under his wing and protected me on the set," Fields said.

Fields was 17 and had just graduated high school. During one scene in the picture, he just couldn't seem to please the director. After several takes, Yeaworth was exasperated and told Fields he wasn't giving him what he needed. McQueen held up his hand and played the unfamiliar role of peacemaker.

"Wait a minute, Shorty," McQueen pleaded. "Bob and I worked at the Neighborhood Playhouse together, and we both speak the same language. I think I know what you're asking him to do, so let's take a break so that I can tell him what you need." Yeaworth smiled and readily agreed. The two actors walked away and out of earshot from Yeaworth, and Fields said McQueen spoke with an intensity he'd never seen before.

"Fuck 'em! Keep doing what you're doing, Bob," McQueen said. With that the two men walked back to the set and took their places. "I think we've got it now," McQueen smiled.

Yeaworth called for action, and they shot the scene in one take. "I think that tells a lot about Steve," Fields said. "He was very street smart. He knew how to handle people and certainly people who had no background in the movie business. He could handle the director, fix that moment, dissolve an impasse, which to me illustrates his sophistication. Steve figured out how to handle the director; the director didn't handle Steve. So I loved him for that."

Love-hate was perhaps the best description of McQueen's relationship with actress Aneta Corsaut, who was best known for her long-running role as schoolteacher Helen Crump on *The Andy Griffith Show*. McQueen and Corsaut engaged in an affair—that is, until Neile showed up on the set. "I think Steve seduced her

[Corsaut], and it was no big deal," Fields said. "When you're in the middle of nowhere for weeks, you've gotta do something. Then I remember Neile visited, and Steve was very attentive to her. He went on the alert. He didn't want to get caught and was on his best behavior."

Howie Fishlove said McQueen didn't need to hide because Neile knew all about his past indiscretions. "They had just gotten married, and those two were lovebirds. She would sit on his lap all day, every day, on his actor's chair. One time Neile had complained about his behavior before they met, and she just yelled out, 'He thought he had a golden cock!' I thought it was kinda funny because I'd never heard a woman talk like that before."

Neile's presence and Steve's need to upstage Corsaut caused friction between the two stars. Fishlove recalled, "Those two hated each other. They didn't get along, and we had to separate them many times. I think he was trying to upstage her, and she got really upset. We had to stop shooting several times because they did not like each other at all."

Corsaut never discussed her relationship with McQueen but did tell writer Lee Pfeiffer the production had a hellfire-and-brimstone edge and its star was anything but a saint. "Everyone connected to [*The Blob*] was so religious. The producers, the director," Corsaut said. "I remember Steve McQueen drove the producers crazy. He was more of a maverick in those days, real hell on wheels. Every day the filmmakers would go into prayer meetings—they would pray to everything, including the makeup brushes! They would always finish by saying, 'And save us from Steve McQueen!'"

Not only did they pray to be delivered from McQueen, but they also prayed for his salvation. Russell Doughten said when Yeaworth wasn't witnessing to McQueen, he and several others picked up the slack. "It was easy to tell Steve was not saved. He was materialistic, hedonistic, and profane, like most people. He would talk to me about the Bible; sometimes he'd argue, but he wasn't vehement. He knew he was a sinner. He wasn't trying not to be a sinner. Obviously it didn't take at the time," Doughten said.

When the movie went a week over schedule, Harris asked everyone to work for free to make up the $10,000 overrun. Everyone agreed but McQueen, who adamantly refused. This upset Doughten, who had a heart-to-heart with the actor. "I talked to him about materialistic things and how he was making those possessions more important to him than a relationship with Christ. I think that his time with us on *The Blob* showed him how true Christians lived, acted, and worked. Steve let it be known his intentions were to go to Hollywood and become a big star and that nothing was going to get in his way. Frankly, I saw him entering the wilderness of the world, and it swallowed him up for a long time." Doughten said his last act was handing over his well-worn Bible to McQueen. He specifically dog-eared a page and underlined the verse for John 3:16.

The only thing Biblical about *The Blob* was its box-office take—$6 million net profit. Paramount Pictures, who paid $300,000 to distribute the film, was surprised by its success and initially bought it for the bottom half of a double bill with *I Married a Monster From Outer Space*. When the numbers came back, they flipped the bill and devoted all their promotional energy to *The Blob*. It was a wise decision, and the reward was that it became Paramount's most profitable film for 1958.

Like the Hula-Hoop, coonskin caps, and TV dinners, *The Blob* crossed over into the realm of 1950s pop culture. That was in large part due to the kitschy title song (written by Burt Bacharach and Hal David under the phantom group The Blobs). The song, which ultimately sold three million copies, was a glorified radio jingle for the movie. The lyrics, cautioning audiences to "beware of the Blob," "a splotch, a blotch" that "leaps and slides and glides" also encouraged everyone to view the picture as campy fun.

The Blob also provided grist for comedians and television personalities who found the gelatinous ball of goo too hard to resist as a punch line. Steve Allen, Jack Benny, George Burns, and Bob Hope mentioned *The Blob* every time they needed a sure-fire laugh from audiences. Harris didn't mind all the jokes because he laughed all the way to the bank. "The song, the jokes, the poking fun of my picture all translated into a golden flow of revenue at the theater box offices," Harris said in 2009. This might have made McQueen just a tad envious. He called Harris a few weeks after the film was released and hinted that had he known how big the picture was going to be, he'd have held out for a percentage of the action.

"You wouldn't have gotten it, Steve," Harris said, laughing. Contrary to popular belief, McQueen was never offered $2,500 or 10 percent of the profits. That was a rumor he circulated to several industry reporters perhaps to deflect the film's 'so bad it's good' quality or to hide that he signed a very lopsided deal. Harris also confirmed that McQueen not only signed for a flat rate of $3,000 but gave Harris an option for his next two pictures—*The 4-D Man* and *Dinosaurus!* Harris said, however, he had no inclination to enforce the contract. "Steve was a star without really being one at the time. He was a really revolting star, but I liked him. I picked him for the movie, and I liked him. But he was a serious pain in the ass. There was just no way I was going to make two more movies with him."

McQueen, like everyone else associated with *The Blob*, thought the movie would quickly rocket into obscurity. "We knew we were making a B-class movie, if that," offered Howie Fishlove. "It's not a very good film. It's slow, and there are several errors in the picture. I didn't think we'd even be talking about it after that summer. It's mind-boggling that we'd even be discussing this movie after all these years." Fishlove said McQueen was even reluctant to discuss the movie two decades later when he was an extra on *The Hunter*, McQueen's last film. "I walked up to Steve during a break and reintroduced myself. After a few minutes of chit-chat, I said to him that the editor of the film sent me a blooper reel and offered to send him a copy. Steve said under his breath, 'Burn it.' I objected, 'Steve, you might like to see it.' He said, 'Burn it.' He wasn't kidding around."

After six years on the movie and drive-in circuit, Harris sold *The Blob* to television, where it enjoyed a revival with younger audiences. The film's popularity and camp appeal slowly grew over the years thanks to a big nod in 1978's *Grease*, and like its unconventional monster, it just wouldn't die.

The Blob has morphed into a cult classic with a devoted following that defies logic. Forty years after the motion picture was shot, a nonprofit community group in Phoenixville, Pennsylvania, restored the Colonial Theater (where the film's climax was shot) in 1997. Its biggest gate was in July 2000 when *The Blob* made a triumphant hometown return. Since then, the town has held the annual BlobFest every July to celebrate the most famous product the town has ever produced. A collective scream at noon by audience members officially signals the commencement of the daylong festival.

"In my lifetime as I wander through various meetings and speeches, I haven't met one person who didn't see the film or didn't remember exactly where they were when they first saw the picture. Now that's an icon," Harris said.

While McQueen ranted for years that *The Blob* was a professional embarrassment, there's no denying what the film did for his career—it ultimately brought McQueen to the attention of Dick Powell, who headed up Four Star Studios in Los Angeles. He asked to see a rough cut of the picture. Based on McQueen's performance and a begrudging recommendation from Harris ("He's a temperamental jerk, but he's worth it"), Powell ultimately cast him in the CBS television series *Wanted: Dead or Alive*.

From here on, McQueen could forget fighting a not-so-special-effect movie monster and get to play a character he could immerse himself in. As Josh Randall, the bounty hunter, McQueen would play a character with a dichotomy he could empathize with, torn between ruthlessness and a good-natured heart. This was not unlike McQueen himself, even if the good side was sometimes difficult to spot and the ruthlessness often overzealous. This would be the star vehicle that made Steve McQueen a household name.

11

GO WEST, YOUNG MAN

THE BLOB DIDN'T MAKE STEVE McQUEEN AN OVERNIGHT STAR or place him high on any studio's list, but it did garner his name above the title billing in his next motion picture—a low-budget bank heist drama called *The Great St. Louis Bank Robbery*.

The United Artists film (the first of four that McQueen did with the studio) is based on a true incident in which four outlaws from Chicago attempt to rob the Southwest Bank in St. Louis for more than $140,000 in April 1953. Once inside the bank, their scheme quickly unraveled, and pandemonium erupted as the robbery went awry. Approximately 100 officers arrived shortly after the call, and police tear-gassed the building while drawing the attention of thousands of curious onlookers. Four years later, Charles Guggenheim decided he wanted to immortalize the robbery for the silver screen.

The Oscar-winning documentary filmmaker stepped out of his comfort zone to produce his first feature, and he signed McQueen in October 1957 to star as George Fowler, a college dropout who is talked into becoming the getaway driver. Guggenheim enlisted John Stix to direct the black-and-white picture on location in St. Louis.

Stix was a highly respected Broadway director (*Too Late the Phalarope*) and a fixture at the Actors Studio, where he was well acquainted with McQueen. According to actor and Actors Studio alumnus Bob Heller, Heller himself was Stix's first choice as George Fowler. Before Heller signed the contract, Stix discovered the unfortunate fact that Heller could not drive. "I was born and raised in Brooklyn and there was never a need for me to drive, but it was necessary for the movie," Heller said more than five decades later. "Oh, how things might have been different."

To keep the film as authentic as possible, Stix also hired some of the men and women from the St. Louis Police Department, as well as local residents and bank employees, to play the same parts they did in the actual robbery attempt. He also lured Melburn Stein to play himself and re-create the shooting. Stein said he "didn't get paid one red cent" for his participation in the film because his superiors felt the movie would reflect positively on the police department.

Stein turned out to be a natural and pulled off his speaking role flawlessly in a single take. However, he found McQueen didn't offer much in the way of acting tips or conversation. "McQueen was as cold as a cucumber. He might have been able to convey a lot in movies by not saying much, but I quickly discovered he didn't have much to say off camera, either. I don't know if he was nervous or if he was indifferent. Let's just say he wasn't much of a conversationalist," Stein said. "I've discovered over the years many people have a hard time becoming friendly with an officer in uniform. Given McQueen's reform school background and his history with police, it's easy to see why he kept his distance."

To give McQueen his due, he had the weight of the picture on his shoulders, and it was a confusing shoot. Guggenheim and Stix employed multiple cameras, using a lot of movement with large crowds watching the actors' every move. Because of the film's low budget, scenes had to be shot guerrilla-style, and there wasn't the money or luxury of retakes in the 33-day shoot. *The St. Louis Post* also reported that someone stole the wardrobe of the entire cast, including McQueen's outfit. Filming was halted for an entire day until the clothes could be duplicated.

Though McQueen's character was fairly weak, he made the part believable and exhibited all the signs of the great things that were to come in his career. His performance deftly combines elements of innocence, bitterness, madness, and despair, and all are convincingly portrayed. The film, however, is deeply flawed. It is 75 minutes of careful preparation and 10 minutes of abrupt violence during the bank robbery. It was too static for most who saw the picture. "The pacing is far too slow and the neurotic clashes of the four thieves make the actual robbery anticlimactic and slightly absurd," noted Howard Thompson of the *New York Times*.

Stein, who is in his nineties and still lives in Missouri, conceded it was not a stellar production. "Frankly, I didn't think McQueen was all that great. I can't say I was pleased with the picture, either, because it contained too many historical inaccuracies. But there isn't a day that goes by when somebody doesn't ask me about the robbery or Steve McQueen."

Even McQueen admitted *The Great St. Louis Bank Robbery* failed to live up to its billing. "The only great thing about this one was the title. Most of the gang gets wiped out while I surrender to the cops. Nothing really worked in the film, but it was another screen credit. And each screen credit helps you get the next one. You're young and you're hungry and you grab at what comes along."

McQueen's professional frustration boiled over into his personal life, and his foul mood on *The Great St. Louis Bank Robbery* could be chalked up to the fact that his marriage to Neile was hanging by a thread. Infidelities aside, the bicoastal newlyweds rarely saw each other during the first year of their marriage. When they did, their sleeping arrangements were often disrupted by Thor, Steve's unruly and ill-mannered German shepherd, who was not potty-trained and relieved himself wherever he pleased. Steve also racked up thousands of dollars per month in long-distance calls, which often ended in slammed phone receivers and hurt feelings. "It was the one and only terrible period of our marriage," Neile said. "We were married and thousands of miles apart. We didn't know each other too well, and the minute we were separated all the insecurities came flooding."

However, it was the disparity of their paychecks and McQueen's ego struggling with the fact that his wife was the main breadwinner that were the true underlying problems. A joint filing of their 1957 taxes showed that Steve made $6,000 a year compared to Neile's annual take of $50,000. Steve was an unabashed chauvinist who felt that women should be "at home tending to the kids during the day and cooking and making love to her man at night." Yet there was no denying that it was Neile who brought home the bacon. "It didn't bother me. I knew that eventually he'd take over, no question about that," Neile said. "I didn't care about money anyhow. I never saved any, and we were just sharing. But it didn't sit well with him; he's not the type. He just can't let his wife support him. And he didn't want me alone at Las Vegas without him, and his career hadn't begun to move into high gear." McQueen was a man who saw women as unreliable or at best not to be fully trusted. He wanted to be self-sufficient and in charge of the money. That was his way of being secure and ensuring that if anyone would do the walking out or abandoning, then it would be him.

It was the first time the word "divorce" crept into her consciousness, although she wasn't quite ready to throw in the towel. After one particular blowout, Neile received an apologetic letter from Steve. In it he spelled out how much she meant to him and how they were going to have a fabulous life together. Steve wrote, "I like you, baby. Love is one thing, but I like you very much. You're part lover, part friend, part mother, part sister—above all, we're pals." She in turn purchased a St. Christopher medal and had a special inscription engraved on the back: "To part is to die a little." Steve wore the medal around his neck for years—it even appears in a few of his films—and considered it his talisman. It was a sacrament of their marriage, which was extremely important to him despite his warped view of fidelity. Reporter James Gregory asked McQueen of its origin. He replied, "That's from the old lady," he said proudly. "She had a job dancing in Las Vegas for $1,500 a week, and I was out of a job and had to go scrounging for work. She knew I felt like a gigolo, and she thought this might help." When they eventually split up, this medallion disappeared from view and was never seen in photos from the period after *Le Mans*. No doubt it contained deep meaning for McQueen.

It did bring him luck, but it was Neile's phone call to Hilly Elkins that helped her husband immeasurably. The call wasn't so much a favor as it was a plea to save their marriage. Steve was driving her crazy and needed work as quickly as possible. It is a credit to Neile how much she helped his career; despite her busy workload, she found the time to help him. This dedication and belief in McQueen was one of the chief reasons he was able to genuinely open up and trust someone.

A whiskered and scruffy McQueen, who sported a sweatshirt, blue jeans, and Army-style butch cut, met with Elkins for lunch at the famous Polo Lounge inside the Beverly Hills Hotel. Elkins had lent McQueen his motorcycle and hadn't seen hide nor hair of his bike, nor McQueen for that matter. "Where's my bike?" Elkins asked after they exchanged the usual pleasantries. McQueen sheepishly explained that he had jumped over a hill and broke it in two pieces. Elkins figured if he were ever to get his money back, he'd have to find employment for the irresponsible son of a bitch.

Elkins got McQueen a screen test with CBS, and in his words, "The executives flipped." McQueen secured a role on *Tales of Wells Fargo*, a part that paid $400 for three days' worth of work. To his surprise and against all his preconceptions, Elkins discovered that McQueen was a natural, an untrained, unselfconscious, unmannered presence the camera just happened to love. Elkins was electrified by McQueen's authenticity, how his stillness and silence could speak volumes. Those thoughtful eyes and cool demeanor somehow expressed intense feelings without having to utter a word. Whatever acting technique McQueen lacked on the stage, he had it in spades on film.

After *Wells Fargo*, Steve was headed back to New York where he was supposed to head the cast for a new Irving Wallace play called *The King of 36th Street*, but those plans were placed on hold by an unexpected turn of events. Elkins successfully landed McQueen a guest spot on *Trackdown*, a Four Star western starring Robert Culp (whom Elkins also managed) as Texas Ranger Hoby Gilman. The three studio heads—Dick Powell, Charles Boyer, and David Niven—recruited Culp from Broadway a year before and placed him in the CBS series to great success; they were hoping that history would repeat itself.

Elkins talked the William Morris Agency into signing a contract with McQueen on February 14, 1958. They had assigned Stan Kamen, one of the firm's shining stars, as Steve's agent. Kamen proved to be instrumental in the first half of McQueen's Hollywood career, sensing in him real star potential. He recognized in McQueen what many others would come to realize over the years—he had an indefinable and unattainable quality. *Bullitt* costar Robert Vaughan would later sum this up perfectly: "He had what we refer to as the X-Factor."

Elkins and Kamen went to bat for McQueen, and this was exactly what the star-in-the-making needed—someone to put all his efforts into putting him forward, to smooth out those rough edges and champion him.

McQueen was ultimately selected by *Trackdown* producer Vincent M. Fennelly. Although the name of the show is now obscure, there is one name that certainly isn't—Josh Randall. This was the role Steve portrayed, a frontier bounty hunter who brandished a sawed-off Winchester. Fennelly kept coming across wanted posters on *Trackdown* and decided to develop stories about the men on the posters and called in writer John Robinson to help flesh out the idea. The two cleverly devised a spin-off of the half-hour pilot episode, *The Bounty Hunter*, which aired March 7, 1958. It became *Wanted: Dead or Alive*, and it debuted on September 6, 1958.

The series distinguished itself by making the lead character, Josh Randall, the heavy. He was a heavy by the very fact that he couldn't win. Criminals didn't like him for obvious reasons, some lawmen despised him because he operated by a different set of rules, while others who knew him highly respected him. He had to walk a fine line to win over the audience, which appealed greatly to Fennelly. "You know, a bounty hunter is sort of an underdog," Fennelly said. "I picked [McQueen] because [Randall] was a little guy. Everyone's against him except the audience. And McQueen was offbeat. He wasn't the best-looking guy in the world, but he had a nice kind of animal instinct. He could be nice but with some sort of menace underneath."

What makes Randall so unique is that he prefers to bring the bad guys back alive whenever possible, and it's his inherit decency while doing a job every-body scorns that makes *Wanted: Dead or Alive* so appealing. Several episodes emphasize this ethical code and sense of justice—notably in the first season in *Rawhide,* "Breed" and in the second season, "The Hostage" and "Twelve Hours to Crazy Horse."

The series also explored the darker side of Randall's work when, in the third-season episode "Bounty on Josh," Randall is wounded by an unseen stalker and the tables are turned. How does it feel to be the hunted and not the hunter? This episode is a chilling study, and Steve is at his best, with every moment, every twitch and shrug, every expressive glance revealing his thoughts more surely than words ever could.

But at the start of the series, McQueen was not so sure he wanted to get stuck in a Hollywood television factory. Success on the small screen wasn't his ultimate goal; he wanted to make it big in the movies. He was also quite aware that there was a clear line of demarcation when it came to television vs. films. Movie stars were not groomed from the "small box," nor did television stars ever make the leap to the silver screen. But McQueen liked the character of Josh Randall, with whom he seemed to identify. "[Randall] seemed to be a loner," McQueen said, "a guy who made his own decisions, and he didn't have a big star on his chest. This appealed to me." In Josh Randall, McQueen would find a character who would mirror his own personality: the outsider with a strong sense of justice and self-respect, a somebody's-gotta-do-it attitude, and a sensitive and occasionally comic side that would manifest itself.

Culp knew McQueen from New York and was one of McQueen's biggest allies when he was getting panned in *A Hatful of Rain*. The two raced bikes, competed for the same girls, and were also managed by Hilly Elkins. But McQueen was all business when the director called for action. Friend or foe, McQueen would take no prisoners when it came to his career. He would always try to steal the scene out from under his costar's feet. "We were loading our guns in a scene, and there was a way that he did it where the camera instantly took notice of what he was doing. And so did I. I told myself, 'I need to watch out for this guy.'" Culp didn't need to watch out for McQueen any longer—the pilot was approved for a new series, now titled *Wanted: Dead or Alive*, on CBS for the fall season of 1958.

Four Star also insured its new star for $1 million. The Method had come to television, and Steve McQueen was to become its newest star.

The stars seemed to be aligned for the McQueens as Neile's six-month run at the Tropicana came to an end in February 1958. With Steve's career in high gear and a fee of $750 per episode, he and Neile rented a home at 5013 Klump Street in North Hollywood. Though Neile continued to work, she knew in the back of her mind that if their marriage was to succeed, she'd have to ultimately give up her career. The couple found common ground when they decided to have a family. "Steve had the avant-garde view of women that their place was in the kitchen, if they were lucky," Hilly Elkins ruefully remarked, who saw a portion of his income go out the window with Neile stepping down from show business. "That's what he wanted Neile to do—raise a family."

It was on the set of *Wanted: Dead or Alive* that McQueen developed his legendary status in Hollywood as being "difficult." To others who liked to put it more bluntly, he was a major pain in the ass. It was a reputation that did not waver throughout his career.

Psychologist Peter O. Whitmer said McQueen's lack of interpersonal trust, the most and best utilized of all the facets of Attachment Disorder, was in full bloom in Tinseltown. "Hollywood: The land where they kill you with kindness and then tell you that you'll never eat lunch in this town again," Whitmer said. "Deals are broken behind your back, while your spouse is stolen before your eyes. The single most hyperkinetic, club-wielding, cutthroat, competitive, pinball-machine-of-life industry ever, where just one slogan of disdain—or challenge—is, 'What have you done for me lately?'

"Stars—they glitter, they glow, they shine; their trajectory can illuminate with incandescence and then extinguish in a heartbeat. Next, please!

"At first glance, the film industry seems to be the place of last refuge for any-one with a deep-seated and hostile sense of skepticism bordering on a paranoid delusion toward the intentions of all others.

"Then again, this psychology may just be the stuff of the fittest. What would Charles Darwin have said, other than that 'smiling'—Steve McQueen's métier—'is man's polite way of showing his fangs.' And the fangs of anyone raised on a steady diet of abandonment, disillusionment, flux, and change in their human world will be more than slow to trust others; they will forever sleep with one eye open.

"Regardless, it was Steve McQueen's sense of never trusting fully those who had the potential to alter what he wanted from life that pulled his emotions within himself and provided him with his star quality of the American rebel."

• • •

Wanted: Dead or Alive received the official green light from Four Star Studios in April 1958, and filming commenced three months later. A Western Union Telegram from Dick Powell on July 24, 1958, started the series on a classy note:

> *Dear Steve,*
> *Welcome to the fold. Glad you are with us. I know your show will be a huge success.*
> *Dick Powell*

McQueen appreciated the gesture but started the very first day on the job by firing a horse and three stuntmen. Steve told reporter Henry Gris, "They gave me this real old horse they had put on roller skates and pushed onto the sound stage. I went to Dick Powell and said, 'Listen, let me pick out my own horse. We're going to be doing this series for a while; I'd kind of like a horse I got something going with, you know?" McQueen visited a friend who raised quarter horses. They looked at a sorrel, a dapple gray, a white palomino, and a black horse named Ringo. McQueen got a taste of Ringo's feisty quality when he got bucked off on his first ride. He thought the horse was perfect. The first week of shooting, Ringo kicked out several lights and bit all the other horses. It also stepped on McQueen's foot, who retaliated by balling up his fist and punching the horse in the snout.

McQueen explained their complicated relationship. "For three long years, that horse and I fought like fanatics, both of us bent on winning. He'd step on me on purpose again and again. And I'd punch him each time for stepping on me, but he would do it again. We never did compromise, and I sort of liked the idea that he would never compromise. The son of a bitch, no matter how much he was paid back in kind, he stood his place. And we really loved each other, but he never surrendered."

McQueen sought the help of another friend for the series' other main prop—a specially designed .44-40 sawed-down Winchester Model 1892 rifle created by artist Von Dutch.

"I call it a Mare's Laig, kinda like a hog's leg but not so mean," said Josh Randall, who introduced the weapon in the *Trackdown* pilot. "If I have to use it, I wanna make sure the message gets to where I'm pointing." A line in one of the episodes had Randall reply to a comment on the size of his weapon, "I'm just a little bitty feller. I need a big gun."

Three stuntmen also got the message from McQueen that first day when they were summarily dismissed. The third, stuntman-turned-actor Richard Farnsworth, had the audacity to needle the star for rolling the back of his cowboy hat. "You're making that hat look like a tortilla," he teased McQueen, who gave the gentle cowboy the pink slip. The two later became good friends.

Stuntman Loren Janes had just finished another job when he was summoned by Tommy Carr, a veteran director at Four Star Studios, to try and handle its very difficult new star. Janes was a world-class athlete and Olympian and was considered one of the best stuntmen in Hollywood.

When Janes arrived at Four Star, he was promptly handed western attire—the very same attire that McQueen was wearing—and told to check in with Carr. Janes felt the penetration of those baby blues searing through him as he and Carr discussed the next scene—a stunt that required him to jump on a horse and perform a Pony Express mount. When they finished their conversation, Janes went to fix himself a cup of coffee. As he walked past McQueen, he heard his fingers snap and demand, "Coffee. Black." It was a reminiscent of an Old West showdown.

"Coffee—black?" Janes asked aloud, then turned to face McQueen. Janes' eyebrows furrowed as he met McQueen's intense stare. "Let me explain something to you. I guess you must be new around here. Are you Mr. McQueen?" McQueen shot Janes a look as if to say, "Who else would I be?" Janes continued with the charade. "I'll have you know that I'm your stuntman, and I'm here to make you look good, to make you look better than you can make yourself look, and I've got a helluva reputation. I don't want you blowing my close-ups. I'm not a servant to anybody. I don't fetch coffee or anything else. Nobody orders me to do anything." McQueen was momentarily stunned and backed off. Janes, like McQueen, was a former Marine and was nobody's patsy. Explained Janes, "I think one of the reasons why he liked me was that I put him in his place. He didn't like for people to kowtow and brownnose him. They didn't last long." Janes' friendship with McQueen lasted for 22 years, and he worked with McQueen throughout his entire career, right up to his last film, *The Hunter*.

Although he ultimately made peace with the stuntmen on the show, McQueen still waged war with the writers, directors, and *Wanted's* main producer, Vince Fennelly, who was by one person's account snide and short-tempered. "[Fennelly] was a reformed alcoholic and was not to be trusted as a producer," said Robert Culp. "He hated both me and Steve McQueen. Depending on the given day and circumstance, I don't know who he hated more."

McQueen's push for realism grated on everyone's nerves, and he created many enemies on the set. The studio usually churned out an episode every three days, but McQueen didn't care about toeing the line or meeting deadlines. "They'd roll the cameras before I was ready. Everybody was jumping on me, trying to change me as an actor," McQueen recalled. "So finally I just said, 'Stuff it,' you know. I gave my gun to the assistant director and said, 'Here man, *you* do it.' Then I went home to my old lady and said, 'Hey, baby, let's go to Australia.'"

Only the intervention of Dick Powell kept McQueen from packing his bags and heading to the Outback. McQueen agreed to come back to the set, but he insisted on playing Josh Randall his way. McQueen revealed to reporter Charles Witbeck that he based Randall on an actual person in his past. "You know where I got my idea of Randall? From a cop I once knew as a kid in New York," McQueen said. "There was no monkey business with him. When he said he'd shoot, he meant it. Well, I think of him, and pretty soon I'm Josh Randall." McQueen insisted on having a hand in all scripts, his wardrobe, his horse, his gun, and his character's motivation. It took nearly a half-dozen episodes before McQueen fully settled into his character's skin and knew exactly what he was doing. After that, he owned the character; he *was* Josh Randall.

In part due to McQueen's lack of formal education and his dyslexia, which he kept quiet, he had a hard time pronouncing certain words and memorizing large chunks of dialogue. Every line he spoke was terse, sharp, and bordering on proverbial. He also weeded out scripts that were heavy clichés and often based his character's decisions on real-life scenarios. For example, one script called for Josh Randall to fight several men at a time and dispatch them with a few punches like most western heroes of the day. McQueen felt it was bullshit and referred to an incident he had in the Marines. "I remember once there were these two guys who always stuck together. One kept provoking me. One day we had a real argument, but his friend was standing there, so I bowed out. But I got him alone the next day. I waited for him in the toilet, and I said, 'Hey, you,' and he turned around and I punched and kicked the hell out of him. And the other guy never bothered me. I made my point."

McQueen also made his point to viewers. The show was an instant smash when it debuted in September 1958. Strategically slotted behind *Perry Mason* on Saturday nights, the series ended up in the top 10 in its first season. With more than 40 westerns on the networks and in syndication, *Wanted: Dead or Alive* separated itself from the pack. The show drew much attention for its violence. "Like most whodunits, it is stronger on physical movements—fistfights, gunnings, riding that away—than it is on plot," wrote the *San Francisco News*, while the *San Francisco Examiner* opined: "For blood and thunder fans: great! For the squeamish: appalling!" McQueen defended the series' violence to *The Hollywood Reporter*, explaining, "The fans don't care if there is violence in their TV western fare—what they want most is action, and the action must be sustained or there is a quick twist of the dial."

One review that didn't see the light of day for more than four decades was written by the Federal Bureau of Investigation, which kept a dossier on political dissenters and activists, political leaders, and most major Hollywood stars during J. Edgar Hoover's term as director for nearly half a century. *The Hollywood Reporter* article was clipped by an agent along with a handwritten comment, "Gangster Glorification Movies." It was the FBI's earliest dated piece on McQueen, and the agency kept tabs on him for the next two decades.

One of the millions of viewers who tuned in on those Saturday nights was a 51-year-old aircraft parts salesman from Long Beach, California. While he nursed a beer or two during the half-hour drama, he peered suspiciously into the TV set and sized up the actor playing Josh Randall. The resemblance was haunting. "I wonder if that's my boy?"

William McQueen had finally resurfaced. The two men were separated by a matter of inches through the television set, but in reality, they were literally separated by miles and an ocean of time. Who stared back at William was an actor on the verge of superstardom. As William watched his son, he would have seen before him the person he had abandoned as a baby. Over the years Steve had gone through a great deal of pain. He had grown up the hard way and had developed a highly complex character with deep flaws and anxieties. William played his part in this when he left him. A fatherly influence could have made growing up easier and given the young man a firmer sense of direction. However, it was not to be. Instead, Steve would wonder where his father was and why he had simply walked out on him. He had unfinished emotional business and deserved closure. Steve could not shut this door until he had the answer.

He needed to confront his father just once in his life and ask, "Why?"

12

IN THE NAME OF THE FATHER

FINDING A MEASURE OF PEACE was a constant theme in Steve McQueen's life. He had never been given the chance to find a sense of calm or comfort either in his surroundings or in himself. McQueen tried but was always looking in the wrong places. He would disappear on a camping trip, jump in his pickup truck, and travel cross-country, or he would pick up a motorcycle and ride off into the desert for days at a time. Often he wouldn't bother to tell anyone where he was headed. He needed this sense of freedom and control to discover a space where he could find himself.

In his search for solace, McQueen would temporarily give up acting, having banked enough money to retire by the mid-'70s. He simply was not as hungry for the fame as he used to be, and he scaled back his visibility. He had tried for his entire adult life to grab the brass ring and be somebody, to be a success. He had pushed for this with such passion that he lost touch of the reassurance and comfort of the simple pleasures of life. In his late forties, he tried anonymity to escape the limelight, growing out a full-length beard, tending bar at a funky Agoura Hills restaurant, donning a hard hat and tool belt and sneaking around as a telephone repairman, or downing beer with the locals at a dive, insisting that he was a construction crew boss, even though such desire for being just a normal guy was often at odds with his ego.

McQueen had touched the hem of greatness and breathed in the air of success from the summit of stardom. But it was not fulfilling. He perhaps found true peace much later. He would take pleasure in the simple things once more, collecting things from the '30s—toys, gas station signs, jackknives—anything that might transport him back to a time when things could be rewritten to a perfect childhood that had never been and could never be.[1] McQueen finally stripped things back to the simplest form and found inner solace in Santa Paula, California. He would sit on the porch of his ranch house, with only the wide-open land, a cold beer, and a setting sun before him.

Before he could get to the end of that journey, however, he would have to come to terms with himself and the root of his pain—coming from a broken home and the rest of his past. Studies show that most children of abandonment suffer from low self-esteem and have difficulty expressing their emotions. They may project and ascribe anger and resentment toward the absent parent or conversely idealize everything about them. Often McQueen did both, alternately cursing his father for abandoning him and at other times casting him to the media as a World War II hero.[2] "My father was a Navy flier at one time, back when flying was a sketchy thing," he said in an August 1964 *Photoplay* article. "He fought the Japanese in China in 1939 with General Chennault, and he did a lot of adventurous things like that. Although I didn't know much about him, I had heard that he was a *full* swinger, a guy who really had a love for life." The truth was a lot less romantic, and when the truth did not suit Steve's needs or defend him from his feelings of rejection, then a reimagined history certainly would.

Although his bitterness toward his mother was duly noted by family, friends, and associates, Steve's hatred for his father was not as evident, but it was certainly just as strong. Julian was omnipresent in New York when Steve was living there, embarrassing him so often that he would come to expect it. She was largely absent for the important parts of his childhood, but ironically, she was everywhere now. He would find this stark reminder of unhappiness impossible to hide from and something to be reluctantly confronted. By contrast, Steve's feelings toward his father could often be hidden from view simply because he was physically absent. Steve did not have to confront these feelings head-on. However, the end result was that the trauma of this would go unnoticed, yet it would be magnified as it quietly smoldered. Steve's usual flippancy flashed to rage when reporter Tom Hutchinson asked him on a June 1969 press junket in London, "What if you could meet your father right now?"

"I'd probably kill him," came back the reply. The answer stunned Hutchinson, who was momentarily taken aback, and McQueen was forced to retract his initial response. "No, that's the wrong thing to say. I wouldn't kill him—I'd feel sorry

---

1   It's worth noting that Steve's mother, Julian, was a lover of antiques and became a dealer in her later years while living in San Francisco.

2   Military records show that William McQueen was a civil servant stationed at Will H. Point in Seattle during World War II. He drove a truck.

for him because he missed out on me, on me growing up, as much as I missed out on him. He was foolish in what he did."

Psychologist Peter O. Whitmer explained, "Emerging from the total gamut of childhood and adolescence, including the time Steve McQueen was starting his career in New York City, until her death, his mother was a real-life figure. She was, in her real life, a case in pathology and a cause of some pathos for Steve. On the other hand, his father made an easier target for his anger by *not* being present. His father could provide no argument to his son for his wrongs, hence the young McQueen's relentless and burning hostility toward him. Similar dynamics are often found when adopted children, not knowing who their biological parents are, enter their teens. There appears to be some genetic determinant to this emotional confusion. What is known and well-researched is that the closer a relative is as regards kinship, the more powerful the emotions toward them."

It was Neile's pregnancy with their first child, Terry, that triggered Steve's on-again, off-again quest to find William McQueen. The official search began a decade before when Steve was a troubled teen. "I was 16 and getting into all sorts of trouble. I didn't have much to go on. When I was in the Marines, I tried the Navy files, but nothing happened."

Gene Lesser, who was McQueen's roommate in Greenwich Village, remembered meeting up with McQueen again in Los Angeles in 1957. Lesser said after the two finished dinner, McQueen enlisted him to help him track his father. "We planned on it the next day, and we got in his car and drove to Ojai looking for him.... This was at night," Lesser said. "He drove up to a house he recognized, knocked on the door, and a woman answered. He asked her if she knew his father, and she said she had no idea. That was a subject that was on his mind all the time."[3]

After months of working with detectives and putting out feelers, which included pool halls, bars, gin joints, and veterans' organizations, McQueen received a phone call from a woman who identified herself as William McQueen's "lady friend," Mary Jane Wyckoff. She said she had information about Steve's father, whom she called "Terry." Steve and Neile made the short drive to her Echo Park apartment building. The two inhabited the same orbit for almost a decade but didn't know how close in proximity they were to each other. How could a man abandon the mother of his child and newborn son? Why did he leave? Where did he go? And how was he able to elude everyone for almost three decades?

---

3   Although Lesser said McQueen was looking for his father, it's quite possible he was hunting down stepfather Hal Berri, who owned a well-known home in Ojai called Casa de Paz—"House of Peace."

Steve was on the verge of putting his greatest anxieties to rest and finally getting the answers he deserved. He had waited decades to tell his father exactly what he thought of him, and now he had his chance.

The mystery of where William McQueen was during those missing years has remained unsolved for more than a half century. However, after searching through government documents, voter registrations, city directories, military records, and William McQueen's death certificate, this author can, for the first time, provide a clearer understanding of those missing years. His story has never been told until now.

When William McQueen deserted his wife and son, he ended up in the city where he spent most of his life—Los Angeles. According to a 1930–32 city directory, William McQueen moved to an apartment complex at 3700 Sunset Boulevard in the Silver Lake section of the city, the same neighborhood where almost 10 years later Steve resided with Julian and Hal Berri. William lived at the location for a year and then moved to 2006 Ivar Avenue in Hollywood, where he was listed as a "service station manager" for the next two years.

According to Harold Eddy, who grew up next to the Thomsons and now owns Claude Thomson's home, William and Julian lived in Slater briefly—in a back house where a grain silo now stands. This claim can explain why in 1932 Julian is not listed in the Beech Grove city directory and then in 1933 they are listed as McQueen, Wm (Julian) in the Beech Grove city directory, residing at Victor and Lillian Crawford's 311 N. Drexel Avenue home, where he is listed as an "aviator." Did William McQueen make an attempt at reconciliation with Julian?

If there was some sort of reconciliation, it didn't last long. By 1934 Julian is again listed as single woman in the Beech Grove city directory as McQueen, Julian at 311 N. Drexel Avenue, while William washed up on the shores of San Francisco, where he found employment with the Dollar Steamship Line Inc. The company owned the largest fleet of passenger and cargo liners operating under the U.S. flag. Despite being launched right as the Great Depression started, the Dollar Line managed to stay afloat during the early 1930s with a $5 million government bailout loan and an increased mail subsidy.

A statement of service showed that William sailed on the USS *President Hoover* (12/27/34 to 2/14/35; 2/21/35 to 4/10/35; and 5/18/36 to 7/2/36), USS *President Van Buren* (5/22/35 to 9/11/35), SS *Mariposa* (12/5/35 to 1/27/36), and the USS *President Coolidge* (2/20/36 to 4/11/36 and 8/6/36 to 9/23/36). The document also shows that William served in several capacities, including ship steward, waiter, and elevator operator.

William Terrence McQueen (right) with a friend in Calcutta, India, circa 1920. William abandoned his wife and child when Steve was six months old. He died of cirrhosis of the liver in November 1958, a few months before Steve would finally catch up to him. *(Courtesy of Terri Carol McQueen)*

Long thought to be a barnstorming pilot, William McQueen was actually a Merchant Marine. Here he is on a vessel sailing out at sea. His job cost him many relationships, including one with Steve's mother, Julian Crawford, and later, Alma Doris Moody. *(Courtesy of Terri Carol McQueen)*

PHOTOGRAPH

Applicant to affix his signature
partly across photograph.

A head shot from William McQueen's Merchant Marine file, dated September 20,
1937. At the time he was 30 years old and a cabin steward based in the Port of San
Francisco. Although Steve was not a dead ringer for his father, he and William shared
the same slender build and other similar features: a large forehead, small ears, thin lips,
and blue eyes—piercing blue eyes. (*Courtesy of the United States Coast Guard, National
Maritime Center*)

Alma Doris Moody was the great love of William
McQueen's life and "the woman who got away." After a
year-long courtship, Doris was with child. She gave birth
to Terri Carol McQueen on May 5, 1940, at Kings County
Hospital in Seattle, Washington, which makes Terri Steve
McQueen's half-sister. (*Courtesy of Terri Carol McQueen*)

An acting headshot of Terri Carol McQueen taken in 1963, the same year that Steve McQueen became a breakaway star in *The Great Escape*. Terri tried contacting her famous half-brother when he made *Bullitt* on location in San Francisco but was rebuffed. (*Courtesy of Terri Carol McQueen*)

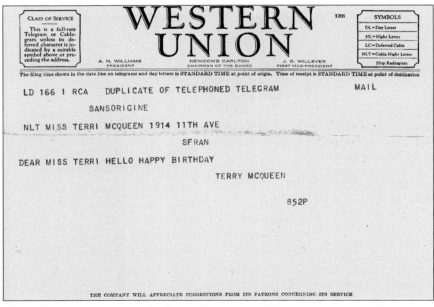

This undated Western Union birthday telegram from William McQueen to Terri was one of many correspondences he sent to his daughter. It remains one of the few prized possessions Terri has from her late father who, like Steve, she never knew. (*Courtesy of Terri Carol McQueen*)

Although Steve McQueen's birth certificate does not list the hospital where he was delivered, he was most likely born at St. Francis Hospital in Beech Grove, Indiana. Built in 1914 by the Sisters of St. Francis of Perpetual Order, the 75-bed hospital believed that human needs should be met in a holistic manner, which means Steve's birth must have been a physically grueling ordeal for his mother Julian. *(Courtesy of Beech Grove Public Library)*

A copy of Terrence Steven McQueen's birth certificate issued by the Marion County Health Department in Indiana. Note the incorrect spelling of McQueen's first (Terrance) and middle (Stephen) name as well as his mother's (Jullian). He continued to spell his name a variety of ways due to his dyslexia. *(Courtesy of Marion County Health Department)*

MARION COUNTY
HEALTH DEPARTMENT
making a difference

NON-CERTIFED COPY OF BIRTH

Marion County Health Department records show:

NAME AT BIRTH	TERRANCE STEPHEN MCQUEEN
DATE OF BIRTH	MARCH 24, 1930
PLACE OF BIRTH	MARION COUNTY
PARENTS NAME	WILLIAM & JULLIAN MCQUEEN (CRAWFORD)
FATHERS STATE OF BIRTH	TENNESSEE
MOMS STATE OF BIRTH	MISSOURI
FILE DATE	APRIL 3, 1930
CERTIFICATE NO.	187
DATE ISSUED	Tuesday, November 01, 2005

Main Street in Slater, Missouri, probably in the 1940s. Slater was the boyhood home of Steve McQueen and where the actor spent a majority of his childhood. He left for good at the age of 14 and ran off with a traveling carnival. *(Courtesy of Slater Main Street News)*

A period photograph of the Thomson homestead on the outskirts of Slater, Missouri. The home was owned by Steve McQueen's great-uncle, Claude Thomson, a prosperous hog farmer. Over time Claude grew to love Steve like a son, filling the role of surrogate father in the absence of the real thing. *(Courtesy of Slater Main Street News)*

Orearville School, the one-room schoolhouse where Steve McQueen received a majority of his early education, was later converted into a small chapel and still sits on Front Street in Slater, Missouri. *(Courtesy of Veronica Valdez)*

According to Steve McQueen, his stepfather, Hal Berri, was an alcoholic and a bully. The two locked horns from the moment they met, resulting in several beatings for McQueen. Ironically, Berri was killed by a drunk driver in January 1950. *(Courtesy of Lowell Boardman)*

The 1946 Boys Republic baseball team. Steve McQueen is seated on top row, fourth from right. This is the earliest known photo of the actor. He often credited the reform school for turning his life around, and paid frequent visits to youth to encourage them. He also set up an annual scholarship in his name and bequeathed $200,000 to them in death. In return the Boys Republic built a recreation center in his honor. *(Courtesy of Boys Republic)*

Sharing a laugh with a pair of Marine buddies upon his July 1947 platoon graduation, Parris Island, South Carolina. McQueen served a three-year stint and often told reporters he was busted down to private seven times to enhance his rebel status. However, his military file showed he was a competent soldier and McQueen ascended in rank rather quickly despite not serving in the Marines during wartime. (*Courtesy of Bonham's Auctioneers*)

After completing boot camp, McQueen's natural aptitude for engines landed him a job as a tank crewman/driver. His first assignment was to the Second Amphibian Tractor Battalion, Second Marine Division, Fleet Marine Force in Quantico, Virginia. He later transferred to the United States Naval Gun Factory in Washington, D.C., where he served in the 1st Guard Company, and received his final assignment as a tanker at Camp Lejeune, North Carolina. (*Courtesy of Bonham's Auctioneers*)

Preparing for *Peg O' My Heart*, a summer stock play staged in East Rochester, New York. McQueen snared a minor role in this 1952 production as an English squire starring opposite Margaret O'Brien. *(Courtesy of Academy of Motion Picture Arts and Sciences)*

McQueen's inauspicious film debut was as an extra in *Girl on the Run*, a 1953 burlesque thriller and murder mystery. Directed by Arthur J. Beckhard and featuring lots of "Girls and Guns," McQueen appears in two scenes as an uncredited extra, and he was given no dialogue. The actor never commented on the picture, and his appearance was first discovered nearly four decades later by filmmaker Mimi Freedman when researching the 2005 documentary *The Essence of Cool*. *(Courtesy of Steve Kiefer)*

Steve McQueen won this 1948 MG TC Roadster in a high-stakes poker game. The vehicle met an early demise when he drove it into an excavation hole on Sixth Avenue in Manhattan. *(Courtesy of John Waggaman)*

Using a bus stop sign as a barbell in his New York City apartment with dancer and first wife Neile Adams in the background. *(Courtesy of Academy of Motion Picture Arts and Sciences)*

Steve, Neile, and Julian McQueen inside of Jim Downey's Steakhouse, located in the heart of New York City's theater district. Julian (right) was a constant source of heartache and aggravation for her son; she abandoned him throughout his childhood. *(Courtesy of Linda Lukens)*

Steve McQueen and Paul Newman share a light moment on a New York City rooftop in this rarely seen publicity photo from *Somebody Up There Likes Me*, 1956. McQueen was a $19-a-day extra while Newman was given top billing. It took McQueen 18 years to finally catch up to Newman when he starred in 1974's *The Towering Inferno*. *(Courtesy of Brian O'Mahony)*

Actors Studio instructor and guru Lee Strasberg and Steve McQueen having a colorful conversation, 1957. Some say McQueen's presence was disruptive to many in the Actors Studio and that Strasberg eventually had to cut him loose. *(Courtesy of Academy of Motion Picture Arts and Sciences)*

From *A Hatful of Rain*, featuring Harry Guardino and Steve McQueen in the 1956 Broadway play. McQueen lacked the inner techniques to make the role of Johnny Pope his own and was unable to deal with *Hatful*'s drug aspects. He was eventually replaced by actor Peter Mark Richman. *(Courtesy of Kandee Nelson)*

On the set of *The Great St. Louis Bank Robbery*, 1957. McQueen plays the getaway driver of a botched real-life heist in his first above-the-title billing in a movie. McQueen said of the picture, "The only great thing about this one was the title. Most of the gang gets wiped out while I surrender to the cops. Nothing really worked in the film." *(Courtesy of Academy of Motion Picture Arts and Sciences)*

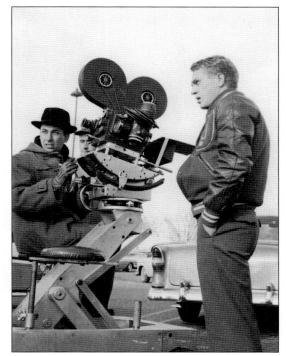

Billed as "Steven McQueen," the fresh-faced 27-year-old (with actress Aneta Corseaut) played the role of a teenager in *The Blob*. McQueen ranted for years the movie was a professional embarrassment, but *The Blob* has morphed into a cult classic with a devoted following that defies logic. *(Courtesy of Donna Redden)*

Bounty hunter Josh Randall in CBS's hit series *Wanted: Dead or Alive* was the star vehicle that made Steve McQueen a household name. McQueen portrayed a character with a dichotomy he could empathize with, torn between ruthlessness and a good-natured heart. *(Courtesy of Donna Redden)*

With Frank Sinatra in 1959's *Never So Few*, a World War II film set in Burma. Sinatra generously instructed director John Sturges to "give the kid all the close-ups," which allowed McQueen to turn the wisecracking, scene-stealing supply sergeant into a memorable performance. As Sgt. Bill Ringa, McQueen played a forerunner of the roles he would later portray in almost all of his movies— cool, understated, and extremely at ease with a gun in his hand or behind the wheel of a fast-moving vehicle. (*Courtesy of Donna Redden*)

Recognizing McQueen's star power, comedian Bob Hope enlisted Steve on a 1959 Christmas USO Tour in Alaska. The two performed a live comedic skit called *Operation: Eggroll*, in which they played Japanese soldiers about to be taken captive by the Americans. The now–politically incorrect skit was later aired on *The Bob Hope Buick Hour*. (*Courtesy of Donna Redden*)

The Magnificent Seven was an early career milestone and McQueen's first real shot at stardom. With director John Sturges' promise of being generous with the camera, McQueen schemed to steal the movie out from under its star, Academy Award–winner Yul Brynner. He not only achieved this goal but did so with approximately a dozen lines of dialogue and several other costars nipping at his heels. *(Courtesy of Photofest)*

McQueen was every ounce the ugly American when he flew to London to film *The War Lover* in September 1961. However, England has fervently carried a torch for him ever since his 1980 death, and it is arguably the most rabid country when it comes to McQueen's current fan base. *(Courtesy of Donna Redden)*

McQueen with Hilly Elkins going over the script for *The War Lover* at the Savoy Hotel in London, England, 1961. Elkins was McQueen's first manager and was instrumental in the actor's career arc, nabbing him key roles in television and movies. *(Courtesy of Elisabeth Osborn)*

In his breakout role as Captain Virgil Hilts in 1963's *The Great Escape*. Revving up his Triumph TR650 motorcycle, McQueen's jump over a 14-foot barbed-wire fence (performed by stuntman Bud Ekins) was the most breathtaking leap of faith ever seen on film and catapulted him to superstar status. *(Courtesy of Photofest)*

Although this may have satisfied William's wanderlust, it was not steady work. In 1934 and 1936, maritime strikes crippled Dollar and took it out of action for more than three months at a time. The strike made it unprofitable to operate the ships, and Dollar was forced to pay other carriers (mostly Japanese lines) to carry its passengers. In November 1936, Dollar filed for bankruptcy, and another ship was sold up to meet debts. Eventually, the Dollar family passed ownership of the line to the U.S. government in a swap for canceling all their debts. That's when William McQueen decided he probably needed a more permanent line of work.

William landed a job as a cabin steward with the Department of Commerce in the Bureau of Marine Inspection and Navigation in San Francisco. He was join- ing the Merchant Marine. William's enlistment date was March 24, 1937, which coincidentally fell on his son's seventh birthday. He listed on his application as his next of kin Paul Z. Sedam of 2429 N. Alabama Street, Indianapolis. Sedam was a childhood friend with a colorful teenage past that included grand larceny, as reported in *The Indianapolis Star*. Why William chose to list a friend 2,000 miles away and not his mother[4], his father's aunt, Jennie McQueen Totten, and cousin Oren M. Totten, who lived nearby, or Edwin or Eloise Wilson, friends from Hollywood with whom he boarded for two years at their Culver City address, was a curious choice. But it wasn't curious to Mike Sedam. "My dad and William McQueen were like Butch Cassidy and the Sundance Kid, riding the rails, com- mitting petty crimes, and raising a lot of hell. The two were thick as thieves," Sedam said. "They were both Merchant Marines, drinking and smoking buddies, and if they had a girl in Shanghai, then they shared her, too. That's how close they were. William listing my dad as next of kin was his way of saying, 'I take care of you, and you take care of me.' That pretty much defines their relationship."

Sedam said his father, Paul, died in May 1984.[5] Over the years, Mike learned bits and pieces about his dad's exploits with William McQueen. Their adventures usually involved booze, jazz music, marijuana, and women. "It was the post-Depression era, and it was a time to live it up. I remember my dad told me they once smoked dope with Nat King Cole on a cruise ship. They pretty much spent all of their money on booze and women, and their main goal in life was to have a good time. The lifestyle they held to was, 'Live life for all its worth, and grab all the gusto you can.'"

---

4   All traces of Caroline McQueen end in 1923. It's possible she died prior to the 1930 Census and could have been a reason why William McQueen joined the U.S. Marines in 1927.

5   Paul Sedam was a set artist and painter for Fox studios in San Francisco after his tenure in the Merchant Marines.

One of the women William and his father shared, Sedam claimed, was Julian. He believes she joined William on the West Coast after she deposited Steve with Uncle Claude in Slater in the mid-'30s, only to resume the good times. "They were the Three Musketeers instead of the Dynamic Duo," Sedam said. "If William was shipping out to port and my dad was on land, well, he sort of had his way with Julian and neither man was the wiser."[6]

Sedam also claims that William and Steve had met once before when Steve was a teen but that William turned him away. "From what I understand and what was told to me from my dad was that Steve had visited William's apartment at one time. Steve asked for 'Terrence' McQueen (his middle name) instead of 'William,' and being the bum that he was, William turned the kid away." Each was oblivious to who stood opposite him, and Steve's next chance to meet his father would not come until years later.

A handful of pictures, a birth certificate, a telegram, and a fingerprint file are the only physical proof of William Terrence McQueen's real existence. The photos, which have been tucked away for more than five decades, show physical similarities between father and son—they have the same head, ears, lips, nose, and intense gaze. The two shared almost identical builds as adults: William was listed as 5'10¼", 160 pounds, medium build, white complexion, light brown hair, and blue eyes. And indeed, they were piercing blue eyes.

A record of certificate (E37188) was issued to William Terrence McQueen on March 25, 1937, and he was made an "Ordinary Seaman" by the Department of Commerce. William was based in the port of San Francisco and for the next several years took several coast-wide trips to Long Beach, California; Honolulu, Hawaii; Port Arthur, Texas; Lake Charles, Louisiana; Kodiak, Alaska; Baltimore; Seattle; and once to Calcutta, India. It was in San Francisco where William met a waitress named Alma Doris Moody. The 25-year-old brunette was slender and olive-skinned, with brown eyes and a Roman nose.

The two met at Joe Kelly's Restaurant, a lively nightclub on 76 1st Street near the Bridge Terminal. Their romance revolved around the heartbeat of that magical city—the music, the nightclubs, and the dancing. William wooed her with enchanting stories of his travels to far away and exotic places, and he often quoted poetry to her. William's favorite poem was the 1859 translation of "Rubaiyat of Omar Khayyam" by Edward FitzGerald, a hedonistic anthem whose basic tenets were *carpe diem*, wine is the water of life, fate, and the inevitability of death. The

---

6   Mike Sedam said he actually met Julian once when she lived in San Francisco sometime in the late '50s. He said his dad asked Julian for a cash loan.

poem grabbed both English and American audiences when it was first published, and it served as a religious proxy for a man who grew up mostly fatherless, lived through the Depression, Prohibition, and World Wars I and II. William's affinity for quoting "Khayyam" should have been a harbinger for Doris of what life with William would be—a life of love, heartache, pain, and continual disappointment.

William pursued Doris vigorously, with weekend trips to his favorite spot in Big Sur, California; taking her canoeing in the moonlight at Golden Gate Park; and, on another occasion, proposing to her after he dove into the water to bring her a swan. Her wedding ring was a band of rubies, which was Doris' birthstone.

Their romance swiftly kicked into high gear, and William moved in with Doris. They were listed as "McQueen Wm T (Doris) mariner 1520 Melrose Avenue" in the 1940 Seattle city directory, although a marriage license has not been found. Doris was soon with child. According to a State of Washington Department of Health Certificate of Live Birth, Doris had the child at 3:37 PM on May 5, 1940, at King County Hospital in Seattle, Washington. Her name was Terri Carol McQueen—Steve McQueen's half-sister.[7]

Terri McQueen, who turned 70 in 2010 and lives in the Midwest, said that like her famous half-brother, she never knew her father, either. "I guess we were kindred spirits in that sense, you know, sharing the same grief and secret heartache of not knowing our father," Terri said. "Every little girl wants to know her daddy, and I've always carried that with me."

She also has regrets about never getting to meet her famous half-brother. Terri said she once tried to contact him on the set of *Bullitt* in San Francisco, asking an assistant to pass a note to Steve regarding who she was. Sadly, either McQueen did not believe her, did not care, or most likely did not want to open a door to the past that held so much pain for him. "I was just totally ignored, but he knew I existed," Terri said. "He wanted no part of those bad memories, and I don't blame him. I really don't."

She also admitted, "There is a sadness regarding the truth of who I am and the fact that I wasn't recognized when Steve was alive. I'd have given anything to have met him. He was the big brother of my dreams, dreams that were never shared and could never be shared."

Through Doris, Terri learned that her father was heavily involved in the jazz and Hollywood scene. She later discovered through her mother that William befriended some heavy-duty people, such as singer Hoagy Carmichael and actor Dick Powell. Terri said that Carmichael wrote a song for her in honor of her birth,

---

7   William Terrence McQueen is clearly listed on Terri C. McQueen's birth certificate as her father.

while Powell[8] sent Doris $100 when Terri was born. Terri said William was drawn into jazz music's darker elements and yet tried to shield Doris from following in his footsteps. "Mom told me he was very much into the whole musician and drug scene but didn't want Mom to drink and wouldn't allow anyone to tell dirty jokes or curse in her presence," Terri said. "In her own way she rebelled against this, because all of her friends drank."

In an effort to be closer to the mother of his child and his daughter, William put in for a transfer and moved to Seattle in late December 1941, a few weeks after the Japanese bombed Pearl Harbor. He reported for duty at the United States Army Transport Service at Will H. Point in Seattle. Military records show William was designated a civil servant and received a base salary pay of $1,122 a year as a "mess man."

Terri said her mother was also a restless spirit and longed for big-city life. She said Doris placed her with her grandmother in Spokane, Washington, and moved back to San Francisco a year after she was born. William soon followed, hot in pursuit, trying to woo her back. Terri said after several years of back and forth, her parents simply could not come to terms on marriage. She said it was a courtship that broke three people's hearts—those of William, Doris, and herself. "Mom was not interested in having a husband who was gone all the time. Dad was an adventurer and would not give up the open water until it was too late. She married another man when I was seven years old and terribly discouraged me from contacting Dad. I complied out of respect for her."

William sent exotic gifts, letters, and telegrams to both Doris and Terri whenever his ship docked, but they were either tossed in the trash or ripped to pieces. Only one of those Western Union telegrams survived Doris' bitterness. Along with a few photographs of William, the telegram remains among Terri's prized possessions.[9] Despite Doris' hard feelings and subsequent marriages, she revealed to her daughter before her 2002 death that William was indeed the love of her life.

"He was mine, too," Terri said.

William McQueen resurfaced in Southern California in 1949 in Wilmington at 428 Fries Avenue, a 12-room boarding house where he lived for about a year

---

8   Terri McQueen's photo collection includes a picture of Dick Powell. Powell's friendship with William McQueen is especially curious since Powell ran Four Star Studios when Steve filmed *Wanted: Dead or Alive*. Did Steve know that Powell had a connection to his father? Unfortunately, both men took that information to the grave.

9   Another of Terri McQueen's prized possessions is a handwritten copy of Sara Henderson Hay's poem "Field of Honor" by her mother, Alma Doris Moody. It was a poem she most likely reverted to when thoughts of reconciling with William McQueen emerged.

and a half before serving his last back-to-back sea voyages on a tanker bull, the USNS *Cedar Creek*. It was in Wilmington where he found employment under Charles Gabriel Bakcsy, a Hungarian immigrant who ran the West Coast Rigging Company in the San Pedro Harbor. Bakcsy's daughter, Esther McBurney, was nine when she met "Captain Ring." She would discover during the interview for this book that he was actually William McQueen. "My dad owned a ship, and he employed a lot of Merchant Marines. You've heard the expression *drunken sailor*? Well, many of these men were alcoholics and had serious problems. When these men came to shore, my dad took care of them. He'd make sure to hold on to their money and not give them any until they sobered up. They had hard lives, and many of them ended up in the boarding house my father ran. When the men couldn't afford to pay for a room, they stayed up in the attic. I know it sounds like *The Grapes of Wrath*, but those were hard economic times and it was better than being on the street."

McBurney said William McQueen was memorable to her because of his gentle nature, often escorting her to and from Fries Elementary School. "He was a kind man," she recalled. "My school was a good half-mile from my house, and he'd meet me almost every day. He was very protective of me and my sisters. He was always worried that I was hungry, so he would buy me a hamburger and a pint of milk on the way home from school. He was a real gentleman because he respected my dad."

She also witnessed another side of William—a sad and helpless man in the throes of gut-wrenching alcoholism. McBurney recalled several violent outbursts whenever he had too much to drink. "There were times when he had the DTs [delirium tremens], and Mom would have to go over and hold him down. Of course, I was scared to death. I stood out front and could hear him scream. He saw snakes and bugs on him and on the walls, and [he] couldn't get a hold of himself. It happened more than once."

When he gathered up the strength and sustenance, William relocated across the Los Angeles River in 1951 to the coastal neighborhood of Alamitos Beach, a section of Long Beach, California. It was an ideal place for a seaman to retire—a beautiful tree-lined community with its grand Ocean Boulevard and its open view of the Pacific Ocean, as well as its mix of family restaurants and neighborhood bars, dance halls, and The Pike—a Coney Island–like amusement park at the end of the Red Car Electric Line on the water. William McQueen's name showed up in the Long Beach city directory that same year, and his listed occupation was "aircraft salesman."

Long Beach was a boom town post–World War II and a municipal haven for those seeking steady employment. The city boasted the Long Beach Harbor, a Veterans Administration Hospital, a naval base and shipyard, approximately 650 manufacturing plants, and a substantial acceleration in aircraft-frame building due to the impact of defense mobilization.

Father and son lived only a relatively short distance from each other but were emotionally separated by circumstances. Steve had no idea of William's whereabouts or his proximity, and vice versa. It appears as if William did not want to be found, because he used slight variations of his name in subsequent city directories. At times he used Terry McQueen, W. Terry McQueen, W. McQueen, and Terrence McQueen.[10] Mike Sedam said his father, William's best friend, also played the name game. "It could have been used to avoid women, or it could have been the law, too," Sedam said. "My dad racked up a bunch of DUIs in the early '50s, and we left California for seven years. He'd flip-flop on a name a time or two, so that's why William probably used a few different names."

William also had three different addresses in the span of seven years—always as a renter, never an owner. His liberal use of aliases and the shuffling of addresses was just enough to throw his famous son off his scent, whether it was done by design or not. His last address was 284 Gaviota Avenue in Long Beach, California. He was living as a boarder in the home of Richard and Mary Jane Wyckoff, a young military couple who took in William during the last ailing years of his life. Mary and William were lovers, which made for an interesting living situation. Mary and Richard separated for a brief period, and she moved to an Echo Park apartment building, which is where she was when she called Steve McQueen with information about his father.

When Steve and Neile showed up, Wyckoff graciously ushered them in. Steve's moment was approaching. He was on the verge of fulfilling that empty void in his life nearly three decades in the making. However, Steve was once again denied. Wyckoff politely told Steve that his father had died three months earlier but spent every Saturday night parked in front of the television, watching *Wanted: Dead or Alive*. And almost faithfully, William would wonder aloud, "I wonder if that's my boy." Fate had dealt another cruel hand. William had been able to see his son, but Steve was now forever unable to confront his father. Wyckoff excused herself and ducked into a bedroom where she produced a picture of William and a Zippo lighter engraved, "T.McQ". When Neile saw the photo, her gut told her

---

10 It's also interesting to note that Steve's mother played this game as well, who, in addition to Julian, used Julia Ann, Julien, and Julie.

it was Steve's father. He was crestfallen and years later told friend Bud Ekins that he pitched the lighter into the weeds.[11]

Pat Johnson, one of Steve's closest friends, revealed that his father's death haunted him to his dying day. "He really wanted to meet his father, wanted to talk to him. This was a source of great frustration for him because there were so many things left undone, unsaid, that were never resolved, even to the time of his death. He always felt this emptiness. He often mentioned to me that he wished he had a chance. One of his great regrets in life was that he wanted to be able to go up to his father and say, 'Look what I've done with my life, and I didn't need you.' He told me that his father was a no-good bum. A drunken bum. Period." All his life, Steve had sought approval, and his father's blessing would have no doubt touched him deeply.

"Psychologically, there is a Spanish [phrase] that captures McQueen's emotions at this time. It is *olla podrida*. Literally, this means a 'rotten pot' or an incongruous mixture," said psychologist Peter O. Whitmer. "In Steve's case, it seems appropriate, as I see his motivations toward wanting to find his father as weird, unsettled, and a primarily nasty and angry stew of emotions. It began at ground zero of his psyche—especially so with a father-son dyad.

"The fact that the abandonment happened before the acquisition of language—the nonverbal dimension of this—allows it to color everything else as he developed. It can be thought of as a 'cognitive/emotional filter'—his every life experience is sieved through this filter.

"The fact that Steve never did have the chance to put a living image, with eye contact and a handshake, on this 'nasty stew,' yet came so close to doing so, undoubtedly stirred it up to a foam. He might have kept it bottled up, from the outside looking in, but the best prediction would have him in a hyper-emotional, itchy-trigger-fingered mode for weeks, perhaps months."

William McQueen's story has a profoundly sad postscript. He withered away in his last days at County Harbor General Hospital in Torrance, California, finally passing away on November 11, 1958. An inventory and estimated value of assets prepared by the Los Angeles Superior Court listed his total assets as $300.[12] He was declared insolvent, and the county picked up the tab on his

---

11 Though McQueen repeated this story to Ekins, the truth is that he kept the lighter. Upon Steve's death, daughter Terry discovered the Zippo lighter in his jewelry box where it remained in her possession for years. It was the only legacy left to the grandchildren from their paternal grandfather.

12 The court discovered that William McQueen had six $50 traveler's checks stashed away in a drawer when he passed.

hospitalizations for 1956 (11 days), 1957 (11 days), and 1958 (four days), which totaled $1,711.63.

The coroner listed William's cause of death as "Hepatic failure" due to "Chronic alcohol toxicity." In layman's terms, he died of cirrhosis of the liver.

With no legal family members to claim him,[13] Richard Wyckoff was listed as William's next of kin on the death certificate.[14] William's body was shipped from the county morgue to All Souls Cemetery in Long Beach. The cemetery, which is sponsored by the Catholic Church, gave him a proper burial but placed his casket in an unmarked grave. A pauper's death marked the end of his life. More than 50 years have passed, and his grave still does not have a headstone. His body remains anonymous for eternity—anonymous to Steve as much in death as in life.

---

13 Although Oren McQueen Totten and his family lived in the Lakewood section of Long Beach, California, from 1944 until his death in 1964, his daughter Joan Totten Wright stated she had never heard her father even mention William Terrence McQueen. Nor was she ever aware of the public death notice posted by Marnsett and Peek Mortuaries in the November 16, 1958, edition of the *Independent Press-Telegram* (Long Beach). William was one of 48 charitable burials for the week of November 7–14, 1958.

14 William T. McQueen's death certificate lists his marital status at time of death as "divorced." This is the only public record confirming that Bill McQueen was at one time legally wed.

13

RAT PACK CONFIDENTIAL

SIX MONTHS AFTER HE TRACKED DOWN HIS FATHER, Steve and Neile started their own family with the birth of daughter Terry Leslie McQueen on June 5, 1959. Steve was a man of his times and was disappointed his firstborn was a girl. However, his tune changed over time. "I was a little hacked when the old lady bore me a daughter, but this kid is really gonna be a gas. I wanted a boy, but now I want another girl."

Terry, whom Steve referred to as the apple of his eye, took after the Thomson side of the family and had an uncanny resemblance to Julian—fair hair, blue eyes, and lean body. She also shared the same humor and energy as her father, and she inherited his naturally rebellious spirit. "My father was goodness personified," Terry recalled before her 1998 death. "We used to spend every weekend together. He loved motorcycles, of course, so me and my brother learned to ride when we were little."

Eighteen months after Terry's birth, Steve was blessed with a son. Chadwick Steven McQueen was born on December 28, 1960, rounding out the McQueen family. This would provide Steve with an anchor and something to aspire to—although his family life had been painful when growing up, his family would enjoy something far more wholesome. Chad said Steve was a great father and role model. "He was more of a real, hands-on father than a lot of my regular friends' dads. I mean, I never saw *their* old men park the truck, hop over a fence, and play lunchtime kickball with the elementary-school crowd, which Dad did all the time.

"When I was six and doing wheelies on my bike, he said, 'It's time, son,' and boom—[he] started me on motorcycles. My first was a Benelli, an Italian bike. Suddenly I had something cool to do with my old man every weekend."

Chad said his father also had a superior take on discipline and was wise in the ways in how he dispensed lessons to his son. "One time when I was really little, I found some shotgun shells that my friends and I were going to hit with a hammer, but luckily my mom caught us before we could. Instead of giving me a beating, Dad did a very smart thing: He took me outside and loaded both chambers of an over-and-under shotgun, held the butt about four inches from my shoulder, and had me pull the trigger. I got the shit bruised out of my shoulder but suddenly understood the power of a bullet."

In time, Steve's family became his religion, his anchor to reality, and he protected them at all costs. "I believe in a lot of love, security, and discipline," Steve said. "I'll never be able to see my father in this world, but at least I can be a good father to my own kids. Maybe it didn't turn out too badly after all. I lost my father, but I found myself."

He also found himself as an actor. McQueen used *Wanted: Dead or Alive* as a proving ground to find his acting personality and the opportunity to experiment with the camera. The biggest conclusion he drew was that acting was the art of doing; it was mostly a physical art form, and he discovered a look or reaction was much better than a piece of dialogue or a throwaway sentence. "I admire Gary Cooper—he's an actor who never studied in his life," McQueen said. "He has something—he's gifted with a casual manner that I have to work for. I work like hell to get that simplicity that is natural to him."

McQueen didn't have to work as hard to alienate his crew and castmates. That came naturally, as he developed a truculent reputation on the set. His famous ego clashes and the artistic control he sought over his on-screen persona often echoed the drive and energy of his itinerant youth. As the popularity of the show grew, so did Steve's power and status. Over time, McQueen wrestled control away from producers, directors, screenwriters, actors, and anyone he perceived to be an enemy. At times he was willing to admit his transgressions. "One mistake I made was forgetting about the dignity of my directors. I'd get into a scene, and suddenly I'd be tellin' the other actors how to play it. Then I'd have to go over and apologize to the director. But one thing was for sure, I *understood* the character of Josh Randall," Steve said.

Shortly after Terry's birth, Steve and Neile appeared in *Alfred Hitchcock Presents*' "Man From the South," penned by the acclaimed writer Roald Dahl. "It was a grand old time on that," Neile said. "There were no problems. The script was so tight. I'd just had the baby, Terry, and all I could think of was, 'How do I look?' All I kept thinking was, 'God, I hope I don't look too fat.'"

In one of the most intense episodes of the entire series[1], McQueen portrays a down-on-his-luck gambler in Las Vegas who makes a bet with Peter Lorre that he can strike his lighter 10 times in a row. If McQueen wins, he collects the keys to Lorre's new Cadillac. If he loses, Lorre gets to chop off McQueen's little pinky.[2] McQueen turned in a most memorable performance, and his strong personality overshadowed Neile's turn in a small role as his love interest.

Success on a network television show was fine for other actors, but not for McQueen, who had a fanatical drive to succeed in films. Just a few years later, when McQueen was indeed a movie star, he worked hard to shed his television past. McQueen publicist David Foster remembers a time when he, Steve, James Garner, and James Coburn were invited to actor James Cagney's home. It was a summons from on high, as Cagney was one of McQueen's boyhood idols. After dinner, the actors moved to the living room to talk, all sitting at Cagney's feet while he relaxed in a recliner. Cagney took a liking to McQueen and made a special point to compliment him. "Yeah, yeah, kid. I see you on TV," Cagney said in his inimitable voice. "I catch you on that western." It wasn't exactly what McQueen wanted to hear. "Uh, Mr. Cagney," McQueen stammered, "I'm into movies now. Yeah, movies."

In McQueen's best interest, a verbal agreement was made with Dick Powell at the start of *Wanted: Dead or Alive* that if a movie role came along, every possible attempt would be made to work out a schedule to allow him to make the film. Such an opportunity arose during the series' first hiatus in late April 1959.

Never So Few, a World War II film set in Burma, features an all-star cast of Frank Sinatra, Gina Lollobrigida, Sammy Davis Jr., Peter Lawford, and Charles Bronson. At the helm of the $2 million production was John Sturges, who was perhaps the finest action director of his time (*Bad Day at Black Rock, Gunfight at the O.K. Corral*). He proved to be a key figure in McQueen's career trajectory, and he was the first of many mentor-surrogate fathers McQueen adopted throughout his life. Sturges was largely respected by the industry because he was straightforward and honest. He understood talent, and he came to his sets thoroughly prepared. "John possessed an incredible mind. Like an architect, he was very precise. He planned his movies out in great detail, which is why his pictures turned out so well," said Jim Harper, who was Sturges' business manager for half a century. "A

---

1   The episode was so intense that CBS postponed its original January 1, 1960, air date, stating the material was "macabre" and wasn't appropriate for the holidays.

2   The story was also the basis for the Quentin Tarantino–directed segment of the 1995 film *Four Rooms*, starring Tarantino in the McQueen role.

star is like the foundation of any building, and Steve McQueen was the cement for some of John's best work."

But McQueen was not part of the equation when Sturges started second-unit shooting in Ceylon (now Sri Lanka). Set up as a loosely assembled Rat Pack travelogue, Sinatra dispensed prime roles to buddies Sammy Davis Jr. and Peter Lawford. Davis was awarded the flashy role of Corporal Bill Ringa, but his name was quietly stricken from the roster when he unexpectedly blasted Sinatra in a radio broadcast from Chicago's Chez Paree. "Talent is not an excuse for bad manners," Davis told host Jack Eigen. "I don't care if you're the most talented person in the world. It does not give you the right to step on people and treat them rotten. This is what [Frank] does occasionally."

Davis' comments infuriated "Sir Francis" because they were more than just friends; Sinatra helped break color barriers in Las Vegas and Hollywood in an era of segregation, and he lobbied for Davis in the role of Corporal Ringa. In one fell swoop, Davis managed to offend one of his biggest benefactors and talked himself out of a $75,000 payday.

Defending Davis, Hilly Elkins said, "The comment just came off wrong. I mean, Sammy adored Frank. He just adored him. But as the last concert tour they did together will tell anyone, Frank was Frank and you didn't fuck with him."

Davis wasn't the only person singing the blues. Sturges had shot four weeks worth of film using Davis' body double in several key shots. He had to ditch that footage and was also at a loss as to who should replace Davis. It was Sturges' wife, Dorothy, who initially brought McQueen to her husband's attention, according to Jim Harper. "John had to fill that spot with a piece of inspired casting, and he did, thanks to his wife, Dorothy. She spotted Steve on *Wanted: Dead or Alive* and mentioned to John that a charismatic young man on television just may serve the picture well," Harper said.

Sturges was dubious when agent Stan Kamen pitched his client as "Hollywood's next Bogie," but McQueen lived up to the hype when he walked into the director's office. "I've always had good luck seeing people in person, and he looked just right to me. He didn't particularly impress me on *Wanted: Dead or Alive*. He looked good in person. You could see that on the screen, and when you meet an actor, you look for that quality. Steve looked like a movie star, which he turned out to be," Sturges said.

Assistant director Robert Relyea remembered receiving a mysterious telegram that read, "Chicago replaced by Detroit." It was code for Steve McQueen was in, and Sammy Davis Jr. was out. McQueen's salary was $25,000, three times less the amount than Davis' fee, but he was finally in the club. In his first big-budget film, Steve McQueen was ready to grab the movie world's attention.

Equally as important as Sturges' casting approval was the blessing of star Frank Sinatra, who immediately liked his young costar. McQueen, who was as streetwise as they come, paid proper tribute to Sinatra by acknowledging his position. He was deferential to Sinatra but certainly no pushover. Sinatra, no matter how big or small, tested everyone's mettle. With McQueen, he slipped a firecracker in the loop of his gun belt while reading a script. When it went off, "I jumped about three feet in the air, which naturally delighted Frank," McQueen recollected with a smile.

The feisty upstart showed he was game as hell and quickly grabbed one of the prop Tommy guns. McQueen jammed in a clip of blanks and yelled at Sinatra as he was walking away. "Hey Frank!" When Sinatra turned around, McQueen squeezed the trigger and emptied the contents of the gun. Sinatra tap danced like a cat on a hot tin roof while the cast and crew fell silent. This kid McQueen was either supremely stupid or sported a pair of bocce-sized brass balls. The two men stared at each other, neither blinking. McQueen observed, "The whole set just went dead still. Everybody was watching Frank to see what he'd do. He had a real bad temper, and I guess they all figured we were going to end in a punch-out. I wasn't sure myself, as we stared at each other. Then he just started laughing, and it was all over. After that, we got along just fine. In fact, we'd toss firecrackers at each other all throughout the picture. Off camera, that is. I'd done the right thing. Once you back down to a guy like Sinatra, he never respects you."

When they finally stood face-to-face, Sinatra recognized a kindred soul. "You gas me, pal," Sinatra said.

"That's funny. You gas me, too," McQueen smiled.

Sinatra and McQueen carried on throughout the picture by using pyrotechnics as a constant source of entertainment. One of them ignited a can of paint, which caused considerable damage to a set, while MGM brass made a preemptive strike by contacting the Culver City Fire Department not to be too alarmed if they saw smoke on the back lot. The frivolity came to a momentary halt when McQueen tossed a powerful cherry bomb in Sinatra's dressing room and shut the door. The burst was so powerful that it knocked out the wardrobe man's hearing aide.

Relyea likened the situation to an older, wiser brother (Sinatra) showing the younger brother (McQueen) the ropes of the business. "[Frank] thought Steve was funny, in the sense of his energy level," Relyea said. "I have a hunch Frank said to himself, 'I remember when I had that much drive and desire to get that much attention.' In turn, Sinatra gave Steve the camera."

Sinatra was strictly a 9-to-5 guy when it came to filming movies. He disliked the medium and had less respect for its execution. Contractually Sinatra was out the door at 5:00 PM, more often than not with a tumbler in his hand and a showgirl on his arm. On those days when his scenes weren't completed, Sinatra generously instructed Sturges to "give the kid all the close-ups." Wisely, McQueen made the most of those moments. He turned the wisecracking, scene-stealing supply sergeant into a memorable performance. In *Never So Few*, McQueen played a forerunner of the roles he would later play in almost all of his movies—cool, understated, and extremely at ease with a gun in his hand or behind the wheel of a fast-moving vehicle.

Sinatra's largesse toward McQueen extended beyond MGM's back lot. In January 1960, he invited Steve and Neile back east to spend a gala-filled week with him and his entourage. The McQueens were taken backstage to Sinatra's homecoming concert in Atlantic City and accompanied him to the *Never So Few* premiere at Radio City Music Hall. Naturally, the firecrackers and cherry bombs came out again. McQueen tossed them from his hotel window and had to do some pretty fast talking, despite the heavy aroma of gunpowder, when the police showed up at his door. "Steve had a gift for talking the police out of arresting him," said friend Steve Ferry. "In California, he got in a lot of trouble because he didn't carry anything in his pockets, and he didn't carry his driver's license. He always talked himself out of it. He charmed the people."

Hanging around Sinatra opened a picture window into the A-lister's lifestyle, which included private jets, limousines, red carpet events, screaming fans, opened doors, and plenty of respect and fawning admiration. McQueen got a glimpse of the good life and was instantly hooked.

"I want some of that," he whispered to Neile.

No matter how much of a big shot he felt while hanging around Sinatra, McQueen felt compelled to repay an old debt. Before the *Never So Few* premiere, he escorted Sinatra and Peter Lawford to Louis' Tavern in Greenwich Village for what he billed as "the tastiest veal in New York City." As always, he was greeted by Sal, the cook who had fed him on many nights when he was just another starving artist. "Ah, Desperado!" Sal clasped his hands high in the air. After they exchanged greetings, McQueen made sure that Sal was properly introduced to the biggest Italian icon of the 20th century. Judging from Sal's ear-to-ear grin, the debt was paid in full.

Never So Few opened to middling reviews. The film was widely criticized for failing to live up to its epic stature, its lack of plot, and zero chemistry between Sinatra and Lollobrigida. However, their loss was McQueen's gain. One thing all critics agreed on was that a movie star was suddenly in their midst. *Variety* noted, "Steve McQueen has a good part, and he delivers with impressive style," while the *New York Herald Tribune* assessed, "Steve McQueen looks good as a brash, casual GI. He possesses that combination of smooth-rough charm that suggests star possibilities." *The Hollywood Reporter* boldly predicted the picture "provides a catapult to stardom for Steve McQueen." Less than a year later, no one could argue with that declaration.

Sinatra, by all appearances, had big plans for McQueen. He had extended an offer to McQueen to costar with him in *Ocean's Eleven*, another Rat Pack film with Dean Martin and Sammy Davis Jr., who was back in Sinatra's good graces. Sinatra also wanted to direct McQueen in *The Execution of Private Slovik*, the story of the only soldier in U.S. history to be executed for desertion. Both were tempting offers, and Sinatra wasn't a man who usually took no for an answer. McQueen was at a crossroads, but it appeared as if Hedda Hopper, who was one of the most powerful women in Hollywood, was going to make the choice for him.

The former actress-turned–Hollywood gossip columnist took a liking to the "feisty little bastard" well before he became a household name, and the two became fast friends. Her position in the media would make her a powerful ally, too. Steve often sent her birthday cards and letters (often addressing her as "Slim") from location, and he never failed to feed her tidbits on his career. In return, Hopper kept his name in national circulation with her six daily columns and a Sunday column for the Chicago News Syndicate. She was a powerful figure and was vicious in her dealings with those who dared to cross her. McQueen was a pussycat in her presence, often charming, flirtatious, and always deferential.

When Hopper heard about McQueen's run-in with the law back in New York and possible future plans with Sinatra (whom she beat up in print for leaving his first wife for the sultry Ava Gardner), she decided it was time to step in.

Hopper heard about the openings Sinatra had offered McQueen, including two film roles and a mini-showcase in a nightclub act, where his repertoire included impressions of Walter Brennan, Cary Grant, and Marlon Brando's famous speech from *Julius Caesar*. Comedy never provided McQueen's strongest screen moments, so one can only imagine whether this would have been funny for all the wrong reasons. For the up-and-coming star, this could have been career suicide. Hopper dutifully smiled and then flipped her notebook shut. She decided it was time to go off the record.

"Do you want to be a movie star or a Frank Sinatra flunky?" she asked McQueen point blank. It was a rhetorical question, one that McQueen thought about long and hard. On one hand, he was offered membership into the most exclusive club, the Rat Pack, and had the blessing of the world's most powerful entertainer, and with it came glamour and opportunities. On the other hand, he would never be the main attraction, just a subordinate to Sinatra and subject to his whims and temper tantrums with the risk of falling out of favor at a moment's notice. This was not to be McQueen's destiny, and this route could never fulfill his star potential. He finally shook his head and got the message. Hopper was on his side, and he appreciated the sage wisdom.

McQueen never forgot her kindness and how her advice shaped his career. Years later when he was in Taiwan filming *The Sand Pebbles*, the news of her death affected him greatly. Shortly afterward, he paid for two unsigned tributes on the back pages of *The Hollywood Reporter* and *Variety* magazines. The tribute read: "To a great lady—Hedda Hopper."

McQueen's next film would prove that he didn't need to ride Sinatra's coat-tails, or anyone else's for that matter, to make him one of the most powerful stars of the next two decades. He was ready to take all the limelight for himself, although this would still require hard work and lots of scene stealing. He would create one of his most memorable performances against stiff, "bald-headed" competition. But as always, McQueen had the desire and determination, as well as several tricks up his sleeve.

14

SILENCE IS GOLDEN

SEDUCED BY THE GOOD LIFE COURTESY OF FRANK SINATRA, Steve McQueen returned to the second season of *Wanted: Dead or Alive* a reluctant man. He had tasted the high life of a megastar and liked it. Being saddled as a television star simply wasn't enough for the ambitious actor; he ached for the next level of fame. Actor Cliff Robertson remembered seeing McQueen on the Columbia studio lot at the time and sensing his desperation to enter the big leagues. "[Steve] wasn't a member of the studio, but he used to have a motorcycle out in front. He'd strut around, and we used to say, 'Well, there goes another guy doing *Waterfront*.' Jesus, did he want to be a movie star."

McQueen detested the monotony of the series and said it wasn't conducive to his internal alarm clock. "You don't have any idea what a rough grind it is, doing a TV series. I had to be up at 5:00 AM, to the studio at 6:30 AM.... Then [I] worked all day on the set and usually didn't get home until 9:00 PM. Sometimes, under deadline pressure, we'd film a whole episode in a single day!"

Four Star also farmed out McQueen on the road for state fairs, festivals, and rodeos. Hilly Elkins recalled McQueen's first promotional visit was a rodeo in some "godforsaken little town" in Texas. Elkins asked what McQueen's plan was to entertain the masses. "I don't know," was his response. The two quickly devised a scheme. A coin would be tossed in the air while Steve rode on his horse and took aim at the coin with his Mare's Laig while Elkins threw the houselights. Elkins remembers the execution well. "We did it exactly according to plan—threw the coin, put the lights out, shot at the coin, ran out, got into the car, and drove home. To this day I don't know if he hit or missed the coin," Elkins said.

McQueen also made a memorable appearance at the Vinton Dogwood Festival just outside of Roanoke, Virginia, where he accepted the town's invitation to be its 1959 parade marshal. Festival organizers nearly had to put a bounty on the actor's head after he arrived in town.

The festival was a big draw for flesh-pressing, backslapping politicians, and it represented everything McQueen hated. In his duties as parade marshal, McQueen was required to ride a horse through Vinton and chat up the townspeople, but he darted in and out of the daylong activities with a friend in a local bar. Wallace Cundiff, that year's committee chairman who helped select McQueen as parade marshal, said almost 50 years later, "I think McQueen, like his character Josh Randall, preferred the company of common folk and a quiet place to wet his whistle. I can't honestly say he was our greatest parade marshal, but the rascal sure made a lasting impression."

Stuntman Fred Krone said McQueen's growing hatred of the show was understandable. "Four Star Studios, who produced the show, pushed Steve an awful lot. He worked many hours—and all the production cared about was getting film in the can, developed, and onto the next," Krone said. "Steve had a healthy ego. He could be moody and a pain in the ass, and [he] had to be put in check every now and then."

Krone referred to the time when McQueen reported to the set five hours late. A phone call was placed to Four Star head Dick Powell while the cast and crew toiled around, waiting for the show's star to show up. When McQueen casually strolled in, he calmly sat in his chair, and the makeup artist began powdering his face. A few minutes later, Powell appeared and asked to have a chat. The two men walked outside but weren't exactly out of the crew's earshot. Powell, who was one of Hollywood's few power players and a true gentleman, explained to McQueen in simple terms he was never to pull that stunt again.

"We are a bakery, and you are the product," Powell said calmly. "We tell you how you're wrapped, presented, and sold, and that's how the cookie crumbles." Krone said it was the only time he ever saw McQueen humbled. Powell did, however, make a concession for McQueen by pushing the start time of his shoot an hour later to 7:45 AM. "I've got a mental block about getting up early," McQueen explained. "I have had it since I got out of the Marines."

At times, McQueen smoked pot between takes to relieve the tedium. Actor James Coburn, who was a guest on the show a few times, recalled, "It would take 15 minutes to set up a shot, and Steve was off on his motorcycle for 30 minutes. He was causing the producers a lot of anxiety because those spare 15 minutes cost them money. On a couple of those trips, he would take me to the dressing room, smoke a joint, and come back." What the producers failed to understand was the importance of keeping McQueen's interest alive and his ego placated. He thrived on approval, and fighting was a way to get the outcome he wanted.

Actress Mara Corday said McQueen's impossible behavior sometimes drove others to substance abuse. "He was an egomaniac at the time—the most unprofessional actor I've ever worked with," Corday said. "He'd go off and ride his motorcycle. We'd all sit around waiting. Director George Blair was a recovering alcoholic. We were getting way behind schedule because of McQueen's delays. Steve proclaimed, 'Hey, I'm enjoying my bike better than a little TV show.' I noticed George's breath had alcohol—and by the last show, Steve McQueen was directing it!"

The success of the series put Steve in a position of power, and he demanded his fingertips touch everything, from scripts to choice of directors, casting, and even wardrobe. He eventually ran off *Wanted's* first producer-writer, John Robinson, who was an integral part of the first two seasons. McQueen had a personal relationship with Robinson, having invited him and his wife over to the house many times for dinner. On the set, however, it was a different story. McQueen constantly undermined and questioned the mild-mannered Robinson in front of the entire company. Rather than bump heads with McQueen, Robinson quietly opted out of the series, taking sick leave at the end of the second season; he never returned. This epitomizes the duality of McQueen—he could be thoughtful and friendly but incredibly mercenary when he thought he needed to be. He could be ruthless and unforgiving if he thought his career could be affected. This determination had its benefits, though. It ensured few people would stand up to him and enabled him to test people's loyalty. However, the reputation he created would prove to be a double-edged sword; later in his career, this would ultimately put him at risk of losing a sense of proportion and moderation.

Psychologist Peter O. Whitmer said there's a good explanation for McQueen's Jekyll and Hyde personality. "McQueen's hyper-competitive, combative drive for success as an actor was somewhat of a different game with different rules than his marital life," Whitmer said. "He could keep score to gauge how he was progressing in the films. Salary, billing, the 'body count' of fallen actors, writers, producers—anyone who got in the way of his forward progress—was, in Steve McQueen's mind, the measure of the man. However, only so long as he kept up his career momentum could he continue to tell his inner insecurities that they were wrong and keep them at bay. His emotional reaction to whomever he perceived as giving him an 'assist' were perfectly acceptable and often bountiful, as they fed into this scheme, his ego. Just don't cross him. He's both fragile and volatile."

Occasionally Steve's puckish humor surfaced and provided a good laugh every now and then. In an episode titled, "The Tyrant," Josh Randall was set to be executed by a firing squad for a murder he didn't commit. It was a complicated scene involving three cameras and nearly 100 extras. Segment director Donald McDougall had rehearsed the scene nearly a dozen times. McQueen arrived on the set pedaling his bicycle, wearing a black leather ankle-length duster coat and sipping a chocolate milkshake. Three makeup artists rushed in for a quick touch-up on McQueen's bruises and blood. The actor took his place and nodded to McDougall that he was ready.

A sudden silence fell over the scene as the director called for "Action!" McQueen magically transformed into a dazed and dying prisoner as a squad of soldiers dragged him through the square, past the townspeople, and viciously slammed him up against the adobe wall, ready to execute him. The three cameras cranked away, carefully maintaining focus, knowing there would not be time for a second take.

"Lock and load!" said veteran actor William Forester, who began the traditional countdown to the final command fire.

Screenwriter Tom Gries called for a last-minute reprieve at count four, but on count three, in front of everyone, Josh Randall suddenly burst out of his dazed stupor and stood erect with the McQueen shit-eating grin spread across his face and performed a broadly animated masturbation gesture in front of the camera. David Ross, who was visiting a friend on the set recalled, "You could hear a pin drop as a sudden hush fell over the crowd, which lasted all of 30 seconds before the actors, crew, and yes, even the director, broke into gales of laughter."

Ross found it ironic that the episode was aired on Halloween 1959.

• • •

Screen icon Bette Davis once asked Steve McQueen why he would he risk his life and his career by tooling around Hollywood on a motorcycle.

"So I won't forget I'm a man and not just an actor," McQueen replied. Davis smiled and did so knowingly, for she knew the industry could be dangerously all-consuming. McQueen understood that he needed an outlet and friends outside the movie business to keep his sanity. He needed to have something on standby to allow him to escape to his own world. A car, a motorbike, a young starlet—all of these would provide ways for him to disconnect from Hollywood when he had to. He was never truly at ease as an actor, so these other activities helped him keep hold of the reality he had created for himself.

McQueen was fascinated by anything with a motor and wheels from an early age, and that fascination developed passionately during his life, so much so that his racing exploits are as much a part of his legacy as his films. In his 50 years, he competed in motorcycle and car races in the United States, England, France, and Germany. He flew antique airplanes, executive-produced an Oscar-nominated motorcycle documentary (*On Any Sunday*), and risked his career on *Le Mans*, known today by motoring enthusiasts as the definitive racing film. He also collected and restored hundreds of antique bikes and cars, and these vehicles have formed a cottage industry of their own. McQueen and his machines were inextricably linked. Psychologist Peter O. Whitmer said, "There was a sexualized relationship between Steve and the bike, the automobile, the biplane, and anything with a machine. Unlike the human, it would pretty much do—with total positive regard, never talking back—what he could make it do. It was a hyperextension of our own deepest fantasies of grace and power and finesse, usually displayed in a competitive arena. It was an issue of power and control and personal skill and creativity, bringing about the whole union—the yin and the yang of the Tao."

McQueen's appreciation for wheels started around the age of 12, when he and an older buddy successfully pieced together a potent street machine. They did so by joining together a Model A frame with a Ford 60 engine. "It had an Edelbrock manifold," Steve recalled. "We could accelerate with a J-2 Allard, which was *the* going sports car around there at the time. Our rod didn't handle for beans, but when the engine stayed together, that machine had *stark* acceleration. It was a real jumper."

With money from the television series, McQueen's fascination turned into a full-time hobby with the purchase of a 1958 Porsche Speedster. It was his first factory-purchased automobile and doubled as his racing car on weekends. Steve's first competition was for the Sports Car Club of America at an event held in Santa Barbara on May 30, 1959. He joked that the worst possible thing happened to him: "I won. That *really* got me hooked."

Neile said of that first victory, for which he was awarded an engraved Sheffield Pewter tankard, "Steve was so proud of this. He talked about it for weeks to anyone who would listen!" He also participated in several other races that year at Del Mar, Willow Springs, and Laguna Seca, taking the checkered flag in two of those instances.

Driving legend Bob Bondurant was at the Santa Barbara race and said McQueen made a lasting impression on him. "I had enjoyed watching him on *Wanted: Dead or Alive*, and when we met that day, he was quite congenial and much more interesting in person," Bondurant said. "We talked about cars and

Indian motorcycles, which were also my first passion. I believe his handling of motorcycles helped him as a race car driver because the handlebars of a bike are close, just like the steering wheel of a car. Not all actors know how to race, but he most certainly did."

McQueen won the respect of his peers and was named 1959's Rookie of the Year by the American Sports Car Association. It was one of his proudest accomplishments.

A few months after the Santa Barbara race, McQueen traded in the Porsche for a Lotus Mark II, a serious racing machine. The car was primarily designed to compete in the 1100 cc class where it was one of the most successful cars during the mid- to late-1950s. He enjoyed several good battles in it, winning a few races along the way. McQueen said of the machine, "In that Lotus, I really started to become competitive. I was smoother, more relaxed. The rough edges had been knocked off my driving. I was beginning to find out what real sports car racing was all about."

McQueen wasn't academic or highly literate, but he was inherently intelligent and eager to learn, and he was curious and anxious to learn from the best. When the legendary racing driver Sir Stirling Moss came to the United States, McQueen sought him out. "I met Steve back in 1959 in California. He was keen on racing bikes and cars, and he had heard that I was going to be at a particular race," Moss said in 2009. "I suppose in those days when you were in the know and somebody came to town, it was quite easy to track him down. Steve found out I was staying in Beverly Hills and invited me to stay with him and his wife, Neile. At the time, I'd never heard of Steve, but he was so friendly and persuasive, it was hard to say no." It was a friendship that grew over the years, and Moss became extremely close to both Steve and Neile. In fact, Neile often stated that she felt Moss had a little crush on her, though in an innocent and complimentary dimension as opposed to flirtatious, often sending them both charming letters. McQueen and Moss had a mutual respect and appreciation for one another. Moss never treated McQueen like a big movie star because they were peers on the racetrack. McQueen was not the big shot from the studio anymore; he was on an equal footing with Moss as the seasoned professional. Perhaps that is what McQueen found most enduring; he would regularly grow weary of the mendacity of Hollywood and liked the raw intensity of the racetrack where he was first or nowhere.

McQueen was just as fierce on the motorcycle circuit, said stuntman-turned-director Hal Needham, who raced against McQueen on many weekends. "One time during the middle of a race, his motorcycle broke down and he could not start it because of a bad spark plug. I drove past him and stopped. I had a wrench and a spark plug, and in less than a minute, he was back in the race," Needham said. About five races later, the opposite situation happened to Needham, who needed a helping hand when his bike suddenly conked out and McQueen came roaring past. However, there was one exception—McQueen didn't stop to help. When the race was over, Needham mentioned the snub after the race. "I said, 'Thanks a lot, Steve, for helping out your buddy. I'll remember that next time your bike breaks down.' Steve said, 'I'm sorry, Hal, but I was running second and I just couldn't afford to stop.'" Needham couldn't stay mad at McQueen because he understood and admired his competitive spirit.

Be it a bike or a car, racing was something that was real and tangible to McQueen, who thrived on competition. "You see, around the studios, everybody waits on me," McQueen explained. "They powder my nose and tell me what they think I want to hear. After a while, you're convinced you are superhuman.

"But when you're racing a motorcycle, the guy on the next bike doesn't care who you are. And if he beats you in the race, well, it means he's a better man than you are. And he's not afraid to tell you that you're lousy.

"Racing keeps my equilibrium intact. It makes it difficult to believe I'm God's gift to humanity."

Whitmer said McQueen's thrill-seeking nature was a large part of his psychological makeup and a major trait of Attachment Disorder. "The accepted clinical interpretation is that early developmental psychological experiences—the punitive family life, the inconsistent parenting, the constants of chaos in flux—directly impacts the endocrine system [especially the androgen-estrogen balance, determining male or female secondary sex characteristics], and secondarily, their neurological wiring," Whitmer said. "As they grow older, this renders them under-stimulated from baseline, in comparison to the normal population, and as a consequence, in order to feel 'normal,' they have to go to extremes and inundate themselves, overload themselves with what the average person would perceive as frightening, dangerous, crazy-making activities. [It's] life on the edge."

McQueen needed racing because it was a great equalizer for him. He had only himself to rely on, and his ego would have to take second place if he wanted to finish in first. Bud Ekins, a racing legend who ran a Triumph dealership on Ventura Boulevard, certainly never thought McQueen walked on water when he came in to inquire about a Triumph 650 cc. "I recognized him from *Wanted: Dead or Alive*, but I had worked with movie-industry types and certainly didn't look at them through rose-colored glasses," Ekins said in 2006. "Steve wasn't magical or special; he was just a fellow human being. In fact, he was a bit of a nuisance and invariably picky, even with technical matters he did not understand. I think he liked that I didn't give him preferential treatment."

Bud's brother, Dave Ekins, said he thinks their meeting was no accident. "Steve and Bud were both born the same year, and they lived parallel lives—early delinquents graduating into reform school and later self-made men who liked their booze and their talk straight. Of course, they loved their machinery and the freedom of the road. I believe they were destined to find each other."

Their friendship lasted more than two decades, three wives, and hundreds of verbal barbs. If Neile was the seminal female relationship in his life, then Ekins was her male counterpart. "Now, Bud is my friend in the fullest meaning of the word," McQueen once told a reporter. "He's got two kids, and I've got two kids. The old ladies hang around each other. We're pitching our kids off to get married when they grow up."

Ekins in turn was equally impressed with McQueen's respect for machinery and his innate curiosity. McQueen devoured manuals and history books on bikes and eternally peppered Ekins with questions. "When he got on a motorcycle, he wanted to know the complete history of the bike from the beginning. Why did this company do this? Why did this company do that? Of course, I gave him 30 years' knowledge in a year. He pretty well knew it, too. He was a good student."

McQueen was also an excellent student of the Hollywood game and adapted quickly. McQueen had now generated a great deal of interest in himself from the film industry, and he challenged the conventional wisdom that television actors couldn't make the leap to the silver screen. "I think it's ridiculous to say that somebody from TV can't make it in pictures," McQueen said to reporter Bob Thomas. "The movies have been at a standstill for the past two years. They've got to start moving or else."

Hedda Hopper noted in an April 29, 1959, column that producer Robert Webb (*Love Me Tender*) bought a property called *Terror at Webb's Landing*, a gripping kidnap story set deep in the Florida swamps, specifically for McQueen. "It will star Steve in it later this year when other commitments allow," Hopper wrote. It's possible the item was a plant by McQueen to let CBS know there was interest in him outside of the TV realm, or it was a trick to get more money from his contract. Whatever the case was, CBS wasn't budging. When United Artists producer Walter Mirisch called Hilly Elkins to check on Steve's interest and availability in a new film directed by John Sturges, it was a project McQueen simply couldn't ignore. Nor could he ignore the $65,000 payday. Come hell or high water, McQueen was going to be in that picture.

Elkins read the script, which was a reworking of *The Seven Samurai*, a Japanese film classic directed by Akira Kurosawa. Sturges had planned to turn it into a western titled *The Magnificent Seven* about seven gunmen hired to protect a Mexican village. The immediate problem was how in the hell was he going to get McQueen out of his Four Star contract? Elkins was concerned about McQueen's limited speaking part—it had just seven lines of dialogue. McQueen would never be satisfied to be a small fish in a big pond, so if there were few lines then he would have to ensure his part was big enough in other ways. Elkins placed a call to Sturges, who acknowledged the part wasn't very talky. "I know, Hilly, but I promise I'll give him the camera." Sturges was one of the few men in the industry whose word was as good as gold. He had helped McQueen in *Never So Few* by doing precisely that—giving him the camera. McQueen agreed to play the role of Vin, the movie's hotshot gunslinger, but Four Star Productions had to sign off first.

Sturges was going to shoot the film on location in Cuernavaca, Mexico, in late February 1960, which would overlap with *Wanted*'s tight shooting schedule. Elkins went to see Dick Powell, who steered him to business executive Tom McDermott, a person whose reputation preceded him. "Tom McDermott, may he rest in peace, was out of New York and was a tough guy, a tough Irishman, and knew what I was coming into his office for," Elkins said, who tried to appeal to the business side of McDermott by telling him the movie would draw more attention to the series. "Give him a couple of weeks compensation leave. I know that in the spirit of Dick Powell, you're going to help us out," Elkins said gently. McDermott's face turned beet red. "Don't start that Mafia approach with me, kid! He's got a deal, he's got a contract, and that's what he's going to be doing," McDermott said. "Hey, listen kid. When we need your help, we'll call you." That was Elkins' dismissal, who politely nodded and left quietly. When Elkins got back to his office, he called McQueen, who was in Hartford, Connecticut, making another dreaded personal appearance on behalf of *Wanted: Dead or Alive*. Elkins explained the situation and was as succinct as possible—have an accident. "I felt comfortable advising Steve on that level because of his racing and driving skills, and I knew he'd be careful but convincing. But I had no idea he would take it to the level that he did," Elkins said. Once again, McQueen would pull out all the stops to feed his ambitions.

With wife Neile in the car, McQueen drove his rented Cadillac into the side of the Bank of Boston, narrowly missing a police officer, and smashed the car into actual bricks and mortar. The incident made the papers, and McQueen came back to Hollywood in a neck brace. McDermott called Elkins and said he wasn't buying the story. Elkins' duties called upon him to sometimes act with feigned innocence. "Hey, look. It was an accident, he's got a neck problem and he can't do the show, he can't do the movie. We've got a problem," Elkins said. McDermott knew when he was licked. He called Elkins into his office and signed off on the movie, "Okay, look. This isn't what we like to do, but you get this round. We'll let him out early to do the picture." Elkins had some unfinished business. "Thank you, Mr. McDermott. That was then, this is now. There's another requirement, and that is you double the salary."

"You motherfucker!" McDermott screamed, followed by a string of epithets. No matter how many obscenities Elkins heard that day, he got McQueen the raise, and more important, he got him the part. "The rest, of course, is history," Elkins said.

Four Star not only obliged McQueen by releasing him to do the movie and giving him a hefty pay raise, the $150,000 a year he had dictated—they also added actor Wright King to the cast as Josh's sometime partner, deputy sheriff Jason Nichols, who carried the show for nine episodes. "Those were difficult circumstances," King said. "The producers took his scripts and split his lines and gave me half. That's not a good way to work. I was kind of tentative coming on as a character. [Steve] wasn't too happy, and I wasn't either. Finally, I think it kind of straightened out."

Wright, who had a prestigious theater background, said McQueen's acting style inadvertently rubbed off on him. "He said to me once, after we had been working together for a while, that he had been watching me and he thought I was getting more and more like him. I told him that it wasn't true! I had never imitated anyone, and I wasn't going to start with him. I saw that episode he was talking about years later, and he was right." Wright shouldn't have felt bad. Decades later, McQueen would not be remembered as the unrefined actor he once was; he would gain recognition in his own right and influence an entire generation of actors with his inimitable style.

The Magnificent Seven was a milestone in the early portion of McQueen's career and his first real shot at stardom. With Sturges' promise of being generous with the camera, McQueen schemed to steal the movie from underneath its star, Academy Award–winner Yul Brynner. That was a daunting task; the Russian-born actor was at the top of his career with his shaven head, deep voice, and intensity. He was naturally a commanding and intimidating screen presence. He also had on his résumé one of those little gold statues called an Oscar, courtesy of his star-making turn in *The King and I*. Brynner had what McQueen wanted—the starring role, power, and status. He was also equally as competitive as McQueen. Standing 5'10", Brynner was reportedly concerned about being overshadowed by Charlton Heston's physical presence in the film *The Ten Commandments* and prepared for the role of Ramses with an intensive weight-lifting program. However, this giant of the screen underestimated one thing—the McQueen factor.

In addition to Brynner and McQueen, Sturges rounded out the cast with actors Robert Vaughn, James Coburn, Charles Bronson, Horst Buchholz, Brad Dexter, and Eli Wallach. As the movie unfolded, it turned out that McQueen wasn't the only one with larceny on his mind. Brynner may not have fully realized it, but he had been dropped in a literal piranha tank full of hungry actors looking to take the limelight from him. The entire cast was looking to usurp Brynner once they got a gander at his luxury coach, his entourage (a personal secretary, two gofers, and a barber to ensure the famous Brynner noggin was clean-shaven), and his ego. "Yul was the king," James Coburn said. "He had this whole entourage, but he didn't like anyone walking within 10 feet of him. He had this ambience around him. He liked to have his cigarette lit for him at the snap of a finger. Movie star treatment."

While Brynner and Buchholz were ensconced in private homes and treated like kings, the rest of the cast was treated like paupers and put up in a dive motel called Posadas Jacarandas. Soon enough, little cliques formed—McQueen and Bronson buddied up, rekindling their camaraderie from *Never So Few*, while Vaughn and Coburn were already friends. (Vaughn had recommended Coburn for the part.) Sturges quietly approved, knowing those conflicts would translate to onscreen tension and benefit the picture.

Vaughn said McQueen had fun at the hotel, participating in spirited poker games, drinking lots of margaritas, and ogling the señoritas. But on the set it was clear McQueen had an agenda. "I think Steve always felt the world was against him and that he was battling it all by himself," Vaughn said. "And as he became more internationally famous, successful, and wealthy, that continued to increase. It didn't decrease; it went the other direction. For some reason, unknown to me to this day, he was very friendly toward me. He was paranoid about Yul Brynner, who was the star of the picture. One time he said to me, 'Did you see how big Brynner's horse is?' I said, 'No, as a matter of fact, they're calling my horse Elefante.' I think my horse is bigger than his. He said, 'No, Brynner's horse is a lot bigger!' He was angry about this. Shortly after that, he came to me to talk about Brynner's having a white-handled gun or something, which he hadn't noticed originally. He thought it might take away from him. He plotted every day to best Yul Brynner."

The first scene filmed for the movie, where the seven men cross a stream on horseback, set the tone for the rest of the shoot. Brynner was always first, followed by the rest of the cast in single file, who in his mind merely filled out the landscape. When Sturges called for action, Brynner hit his mark while the others went off script. McQueen, making the first move, took off his hat and dipped it in water. Bronson unbuttoned his shirt, Dexter adjusted his guns, and the rest instinctively followed suit. "Catching flies" is what Sturges called it, and he quietly encouraged the competition.

Shaking shotgun shells, flipping a coin, fussing with his Stetson, tugging at his bandana, and whistling through his teeth were all part of McQueen's bag of scene-stealing tricks, which Brynner grew to despise and are part of the film's legend today. Hilly Elkins said McQueen was inspired when he literally brought Brynner down to size. "Steve and Yul Brynner weren't that tall. In one of their scenes, Brynner built himself a little mound of dirt to stand on to appear taller. Steve is circling saying his lines. Every time he passes Yul, he kicks away at the dirt pile Yul is standing on, so throughout the scene, you see Yul is getting smaller and smaller. By the end of the scene, Yul is standing in a hole!"

Brynner summoned one of his assistants to keep a running tally on McQueen's ad-libs and improvisations. But Brynner hit the roof when it became apparent that McQueen had leaked information to *Movie Stars & TV Closeup*. The headline of the article screamed, "McQueen vs. Brynner—Battle of the Hotheads." Brynner grabbed McQueen's arm to turn him around. "There's a story in the paper about us having a feud. I'm an established star, and I don't feud with supporting actors. I want you to call the paper and tell them the story is completely false," Brynner ordered. McQueen told Brynner what he could do with his orders.

When McQueen didn't have his eye on Brynner, he turned his focus to the local ladies, who found the fair-haired gringo most attractive. "Mexican girls who had never seen *Wanted: Dead or Alive* or didn't know anything about Steve were extraordinarily attracted to him," Robert Vaughn said. In his autobiography, *A Fortunate Life*, Vaughn wrote of a memorable visit to a local brothel on Good Friday 1960, where he was joined by costars Brad Dexter and Steve McQueen. "The blonde madam instantly recognized Brad and welcomed us like visiting dignitaries at an embassy cocktail party. Rounds of margaritas began appearing, along with many beautifully coiffed and gowned ladies, any of whom could have passed for a finalist in the Miss Universe pageant. Brad left with a pair of dark-haired beauties as still more margaritas arrived," Vaughn wrote.

With Dexter's departure, the madam had gently pressured Vaughn and McQueen to make their selections. With a wide-eyed grin, McQueen announced to the madam the remaining seven should stay put because, "We are the Magnificent Seven!" McQueen and Vaughn were escorted to a lanai with many large pillows and the seven ladies. While the libations flowed freely, their libidos did not. "I can only say that, due to the effects of the tequila, we did a hell of a lot more laughing than humping," Vaughn recalled.

Their laughter quickly turned to sorrow when they discovered they didn't have enough money between the two of them to cover the $700 bill ($100 per lady). Vaughn, who had about half of that amount on him, didn't know of McQueen's famous habit of not carrying any money on him. He was horrified when McQueen asked, "Hey man, could you loan me some *dinero?*"

The madam, who didn't speak English very well, did understand she was about to get stiffed. She snapped her fingers, and a huge bouncer appeared in the room. He grabbed Vaughn's money and then asked how the two men planned to pay for the rest. McQueen thought he had the solution when he pulled out a Diners Club booklet from his wallet, which offered restaurant coupons. The joke didn't go over so well, and suddenly the bouncer had several reinforcements. Vaughn and McQueen looked at each other for a split second and bolted for the door. Vaughn jumped 12 feet off of a balcony, vaulted over the front wall, and caught a cab back to the motel. McQueen didn't get nearly as far and promised to pay the madam back, with a generous tip for all the ladies, the bouncer, and his seven henchmen. Vaughn said that McQueen reported to work the next day 45 minutes late and was severely hungover.

When McQueen recovered, he tried to topple the King from his throne. McQueen thought Brynner's bald head and pointy ears resembled a pig. Vaughn said McQueen was a gifted ventriloquist and would "oink" whenever Brynner was on the set. The others quickly caught on and joined in to the point where McQueen no longer needed to egg them on.

Director John Sturges acknowledged there was definite friction between his two stars and did nothing to dissuade the tension. "They're dissimilar characters. Yul was like a rock, while Steve was volatile," Sturges said. "Steve probably figured that Yul was being a big star and that he wasn't willing for anyone to catch flies. Yul probably thought Steve was being an undisciplined smart aleck, always trying to catch a fly."

Costar James Coburn said there wouldn't have been a rivalry had Steve not pushed one. "Steve wasn't what you would call a giving guy. He had a lot of power and presence. He loved to play. It was in his nature. An abandoned child always tests everything, and he tested Yul," Coburn said.

As partial atonement, McQueen helped Brynner with his gun draw. Coburn felt it was done out of sabotage, not as a friendly gesture. "Steve, who was an extraordinary draw, gave Yul an ordinary move to draw the pistol and put it back in the holster," Coburn said. "It's been done a thousand times, and Yul used it.

So Steve was very proud that he conned Yul into a simple move, while he did this fancy thing with his pistol."

Character actor Joseph Ruskin said Brynner's hubris ultimately worked against him. The limos, the entourage, the trailer, the trophy wife, the above-the-title-billing all served to make the King fat and lazy. Ruskin said at the end of *The Magnificent Seven*, Brynner sensed the film had gotten away from him. "Brynner demanded several retakes and wanted to cut out the other actors in the script," Ruskin said. "I think he finally caught on near the end that he was not necessarily the reason why anyone was going to see the picture—that distinction belonged to Steve McQueen."

Indeed, it was McQueen who resonated with audiences and walked away with the movie. As any fan of the movie will tell you, this is not surprising. McQueen does his best to stand out in every scene, moving about, catching the audience's eye, while Brynner just stands there and expects the viewer to instinctively follow him, which just does not happen. Again, McQueen proves he is a master of props, using his hat, shotgun, shells, and pistol to devastating effect. This is not just simple bravado to catch the viewer's eye—he actually creates the impression of a real cowboy fully aware of the instruments of his trade. It's this quality that raises his performance as Vin to a level where he is completely convincing. To top it off, McQueen puts all his knowledge and experience to full use, creating perhaps his greatest moment. When the bandits attack the village in the climatic battle, McQueen starts his horse off at a gallop and delays mounting it until the horse is nearing full speed, running alongside as the beast accelerates to amazing dramatic effect. This sums up why McQueen stood out in the film. He not only looked and acted the part of a cowboy—but he also became one.

James Coburn said McQueen accomplished his goal through a combination of sheer will, underhandedness, and finesse. "Steve never took his eyes off the prize, and me, Charlie, and Bobby were so busy hating McQueen that he literally stole the movie from everyone. He'd quietly walk up to Sturges and say, 'Can I make this line change? Can I do this to my character?' We'd look at him and say, 'What a kiss ass.' But you know what? He emerged as the star of the picture." Once again, McQueen had played all the right moves.

Costar Eli Wallach said despite McQueen's opportunistic and underhanded ways, nobody had grasped the film's flow and poetry quite like McQueen did. "Even then he had the raw skill. His chief talent lay in being observant," Wallach said. "He could always find in an earlier scene what had led logically to his actions just then." Wallach was astounded that McQueen, whom he had mentored years earlier at the Neighborhood Playhouse, was so instinctual when it came to film.

Wallach watched in amazement when McQueen once asked Sturges to cut some of his dialogue. "Please, movie acting is reacting," McQueen said. "Silence is golden on the screen."

According to Wallach, "What McQueen had learned to do was what separates the true artist from the ham—to watch and, above all, to listen. McQueen was the best reactor of his generation."

The only roadblock in Steve McQueen's bid for stardom and a career on the big screen was the small screen. *Wanted: Dead or Alive* had given McQueen a degree of fame and opened many doors for him, but the series could only take him so far. He was going to go all the way. McQueen was not the type of man to let sentimentality and goodwill rule him by staying with a show that had served its purpose. It was not even a case of McQueen having outgrown the show; it was that he was too big of a personality for the small screen from the outset. Some would probably argue that his ego had always been too big for a television series. If he was to succeed, he would have to excise himself from the show, but he was not the only forceful personality in town. The producers had a hit prime-time show on their hands, and they would not go down without a fight. However, McQueen had made up his mind, and when diplomacy and ruthlessness didn't work, he had a few tricks up his sleeve. He would break loose no matter what. Nothing would stand between him and superstardom.

15

FREEDOM

STEVE MCQUEEN ONCE FAMOUSLY SAID that stardom equaled financial success, which ultimately equates to freedom. "I've spent too much of my life feeling insecure. I still have nightmares about being poor, of everything I own just vanishing away. Stardom means that can't happen."

Psychologist Peter O. Whitmer said that was "magical thinking" on McQueen's part. "Like believing there is a pot of gold at the rainbow's end, McQueen's 'take,' linking stardom and freedom, was childishly simplistic," Whitmer explained. "It was more a reflection of his inner wish for a simple, logical, predictable—free and safe—world, and he did not put into this equation the price of paradise. It is always there. Regardless, he did show some awareness of his true psychological colors in mentioning '...nightmares about being poor.' He had a handle on what really made him tick; he had moments of being psychologically minded. And tapping into this knowledge base helped his skill as an actor. But the pain must have been extreme."

McQueen often preached this, but it is not clear whether he could actually believe in this or draw comfort from his statement. He would achieve great fame and financial security, but he would always live his life scared that it would all disappear in a flash. To an extent, he was ruled by his anxieties. He would stiff studios for wardrobe items, hoard masses of collectibles, and develop a reputation for never paying for anything. This all boiled down to insecurity, that after achieving so much he could end up with nothing again. When you have started with so little and fought so hard, ending up with nothing again must have terrified him.

With his new raise from Four Star Productions and the money he earned on *The Magnificent Seven*, the McQueens moved from their Skyline home address and purchased a $60,000 home at 2419 Solar Drive in Nichols Canyon, just north of Hollywood Boulevard. Steve also upgraded his street ride to a 1956 racing green Jaguar XKSS. McQueen paid $4,000 for the rare automobile, which had a 250-horsepower engine. He collected so many speeding tickets in the Jag that he had his driver's license suspended twice. Out on the open road on his way to Phoenix, he put the car though its paces and brought it up to 120 mph when he saw flashing lights in the rearview mirror. It was the cops. Neile, who was six months pregnant, was a convenient alibi when cops questioned why he was driving like a maniac. McQueen explained that his wife was in labor and needed help. The police dutifully escorted them to a nearby hospital, where a nurse rushed out to help Neile. After the officers left, Steve informed the nurse that it was a "false alarm" and led Neile back to the car. "Neile was pissed!" Steve recollected to writer William Nolan. "She didn't speak to me for the rest of the day. But, by God, it worked. I didn't get the ticket!" McQueen sold the car in 1969, but nostalgia got the best of him, and after lengthy and often heated negotiations, he repurchased it in 1977 for considerably more, owning it until his 1980 death. It was sold in a 1984 auction for $147,500. Today it is worth millions.

Their new address also inspired a name change for his production company—Solar Productions. Formerly titled Scuderia Condor Enterprises, McQueen announced to Hedda Hopper that his first picture under the Solar banner was a racing picture titled *Le Mans*. McQueen wanted to shoot the movie entirely on location in France and was pushing for sex kitten Brigitte Bardot to costar. It would take McQueen a decade and full leverage of his star power to get the picture off the ground, and when it did, the toll it exacted was enormous.

Four Star Studios announced on May 3, 1960, that *Wanted: Dead or Alive* would return for a third season. Steve had not grown sentimental toward the series that made him a household name, nor had he mellowed, according to Richard Donner, who directed six episodes of *Wanted: Dead or Alive*, including the finale, "Barney's Bounty." Donner, who studied with McQueen at the Neighborhood Playhouse, said his former classmate did not make his transition from New York to Hollywood an easy one. "One day I was shooting a Westinghouse commercial with Lucille Ball, Desi Arnaz, Bill Frawley, Vivian Vance, and Betty Furnace," Donner said. "Bottles of vodka had been emptied well before noon, making the Desilu actors a tremendous handful to work with. Ed Adamson, who was visiting our sales manager, came over to me and said, 'Boy, if you can work with that crowd, would you work with Steve McQueen?'"

Donner replied yes, but McQueen said no. He balked on the grounds that Donner was an actor, not a director. Adamson enforced his authority as the show's producer, thus purposefully trumping McQueen, who was bristling. The uncooperative star got back at Donner by giving him a baptism by fire. Donner reported to the set on a Friday and was saddled with a technically difficult shot. When he was ready, McQueen balked again—that it's not how a gunfighter would handle the situation. Donner was open for suggestions. "You're the director," McQueen snickered. "You figure it out." The day was wasted, and Donner figured McQueen would continue to sandbag him, so he drove to McQueen's house the next day, fueled by alcohol, and announced his resignation. "Nobody quits my show," McQueen replied.

"Well, Steve, you will have to give me a hand," Donner said. Years later, Donner talked about that confrontation. "[McQueen] turned his attitude around and was tremendous. We did that show, and I ended up directing about [six] of them. That was my start." The episode "Journey for Josh" is considered by many fans as one of the series' best. Donner later went on to have a hugely successful career in feature films, including *Superman* and *Superman II*, four *Lethal Weapon* movies, *The Goonies*, and *Maverick*.

The fading genre of westerns and CBS' decision to move *Wanted* from its Saturday night slot to Wednesdays spelled the death knell for the series. Oddly enough, the show was No. 2 in its time period (losing out to *The Price Is Right* but edging out *Ozzie and Harriet*) and held a 29.2 share in the ratings.

Publicist David Foster said no one associated with CBS or Four Star Productions was sad to see the series come to an end. "There's two ways to get what you want. One is to kill them with kindness, and that was never Steve's style. Two is to be angry and bully. That's why the show didn't stay on the air, because it was just too painful for all those people to work under those circumstances," Foster said. "On a film, if someone is unhappy, you only have to work with them that one time and they're gone after three months. On a series, where it's a continuing relationship, week after week, it's just a killer. I don't care how popular that show might have been, it just couldn't go on."

Lasting 94 episodes, *Wanted: Dead or Alive* closed out its CBS run on March 29, 1961. Twenty-six years later, a modernized feature-film version of *Wanted: Dead or Alive* was released with Rutger Hauer as Josh's great-grandson Nick Randall. That same year, Four Star International created a colorized version for syndication and videotape. The show enjoyed a revival in France, Spain, Italy, Greece, and several other foreign countries, which globalized McQueen's name in the late 1980s.

McQueen didn't exactly cry into his beer when he got word the series was canceled. He reportedly whooped with delight and did a pirouette that would have made his former dance instructor, Martha Graham, proud. Neither did he need to worry about employment. MGM tendered an offer to him to star along with the studio's flagship artist, Debbie Reynolds, in a light comedy called *Champagne Complex*. The improbable plot would have cast McQueen as the youngest vice president in U.S. history, engaged to a woman who has an uncontrollable desire to take her clothes off whenever she drinks champagne. McQueen took a pass in favor of another MGM sexy comedy romp called *The Honeymoon Machine* (after Cary Grant rejected the part) about two Navy men who hatch a scheme to win big by figuring out a casino roulette wheel using their ship's computer. Lots of mayhem ensues when their admiral intercepts the signals and misinterprets them as attack warnings. Based on a 1959 Broadway play called *The Golden Fleecing*, McQueen relies on costars Jim Hutton, Paula Prentiss, Dean Jagger, Brigid Bazlen, and Jack Weston to do most of the comedic lifting. Manager Hilly Elkins saw the play on Broadway and, sensing its enormous potential, felt it was an opportune time for McQueen to incorporate comedy into his acting repertoire. McQueen learned quickly that comedy was a unique art form to master. "I will take full credit for that one," Elkins said. "It was a dumb move. It was a dumb move for both Steve and me. We were looking the other way, and we should have passed."

Elkins was tapped for double duty on the picture—babysitting both McQueen and his female lead, actress Brigid Bazlen. Dubbed "the next Elizabeth Taylor" when she was just a teenager, Bazlen had two blockbusters under her belt—*King of Kings* and *How the West Was Won*. At 5'4" and weighing 87 pounds, with haunting, dark amber eyes, it was like asking the fox to guard the henhouse. "My job was to keep [McQueen and Bazlen] from killing each other, either with fisticuffs, verbal attacks, or fucking," Elkins said, laughing. "It was a choice, depending on the mood of the two kids."

Not only was it a miserable production, but McQueen also knew he was putting forth a clumsy and painfully strained effort. He simply was not adept at comedy, and he walked out of an early screening of the picture. He was disgusted by his performance and didn't like the movie much better. His instincts ultimately proved correct. *The Honeymoon Machine* was both a box-office and critical failure when released on August 16, 1961. *The New York Herald* said McQueen "confused posturing with entertaining," while *The Saturday Review* suggested he go "back to TV westerns and selling cigarettes."

Bazlen never made another movie and ultimately gave up performing. McQueen decided comedy wasn't his forte and decided he should get back to what he did best—action. Luckily he found himself in demand when it came to the genre when Paramount offered him $100,000 to star in *Hell Is for Heroes*.

Taken from the Robert Pirosh script *Separation Hill*, the World War II film is an ensemble piece. In addition to McQueen, the rest of the cast included James Coburn, Bobby Darin, Fess Parker, Nick Adams, Bob Newhart, and Harry Guardino. Playing a psychopathic loner incapable of getting along with other soldiers in this war drama, McQueen's characterization of Reese is one of the most underrated and powerful performances of his career. That's largely due to the fact that Pirosh, a former WWII Master Sergeant, saw action in the Ardennes and Rhineland campaigns and parlayed his experiences into inspiring and profitable films. He won an Academy Award in 1949 for *Battleground* and another Oscar for 1951's *Go For Broke!*, which was his directorial debut. Pirosh said he and McQueen clicked—at first. "Steve was very stimulating to work with during the script stage. He was fun, and he had some terrific ideas that helped me develop the Reese character," Pirosh said. "He came up with little bits of dialogue. I thought the guy was great. He was going to give a great performance, and I was going to get some credit for it." A week later, Pirosh changed his tune.

In what became a ritual on almost every one of his pictures, McQueen felt that his role had not been clearly defined and wanted a script revision to beef up his part. Pirosh adamantly refused on the grounds that the film was about a band of brothers, not a singular hero. But brotherly love was not on McQueen's agenda. He would not be satisfied until he felt he was given enough material and screen time of high enough caliber to establish him as the star of the picture and distinguish himself from his screen peers. Costar James Coburn said McQueen once griped to him, "Why can't they do a story about one guy—me?" Coburn laughed at the memory of McQueen's selfishness, which he knew stemmed from his pained childhood. "He wanted to be totally alone as the star and didn't want anyone to be around," Coburn said. "Steve wanted the film to be about him, and he got as close as he could get."

When McQueen and Pirosh reached a stalemate, McQueen had him removed. Paramount dismissed Pirosh (no small feat considering Pirosh had won an Oscar) and shut down production until McQueen's part was spruced up and a new director could be located. Once again, McQueen had laid down his ruthless authority to get what he wanted. He was self-serving in the utmost, but he knew that success would not be handed to him on a plate. He pushed for everything he could get. Upon McQueen's approval, Don Siegel (*Invasion of the Body Snatchers* and later *Dirty Harry*) was hired to helm the picture.

Siegel was one of the darlings of France's cineastes of the '60s. His pictures had style, flair, and an uncommon sense of humor. The director also had an innate understanding of actors and tried to be accommodating, even on a picture as trying as *Hell is for Heroes*. Parker, Coburn, Newhart, and Darin all had simultaneous projects during the making of the film. They repeatedly showed up at the last minute to do their lines without makeup and little or no rehearsal. This would inadvertently benefit McQueen, whether he realized it or not. This resentment he harbored would enhance his portrayal of Reese and galvanize his brooding detachment. Because the other actors were preoccupied, McQueen could devote his entire energy into making sure that the picture worked for him and him alone.

However, McQueen was still infuriated and felt the movie lacked professionalism. "[McQueen] walked around with the attitude that the burden of preserving the integrity of the picture was on his shoulders, and all the rest of us were company men ready to sell out to the studio bosses," Siegel said. "One day, when we were sitting together on the set, I told him that his attitude bored me, that I was as interested in the picture being as good as he was, and that when this fact sunk through his thick head we would get along. I could see he was angry. But I decided that if he stood up and came for me, I would hit him first as hard as I could and hope for the best."

Siegel didn't have to resort to such measures, but he learned quickly to cater to McQueen's massive ego. With McQueen there were usually only two ways to deal with him when he turned on the ego—you either backed down completely, or you stood up fiercely against him and braced yourself. However, Siegel discovered a novel and low-risk approach. "I found one way was to play Steve as a professional, a real pro who was surrounded by amateurs," Siegel said. "Certainly, with our cast, which came from all walks of life in the entertainment world, there was hardly a professional aura, and that made Steve stand out all the more." Coburn said he thinks that Siegel was a passive Svengali who was putting McQueen on. "He would say to Steve, 'Sure, go ahead and do that. You want to shoot when? Sure, we can accommodate that.' When Steve wasn't around, he'd shoot something else. He was very, very easy. There was no opposition. If there's no opposition, there's no conflict."

Conflict was something that McQueen seemed to often purposefully seek out. Perhaps it was a way of releasing the pressure he was under to become a star, or perhaps it was simply to stamp down his authority, satiate his ego, and assert his power status like a silverback gorilla. When McQueen wasn't causing headaches for the directors, he was tangling with his costars, especially Bobby Darin, who was jockeying for top billing in the picture. Adding to the dissension was Nick Adams, who leaked stories about the infighting to a publication in exchange for a feature article on his next film. Unfortunately, the unit publicist was blamed for the leaks and was fired. James Bacon, the colorful Hollywood columnist and sometime film extra, visited the set and quickly assessed the situation. He told Darin, "McQueen was his own worst enemy."

"Not while I'm still alive," Darin famously quipped.

Comedian Bob Newhart wrote in his 2003 book, *I Shouldn't Even Be Doing This!*, that McQueen went out of his way to alienate everyone before the cameras even rolled. "He met with the cast and told us, in his trademark low-key fashion, how things would go during filming. 'Man, I like you guys. But I'm not supposed to like you in the movie, man, so I've got to live apart from you guys and not have anything to do with you during the shoot.' We all told McQueen that was fine with us, man."

The conflict seemed mostly internal, said Sonny West, who was an extra in the film. "He was intense, a loner, and gave off a vibe that made it obvious that unless he expressly invited you to speak to him, you shouldn't," West said. "When McQueen wasn't shooting a scene, he pumped weights, often joined by James Coburn, with the intensity of someone trying to work off a lot of pent-up energy."

The pent-up frustration came from inside him, always smoldering away as he ascended Hollywood's ranks. However, McQueen's personality cannot shoulder all the blame, because these difficulties were also exacerbated by the film's low budget and shooting in the forests of Redding, California, which often reached triple-digit temperatures. The studio's budget restrictions resulted in phony-looking props, malfunctioning firearms, and the same German soldier having to be killed several times. In the last battle scene, McQueen can be seen experiencing multiple failures firing his grease gun, which were due to problems with the low quality of blanks.

To offset the heat, most of the filming took place at night, which left McQueen with plenty of free time during the day. That gave him opportunities to orchestrate chaos. Coburn recalled, "He created this great big storm of people running and solving McQueen's problems, which were all ridiculous, silly things. He just loved to have people rushing around, feeling that strange need he had. And when he'd had enough, he'd go off into the desert by himself on his motorcycle."

The studio also rented three cars for McQueen, all of which he wrecked on wild rides through the forest, including a Mercedes 300 SL. Paramount executives fired off a missive to McQueen stating if he wrecked another rental car, it would be deducted from his six-figure paycheck. They had found one of his sweet spots—his wallet. No more cars saw the salvage yard, but the film was about to experience the wrecking ball.

The script rewrites, production delays, and McQueen's slew of trashed auto-mobiles inflated the budget from $900,000 to $1.9 million. Paramount executives were planning a trip to Redding and threatened to shut down the picture for good. McQueen knew that a shutdown to a picture with his name attached as its star would have had serious repercussions on his career and could damage the momentum he had built. When the upper brass appeared on the set, Steve knew their mission and took swift action. When they approached, he calmly pulled a branch from a tree and drew a line in the dirt. He announced, "Anyone who steps over that line gets the shit knocked out of him." The suits got back in their cars, drove off the set, and went back to Los Angeles, allowing the movie to finish.

Hell Is for Heroes wrapped in late summer of 1961, almost four months after principal photography. The film opened to enthusiastic reviews when it was released on June 26, 1962. Critics raved about McQueen's virtuosity, and it was clear that his self-promotion had worked. *Variety* wrote, "McQueen plays the central role with hard-bitten businesslike reserve and an almost animal intensity, permitting just the right degree of humanity to project through a war-weary-and-wise veneer." The *New York Times* agreed, as it assessed, "An arresting performance by Steve McQueen, a young actor with presence and a keen sense of timing, is the outstanding feature in *Hell Is for Heroes*."

Despite outstanding reviews, Paramount had zero faith in the picture and released it as a double feature with *Escape from Zahrain*, where it sank. Although *Hell Is for Heroes* hardly rivaled the box-office receipts of *The Longest Day*, the gritty little WWII film has developed a cult following. Audiences like its stark and authentic look, connecting with its anti-war message.

A year later McQueen, who was in Germany on the set of *The Great Escape*, received an enthusiastic telegram from an ardent admirer. It read:

> *Dear Steve,*
>   *I want to congratulate you for your performance in* Hell Is for Heroes. *It's the most perceptive and realistic performance of any soldier in any war film I have ever seen.*
>   *Regards,*
>   *Stanley Kubrick*

It was praise of the highest kind indeed, but Kubrick's endorsement wasn't enough to sustain McQueen. With a canceled television show and a string of unsuccessful films under his belt, McQueen needed a hit badly. "I'd made eight films up to then, and only one, *The Magnificent Seven*, was any good. I just wasn't making the right connections—so I tried doing a film in Europe."

The situation was indeed ironic: one of the most original American figures of the 20th century cinema had to fly across the pond in order to catch his big break. This time it would be worth it, though. He would costar with some of the biggest names in cinema, including classically trained actors. Of course, "costar" for McQueen simply meant more actors who threatened to take the limelight from him. If he was going to make the most of his chance and truly break through, he would have to once again demand the favor of the camera lens and fight those around him to command the screen by any means necessary.

16

GOD SAVE McQUEEN

ENGLAND HAS FERVENTLY CARRIED A TORCH for Steve McQueen ever since his 1980 death, and it is arguably the most rabid country when it comes to McQueen's current fan base.

It's an interesting enigma. England is a country that prides itself on its impeccable manners—and McQueen was every ounce the Ugly American when he flew to London to film *The War Lover* in September 1961.

On the surface, McQueen was the antithesis of an Anglophile. So why does Britain hold him so dear? There is no one simple answer. One possible explanation stems from the fact that many people often use national stereotypes as a way of playfully mocking one another. However, one British stereotype in particular rings true. The British are extremely polite to the point of being over the top. The classic anecdote runs along these lines. An English couple patronizes a restaurant. They order their food, and when it arrives, the lamb is virtually raw and there is a rat in the soup. The couple looks at each other and says, "This is frightfully terrible. How dare they serve us this dreadful meal, dear?" However, when the waiter comes past and routinely asks how their food is, they reply in unison, "Delightful, thank you kindly." As a nation, the British are polite and often far from outspoken. With this level of reservation ingrained in the national consciousness, perhaps they see the opposite in McQueen and cannot help but find it compelling. If he wanted something, he didn't ask—he simply took. If someone got in his way, he didn't say sorry—he said, "Screw you." He was someone who would speak out in situations where polite people never would. He would break the rules, while Brits would proudly adhere to them. They had to admire someone as free, liberated, and self-confident as McQueen.

Second, the British always root for the underdog. Steve epitomized the fighter, the one who had to struggle and battle for everything in life. He is someone they could identify with and support. McQueen's gung-ho spirit was immortalized in the fence-jumping scene on his motorbike in *The Great Escape*. This was a potent symbol of rebellion against the German machine that would forever seduce British fans and place McQueen high in their esteem. The quintessential Englishman, Lord Richard Attenborough, said, "His whole being is so alive and vibrant! You really did feel that he might burst out and walk down the aisle at any point and walk off the screen."

Then there are the cars and motorbikes. Great Britain is a nation of motoring enthusiasts, so it is no wonder they adore Steve, the man synonymous with cars. How could they not fall for Steve in his Jaguar, which was custom-painted in British racing green? McQueen and Stirling Moss, one of the most famous racers of all time, not only raced competitively—they also became firm friends. McQueen returned the favor to British motor sports with his undeniable dedication to the Triumph through the motorbikes he owned and the numerous photos of Steve proudly wearing a Triumph motoring T-shirt. In fact, fashion and clothing demonstrate another link between Steve and England. Steve's white Baracuta jacket was integral to his image as the sex symbol of the '60s. He was a British icon.

There is an image that perfectly sums up both the respect and the affection given to McQueen. The British poster for *The Great Escape* proves the affinity they felt and continue to have for McQueen. On the artwork for this poster, McQueen is shown sporting the RAF bomber jacket complete with insignia. In the film he is, of course, an American pilot, but the British redefined him as theirs. The nation adopted him as their son. Not bad for a man who was abandoned by his own father.

Steve may have arrived in London as the Ugly American, but he left an indelible mark on the people he worked with and the nation as a whole.

• • •

The War Lover is based on the Pulitzer Prize–winning novel by John Hersey, a work that McQueen said he devoured upon its initial release. "When I read this book about four years ago, I found the central character fascinating. I knew that when they made the film, I'd be gunning for the part," McQueen said. And he scored a direct hit. Warren Beatty was originally offered the starring role but turned it down to work with director John Frankenheimer and writer William Inge in *All Fall Down*.

In addition to McQueen, the cast featured Robert Wagner, Shirley Anne Field, and a young Michael Crawford. McQueen portrays Captain Buzz Rickson, a reckless B-17 pilot in England who finds himself pitted against his copilot, played by Wagner, and battling for the love of Shirley Anne Field.

Columbia Pictures, which financed the $2.5 million picture, rewarded McQueen handsomely by giving him top billing, a $75,000 payday, and treating him with the majesty reserved for visiting royalty. Unfortunately, he acted like someone of rather less noble blood. Even though the red carpet was rolled out for him, McQueen didn't walk down it with grace and good manners. At the end of his four-month stay, he had totaled a studio-owned automobile, raced in his off-hours and smashed up his face, taunted his female lead, poured beer on an extra's head, sprayed mud on an executive with his motorcycle, and was kicked out of a plush suite at one of London's swankiest hotels.

Perhaps McQueen's bad-boy behavior stemmed from the fact that he resented having to fly across the pond to make a picture. He told Hedda Hopper, "I'd like to see more films done here in Hollywood," McQueen said. "I blow my horn about it. They're going to have to come to some sort of compromise so we can shoot more films here. I like this industry and don't like to see it taken to Europe—but I'm forced to go there to work."

Steve bunked at the world-famous Savoy on The Strand in the heart of the West End theatre district. Manager Hilly Elkins had an adjoining suite with a living room connecting the two bedrooms. He said the disparate room temperatures were a metaphor of sorts. "Steve liked his room very hot, and I liked mine cold," Elkins said, laughing. "It was about 90 degrees in his bedroom and 50 degrees in mine. We had this neutral living room in which we met to work on the script."

When not working on the script, the McQueens behaved like typical tourists. Neile shopped for antiques (they bought a pair of 17th-century dueling pistols), while Steve was fitted for several suits on London's Savile Row, where he discovered the tailors lived up to their worldwide billing. ("When I got an English suit, I liked the way it looked and said, 'This is fine. Give me five more.'") Steve and Neile also went for relaxing weekend drives in the English countryside in his newly acquired Land Rover. McQueen relayed a story to entertainment columnist Sidney Skolsky about an encounter with an English farmer. "On Sundays, Neile and I have been driving out in the country around Surrey, Hampshire, Kent, and Essex. It's really beautiful," McQueen said. "I was out looking at some of the soil when a local farmer asked me what I was doing, and I explained to him that I was just feeling the soil, as it was certainly fertile and rich. When he found out I had been a farmer, we spent a good hour and a half discussing crops. I must say, it was kind of refreshing after talking films five days a week. And you know, you can grow anything in this soil because it's always very damp. The soil is constantly left with a very rich silt on top. [It will] grow everything but money, that is."

Typically, McQueen could not simply do his job, learn his lines, and play the scenes. He needed further extracurricular stimulation. England's robust racing scene excited McQueen, and he quickly resumed his relationship with the country's most beloved driver, Stirling Moss. "When Steve was making *The War Lover* in England, he rang me up," Moss remembered. "Our conversation was fairly simple—girls and cars. Yes, in that order. I also taught Steve some advanced skills in motor car racing. He was very keen to learn, interested to listen to advice and take it, which I consider very intelligent. Some of the film stars who raced back then weren't very fast, but Steve was quick. There wasn't much difference in some of our times—only a second or two. If Steve had buckled down and given up acting, he would have become a very competent driver."

Moss encouraged McQueen to buckle down long enough to compete in a Formula Cooper race on October 1, 1961. The event was sponsored by the British Racing & Sports Car Club at Brands Hatch, a famous motor racing circuit in Kent, just outside of London. McQueen raced the same Mini Cooper that Sir John Whitmore had used to win the British Saloon car championship, although McQueen didn't fare as well. He took a respectable third-place finish behind Vic Elford and Christabel Carlisle. He could accept his loss to Elford, but a loss to Carlisle, who was female, was hard to swallow. That particular defeat drove McQueen crazy, according to manager Hilly Elkins. "He hit the roof and wouldn't come down for days," Elkins said. "He couldn't believe that he had lost to, in his own words, 'a dame.' Yes, he was a little hot."

McQueen was also introduced to another key racing figure at Brands Hatch—John Cooper of the Cooper Car Company. McQueen took racing lessons from Cooper on weekends, blowing off a *Life* cover story in the process, and eventually purchased a brown 1961 Austin Mini Cooper S and a Formula Cooper Jr., for which he paid $6,800.

John Cooper Jr. was seven years old when McQueen spent the night in their home in Surbiton. "I had no idea who Steve McQueen was, nor did I care," he told the *Daily Mail* in November 2009. "So when he came to stay at our house in Surbiton—not somewhere you would automatically expect to find a Hollywood star—I was miffed, to say the least, to be turfed out of my bedroom. The spare room was deemed too small for Steve."

The Mini Cooper also provided a moment of comic relief, said Liz Charles-Williams, who was McQueen's personal secretary on *The War Lover*. "I had a 5:00 AM phone call one morning. It was Steve to say that he had been robbed of his brolly [umbrella] and his bowler [hat]. I asked him where he left his brolly and bowler, and he replied that he had left them in the car. I asked, 'So where's the car?' Steve replied, 'The car? Oh, that's been stolen, too.' I think of Steve every time I see a Mini Cooper."[1]

Columbia executives did not think McQueen's racing activities were amusing. When producer Arthur Hornblow caught wind, he warned McQueen that the $2.5 million production was on the line. Hornblow, though, was no match for McQueen's persuasive charms. McQueen ended up not only convincing Hornblow that racing was safe but also talking Hornblow into becoming a spectator who eventually cheered McQueen from the stands.

Steve basked in Moss' attention, and they spent time together on and off the racetrack. "I would follow Stirling around the course. He'd signal with one hand, and there I was hanging on for dear life," McQueen said. "Following Moss is like taking your first drink of sake!" The drinking story wasn't just an analogy. Moss was McQueen's pub partner, and the two enjoyed the delights of the big city. McQueen confessed to a reporter with *The Sunday Express* that he was still feeling the effects of the night before. "Man, I'm still a little drunk," said McQueen, who was shirtless and sipping on a glass of tea. "Went out last night with Stirling Moss and got stoned. When I woke up this afternoon, I took a great big swig of that pitcher of iced tea and got stoned all over again. Oh, this is a city. I dig London."

McQueen also introduced Moss to entertainer Sammy Davis Jr., who had just opened *An Evening with Sammy Davis Jr.* at the Prince of Wales Theatre in London. McQueen and Davis were friendly but highly competitive when it came to who was the Best in the West. The two often engaged in fast-draw competitions, and sometimes their duels got heated. "It bugs him when I occasionally outdraw him," McQueen said. "Stirling Moss and I went 'round to his dressing room the other night, and we started competing for fast draws. Man, we had Moss scared. He was in the corner."

Moss was also present when McQueen dashed down the hall of the Savoy when a curtain caught fire in his room. McQueen was playing the hospitable host, cooking eggs on a hot plate for his guests, when things went awry. "I quick-hopped into the hall to grab a fire extinguisher and ran smack into two dignified old English ladies," McQueen said. "I was barefoot, in my shorts, with no shirt on, and they let out a yell and reported to the manager that a naked man was running amok in the hallway." Neile told Hedda Hopper about that night at the

---

1 The 1961 Austin Mini is owned by Lee Brown and is housed at the Petersen Automotive Museum in Los Angeles.

Savoy. "Somebody hollered fire, and Steve lunged out of our room minus his Levi's to find an extinguisher." Movie star or not, complaints were lodged about the "McQueen Endowment," and he was asked by management, couched in British niceties, to vacate the premises. The studio brass asked production secretary Liz Charles-Williams to locate a new residence for its star. Williams said despite McQueen's hell-bent-for-leather persona, he was a gentleman. "During the course of a couple of afternoons reviewing houses, Steve asked me about my family as we rode along in a taxi," Williams recalled. "I told him during the World War II bombings of London, my father used to devise quizzes on the subject of the Old West to keep us entertained. His favorite film cowboys were William S. Hart and Gary Cooper, and after *The Magnificent Seven*, Steve immediately became number three!"

McQueen was so moved by the story that he consigned famed Mexican silversmith Edward H. Bohlin to make Williams' father a pair of spurs. They were inscribed, "For Bill from Steve McQueen." Williams said, "My father was simply thrilled. It was just one of the kind deeds Steve did for so many people during his short life."

Williams' initial selection didn't suit the McQueens well, according to Neile. "That winter was called the worst in 50 years. The first house we moved into was the house Elizabeth Taylor was renting when she got sick. I didn't know how she could stand it. It was [a] terribly dreary, very dank, and musty place. We packed up three days later and went to the Mayfair Hotel." Williams eventually found the McQueens a home at 80 Chester Square in Westminster, once owned by former British Prime Minister Lord John Russell. The rent on the four-story Victorian mansion was $300 a week, which was generously picked up by Columbia. It was from this address where McQueen corresponded with Hedda Hopper (whom he had affectionately nicknamed "Slim") on October 17, 1961, detailing his experiences in England:

> *Dear Slim,*
>
> *Neile and I are having a ball in London—to us it's sort of like babes in toyland.*
>
> *Gave your best to all the doormen at the Savoy and the Dorcester. The English people have a great deal of dignity which I have learned to respect, although it's taken me nine weeks and I've just got my first jar of peanut butter.*
>
> *I've done a bit of racing at Oulton Park, Brands Hatch, etc., and plan to race at Crystal Palace, Silverstone, Goodwood, and Aintree. They race like hell over here and they are very fast, but there's a great deal to learn about engines,*

suspensions, etc. By now I guess you know about my crash and race at Brands Hatch. Just bumped my head, got a scolding from my wife, patched the car up, and was able to finish third in the main event.

We have rented a beautiful four-story house at 80 Chester Square in one of the elite parts of London. It belongs to an English diplomat, and the servants make me nervous as hell. I find myself wanting to get up as soon as they come into the room!

Let me hear from you, Slim.

Love,

Steve McQueen

After a few weeks, Williams became a permanent part of McQueen's employ when she was fired by the studio after someone signed her name to a telegram requesting Air Force uniforms. "I was fired despite denying any knowledge of the telegram. I ended up in tears at the foot of the staircase in Steve's home crying about how cruel it all was and that I would miss working on his film." The next morning, a messenger delivered a red rose with a note from McQueen written in red ink. "I am writing this in my blood so that you'll know that I mean it. As a man once said, 'It's the little things that count.'" Williams was hired as McQueen's personal assistant for the rest of filming. She also witnessed a different side of Steve that he would show to only a select few whom he trusted, proving he was not always the ruthless and power-hungry star. She said McQueen was a fiercely loyal boss. "During filming, we were on location at a muddy airfield, and when he had a free moment, Steve would often get out one of his scramble bikes and do wheelies. One day Steve said, 'This one's for you, Liz,' as he sprayed mud on the crew member who had taken 'my' telegram to the head of Columbia. Steve didn't forget that."

He brought the same piss-and-vinegar intensity to his role. "I have to stay in character," McQueen said. "I always try to immerse myself in the role I'm playing, and Buzz Rickson is no shrinking violet."

"Shrinking" was the operative word where it concerned costar Robert Wagner, who wrote in his memoir, *Piece of my Heart*, that McQueen was not an easy man to be around. "I found Steve very self-conscious and very competitive, even about small things," Wagner recounted. "For instance, Steve was about 5'9", smaller than me, so he made sure never to have his wardrobe next to mine where anybody could see it. It's the sort of thing that strikes me as a wasted effort—why not use that emotional energy for something constructive? Steve was such a complicated man—always looking for conflict and never really at peace."

Wagner was nursing a broken heart over his impending divorce with Natalie Wood, who threw him over for Warren Beatty. When McQueen wasn't busy playing the superstar, he lent a much-needed shoulder of support when he realized that Wagner was a straight shooter who wasn't going to engage in reindeer games on the set.

Costar and female lead Shirley Anne Field, a British model turned actress, was one of McQueen's few female counterparts who held her own with the volatile star. She told journalist Mark Mawston in 2009 that she found McQueen's behavior on *The War Lover* reprehensible. "Steve used to get in a fury if Robert [Wagner] and I were on a magazine cover, which there were many of. He was very aggressive, Steve. An example of that was when I was doing a love scene with RJ [Wagner] and there was a commotion, and I looked up to see Steve pouring beer over an extra's head out of shot. I said, 'Steve, what are you doing?' That's why Mr. Leacock liked me, because I wasn't afraid of Steve. I couldn't fight him, but I could stand up to him. After 12 years[2] in TV, he wanted to be a big movie star. That trick of stealing a scene is called 'pulling focus.' Robert was very good with Steve McQueen, very calm and patient, whereas I was furious."

The two stars clashed, and it eventually became physical. Field said in one of the love scenes, they were supposed to end up on a sofa. She said that McQueen, however, got her there a little faster than she had anticipated. "Steve threw me so hard that I went up and over the sofa and out of the shot altogether. It took ten takes! I still have the scar on my lip," Field said.

Field, who was bleeding profusely, retreated into the arms of the picture's makeup man. While he was patching her up, he whispered in his Cockney accent, "Bite his bleedin' lip." Field says she took his advice. "So the scene started and I did just that, and it went along 'Bang!' and it was over. You see, I had to fight for attention in my early days when I was surrounded by 400 others. He just looked at me, knowing what I'd done, and I said, 'It takes one to know one.'"

For his part, McQueen had felt that Field was "pulling focus" as well. He bitterly complained to director Philip Leacock that the stage-trained actress was overplaying his understated style of acting. "She's cutting my balls off," McQueen said.

Mike Frankovich Jr., the son of Columbia Pictures president Mike Frankovich, was in charge of publicity on the set of *The War Lover*. He said McQueen didn't play nice and unfortunately lived up to the stereotype of a brash Yankee. "He was bullying Shirley Anne and playing a little bit of the Ugly American. She developed an intense dislike of Steve, and quite frankly, that was fostered by McQueen. He

---

2   Field was off by nine years. McQueen was on *Wanted: Dead or Alive* for three seasons.

often goaded her, 'We Americans, we're real movie actors. Here, you don't know how to act in movies,'" Frankovich said. "He could turn his character on and off. At certain moments, he could become the little boy with that side grin of his—then, boom, he's back in the driver's seat again as an actor, totally immersed in what he's doing. That suit of clothing that he could put on once the cameras were rolling was amazing."

A technician on the picture, who requested anonymity when speaking to *Photoplay* reporter Ken Johns, said of McQueen, "He's a quiet chap. Never mixes well. He likes to be alone. He doesn't eat in the studio restaurant; instead, he prefers to eat alone in his dressing room. But he's a good worker. He knows what he's doing."

There was a simple reason why McQueen didn't socialize much—he felt he had nothing in common with anyone on the set. "My trouble is I say what I think too often," McQueen said. "I never mix with actors much. I'm not interested in actors' talk, and they're not interested in racing cars, so what the hell can we talk about?"

McQueen did enjoy working with director Philip Leacock, a veteran of British cinema (*13 West Street*). "I have great respect for Phil Leacock," McQueen told a reporter. "He is a very kind and sensitive man, has great patience with artists, and has a great feeling for scripts and the story as a whole, and [he] knows what he wants."

The War Lover was shot throughout England and included several locations: RAF Bovingdon in Hertfordshire, RAF Manston in Kent, and Cambridgeshire and Shepperton Studios in Surrey. It was at the Bovingdon Air Strip where three B-17s landed, resurrected from an Arizona junkyard, which gave McQueen a moment for pause. "The British who were there, crew, actors, technicians, etc., who remember back to World War II, seem to reflect the era of destruction that is not yet forgotten in the English people," McQueen recalled.

The movie was emotionally and physically stressful for McQueen, who perhaps got too personally involved with his role. "This character is a kind of schizophrenic," McQueen said. "He revels in war and destruction. He lives for killing. I've got too involved with him. By the time I get home at night, after a day's work, I'm physically and mentally exhausted." It was very clear in a December 5, 1961, letter to Hedda Hopper that McQueen was yearning for his homeland:

> *Dear Hedda,*
> *Just a note to let you know I am still alive. Neile is fine and the kids are growing like weeds.*

*We are working very hard on the film and if the rushes are any indication
of us having a good movie, the census of opinion from the Cutters, Assistant
Directors, and our Producer, it looks as though we might have something kind
of interesting.*

*England's fun, Hedda, but I miss California very much. I am an American,
and I never realized how deep-rooted this was until I was a foreigner in someone
else's land. We have a great country there, and you don't realize how great it
really is until you are away from it for a while. This might sound a little hokey,
but it is exactly the way I feel.*

*It pretty well rains all the time now, and yesterday, last night, I got caught
for three hours in a fog coming back from Shepperton Studios, the traffic piled
up for three miles and I was getting hungry, but having my Land Rover I put it
in four-wheel drive and cut across a farmer's ploughed-up field and made it on to
the next highway. I told Neile that Land Rover would come in handy one time.*

*Sometimes when I get home from work if I have got a few hours to spare,
Neile and I go down to the market along the Thames and have fish and chips. In
the evening, if it's not raining, it's kind of pretty sitting there watching ships going
down the Thames. I should be back home about the middle of January, and I'm
going to make a beeline for Palm Springs and do nothing as hard as I can.*

If you get time, Slim, drop me a line, as we are yearning for news of home.
Love,
                    Steve

That Christmas, the McQueens hosted a special party for American actors
and actresses unable to go home. It was a star-studded affair, with Robert Wagner
teaching party-goers the Watusi; John Dankworth and Cleo Laine providing the
music; famous race car drivers, including world champion Graham Hill; and
Lionel and Joyce Bart, who danced for everyone.

Near the end of filming, McQueen's racing intersected with the picture when
he had a near-fatal accident at Brands Hatch, which resulted in a badly cut and
restitched lip. Leacock filmed around the injury, allowing McQueen to wear his
pilot helmet and oxygen mask to hide the injury.

When the picture wrapped, McQueen discovered that film executives
in England did not turn a blind eye when it came to pinching their property.
McQueen was still part-hustler at heart. He already had more money than he
could have hoped for, but he never knew if one day it would all just disappear. So
he took whatever he could whenever he had the chance. McQueen was billed for
a list of missing items, but the notoriously tight-fisted star balked in a four-page
correspondence to 13 different parties, including the William Morris Agency;

Mitchell, Silberberg & Knupp (McQueen's attorneys); the film's unit accountant; and U.S. Air Force security police:

> *With the completion of* The War Lover, *it has been called to my attention that there are several items that have been checked out to me, and so that I will not be charged for them, I should like to clarify the position regarding these said items:*
>
> *One pair of flight boots, one light blue crew-neck sweater, and one dark blue crew-neck sweater, which I am sorry to say I know nothing about. There was also the case of the two teapots that where [sic] purchased for me so that I should be able to have tea early in the morning. Unfortunately, one teapot was stolen from my dressing room before it had even been taken out of the box, and this I reported immediately [when] I discovered there had been foul play. The other teapot was confiscated by one of the Assistant Directors in making tea for the crew in the morning before they started production. This was quite alright by me, [but] as for the other teapot, again, I know absolutely nothing about it other than that it was quietly removed from my dressing room on or about December 12th, along with [the] miscellaneous cups, saucers, and spoons.…*

The situation was eventually remedied by waiving the cost of the boots and sweaters, but McQueen was docked $7.50 for the missing teapots. Despite the fact that his attorney fees must have cost a small fortune, McQueen saw to it that he won the battle of one-upmanship.

The trip back to the States was a fitting ending for the McQueen family. Their first plane had a leak in the jet fuel system and was forced back to the terminal to land; the second plane had flown through a fallout cloud caused by Russian nuclear tests and had to be decontaminated. The third plane finally brought them home to Los Angeles, where Steve kissed the ground and vowed he would never do another movie overseas.

McQueen also kissed good-bye his working relationship with Hilly Elkins over a petty misunderstanding. Elkins visited Paris for a weekend while retaining a room at the Savoy at Steve's expense. McQueen, who was thrifty with a dollar, grew more mistrustful of others as his star began to rise. His paranoia forced him to always push, testing others to see how far their loyalty stretched or how long it would take before they were ready to throw in the towel. "There was always a testing in that relationship," Elkins admitted. "How big am I really? How much shit can I get away with? He wanted to get my opinion on a project before his got his opinion out on the table, threatening in a benign way to do something that was off the wall. When push came to shove, he backed down. We were very close. We spent a lot of time together and I enjoyed it.

"Steve was very quixotic and had very wide mood swings. [We were] capable of having enormous fun. We were two juveniles fucking with the system and having it work. We would spend a week on location and mostly had laughs until someone fucked up."

Babysitting McQueen and other stars of his mercurial temperament was not satisfying to Elkins, who felt unfulfilled in the management area. Elkins turned to Broadway producing and struck gold immediately with the Garson Kanin play *Come on Strong*. Productions of *Golden Boy*, *The Rothchilds*, *A Doll's House*, and *Oh Calcutta!*, the longest-running revue in Broadway history, followed. Elkins was one of the most successful producers of all time, and he has remained a key player in Hollywood for more than five decades. He said McQueen was a mercurial man whose paranoia kept him from fully enjoying his life. "Steve had a very interesting, self-involved and eccentric, loveable quality about him," Elkins said. "He knew he was a good actor, and he was able to communicate that on the screen. When people ask me who of today's actors I would compare him to, the answer is unfortunately no one."

On January 2, 1962, McQueen renewed his deal with the William Morris Agency. Agent Stan Kamen developed a system that fielded calls and read scripts, farming out the most promising projects to wife Neile, who played a vital role in some of her husband's most famous films.

• • •

The War Lover was released in October 1962 and was met with mixed reaction. In Britain, where it premiered in June 1963, it was a smash and propelled McQueen to movie stardom in that country. "McQueen was a hero to almost all Englishmen of that era for a very personal reason," observed Liz Charles-Williams. "Most Englishmen are very reserved and quiet, but Steve did things in public that they secretly wished they could do in private."

Indeed, McQueen has left a firm legacy in Britain. He is deeply ingrained in the public consciousness. Car enthusiasts still talk of the actor turned racer—or more affectionately, the racer turned actor. Every time a new star emerges today, the British media uniformly refer to them as potentially the "new Steve McQueen." Even though invariably none of these new actors lives up to McQueen's hype, it underscores one thing—McQueen is still the defining man's man, the yardstick of a sex symbol, the ultimate actor that still resonates with modern views. McQueen still resonates even in everyday elements. Baracuta jackets are still sold in Britain, only now they have a paper tag proudly bearing his image and stating they were the jacket of choice of the Hollywood star. Often British magazines will feature

McQueen's face on the cover, nearly three decades after his death, always with the word "cool" included somewhere. The reason? McQueen still sells in England. He defines determination and greatness, and his image will always move copies. The national holidays also succumb to McQueen mania. *The Great Escape* is a national favorite and airs on television every Christmas in England; it has become as quintessentially British at Christmas as turkey and sprouts. McQueen's popularity is as high as ever there.

McQueen gave the British public indelible images as Buzz Rickson, courageously piloting his Flying Fortress in an attempt to avert an inevitable crash, and as Virgil Hilts, attempting to jump the fence to freedom. In both of these on-screen moments, his character crashes. But at least he fought and tried to win against the odds, and he gave it everything he had. The British were left with these stark scenes of valor and courage, and they would always hold McQueen close to their hearts.

In the United States, it was a different story. *The War Lover* didn't do quite so well, with one critic calling it, "a curious mixture of authentic and phony." *The Washington Post* felt the picture "goes to remarkable trouble to avoid what it is talking about."

Even though *The War Lover* was a flawed picture, McQueen was intense and commanding in his performance as an arrogant, cruel, war-mongering misfit who was incapable of love. His portrayal of Buzz Rickson is one of the best of his early career, and the film made him an international movie star in every other country but his own.

McQueen knew he needed that one defining picture. It was to arrive soon, and he would do everything he could to make it as successful for him as possible. He would dominate the movie, shamelessly steal scenes from his costars, mesmerize the camera, and make the film his own. He was on the precipice of global superstardom. He was desperately close to entering the Hollywood elite, but before he could break into that echelon, he would first have to perform a high-octane breakout. His career-defining moment would come from a barbed-wire fence, a motorbike, a steely look of determination, and the most breathtaking leap of faith ever seen on film.

17

HE'S ALIVE!

Safely back on U.S. soil, McQueen wasted no time switching gears from movies to motorcycles, and he dove headfirst back into his racing activities. McQueen was smitten with anything motorized or that had wheels, and he had an extreme fondness for motorcycles. In 1984 when his estate was auctioned off, aficionados from the biking world flocked to the event in Las Vegas along with McQueen fans from all walks of life. These particular fans were after one thing—or rather one of 100 things—to try and get one of the bikes McQueen once owned. His collection was truly astounding, featuring more than 100 motorcycles. He had everything from the vintage to the modern day and every marquee, including Husqvarna, Kawasaki, Harley-Davidson, Triumph, Ace, and Norton. Plus McQueen had a special fondness for Indian bikes. McQueen did not just enjoy these motorcycles as a passing hobby—he lived and breathed them, often making bikes from scratch using parts from his collection.

The importance of motorcycles is fundamental not only to McQueen's image and personality but also to the legacy he left behind. The motorcycle was instrumental in establishing him as a star; his *Life* and *Sports Illustrated* magazine covers are among the most famous cover photos of all time and helped cement his status. Motorcycles also provided the foundation for his lifelong friendship with Bud Ekins, whose Triumph dealership and garage was the setting for many good times for McQueen. However, along with image and friendship, these vehicles gave McQueen something else—a release. Everything about them allowed him to forget his troubles and worries. The intricacies of their construction, understanding how each one operated, and the hard work of maintaining them allowed him some much-needed escapism. Not only did McQueen enjoy the discipline of being an enthusiast—he also felt the need for speed. Taking off at high speeds with no warning to family and friends provided a potent cathartic release when he needed to find his own space.

McQueen regularly raced competitively. Why would a movie star let himself get out of his depth and risk injury? The answer was that concern about injury and keeping studio executives happy were not high on his agenda, and he was an extremely competitive person with something to prove. Immersing himself in the racing world meant he was just another guy and no longer a Hollywood hotshot. It was his great equalizer, forcing him to prove himself and earn respect. The final scene of *On Any Sunday* clearly shows just how much pleasure he took from riding. The smile on his face as he races up and down the beach shows a genuine sense of childlike glee coupled with an inner solace.

McQueen entered the Four Aces Moose Run, a cross-country motorcycle race, in early March 1962. The race covered 150 miles of California desert trail. McQueen placed 45th overall (out of a field of 193) and third in the Novice division despite a rocky start. "Had a bit of a problem early in the race," McQueen said. "Some of the riders resented the fact that I was an actor. They didn't trust my motives for being there, so they blocked me at the start. Still, I did okay."

Two weeks later, he traded his Triumph 650 cc for a 1000 cc Austin-Healy Sprite for his first taste of international competition in the Sebring 12-Hour Race on March 23, 1962. McQueen ran an individual race and later teamed up with Stirling Moss, Innes Ireland, and Pedro Rodriguez, who represented the British Motor Corporation. McQueen's first race, a three-hour solo grind (which covered 239 miles) was his longest uninterrupted stint behind the wheel. Both his hands were blistered afterward. He was also the only one of 10 Sprite drivers who didn't make a pit stop for gas in the three-hour test. A mechanic for BMC asked McQueen as he climbed out of the heated auto how he kept such close track of his fuel.

"I never looked at the gas gauge," McQueen answered honestly. After McQueen finished a pleasantly surprising ninth place in a field of more than two dozen, John Cooper immediately asked McQueen to become an official member of the BMC team. Once again, McQueen was at another crossroads that could change the course of his life forever. McQueen said the decision was agonizing. "They gave me a weekend to make up my mind," he said. "I spent two full days in a sweat, trying to decide whether I wanted to go into pro racing, earning my money on the track, or whether I wanted to continue being an actor. It was a very tough decision for me to reach, because I didn't know if I was an actor who raced or a racer who acted. But I had Neile and our two children to consider, and that made a difference. I turned down the BMC offer. But I came very close to chucking my film career. I hadn't done anything really important or outstanding on the screen, and I was tired of waiting for the 'big picture,' the one that hopefully would break me through." But fate intervened when John Sturges called with an action vehicle called *The Great Escape*. This one would be different.

Plenty of scripts had been filtered to McQueen, who had contemplated several offers at the time, including *The Victors* with Warren Beatty (which would have placed Hollywood's greatest lotharios together on the screen) costarring Ava Gardner and Simone Signoret; a TV version of *Beauty and the Beast* featuring Sophia Loren with Aaron Spelling assigned to write the script; *The Kimono*, an English story by H.B. Bates; and *Smile for a Woman*, an artist who is asked to make a copy of the Mona Lisa, with *Honeymoon Machine* costar Brigid Bazlen and Michael Gordon as director.

But McQueen had a loyal streak in him, especially when it came to Sturges, who had generously given him some great close-ups and shots in both *Never So Few* and *The Magnificent Seven*. He had trusted Sturges in the past, and it had paid off. "He started me in this business, and I owe him everything," McQueen said. "If he wants me, I'm his."

The progression from working actor to recognizable face to star took giant leaps with the films he made with Sturges. *Never So Few* introduced him to the big leagues. *The Magnificent Seven* gave him an opportunity to set himself apart in a first-tier cast and gave him some fantastic, star-making shots. However, *The Great Escape* would be the movie that finally turned Steve McQueen into an international movie star. Again he would be immersed in an all-star cast of seasoned actors, but he would rise head and shoulders above them all and emerge as the true star of the film. Surprisingly, it was a film he entered into with much trepidation.

The Great Escape is a World War II epic adapted from Paul Brickhill's 1950 novel, itself based on a true story recounting the largest Allied prison break of the war, which took place on March 24, 1944. Given that McQueen was born on March 24 and was 14 when the real escape took place, it almost seems that he was cosmically fated to star in this picture. Brickhill had received several generous film offers from studios but had the nagging suspicion his book would be decimated into a fictional account and given the Hollywood treatment. He agreed to meet with Sturges shortly after the book was published in 1950 and was struck by the director's sincerity. Sturges assured Brickhill that under no certain terms would the story be changed. The two men shook hands and struck a deal, but it took almost a dozen years to see it come to fruition. Today it is hard to imagine the film as anything but a major blockbuster, but as a claustrophobic ensemble piece with no female characters or battle scenes, a threadbare script, and an epic concept, Sturges didn't find many takers. *The Magnificent Seven's* financial bonanza meant Sturges could finally write his own ticket, and United Artists, which practically stole Sturges away from MGM, agreed to underwrite the project. "I waited until I had enough prestige as a director," Sturges said in 1991. "If you make successful movies, big hits, and you come up with something they may not like, they may hate it, but if you want to do it, they start to think, 'If we don't let him do what he wants, he'll go to another studio that will let him and we'll lose him.' That was the case with *The Great Escape*."

United Artists gave the project the green light and a very tight budget of $4 million. With the picture being shot entirely on location and with an unfinished script, Sturges was walking the tightrope.

Aside from working again with Sturges, the only bait in the 64-page first script for McQueen was a thrilling motorcycle chase in the finale. That prompted McQueen to pay a visit to Bud Ekins at his Sherman Oaks shop. Ekins remembered, "I had known [McQueen] about two years and one day in 1962 he says, 'Gonna make a movie in Germany. Gonna have a motorcycle in it. Called *The Great Escape*. I steal a motorcycle, and we have a big chase sequence. Wanna come to Germany and double me?' I thought, 'Bullshit. Never happen.'"

A week later, Ekins received a phone call from the actor. "Gotta suit? Well, put it on. I want you to come down and meet the director. I'll pick you up." Ekins laughed at the memory of McQueen picking him up in his Jaguar wearing blue jeans and a T-shirt. Sturges was wearing the same attire. "He'd do weird things like that, just to put me on. Nothing harmful—he'd just twist things around. I don't know why. Anyway, I get there and Sturges opens the door and Steve says, 'This is Bud.' He looks at Steve and me and nods his head. Hell, in a few weeks, I was in Germany."

For his part, McQueen was paid a hefty $100,000 to secure his name to the picture while the rest of the cast was assembled. Eventually, the cast was rounded out by James Garner, Charles Bronson, James Coburn, James Donald, Richard Attenborough, David McCallum, and Donald Pleasance.

McQueen departed from California on May 30, 1962, and he, Neile, Terry, and Chad stayed in a rented chalet in Deining, Bavaria, about a 45-minute drive from the studio. The drive allowed McQueen to decompress and think about his role, but he used the Autobahn as his own personal racetrack. Sometimes he'd cut through private farmland with no paved roads. Often he would arrive at the set with German officers in hot pursuit. One day police set up a speed trap near the studio, and several members of the crew and cast were ticketed. The chief of police told McQueen after he was nabbed, "Herr McQueen, we have caught several of your comrades today, but you have won the prize for the highest speeding." McQueen was arrested and briefly jailed.

According to almost everyone who was around McQueen, he was unusually anxious. Ekins said the British actors—Richard Attenborough, James Donald, and Donald Pleasance—made McQueen uneasy. "I can tell you that some of those heavy-duty English actors on *The Great Escape* really scared the shit out of Steve," Ekins said. "All those English guys were stage people, and they had a different presence than McQueen." Ironically, a few months before, McQueen had been goading Shirley Anne Field in *The War Lover* that the American actors held the upper hand when it came to cinematic supremacy. His fear was that he would be exposed as inferior and upstaged by these professionals, although this fear was unfounded because he was a talented actor. Yet it still affected him enormously. To realize his ambitions, he could not afford to let himself be relegated to just another cast member. He had stiff competition from these actors and would have to find a way to outdo them in order to succeed.

Lord Richard Attenborough, who later befriended McQueen, said it was an ironic situation. "The Americans expected the British actors to be a bit snobbish, because the British actors back then were held in such high regard. It's funny because ever since [Marlon] Brando came on the scene, the Americans were way ahead of the British cinema. The British cinema was a bit talky, whereas the American films relied primarily on expressions and emotions. It was just more realistic. Little did the Americans realize that we were just as much in awe of them as they were of us."

The two camps—the Yanks and the Brits—were embroiled in an intense macho rivalry, and they naturally split into separate groups during lunch and shooting breaks. McQueen didn't exactly foster international relations or show much ambassadorship by skidding around the Brits on his bike.

Attenborough said national honor was at stake when McQueen rolled up next to him on his Triumph, gunning the throttle. "Wanna ride?" McQueen asked. Attenborough paused, and for good reason. He had been in a motorcycle accident 30 years earlier, which resulted in a trip to the hospital. Putting on his best actor's face, though, Attenborough smiled and said, "You bet." His affirmation was an acceptance of the metaphorical olive branch, but the motorcycle ride was something Attenborough never forgot.

"The next 15 minutes were the most terrifying I can remember as I clung on for dear life, but they cemented a deep friendship," Attenborough recalled, who has remained protective of McQueen's memory for three decades. "I've never been more delighted and thrilled to get off any vehicle of any kind!" This moment proved to be a turning point, and Attenborough affirms that McQueen "was a perfectionist in every sense of the word. All those rumors about him being hard to get along with are scandalously untrue. I can remember rehearsing with him for weeks, because we had a lot of scenes together. Not one incident of ugly behavior sticks out in my mind. I admired his integrity."

W.R. Burnett, the on-location screenwriter, certainly did not hold the same sentiment. He bore the brunt of McQueen's anger when the actor felt his role had not been fully developed. "McQueen was an impossible bastard. A third of the way through the picture, he took charge," Burnett said. "I had to rewrite scenes and rearrange them. Oh, he drove you crazy."

"Where's my *thing*?" McQueen asked Robert Relyea, Sturges' assistant director. "I don't have a *thing*." Relyea said everybody had a thing—a gimmick, a film characteristic that made them stand out. Charles Bronson's character was the Tunnel King, and his *thing* was battling claustrophobia. James Garner was the Scrounger, and his *thing* was using his charisma to secure items the operation needed from the Germans. James Coburn's thing was his mysterious suitcase, which served no useful purpose but at least gave him a film identity. Richard Attenborough was Big X, and he was the brains of the operation. Relyea said McQueen keenly recognized that his part was minor and underdeveloped. That's no surprise given that his character, Captain Virgil Hilts, was based on an amalgamation of several real-life people. Despite the fact that most of the people were real life heroes, McQueen still had no *thing*.

McQueen's personality was such that he would never allow himself to be disadvantaged if he could help it. He would demand parity with his costars as a bare minimum and was seldom satisfied until he had preferential status. To McQueen's credit, he demanded this and got it. "John Sturges was good to me and helped me tremendously in my career, but bless his heart, whenever he got a script, he dismantled it and took it apart," Relyea said in 2010. "He got away with it a number of times, and sometimes he didn't. When you mix that with an insecure actor, which Steve was, it invited trouble. Steve correctly figured out, 'What am I? What's my thing? I'm not anything.'"

McQueen wasn't the only actor who had problems with the script. Actor Richard Harris bailed on the picture 10 days prior to shooting, partly because *This Sporting Life* was behind schedule but also because he was displeased with the diminished role of Big X after script changes had been made. Richard Attenborough, a former Royal Air Force pilot, was cast on short notice and proved to be one of the movie's bright spots. Sturges eventually employed six writers and went through 11 drafts, and the script was still a work in progress at the time of principal photography. "I'm not proposing that's a good way to make a picture, but it was the right way to make this one," Sturges later said.

Adding to McQueen's consternation was the fact that close friend Stirling Moss had been lying in a hospital bed since April 23, 1962. That's when his Lotus Climax crashed at 110 mph in the Glover Trophy race in Goodwood. The accident left Moss in a coma for a month, partially paralyzed, and prematurely ended his racing career after 66 Grand Prix victories. McQueen was despondent and tense about Moss' condition for the first month of filming. He finally received word from Moss in a June 28, 1962, letter:

> My dear Steve,
>
> Thanks very much for your letter, which was most welcome.
>
> Unfortunately I am not sure that Neile will still love me because I am a bit broken up. I also happen to have a little bit of a scar down the left hand side of my face, which I am glad to be able to report does not really show that much. However, please tell her that I still love her.
>
> The new film sounds as though it could be good. It has a jolly good name, and if it has the same director as The Magnificent Seven and if you behave yourself, he may not make a mess of it!
>
> Thanks very much for your kind offer of a room. This is most appreciated but unfortunately I shouldn't think I shall be able to take you up as much as I would like to, the reason being that I hope to get off to Nassau soon and back to racing in the not too distant future. If I don't get back to racing, I guess I'll be selling matches on the street corner!
>
> In closing, I send both of you my very best wishes, and one of you my love.
>
> Yours sincerely,
>
> Stirling Moss

Although Moss' letter was cause for celebration, McQueen still acted as if he had a dark cloud hanging over him. This was the most important picture of his career, and his top-billed role was ambiguous and not well-defined. In a move to placate the actors, Sturges showed them the rushes of the first six weeks of shooting in mid-July. The rushes fueled McQueen's paranoia that he was not the star of the picture. After a thrilling opening sequence, his character virtually disappears from the film for 30 minutes. There was good reason for it. Heavy rains (and in some instances sleet and snow) had forced the schedule to shoot interiors from the middle portion of the picture first. Adding insult to injury was that McQueen watched the charismatic Garner, in a white turtleneck and blue aviator uniform, oozing charm and looking every bit the movie star. McQueen felt especially competitive with Garner because they were both products of television, jockeying to make the transformation to the silver screen. McQueen had grave misgivings that he would be overshadowed. Sturges admitted the half-hour gap was a problem but promised to fix the situation. After all, he made McQueen.

"Nothing doing," McQueen told Sturges. He was ready to up the stakes and make demands until he got his way. Accordingly, he walked off the picture for six weeks.

Garner recalled the incident. "Steve went out of there so angry that he was going to leave the picture. He wanted to reshoot everything. And we were hurting for money and time. So a couple of days later, John Sturges came to me and said, 'Jim, you're the star of the picture and Steve is out.'

"I took Steve and the other costar, Jim Coburn, to my house in Munich and we went through the script, discussing several scenes, and I said, 'What's your problem, Steve?'

"'Well, I don't like this. I don't like that.'

"I said, 'This is silly. You don't like anything.' We finally figured out that Steve wanted to be the hero but didn't want to do anything physically heroic. He didn't like the part where the little Irishman climbed the wall and was shot and he then had to pull him down.

"So they changed the script to make him the hero by the way he had escaped and was captured, but when he came back, he had information about the area. Oh boy, what a hero, and he didn't have to do much at all!"

This may appear to be a contradiction—he wanted to be a hero but not perform obvious acts of valor. However, as a person riddled with his own contradictions, this move was actually McQueen's masterstroke. He knew that the essence of the character was his status as the antihero who cares only about himself; he has a keen sense of detachment and is someone who strives only for self-preservation. The expansion of character that he demanded allowed him to become an accidental hero, initially serving himself but achieving a great feat in both defying the Germans and helping the escape effort. He therefore receives all the accolades but no stigma from being a self-righteous two-dimensional hero.

After six weeks of shooting around McQueen, Sturges was fed up. He called agent Stan Kamen to tell him "his boy was off the picture." Almost 24 hours later, Kamen flew to Munich to iron out the situation with McQueen, who wore a tie when he went to meet with Sturges. Such formalities must have been an attempt to demonstrate and underscore his seriousness. "Look, Steve, when I made *The Magnificent Seven*, you did what I told you to do and it came out fine," Sturges said. "But you believed in the scenes, and you believed that when I staged them, they were good. Now all of a sudden you don't believe me. And if you don't believe the scenes, then you're going to be lousy. I don't want you to be lousy. And frankly, Steve, I'm getting tired of arguing with you. If you don't like this part, to hell with it. We'll pay you off, and I'll shift to Jim Garner."

McQueen's eyes grew wide and he knew Sturges meant business—he said exactly what McQueen had feared, and the visceral attack stung. But McQueen wasn't going to sabotage this opportunity only to see James Garner come out as the beneficiary.

McQueen's bluff had been called. His temper tantrums and mind games had hit a brick wall. Sturges was one of the few people who knew that he had to stand up to McQueen. McQueen must have known at this moment that he was risking it all. On one level, he was losing the respect and approval of a pseudo-father fig-ure in Sturges, who had helped his career. And all McQueen was doing in return was making his life hard. McQueen had definite trust issues, always assuming people were conspiring against him, so he must have struggled to believe the director when he said he had his best interests at heart. Second, McQueen was ultracompetitive, and Garner was about to be handed the picture. McQueen had developed an enormous chip on his shoulder over the years of being passed over for actors such as James Dean and Paul Newman. Now Garner was going to do the same. There was no way his competitive streak would allow this.

McQueen had agreed to do the film as his last big chance to break into the Hollywood elite. In those days, you either broke in after a few years, or you floundered in the B-list. His time was running out, and he could not afford to be attached to a troubled picture as the fired star. After flying halfway around the world in a bid to make a film to put him at the top, he could end up virtu-ally blacklisted as difficult to work with. This was not some small-stakes poker game from back in Slater—this was life-changing stuff. It was time to make a compromise, put his inflated ego to one side and do the unthinkable. He had to trust someone.

Ten minutes later, McQueen and Kamen emerged from the other room, and Kamen spoke up first. "Steve wants to stay in the picture. He'll do exactly as you say." It was one of the few times McQueen ever backed down in his career. But it would prove to be one of the best moves he ever made.

Although they were over the worst, the roller-coaster ride was far from over. Two days later, McQueen blew his stack when he discovered a revised script did nothing to beef up his part. Sturges made a preemptive strike and called Kamen. Sturges instinctively knew that McQueen would understand only absolutes, and empty gestures would not work. He told Kamen, don't bother coming back to Munich—his boy was out.

It was only through the intervention of United Artists, who felt McQueen's participation was vital to the picture, that kept McQueen in. It sprang for the extra money to hire another writer, Ivan Moffat, to deal with McQueen's demands. Moffat, Oscar-nominated for *Giant*, was dispatched from England and immediately reported to the set. Moffat was part of director George Stevens' documentary film unit covering the Allies in Europe, and his temperament was perfectly suited for McQueen's volatile nature. This was an important development for McQueen because Moffat was responsible for several of McQueen's best moments in the picture: flipping the baseball up against the wall to pass the time in the cooler; getting conned by English officers to become an advance scout for the operation; rolling a baseball out to test a blind spot between the guard towers; and the career-defining motorcycle sequences at the end of the picture.[1] "Steve loved the cooler set because that was exactly the guy he wanted to be—the loser who wins. And it worked," Robert Relyea said. "The movie even ended with McQueen in the cell, bouncing that ball against the wall and catching it with his glove. The audience figured out even though McQueen's character had sacrificed himself, he would never give up."

McQueen finally had his thing.

Steve wrote to Hedda Hopper on August 8, 1962, just days after he returned to the set. He kept mum about his six-week walkout:

> *Dear Hedda,*
>
> *Just came back from location for a few days. Then back to the Alps and more locations with the motorcycle.*
>
> *Neile and I are off to Paris. I promised Neile a new wardrobe for her anniversary, so we will be sitting at all those fashion shows. I promised Neile I would wear a tie, so all is well.*
>
> *I am going to export some German driving gloves for all the sports-car minded people in the U.S. under the Steve McQueen banner. So it looks like I am going [into] the glove business.*
>
> *Terry, my daughter, speaks German, and I must say it is a little embarrassing when she has to interpret for me. She has picked it up playing with the children in the village, and I have asked her please not to talk German at the dinner table, as I don't know what she is saying.*

---

1   McQueen's demands to spruce up his role added 18 minutes to the film's 172-minute running time. He also emerged with more screen time than any of his costars, clocking in at 43 minutes in total.

Other than that, old girl, I have just been plain working and hope to be back in the U.S. in about three weeks. Then four months off, a vacation in Palm Springs, a camping trip with my family, and back to work preparing Soldier in the Rain *with Blake Edwards and Marty Jorrow, as this is the project that Mr. Edward's company and mine are doing together.*

Neile sends her love, and the children, and I would give half of my domain for one hot, juicy Californian Hamburger with raw onions. Wiener Schnitzel is starting to come out of my ears.

> *Love,*
>
> Steve

With renewed vigor in his growing role, Steve felt there was cause to celebrate. Jack Linkletter, the son of famed broadcasting personality Art Linkletter, recalled visiting the set to collect interviews from the cast for his television show, *Here's Hollywood*. On a free night, McQueen rounded up three motorcycles, and Linkletter, James Garner, and McQueen rode to nearby Obermensing for a folk festival. Linkletter said everyone was in a festive mood. "We arrived at the folk fest with lots of carnie offerings, bumper cars, etc. From a big tent we heard classic oompah music. Inside, we found picnic tables, the locals, many in leather pants, the band, and lots of beer," he said. "Steve and Jim were recognized immediately, and room was made at a table with a policeman, a dairyman, and others. While we didn't understand German, we were soon singing along as if we knew the words, and Steve was standing on the table—everyone loved it."

McQueen was also in good cheer when the production moved to the town of Fussen near the Austrian border for the post-escape sequences. The scene would require a chase sequence culminating in a big stunt. McQueen was such a racing enthusiast that in the chase scenes he actually plays one of his own Nazi pursuers, dressed in full costume and unknown to the viewer, in pursuit of himself as Hilts. The magic of editing allowed McQueen to get even more time racing on his motorcycle.

The end stunt was a different matter entirely, though. Even though McQueen was an accomplished motorcycle rider, insurance restrictions from the film's bonding company prohibited McQueen from making the jump, so Bud Ekins was tasked to perform the dangerous stunt. Before going overseas, Ekins shipped two Triumph TR6 Trophy Birds and converted them to look like World War II German-era bikes.

Ekins also had to figure out how to jump a motorcycle over a barbed-wire fence in the middle of the German countryside without a ramp. The problem was partially solved when Sturges figured out the area's wallows could serve as a natural ramp for the bike. But on Ekins' first attempt, he got up 2 feet in the air and 10 feet in length. As Ekins stood staring at the German soil, he came up with an idea—dig a ramp out of the dirt. "The ramp was shaped like a spoon. You come and you drop, which drops your suspension, then you come around and you lift up," Ekins said. "The way we designed it was that you would land uphill, taking off downhill. We maxed out at 14 feet high and 65 feet long."

The jump scene was one of the last shot during principal photography on *The Great Escape*, and cast and crew had lined up to watch the iconic action film stunt. McQueen was on the sideline holding his breath as Ekins revved up the Triumph and accelerated toward the wallow. As planned, he hit the ramp at full speed and sailed up and over the fence. "When I was in the air, it was dead silent," Ekins said. "It was hard. [The Triumph] just went bang, then it bounced. I made it on the first pass. I filmed it. That was that."

Yet it was more than that—it was the most famous motorcycle stunt ever performed in a movie.

Everyone on the production cheered wildly for Ekins, and McQueen was the first person to extend his hand. "That was bitchin'!" McQueen said proudly.[2]

Although it was Ekins behind the wheel, it was McQueen in spirit, on camera and in the hearts of the viewers. This movie moment would define his career and cause audiences to give standing ovations across the world.

The film's July 4, 1963, release made *The Great Escape* an instant American classic. The *New York Herald* wrote, "A first-rate adventure film, fascinating in its detail, suspenseful in its plot, stirring in its climax, and excellent in performance. Steve McQueen plays a familiar American war-movie type—brash, self-interested, super-brave emoter. For sheer bravura, whether he's pounding a baseball in his catcher's mitt in solitary or stumping cross-country on a motorcycle with scores of Germans in pursuit, Steve McQueen takes the honors." Arthur Knight in *Saturday Review* called it "the most exhilarating and sobering adventure of the year."

Life knighted Steve as "the next big movie star," while *Time* declared him "the next John Wayne." One scribe wrote, "Not since the exciting days of Bogart, Gable, Tracy, and Wayne has there been such a success story as that of McQueen."

McQueen's decision to trust Sturges and stay on with the picture, along with his own competitive and strong-willed nature that forced him to secure such a major role, had hit the jackpot. The movie was a worldwide smash. Audiences from around the globe, including Germany, England, France, Japan, Canada, Australia, Finland, Norway, Portugal, Sweden, Hong Kong, Denmark, Turkey,

---

2   Elkins was paid $750 for the stunt.

and the Soviet Union—where McQueen was the first American ever voted Best Actor in the Moscow International Film Festival—also fell in love with the American superstar. Artist/muralist Kent Twitchell, who was a U.S. Air Force serviceman stationed in England, said McQueen's appeal crossed international borders. "When *The Great Escape* first came out in movie theaters, every Saturday night the Mods and the Rockers would pack the theaters just to see the jump. As McQueen soared over that fence, these British kids would go bananas and stand and cheer wildly, even though they had seen the movie several times."

The film had it all, including a great story, a terrific cast, thrilling set pieces, and an amazing score. As John Williams' score for *Jaws* would prove, simplicity can be amazingly effective. Elmer Bernstein's score for *The Great Escape* was indeed simple, yet it is irresistibly infectious. It gives the film an undeniable sense of defiance against adversity. Today the score itself has taken on a life of its own and is known, repeated, and whistled around the world to symbolize courage.

James Garner said he got an inkling that McQueen would emerge as the film's star when Sturges called him at his home during postproduction. Garner recalled the conversation. "[Sturges] said, 'Jim, I have to tell you, the two best acting scenes in the film with you and Donald Pleasance are on the cutting room floor. I have to stay with McQueen and the bike.' Hey, it made the picture. Sturges was absolutely correct, but as far as acting went, it was out the window." This was surely a double win for McQueen—he had stolen the film and trumped his costars at the same time.

Costar James Coburn said even though McQueen could be ruthless at times on *The Great Escape*, his razor-sharp instincts served him well. "Steve liked to watch the scene being rehearsed and watch how the other actors would act so he would know all the boundaries to watch out for. The British would always base their character on what the character would do, whereas Steve would base his character on what Steve McQueen would do. And, strangely enough, it worked for him. That personality, that character is what he created, and everybody in the theater wanted to see it.

"It didn't cause other people happiness, but it did cause him to be a star, so you can't fault that. He was a very complicated, complex guy, yet he was very simple. Very simple and straightforward. He was selfish, but I don't think he thought he was being selfish. I thought he was doing everything for the good of him. That's not selfish but self-protective. I think that stems from being an abandoned child. It was all a test, a psychological thing.

"The role in *The Great Escape* wasn't originally built around him. He had to develop it. He wanted that separation from the other men. He was in the cell and always had to be brought in as a separate prisoner. He was always an individual, which was very clever of him," Coburn said.

Robert Relyea said McQueen's actions should have led to disaster but that Sturges got very fortunate. "I understood his stance, but I didn't respect it because he stopped the whole picture," Relyea said. "Steve had to have his thing, and to be honest, he was right. Out of solitary confinement, he found his thing, which led to a lot of the best moments in that film.

"Whatever could go wrong on that picture went wrong, but it turned out okay. We just persevered. We got lucky."

Director John Sturges said his temperamental star was worth his weight in gold despite all of the headaches during production. "When you find somebody with that kind of talent, you use him. Steve is unique, the way Cary Grant is unique or Spencer Tracy or Marlon Brando. There's something bubbling inside of him; he's got a quality of excitement that he brings to everything he does.... That's why you can't take your eyes off him. He's alive!"

The Great Escape was one of the top-grossing films of 1963.[3] The film helped put United Artists firmly on the map as a studio, and it minted a throwaway kid into an international movie star. In 2001, the picture was selected as #19 on the American Film Institute's list of the 100 most thrilling American pictures of all time, and it is a sentimental favorite of veterans all over the world.

In Hilts, McQueen had crafted one of the great screen characters. Hilts is not just a hero; he's an antihero. McQueen's Hilts transcends the prototype of the strong and silent martyr. He is self-serving and on the surface only wants to help himself. McQueen managed to subtly underscore this with a courage and valor that goes unspoken. In classic McQueen style, his actions speak louder than any words. McQueen plays the tough guy with machismo in abundance, yet he manages to convey compassion. The character and icon he created can be indefinitely deconstructed, but as with many things about McQueen, it is the simplest things that carry the most credence. The character, the stare, the baseball and mitt, the motorcycle, and the jump all added up to some of the most startling images on the screen. Everyone from the oldest man to the youngest child can sit glued to the screen and roar with delight when he defies the odds—and gravity—to jump the fence and define history.

---

3 *The Great Escape* grossed approximately $20 million domestically. Adjusted for inflation, that is equivalent to $187 million in 2010 dollars.

18
THE JUICE

ONCE AN OUTSIDER, STEVE MCQUEEN had finally clawed and fought his way to the top of the Hollywood ladder. For the first time in his life, he was able to look forward instead of watching over his shoulder. "I've looked at the world through blackened eyes, through the sights of a rifle, through the portholes of ships, through the peephole of a gambling casino, through the bars of a jail. I'll make it now," he said months after *The Great Escape* was released.

His rough-and-tumble childhood left emotional scars, but it also provided him with the hunger and raw determination to become a star. Suddenly, every wish or fantasy he had ever envisioned for himself had been granted a hundredfold—cars, homes, motorcycles, choice scripts, top directors, profit participation, exotic film locales, sexy costars, klieg lights, limousines, glitter, and the adulation of millions of fans from around the world. But all of those things paled in comparison to what McQueen really craved—absolute power, or as he called it, "the juice."

McQueen was one of the first film stars in Hollywood to demand and get $1 million per film. He was also the first to demand and get total approval of his film's producer, director, writer, and costars. Now that he had the "juice" he was going to squeeze it until it was wrung dry. "I've been through it all a million times," he said when a reporter queried him about his need for total control. "For years those guys in the big offices have been sitting on me. It's about time I was doing the sitting."

Being humble and grateful for what he had achieved in his career so far and appreciative for the breaks he had been given was not in McQueen's nature. All his life he had to fight, and he believed that unless he used any means necessary, nothing would be given to him. McQueen's ruthlessness would grow and take hold that by the apex of his career he had lost his sense of moderation completely.

Many of McQueen's closest friends recount stories of the generous and friendly Steve. This is only half the story, and these were often the exception and not the norm. For every warm and kind anecdote, there were many more that resulted in someone losing out because Steve felt threatened. It may have been a director being kicked off a set because he did not placate McQueen's ego, an actor or actress who was too tall and lost a part, or a loved one being hurt. In the end, McQueen would use his power to serve only himself.

This is not to say he was a fundamentally terrible man—to label him that would be to ignore all the hardships he endured that made him who he was. The reality was that McQueen was a highly flawed human being. He had been prepared to be cruel and unflinching, so why should he be any different now that he was at the top? McQueen's desire was not appeased by success—it was only fueled by it. To remain in the elite and eventually become Hollywood's No. 1 actor, he needed to be even more cautious, more paranoid, and completely merciless. Otherwise, as he saw it, it would all vanish and he'd be back to nothing again. Moreover, for the first half of his life, McQueen felt that he was no good and those around him mostly thought he would amount to nothing. He had proven them wrong the only way he knew how—with unabated ambition.

It would become easy to forget that it was not just his own hard work but the faith and care of others that were also instrumental in his rise. Among others, Hilly Elkins, John Sturges, Stan Kamen, and most important, his wife, Neile, always went above and beyond to help McQueen's career. He had unquestionably worked hard to reach the top, but many others played a part in his success. Eventually all of them and many more would ultimately be pushed out, even his wife, in McQueen's pursuit for full autonomy. The historian Lord Acton once said, "Absolute power corrupts absolutely." This would encapsulate McQueen at the zenith of his fame as he was about to lose control in his pursuit of autocracy. *Le Mans* would eventually prove the tipping point where fame, great wealth, and influence over other people would no longer be enough. While everyone around him was getting hurt, he failed to see that he was ultimately hurting himself and losing them. While everything he did was to reinforce his status and identity, the truth was that he was losing the very identity he sought to enhance.

• • •

In Hollywood where appearances are everything and the only truth is aesthetic, McQueen was compelled to show the world that he had arrived. In February 1963, he and Neile moved from their Nichols Canyon residence and purchased a three-and-a-half-acre country-style stone mansion at 27 Oakmont Drive in the exclusive neighborhood of Brentwood.

McQueen recalled the moment when they first laid eyes on their new residence. "We had to get out of our other house because it was too small, and we started looking around, and this real estate lady, a very nice one, said she knew a house we'd love and she might be able to get it for us. You couldn't get her to mention price. So we went through this electric gate and started swinging around the mountain with the rock wall along the side and all these trees, then [we] came up top and through this big stone archway into this medieval Spanish courtyard, and my eyes are going like a cash register, registering dollar signs. The higher we went, the further they clicked, and when we got to the top of the archway, I simply said, 'Let's go home. We can't afford it.' 'Just look at it,' the real estate agent said. Ten minutes later, we bought it.'"

Built in 1942, the 5,560-square-foot house is a Spanish, Mediterranean, and modern architectural wonder. The five-bedroom home features an imposing front gate (15-by-30-foot), a winding stone driveway, an Olympic-sized swimming pool, a courtyard the size of a football field, a tennis-court-sized den, a custom pool table in the sunken living room, an outdoor playhouse for the two kids, and a panoramic view of the Pacific ocean. The massive garage (which doubled as McQueen's workout room) was soon filled with goodies, such as a GT Lusso Berlinetta Ferrari, Mini Cooper, Jaguar XK-SS, Shelby Cobra, Land Rover, Lincoln Town Car, and a three-quarter-ton International Travelall to haul his motorcycles on weekend trips to the desert.

Actor Edd Byrnes, who had a passing acquaintance with McQueen, said the newly minted superstar was nervous about the quarter-million sticker price on the home. "I bumped into Steve outside of a Sunset Boulevard boutique, and he wanted to show me his new home in Brentwood," Byrnes recalled. "So I followed him in my car and, lo and behold, what a house! He confided to me, 'I have no idea how I'm ever going to pay for this place. You'd better believe I'm not gonna be late for work one single day.'"

McQueen was the king of "The Castle" with an old lady and two kids. His court also included talented henchmen, who were at his beck and call and largely shielded him from the public. They included Stan Kamen (William Morris Agency), Bob Schiller (Guild Management), and Rick Ingersoll (Alan, Ingersoll, Weber Public Relations). His reign went unchallenged for the next decade.

By all appearances, it seemed as if McQueen intended to pay off the Castle's mortgage by accepting three film offers in the span of a year: *Love with the Proper Stranger, Soldier in the Rain,* and *Baby, the Rain Must Fall.*[1]

Love with the Proper Stranger was Steve McQueen's first romantic lead in a film and his most ambitious role to date. The movie established McQueen as a bona-fide sex symbol and expanded his fan base, which included millions of admiring women. "*Love with the Proper Stranger* was really the first time where you saw a three-dimensional Steve," Neile said. "It showed all the aspects that made him really appeal to women so much, because it showed this macho man who dared to be vulnerable."

Shot entirely on location in New York City in the spring of 1963, McQueen made a triumphant return to the Big Apple from his days as a struggling young actor. He was both sentimental and grateful for the opportunity. "For a few days, we were filming scenes on East 11th Street, which is near Third Avenue," McQueen said. "Well, I used to live a block away on East 10th Street when I worked as the driver of a TV and radio repair pickup truck. You know, it was a strange feeling to be playing scenes for a movie camera on the streets where I used to play ball. But I can't say I was unhappy in those days, despite the shabbiness and congestion of the neighborhood. And yet, seeing the old and familiar streets gave me a fuller appreciation of how lucky I have been."

Producer Alan Pakula and director Robert Mulligan, fresh off the success of *To Kill a Mockingbird,* selected McQueen to portray Rocky Papasano, a young, struggling musician who impregnates Catholic girl Angie Rossini, played by Natalie Wood, after a one-night stand. Rocky doesn't quite remember Angie but eventually attempts to do "the right thing" and asks the strong-willed Angie to marry him—a proposal she turns down. The two then decide to raise money for her abortion, but Rocky cannot stand the back-alley conditions that Angie must endure. By the end of the film, Rocky shows up at her work holding a picket sign, "Better Wed than Dead." This is one of McQueen's rare offbeat roles, with his New York Actors Studio training put to excellent use. Mulligan, who directed McQueen in his groundbreaking television performance in *The Defender*, felt that the right comedic vein hadn't been tapped in the actor. "He had a wonderful comedic talent and wanted to show it and let it come out," Mulligan said.

---

1   McQueen waded through several offers at the time. They included a remake of *Vivacious Lady* with
    John Sturges directing; Robert Aldrich's *Two For Texas* with Dean Martin and Gina Lollobrigida;
    and *I Love Louisa* costarring Shirley MacLaine in a Walter Mirisch–financed picture.

Despite a budding reputation for bedding his female costars, McQueen declined the not-so-subtle advances of costar Natalie Wood, whose relationship with Warren Beatty was quickly unraveling. Wood tried every trick to make a play for McQueen, including dangling her leg outside her trailer door, pretending she was talking to someone else while he passed by, and long seductive stares. "Natalie began to flirt openly and charmingly with Steve," said screenwriter Arnold Schulman. "But neither Steve nor his wife took it seriously."

McQueen often told Neile of Wood's latest exploits, and the two shared a laugh, though privately Neile wasn't so amused. It was not McQueen's loyalty to his wife or professionalism that enabled him to resist. Surprisingly, it was his loyalty to Robert Wagner, who was in the middle of a divorce with Wood, and the fact that he genuinely liked Warren Beatty.

Photographer William Claxton, who was hired by Paramount Studios to shoot publicity stills for the movie, said the two stars were polar opposites in terms of temperament. "I shook hands with Natalie Wood and got my first live close-up of her beautiful face. Her dark brown, friendly eyes met with mine, and I knew that we would be friends," Claxton said. "I then turned to meet her leading man, McQueen. He didn't offer his hand; he just stared at me with his intense, steel-blue eyes. Later he would say to me, 'Clax, I really zapped you with my look, didn't I?' His look was chilling. I felt that he knew everything about me in a split second. I thought, 'Oh shit, what have I got myself into with this guy?' He was both seductive and threatening. Time would prove that my hunches, instincts, whatever you want to call them, were right about this unusual actor. He was street-smart, animal-like, nonintellectual, and hip. In fact, he brought new meaning to the word hip; he was super-hip."

Claxton eventually gained McQueen's trust and developed an easy friendship through their common love of sports cars, motorcycles, and jazz music. Claxton sensed McQueen was uneasy with still photography and had to be eased into becoming comfortable as the subject of his camera. "I studied him, watched his moods, and learned just when to push the shutter release. He liked the pictures and soon learned to trust me—I found out pretty quickly that he didn't trust many people," Claxton said.

The shutterbug often accompanied McQueen on location in New York whenever the star had free time, and the two roamed the city. McQueen showed Claxton where he had lived, where he met Neile, and various places he'd worked. He also stopped on the Lower East Side and studied the homeless, often staring at them intently. Claxton asked why he was so fascinated with the derelicts.

"Oh man, that could be me," McQueen revealed. "I just barely missed being a bum."

Claxton noted that McQueen was riddled with insecurity regarding his lack of education, and he made sure never to do "an education number" on McQueen. "He would ask questions about things, and I would try to answer him. He liked that," Claxton said. "One time I reminded him that I, too, was learning from him, he was so street-smart. But he had his paranoid moments. He liked to wait until it was almost too late to enter a situation, then go in at the last moment, maybe dressed incorrectly, but [he would] still win everybody over.

"As a film actor, he knew the power of his own charm; he studied it and incorporated it as a tool. He used that little-boy found-me-out thing beautifully. I studied his gimmicks. I was allowed to go to the rushes, and I learned a lot about acting. But I didn't dare to criticize him. My aim was to take good photographs.[2] I enjoyed this relationship with such an interesting guy."

Love with the Proper Stranger was released Christmas Day in 1963, and its box-office returns received a nice holiday boost as well as good tidings from critics. "Steve McQueen is probably a better performer than we are allowed to appreciate," observed *The New Republic*, while the *New York Herald* raved, "McQueen is first rate as the musician." *The Saturday Review* lavished high praise on McQueen by stating he "is just about the best actor in Hollywood today. He always seems to believe in what he's doing and saying, manages humor and emotion without evidence of perceptible strain, and for modesty, offhandedness, and all-around ability, could probably offer Marlon Brando a few lessons. Attention, as they say, should be paid to Mr. McQueen."

Unfortunately, the Academy Awards nominating body felt otherwise, who gave Natalie Wood a nod for Best Actress while entirely overlooking McQueen's performance, although he did receive a Golden Globe nomination for Best Actor.[3] It wasn't the last time he would be snubbed by the film establishment. Success of every kind was flowing profusely for McQueen, yet award recognition would mostly elude and frustrate him.

Soldier in the Rain was a military comedy-drama based on a much-loved William Goldman novel. "I hadn't done any comedy since *The Honeymoon Machine*," Steve said. "I felt it was time to do something different. But the picture

---

2   *Steve McQueen* by William Claxton (Arena Editions, 2000) catches a '60s icon in full flight, including some of the most candid and enduring images of McQueen during the happiest period of his life. Claxton is considered by many as the definitive McQueen photographer.

3   *Love with the Proper Stranger* received a total of five Academy Award nominations but came away with nothing on Oscar night.

just didn't come together. I really don't know why, because all the right elements were there." Indeed, the picture had all the earmarks of a blockbuster: a formidable cast, featuring Jackie Gleason and Tuesday Weld; a distinguished director in Ralph Nelson (*Lilies of the Field*); and producer Blake Edwards (*The Pink Panther*), who cowrote the screenplay with Maurice Richlin.

The $1.5 million production commenced on June 10, 1963,[4] and the movie was set up through Allied Artists. It was the first McQueen film to feature the Solar Productions banner. It was a major accomplishment for McQueen, who had a ninth-grade education. McQueen's share paid him a handsome $300,000 salary and profits after the film's break-even point. McQueen could afford to be generous, and in an uncharacteristic move for the power-hungry star, he gave away his top billing to lure costar Jackie Gleason, despite usually fighting for preferential billing at all times. But that's where the respect ended. As soon as McQueen stepped on the set in Fort Ord, California, he let it be known that he was calling the shots. "It was Steve McQueen who everybody was in fear of," said costar Tony Bill. "Ralph Nelson, the director, was an extremely kind and gentle man, but it was very clear that he was not in charge of decision-making on the set. It became very clear that was going to be Steve McQueen's call."

It was Bill's second movie, and McQueen decided that he wasn't a threat. If Bill had been a threat, then he would have no doubt left the set quicker than McQueen removed "free items" from his own dressing room. The Oscar-nominated Gleason, television's King of Comedy, was the man in McQueen's sights. Gleason had talent to match his size and ego. "I have no use for humility. I am a fellow with an exceptional talent," Gleason once famously said. McQueen decided to test "The Great One" and soon found out his physically imposing costar was also nimble of mind. "McQueen had just become a big star off of *The Great Escape*, so he was really having that heady feeling of stardom and [was] prone to showing up late on the set," Tony Bill recalled. "Jackie Gleason found himself in the position of being on the set, waiting for the arrival of a young Mr. McQueen. Gleason, being a consummate professional and extremely experienced performer, started getting annoyed with this. Shortly after we started filming, I guess he let it be known that he would no longer show up on the set before McQueen. Steve got wind of this, and there was a short-lived stalemate between the two of them. That was worked out as the movie progressed."

---

4   *Soldier in the Rain* was filmed three months after *Love with the Proper Stranger* but released to theaters a month before.

McQueen then turned his arrogance on director Ralph Nelson, who planned on filming master shots. McQueen told Nelson, "Well, I don't do master shots."

Off camera, McQueen was certainly not bothered about getting up close and personal, as costar Chris Noel remembers. "Steve was incredible. He was a fascinating and sexy actor. Very, very intense. Gorgeous eyes. I had a major crush on him, and early in the shoot he invited me into his bungalow and said, 'Baby, you're adorable,' and began kissing me. I told him, 'No, Steve! You're a married man.' He responded, 'You don't understand. I've been to bed with every one of my leading ladies!' Over time he wore me down, and who was I to break his streak?"

Though Noel adored working with McQueen, she got the cold shoulder from her other costars. "Tuesday Weld was bitchy and didn't like me," she recalled. "I even had to darken my hair because of her! And Jackie Gleason liked only who he chose to like. He wasn't friendly. I'd say hello to him, and he'd grunt something back. He didn't like rehearsing either. But I got used to it. I liked working with Steve McQueen so much that it didn't bother me how everybody else was."

When Neile visited the set, the reality that Steve was married hit Noel square between the eyes, and she stopped seeing McQueen. "Neile was a very sweet person and a good girl. I was raised in a small Florida town with proper morals, and I'm a good girl, too," Noel said. "I knew what I was doing was wrong, and so I eventually said to Steve, 'We can't continue doing this. It's not right.' Steve was an incredibly exciting and sexy man, and there aren't a whole lot of people out there that are exciting. Most people are complacent and don't know how to step out of their comfort zones or how to move forward. He was always moving ahead in a way that many others never managed."

Soldier in the Rain did nothing to move McQueen's career ahead. He gave one of the oddest, over-the-top, most unsubtle performances of his career and was plainly miscast as Sergeant Eustis Clay. "McQueen, one of the more exciting actors around, is totally suppressed as a mush-mouthed stupid devoted to dawg and buddy to the point of tears," wrote Judith Crist of the *New York Herald*. The *Los Angeles Times'* John L. Scott wrote, "*Soldier in the Rain* is a strange film comedy-drama about life in the peacetime army...a disjointed production that must be classed generally as a novelty." And Archer Winston of the *New York Post* predicted that *Soldier in the Rain* "should set back [McQueen's] blossoming career one giant step."[5]

---

5   *Soldier in the Rain* also suffered from poor timing. It was released on November 27, 1963, just five days after John F. Kennedy's assassination. The country was in mourning and simply in no mood to laugh. The film sank quickly into oblivion.

Feeling that the third time might be the charm, McQueen worked once more with Mulligan on *Baby, the Rain Must Fall*, which was his last black-and-white film. Based on Horton Foote's 1954 play *The Traveling Lady*, the film matched McQueen with well-respected actress Lee Remick. McQueen had worked with Remick before, though it's doubtful she remembered him, according to actor Robert Loggia. "Steve and I worked as extras in a live TV show, a Kinescope deal, with Lee Remick, and they needed three guys—one in the Army, one in the Navy, and one in the Air Force—to stand on a podium in uniform. Lee was the star, and McQueen and I were peons," Loggia said.

No doubt the contrast in their careers resounded favorably for McQueen. He often took pleasure and reassurance from surpassing actors from his early days. She was a somebody, while he was a nobody. At the start of his career, he would have killed to have even a small part in the sort of productions she was routinely offered. Since then she had grown in stature, but McQueen had moved into top gear and thoroughly eclipsed her as a big box-office star. This was the McQueen show, and she was just a costar.

McQueen failed to impress his enthusiasm for the picture upon Remick. "I was curious what he was like. He was friendly and nice and funny and odd. He wasn't just your ordinary run-of-the-mill actor," Remick said in a 1991 interview. "I don't think he liked acting very much; that's the feeling I got. I didn't feel his heart was in this movie. He liked action movies better. This was a little too delicate and soft and tender for his taste. He did it very well, however."

As with many of his leading ladies, McQueen ended up in bed with Remick, according to Neile. She claims in her memoir that Steve felt lonely and isolated in Texas and admitted as much, "There was no reason for me to find out except for his compulsion to tell me. Not to hurt me—just to make it all right. For him." Remick denied the claim to this writer a few months before liver and kidney cancer took her life at 55. "Oh, no. Really, now," Remick replied. "Those are [Neile's] words, not mine, so I can't comment on that except to say that it's not true."

In the film, McQueen portrays Henry Thomas, a parolee who returns home from prison and is received by his hopeful wife, Remick, and their young daughter. The three try to start over again as Thomas takes on a singing career. McQueen, who had a tin ear and was not very musically inclined, did give the part his all, according to guitarist and technical adviser Billy Strange. "[McQueen] expels so much energy it's wild. He's got the bile going in this part. He falls into a category of 20,000 hillbillies that I have known. He is aggressive in a part but not aggressive to work with. He'll try anything you suggest. He's not worried about his image."

McQueen certainly did live up to his image when it came to his status as a cheapskate movie star. A document from the American Motion Picture Academy shows McQueen billed almost everything he could to the film's production when he arrived in southeast Texas in September 1963:

- 1 set of barbells $38.45

- 1 abdominal board $19.95

- 1 Gibson guitar and case $338 (case was $47)

- 1 exercise bench $29.95

- 1 pair of dumbbells $27.95

- Valet $115.23

- Car $24.97

- Sid Kaiser $256.02[6]

- Restaurant $234.32

- Long-distance phone calls $346.86

- Nurse $29.46

- Doctors $40

- Cash $170

- Organic foods $74.24

- Freight charges for six shipments of food $209.97

- Limo service to pick up family on Nov. 7 $32

- Return of Cobra via Tandem $727.06

- Barber air fare $228

- Limo service from Steve McQueen's home to Union Station $21

- Expense money $25,000

6   Sid Kaiser was a well-known drug dealer in movie and music circles and this was most likely a payment for marijuana or another illegal substance. Columbia dutifully picked up the tab.

One item that didn't show up on the expense report was a high-end convertible loaned to the production from Ford. William Claxton was with McQueen on a long stretch of Texas highway when the car, which had approximately 30 miles on the speedometer, met its untimely demise. McQueen had the day off, and he was ready to unwind. "We smoked some dope and then drove way out in the country," Claxton said. "Once he saw a clear road, he just floored it until the car started heating up. I said, 'Steve, I smell the car.' And he said, 'Yeah, I know, don't worry about it.' We were probably going over 100 mph when smoke started coming out from under the floorboards and it became hot. I said, 'Steve, this motor's on fire.' He slowed the car down to almost a stop, and I was the first out of the car, followed by Steve. It burned right down to the ground, while he just sat laughing. The headline in the local paper the next day was, 'Steve McQueen Escapes Death as Car Burns.'"

The headline wasn't as serious as the news bulletin that came across a local police car radio on November 22, 1963, while McQueen was on location in Columbus, Texas. "The president has been shot!" cried out one of the state troopers. Claxton recalled, "The entire cast and crew gathered around the radio. Everyone was stunned, of course. A pall was cast over the entire group. Lunch break was called, but very few of us could eat. Steve took the news of the assassination of President Kennedy very hard.[7] The producer, Alan Pakula, decided to fold up the set, leave Texas, and head back to Hollywood where they would have to re-create the set on the sound stage. Peggy and Neile met Steve and me at Los Angeles airport, and we parted ways with sadness."

The film had a downbeat tone about it. The subject matter of a released prisoner trying to rebuild his family's life on the back of a failed career and unrealized ambition is inherently somber. Despite this, though, it is likely that JFK's death permeated the filming. The sadness and emptiness of a shattered dream and uncertain future must have certainly influenced the actors and filmmakers alike, translating to a melancholy picture. The tone of the film and the timing of its release meant lackluster reviews and a weak box-office showing in January 1965. *Variety* assessed, "Its somber, downbeat story meanders and has plot holes that leave viewers confused and depressed." *The New York Times* wrote, "There is a major and totally neglected weakness in this film that troubles one's mind

7   McQueen had actually met JFK in 1960 through Peter Lawford and Sid Kaiser, who was the manager of the Hollywood Coordinating Committee for Senator Kennedy's presidential campaign. Neile McQueen recalled in 2010, "I'm standing next to Judy Garland and Marilyn Monroe. I remember walking into the living room and Joe Kennedy was there. I said hi, he said hello. I asked if he thought Jack would win. He looked at me like I was out of my mind and said, 'Of course he's going to win!'"

throughout the picture and leaves one sadly let down at the end." *The Saturday Review* opined, "Steve McQueen, ordinarily a vital performer, seems rather cast down at having to play someone who fails at becoming Elvis Presley,[8] and neither he nor Horton Foote ever makes clear what has instilled in him such a sorry ambition."

Of the three films McQueen shot in 1963, only *Love with the Proper Stranger* commercially panned out. After the success of *The Great Escape*, he was ready for a glittering career full of box-office smashes. Exhausted, he took a year's hiatus from the film industry, no doubt to take stock and plan his next career move—after all, he had worked too hard to blow it now. When he returned, the break seemed to do the trick. He didn't come back with just one hit—that would not be the all-or-nothing McQueen that was adored by fans the world over. He returned with no less than five back-to-back worldwide hits, a feat that no other movie star accomplished in his lifetime.

Despite the recent setbacks and misguided film choices, McQueen was about to enter his own golden era. If the '50s were all about McQueen learning his craft and the early '60s were about his rise to stardom, then the rest of the decade would mark his full ascension to power and dominance. The string of back-to-back hits would see him achieve everything he wanted, though there would be costs along the way. The actor who once would grab any chance he could to get a role would now have producers begging for him to simply read a script. McQueen would play the roles of the loner card shark, a naive half-breed who evolves into a killer, the reluctant war hero, a white-collar bank robber, and a laconic cop—roles that would extend his range of characters to a level unsurpassed, so much so that his performances have formed the archetype and are referenced by actors even today. He would consolidate his image as the leading man of the era, the action star of the century, and most important, he would be crowned global cinema's "King of Cool."

---

8 Presley bodyguard Sonny West said his employer openly wished for the Henry Thomas part but was stuck doing mindless musical travelogues under the direction of his manager, Colonel Tom Parker.

19

THE THREE FACES OF STEVE

STEVE MCQUEEN'S PUBLIC PERSONA was always at war with the private man. He found that his atomic fame wasn't conducive to his personal happiness despite the fact that on the surface he was a man who had it all: a doting wife, two healthy children, wealth beyond his wildest imagination, and the adulation of millions. Striking a balance was always hard for McQueen, who was a man used to living between extremes. Every aspect of him seemed to embody contradictions. He was often candid but also deflective when it came to the truth of his upbringing. He enjoyed the spoils of stardom but wasn't emotionally equipped to handle the attention that came with it. He often espoused the joys of domesticity but was a sexual Olympian and not exactly a role model for intimacy or monogamy. He was academically deficient but was streetwise and highly intelligent, forming his own successful production company and often outsmarting movie moguls, executives, and costars. He was contradictory to the point where he would be dubbed tight-fisted and cheap but gave generously of his time to Boys Republic and donated to many charitable causes, often anonymously. He outwardly denounced illegal substances but tried to fill his emotional potholes with drink and drugs. He had an angel on his shoulder, but the devil was always on his back. McQueen's sudden rise to stardom made him feel a loss of control, and consequently he created crises when life became too stable or tranquil. Fame had made him an icon, but there were always three Steves—the unloved kid who remained unsure of himself; the confident, reckless, and indulgent movie star who was the essence of cool; and the rational and responsible adult.

In the midst of all the sanctioned madness, McQueen also created outlets for himself, such as automobile racing, motorcycle rides in the desert, family camping trips, weight training, and as he became more established in the film industry, acts of philanthropy and civic participation. His lesser-known outlets were as beautifully simple and down to earth as sharing Mexican food with his motorcycle buddies or winding down an evening with a joint. In typical contradictory McQueen fashion, he still spent much of his free time in the limelight, such as a trip to a nightclub to soak up the atmosphere and hold court.

His favorite nightclub was the world-famous Whisky A Go-Go on the Sunset Strip. The Whisky quickly emerged as the hot spot on The Strip when it opened for business in January 1964. It soon became the central headquarters for hipsters, musicians, and bands looking to launch their musical careers. The first act to get a big break at The Whisky was a rhythm and blues rocker named Johnny Rivers.

Johnny's frantic sound, a mixture of upbeat blues, R&B, and rock 'n' roll covers, attracted celebrity-studded sold-out audiences, including McQueen. "I remember the Beatles coming and the Stones and Bob Dylan playing pool upstairs," Rivers said in 1999. "And I didn't recognize half the celebrities. People'd say, 'That was Gina Lollobrigida dancing out there with Steve McQueen.'"

McQueen, Jayne Mansfield, Johnny Carson, Rita Hayworth, and Lana Turner were just a few of the personalities who showed up for Rivers' legendary performances. McQueen soon installed himself as a regular and befriended co-owner Elmer Valentine, who gave him the best booth in the house and introduced him to an endless supply of nubile beauties.[1] "He drove up on his motorcycle," Valentine told author Penina Spiegel. "He was cruising—but I could tell right away he was a loner. I treated him nice, gave him the best booth, introduced him to all the girls. Steve would only drink beer. He was real narrow-minded about drinking. A person would have a drink, [and] Steve would look at him and say, 'That's a boozer.'"

He wasn't as narrow-minded where it concerned other illegal substances. Actress Mamie Van Doren recalled an LSD-laden tryst that started at the Whisky and ended up in bed at the home of hairstylist Jay Sebring.

Van Doren was a reigning sex symbol in the late '50s and early '60s, and studio honchos had her pegged as the next Marilyn Monroe. In 2005, she recalled the night she met Steve McQueen and the two danced the night away on the Whisky's tiny dance floor. McQueen kept his flirting like his on-screen dialogue—short and to the point. After a few minutes of polite conversation, McQueen suggested they go to her place. Van Doren had a strict no-sleeping-with-married-men rule, but

---

1   McQueen's association with the Whisky A Go-Go was duly noted in his FBI file. "Among its clientele are well-known legitimate people, as well as entertainment celebrities and in addition, pimps, prostitutes and other notorious characters," wrote a Los Angeles field agent. "It is probably the most popular spot on the Sunset Strip."

minutes later the two were standing on her balcony, swilling beers and watching the city lights below. "He had one thing on his mind—jumping into bed with me. He didn't need a second wife," Van Doren said. "But hell, it was the '60s!" The two embraced in a passionate kiss just a few steps away from the bedroom. Their romantic evening screeched to a halt when Van Doren's young son from her second marriage wouldn't settle down. Undeterred, McQueen called two nights later and invited Van Doren to a party at the Benedict Canyon home of friend and hairstylist Jay Sebring. Van Doren accompanied him and described the scene as a mod-style party that was in full swing, with people splashing around the pool while others wandered around the Tudor mansion, drinking, smoking pot, and thoroughly enjoying themselves. McQueen summoned Van Doren into the bathroom to drop some acid. Van Doren said they were heady days and hallucinogenic times, and acid wasn't hard to find. "You could get LSD over the counter then. Also amyl nitrate. You could get that as well if you said you had a heart murmur or something. I had a carpenter who was always doing LSD. I asked him about it because I thought it sounded like Lucky Strikes. Cary Grant said his doctor was giving it to him for his problems. Everyone had a problem back then," Van Doren said.

McQueen didn't take any ordinary acid—he had Sandoz[2], the strongest and most potent form, because he was always on the quest to take things to an extreme. Van Doren was guarded because she liked being in control of her faculties, but McQueen's persuasive charms eased her fears.

"No bad trips on this shit," Steve promised. "It's made by a pharmaceutical company. It's the best. It makes sex a totally new experience."

He placed the pale yellow tablet in her hand, gulped down one himself, and chased it down with a beer. She took hers with a glass of red wine. As they made their way into the bedroom, McQueen enlightened Van Doren with a bit of movie trivia.

"Do you know whose bedroom this was?" McQueen said.

"No."

"It was Paul Bern's and Jean Harlow's. This is the room they were in when she found out her husband was impotent."[3]

McQueen took Van Doren in his arms and kissed her neck and face.

"At least it's not something in the room," Van Doren quipped.

---

2   Sandoz Laboratories introduced LSD as a psychiatric drug in 1947. It was believed to be the strongest form of the hallucinogenic drug because it was produced in a pharmaceutical lab.

3   Harlow's husband was German-American film director Paul Bern, who committed suicide in 1932. It was believed that he took his life because he was impotent.

She recalled of that psychedelic lovemaking session, "There was a flash of red light, like a skyrocket across the room. Following that, there was another, and another. Soon, the room was crisscrossed by tracings of colored lines of light."

Van Doren expounded on that evening in her 1987 memoir, *Playing the Field*. "I could feel the crinkle and crush of the bedspread beneath us as we lay in a tangle of arms and legs, creating our own special tempo, our own frantic rhythms. From the haze of our lovemaking, I could hear music in the house, guitars mimicking the beat of our bodies. My own voice, as I cried out, sounded as though it was someone else's.

"We encouraged each other to longer, more desperate fulfillments after the tidal wave of our first climax. The moments were too short, too long. We were all time, all beginning, quick thrusting, widening, our bodies each other's receptacle, and death and life were at our side. We kept on and on through the psychedelic night."

Van Doren had an addendum to the story in 2005. She said that while Steve slept soundly, she looked up into the full-length mirror above the bed and saw the ghost of Paul Bern. "He appeared middle-aged and was naked except for a sequined mask over his eyes," Van Doren said. "As I watched him, he stepped out of the mirror, put a gun in his mouth and pulled the trigger. His head exploded everywhere, and this multicolored confetti scattered all over Steve and me. I started screaming, and I could see this body twitching at the foot of the bed while confetti was still coming out of its head. Steve was shouting at me to hold on, but I was hallucinating. Then Jean came out of the mirror, stepped over her husband's twitching body and smiled. She told me the blondes, brunettes, and redheads in Hollywood were all the same, 'like horses running back into a burning barn. We'll burn up, but we can't stop ourselves,' she said. 'You can come over now with me if you want.'" Van Doren screamed and grabbed a vase from the table and tossed it at the mirror, smashing it to bits. She admonished Steve for not being able to see the blood and Bern's twitching body at the foot of the bed. To appease her, McQueen got out of bed and kicked 'the body,' which turned out to be a pile of clothes.

According to Van Doren, it took weeks to clear the macabre images from that night. She said the two continued to see each other "when Steve was having problems with his marriage." Van Doren said she never took LSD with McQueen again, but he did introduce another equally potent drug into the bedroom—amyl nitrate. "As we were about to reach a climax, Steve would crack open one of the glass vials of amyl nitrate and inhale the deep vapors."

During more sobering moments, Van Doren realized that McQueen was a lot like her father. "My dad was a mechanic and rode an Indian bike just like

Steve, who was a grease monkey at heart. He was a lot like all the mechanics I knew—he preferred T-shirts and jeans and always had a little grime and grease underneath his fingernails. He was just a guy in the movies and treated it like a regular job." Their relationship came to an end when Van Doren realized that Steve wasn't going to leave his wife or kids. "Our purely sexual attraction began to wane, although he was a man of great charisma and imagination who was wonderful in bed. But in the end, my dislike of drugs won out over passion. I was not comfortable with the experience of my faculties being out of control, and I always feared a return of those bizarre hallucinations. Steve was constantly on the edge and looking for something higher. He was on drugs a lot, and I just did not like them at all. It ended up spoiling our relationship."

McQueen also embarked on an ongoing affair with stripper, burlesque dancer, and stag movie superstar Candy Barr. The curvaceous, green-eyed blonde was the toast of the bump-and-grind circuit and romantically linked to mobster Mickey Cohen and Dallas nightclub owner Jack Ruby (who killed President John F. Kennedy's assassin, Lee Harvey Oswald, in November 1963). She and McQueen engaged in several sexual trysts in the apartment of a television director, who loaned the two his pad whenever she had an engagement at the Largo Club on the Sunset Strip.

John Gilmore said McQueen also reconnected with former girlfriend Dianne Rico, who moved from New York to Los Angeles in the '60s. "Though I had long since broken off my relationship with her, Steve was continuing to see her, sneaking into the back window of a room she had on Sunset Strip so no one could spot him," Gilmore said. "Though Steve was married, he was getting all he could get from any female he'd pick up or revisit 'used ones.'"

Gilmore said one night after Rico met him secretly behind a bar in Santa Monica, McQueen gave her a glimpse into his psyche. "[McQueen] confided to her that he felt like he'd gone to bed a flop and a failure and awoke to hard success," Gilmore said. "It was like Brando's line in *Viva Zapata* about a monkey in silk still being a monkey. McQueen never thought he could be that person everyone was seeing on the silver screen. He was afraid his life was going to collapse on top of him. He was empty, he said; it was the reason he needed so many things—so much dope, so many girls, cars, motorcycles— you name it, he needed it. His life was a hole that had to be filled."

McQueen frequently trolled the Sunset Strip in one of his high-end sports cars and picked up women hitchhiking, at bus stops, phone booths, supermarkets, and restaurants. There was no promise of courtship, roses, candlelight dinners, or follow-up phone calls the day after. "Get in. Shut the door. You know who I am, right? I don't like to talk—you can see me talk in the movies. But if you're up for some fun and games…" McQueen usually took his women to a rented office in Santa Monica that had concealed parking. It was used as a crash pad for nocturnal one-shot situations where he could indulge his desires and take anything he wanted to the extreme.

McQueen's promiscuity is a core component of Attachment Disorder, according to psychologist Peter O. Whitmer. "*Love with the Proper Stranger* seems a more psychologically apt title to Steve McQueen's promiscuity," Whitmer said. "More satyriasis, this is an unbridled need for constant sexual activity, named after the mythological Greek beast the satyr, constantly in heat, constantly rutting. Here is the steamy side of indiscriminate socializing. This goes on with no impulse control and no sense of delay of gratification. The desire is ever present. So, too, is the 'object.' And in cases such as this, that is all they are—animated yet nameless sexual 'objects,' each indiscriminate from the other, a virtual sexual smorgasbord.

"One school of thought says, essentially, that 'opportunity creates the thief'; that many individuals placed in the same circumstances would react the same way, [yet] very few are afforded this chance. Just as powerfully addictive as chemicals, the reward center of the brain is stimulated by sex, and it needs an ever increasing supply of stimulation. Here is the metaphor of women being 'drugs with legs.'

"Also behind this behavior was McQueen's archaic view of women as chattel—things, not people—a perspective taught him well by his mother."

The public persona McQueen created for himself was largely at odds with the private man. He was the rebellious movie star who also happened to be a loving husband and a father. He once told a reporter, "When I'm not making a picture, I spend all of my time fixing my car. My wife doesn't have to worry about other women; she knows where to find me." That was not the reality, though. That was the media-friendly image a movie star needed in that era to avoid scandal. As long as Steve came home at night, he was forgiven for his transgressions, but those in his inner circle knew the real score. "To Steve, the world was just a giant sexual supermarket," Bud Ekins said. "He constantly had women chasing him, and he couldn't say no. Steve just couldn't control himself. When he saw something he wanted—a woman, a motorcycle, a car—he'd go for it. Everything he did was extreme. He liked an extreme amount of sex, an extreme amount of marijuana, and an extreme amount of cocaine."[4]

---

4   McQueen shouldn't be singled out as a philandering movie star. Many actors from his era, including Paul Newman, Marlon Brando, Elvis Presley, Clint Eastwood, and Bruce Lee, all engaged in extramarital affairs. As comedian Chris Rock once famously said, "A man is basically as faithful as his options." McQueen had a lot of options.

However, McQueen cannot simply be viewed as a hedonist megastar. His behavior requires context to fully understand it. All his life he had to fight, but now he was getting things much easier, and he planned to take full advantage of this newfound access to everything that would have otherwise been denied to him. "I did everything in a hurry. I got married in a hurry, and I've spent every free moment from films hurrying around racetracks both in the U.S. and abroad, on motorcycles and then the fastest cars I could find," McQueen said. "I have a million plans—movies to make, movies to direct and produce with my own company. I want to go places, and I want to go fast. I've hurried all my life. It's a way of life for me."

Neile McQueen says it was something else nagging at him—the notion of losing it all. "He's deeply concerned about being poor again," she revealed. "He's got the brass ring right now, but he's afraid it might be snatched away. When things are going too well, he worries. It's the fear of being poor and lonely again, of everything good vanishing."

Steve's dark side was often tempered by his concern for youth and his quiet benevolence. Growing up, he had so little support or guidance from adults and resented authority. Childhood and the struggles of being young and disadvantaged were things he could fundamentally understand and relate to. It is too easy to dismiss McQueen as someone who was selfish and mean; indeed, he did many kind acts. He was no saint and often a sinner, but he did give something back to those around him. He knew that his own life could have ended very differently and knew the value that care and compassion could make in a child's life. Accordingly, he was an incredibly passionate and caring father, compensating rather remarkably for the lack of parental care he had and successfully breaking the cycle of the abused parent/child syndrome.

Heading back to the Boys Republic was a way for McQueen to dip into the spiritual well when things got too overwhelming. In 1963, he established the Steve McQueen Fund at the Boys Republic, a generous four-year scholarship to the best student. He also purchased and distributed the school's famous Della Robbia Christmas wreaths annually and regularly frequented his old alma mater for sit-down chats with the kids. He took time to talk to them one on one on their level, showing interest in their hopes and aspirations as well as imparting advice and guidance. "I go back when I can. I just sit down and talk to the boys; that's the best way I can function with them," Steve said. "Boy, they're smart and bright. They know the scam. But they have a hard time adjusting to school, just as I did. It's different from the streets. You've got to learn to get along. But they make it. Insecurity is a pretty good motivation."

Boys Republic director Max Scott said McQueen's visits to the campus were uplifting to the students and gave them hope. "He never stopped by my office," Scott said. "He'd just go straight to the cottage, and [he] sat on the floor of the room, which was jammed with students, while the temperature hovered close to 100 degrees.

"He also enjoyed the Activity Center, shooting pool with the students, fielding their questions about whether he worked on the farm or if he had been assigned to the kitchen, what he liked most or least about the program, etc. Almost immediately, Steve would turn the attention back to the boys, asking what they were currently doing and if they were making the experience a positive one in terms of their futures.

"Once he ventured over to our print shop where the students had been making turquoise Indian-style bracelets. Steve purchased over $1,000 worth, although the jewelry was quite poorly made and of little value. They were thrilled.

"Following his visits, they would write to him and, without exception, he answered their letters. Steve would call me asking for information about the letter-writers so he could write a meaningful, personalized response."

McQueen correlated Boys Republic to almost every aspect of his life, according to former roommate Arden Miller. "I saw Steve again at a Boys Republic fundraiser in 1963, and it was the first time in almost 20 years," Miller said. "We shared some laughs, and he told me about a movie he'd just completed called *The Great Escape*. 'You've gotta see it,' Steve said with a glint in his eye. 'It was just like escaping from Boys Republic on those nights when we went into Pomona.'"

His humanity also entered the realm of civil rights when he was scheduled to appear at the March on Washington on August 28, 1963, in support of Dr. Martin Luther King Jr. An FBI agent noted in an August 1, 1963, memo to Bureau Chief J. Edgar Hoover that McQueen and approximately 60 to 90 movie personalities[5] had planned to charter a Lockheed Electra airplane for $14,000.

For whatever reasons, McQueen did not participate on the March on Washington, but he did express his opinions on politics and race to *Variety*. "Though actors who mix into politics want to do good, they must be sure that the stand they are taking is valid. We have a lot of kitchen cleaning to do in Hollywood, and I think we are doing it. As for the problems of employing Negroes, I think you should use a Negro actor because he is good at his craft and not simply because he is a Negro." These weren't mere words; McQueen

5   They included Charlton Heston, Marlon Brando, Debbie Reynolds, Kirk Douglas, Burt Lancaster, Sidney Poitier, Gregory Peck, Eartha Kitt, Dick Gregory, Paul Newman, and Joanne Woodward.

often put action behind them. He went to bat for several black actors and placed them prominently in his movies, most notably Georg Stanford Brown in *Bullitt*, LeVar Burton in *The Hunter*, and Rupert Crosse in *The Reivers*. Notably, Crosse was fortunate enough to be one of the few taller costars that McQueen would allow to work with him. For McQueen, endorsements do not come much bigger. Steve also acted as Hollywood's goodwill ambassador by welcoming South African expatriate and trumpeter Hugh Masekela when he played the Whisky A Go-Go.

McQueen also engaged in local politics when the Los Angeles City Council revealed its master plan for the Santa Monica Mountains in July 1964. The controversial plan called for tall structures, high-density subdivisions that would have doubled the area's population, no park, and a freeway running through the mountain. Several high-profile residents such as McQueen, James Garner, Eva Marie Saint, Betsy Drake, and film producer Martin Jurow were resentful of the encroachments to their wooded dells. They voiced their opposition in a verbal shootout with the council, specifically 11th District Councilman Karl Rundberg, who was openly hostile to the group of thespians.

McQueen rose to protest the plan during the meeting and was promptly ruled out of order. "I'd like to ask the learned councilman [Rundberg] what it is going to cost to build freeways through this mountain area." Karl Rundberg, who was known for his ill manners, shot back angrily, "Well, Mr. Whatever-your-name-is, that is a question that should be put to the planning department, not me."

Rundberg doled out the same treatment to James Garner when he stepped up to the podium, suggesting Garner and McQueen should stick to acting and leave the politics to the professionals. Garner almost came to blows with Rundberg at the end of the meeting, but McQueen didn't get mad—he got even. He placed his full public support behind environmentalist Marvin Braude in the 1965 Los Angeles City Council race and helped to unseat incumbent Rundberg. It appeared as if the civic lessons McQueen learned at the Boys Republic served him well.

McQueen's political clout shot through the roof when he received a phone call from Peter and Pat Lawford on behalf of the National Democratic Party, asking McQueen and Natalie Wood—the year's hottest screen couple—to cohost a fundraiser for President Lyndon Johnson's reelection campaign against conservative Barry Goldwater. Steve danced the Watusi with the First Teenager, Luci Baines Johnson, at the celebrity-studded barbeque called the Young Citizens for Johnson. Their dance-floor antics were captured by several photographers and made the front page of the *Los Angeles Times* and the evening news around the country. Years later, these images encapsulated a pop-culture moment.[6]

Johnson later thanked McQueen in a November 19, 1964, correspondence:

> *Dear Mr. McQueen:*
>
>   *Mrs. Johnson joins me in thanking you for your valuable participation in the campaign. A great deal of the success we achieved on November 3 was due to the time and talents that responsible citizens such as you gave to the effort.*
>
>   *The unity of the American people, demonstrated in this election, is both a great trust and great opportunity for us all. I pray that we may work together, as we have voted together, to keep our country safe, strong, and successful as we continue our responsible efforts to assure freedom's victory in a world of peace.*
>
>   *With warmest best wishes,*
>
>   *Sincerely,*
>
>   *Lyndon Johnson*

With "time out for good behavior," the McQueens hosted an August bash at the Castle and went all out by hiring Johnny Rivers as the musical guest and a Whisky dancer who gave free Watusi lessons to anyone who desired. It was a who's who of Hollywood that included A-listers such as Lee Marvin, Kirk Douglas, James Garner, James Coburn, Janet Leigh, Norman Jewison, Tuesday Weld, George Hamilton, Eva Marie Saint, John Cassavetes, Sharon Tate, Jay Sebring, and Robert Vaughn, who recalled a poignant exchange with McQueen in his memoir, *A Fortunate Life*. "It was a spectacular event, one that proclaimed the arrival of Steve and Neile McQueen as important figures in Hollywood. Around midnight, I found myself on the patio looking at the ocean. Steve joined me, and we had a chat. Then there was a long pause, not unusual in a conversation with Steve. Finally I said, 'When you were in New York in the '50s, living in a cold-water flat and courting Neile on your bike, did you ever think you'd end up this way?' There was another pause and, without looking at me, Steve replied, 'What makes you think I'm going to end up this way now?' After another pause, he walked away. I'll always miss his unique way of looking at life."

In September of that year, McQueen was picked to be a member of the United States team in the International Six Days Trials held in East Germany. There, McQueen and the four other members—Bud Ekins, Dave Ekins, Cliff Coleman, and John Steen—comprised the U.S. team that competed against top

---

6 This could also be the reason why President Richard Nixon inexplicably placed the normally non-partisan McQueen on his infamous "enemies list" almost a decade later.

racers from around the world.[7] The grueling cross-country race consisted of 250 miles every day for six days, taking racers through mountainous terrain and woods as well as along narrow paths and trails.[8]

When the team arrived in London, they partied to Olympic proportions, according to Bud Ekins. "One party, [Steve] had so many girls on his arms—good lookers, too—that he would forget which one he was with. He'd say he was going to leave, had a blonde on his arm, leave her in the hallway, go back into the party, start talking to another blonde, then bring her out into the hallway, and bump into the blonde he left in the hall. He did that many times that night," Ekins said.

The team rolled on into Erfurt, East Germany, where the communists got a taste of real power, said Dave Ekins. On the day before the race, all the teams were required to attend a dinner hosted at the Erfurt University gym. The meal consisted of cold cuts surrounded in eel. Everybody was about to dig in when McQueen, who was repulsed by the fish eye, stood up and waved the waiter over to his table. "Where does the jury eat?" McQueen asked. He was told they were dining at the elegant Erfurt Hof Hotel, which was just down the road. With that, McQueen stood up and told his teammates to follow his lead. Ekins recalled in amazement, "Our British and Swedish counterparts, who had watched the scene unfold, marched out as well and followed us to the Erfurt Hof Hotel for a grand dinner. We ate there the next day, and the rest of our meals were Western-style. The communists were forced to shape up their act because Steve was the only one among 300 contestants who said, 'I'm not going to eat that shit.' This is the kind of force the guy had."

McQueen also performed wonders when it came to thawing out Cold War relations. Ekins said that Steve charmed the female guards who were supposed to keep watch on the American capitalists. "The event was manned by the reserve military, and about 20 percent of them were females," Ekins said. "Steve and Bud partied and had their bit of fun, but they later paid the price in the race."

The first three days, Steve won bonus points toward the coveted gold medal, but at the end of the third day, he was unfortunately sideswiped by a spectator and sent down a steep ravine, cutting up his face, injuring his leg, and wrecking his motorcycle. He was forced out of the race. Ekins also broke his leg the same day.

Following the Trials, McQueen made a visit to Paris for the French premiere of *Love with the Proper Stranger*, and he struck an exclusive deal with *Paris Match*

---

7   Steen served as an alternate and earned a silver medal in the race.

8   Ekins said the team did not have to qualify or compete for the Six Days Trials. "The event was run by the Federation International of Motorcycles in Europe. We applied, paid the entry fee, and got in and rode."

magazine to follow his exploits, which included disco-filled nights; five-star restaurants; a department store promotion; a charity event; and an event where *Tele-7 Tours*, France's leading television magazine, gave him its prize for most popular foreign actor for *Wanted: Dead or Alive*.[9] This visit was such a triumphant success that he was obliged to don a disguise in the form of a mustache and goatee to walk the streets during the daytime. "It was really the first time I had ever experienced the paparazzi up close and personal," said Dave Ekins, who along with the other Trials teammates, pulled double duty as bodyguards. "That sort of fame was unnerving and gave me a good idea what must have been going on in Steve's head."

It didn't seem to bother McQueen, said publicist David Foster, who had a room next to the McQueens at the Le Creux Hotel in Paris. "It was a great week. The only part of that trip that was disconcerting to me was that [McQueen] was trapped in that hotel for two days. He was the single biggest movie star in France," Foster recalled. "Every time he walked out, thousands of kids would mob him. It was worse than the Beatles. He kept saying, 'I can't believe this is happening to a kid out of reform school. Can you believe this, Foster?' We thought that was so funny. It was a very happy time."

McQueen had now confirmed himself as part of Hollywood's elite. To maintain his momentum, he would have to keep up the pressure on himself and his image. This required making more films. After a year out of the studio, he would return and start to shoot *The Cincinnati Kid*. He was up against formidable Hollywood royalty in the form of costar Edward G. Robinson. McQueen would once again reveal his competitive streak and find a role that enhanced and consolidated his image of the intense loner, willing to do anything to reach the top. However, while this role would bring him further acclaim, it would also lead to rivalry, more battles, more wild stories, and even more women. Soon McQueen would find himself even closer to the edge.

---

9   France started syndication of the show on May 25, 1963. The series was a smash, and the French were crazy for McQueen's unique brand of cowboy cool.

20

THE BIG LEAGUES

AFTER A YEAR'S SABBATICAL FROM THE FILM INDUSTRY, Steve McQueen was ready to resume his acting career in late 1964. Of course, he was well compensated for stepping in front of the camera again—a then-staggering sum of $350,000.

McQueen chose *The Cincinnati Kid*, a card-shark drama, for his big-screen return. The script was based on the Richard Jessup novel about an up-and-coming stud poker player who is looking to topple Lancey Howard, aka The Man, who was an old and weary card champ.

McQueen is surrounded by an all-star cast that included Edward G. Robinson, Ann-Margret, Tuesday Weld, Karl Malden, Cab Calloway, and Joan Blondell. However, producer Martin Ransohoff knew who the star was and who would be the draw for cinema-goers. Ransohoff rolled out the red carpet and got MGM to spring for a luxurious 10-by-50-foot motor home that came with a bedroom, dressing room, full kitchen, wall-to-wall carpeting, and a living room filled with masculine-looking furniture in a heavy Spanish motif. McQueen used the quarters for lunch and scene breaks, conferences, bull sessions, and a place to entertain his costars. McQueen may have been playing the "kid" in the film, but on set he was "the man."[1]

Now that McQueen had almost full autonomy when it came to his pictures, he tried to recruit childhood idol Spencer Tracy to play Lancey Howard. It was an unfortunate career miscalculation for Tracy, who turned down the role, because it would have been great for an older actor. Edward G. Robinson, who later took the job, turned in a phenomenal performance. Tracy graciously turned down McQueen in an October 24, 1964, letter:

---

1 The crafty star even got producer Martin Ransohoff to spring for approximately 50 pairs of tailored jeans. It was eventually discovered that McQueen donated the clothes to Boys Republic.

Dear Steve,

 I'm sorry, too, that it didn't work out. I had felt from the book that it could develop into a very interesting part and a wonderful situation between them, but somehow the old man never came to life for me, and when you're my age, you just cannot play someone you don't comprehend. I think you are very wise to go ahead, for while it's not the book, it's a damn fine part. Many thanks for your notes. In another time I hope. Good luck.

 Sincerely yours,

  Spencer Tracy

As was the case with most of McQueen's films, the production had a troubled history from the outset. Before the picture was through, the toll included two screenwriters, a maverick director, useless footage, and a month-long shutdown that cost MGM Studios a hefty six-figure sum—all of which had nothing to do with McQueen, for once.

The first casualty was celebrated screenwriter Paddy Chayefsky (*Network*), who had a reputation as a wordy writer. McQueen asked Ransohoff to give Chayefsky one bit of advice. "Tell Paddy when he's writing that I'm much better walking than I am talking." Chayefsky, by all appearances, didn't heed the advice and had a different interpretation of the mystique present in New Orleans' culture of jazz, Creole, and the mighty Mississippi. Chayefsky turned in a character-driven piece rather than the action movie that Ransohoff had envisioned as a "gunfight with a deck of cards."

"What is this, Paddy?" Ransohoff asked.

"Let's do something else," Chayefsky replied.

The two men parted amicably, and Ransohoff enlisted Oscar-winner Ring Lardner Jr. (*M*A*S*H*) to rewrite his vision of the film. When Ransohoff had a finished script, he faced another big obstacle when he hired Sam Peckinpah to helm the picture. The iconoclastic director had a reputation for being wild, reckless, egotistical, and stubborn. His dislike of producers was inherent, which meant he and Ransohoff were doomed from the start. Peckinpah insisted the film be shot in black and white, while Ransohoff held the belief that the climatic scene near the end of the movie demanded the audience be able to read the color of the cards. Moreover, films that were shot in color almost guaranteed a break-even point after the sale of television rights. Black-and-white movies no longer had the box-office pull of color films, and studios always had an eye toward the bottom line. Yet Peckinpah won that battle, temporarily.

Peckinpah personally rankled Ransohoff by not hiring actress Sharon Tate, whom the producer was grooming for stardom. Recalled Ransohoff, "Sharon screen-tested for the picture and did very well. I liked her very much." Peckinpah wasn't as impressed and awarded the role to Tuesday Weld, another Ransohoff protégée.

Cameras rolled the first week of November, and Peckinpah had pushed his luck too far by not sticking to the script. He had filmed two unscripted sequences that were wildly disparate—a riot scene involving approximately 300 extras, and a nude scene between a wealthy businessman and a black prostitute. Ransohoff envisioned his film going way over budget and ending up with an X rating, to boot. Peckinpah was also a hard drinker, a loose cannon unwilling to compromise. Ransohoff convinced the studio it was in their best interest to fire Peckinpah, shut down the production, and regroup. The studio paid the cast and crew to go home while they searched for a new director.[2]

Agent Stan Kamen felt it was an opportune time to introduce Ransohoff to another client—director Norman Jewison. He was a most unlikely candidate given that he was primarily a television director with a pair of lightweight Doris Day films on his résumé. Kamen, who was vital in McQueen's upward career trajectory, lobbied equally as hard for Jewison. The Canadian-born director had a unique perspective of the situation. "For me, the movie was about winning and losing. Winning is more important in the U.S. than in any other country," Jewison said.

The director found the script "turgid and melodramatic" and thought it needed an injection of lightness, wit, and irony. He insisted on three weeks to rework the Lardner script and enlisted Terry Southern (*Dr. Strangelove*, *Easy Rider*) to stamp his indelible print on the work. Jewison also made a key hire in Hal Ashby, who was arguably the best editor in the film industry and later a director whose movies practically defined the '70s.[3] But Jewison had yet to pass the most important test of all—the McQueen test.

Jewison recalled visiting McQueen at the Castle and found Neile instantly approachable and likable. Her husband was another story. Jewison felt McQueen was guarded, distant, and suspicious. "I didn't mind an actor feeling me out in order to judge the approach I intended to take to the character he was hired to play. But Steve went far beyond that," Jewison said. "He was testing me to determine whether he'd admit me to his private club."

---

2   MGM also gave McQueen $25,000 in cash and sent him to Las Vegas to refine his poker skills.

3   Ashby's film output during the '70s is unparalleled. In that decade he directed *Harold and Maude*, *The Last Detail*, *Bound for Glory*, *Shampoo*, *Coming Home*, and *Being There*.

Back on the set, Jewison sensed McQueen was holding back and did not take direction very well. At the end of one particular day, Jewison and McQueen sat down on the curb of a New Orleans street and had a heart-to-heart talk.

"Steve, I don't know what you want from me. Maybe you're looking for a father figure. God knows I can't be that. But I'll tell you what I can be," Jewison said. "How about we think of me as your older brother, the one who went to college? I'm the educated older brother, and I will always look out for you." Jewison's words struck a chord, and he saw that he had McQueen's full attention. Finally, McQueen nodded, and the two seemed to have an understanding—that is, until McQueen asked if he could see the dailies. Jewison immediately became suspicious.

"Why do you want to watch them?" Jewison asked. "You want to check if I'm doing my job? You want to watch yourself? What I think is that the actor should concentrate strictly on his acting. Watching the dailies can throw an actor off. You should forget the dailies. You should rely on your director for guidance. A certain amount of trust is needed on this movie." McQueen was thrown by Jewison's rational and erudite reply and didn't know how to respond.

"You're twistin' my melon, man. You're twistin' my melon. You're getting me all mixed up," McQueen said. Jewison had no clue what a melon was but asked McQueen to trust him. It was a rare moment and McQueen finally gave in, saying that he would rely on Jewison as his "older brother" to tell him if he was going in the wrong direction. A few weeks later, Jewison assembled some footage for McQueen and allowed the actor to see his performance. He liked what he saw and never brought up the matter again. Jewison said he forgave McQueen's personality quirks because of his fragile soul. "I felt he was hurt badly when he was a child," Jewison said. "He had difficulty in relationships, and yet he had such believability. When I looked through that camera, I would believe him."

Costar Karl Malden was certainly made a believer after an intense scene with McQueen, which defined part of Steve's electric charisma. "Steve McQueen recognized the important challenge when he made The Cincinnati Kid, and I felt that he achieved the big leagues with this movie," Malden said. "I played the part of a professional card dealer called Shooter, dealing in favor of the kid [McQueen] so that he would win the game. He wanted to take some time off to rest, and he asked me to accompany him. Once in his room, he confronted me with the question, 'Are you cheating?' McQueen sprung at me like a tiger. He had the quality of appearing so tense and high that he was ready to explode at any minute."

McQueen's anger toward Malden, it seemed, was quite real. Malden said in another scene he accidentally placed his hand on McQueen's shoulder and incurred his wrath. "Don't ever touch me," McQueen said, stopping dead in his tracks. Malden smiled in return, trying to defuse the situation. It didn't work.

"Do you have a problem with that?" McQueen growled. Malden was baffled. It seemed as if McQueen was genuinely miffed at him, but he couldn't figure out why.

"No, but where did you ever pick that up?" Malden asked.

"I just don't like it."

The two did the scene again, but this time Malden didn't lay a finger on McQueen. Later that year when Malden worked with the temperamental star again in *Nevada Smith*, he eventually learned the real truth from an agent at William Morris. "Years before [1953] when I had been casting *Tea and Sympathy* for Kazan in New York, I guess I had seen Steve for the lead, though I had no memory of him," Malden said. "He didn't get the part and, apparently, he held it against me all that time. I still say he wasn't right for the part." McQueen never forgot when someone tried to outdo him or take what he thought was rightfully his. He had developed quite a grudge from the hard time he had trying to break into acting, and now that he had established himself, he never failed to settle a score, whether it was well-founded or not. McQueen could never let go and simply enjoy his success and fruits of his labor; everything had to have an edge or an angle.

The only actor on the set who equalized McQueen was film veteran Edward G. Robinson, whom McQueen felt was stealing the movie from him. "Steve was a little nervous about Eddie Robinson," Jewison confirmed. "Eddie was a star, true Hollywood royalty. A sign of insecurity is when another actor looks away. And Steve always used to look down on his feet, then look up at you. Then he'd look away again."

But Robinson sensed in McQueen a special talent and realized the irony of the situation. "Once, back at the start of my career, I had been another McQueen," Robinson said. "I'd played the same kind of parts, cocky and tough, ready to take on the old timers and beat them at their own game. I identified strongly with McQueen, and I had a lot of respect for his talent."

Robinson was immensely talented himself and hugely experienced. This brought out McQueen's competitive drive and insecurities about his own acting abilities. He was understandably concerned about being outclassed by one of the all-time greats. McQueen would never admit this though, and he used some of his old tricks. Just as he had done to Yul Brynner on *The Magnificent Seven*, McQueen tried to steal every scene from Robinson. There is a moment when the two characters take a break from their poker game and have a chat. While they talk and fix drinks, McQueen picks up a lemon wedge and sucks it. This is a masterstroke in the use of props and demonstrates McQueen's uncanny ability to know what the camera picks up. With two people on screen, how can the viewer do anything else but ignore Robinson temporarily and focus on McQueen sucking a lemon?

The two actors interface well with each other, especially in the stud poker showdown at the end of the picture. The Kid has had the Man on the run throughout the game, and the finale boils down to one hand. McQueen has calculated in his head all the possible combinations in the Man's hand. However, he does not calculate for a royal flush, a million-to-one long shot, which Robinson uses to gut the Cincinnati Kid.

"Gets down to what it's all about—making the wrong move at the right time," says the debonair Robinson, who strikes a match, lights up a cigar, and tells McQueen, "You're good, kid, but as long as I'm around, you're second-best. You might as well learn to live with it."

McQueen loses the card game, loses the girl,[4] and finally loses a game of pitching pennies at the end of a film to a street urchin. But he came away a grand winner at the box office—*The Cincinnati Kid* earned nearly $10 million worldwide.[5]

The picture's success swept up everyone in its wake. It reestablished Robinson's career, opened up Jewison's future, and cemented McQueen's status as a global star. *The Cincinnati Kid* was the first of his five back-to-back worldwide hits and earned McQueen a slot as a top 10 box-office champ for the next decade.

Steve McQueen was on a roll.

In the summer of 1965, Steve McQueen had planned on attending the Moscow Film Festival in late July. The festival, which was in its sixth year at the time, had awarded McQueen a Silver Prize for Best Actor for his performance as Hilts in *The Great Escape*. McQueen, who had screamed Americana, was strangely adored in Eastern Europe and Russia. But it was not meant to be. The shooting schedule for *Nevada Smith* had been pushed up a few weeks and conflicted with his appearance, so he never stepped foot in Russia.

In *Nevada Smith*, McQueen returned to the Western genre that had made him a household name, and Paramount Studios was willing to pay McQueen $500,000 and a percentage of the profits. The film, written by John Michael

---

4   MGM revised the overseas version, which showed McQueen and Tuesday Weld walking off happily into the sunset. It worked. The film was enormously popular abroad.

5   That amount would be equivalent to $112 million in 2010.

Hayes and based on the memorable character created by Harold Robbins, is a prequel to *The Carpetbaggers*.[6]

The revenge drama was directed by Henry Hathaway (*How the West Was Won*, *True Grit*) and features a glittering all-star cast that includes Brian Keith, Karl Malden, Arthur Kennedy, Raf Vallone, Howard Da Silva, Martin Landau, and Suzanne Pleshette, whose addition to the roster caught McQueen off guard. Pleshette said she and McQueen were at the same Hollywood party when she casually asked him if he knew who the leading lady was in *Nevada Smith*. McQueen pleaded ignorance.

"Me!" said the husky-voiced actress. McQueen's hand slapped his forehead and exclaimed, "God, no. You've got to be kidding?"

The two had known each other since his lean New York days and, like Nancy Malone before her, was an "adopted sister" that McQueen immediately wanted to keep safe. "I was 14 at the time and was with an older man that Steve had known at an actor's party," Pleshette said. "He just thought we were an inappropriate couple and offered me a ride home on his motorcycle. From that day until the day Steve died, he always treated me like a baby sister, and he was always very protective and loving toward me. I was just crazy about him. I don't know for what reasons he decided to become my protector—maybe I reminded him of someone—and it lasted our mutual lifetime."

McQueen's relationship with Hathaway also took on a familial posture, with Hathaway taking up the pseudo-father role. The gruff director set the tone for the actor in a private meeting at Hathaway's Paramount office. Hathaway knew of McQueen's reputation for being difficult and wanted no surprises before he took over the $4.5 million production. Hathaway himself was an established and highly respected director of the old guard from the John Ford era and was certainly not the type to take any of McQueen's bad-boy behavior. "Now, Mr. McQueen, I want you to know something. I'm the boss. Nobody argues with me. I'm not putting up with any shit from you, and if I do get any shit from you, I won't hesitate to deck you," Hathaway said with a shake of his fist. "I don't want any of this star-complex bullshit. We're a family out there. We're making a movie. Going to put in a lot of long hours. The crew's working just as hard as you are. If you've got some ideas, I'll listen. But don't you get bullheaded and scream and holler at me, because I'll holler and scream back. I'm the meanest son-of-bitch that ever was!"

---

6   *The Carpetbaggers* was a 1964 film starring George Peppard with Alan Ladd in the Nevada Smith role.

After a long pause, McQueen smiled and offered his hand to Hathaway. "All right, Mr. Hathaway. You've got a deal. That's it, Dad."

Hathaway never had a problem with the superstar, who reported to the set a half-hour early every day and often asked the director if his takes were good enough. Hathaway in turn called Steve "son." It was unprecedented and unlike any other relationship McQueen had ever had with another director, including John Sturges. Psychologist Peter O. Whitmer said the dynamics between Steve McQueen and Henry Hathaway may well have been fleeting and compressed in time and place. Regardless, they affected Steve's behavior in a positive and productive way.

"In the interpersonal style of Hathaway, McQueen found a new 'equation' for a relationship," Whitmer said. "If he did not try and manipulate the man with his side tactics, then he found more than a clean slate—he found unconditional positive regard and a parental-like appreciation of his talent and ability to walk the straight and narrow and deliver the goods. Hathaway liked that, and McQueen liked the fact that Hathaway liked that. It was a win-win deal.

"Here was one relationship that could not only *not* be 'tinkered' with, it could *not* be denied. Hathaway was at the pinnacle of Steve McQueen's industry. Like an orchestra's conductor and his numerous musicians, there is but one director… and hundreds of actors.

"Steve McQueen looked at Hathaway and saw—perhaps just for one brief filming moment—an older person possessed of 'good.' [He was] successful, manly, a straight shooter who was above playing games. This made things simple for Steve. Plus, here was someone established and widely known who saw through to the polished diamond that McQueen could be when he wanted to."

The first portion of *Nevada Smith* was shot in the bayous of the Atchafalaya Basin and in the prison compound of Fort Vincent in Baton Rouge. While there, McQueen and the crew encountered leeches, spiders, snakes, and lots of mud. Several crew members got spooked and even quit the movie when they witnessed the local reptile community up close.

Hathaway recognized that McQueen was a free spirit who was often restless and couldn't be confined to the backwoods and river banks. Understanding McQueen perfectly, Hathaway arranged for him to be given something with a motor—a small boat to putter around with when he wasn't working. Suzanne Pleshette thought it was a brilliant move. "Henry Hathaway was difficult, but he was a great psychologist and a wonderful filmmaker," Pleshette said. "He really knew how to handle Steve, knew how to make him comfortable. What every good professional director should know. He knew that Steve had a lot of energy. That was the wonderful thing about Steve; he had this sense of energy, always going, a wonderful sense of physical ability to react quickly, which is very appealing about him as an actor. When we were out in the swamp, Henry knew there was no way that Steve could just sit still on this raft with the rest of us. He kept Steve's energy up and didn't make him feel he was trapped, which was always so dreadful for Steve."

Pleshette was referring to a sequence where McQueen's character, Max Sand, is sent to prison. The setup clearly upset him, Pleshette said. "It seemed difficult for him, that sequence. He was sharing some feelings with me that night that led me to believe he was incarcerated at some time in his life. That was difficult for him to be in a similar situation, even as an actor knowing that he could leave."

What McQueen found even more difficult was a love scene between him and Pleshette where the two had to lock lips in a big-screen kiss. "It was the hardest thing for us to do," Pleshette said, laughing. "It was so awkward; we didn't know where to put our lips. We never thought of each other that way, and we were just terrible at it." Pleshette knew of McQueen's habit of bedding his costars, and she teased him mightily about his pucker power. After the scene was finished, she told him, "You are the absolute worst kisser in the world!"

Nevada Smith was a plodding, straight-by-the-numbers western with McQueen's performance taking a step back, artistically speaking. The picture did well financially despite the fact that McQueen was essentially miscast. He turned in a good performance, but he was still a 35-year-old man playing an 18-year-old half-breed who gradually matures despite adversity. It is quite a bizarre role in this respect. McQueen manages to just about pull off the age gap mainly due to his nature. The energy and restlessness of McQueen were perfect for the part, because he was still a child at heart.

Stuntman Loren Janes, who doubled McQueen on the picture, said Steve admitted he wasn't crazy about his performance and probably acquiesced too easily to Hathaway. "There were things about the picture that he didn't like, things he wanted to change but wasn't able to." Film critics seemed to agree that McQueen wasn't at his finest. Wanda Hale of the *New York Daily News* called it a "tedious Western with too little suspense." *Variety* wrote, "Although excess footage is a prime heavy in the film's impact, McQueen's erratic performance also detracts." *Time* magazine opined, "Steve McQueen, unmistakably modern, looks as if he would be more at home in the saddle of a Harley-Davidson than on a horse."

Whatever McQueen or the critics felt about *Nevada Smith*, it proved amazingly popular with audiences, grossing $12 million[7] in the United States alone. Overseas it fared even better, establishing McQueen as the modern-day American

---

7   If adjusted for inflation, *Nevada Smith*'s box-office gross amounts to $129 million in 2010 dollars.

hero. In Japan, audiences were taken with the story of honor and revenge that echoed their own samurai films, as hero Max Sand hunts down his parents' killers. Mounted police in Trinidad were called four times in one day to quell the crowds outside a theater where people were ready to break down the doors to see the film. No other film star during his box-office reign caused such a frenzied reaction.

"Real stars, like Steve McQueen and John Wayne, are worth their weight in gold," said one producer. Scripts came pouring into the William Morris office to the tune of 20 per week, while studios were offering up to 50 percent of the gross if McQueen would sign his name on the dotted line. McQueen, it seemed, had the Midas touch.

• • •

Steve McQueen was a person trying to live many lives at once—a Hollywood star, a racer, a Casanova, and a family man. However, he was never able to sustain all of these personas at the same time. Something would always give. He had just about found a comfortable groove for himself where everything was in balance on many levels, but fortune is frequently followed by tragedy. On October 14, 1965, Steve and Neile were preparing to leave Los Angeles for the New Orleans premiere of *The Cincinnati Kid* the following day when they received a distressing phone call. Julian had suffered a massive cerebral hemorrhage and lay comatose in San Francisco's Mount Zion Hospital.

After Steve started his own family, the strained and complex relationship between Julian and Steve had finally reached a point where they could communicate again. His stardom made Julian proud—she often saw each film at least twice. Her apartment was filled with pictures, magazines, and articles about her famous son. Plus she doted on his children.

McQueen's sudden wealth had allowed him to subsidize Julian, who migrated to San Francisco's North Beach in the early '60s. It was the West Coast version of Greenwich Village, filled with artists, beatniks, coffeehouses, and smoke-laden atmospheres.

He sent her money through a business manager, paid the $90 monthly rent on a small Houston Street apartment, and set her up in a boutique shop. Steve periodically sent pictures of six-year-old Terry and four-year-old Chad, but the photographs rarely contained letters. He had also designated a room for Julian at the Castle when she visited on the rare occasion, but her stopovers never lasted long. Inevitably Julian would get antsy after a few days and spoiled their visits by getting tipsy. It was often too much for Steve to bear; he was still bitter toward Julian, according to publicist David Foster. "[Steve] took great care of his mother, but every time he mentioned her, it was with great hostility and anger. 'That bitch! That drunk! She fucked up my life. She never gave a shit about me—here's another check.' It was a very complicated relationship."

McQueen still found it hard to discuss Julian with anyone, let alone reporters, and he clearly drew a line of demarcation for those who probed. "Whatever thing I've got with my mother is a private thing and I'm not about to discuss it with anybody," McQueen said to *Photoplay* magazine. "If it means hurting her feelings to give a good story, I know which I'm going to choose."

Julian's life had often been defined by men, but at the end of her life she was no longer interested in the opposite sex. The once striking blonde from the Midwest was now older, and time and drink had taken their toll on her, but not her zeal for life. Friends described her as loyal, creative, and always laughing. She enjoyed visiting with friends and acquaintances and hand-stitching clothes for her grandchildren, and she planned on going into the travel business with one of her friends.

Aside from the odd personality quirks—crash diets, herbal remedies, and inventing odd knick-knacks and crafts—friends noticed that Julian had started behaving strangely the previous month. Two weeks before her collapse, she was irrationally irritable, often complaining about another neighbor's cat and baby.

When Steve received the phone call that Julian's life was in peril, he and Neile immediately canceled all of their plans and caught a midnight flight to San Francisco. The two didn't talk much on the plane. Steve had talked to his mother during the week, and she'd been having a ball driving her used $400 convertible Volkswagen, courtesy of her son.

Whatever hostilities he had toward Julian, Steve put them aside. He kept vigil, never leaving her bedside. Neile recalled, "Steve kept hoping that she would recover. He had so much to say to her, but now she was dying and slipping away. Unfortunately, she never recovered and, at that point, he just sat down and sobbed." Friend Pat Johnson elaborated, "Steve had this love/hate relationship with his mother. He felt that she deserted him, that she turned her back on him, and yet she loved him and did the best that she could. She just was not maternal. There were a lot of things he wanted to say to her that were never resolved. He regretted the fact that he had never opened up to her, just as later in his life he regretted that he had never opened up to the public in general. In fact, his relationship with all the women in his life was probably influenced by his mother."

During the bedside vigil, a fan had shyly approached McQueen in the hospital for an autograph. His chest suddenly heaved with anger, and just as quickly he caught himself. He shook his head no and gently said, "Sorry, but the timing isn't too good." Steve stayed with Julian until 5:00 AM, hoping she'd regain consciousness. She never did. On October 15, 1965, 55-year-old Julian Crawford McQueen Berri died.

When Steve and Neile went to Julian's apartment to gather up her possessions, they found on a sewing table a dress Julian had been making for granddaughter Terry. "[Steve and Julian] were so similar in temperament, both terribly independent, both with a wonderful lust for life, so of course they butted their heads and sometimes had their problems," Neile said. "But Steve loved her deeply and was deeply aware that she was the last remaining member of his family."

Steve didn't have the emotional strength to make the funeral arrangements, so the task fell to Neile. He did summon up the wherewithal to issue a mandate to Julian's friends. "No interviews about my mother's death. No interviews. No reporter's going to be allowed to know anything." Fans felt McQueen's loss and sent flowers in her honor. He respectfully requested all donations be sent to Boys Republic.

Julian was buried in a shaded plot in Gardens of Ascension, Forest Lawn Memorial Park, in Glendale, California, on October 20. Attendants included Neile, Terry, Chad, agent Stan Kamen, and publicist David Foster and his wife, Jackie. There was no priest, minister, clergyman, or anyone with a religious affiliation. Only Steve spoke. "Julian liked shade," Steve said. "She would have liked this spot…shady with no sun." With tears streaming down his face, Steve stood next to his mother's casket, folded his hands and prayed. "Steve may have been a bastard, literally, but he cried at the funeral," Foster said. "He was a lost soul."

After three-and-a-half decades, Steve was finally forced to accept the finality of his complicated relationship with William and Julian. His parents had passed, but Steve's pain would remain. Though separated by a distance of only 30 miles, each parent was buried in wildly disparate locales—William in a pauper's grave in Long Beach, while Julian rested in the cemetery equivalent of the Taj Mahal. Both of Steve's parents were now gone, and he was forever physically cut off from his roots and his past. The heartache of not being able to fully reconcile with his mother or meet his father left Steve with a pain he would carry around for the rest of his life. McQueen was finally starting to make some sense of his life, but this was cruelly denied. Their deaths did not provide closure; they were open wounds. Steve had power, fame, fortune, and success, but none of these would change the fact that he was an abandoned kid who had just been abandoned again. Almost every relationship he had would be influenced by this void. Though McQueen tried to hide it away inside himself, the repercussions of this trauma would occasionally manifest itself throughout his life.

21

TOP GEAR

BY THE MID-'60S, STEVE MCQUEEN HAD THE WORLD by a golden string. There was only one thing that seemed to elude him—the respect of his acting peers. His next picture, *The Sand Pebbles*, eradicated the notion that McQueen was a personality suited only to action vehicles. The emotionally charged and tragic role also silenced his critics and established him as a highly talented actor with an impressive range and ability. When the epic film was released a year later, McQueen's peer group suddenly realized a great actor was in their midst.

"I'm an interpreter," McQueen said. "I represent a whole lot of guys my age who finally looked around and said, 'Hey, somebody's been lying to us.' Guys who suddenly found out they're a lot smarter than some of the head honchos sitting up there pushing buttons in the front offices."

McQueen had planned to deliver a one-two punch to cinema lovers with *Day of the Champion*, a race film about the Formula One circuit, and *The Sand Pebbles*, an action-drama about an enlisted Navy man in war-torn China in the '20s.

Day of the Champion was firmly rooted in turmoil and was one of the few races that Steve McQueen ever lost. McQueen and director John Frankenheimer were on the same page when they wanted to adapt Robert Daley's *The Cruel Sport* into a movie called *Grand Prix*. Daley was quite receptive to the idea, and Frankenheimer commenced negotiations with McQueen. A few days later, McQueen bumped heads with producer Ed Lewis, who was going to make the film with Frankenheimer. McQueen then contacted John Sturges, who was not only his mentor but also someone he could connect with as a racing enthusiast, and they began silent negotiations with Daley. "Sturges believed that you should always base your movie on something—didn't matter if it was a foreign film, a book, a newspaper article, or a poem; he felt basing a film on something added legitimacy, and no one could say you stole the idea," said Robert Relyea, who was Sturges' assistant director and was responsible for setting up the production.

A bidding war erupted between the Mirisch Corporation; United Artists, who produced *The Great Escape*; and Warner Brothers, who was more established and had stronger financial backing and better distribution. Warners tendered a substantially higher offer to Sturges and McQueen, and the picture was officially green-lighted...but not before Frankenheimer scored a deal with MGM. The race was on, and the checkered flag had been waved between the two rival parties. The rivalry would prove to be a contest with more drama than most speedway clashes.

Sturges and Frankenheimer attended a benefit dinner in Hollywood the night before both deals were announced. Frankenheimer was an ardent admirer of Sturges' work and pulled up a seat next to the veteran director. Sturges quietly picked at his food while Frankenheimer excitedly told him and the entire table about his next project—a car racing feature.

"We're calling it *Grand Prix*," Frankenheimer said, not having a clue that his idol was poised to make a similar picture. "I'm basing it on a fantastic book of photographs I discovered called *The Cruel Sport*." Sturges kept a poker face the rest of the evening and remained silent.

Sturges had cut his deal with the author's literary agent while Frankenheimer had dealt directly with Daley. Neither Daley nor his literary agent communicated with each other about the deal. The following morning, both projects were announced in the trades with each citing *The Cruel Sport* as its source material for the respective films. "No one in Hollywood wants to make a movie on the same subject at the same time as another studio—especially about racing," said Robert Relyea. There might be enough of an audience for one film, but the market could not bear two. It became an ugly fight to see who could complete their film first.

The two crews faced off at the 1965 Grand Prix Race in Monaco in late May. McQueen and Sturges were there to recruit drivers, while Frankenheimer gathered a small film crew and got the upper hand. Sturges retaliated by getting studio head Jack Warner to spring for a full-page trade ad announcing principal photography for *Day of the Champion* at Nürburgring, Germany, where he shot loads of racing footage of a man in a green helmet. He also began constructing a script with Ken Purdy, a well-known sportswriter. The two competing directors were flying all around the world, hiring racing crews away from each other and trading personal insults the entire time. In wasn't long until the tension spilled over physically, resulting in an altercation in Monte Carlo, where the two crews faced off, calling each other out for a fight.

While Sturges was preoccupied with *Day of the Champion*, the time had come for McQueen to film *The Sand Pebbles* in Taiwan, but Sturges told McQueen that he had a handle on everything. "You go to Taiwan, and I'll set up the picture," Sturges said.

McQueen was no doubt thriving on the rivalry to get his racing picture made, and his competitive nature probably went into overdrive. His personality was such that he would throw all his energy at something if he believed in it, and few things could hold his imagination and desire as much as being paid to make a racing picture with almost total autonomy. But now he was forced to take his focus and attention away from his pet project and step back in time to a period film in an unbearable climate. He also had to relocate his whole family for several months.

Jake Holman, McQueen's character in *The Sand Pebbles*, was the embodiment of the loner; he was a rebel at odds with himself and his environment. Holman is arguably McQueen's most complex character up to this point—an unlikely hero who finds it easier working among the gears and pistons of an engine room than he does fellow sailors. McQueen perfectly conveys the character's unease as a sailor at war, conflicted between doing his duty on the boat yet wanting to explore a possible future with the missionaries. Never before had he been challenged in this way. The role stands as one of McQueen's finest, showing his ability to combine action, romance, and tragedy in a thoroughly believable and moving performance.

The Sand Pebbles is based on Richard McKenna's first novel, which spent 28 weeks on the *New York Times* best-seller list in 1962. Academy Award–winning director Robert Wise, who had just won Oscars for Best Picture and Best Director for *The Sound of Music*, had optioned the book the year it was released.

Following *The Sound of Music*,[1] 20th Century Fox gave Wise the red-carpet treatment, and the musical practically bankrolled *The Sand Pebbles'* $8 million production along with McQueen's $650,000 salary. With each film, McQueen's salary had increased substantially; less than 10 years before, McQueen could barely get a paid acting job, and now he was getting more than half a million per film. Wise felt McQueen was the perfect choice for Jake Holman. "I've never seen an actor work with mechanical things the way he does. He learned everything about operating that ship's engine, just as Jake Holman did, in the script," Wise said. "Jake Holman is a very strong individual who doesn't bend under pressure,

---

1 The movie grossed a then-staggering sum of $165 million in 1965 and cost $8.5 million. At the time of its release, *The Sound of Music* was the most successful musical in history until *Grease* in 1978.

a guy desperately determined to maintain his own personal identity and pride. Very much like Steve."

The Sand Pebbles was the first major American film shot entirely in Taiwan. Wise brought with him a 111-man crew, with 47 speaking parts and 32 interpreters, and he recruited thousands of extras for several crowd scenes. He also had the studio build the most expensive prop ever for a film—a $250,000 re-creation of a 1920s gunboat called the *San Pablo*. As was the case with almost all water-related films, *The Sand Pebbles* was plagued by a series of unpredictable weather and tides, cost overruns, and production setbacks, which turned the original 80-day shoot into an seven-month ordeal. It was without a doubt the most difficult assignment in McQueen's career. "Anything I ever did wrong," Steve confessed, "I paid for in Taiwan."

The McQueen family flew to Taiwan in late November 1965 and spent a few weeks at the Grand Hotel in Taipei before settling into a rented villa outside the city. McQueen extended greetings to his two costars—Richard Crenna and Candice Bergen—before cameras rolled. Crenna recalled, "Steve and I had a wonderful relationship. I first met him prior to arriving in Taiwan to shoot *The Sand Pebbles*. Later, while settling into the hotel there with my wife and children, the phone rang. It was Steve. 'Hey, Dick,' he said. 'I'd like to come over and shuck.' I looked over at my wife and said, 'What the hell is *shuck*?' He wanted to see how we would fit together in the great scheme of things and whether the filming was going to be a collaborative effort or a competition. After talking for about 10 minutes, I saw him relax, and we realized that we had quite a journey ahead of us on the film.

"He was complicated in the sense that he was ambitious but had insecurities that manifested themselves in interesting ways. He was a superlative actor, and without a doubt, *The Sand Pebbles* was my favorite Steve McQueen picture. He had never been better than he was in the film. You hear the comment 'born to play this role.' [McQueen] was born to play this role."

Actress Candice Bergman said McQueen took on the role of her protector and included her in many family activities when the two weren't filming. She said that experience gave her an up-close look at McQueen, who was a man of many moods. "Steve clearly suffered emotionally in life. He had experienced a painful and difficult childhood, and he was a textbook case of that kind of neglect," Bergen said. "He grew up in Boys Town [Republic], and I think he carried the pain with him all his life. The hostility and resentment he felt caused tremendous mistrust and anger, and he was constantly testing people. He really simmered, which made him such a complicated, interesting, and appealing presence on screen.

"He was compelling in the role of Jake Holman because you saw him experiencing the dilemmas of the role, which he communicated powerfully. He was also unpredictable, and that's what was so charismatic about him on screen. He projected a tremendous sense of threat and menace. You just didn't know with him, and he could turn on a dime either way. He could be unbelievably endearing and then so mistrustful."

The movie got off to an ominous start with the Keelung River, where the *San Pablo* was supposed to dock, at low tide, and the cast and crew sat around waiting for two weeks. Torrential rains also added another three weeks to the production, and sometimes the cast and crew got up to a handful of daily assignations. Several members of the crew were dumped into the same river when a 15-foot camera boat sank, which held some very expensive equipment, including a sound control panel, setting the film's schedule even further back. Despite the run of bad luck, everyone seemed to make do, according to extra Steve Ferry. "We spent a lot of time together," Ferry said. "We were all trapped on a little boat, and we amused ourselves as best as we could: playing, diving, swimming, all those warm-water things."

McQueen also observed and explored the people and the landscape of the Orient. "The thing is, everything is different over there. I mean all of life from top to bottom," McQueen said. "It was wild. Like they say, 'That's a nice shirt you've got on,' and what they mean is, 'There's a spot on it.'" Steve and Neile also discovered an orphanage run by Catholic priest Edward Wojniak. The orphanage assisted young girls, who were mainly prostitutes heading into a life of indentured servitude in the sex trade. McQueen donated $25,000 to the mission and continued to support it throughout his lifetime. Stuntman Loren Janes revealed, "Steve supported that mission even after Father Wojniak's death [in the late '70s]. [McQueen] sent them money; he sent them clothes; he sent them autographed pictures. And remember, he didn't sign pictures. He just reached out to help. Steve was a very generous man. He would give the shirt off his back to anyone who needed it."[2]

Janes also recalled a stolen moment on the *San Pablo* with McQueen, where the two feasted on 'American contraband' away from the cast and crew. "I brought a bunch of bananas to the set. Steve had the studio send him jam from California," Janes said. "Our favorite sandwiches were peanut butter, banana, and jam sandwiches. Over in Taiwan, we were eating Oriental food every night, and we were getting sick of it. The jam finally arrived, and Steve and I sneaked into

---

2   McQueen also donated $50,000 to go toward earthquake relief victims in Peru in October 1966.

one of the little rooms on the ship because we didn't want to share our bananas and jam with anyone. In fact, Steve stole a loaf of bread on the ship, and I got the silverware and we sliced the bananas into big, thick chunks. We ruined our wardrobe and we had to go change because we got jam stains all over us. We were so sneaky about it. We didn't have to steal the stuff, but it was more fun that way."

When filming did commence, Wise found himself tested and sometimes exasperated by McQueen, who tried to take control of the picture by insisting on shooting scenes differently. Finally, Wise came up with a solution—he shot two versions of almost every scene. If McQueen liked his own version better when the film was in the editing process, then Wise would accommodate him. This tedious procedure prolonged filming and swelled the shooting budget.[3] Wise said of his star, "The thing with Steve was you never quite knew what his mood was going to be. Once I was trying to line up a dolly shot. It was difficult, and then all of a sudden, I felt a tap on my shoulder and it was Steve. He said, 'Now, Bob, about this wardrobe,' and I blew up. I said, "Steve, for heaven's sake." I used a little stronger language than that, frankly. 'Please don't bring that up now, I'm in the midst of something difficult. Let's talk about it tonight.' Well, he was really hurt, and he didn't speak to me for three days. Here I was directing the star of the film and he took directions and he was in the scenes and he would listen to me, but he did not speak one word to me for three days. When Steve saw the dailies and how good he looked, he decided to talk to me again. As a matter of fact, Steve never gave me a hard time again."

McQueen knew his strengths and played them to his advantage to produce some amazing scenes. The unforgettable scene where he enters the engine room for the first time and introduces himself to the steel mass, "Hello engine, I'm Jake Holman," is a remarkable moment. He interacts with the engine as though he had constructed it himself. This quality of acting gives his performance an incredible authenticity. Although McQueen fell back on his use of props, he also managed to extend and refine his acting range considerably. In the scene where his character shoots his friend Po-Han in a mercy killing, he raises his rifle, adjusts the sight, takes aim, and then pauses to reflect. McQueen is stunning, and his pause feels like an eternity before he decides on what he *must* do. At this moment, he reveals his own character's vulnerability and internal conflict while ratcheting up the tension for the audience to an unbearable level. It is a landmark moment in McQueen's career. Never before had he been presented with an opportunity to convey such depth. It is an achievement both for the film and McQueen himself,

---

3   Incidentally, not one of McQueen's takes made it into the final version of *The Sand Pebbles*.

not only because of the caliber of the performance he delivers but also in the way it shows how he was able to channel his own emotion into his character.

Stand-in John Norris recalled an intense scene McQueen experienced with costar Candice Bergen, in which she tries to persuade Jake Holman to go AWOL. While the lighting, sound, and cameras were being attended to, McQueen and Bergen were off in makeup, and Wise was running the stand-ins to go through the scene. Norris recalled when the two actors arrived on the set, "Steve was uneasy with everyone around. Mr. Wise asked all nonessential people to leave, but Steve signaled that I should stay. Surprisingly, there seemed to be a little tension about the kiss," Norris said. "At the suggestion of going AWOL, his response was supposed to be something to the effect of, 'Do you know what they will do when they find me?' I think there was supposed to be a pause before Steve continued the dialogue, but Candy responded, 'What?' Steve never missed a beat and said, 'They would cut my fucking balls off!'" Everyone howled with laughter. This broke the tension, and the scene was reshot. I think Candy still had a smile on her face."

The smile was wiped from McQueen's face when he received a long-distance phone call from James Garner, who informed Steve that Garner had been signed to star in *Grand Prix*. It was a magnanimous gesture on Garner's part, but McQueen didn't see it that way. He was the only actor who had the necessary tools and chutzpah to play the lead in a realistic movie about car racing and felt Garner was encroaching on his territory. When the phone call ended, the blood rushed from McQueen's face. The following day the announcement along with Garner's photo appeared in a Hong Kong English-language newspaper. McQueen was livid.

Constant delays on *The Sand Pebbles* had pushed back the start date for *Day of the Champion*. Frankenheimer had gained considerable ground on *Grand Prix* while Sturges shot second-unit footage and stockpiled more than a million feet of film.[4]

A week before principal photography was scheduled to begin on *Day of the Champion*, Robert Relyea received a midnight phone call from studio head Jack Warner, who was in Monte Carlo. Warner enjoyed high-stakes gambling and never failed to tell Relyea when he cleaned up at the tables. Warner made pleasant small talk. Then casually, almost as an afterthought, he said to Relyea

---

4   A Warner Brothers memo shows that 121 canisters of film were shot at Nurburgring, Germany, and Oulton Park in Cheshire, England, for *Day of the Champion*. Said Robert Relyea, "Somewhere in the Warner Brothers vaults is a lot of footage of a man in a green racing helmet driving a green car around and around a racetrack."

before he hung up, "Oh yeah...pull the plug on the racing picture. We're not going to beat them. *Grand Prix* will be the first to the theaters—I don't want to be second. Shut it down."

"But Jack..."

"Send everybody home," Warner said without a trace of emotion. Said Relyea, "It was heartbreaking for me because of all the time I had put into preproduction. We had been filming second-unit shots for almost a year, had a million feet of racing footage in the can, and had spent close to $4 million. For Steve, I'm sure it was worse."

For nearly two years, McQueen didn't talk to James Garner. "Saw *Grand Prix*, man," McQueen said when he finally bumped into Garner at his mailbox. "Not bad." It was the only compliment Steve could muster.[5]

"Steve and I never liked coming in second, and to top it off, we weren't good losers," Relyea said. "Enough time had passed to where we could finally talk about the subject again. I said, 'One day we're going to make that racing film, and it will be the death of us all.' That movie turned out to be *Le Mans*, and I didn't realize how prophetic that statement would be."

The debacle surrounding *Day of the Champion* would bother McQueen for some time, but *The Sand Pebbles* had been a great achievement on many levels and offered up some consolation. The experience also provided a real-life happy ending when McQueen was asked to stand in as best man for makeup artist Bill Turner, who got hitched in a quickie wedding while on location in Hong Kong. Kaori Nara, a Japanese dancer who had a revue at the Ambassador Hotel, recalled, "At the time, I had no idea who Steve was. He seemed normal enough, and I thought he was just trying to help out a friend. Steve sang Bill's praises, but it took the local police to clinch the deal. One night, I was picked up by the local authorities for breaking Hong Kong's curfew laws. I was from Japan and not familiar with their customs. Bill and Steve came to the rescue. Steve's clout as a major movie star was a big part of why I was able to go home that night. A month and a half later, Bill and I married on a ship anchored in Hong Kong. Steve stood in for my father, because I had no family at the wedding to represent me. Bill and I were together for 25 years until his death in 1992. We shared a wonderful and full life together. Many people say that Steve was a macho man, but for me, he was a regular guy—and a gentleman."

---

5   *Grand Prix* zoomed into movie theaters by that Christmas, just in time for the 1966 Academy Awards. The film won three Oscars for Best Effects, Best Film Editing, and Best Sound, and was nominated for two Golden Globes, Directors Guild of America, and American Cinema Editors awards.

The Sand Pebbles finally wrapped in late May 1966 after seven months abroad, several months of delays, and nearly $3 million over budget. McQueen literally kissed the ground when his family landed safely on U.S. soil. The Academy Awards nomination committee kissed him back with a nod for Best Actor and seven other nominations for the film, including Best Picture.

McQueen took the rest of 1966 off, loaded up the family in their camper, and went on a three-week trip to Idaho, Utah, Montana, Canada, the Yukon, Washington, Oregon, and California. McQueen also pursued other projects outside of the movie industry. He talked of partnering with Whisky co-owner Elmer Valentine about opening a Spanish restaurant on the Sunset Strip to be called Rebelion de Los Adolescentes (Teenage Rebellion), but nothing ever came of this idea. McQueen also narrated *The Coming of the Roads*, a locally produced half-hour documentary on conservation. It aired on September 17, 1966, on KABC-TV.[6]

To ensure the success of *The Sand Pebbles*, McQueen embarked on an unprecedented press junket in New York, one of the largest campaigns of the year. It was a road-show campaign, a high-profile marketing strategy including worldwide coverage and several huge premieres usually reserved for only the most epic films, such as *Ben-Hur* and *Lawrence of Arabia*.

David Foster was summoned by Richard Zanuck, president of 20th Century Fox, to accompany Steve in New York for a media blitz. "In those days, publicity in New York helped a picture tremendously," Foster said. "[McQueen] was excited about all of these things. It meant that he had arrived. He didn't enjoy doing them, but he also realized that these things made him a star." Foster lined up interviews with *The New York Times*, *The Saturday Evening Post*, and *The Saturday Review* and appearances on *The Ed Sullivan Show*, *The Tonight Show with Johnny Carson*, and *What's My Line?*, where McQueen did a spot-on impersonation of Walter Brennan to mask his identity to the celebrity panel.

Zanuck had hired a limousine for McQueen and Foster to make the rounds in grand style. By the second day, McQueen had enough of the high life. He had Foster ditch the limo in exchange for a Volkswagen Bug, and he drove them around the Big Apple to all of their appointments himself.[7]

---

6   A copy of *The Coming of the Roads* has not surfaced in more than four decades.

7   Three months later Foster received a phone call from Zanuck querying the fate of the rental car. Foster eventually discovered that McQueen left the vehicle in the parking lot of the hotel and never bothered to tell anyone. Zanuck seethed but picked up the tab.

The Sand Pebbles premiered at the Rivoli in New York on December 20, 1966,[8] to rave reviews and a $30 million domestic gross.[9] Arthur Knight of *The Saturday Review* wrote, "Richard Crenna is outstanding, Candice Bergen attractive, Richard Attenborough effective—and all of them dominated by Steve McQueen, who is nothing short of wonderful in the pivotal role of Holman." *The New York Times* raved, "Performed by Steve McQueen with the most restrained, honest, heartfelt acting he has ever done." *Variety* assessed, "Steve McQueen delivers an outstanding performance and looks the part he plays so well."

The film is one of the definitive McQueen pictures for many reasons. Foremost is his performance, which thrills fans even today. But also contributing to this stature is the fact that the film is so quintessentially epic. *The Sand Pebbles* is a historical epic of the sort no longer made today. McQueen's role in a film of this caliber cemented his leading man status. The picture also has overtones of the Vietnam War and must have connected with audiences in this way, making McQueen's performance all the more potent.

It was a pivotal point in McQueen's development as an actor. McQueen was at his best when playing guys who are struggling to be better men. He had extended his acting range beyond anything he had done before. He was no longer simply the antihero or the loner—he was now capable of playing all of these roles and more, distilling them into a single highly complex character. With his economical use of dialogue and creative license with the script, McQueen ensured that he literally made this character his own. Anyone with any doubt as to his talent need only consider the contrasting roles of Jake Holman, Hilts, Frank Bullitt, Papillon, or Thomas Crown. Over his career, McQueen often sought to challenge his own ability and redefine his own image, succeeding as an action hero, wealthy businessman, a rascal with excellent comic timing, and the coolest cop in San Francisco.

On February 20, 1967, *The Sand Pebbles* received eight Academy Award nominations. And Steve McQueen—along with Paul Scofield (*A Man for All Seasons*), Alan Arkin (*The Russians Are Coming, The Russians Are Coming*), Michael Caine (*Alfie*), and Richard Burton (*Who's Afraid of Virginia Woolf?*)— was nominated for Best Actor. It was the first and only Oscar nomination of McQueen's career. Zanuck, the man who footed the bill for *The Sand Pebbles*, congratulated McQueen with a Western Union telegram:

---

8   *The Sand Pebbles* was released a day before *Grand Prix*, and McQueen and Garner were forced to compete once again. This time McQueen took the checkered flag at the box office by nearly $10 million. McQueen must have felt vindicated in some small way.

9   *The Sand Pebbles'* $30 million domestic gross would be equivalent to $336 million in 2010 box-office dollars.

Dear Steve,
    I couldn't be more delighted with your Academy nomination. Congratulations
on this well-deserved recognition of a great performance.
    Sincerely,
        Richard Zanuck

Three days before McQueen's 37th birthday and three weeks before the
Academy Awards, Grauman's Chinese Theater immortalized McQueen's place
in Hollywood history on March 21, 1967. In front of a crowd of 2,000 fans and
well-wishers, as well as photographers and news crews, McQueen pulled up with
Neile in his Ferrari and became the 153rd star to put his footprints, handprints,
and signature in cement at the Tinseltown landmark. Whether in concrete or
on screen, McQueen had left an indelible impression in the hearts and minds of
audiences around the world.[10]

The 39th Academy Awards were held on April 10, 1967, at the Santa Monica
Civic Auditorium. A red-carpet photo from that magical night of McQueen in
his crisp black tuxedo and tie and Neile in a lilac satin dress shows the couple in
awe of the spectacle and how far they had come together. McQueen, enraptured
under the glare of klieg lights and popping flashbulbs, received a warm greeting
from the crowd; he was clearly the favorite with the people on the street.

It was a British sweep at the Oscars that year, and Paul Scofield took home
the Academy Award for Best Actor.[11] Time has proven that McQueen's portrayal
of Jake Holman is much better-remembered today than Scofield's Sir Thomas
More.[12]

Neile believed it was fate that McQueen didn't win because her husband
would have been impossible to live with if he had actually been awarded the
statue. As some consolation, Steve won the World Film Favorite award for favorite
actor by the Hollywood Foreign Press Association and received the *Photoplay*
Gold Medal Award. In Japan, he was named the most popular foreign star for
the second consecutive year.

With his next pair of roles, McQueen would complete an unbroken run
of five back-to-back global hits. The first of the pair showed McQueen play

---

10 In a mysterious coincidence, Steve McQueen and future wife Ali MacGraw are the only celebrities
    on the grounds whose cement blocks are upside down in relation to the others.

11 *A Man for All Seasons* took home six Oscars, but the ceremony is somewhat infamously remem-
    bered as the year in which *The Good, the Bad and the Ugly* didn't receive any nominations.

12 In 2007, AMC's *Shootout* host Peter Bart asked actor Kevin Costner if there was a great role that
    he'd seen other actors do that he would have liked to have done. Costner replied, "Yeah, there's
    been a lot of them. I love *The Sand Pebbles*."

completely against type and once again demonstrated his acting chops, portraying the one character perhaps furthest from his upbringing—a successful million-aire. The transition and progression in characters is an interesting comparison to McQueen's own rise to fame and power. After that, he would go on to make the most iconic film of his career with its own place in popular culture. This role broke the mold for crime drama and sparked a new trend in cinema—the renegade cop. McQueen's life was hitting top gear and gathering speed at every turn. This film would see this momentum literally spill onto the screen at more than 110 mph through the streets of San Francisco in scenes that had audience members jumping to their feet and cheering.

Steve McQueen was just hitting his stride.

22

SUPERNOVA

These were the halcyon years.

McQueen's rise to stardom paralleled the Beatles' atomic fame, rising from practically nowhere and shooting into the stratosphere like a supernova. McQueen had always been a man on a mission, looking to build his fame and gild his image as a superstar while maintaining a Zen master's composure in the midst of high drama. He molded his public image to fit the hero he wanted to be while giving moviegoers a new cinematic icon—the antihero. "There are just two ways to go as an actor when you deal with the public," McQueen explained. "You either stay yourself, or you become what they want you to become. Some guys will sell out, but I can't be trapped into that way of life." McQueen took this maxim with him through his whole life. As his Doc McCoy character in *The Getaway* put it, "Let's do it my way," which became McQueen's mantra and the only way he could live his life—on his own terms.

McQueen received up to 20 scripts per week[1] from major producers, and Steve's nod meant the picture was a go and whoever was attached could count on a financial windfall. "Steve is the only guy around who can do the kind of pictures that made big stars of Gable, Cooper, and Wayne," said one producer. McQueen was cinematic gold, that rare commodity that would make or break movies and careers in a second.

The glittering success of *The Great Escape*, *Love with the Proper Stranger*, *The Cincinnati Kid*, *Nevada Smith,* and *The Sand Pebbles,* plus McQueen's blue-chip status as a box-office king, brought the spoils. Solar Productions entered into a multimillion dollar, six-picture contract with Warner Brothers, which financed

---

1   Some of the scripts that McQueen passed on during this time were *Marooned, King Rat, In Cold Blood, Two for the Road, The Kremlin Letter, Man on a Nylon String, The Ski Bum,* and *Return of the Seven,* a sequel to *The Magnificent Seven.*

and distributed McQueen's movies. Warner also cracked open its checkbook and paid McQueen a then-staggering sum of $700,000 per picture and 50 percent of the profits.[2] McQueen had skillfully secured a base salary that was incrementally higher than the last, with no exceptions. Not bad for someone who considered himself far from being good with numbers.

This arrangement brought not only financial reward but also the elusive and intangible film industry kudos and respect that only a handful of stars could ever hope to possess. McQueen was, in his own words, "the head honcho." He could select his own material, choose the actors and directors of his liking, and reap the profits. Wise and shrewd in all his dealings, he also had the right team around him to push the right buttons. McQueen's business model held the same sentiment as the Beatles' Apple Records. "Solar will seek out new young people in the film industry and give them a break. We will look for fresh ideas and new approaches to producing films," McQueen told the *Hollywood Reporter*, flanked by Solar Vice President Robert Relyea and Staff Production Manager Jack Reddish.[3] McQueen would back up this assertion, too. He would champion and help just as long as these new actors knew their place and would not attempt to upstage him. After all, McQueen was still as competitive and as power hungry as he had ever been.

It was out with the old and in with the new, a maxim that friend Jack Garfein experienced when he had a chance encounter with McQueen. Garfein's fortunes had shifted after he fell out of favor with the Actors Studio and his second film, *Something Wild*, tanked. Garfein moved to Los Angeles but couldn't find work as a director. He thought his fortunes would change when McQueen spotted him walking on the Sunset Strip. "One day I happened to see Steve on his motorbike, and after he had pulled over he asked me what was happening. 'Steve, I really need a job. I've written a good screenplay, and I can't persuade anyone to read it.' Steve agreed to take a look, and I sent it along to my agent, Mike Levy. He didn't believe me at first because Steve was the hottest star in Hollywood at the time." Garfein's script was returned with a note from Robert Relyea, thanking Garfein for the submission. Garfein was crestfallen. "You can imagine I was deeply hurt. If he didn't want to do the fucking thing, he at least could have called me. Or 'Jack, I don't like this,' or 'Jack, let's do something else.' But no, he sent it back with a note from his manager. I was deeply hurt that Steve didn't bother to tell me

---

2 Only John Wayne commanded a higher fee at the time; he received $1 million per picture plus profits.

3 The original slate of Solar Films included *Day of the Champion, Suddenly Single, Man on a Nylon String, The Reivers, Le Mans,* and *Adam at Six* A.M., a non-McQueen film featuring Michael Douglas and Lee Purcell.

personally, and I was never in touch with him again." This story encapsulates the deep emotional and personal impact that McQueen could have upon anyone that crossed his path. His approval or his whims could set off your career or leave you with nothing. That was the force of his natural kinetic energy. He had become the modern-day equivalent of a Roman emperor at the gladiatorial arena—a simple thumbs up or down would change a person's life forever.

McQueen wanted a clean slate and no reminders of the past. He had taken his share of pain and hardship and now had accomplished more than he could have dreamed. Accordingly, McQueen wanted two things. First, he wanted to leave that past behind. Secondly, he wanted to believe that he was a completely self-made success, that he alone had achieved the impossible. His ego and nature demanded this despite the fact that his agents, wife, and colleagues over the years had all played their part. Garfein was one of many whom McQueen conveniently forgot when he was a success and had pulled up the ladder after himself. He was also looking to shed his film persona as a loner, rebel, and misfit. "I've played a lot of losers," McQueen noted, "but now—unless I get a really great script—I'm through with that. It took me a long time to realize that I wasn't a loser myself." His next role, a bored business tycoon who turns to bank robbery and courts the insurance investigator assigned to bring him in, was anything but a loser. The real-life winner was now ready to play one on screen.

The Thomas Crown Affair was the only film that McQueen had to fight to be cast in after he was an established cinema superstar. Lawyer-turned-screenwriter Alan R. Trustman had created the role of Thomas Crown with Sean Connery in mind, who later declined because he was just wrapping the James Bond feature You Only Live Twice. Trustman felt Rock Hudson, Richard Burton, and Jean Paul Belmondo were also excellent candidates.

Director Norman Jewison, who worked with Trustman for 15 months to flesh his 30-page treatment into a script, didn't feel McQueen was right for the part. But Jewison was in a strange predicament—he was the hottest director in Hollywood[4] and held in his hand the hottest script in town, and yet no one was available to play the part...that is, except for Steve McQueen, who wanted to do it very badly. When McQueen called Jewison asking to pay him a visit, Jewison suspected it wasn't a social call. "If you're calling about Thomas Crown, you can forget it," he told McQueen. Jewison's directorial duties with McQueen on The Cincinnati Kid had taught him that McQueen responded only to absolutes, and reasoning and logic were out of the question. Undaunted, McQueen showed up

---

4   Jewison had just won the Academy Award for In the Heat of the Night.

at Jewison's Brentwood home to plead for the part. Jewison was resistant at first but admitted McQueen eventually wore him down. "You're not right for it, Steve," Jewison said. "My God, this man wears a shirt and tie, he's a Phi Beta Kappa, a graduate of Dartmouth." "That's why I want to play the part," said McQueen, whose hat-in-hand demeanor and impassioned plea took Jewison by surprise. Jewison reflected later that, "I think he wanted to grow up; he wanted to play a part that he had never played before, and maybe, in a secret desire deep within him, he wanted to be Thomas Crown—you know, who was so bright and erudite and cultured and sophisticated and chic and smart and a Bostonian from an old family… all the things Steve wasn't."

Despite his insecurities about playing the part, McQueen examined Thomas Crown through his prism and decided he could tackle the role. "I felt it was time to get past those tough, uptight types," McQueen said. "This dude wants to show he can beat the establishment at its own game. He's essentially a rebel, like me. Sure, a high-society rebel, but he's my kind of cat. It was just that his outer fur was different—so I got me some fur."

The fur flew when Trustman discovered that McQueen had been cast as Thomas Crown. "At the time, he was a decent character actor with a limited range, beautiful moves, and a reputation for being difficult," Trustman said. "There was no way he could play my distinguished Bostonian, but they cast him and that was it."

Even though McQueen was playing against type, his name on the contract almost ensured instant dividends for everyone involved, including Trustman, who had a piece of the picture. After he got over the initial shock, Trustman rolled up his sleeves and tailored the script to McQueen's acting style. He insisted that United Artists, who was the studio behind the film, assemble every piece of movie and television footage available on McQueen so he could make up a checklist of the actor's strengths and weaknesses. "I discovered that if he was comfortable and stayed within a certain range of characterization, he was terrific," Trustman said. "The moment he became uncomfortable, you could squirm watching him."

Based on his checklist, Trustman's rewrite made McQueen a better fit for the role by making the character much more laconic. When Trustman met McQueen to explain the character of Thomas Crown, he told McQueen he could be the new Humphrey Bogart. "You are shy; you don't talk too much. You are a loner but a person with integrity. You're quiet; you're gutsy as hell. You like girls but are basically shy with women. You have a tight smile, and you don't show your teeth, but it's a small smile around your mouth and you never deliver a sentence more than five or 10 words long because paragraphs make you lose interest or something goes wrong with your delivery. As long as you can stay with that, you can be No. 1." Trustman later expounded, "The reason why my movies made money, I'm convinced, is not that my scripts were brilliant but that they were good. A movie is made by force of personality that dominates the movie, and if he has a clear idea of what he wants and gets it on film, you've got a strong central character and a terrific picture. I went over this with McQueen, and he dominated *The Thomas Crown Affair*."

McQueen threw himself into the part with uncommon restraint, finding a way to get comfortable in his three-piece suits and learning polo within a matter of weeks. His natural athletic ability, competitive nature (McQueen played until his hands bled), and steely determination paid off. Widow Barbara McQueen, who had played polo for years, marveled at his mastery of the game. "Polo is a game that takes years to learn, but Steve really had it down. He looked like he belonged on the field, which is amazing considering how much he disliked horses."

While McQueen busily prepared for the role, Jewison was occupied with testing female leads for the role of Vicki Anderson. McQueen lobbied hard for actress Camilla Sparv[5] and Brigitte Bardot, whom McQueen had been chasing for *Le Mans* since 1959. According to Jewison, Sparv didn't test well and Bardot's agent pushed for the locale to be switched from Boston to Paris. Sharon Tate, Raquel Welch, Candice Bergen, and Suzanne Pleshette were also considered, but actress Faye Dunaway, a relative newcomer,[6] trounced the competition. Years later, McQueen dubbed her "The Great Lady," and Dunaway was equally enamored with her new costar. She recalled in her 1995 memoir *Looking For Gatsby*, "It was my first time to play opposite someone who was a great big old movie star, and that's exactly what Steve was. He was one of the best-loved actors around, one whose talent more than equaled his sizeable commercial appeal. Steve, I loved. He was darling. He was daunting. Steve McQueen was an absolute professional, and he knew what was necessary technically to achieve his performance every time he went in front of the camera."

Dunaway had seen the side of McQueen that strove for excellence and became a screen legend, but she could also see his vulnerability from a woman's perspective. "Steve was all sinewy and tough, but at the same time he had such vulnerability. He definitely had archaic notions about women. If he said it once to me, he said it a million times, 'A good woman can take a bum from the streets

---

5 Sparv was married to producer Robert Evans from 1963 to 1965. Years later, McQueen had his eye on another one of Evans' wives—actress Ali MacGraw.

6 *Bonnie and Clyde*, the movie that made Dunaway a star, had not been released when Jewison tested her for *The Thomas Crown Affair*.

and turn him into a king.' He believed a good woman was terribly important in a man's life. Steve had so much charisma, and he seemed to trigger those nurturing instincts in women. He was a chauvinist—notoriously so—but a chivalrous one to me. There was a strange dynamic between us. We'd both grown up on the wrong side of the tracks, but by the time I appeared in *Thomas Crown*, I'd shaken off anything that might hint of that. I could walk into an art auction or the polo club with absolute confidence. Steve, on the other hand, never stopped feeling he was a delinquent and any day he'd be found out. For my part, I saw him as such an icon. That shade of distance between us ended up working well in creating the relationship between Vicki and Crown. That's what they call chemistry, [and] Steve and I had that in spades."

Three months before principal photography commenced, Trustman's script and a request to shoot the film at the FBI headquarters in Boston caused problems. The Bureau was outraged by the film's portrayal of them as bumbling, incompetent idiots led by Faye Dunaway's character, who is a private investigator for an insurance firm. It refused the request from Walter Mirisch and United Artists in this March 17, 1967, memorandum:

To: Mr. Wick

From: M.A. Jones

Subject: Request for Bureau Cooperation in Filming Scenes for Proposed Motion Picture The Crown Caper

Mr. Deloach has received a letter dated 3/17/67 from [deleted] of the Motion Picture Association of America, Inc., requesting permission to photograph the Boston office in connection with the proposed captioned motion picture being produced by Walter Mirisch. It is noted that on 2/24/67 the Boston Office was contacted in this regard by a Mirisch representative who was told his request would have to be referred to the Bureau. Steve McQueen *will star in this film, which is written by Alan R. Trustman.*

McQueen indicated he planned to participate in the March on Washington in 1963.

This screenplay has been reviewed in the Crime Research Section. It involves a bank robbery in Boston conceived by Crown who hires five others to commit the robbery and then secrets the remaining proceeds in a Swiss bank. The investigation by the Boston FBI Office, headed by Edward Rock, makes no progress until the bank's insurer assigns a beautiful young investigator, Vicky [sic], to work with the FBI. Vicky completely dominates the investigation and through her efforts identifies the subjects and furnishes this information to the FBI. Sex is both explicit and implied throughout the story and is especially apparent in the romantic relationship between Vicky and Crown. Rock is fully aware of the methods being used by Vicky to extract admissions from Crown. The story ends when Vicky and the FBI are outwitted by Crown, who flies to Brazil, leaving a final invitation to Vicky to join him in the country.

OBSERVATIONS:

This is an outrageous portrayal of the FBI, which depicts a Bureau bank robbery investigation being taken over by a young girl who uses her physical charms to conduct her mission. No doubt the producer sees this film as a great money-maker at the box office as a result of its great emphasis on sex and the use of the FBI's good name.

RECOMMENDATION:

That we have absolutely nothing to do with the proposed film and that [deleted] be so advised.

Shooting began in June 1967 in and around the Boston area, which included Beverly Farms, Crane Beach, Ipswich, and Hamilton, Massachusetts. It was the "Summer of Love" according to pop-culture historians, but McQueen, perhaps one of the biggest lovers of them all, was firmly ensconced in a Beverly Farms beach home with his family, where on Sundays they would hold clambakes on the beach, ride bikes, and explore the local scenery. It was the last time the McQueens experienced a film locale as a united family.

Sketch artist Nikita Knatz recalled a lobster clambake for the cast and crew at the start of the picture. He said that McQueen, though he was playing an urbane and sophisticated character, was a little out of his depth when it came to eating the crustacean. McQueen announced, "It looks like a big bug to me," a line he parodied in *Tom Horn*. Knatz said, "They bring in these lobsters in crates, and McQueen picks one of them up the wrong way and it snaps at him and he tries to shake it off and can't. He starts laughing at the stupidity of it because he knew better than to stick his finger in there. Then he just hits himself in the head with this lobster and [McQueen's son] Chad just roars with laughter."

McQueen was also feeling a little out of his depth when it came to filling the shoes of Thomas Crown, and his anxiety was apparent to the crew. "He was very nervous about the role," said director of photography Haskell Wexler. "I never really talked to Steve about anything but cars. We went tearing away from the set in a dune buggy one day, and the engine literally blew up. I spent about 40 minutes with him just stranded. It felt like in those 40 minutes, that's when I got to know the real Steve McQueen. I think he just wished that day he didn't have to go back to the set and be Thomas Crown."

Boston cop Ed Donovan, who stood in for McQueen for two days, said the star was just as uncomfortable in his three-piece suits as he was. "At the time of my assignment, I had to wear a suit and a tie, and in his role as Thomas Crown, McQueen was required to wear three-piece suits all day," Donovan said. "He asked me if I ever became accustomed to it. 'Never,' I replied. 'I can't wait to take them off at the end of the day.' Steve was like me—he was more comfortable in blue jeans and a T-shirt even though he cut quite a striking figure in his expensive suits."

Donovan, who was in the throes of an alcohol and pill addiction, said he came to the set with a major hangover, a fact that didn't go unnoticed by McQueen. "I didn't take my big assignment as his stand-in as seriously as I should have. The '60s were some of the busiest drinking days of my life. Thoughts of suicide continuously ran through my mind due to depression. I was not only drinking but was taking quaaludes as well. I certainly did on that day. I felt I had to appear tough. Of course, who was more macho than Steve McQueen? Well, he noticed my hands were shaking and walked over to me. 'How you doing? Have a rough night?' No one else knew my torment except McQueen.

"I admitted, 'Frankly, I could use a stiff drink right about now.' He just smirked and said he could use one as well. I think McQueen respected me because he knew I was a blue-collar worker. I felt he didn't completely trust people and was somewhat of a loner like myself. He recognized that I was uncomfortable as a cop, needing help. Though I was outwardly macho, I was lonely inside."

After he retired from the Boston Police Department, Donovan followed in McQueen's footsteps and became an actor, compiling an impressive list of credits. Years later Donovan said he was amazed by McQueen's dedication on *The Thomas Crown Affair*. "McQueen cared deeply about his craft and was always on the set watching and learning. Many actors disappear or go into their dressing rooms when they're not shooting, but not McQueen. He was the kind of actor who wanted to make sure everything was perfect. He wasn't just part of the scene—he felt he was a part of the movie," Donovan said.

But McQueen wasn't always easy to handle. Jewison said McQueen was street-smart and had a quick mind. "If you were an insecure director, he could make you miserable. He was affected by the moon and would just take off for days. He was very strange." And cheap. Writer Alan Trustman said McQueen had agent Stan Kamen bill producer Walter Mirisch a "$250 rental fee" for the use of his personal watch in the film.

The director recalled the time McQueen took off in the film's iconic dune buggy as the crew was about to film a scene at the beach with Steve and Faye

Dunaway just before sunset. While McQueen performed wheelies in the dunes at Crane's Beach, the cast and crew watched the sun go down and lost their light. When he returned, McQueen was oblivious and Jewison was fuming.

"What's up?" McQueen asked flippantly.

"It's too late. You cost us the scene, that's what!" Jewison exploded as the crew loaded up the trucks and called it a night. McQueen was taken aback.

The next day when Jewison arrived, he brought with him a long seagull's feather he found on the beach and stuck it in McQueen's cap. McQueen was suspicious and squinted at the director. "What's that for?"

"On days when you wear the feather, you're the chief," Jewison said sarcastically. In the next motion, he took the feather out of McQueen's cap and placed it into his. "But most days, I wear the feather, and that means I'm the goddamned chief."

Jewison was the chief, more so than any of McQueen's directors, and Jewison knew how to handle McQueen using a stern-when-necessary-and-subtle-when-needed approach. Jewison stripped McQueen away from his usual screen habits by pushing the star into foreign territory. "Thomas Crown has no McQueen signatures in it at all," Nikita Knatz said. "Jewison had McQueen doing what he wanted to do all along. The chess game—it looks like McQueen ad-libbed it. It was all predesigned by Jewison. He took Steve out of his element, [using] high-fashion suits, Phi Beta Kappa key, brandy snifters, cigars. Jewison really directed the man."

However, *Thomas Crown* is not simply McQueen out of his comfort zone. The exceptional performance marks a point in McQueen's career when he was able to learn from this experience and add these new elements from playing such an unusual character to his formidable arsenal. The usual McQueen traits are still in place, though. There is the economy of dialogue and his method of using an expression or gesture to speak volumes. Many times during the scenes with Dunaway, McQueen shrugs, looks down and then up into her eyes. The safe thing would have been to deliver a great line in retort to her, but McQueen knew that less was more and let his blue eyes do the talking. One of the real pleasures of the film and McQueen's performance is when he takes his dune buggy for a high-octane spin over the beach. The classic McQueen smile is real as he scares seagulls and leaves his tracks in the sand. He's happy just being himself and being natural. This is the real McQueen being the real McCoy.

The combustible energy between McQueen and Dunaway made for *Crown's* best moments, most notably the movie's key scene where a game of chess is used as a metaphor for the sexual dynamic brewing between the two characters.

"Do you play?" Crown asks.

"Try me," Vicky replies.

The six-minute scene is a prelude to one of cinema's most romantic kisses, which had women around the world swooning. It transformed the once-rugged McQueen into a debonair matinee idol, so much so that when the picture was released, the Belles of Memphis, a group of southern college women, voted McQueen "the sexiest man in America." It was also a milestone in cinema for being the first kiss on screen that vividly depicted the use of tongues, which earned the film a mature rating.

Reprising Crown's dapper look at the world premiere at Boston's Sack Hall on June 18, 1968, McQueen sported a black tie and white jacket. When Steve and Neile showed up at the last minute, Neile was escorted to her seat by two deputies while her husband's presence created a frenzy with the crowd, who blocked the aisles to get a glimpse of the star up close. Quick-thinking members of Boston's finest hoisted McQueen above the crowd and carried him on their shoulders as they entered the theater, with Steve laughing at the absurdity of it all and looking every bit the movie star.

The film's style over content—multi-image screen techniques, McQueen's and Dunaway's wardrobes, Haskell Wexler's dazzling cinematography, Hal Ashby's slick editing, and Michel Legrand's lush theme, "The Windmills of Your Mind"—swept audiences away. The $4 million production brought back $14 million in the U.S. alone, making it McQueen's fourth hit film in a row.[7]

The Thomas Crown Affair was also a big critical hit, thanks to a June 30, 1968, press junket arranged by United Artists that brought 40 of the biggest entertainment reporters to the Beverly-Wilshire Hotel. The studio accommodated McQueen ("I don't like talking that much and answering the same questions") and picked up the tab whereby reporters received a free ticket, meals, movie screening, and an interview with McQueen, who sat for 20 minutes with 10 writers at a time at a roundtable discussion. With five press agents on hand, McQueen fielded questions on his film career, racing activities, staying in shape, future movies (McQueen pushed *The Reivers* over *Bullitt*), hippies, the multi-image process used in *Crown*, and his new image as a Boston millionaire who robs banks for kicks. Before the three-hour junket ended, McQueen obliged everyone with a photo-op and a handshake. The payoff was huge, and McQueen received some of the best notices of his career. Kathleen Carroll of the *New York Daily News* wrote, "A polished McQueen, minus his motorcycle's mumble, shows a

---

7 *The Thomas Crown Affair's* 1968 box-office take would be equivalent to $139 million in 2010.

whole new facet of his active personality. He is cast most successfully." *The New York Post* observed, "McQueen, dashing with verve, unlimited energy and bright, inquiring eyes, makes you wonder if he's hatching something akin to a turkey." *The Saturday Review* claimed, "Steve McQueen is no underworld hoodlum with dreams of glory but is himself a member of the Establishment—an impressively successful investment banker."

Success was had by everyone involved. McQueen played against type, and it had paid off. He had lobbied hard for the role and had done a great job. Now his critics could not typecast him as strictly a blue-collar actor. He could play the rebel and the loner, but now he proved he could also be the suave business-man. People had told McQueen he could not pull it off, but he had proven them wrong. It was another personal victory essential to his fragile ego and his desire to always prove himself.

Almost three decades later, Pierce Brosnan and Rene Russo starred in a suc-cessful remake of the sexy caper film in 1999 with Crown as an art thief. Curiously though, *Thomas Crown's* most enduring legacy has been on the fashion world. Just as Rudolph Valentino had popularized the wristwatch in the '20s, McQueen introduced British menswear to the U.S. market thanks to top English tailor Douglas Hayward, who created a line of smart-looking three-piece suits with two-button jackets and snug waists that captured Crown's affluence and set off the star's angular frame to perfection. His accessories—the Patek Philippe pocket watch, blue-lens tortoiseshell Persol sunglasses,[8] and perfectly snipped hair—have created a timeless image of opulence. McQueen's look and the Crown persona have inspired such designers as Ralph Lauren, Dolce & Gabbana, Tommy Hilfiger, John Bartlett, and Tom Ford. And celebrities including David Beckham, Daniel Craig, Kevin Costner, Christian Bale, Ashton Kutcher, and Jason Statham have adopted McQueen as their fashion icon.

McQueen has left an indelible mark on style and fashion. He managed to achieve an impossible blend of understated and effortless cool. Early in the '60s, he pioneered the white Baracuta Harrington jacket with upturned collar. Later, he made the Belstaff Trialmaster jacket an icon in its own right. After popularizing immaculate suits in *The Thomas Crown Affair*, McQueen would go on to make the most unlikely items extremely fashionable—Italian loafers, a trench coat, and a certain blue turtleneck sweater. Only McQueen could turn all of those items into global trends and a smash film that would benefit from the greatest on-screen car chase of all time.

---

8   The Persols McQueen used in *The Thomas Crown Affair* were sold at auction for $70,000 in 2006.

23

TODAY HOLLYWOOD, TOMORROW...THE WORLD!

THE YEAR 1968 PROVED TO BE one of the most volatile years in 20th-century America, starting with the assassinations of Martin Luther King Jr. and Robert Kennedy. A hail of bullets and tear gas from the National Guard marred the Democratic National Convention in Chicago, while on the other side of the country, the Black Panthers in Oakland began baring their claws and flashing their shotguns. Anarchy and confusion were everywhere. Thousands of college students openly and defiantly burned their draft cards to protest the Vietnam War. Revolution was in the air, and the youth of the day threatened to topple the government.

While the world seemed in disarray, McQueen's life seemed to go from strong to stronger. That year saw *The Thomas Crown Affair* turn Steve McQueen into a matinee idol, and *Bullitt* became a pop-culture sensation. McQueen stood alone high atop the Hollywood mountain, scaling heights that had rarely been navigated. In the Solar offices, a sign read, "Today Hollywood, Tomorrow...the world!" By year's end, McQueen had pretty much fulfilled the destiny of that slogan. However, it carried the same duality of similar words uttered by James Cagney in *White Heat*—"Top of the world, Ma!" McQueen was indeed at the summit, but that would also mean a longer and harder fall if McQueen was ever toppled.

Fans went crazy just to get an autograph or see McQueen in the streets. Reporters scrambled over each other to secure an interview. Flashbulbs lit the night sky every time McQueen went out in public. Simply calling McQueen a big Hollywood star at this point in his career fails to successfully capture the height of his fame. Fundamentally, he was one of the most popular and well-known faces on the planet. Fame was hard to deal with for someone like McQueen, and he turned more and more to the things that gave him pleasure—his friends, cars, bikes, family, drugs, and women. The problem was that McQueen had been so successful he had essentially created a monster that he had to continually feed. He could not afford to fail; he could not have any box-office disasters. He was invincible. However, McQueen always felt that everything could disappear as quickly as it had arrived, and this anxiety would both drive him forward and trouble him in equal measure.

If 1968 was a benchmark year of unrest, tumult, and change, then those traits also spilled over into the McQueen household. Despite the exterior veneer of success and being the man who had it all, McQueen was going through changes and negotiating insecurities. Neile noted that as her husband was fast approaching middle age, he adopted the lifestyle of the hippie culture in his dress, attitudes, and beliefs. It was a time of the flower children, the sexual revolution, and the drug culture, and it mightily clashed with Steve's midlife crisis. "It all came at the same time and conspired to throw him off-kilter, off-track, and suddenly the premium on happiness was incredible," Neile McQueen said. "If he wasn't happy, it was because, 'I can't go out and be free and fuck around.' Then he was blaming it on me, although he knew in his heart it wasn't right. But his head couldn't get it quite together.

"Our marriage started cracking about the time Woodstock became a mecca for California flower children. These hippies had a style with which Steve truly identified. He'd been the same kind of kid, only at a different time. Instead of frolicking at Woodstock, he'd been confined at the Boys Republic."

McQueen in the '60s symbolized cool and alpha-male energy. His self-image demanded that he could not be left behind and he could not feel old as the times evolved around him. Eventually the emotional dam broke when McQueen received an anonymous phone call one early January morning. The person on the other line cryptically told McQueen, "There's a new book out now that lists all the celebrities in Hollywood who are homosexuals. I thought you'd like to know your name is on the list." McQueen's face turned flush-white as he put down the phone. Neile watched his good mood flash from happiness to seething anger.

It was an attempt at a smear campaign against him that was typical of what could happen to big stars in those days, and it still happens today. Though the rumors were unfounded and ultimately not taken notice of, the subject matter struck a nerve with McQueen, who defined himself as a man through his sexuality.

Neile suggested that they call a friend in the FBI[1] to trace the underground publication, but after a few weeks of dogged pursuit, nothing was found. Neile dropped the subject after a while, but the insinuation was too damaging for Steve's fragile ego, and he acted out by becoming more sexually acquisitive than he had been in the past. After all, McQueen was highly competitive and difficult by nature; if he was told he could not do something, he placed all his energy into seeing that he could. This situation was no exception. If there were rumors about his sexuality, then he would simply up the ante and gain even more notches on his bedpost. McQueen had been happily betrothed since 1956, but he no longer found happiness in his domesticity. He wanted it all—a loving wife and stable family unit—but those things were at odds with both his ego and libido. Living with these conflicted desires was causing him to slowly unravel, and it spelled the beginning of the end of his marriage to Neile.

Bullitt is the defining movie of Steve McQueen's illustrious film career, but surprisingly, it was a project that he had to be talked into. The thought of playing a police detective frightened him. "No way am I playin' a cop," he told Neile, who subtly floated the idea past him while stylist Jay Sebring cut his hair. "Those kids call 'em pigs, man. What are you trying to do to me? Why, those kids would turn on me so fast it'd make your head spin!"

With Neile and Stan Kamen's gentle prodding, over time McQueen changed his mind. He decided that an honest portrayal of a cop might help recast the image of law enforcement and bridge the gap between the counterculture movement of the '60s and the establishment. "Hippies have gone too far. They're one of the reasons we're losing the unity of this country," McQueen said. "We've got to get together, and they've got to help. Their lack of concern is dangerous, and so is their conformity." In reality, this was an extremely brave and ultimately clever part to play. In the character, McQueen was able to play the cop role against type and create a highly nuanced and complex character who was not a clear-cut cop but his own man with his own rules and integrity.

Adapted from Robert Pike's 1963 novel *Mute Witness*, the book had originally been bought by producer Phil D'Antoni with Spencer Tracy in mind. But with Tracy's death in June 1967, D'Antoni sold the property to McQueen, who single-handedly transformed a New York cop with a fondness for ice cream into a hip San Francisco detective.

---

1 Ironic considering the Federal Bureau of Investigations had kept a running file on McQueen since 1958.

Solar enlisted the help of *Thomas Crown* screenwriter Alan R. Trustman, whom McQueen came to implicitly trust. "He knows me. I don't know how, but he knows me," McQueen would tell anyone who would listen. Trustman wrote *Bullitt*'s first treatment, but when he handed over the finished product, McQueen found the plot muddled and confusing. That was deliberate, said Trustman. "Do you know what a hook is? A hook is a device you use to keep the audience in their seat. If you go out to buy the popcorn during the picture, you're going to miss one line and you won't understand the movie and the confusion is deliberate. There is an inherent plot, and you don't pull it off on the screen. It's the opposite of television. A television audience gets infuriated if they don't understand what's going on every five minutes. A movie audience is locked into it by the confusion."

Costar Robert Vaughn said he was also confused and turned down the part of Walter Chalmers, a slick and ambitious politician, several times. Vaughn was so confounded by the script that he was convinced several pages had gone missing during the photocopying process. Vaughn recalled, "I told McQueen on two or three occasions, 'Steve, I don't think this is going to be good. This is the first picture you're producing, the script makes no sense, why are you wasting your time?' I requested script changes, and every time they made them, they paid me a little more money. It was my first six-figure payday. I told Steve, 'This picture's starting to look better and better to me!'"

Recruiting a director was much easier, though the method used was unorthodox. Between McQueen, Kamen, Trustman, Robert Relyea, and producer Phil D'Antoni, they assembled a list of 100 possible directors and eventually whittled it down to five. The short list included Trustman's selection of Peter Yates, an unknown English director who had been generating some buzz through a brilliant car chase scene in a little-known heist picture called *Robbery*. The group ranked the directors and phoned the first name on the list. It was busy. The second number rang eight times without an answer, and the group hung up. The third call was to Yates. When it was pointed out that it was 3:00 AM in England and that Yates most likely would be sleeping, McQueen replied, "Good, he'll be home. Phone him." Said Trustman incredulously, "They did, and that's how Peter Yates made it in Hollywood when he got to direct *Bullitt*."

Yates, who did not know of McQueen's reputation for being hard on his directors, found the screen legend a delight. "I was at a great advantage because I had an English accent and Steve took that as a sign that I was more clever than I actually was," Yates said. "I must say, I found him incredibly supportive at all times." Robert Relyea said McQueen always demanded the best of everyone and wasn't so easy on Yates. "Steve was harder on directors than anybody. I remember him bringing Peter Yates and others to tears because he was looping into a new attitude every day. One day he'd walk onto the set, rubbing his hands together, licking his lips saying, 'Oh boy, we're going to do 10 movies together,' and then the next day he'd arrive in a leather jacket, dark sunglasses, his teeth locked, and start the morning off by saying, 'I can't do your job and mine. We've talked about this over and over. I'm going to go into my trailer and when you've worked this out, come and get me and we'll continue.' The director would look around with pleading eyes wanting to know what the hell just happened, and it would just bring him to tears. My advice was to wait 24 hours and the mood would pass. It was so definite that you could set your watch by it. I found it frightening."

Authenticity was McQueen's driving force as an actor, perhaps even more so when he put on his producer's hat. He insisted that *Bullitt* be shot entirely on location in San Francisco, a decision that added another $500,000 to the $6 million budget. "Sure, we could shoot in the studio," McQueen said, "but I think we're getting into an era where pictures are more and more visual. And the audiences are sophisticated. They're not accepting substitutes." It was the first studio movie to be shot entirely on location with an all-Hollywood crew.

Indeed, a shift was occurring in cinema. A European influence had drifted into American films and the nation's consciousness in the '60s. Audiences were getting hipper, feasting on rich offerings such as *Bonnie and Clyde, The Graduate, Blow-Up, Cool Hand Luke, Yellow Submarine, Rosemary's Baby,* and *2001: A Space Odyssey.* McQueen said Solar needed to turn away from the old studio system and get in alignment with the nation's youth. "I think that more so than any other time in the history of motion pictures, people in college are taking their Super 8-mm cameras and going out and shooting film. Before long, in the near future, they'll probably bypass the motion picture industry as far as technique is concerned because there is freedom, and improvisational freedom at that."

For all of McQueen's posturing toward the direction of cinema, Solar still had a lot of freedom under its Warner Brothers deal. But that did not last long. Warner had recently been taken over by Kenneth Hyman and Seven Arts. The production company's original six-picture deal was pretty much a handshake deal with Jack Warner. Robert Relyea said the pitch to the studio boss lasted but a minute. "Warner said, 'Which movie have you decided to make?' I said, 'The cop picture.' He said, 'Why does Steve want to do a movie about a cop when we're having anti-war demonstrations and anti-authority is an all-time high in this country? I said, 'Well, he thinks he can do something different with the cop.' Jack asked how much, and I told him. He asked if he could have it before Christmas and I said yes, if we start immediately. He said, 'Go,' and that was it. That's not a synopsis of the meeting—that was our entire conversation."

Unfortunately for Solar, Warner had sold his share of stock in the studio and retired a few weeks before *Bullitt* started principal photography in February 1968. Hyman looked at the books and determined the film was already a million dollars over budget before one canister of film was shot. "The studio said that because they were trying to get rid of Steve," said director Peter Yates. "They had a contract with Steve, and apparently he spent a lot of money preparing the script. There was never a good relationship between Kenneth Hyman and Steve."

Hyman told McQueen and the Solar brass that Warner Brothers was going to be much more hands-on now, an idea that McQueen found disheartening. Said Robert Relyea, "[Solar] came in with one understanding and then found ourselves in another; it led to misunderstandings on both sides. I don't think Solar was equipped to make that change."

The weekend before principal photography started, Hyman came to the set and told Relyea the movie had to be moved back to Los Angeles and shot on the studio lot. Relyea politely told Hyman, "No, we're not going back."

"Fine. Your six-picture deal is now a one-picture deal," Hyman said. "And when you finish shooting, gather all your things and kindly move off the lot."

On the first day of shooting, McQueen gathered the crew around and announced that the movie was a one-shot deal and the studio was not going to be very supportive. "Let's put this behind us. We won't worry about it," McQueen said. "We'll find a new home. Let's just execute this picture as well as we can."

When studio executives later showed up in San Francisco to check on their investment, McQueen was openly hostile. He made it a point to personally escort them off the set and did so with great relish. "He loved to bust the executives, and he kicked the Warner people out right and left," Nikita Knatz said. "[McQueen] hated authority. He was getting more and more powerful."

Relations were much warmer with San Francisco Mayor Joseph L. Alioto, who rolled out the red carpet for McQueen after he had established with the superstar that the city needed a little quid pro quo. Solar donated $25,000 for Hunter's Point Pool near the Bayview District and thousands of dollars in medical equipment, employed hundreds of local teenagers (many of whom were gang leaders), and infused $2 million into the local economy.

In return, McQueen was given access to the city—including its busiest hospital, the airport, the police department—and he was allowed to run cars at speeds in excess of 100 mph. McQueen visited San Francisco's General Hospital to see crime victims firsthand. One person he met doing the rounds was recovering in the intensive care unit after a motorcycle accident. The patient was surprised by the visit and, knowing McQueen was a biking enthusiast, warned him to "Take it slow, Steve." Not only did McQueen heed the advice, he actually used the line in *Bullitt*.

The city also allowed McQueen to shadow San Francisco Police Department detectives John McKenna and Dave Toschi,[2] who gave the actor an eye-opening education on police work. Keen to prove he wasn't merely an actor but the real deal, McQueen wanted to show these hardened cops that he was tough, too. McQueen was due to be shown the morgue to see the grizzlier side of detective work. That morning he stunned them all by casually crunching on an apple at the start of the tour, showing he was ice cool. He and on-screen partner Don Gordon were taken to murder scenes, riots, drug busts, and the coroner's office. "I wanted to see the inside. I saw more than I ever counted on," McQueen said. "I got my head twisted. I was raised in the streets and never liked cops much. But here I am right in the middle of real police business. Man, it's different from the inside. I see 75 suspects paraded in the lineup; over half of them are armed. Christ! I'm playing a real cop, and I can't imagine going up against that."

Like he did with all of his films, McQueen gave his character, Lt. Frank Bullitt, his own special touch. Although most detectives back in the '60s wore shirts, slacks, and ties,[3] McQueen clothed his character in his trademark understated style of cool—a turtleneck with a tweed sport coat, casual slacks, suede shoes, sunglasses, and a fast-draw shoulder holster for his weapon.

Visual consultant Nikita Knatz said there was no police participation the night he and McQueen went into the bowels of Chinatown to see an underground fight by the White Changs, a local gang. After a confusing and lengthy car ride, McQueen and Knatz arrived at a nondescript warehouse and were escorted to an underground room filled with crates. They thought they were there to see a karate match; it turned out to be a death duel, according to Knatz. "These two old gentlemen come in and they look like bums, but they're the dons. No words are spoken. They sit down on folded chairs around what looks to be a big crate, bigger than the size of a room. Two people enter the crate, one with a raincoat on and the other wearing sunglasses. They go inside the crate and it's nailed shut with a four-by-four piece of wood. Then we hear in Chinese, 'Do it.' With that, one of them comes running toward the other guy and takes him out with one

---

2   McQueen based the role of Lt. Frank Bullitt primarily on Toschi, best known for his assignment to the Zodiac Killer case. Toschi was immortalized again on screen by actor Mark Ruffalo in 2007's *Zodiac*.

3   Toschi preferred bow ties and suspenders.

kick. A doctor is there and checks the guy's pulse. He says in Chinese, 'He's dead.' They bring the body out of the crate, put it in a body bag, wrap it up, shove it in a 50-gallon drum, and take it away. When the winner comes out, it's a dame. A woman! A one-punch fight."

After they were safely deposited back at the airport, Knatz asked McQueen for a response to the evening's entertainment. "It was staged," McQueen said dismissively. A few days later, McQueen wasn't so blasé. During a break in filming, he came to Knatz with a newspaper in his hand and a circled article about a Chinese man's body that had been discovered in an oil drum. McQueen shoved the paper into Knatz's hand and asked, "Does this have anything to do with the fight we saw the other night?" Knatz stayed silent while they exchanged frightened glances. "He got scared because he didn't want any part of it," Knatz said. "He thought he might be subpoenaed as a murder witness. He was very nervous."

In fact, McQueen fostered a nervousness that was parlayed to the set. Outwardly he was the personification of cool. Privately, his close friends could tell he was not the same Steve. "On *Bullitt*, he didn't seem to be in as good humor as he was on other films," said Bud Ekins, who doubled McQueen in some of the shots of the film's chase scenes. "He was bitchy, let's put it that way. He cared more." When stunt coordinator Carey Loftin played a practical joke on McQueen, it almost cost him his job. Loftin donned a pair of sunglasses and posed as a fan. When he got behind McQueen, he asked, "Would you please give me your autograph?" McQueen obliged and signed the piece of paper, never making eye contact. Loftin looked at the autograph and exclaimed, "Oh shit, I thought you were James Garner!" McQueen snatched the autograph out of his hand and ripped the paper to shreds. Costar Jacqueline Bisset said McQueen was definitely out of kilter on *Bullitt*. "It was confusing to me because he spoke in American slang, and I could hardly understand him," Bisset said. "He's a nervous man when he's working. He'd repeatedly come over to me and say, 'We've got to discuss this scene,' and then someone would call him away and we'd never get around to it."

Neile, who was asked by her husband to stay away from the set—he claimed, "It's going to be a heavy location,"—also noticed his foul mood and his growing dependency on marijuana. "The drugs started early on. I had never heard of marijuana. It was hot and heavy around the time of *Bullitt*. He was appearing on the set stoned," Neile said. "He was always so professional. Steve was never late. He was always early on the set, and he always used grass after. He was doing a joint or two, and then it started escalating like mad."

So did his extramarital affairs. San Francisco was the birthplace and head-quarters of the free love movement, where college students, dropouts, and hippies tested the boundaries of permissible conduct by engaging in premarital sex, open relationships, and orgies. It was the era of Haight-Ashbury, Golden Gate Park, the Fillmore Auditorium, the Winterland Ballroom, coffeehouses, head shops, acid parties, and communal-style living, and McQueen was a beneficiary of this new era of sexual expression and freedom.

Neile visited the set on March 24 for Steve's 38th birthday. After a co-celebration party with Robert Relyea, who also turned 38 on the same day, with the cast and crew, Neile shot over to McQueen's Jones Street apartment to shower, change, and prepare him a birthday dinner before he arrived home. When she got out of the shower, she spotted a woman's brush on the dressing table. As she inspected it a little closer, she picked up the brush and pulled out long strands of blonde hair realizing it wasn't hers. She picked up his radio and threw it against the mirror, which cracked in every direction. Neile saw it as a metaphor for their marriage. "That year—1968—proved to be a long, long one. The mirror had cracked and the damage was already irreparable, but neither one of us 'was hip to it.'"

McQueen's mania was most likely due to the fact that his career hung on the success of the picture. It is an old adage in Hollywood that you are only as good as your last picture. The film industry was fickle, and McQueen had to be on his guard and remain hypervigilant. Relyea wrote in his 2008 memoir, *Not So Quiet on the Set*, about how he tried to mend the relationship with the studio by firmly tucking his tail between his legs when he placed a call to Kenneth Hyman. "McQueen said to me, 'Why don't you be a big man and call up Kenny to come up?'" Relyea said. "That was an unmitigated disaster. I couldn't believe McQueen asked me to be nice to this guy."

As promised, Relyea called Hyman and apologized for the rocky relationship. He said he had hoped they could put the past behind them and continue making films together. Relyea capped off the conversation by asking Hyman if he'd like to take a look at some of the rough footage they had assembled. Hyman was not gracious or pleasant.

"You know what, luv?" Hyman said sarcastically. "I think I'll just wait and see it in the theater."

Relyea, a mostly mild-mannered man, uncharacteristically lost his cool.

"Fine," Relyea said. "Fuck you." The phone on the other end clicked dead, signaling the official end of their dicey relationship.

But Solar had one last ace up its sleeve—the film's centerpiece—a 9-minute, 42-second testosterone-fueled car chase through the hilly streets of San Francisco that made the movie an instant classic.

The famous car chase wasn't in the book or in the film's original script, but many people have claimed credit as the midwife. Writer Alan Trustman said that he incorporated it into the script based on a summer he spent drag racing in the streets of San Francisco. "I was looking for something for McQueen to do to keep him busy. I had actually driven most of the locations in the movie, though I did not lay out the chase scene. The car chase was in the first post-McQueen script, right down to the hubcaps falling off and keeping the camera a foot off the ground. I even wrote in a Mustang. To this day, I claim it as the best automobile advertisement ever."

Peter Yates said producer Phil D'Antoni is the rightful godfather of the chase, who pushed for it from the start. "I had just done a car chase in *Robbery*, and I wasn't up for another chase. McQueen was getting ready for *Le Mans*, and he didn't want to do a car chase," Yates said. "In fact, it was only about halfway through filming that we put it in the script at all. Warner Brothers held it like a carrot over our heads, saying, 'If you go over budget any more, you're not going to be able to do the car chase.' It was strategically scheduled to shoot the last three weeks of the film."

Two 1968 Ford Mustang GT fastbacks and three 1968 Dodge Charger RTs were used for the groundbreaking scene. Both Mustangs were owned by the Ford Motor Company and were part of a promotional loan agreement with Warner Brothers. Veteran race mechanic Max Balchowsky modified the Mustangs' engines (325 horsepower), brakes, and suspension to keep up with the 375-horsepower Chargers. Cinematographer William Fraker said the decision to film the chase at high speed was conceived over dinner with Yates at Martoni's, an Italian restaurant and bar in Hollywood that catered to movie and music industry types. The two men discussed Yates' *Robbery* and how the studio wouldn't allow him to film at speeds faster than 65 mph. At the time, directors would under-crank the camera to shoot chases to make them appear faster when the final picture was projected at normal speed. This technique was fine for audiences of the '40s and '50s, but it never looked convincing. So they decided to go for broke on *Bullitt*.

Fraker recalled, "The fastest we went was 124 mph. I was sitting six inches off the ground in the car, going 124, and the centrifugal force of the car wouldn't allow me to move right or left! Steve McQueen is coming alongside, I've got to get his close-up, and I fought and fought, thinking, 'I've gotta get this shot!' Our idea was to take the audience on that trip, which really worked beautifully. The first time I saw it with an audience, they applauded at the end of the chase. It was absolutely sensational."

McQueen and stunt driver Bill Hickman, who drove the Dodge Charger, practiced chasing each other at an abandoned airfield in Santa Rosa to get a feel for one another. Documentary footage shows the two men racing the automobiles, bobbing back and forth, and at times reaching out with their free hand to touch the other car. McQueen had not planned on using a stunt driver, but stunt coordinator Carey Loftin wasn't going to take any chances. The insurance company would be opposed to McQueen doing too much dangerous, high-octane stunt work and, most important, it would put the star at risk. If McQueen was injured, then the picture would be shut down. So Loftin enlisted Bud Ekins to double McQueen to tackle some of the hairier scenes, despite McQueen's insistence on doing the driving all himself. It took Loftin four days to pry McQueen from the steering wheel, who crashed the Mustang at least three times. "Steve was a good driver, but there's a difference between good driving and stunt driving," Loftin noted.[4]

The rollicking pursuit started around Easter 1968 and spanned five San Francisco districts (Bernal Heights, Potrero Hill, Russian Hill, North Beach, and Bayview District) and two other cities (Daly City and Brisbane). Director Peter Yates accompanied McQueen on one of the hill-jumping sequences to keep an eye on his star. After Yates completed the shot, he tapped McQueen on the shoulder and told him he was out of film. McQueen replied, "That's nothing. We're out of brakes." McQueen managed to slow down the Mustang by downshifting and maneuvering the vehicle on a street that inclined upward. When the car came to a complete stop, both men roared with laughter.

Neile had been extremely nervous about McQueen's driving activities and secretly asked Yates to curtail her husband's involvement. Yates made arrangements so that Steve received a late wake-up call on the morning of the most dangerous driving sequence. When McQueen arrived on the set hours later, he spotted Ekins behind the wheel of the 390 GT Mustang, sporting a blue turtleneck sweater and sunglasses with his hair spray-painted blond, driving recklessly down hilly Chestnut Avenue. It took McQueen only a second to realize he'd been had. When the stunt was finished, McQueen ran to the car as Ekins opened the door. "Where'd you learn to drive like that?" McQueen asked, taking the offensive. "I don't know, Steve," Ekins replied. McQueen continued, "You fucker. You're doing it to me again. I had to go up in front of the whole world and tell them that I didn't make the jump over the fence in *The Great Escape*, and now the

---

4   Viewers can determine who's driving the Mustang by looking at the car's interior mirror. If it is up or visible, it's McQueen. If it's down or not visible, it's Ekins.

same thing's gonna happen all over again. I'm going to have to go on the Johnny Carson show and tell him I didn't do it again."

Years later, Ekins said the strength of the driving sequence saved the film. "I've probably seen the movie half a dozen times, and it doesn't make sense to me," Ekins said. "There are holes in it. Terrible holes in that movie. But the car chase was good...It started a whole new thing for car chases."

Bullitt didn't just start a new trend. It became the gold standard for all car-chase films. Over the years, many films have tried, resorting to adding even more action to spice up the chase. Three years later, *The French Connection* tried to repeat *Bullitt*'s success and came close with a pursuit between a car and subway train, although it lacks the artistry and dueling nature of its predecessor. The same could be said for Phil D'Antoni's *The Seven-Ups*, which tried to re-create the magic of *Bullitt*'s chase five years later. *Foul Play*, the 1978 comedy starring Goldie Hawn and Chevy Chase, succeeded in making movie audiences laugh and even forget they were watching a blatant rip-off of *Bullitt*. *The Rock* in 1996 has a San Francisco–based chase, but it is overloaded with explosions and jumps that border on absurd. Other films, such as 1998's *Ronin* and the *Bourne* trilogy, attempt to pay homage to *Bullitt*, trying to emulate the style and specific shots during the particular chase. However, all pale in comparison. The chase is now considered legendary around the world and cannot be toppled. Many lists have been compiled, and *Bullitt* always comes out on top. In Britain, a 2005 television program on the Sky television network listed the top chases, and *Bullitt* was the clear winner. It is no wonder that the film was voted into the National Film Registry in 2007 so that these heart-pounding scenes can be preserved forever.

After three months of shooting, *Bullitt* wrapped in May 1968. Warner Brothers–Seven Arts didn't bother to attend previews or show any support for the film. In fact, when Solar staffers delivered the print to the studio, they were told to immediately vacate the premises. Robert Relyea said security was brought in to change the locks on their former offices and remove their nameplates from the parking lot. "There was nothing subtle about it—we were fired," Relyea said.

Warner Brothers–Seven Arts was amazed that Radio City Music Hall had requested the picture in advance for an October premiere, the first time an action-adventure played in that hallowed venue. The request, while a prestigious honor, meant that *Bullitt*'s postproduction time would have to be cut by a third. And that's where *Bullitt* truly came together—in the cutting room. Editor Frank Keller pieced together a highly stylized yet gritty crime-thriller whose moody look and feel became de rigueur for almost all cop films in the next decade. Keller's deft touches didn't go unnoticed—he won an Academy Award for Best Film Editing on *Bullitt*. It was well-deserved considering he saved the climax of the car chase. When the Dodge Charger overshoots the gas station, Keller's editing ensured this mistake goes by virtually unnoticed.

Composer Quincy Jones was tapped to score the film and sat with Peter Yates during the first screening. After the lights went up, Jones sat in stony silence and then proclaimed, "That's a motherfucker!" Two weeks prior to his start date, Jones burst an appendix and was replaced by Lalo Schriffrin, who not only made the film's score inimitable but made the key decision not to place music over the chase sequence, relying on the sounds of revved-up engines, squealing tires, and crashing metal to keep audience members spellbound and convey the raw intensity of the muscle cars.

Bullitt premiered on October 17, 1968, at Radio City Music Hall.[5] The movie wasn't just a smash; it was a juggernaut. The picture succeeded beyond anyone's wildest dreams—a whopping $50 million in the United States alone.[6] Writer Alan R. Trustman, who had a financial interest in the film, contends that *Bullitt* in the first year of release alone had grossed a staggering $80 million based on his own estimates. "It was re-released in the sixth week of general release, packaged as a double feature with *Bonnie and Clyde*, which the studio owned 100 percent of since they bought out Warren Beatty and everyone else," Trustman said. "Warner attributed half the revenues to each picture for all the costs of *Bullitt* because they didn't have to advertise *Bonnie and Clyde*; everyone was already familiar with that picture. To this day, nobody knows what the picture really grossed."[7]

Critical reaction to *Bullitt* matched its box-office take, and McQueen received kudos for his fresh portrayal of a renegade cop. Archer Winsten of the *New York Post* wrote, "McQueen keeps his cool as only he can, now that Bogart's long gone. The best, most exciting car chase the movies have ever put on film." *Variety* called the film, "an extremely well-made crime melodrama, highlighted by one of the most exciting auto chase sequences in years." And Tom Milne of *The Sunday Observer* wrote, "A curiously exhilarating mixture of reality and fantasy, so actual that at times one could almost swear that the fictional adventures must have been shot with concealed cameras."

---

5 Ali MacGraw said in her memoir *Moving Pictures* that she saw *Bullitt* at its initial Radio City Music Hall run. She wrote that she was spellbound by both the movie and its star, who left her breathless and her knees knocking.

6 Equivalent to a $718 million gross in 2010.

7 Robert Relyea said in 2010 the William Morris Agency requested an audit from the studio, which coughed up a big check to Solar.

The film's success was not just dependent on one car chase. The technical achievement and acting talent of the film are both stellar. McQueen is definitive as the title character cop. All of the other attempts that followed, such as *Dirty Harry* (a role McQueen actually turned down), simply don't capture the same complexity of McQueen's uncompromising cop with his own moral compass and way of doing things. McQueen's less-is-more approach once again works miracles as every shot with him in it is worthy of any photography hall of fame. In *Bullitt*, nothing says more than a silent McQueen looking at the camera, his face portraying his emotions and speaking a thousand silent words.

The supporting cast is also exemplary. Vaughn excels and appears to relish playing the dapper but ruthless politician more interested in serving himself than the public. McQueen once again gave a friend a break, handing Don Gordon a great role with plenty of dialogue and screen time. McQueen's *Sand Pebbles* costar Simon Oakland also gets a choice role as the boss with a conscience. Even Norman Fell gives McQueen a run for his money in his portrayal of the police official who does not say much simply because he doesn't need to, such is his authority.

The film's success swept up everyone involved, from the actors to the crew. Carey Loftin said, "*Bullitt* did wonders for my career. I would get hired for a job and be told, 'We want a chase scene like *Bullitt*.' I'd tell them, 'If you've got the money, I got the time.'"

Director Peter Yates went on to have a long and distinguished film and television career. However, the shadow of *Bullitt* has at times become a detriment to Yates in a personal sense. "I would be hired for a job and be told, 'We want a chase scene like in *Bullitt*.' It's annoying at times because people talk more about *Bullitt* than any of my other films. I've had two films nominated for an Academy Award,[8] and they still want to talk about that damned car chase. That's Hollywood for you."

But no one benefited more from *Bullitt*'s success than Steve McQueen. The film gave him all the power, money, respect, and glory he could ever have imagined. It was also his fifth hit film in a row and his biggest success to date. He had made the rare transition from movie star to producer to pop-culture icon, and everything kept paying off in silver dollars. McQueen had already achieved amazing success, but *Bullitt* really did push him through the stratosphere. The legacy and presence of this role is indelible to this day. *Bullitt* car clubs are a cottage industry in the United States, with the Ford Motor Company still using

---

8   *Breaking Away* and *The Dresser.*

McQueen's footage to sell their cars in their advertising. He literally created the archetypical and quintessential tough antihero cop. Even a simple blue turtleneck would start its own fashion craze. Only McQueen could take an undistinguished garment, completely humdrum if worn by anyone else, and turn it into the essence of cool. McQueen's classic pose in the doorway is famous in its own right and adorns student walls and London art galleries alike. This image of intensity, defiance, and supreme confidence immortalizes McQueen for all time. If the breathtaking jump in *The Great Escape* marks McQueen's transition to the big time, then his role as Frank Bullitt is the one that propelled him beyond cinema and movie stardom. It made him a legend.

McQueen's popularity had reached such heights, but the downside was that his career could only logically go in one direction—south. Pride goes before the fall, and McQueen was more than just proud; he thought he was invincible. Time and history tell everyone that nothing can last forever. It simply can't. In 1968, McQueen was like Icarus, soaring toward both the sun and greatness on golden wings. But how long could he keep climbing before the wax would melt and his wings would give way?

24

STRANGE DAYS

STEVE MCQUEEN WAS ON A HIGHER PLANE NOW. Everything about him had changed in the wake of *Bullitt*—his wealth, his clothes, his manner of speech, how he related to people, and his relationship with his wife. In the span of a decade, Steve McQueen had gone from a bright new star on television to cinema's first rock star. He had received a worldly education that only fame could teach, and he was a willing pupil. He had learned the Hollywood system well, and through his sheer force of will he had outsmarted and manipulated his costars, screenwriters, directors, agents, studio executives, and producers. He had made the successful transition from struggling actor to movie star and now business mogul. The success of *Bullitt* made Steve McQueen not only a world-renowned public figure but also a very rich man.[1] "You know, 20 or 25 years ago, they'd have nailed me up on a cross for doing what I'm doing today in the film industry," McQueen noted. "But it's time someone broke the stranglehold the big distributors have got over the film business. I am fighting them all the time—even now. It is up to the young people to get control now. I am not young anymore, but I'll make a few dents here and there. I am just starting to fulfill one of my ambitions right now." McQueen had always wanted to grab the brass ring, and he had done just that and more. In fact, the brass ring was now sitting comfortably on his index finger. McQueen had made achievements and had success as a businessman and an actor that were previously unheard of, and he had won virtually every battle he chose to fight. However, his ambition was starting to run out of actual achievements and challenges to fuel it. From here on, he would only be competing with himself. This would be the hardest battle, and he did not emerge unscathed.

---

1   Though there is dispute about *Bullitt*'s actual box-office take, the studio claimed $24,950,447 in gross receipts 18 months after its initial release. After the film's production cost of $5,435,303 was deducted, Solar's 42.5 percent of the take amounted to approximately $8.3 million.

His greatest ambition was to become a business tycoon. Solar Productions, with a staff of about eight people, occupied the second floor in a Studio City office on Ventura Boulevard just across the street from CBS.[2] McQueen's tastefully decorated offices resembled an Italian Villa filled with expensive antiques, leather chairs, plush wallpaper and carpets, decorative paperweights, and key lighting. He looked the part of a businessman, too, often showing up in designer suits, laundered shirts, ties, cuff links, and Italian loafers.

In addition to Solar Productions, McQueen opened Solar Plastics and Engineering, which produced accessories for dune buggies and motorcycles. One of the patents McQueen personally designed was a fiberglass Baja Bucket seat to help prevent injuries in case of a roll-over accident. The company also sponsored many of McQueen's racing activities, which weren't cheap.

McQueen enlisted famed car upholsterer Tony Nancy to oversee the Ventura-based operation, which employed approximately 30 people. It manufactured buggy gas tanks, plastic fenders, bike kits for American Eagle, and a buoy system for the Coast Guard. "It was a company that was a quarter-century ahead of its time," said friend Nikita Knatz. "I can't imagine the kind of money it would make in today's car aftermarket."

Steve also had the money and decision-making power to make other people's dreams come true. Filmmaker Bruce Brown approached McQueen in 1969 to finance a motorcycle documentary called *On Any Sunday*. Brown asked him for $313,000. McQueen cut him a check the next day. "He was as good a partner as you could have," Brown said. "He never told me to do this or that—he was just there for support."

McQueen had a unique vision for the films and enterprises he was involved in and the image he wanted to put forward. This was intrinsic to what he could relate to and what he believed in, such as realistic movies, fast cars, motorcycles, creativity, and above all the freedom to do what he wanted. It was as if his maxims were to push things beyond where they could be taken and to be bound by no one. Everything was coming together, and his dreams were becoming a reality.

"If you work, you get the goodies. It doesn't surprise me much. I didn't wake up one morning and find it there," McQueen said. "It was years of hard work, okay? Nobody gave it to me. I feel grateful sometimes, but I'm not sure who to feel grateful to."

---

2   McQueen, in a sense, was coming home, for this was the former site of Four Star Studios, where he spent three seasons filming *Wanted: Dead or Alive*.

The goodies included stocks, bonds, trusts, private holdings, pensions, profit-sharing plans, insurance policies, and limited partnerships; a fleet of high-end automobiles and motorcycles; real estate in Brentwood, Big Sur,[3] a rental home in Leo Carillo Beach north of Malibu, and a second home, a 4,300-square-foot midcentury luxury pad in the prestigious Southridge enclave in Palm Springs. The four-bedroom home was part of a gated community that included full-time guard service, wraparound porch, a triangular-shaped pool, guesthouse, a large carport, and a magnificent view of the San Jacinto Mountains.[4]

McQueen, a symbol of youth and rebellion, was now firmly part of the establishment but on his terms. Experience had taught him that life had its games and he could either play by the rules or be confined by them. McQueen, of course, had his own set of rules.

Closing in on 40, McQueen paid lip service to the idea that he could not go on forever as the rebel, the loner, the antihero, or the movie star. "I've got a feeling I'm leaving stardom behind, you know. I'm gradually becoming more of a filmmaker, acquiring a different kind of dignity from that which you achieve in acting. After all, I'm no matinee idol, and I'm getting older. I don't think I can be doing my kind of thing in the '70s; I want to be on more of the creative side of business…In my own mind, I'm not sure that acting is something for a grown man to be doing."

Neile thought Steve was changing, too. His ego was running amok, his sense of humor was waning, and he was no longer the loose and freewheeling person that had charmed her as well as millions of fans. As she reviewed his press clippings, she noted he became an insufferable bore and took himself way too seriously. After his explosive rise to stardom, suddenly his opinion mattered to others. McQueen wasn't shy when it came to rendering an opinion, which ran the gamut from the direction of '60s cinema ("This is the end of an era, the beginning of the end of movie stars."); breaking the Hollywood system ("Distributors and exhibitors are hungry old dinosaurs who are realizing things are changing."); Vietnam ("If Vietnam falls, the gateway to Asia falls."); conservation ("I believe all of us have the instinct to return to the soil."); racial harmony ("When they understand that black people make love, and they make it good, then we'll be on our way. We've got to learn to live together."); monogamy ("I don't know much about women. The last time I picked one was 13 years ago and I married

---

3   Big Sur was William McQueen's favorite vacation spot, a fact most likely known to Steve.

4   McQueen insisted the beach home was his "crash pad" and that Neile should call first before coming over. He also instructed her to decorate the Southridge home in "bachelor motif" with no "feminine stuff." Surprisingly, she put up no resistance.

her. It's worked out just fine."); hippies ("Cops shouldn't make trouble for the hippies. They've contributed so much that's groovy."); the new establishment ("Soon about 70 percent of the population will be under 30. Then youth will take over."); and the legalization of marijuana ("The world is high-oriented. I say let the grass flow and ban the drugs, the bad drugs."). McQueen saw himself as more than a star, filmmaker, producer, or even movie mogul—he perceived himself as an *auteur*. He felt he was a conduit between the counterculture of the day and the more conservative population who voted Richard Nixon into office.

"I'm half-farmer and half-street people," McQueen said. "I can look at both because I grew up on a farm and on the streets. Out there on the farms, they think, 'All people with long hair are no good.' It takes a very brave man to wear long hair around them." Today some people would dismiss this as McQueen's midlife crisis. But this was more; this was self-imposed evolution in every aspect—outlook, beliefs, lifestyle, and desire. McQueen had always been a man of contradictions, but he was taking this to a whole new level. He was undergoing a metamorphosis. These were strange days.

McQueen's new outlook on life also dictated his choice of film roles. He had the opportunity to follow up *Bullitt* with another blockbuster and continue his run of box-office gold, but his ego got in the way when it came to his selection of projects. He turned down *Dirty Harry, Ice Station Zebra, The Yards at Essendorf, The French Connection,* and *Play Misty For Me.* ("The woman's role is much stronger role than the man's. She's the one you'll remember.") Even one of the most popular films of all time was offered to him on a silver platter—*Butch Cassidy and the Sundance Kid.*

The idea of pairing Paul Newman and McQueen, the two blond-haired, blue-eyed superstars, wasn't a novel idea. In 1967 director Richard Brooks wanted the two to team up for his masterpiece, *In Cold Blood.* Unfortunately, the two were unavailable, working on other projects—Newman was working on *Cool Hand Luke,* while McQueen was on location in Boston for *The Thomas Crown Affair.* Brooks ultimately decided on casting a couple of unknowns—Robert Blake and Scott Wilson—who gave the film a gritty authenticity, resulting in four Academy Award nominations. That same year, 20th Century Fox studio head Richard Zanuck paid a then-record $400,000 for the rights to *Butch Cassidy and the Sundance Kid* with the idea of teaming Newman (whom Goldman had wanted since the project's inception) and McQueen (who made Zanuck a fortune and gave the studio considerable cachet with *The Sand Pebbles*). "These were big, big stars who had never done a picture together before. It was a dream. What more could you ask for than Newman and McQueen?" said agent Freddie Fields, who worked at Creative Management Associates, the agency representing Newman[5] at the time.

"I didn't represent McQueen yet,[6] but because we were friends, I sent him the script directly. McQueen wanted the part, but there was a billing problem," Fields said. McQueen invited Fields to his trailer at the Fox lot to discuss the movie. On the advice of Stan Kamen and the top brass at the William Morris Agency, McQueen said he couldn't commit to the picture unless he was granted top billing.

"I can't take second billing to Paul Newman," McQueen said. Fields was stupefied.

"You've got to be reasonable, Steve," Fields said. "Newman's older than you. He's been around longer. He's made more pictures. He's not as beautiful as you, but you have to give him what he's been getting, and that's first billing. Big deal."

"I can't," McQueen said.

McQueen was used to getting his way and was not prepared to accept playing second fiddle to Newman, whom he had perceived as a rival while he was still trying to break into major films. McQueen actually lost sleep over the deal and woke up with what he thought was a brilliant idea—he and Newman would simply flip a coin. It would be in the hands of the gods. He sailed the idea past Neile, who told him that Newman would never go for it.

In the meantime, Fields came up with an innovative strategy that was pre-approved by Newman where both stars would receive "staggered but equal billing," in which one name would appear first and on the left but in a lower position, and the other would appear on the right but was raised higher than the first name. As a kind gesture, Newman instructed Fields that McQueen could have his pick of the two. McQueen was stymied and asked Fields for his opinion—the lower first or the higher second? Fields told him to go with the first name. With that, McQueen nodded his head affirmatively, which signaled to Fields they had tackled the insurmountable. But by the time Fields reached the front door, McQueen had changed his mind. Fields was Newman's agent, and McQueen couldn't fully trust his advice.

"No, no, man. I don't like it," Steve said, his paranoia surfacing. "Tell Paul I wanna flip coins."

---

5   Agent John Foreman, who signed McQueen years earlier at the behest of Jack Garfein, still represented Newman and served as *Butch Cassidy's* executive producer.

6   Freddie Fields officially became McQueen's agent in 1970.

It was perhaps the biggest miscalculation of McQueen's film career. The Western was the biggest smash of 1969 and grossed more than $100 million domestically.[7] It also introduced the buddy-flick genre, reintroduced Newman as a major superstar, made Robert Redford a household name, and became one of the most enduring classics of modern-day cinema. However, how McQueen would have played the Sundance Kid is open to opinion. If he had exercised his usual flair for upstaging his costars, he may have dominated the film, like he did in *The Magnificent Seven*. Declining the role also meant not having to worry about holding the limelight. Sharing the star billing would also have meant sharing any profits from the picture's success, whereas on all of McQueen's other projects, he alone got the slice of the profits. If Newman's reviews had been better than McQueen's for their performances, no doubt this would have eaten away at McQueen, fueling his insecurities. Furthermore, McQueen had dominated every picture he made, and for the last decade or so, he was the main star. To take this role would arguably be a step back in some ways. One thing was certain though—McQueen would take second place to no one.

After parting company with Warner Brothers, it didn't take long for Solar Productions to find a new home. In early 1969, Solar inked a six-picture, $20 million deal with Cinema Center Films, CBS' newly formed motion picture division.[8] Solar's slate of films included *The Reivers, Le Mans, Adam at 6 A.M., Man on a Nylon String, Applegate's Gold,* and *Yucatan,* a $7 million action-adventure filmed in the heart of Mexico that promised a motorcycle chase to rival *The Great Escape.* McQueen confessed the deal made him more than a little nervous. "When I think of the $20 million invested in my company, I don't sleep very well," he said. "I even have a notebook and pencil by my bed in case I wake up thinking of something."

It appeared to be a perfect match. Cinema Center was part of the new philosophy on filmmaking and wanted to cut away from the old way the studios were run. "In the old days, the studios had story departments that circulated properties among the studio's stable of producers and stars. It became a cumbersome business, and films all seemed to be cut from the same cloth," said Cinema Center President Gordon Stulberg, who was formerly a production vice president at Columbia. "Now pictures are individually crafted. The particular dedication of a filmmaker, actor, or writer is required for success. We encourage producers and others with projects of an individual nature to talk to us."

---

7   That amount doubled *Bullitt's* recorded box-office take.

8   Cinema Centers Films produced 16 films in a five-year span, including *With Six You Get Eggroll, Scrooge, The Boys in the Band, Big Jake, Little Big Man,* and *Snoopy Come Home.* It folded in 1972.

"Cinema Center just got into the film business right when Solar was available," said film executive Bob Rosen. "We were pleased to have the No. 1 box-office attraction in the world." The moment was especially ironic to Rosen, who a dozen years before had been an assistant on the set of *This Could Be the Night*, the MGM movie that was supposed to transform Neile into the next Debbie Reynolds. "She had all of the publicity people to deal with, the hairdresser, wardrobe, and all of the people fussing over her," Rosen remembered. "Steve told me he was up for a new pilot, but I didn't believe him. He didn't strike me as the next superstar."

His next film, William Faulkner's Pulitzer Prize–winning novel, *The Reivers*, didn't provide the best start to this partnership and did few favors for McQueen's image. He had spent a good portion of the decade defining his brash, cool, moody, loner, and antihero characters. After *Bullitt*, McQueen made the artistic leap of faith to go against type. It was a decision that caused him great consternation, according to Robert Relyea. "Steve said to me, 'After *The Reivers*, I'll probably never be hired again,'" Relyea recalled. The comment struck Relyea as borderline humorous given the comment was made on a plane heading to Washington D.C., where McQueen was going to pick up the Star of the Year award from the National Association of Theater Owners, a trade organization whose membership gives awards based strictly on box-office dollars. Relyea dismissed the notion, but McQueen went on the defensive. "You're missing the point," Steve said. "They don't photograph you, they photograph me. And this film will do me in." McQueen went so far as to call it "career suicide," something he reiterated to Relyea many times.

"[McQueen] took insecurity to a new level," Relyea said. "He was totally convinced that he was betraying the public by doing a comedy."

McQueen's history with *The Reivers* predates his Solar Productions deal with Warner Brothers, when he made a verbal agreement to star in the turn-of-the-century comedy with Columbia executive Gordon T. Stulberg. When Stulberg left Columbia in 1967 to take over the reins at Cinema Center, part of his exit deal included several properties, including *The Reivers*.

Solar enlisted the distinguished husband-and-wife screenwriting duo Irving and Harriet Frank Ravetch, who wrote two other screenplays based on Faulkner's works: *The Sound and the Fury* and *The Long Hot Summer*.[9] The biggest stumbling block for McQueen was how to distill his larger-than-life persona into Boon Hogganbeck, a Southern rascal and rogue who shows an 11-year-old

---

9   The couple also won an Academy Award for 1963's *Hud*.

boy named Lucius (played by Mitch Vogel) the facts of life on a spirited jaunt from Mississippi to Memphis in a perky yellow Winton Flyer. It didn't seem to be a problem for the couple. "When we were writing the screenplay, we had only one actor, Steve McQueen, in mind to play the hero, Boon Hogganbeck," Harriet Ravetch said. "If Steve had lived 60 years ago, he would have been the free-spirited Boon."

Despite his misgivings about trying his hand at comedy for the first time since *Soldier in the Rain*, McQueen believed in what was Faulkner's last literary work. "It dealt with our country in the 19th century, the innocent era when people said 'Hello!'" in the street and there was grass everywhere. I'm certainly sympathetic to that and I like Faulkner, but it was a comedy part and I've never had much confidence in myself in comedy. After the life of the party goes, I'll crack a joke and maybe get a laugh, but that's about it."

It was Irving Ravetch, who also served as the film's coproducer, that first suggested Mark Rydell as the picture's director. Ravetch shared the same agent as Rydell, but no one associated with the project knew that McQueen and Rydell shared a past. "McQueen was so peculiar. I told him about our idea regarding Mark Rydell as the director and said, 'I think you two were in the same acting school together,'" Robert Relyea said. "He said, 'I don't remember.' We asked if he'd like to meet with him, and he said no. When we asked if we should hire Rydell he said, 'That's fine.' Well, nobody ever mentioned Mark Rydell and Neile went out together in the '50s and that Steve had stolen her away from him. Neile didn't ever bother to tell me, either. The whole thing was goofy. To be honest, I don't think it affected anything—Steve was just as shitty to Mark as he was to Peter Yates, John Sturges, or anybody else."

The McQueen-Rydell relationship seemed fine at first, with McQueen taking the director's advice on the selection of actors, including Rupert Crosse in a key costarring role. Crosse, who stood 6'5", towered over McQueen. He also had a reported substance abuse problem and had the stigma of "militant" hanging over his head. It was only through the masterful persuasion of Rydell that Crosse got the part of Ned McCaslin, the fun-loving stable hand who is Boon's partner in crime. Rydell remembered, "I had to con Steve into it. They had read well together and had kind of gotten along, and we finally cast Rupert. That took a lot of pushing, because Steve didn't want him. He wanted some little guy."

The director suggested that McQueen throw Crosse a small party at the Castle to welcome him to the fold. What almost ended in disaster eventually turned up on celluloid much to the delight of audiences who later saw the film. "I arrived with Rupert, who was looking around. He had never seen anything like it," Rydell said. "There were only eight of us; we were talking and having drinks. Steve was very big on *jeet kune do*, a form of martial arts. His friend, Bruce Lee, was with us all during the picture. Bruce used to work out with him every day; this was before Bruce became a star.

"Rupert's sitting there and says, 'You're off-balance. You could be knocked down.' Well, to embarrass Steve in front of a group of people was, first of all, wrong. I'm trying to get that through to Rupert. I'm pulling at his pants. I say, 'That's all right. It's not so off-balance.' Rupert says, 'He could be knocked down.' Steve says, 'Oh? Why don't you show me?' I'm thinking, 'Here goes the picture.' I feel it's out the window. Then Rupert unwinds like a praying mantis and stands to his full height—skinny, maybe 160 pounds. Steve goes *pah-toong* and drops down three steps, under a pool table. It turned out that Rupert had a black belt in karate. Steve comes up, red with embarrassment. He walks over to Rupert and shakes his hand. They start to shake, and suddenly they're almost arm wrestling. We used it throughout the film—every time they'd shake hands."

Rydell also selected newcomer Mitch Vogel as Lucius, the 11-year-old boy who comes of age in four days under Boon's tutelage and is exposed for the first time to cheating, lying, brawling, and womanizing. Vogel won out over 4,000 hopefuls who tried out for the part. He landed the role after 13 auditions. "*The Reivers* was a movie that was not only a very special time for me personally but professionally, as well," Vogel said in 2010. "I ended up getting a lot of work as a result of the film, including a regular stint on *Bonanza*. Let's just say when I got the part, it was super exciting."

Vogel said his first day of work was a publicity shoot for the picture on the back lot of the CBS buildings in Studio City. It was a day he'll never forget. "They blocked off the entire back lot of the studio, and there was Steve McQueen, sitting in the Winton Flyer, motioning me to come and join him. Flashbulbs were going off because there were tons of photographers everywhere. We sat in the Winton Flyer for a few minutes posing for pictures, and then he drove it around and finally let me have the wheel. He gave me my first driving lesson because in the movie, my character ends up driving the car. Right away, Steve took me under his wing."

It was an important bonding experience for Vogel, who grew up without a father and was raised by a heavy-handed stage mother. McQueen, who was also fatherless, sensed the void in Vogel and made himself available to the youngster at all times. "Steve was my father at the time," Vogel said. "He was my dad, and he watched over me during the entire time we made that film. He took me for rides on his motorcycle during breaks, was by my side at the hospital when I broke my arm, had me over to his house for a sleepover, and let me hang out in his trailer. I know he cared about me beyond our working relationship, and he was just a very kind man. He was just about the coolest guy I had ever met."

Although Rydell got his way when it came to Crosse and Vogel, he couldn't sway McQueen when it came to his leading lady. Rydell was pushing for Ellyn Burstyn, whom he had known from the Actors Studio, while studio brass had wanted Leigh Taylor-Young. Diane Ladd had also auditioned for the role but was relegated to a much smaller part. McQueen had lobbied hard for Sharon Farrell, a veteran television actress who had worked her way up to feature films, most notably *Marlowe* with James Garner. Decades later she recalled her moxie during the audition process. "When I was up for Corrie in *The Reivers*, I became her. I read 22 times for Mark Rydell. He finally told me they were going with Leigh Taylor-Young. I begged Mark to let me read for Steve just one time. That way, I felt it was a fair shake," Farrell recalled. The two had known each other years before when Rydell was a dialogue coach on television's *Ben Casey*. She had also studied acting with his wife, Joanne Linville. Switching gears, Rydell told Farrell the part called for someone around the age of 23. Farrell was five years older at the time and was not going down without a fight. She fudged the age on her birth certificate and pleaded her case to *Variety* reporter Army Archerd, one of the most respected and influential writers in the film industry. He asked publicly in one of his columns why Rydell would not allow Farrell to read for the part. Archerd's column, combined with Farrell's persistence, finally paid off and won her the part. To her credit, Farrell delivered a standout performance, and *The Reivers* remains one of her most memorable roles.

McQueen recognized in Farrell a kindred spirit. He once told her, "Sharon, we are alike. We're both from the Midwest. You're street smart, not book smart. We even look similar. You have a mole just like me." Out of instinct, she touched the mole on her cheek and in that instant, she said, "Steve McQueen became my hero."

Farrell won the coveted role, which was a huge career disappointment for Burstyn as she recalled in her memoir, *Lessons in Becoming Myself*. "I had done three readings for that film, and Mark [Rydell] let me know I was his first choice for the role, but McQueen had casting approval, so my fourth audition would be for him. In the meantime, Mark asked me to read with the young kids who were auditioning, and I gladly obliged. I felt as if the part were mine...I thought this would be my big break, but Steve McQueen didn't agree. He liked another girl better. I was devastated. I couldn't stop crying for days."

Farrell's casting seemed to be a major point of contention for McQueen and Rydell's relationship, and it became a tug of war about who would direct her. "These two men acted like they were friends, but they were not, and they carried this weird animosity toward each other throughout the entire film," Farrell said.

The relationship with Cinema Center was also tested when the studio posted an advertisement in one of the trades, signaling the start of the production. It featured an intense photo of McQueen behind the wheel of the film's Winton Flyer with a tagline that suggested another action picture: "He's rolling at you again!"

"If we're going to do Faulkner, we're going to do it right," McQueen bellowed at Cinema Center's studio brass. "I'll be a southern hick, I'll dress in overalls, I'll walk knee-high in cow shit—but there will be no car chases!" The final poster showed McQueen in close-up, clad in overalls, a piece of straw hanging from his mouth and one eye closed from squinting in the sun. It read, "You'll LOVE him as Boon!" McQueen wasn't crazy about that ad campaign, either, citing, "I looked like a village idiot in that shot. But you can't control everything." He may not have liked it, but it is worth remembering that this marketing campaign relied solely on McQueen and did not feature any scenes or costars. It carried an important message—McQueen sold pictures.

Principal photography commenced in the fall of 1968 in Carrollton, Mississippi, a tiny town of 250 people situated in the northern-central portion of the state. Robert Relyea recalled one of the first nights in Carrollton when he, McQueen, and Rydell were strolling through the town's main street, marveling at the turn-of-the-century architecture when McQueen suggested they needed more security. Relyea was dumbfounded. Security from what?

"From out-of-control fans like these," McQueen said as a trio of hysterical middle-aged housewives with pen and paper rapidly descended on them. McQueen needn't have worried; they brushed past him and surrounded Rydell, who a decade before had a recurring role in *Days of Our Lives*, but the character had eventually been killed off in a tragic car accident. The women were most thankful he was still alive and requested his autograph. Because the town didn't have a movie theater, they were clueless that the world's biggest movie star was in their midst. "I don't think Steve ever forgave Rydell, or the town," Relyea said. "From that moment until the end of shooting, McQueen would often shake his head and say, 'I don't think this town is right for this movie.'"[10]

---

10 Shortly after production ended, Carrollton named a street near the courthouse Reivers Drive in honor of the film.

Neither did the townspeople recognize Bruce Lee, who showed up in Carrollton in a karate gi with a stack of comic books underneath his arm. Lee was there to keep McQueen in top physical condition, but he tried to get face time with Relyea whenever he could, manically espousing that he could be the next big thing in films if he could get someone to finance his kung fu movies. At the time, Lee's only notoriety was as *The Green Hornet*'s loyal sidekick, Kato. Relyea had finally reached his limit one day when he exploded, "Stop bothering me, Kato, and forget this crap about starring in movies. Just concentrate on keeping our star in shape. And do yourself a favor. Throw away those stupid comic books—they're a waste of time!" Just a few years later, Lee proved everyone in the business wrong by securing a $2 million fee for 1973's *Enter the Dragon*.

One relationship that proved to be a more worthwhile use of time was that of friend Von Dutch when McQueen enlisted him to construct a 1904 Yellow Winton Flyer from scratch. Dutch was paid $10,000 to build the car but was given a tight three-month deadline.[11] Dutch had told a *Los Angeles Times* reporter he worked on the automobile day and night for three months, but according to friend Michael F. Eagan, that was a half-truth. "What he left out of the *L.A. Times* story was that for the first 10 weeks, nothing was accomplished except for the spending of Steve's money," Eagan said. Anyone sent to check on the Winton job during the first two months was told by Dutch that a tarp covering a pile of junk out back was the Winton. The inspectors reported to Steve that nothing appeared to be getting done. As the deadline loomed, Steve was justifiably worried and angry that the Winton would not be built.

Approximately two weeks from the deadline, Dutch's conscience got the best of him as he bolted upright in bed in a cold sweat at 3:00 AM. He knew a movie's start time was on his shoulders and that McQueen, who was one of Dutch's best customers, would be justifiably angry. "Dutch quit drinking and worked like a madman—sometimes 24 hours a day—building the Winton in his backyard," Eagan said. "He adapted new and old salvaged antique chassis and powertrain parts, finishing the assembled car with fine pinstriping. He had Tony Nancy do the rushed but gorgeous leather upholstery, and a plating shop prepared the chrome and nickel work. When Steve saw the Winton, he went bonkers from disbelief. The big yellow open automobile was ready to go and stunning beyond expectations."[12]

---

11 Von Dutch was hired as an on-location mechanic and plays a blacksmith in the film.

12 McQueen called the Winton Flyer "the real star of the picture" and took possession of it after filming ended. It remained in his collection until his death in 1980. The actual car can now be seen in the Peterson Automotive Museum in Los Angeles.

Against expectations, it was the actors and not the automobiles that needed the most fine-tuning. Actress Sharon Farrell said McQueen and Rydell were jockeying for position on the first day of shooting, each man wanting to direct her. "Many times Mark and Steve directed me in scenes, and often I'd have to choose which way to go," Farrell said. "Since Steve was the one who pushed for me from the start, my loyalty was to him, which made Mark extremely upset." Farrell said Rydell often pushed her to the brink, sometimes calling for 40 takes for a single scene. One day she reached her breaking point when she was asked to wear a silly costume, so she knocked on McQueen's trailer door. "It's the kind of thing a real actress doesn't get stressed about, but I was in tears like a big baby and making a mess of my makeup. Steve came to the rescue. He taught me how to stand up for myself and never do anything my gut told me not to do. He told me, 'You can always get what you want, Sharon. Stand firm and remember that you have about three feet around you and that is your space. No one has a right to go beyond that unless you invite them. Think with your body, and listen to your gut. Even when it's over something silly, if you don't feel good about it, then it's not right.' I wiped my tears away and smiled. I've carried that bit of wisdom with me ever since."

Farrell said McQueen's kindness extended beyond the set; he took her for motorcycle rides and taught her how to drive a stick shift, and he freely dispensed dressing tips. "Steve showed me how to dress conservatively, not flashy, but proper like a lady. He wanted me to look classy. Steve also told me to stop smoking Romeo and Julieta Cigars. The cigars were for my cigarette habit and I thought were an improvement. Steve didn't agree."

She says McQueen was a multifaceted person: private, paranoid, controlling but at times very much like his character, Boon Hogganbeck. "Steve was great fun. He could be rascally and charming. In a sense, he was a reiver. One time Steve and I ventured out with our costar Rupert Crosse to a funky, out-of-the-way soul food restaurant. It had everything: sweet potatoes, greens, turnips, grits, fried chicken, and catfish. We sang songs, carried on, and had a great time. Steve and Rupert ended the evening wrestling on the floor of the place."

McQueen saved most of his grappling skills for Rydell, though, as the two continued to butt heads on the set. McQueen made it clear that he was the head honcho and signed Rydell's checks for the next few months. "[Steve] was the main guy in charge," said Richard Moore, who served as the film's director of photography. "I frankly sensed that he felt competitive with Mark. Steve may have thought he was bigger than Mark, looking down his nose to a certain degree."

Relyea thought it was a bad sign when McQueen admonished Rydell in front of the crew a few days into filming by screaming, "I can't do your job and mine!"

"It usually took longer than that for Steve to reach this level of distaste for his director," Relyea said. "But McQueen seemed to have a real problem with Rydell, so a new speed record was established on *The Reivers* for tension between the star and director."

Mitch Vogel said whatever problems existed between McQueen and Rydell, the two men made sure to shield him from it. "The very first scene we shot was singing 'Camp Town Ladies' as we drove through a dirt path through the Mississippi countryside. It was a nice way to break the ice and get to know one another," Vogel said. "Mark Rydell was there the whole time, encouraging us to develop our relationship with each other. It was a lot of fun for me as a 12-year-old boy, and I remember being very grateful to have that kind of experience."

In addition to the simmering personality conflicts, the production was deluged with problems that are not uncommon to films—freak accidents, bad weather, and strange acts of God. "We had horrible weather in Mississippi, and it must have been a nightmare for the director and editor to match the shots," Vogel said. "It would be sunny and bright for two hours, and then it would get cloudy for the next hour, then rain, then sunny again. It changed all the time. We spent a lot of time hanging around the set, waiting for the weather to change so that we could film."

The film was also set back six weeks when Vogel fell off a horse during the crucial racing scene, which was filmed at the Disney Ranch near Santa Clarita. "We were going full speed and the sprinklers at the racetrack went off and my horse got spooked and pulled to the right, and I fell off to the left," Vogel recalled. "I fell on the ground and when I went to stand up, my arm was still on the ground."

A set doctor had asked Vogel to raise his arm three times, which Vogel could not do. The doctor said the arm was probably just sprained and was about to declare him okay until McQueen intervened. "Steve was there when the incident happened, and after the third time the doctor asked me if I could lift my arm, Steve said, 'The kid says he can't move his arm.' At this point, Steve took over and escorted me to his El Camino and drove me to the hospital because he knew something was wrong.'"

Indeed there was something wrong. X-rays showed that Vogel's left arm had snapped cleanly in two. Doctors told Vogel and McQueen that the fracture was so bad that had he lifted his arm, it would have slipped through his skin and been exposed. "Steve stayed with me the entire time—when they took my X-rays, when they took me to the room on a gurney, and [he] even held the bottle when I had to give a urine sample," Vogel said. "He was there for me when it counted, and there weren't many people like that in my life at the time."

When Vogel returned to the set, Southern California had been hit with a two-month barrage of rain, which pushed the schedule back even further. *The Reivers*, which was budgeted slightly above $4 million, ended up with close to $1 million in cost overruns. McQueen wanted Rydell's head and tried to get him fired. CBS president William Paley held firm and told McQueen no. McQueen turned the screws even tighter on Rydell and brought their relationship to the brink during one of the film's key comedic scenes.

Rydell recalled the situation. "We had our big confrontation in a scene where Steve and Rupert Crosse were pushing the Winton Flyer out of the mud. There was mud everywhere, and the two stars were sliding and falling and not having much success at moving the car. I was sitting high atop a crane when McQueen yelled at me. 'Ryyyyydellll, get over here!' As I climbed down from the crane, my heart stopped. The crew stood still. McQueen was a physical presence given to brutality. He'd demonstrated to me many times he was a first-class tae kwon do kicker. When I reached the ground, I stood eye to eye with McQueen. Steve announced loud enough so the crew could hear, "You know, there's only room for one boss on this picture." "Yeah, that's me," I cut him off. Inside I was trembling, but he walked away. If he wanted a fight, I was ready."

By the time shooting was completed, Rydell felt as if he'd been put through the wringer. Even though he openly praised McQueen to reporters at the time, Rydell was a bit more candid a decade after McQueen's death. "Steve was difficult. I've dealt with some major, tough actors. Nobody's had me on the ropes. But I hung in there. I told him I would outlast him. I said, 'When you're furious with me, I'm still going to be here trying. I'm not going to fold. And I'm not going to give in to you, because you're wrong.' It just drove him crazy, but he did finally surrender."

McQueen didn't go down without a fight, though. As Richard Moore recalled, "When things are going bad on feature films, very many times the person that gets sacrificed is the DP [director of photography]. It happens all the time." When Rydell called Moore into his trailer, he instinctively knew it wasn't good. Moore had been replaced on his first film, *The Scalphunters*, by Burt Lancaster. He knew that if it happened again, his career was over. McQueen wanted Moore out and once again took his case to Paley, who vetoed him once again. Moore stayed.

Mitch Vogel's 13th birthday on January 17, 1969, was a cause to rally the cast and crew. Four decades later, Vogel still gets choked up at the memory. "We were at MGM Studios filming the train sequence when the Winton Flyer is introduced in the movie. I was in my trailer studying for school when the assistant director knocked on my door and said, 'Mitch, what are you doing? You're supposed to be on the set. Come hurry up, we need you!' My heart was beating a mile a minute, and I was extremely worried. When I got to the set, everybody was there and they were all smiling. Up on the train platform was a brand new minibike. It was customized and painted by Von Dutch, who also painted my name on the frame. Steve made a small speech about me, and everybody wished me a happy birthday. That was such a special moment in my life.

"Steve always invited me to go riding with him and his son Chad during breaks in the film. My favorite picture of us together, which I still have, is on his motorcycle. He was driving very fast around the racetrack, and I was sitting on the handlebars and honking the horn, which he encouraged me to do.

"He once invited me for a sleepover at the house, where I met the rest of his family—his wife Neile and their daughter Terry. He had such a lovely home; a huge garage with all of these great cars and a big library that had all of his movie scripts, which were leather-bound and embossed. Neile made lunch for the whole family, and they talked and laughed and ate. It was the closest thing to a normal life I'd ever been exposed to. It opened a picture window for me about how I wanted my life to be one day. I often look back and reflect on those good times."

Despite the constant tension, tumult, and setbacks, the final cut of *The Reivers* turned out surprisingly well. It was one of the few good film versions of Faulkner's work and holds up well nearly 40 years after its initial release. "Boon Hogganbeck is the one screen characterization that I believe captures the playful side of Steve's personality," said longtime friend Pat Johnson. "That was the Steve I remember most."

As a comedy performance, McQueen turned in a respectable piece of work and went partway to silencing those who said he could not do comedy. Although Boon was not McQueen's most lucrative or famous character, the role did establish that McQueen had an impressive range and versatility, much more so than he would ever admit or believe himself. But the proof is there on the screen. Moreover, its shows a bravery in playing against type and against what he thought he could achieve. It was further proof that he was a man unafraid to challenge himself and step outside his own comfort zone.

The Reivers opened Christmas Day in 1969 to receptive critical reviews and high praise for McQueen's comedic abilities. "*The Reivers* fills one with a joyous sense of life and laughter," declared Judith Crist of *New York Magazine*. *Look's* Gene Shalit wrote, "McQueen acts as he hasn't before—an artful wily bumpkin," while *Variety* assessed, "McQueen gives a lively, ribald characterization that suggests he will have a long career as a character actor after his sexy allure thins."

The motion picture was also recognized by the industry and was nominated for two Academy Awards—one for John Williams' score, and the other for Rupert Crosse for Best Supporting Actor. McQueen, unfortunately, was ignored. According to Relyea, "Everybody loved Rupert and said Steve was fine, which I don't think is very fair. Steve worked very hard on that picture. When he found out Rupert was nominated, he didn't sulk. He called Rupert and said, 'Congratulations. What can I do to help? I think you've got a real shot at the Oscar.'[13] He didn't mope around like, 'What about me?' He was proud of the picture because he thought he was playing Russian roulette and didn't get shot."

McQueen was so proud, in fact, that he decided he liked the finished product. "To his credit, he came up to me after the picture opened and said how proud he was of it and we shook hands," Rydell said, who went on to have a distinguished directing career, which included *The Cowboys, The Rose, On Golden Pond,* and *For The Boys*. He vowed during McQueen's lifetime to never work with him again, and Rydell kept his promise. With the passage of time, Rydell has grown sentimental toward McQueen, who was a one-of-a-kind talent. "He was a remarkable, exciting personality. Very tortured, very tormented, borderline psychotic, I would say. But he was magic on film. You just can't take your eyes off him," Rydell said.

The Reivers fared well domestically with an $18 million return at the box office[14], but that's where the buck stopped. In France where McQueen had achieved an almost godlike status, the picture opened and closed within the same week. Other countries followed suit. "[*The Reivers*] would be considered a moderate success, but it was just so Americana that it didn't do any business overseas," Relyea said.

For his next picture, McQueen would make a film on his own terms and in his own way. It was a vanity project that had been his dream for more than a decade

---

13 Crosse lost out to Gig Young for *They Shoot Horses, Don't They?* Crosse died of lung cancer in March 1973.

14 That would be equivalent to at least $100 million in 2010 dollars.

and would see him reach a turning point in both his career and his personal life. In return, he was going to give moviegoing audiences exactly what they wanted: cars, high-speed racing, and lots of footage of their favorite leading man. Or, as the poster put it, "McQueen takes you on a drive in country…The country is France. The drive is at 200 mph!"

25
LET IT RIDE

THE '60S HAD BEEN KIND TO STEVE MCQUEEN. Unfortunately, the era of free love, hippies, and flower power had been punctuated by a grisly massacre that rattled the nation and shook Hollywood to its foundation.

On the morning of August 9, 1969, Los Angeles Police were called to the site of a Benedict Canyon home where they discovered five lifeless bodies in what they say resembled a "ritualistic mass murder."

Five people—Sharon Tate, Jay Sebring, Abigail Folger, Voyteck Frykowski, and Steven Parent—were bludgeoned, stabbed, throttled, and brutally slain in the biggest bloodbath of the decade.

Sebring and Tate's deaths shook McQueen to his very core, as he had a personal relationship with each victim. "Jay Sebring was my best friend. Sharon Tate was a girlfriend of mine. I dated Sharon for a while," McQueen admitted in a 1980 deathbed interview.

"Steve and Jay were very much alike and close, close friends," said Larry Geller, who worked for Sebring when he first opened his men's hair salon in Los Angeles in 1959. "The two were both military veterans and self-made men. Jay, like Steve, was very straightforward and honest and wasn't shy about letting you know his true feelings. We worked together, ate together, talked a good many hours alone together. And I'll never forget the first week when I met him, Jay said, 'When I go, the whole world is going to know about it.' I said, 'What? What the hell are you talking about? How do you know this?' He said, 'I don't know how, but I just know it.'" Sebring had no way of knowing just how soon his self-prophecy would be fulfilled.

Neile McQueen recalled in her memoir *My Husband, My Friend* that Sebring had visited the night before the murders when he gave her husband a trim in the living room of the Castle. Sebring wanted to visit with Tate and keep a watchful eye on her while her husband, director Roman Polanski, was in London.[1]

Sebring invited McQueen to dinner at the El Coyote Café on Beverly Boulevard and drinks at the home of Tate and Polanski. Steve turned to his wife for approval. It was an empty and meaningless gesture. He did whatever he wanted, whenever he wanted. By agreeing to go the party, Steve had unknowingly signed his own death warrant.

However, the hand of fate dealt McQueen a trump card that night. Luck was on his side when an unexpected rendezvous with a mystery woman prompted him to cancel his prior plans. That very night, the Manson Family murdered his friends at the party. Ironically, his infidelity had saved him from the Manson murders. When he heard the news the following morning, he realized he had literally dodged a bullet.

McQueen, carrying a gun in the back of his waistband, gave Sebring's eulogy at his departed friend's funeral.

In the days and weeks that ensued, the Hollywood establishment ran for cover. "The shock waves that went through the town were beyond anything I had ever seen before," recalled writer Dominick Dunne. "People were convinced that the rich and famous of the community were in peril. Children were sent out of town. Guards were hired." And McQueen, who already had a cache of weapons[2] took cover, stashing firearms throughout the house, under the sofa, and under the bed. For once, McQueen's paranoia seemed justified. He even opened up his fortress for one famous guest, Barbra Streisand, who was terrified by the killers on the loose. She was escorted by her agent, Sue Mengers, who said dismissively, "Don't worry, honey. Stars aren't being murdered, only feature players."

McQueen, who was the biggest superstar in the world, wasn't taking any chances. He carried a loaded handgun on him at all times, forced Neile to carry

---

1   According to his book, *The Kid Stays in the Picture*, producer Robert Evans says Polanski asked Evans to watch over his wife while he was gone. Evans had planned on joining Tate for dinner but got stuck in the editing room on the evening of August 8, 1969. His last words to her were, "Sweet dreams."

2   McQueen's arsenal included a Ruger .22, a 9 mm Steyr, a .38 Smith and Wesson target pistol, a Beretta over-and-under, a Mannlicher-Schoenauer 7 mm, a Mannlicher-Schoenauer 7 x 57 mm, a Winchester .30-30, a semiautomatic .22, a .30-40 Krag, a short-barreled lever-action Winchester .44-40 rifle, a .44 Colt single-action revolver, a Ruger Blackhawk, a .44 Magnum, a Winchester lever-action .22, a .303 English Army rifle, a .25 caliber Beretta, and a collection of 16th and 17th century Spanish and English dueling pistols.

one, kept a pump-action shotgun[3] at his Solar office, and installed a closed-circuit monitor on the front gate of his home so he could keep a watchful eye on intruders. "He got paranoid as hell. The whole place was locked up tight," said friend Bud Ekins. "Sharon Tate and Jay Sebring were close friends. It hit too close to home."

How close, McQueen eventually learned, was the razor's edge. When Mephistophelean guru Charles Manson and a group of brainwashed followers called the Family, were finally apprehended months after the Tate-LaBianca murders, McQueen would eventually learn that he was literally the name at the top of the list. For once, this was a star billing that he did not want.

One of the killers, Susan Atkins, told cellmate Virginia Castro Graham that she participated in the Tate murders and that they were about to target the world's biggest celebrities. They included Frank Sinatra, Elizabeth Taylor, Richard Burton, Tom Jones, and Steve McQueen.[4]

When the list went public, McQueen was deeply spooked. He dashed off a frantic letter to attorney Edward Rubin of the law offices of Mitchell, Silberg & Knupp. It read:

> *Dear Eddie:*
>
> *As you know, I have been selected by the Manson Group to be marked for death, along with Elizabeth Taylor, Frank Sinatra, and Tom Jones. In some ways I find it humorous, and in other ways frighteningly tragic. It may be nothing, but I must consider it may be true both for the protection of myself and my family.*
>
> *At the first possible time, if you could pull some strings and find out unofficially from one of the higher-ups in Police whether, again unofficially, all of the Manson Group has been rounded up and/or do they feel that we may be in some danger.*
>
> *Secondly, if you would call Palm Springs and have my gun permit renewed, it was only for a year, and I should like to have it renewed for longer as it is the*

---

3   This same shotgun would be later used by McQueen in *The Getaway*, when he chanced upon seeing it at his new Solar office before filming commenced. This weapon was sold by Bonhams in 2008 for $22,800.

4   The "celebrity hit list" was made public by reporter Bill Farr in October 1970, who had covered the Tate-LaBianca murder trial for the *Los Angeles Herald-Examiner*. Farr discovered the story in Virginia Graham's statement to police: cellmate Susan Atkins had bragged about the murders. Farr was summoned to the chambers of Superior Judge Charles Order and was asked how he obtained the information. He refused to name his source and was sentenced to jail for 46 days before he was released on appeal. Farr's case was not resolved until 1976, when an appeals court tossed out Order's contempt sentence.

only sense of self-protection for my family and myself, and I certainly think I
have good reason.

Please don't let too much water go under the bridge before this is done, and
I'm waiting for an immediate reply.

My best,

Steve McQueen

The Hollywood community, which used to be carefree and relaxed, became weary and paranoid, and for good reason. The ever-so-popular "Make Love, Not War" slogan faded into the background. Celebrities no longer mixed with the general public, and in McQueen's case, he closed the drawbridge to the Castle. The tragic deaths, combined with McQueen's escalating drug use, made him extremely paranoid. Not only did he enlist the help of a friend in the CIA to secure his house, he also took defensive measures when driving, suspecting people were following him, and he darted in and out of traffic and took out-of-the-way roads. What should have been a 15-minute ride often turned into an hour-long excursion.

It was not only the end of the '60s but the end of an innocence. Steve McQueen had not entered his fourth decade with any sense of peace or contentment. He had undoubtedly worked hard in getting to the top, and now more than ever he felt, with apparent justification, that it could all be taken from him within the blink of an eye. McQueen looked with suspicion at the world around him. However, he was the master of destiny, and ultimately he was the one starting on a path that threatened self-destruction. It would be himself, not the myriad outside forces that he feared, that took him to the edge.

• • •

Le Mans had been marinating inside his head for a good decade, and McQueen had waited patiently until he had "the juice" to get it off the starting grid. He wanted not only to show his love and admiration for the sport but to introduce racing to the masses. "Some of these men are dealing with the unknown. That gives a man greatness," McQueen said. "I'm making it so my grandmother in Montana who knows nothing about cars will understand."

There weren't many projects in McQueen's film career that he actively chased, save for *The Thomas Crown Affair*. *Le Mans* was his passion, his labor of love, his ode to machinery, and his push into mania. This film was to be, in Steve's terms, "pure."

"I enjoy the fact that we're playing for big marbles. I'm a filmmaker; I feel very strongly about not compromising the film for a business reason. I enjoy the spooky feeling of having it all on my back, but I don't like anyone fucking with my head while I'm doing it," he said.

Le Mans would be McQueen's vanity project, too. No one had said "no" to him in a very long time, and he was determined to make the film his way. His competitive nature was still brewing away; he had not forgotten that James Garner's *Grand Prix* had beaten him to the theaters just a few years ago. McQueen's limelight had been stolen then, and he wanted the last word. If *Grand Prix* had been first to the starting grid, then McQueen was determined to be the one who took first place.

However, with great passion and determination come great risks, and McQueen would risk it all. The film cost him dearly on both a financial and personal level. He lost money and his empire and ultimately severed ties with trusted friends and even shut out the one person who had stood by him since the lean times in the '50s. These sacrifices were made in order to get his film made. Despite the costs, on *Le Mans*, McQueen let it ride.

Le Mans was a disaster in the making with no real story, a foreign locale, expensive props, and an intangible idea that no one seemed to get except McQueen, who himself found it hard to explain. "The emphasis here is on film as a visual—I guess opposed to verbal. We are also interested in reality," McQueen said. The superstar kept telling everyone, "The script is in my head."

The original script was based on a novel by Denne Bart Petitclerc, an American journalist, war correspondent, screenwriter, and author of *Le Mans 24*. Robert Relyea read Petitclerc's book, which novelized the 1967 race of the same name where it was Ferrari versus Ford, old-world craftsmanship versus machine-age efficiency. Relyea suggested to McQueen they purchase an option on the book. "It had always been in Steve's mind that if you are going to make a racing picture, you make it about one race—Le Mans," Relyea said.

Screenwriter Alan R. Trustman said agent Stan Kamen solicited his services, hoping they could re-create the magic of *The Thomas Crown Affair* and *Bullitt*. Trustman, who read an early version of *Le Mans*, said the idea of McQueen losing the race at the end of the movie was a monumental mistake. He made his best pitch at a meeting at the Castle: "In *The Great Escape*, you win. In *The Sand Pebbles*, you die at the end, and your audience loves you and doesn't want you to die at the end, so the picture fails to do the business it should. Thomas Crown wins. Frank Bullitt wins. Steve McQueen is now the top of the heap, with a salary in the millions and all sorts of profit points because he gives the audience what they want. They want him winning!"

McQueen shook his head no and Kamen scowled. McQueen was intent that his character was going to lose, and nothing could change his mind.

"Steve, please," Trustman pled. "We took each other to the top." As soon as the words tumbled out of his mouth, Trustman knew he had made a mistake. No one took McQueen to the top other than himself. Kamen quickly hustled Trustman to the car and berated him the entire drive back to the hotel. "Kamen drove me back to the hotel, calling me a stupid son-of-a-bitch, telling me he had made me, and he could take me down, I had embarrassed him with his most important client, he would never, never, forgive or forget, and I would never work in this town again," Trustman recalled.

Kamen kept true to his word, but Trustman issued an ominous parting shot: "It's Steve. I know the man. And I think he has a death wish about this racing car thing. He'll fire 10 writers, 10 directors, his partner, his lawyer, his agent, and his wife, and die in a flaming car crash on the last day of principal photography, and I don't want to be the first writer to get the axe, and I don't want to see it happen to Steve."

Not everything Trustman said about *Le Mans* came to pass, but a good majority of it did. Trustman captured a fundamental element of what made McQueen who he was—when McQueen believed in something, he would fight to the end and was ready to sacrifice it all. Trustman never worked with Steve McQueen again.

To everyone's amazement, Cinema Center greenlit *Le Mans* and gave Solar $6 million before a director was selected or a finished script was presented. They also rewarded McQueen handsomely with $750,000 and a percentage of the profits. McQueen's star was burning as brightly as ever.

For *Le Mans*, McQueen turned to Relyea and suggested he direct the picture. Though intrigued with the idea, Relyea's gut told him this was a movie best left in the hands of someone young. "My instinct was to find someone with new ideas, maybe someone young, who wouldn't be tempted to make the typical Hollywood racing film." The name that topped Relyea's list was a 22-year-old wunderkind named Steven Spielberg. The Long Beach State dropout had been signed by Universal Studios after his 25-minute short film (shot for $15,000) called *Amblin'* impressed Sidney Sheinburg, vice president of production for Universal's TV arm. Spielberg's only professional credit to date was the 1969 pilot of *Night Gallery* (titled "Eyes" and featuring Joan Crawford). Relyea set up a meeting with McQueen, who then ran the recommendation past the Cinema Center brass. However, Spielberg was deemed "too young" and given the thumbs down.

Relyea's next selection was George Lucas, but it was deemed he lacked the stature to make a feature film. The ball was flipped back to Relyea, who already had enough on his plate as producer. He knew the circles that McQueen ran around directors and decided he didn't have the stomach for it. Relyea took a pass.

McQueen decided there was really only one director who was seasoned and confident, could pass the muster with the studio execs, and "hold his mud." That man was John Sturges. Furthermore, Sturges *knew* racing. The year before he had shot the 1969 Le Mans race and came away with more than 35,000 feet of film. Unfortunately, it was scrapped due to the fact that the Gulf-Porsche team (McQueen's team in the film) crashed their car early in the race and failed to cross the finish line. The design of the cars had changed as well as the course design, and an extra grandstand had been installed at the facility. The tally was such that the footage simply wouldn't match and was deemed useless. This was just the tip of the iceberg in terms of the waste and difficulties that would face this project.

There was also the matter of a storyline—there simply wasn't one that McQueen and Sturges could agree on. McQueen wanted to shoot a pseudo-documentary on the sport of racing, while Sturges opted for a traditional storyline with characters. It was not an issue to Sturges, in the beginning. *The Great Escape* was a prime example of an unfinished script that turned into a masterpiece. "Very rarely do you get a perfect script," Sturges said. "I've only had two. If you want to make movies, that's the name of the game. If you sit around waiting for perfect scripts, you're not going to be a very active film director."

While Solar was prepping *Le Mans*, Cinema Center approved *Adam at 6 A.M.*, the second film under the Solar banner. The movie pushed Solar's operating philosophy of creative extension and gave cachet to the idea that the company was breaking cinematic barriers. Solar also gave the producers, writers, director, cinematographer, and leading lady all a shot at their first feature film.

The storyline revolves around Adam, a disenchanted professor of semantics at a California college who drives cross-country to Missouri to find himself. The $1.4 million production starred Michael Douglas,[5] Joe Don Baker, and ingénue Lee Purcell, for whom McQueen predicted great things. "My partners and I interviewed close to 500 girls for the lead in this picture," McQueen said at a

---

5 Whisky co-owner Elmer Valentine told *Vanity Fair* reporter David Kamp in 2006 that he had personally arranged for Doors singer Jim Morrison to meet with McQueen to discuss the lead role for *Adam at 6 A.M.* Valentine said Morrison, who was in the throes of drug and alcohol addiction, cut his hair and shaved his beard to make a good impression at a lunch meeting. Morrison failed to get the part that was ultimately awarded to Michael Douglas.

September 1969 press conference. "There's a basic honesty and believability in Lee.... I think this girl and the picture are both going to be hits."

Today Purcell is astonished and grateful that McQueen, who was at the peak of his career, was able to devote so many hours to her development as an actress. "Steve McQueen didn't do anything halfway. He was the original multitasker, and he could do just about anything he put his mind to," Purcell said in 2010. "He was a brilliant man. How could he have accomplished so much in such a relatively short amount of time had he not been brilliant? He was driven, ambitious, but he was also incredibly kind and nurturing. He was my first mentor in this business, and up until then, no one had looked out for me."

Purcell, like McQueen, came from a hard-knocks upbringing, and he recognized in her a parallel soul. She had a tough exterior and showed her soft side only to a chosen few. With McQueen, Purcell could let her guard down and be herself. "He told me a few things about his background, no big secrets or anything but enough to let on that we had followed a similar path in life. He was so easy to talk to that I was completely honest about everything," Purcell said. "He would ask me interesting questions that had nothing to do with the role or the film. He was so down to earth. He wasn't like other people."

McQueen saw in Purcell an almost childlike quality, a person who needed protection, and he dispensed wisdom about preparing for the role, diet, exercise, and protecting yourself financially. "I distinctly remember a conversation we had about money and what I should do with it once I earned it," Purcell said. "As I was from a generation that wasn't looking to get rich, he basically explained that money equals freedom and was trying to get me to wake up. He said, 'If you think about the pennies, you'll never get the nickels.'"

When *Adam at 6 A.M.* was released in September 1970, Purcell said Solar pulled out all the stops, and she and fellow star Michael Douglas were treated to an unforgettable press tour that included first-class travel, limousines, five-star hotels, and an unlimited expense account. At the end of the experience, she received a touching note from McQueen praising her performance and a beautiful watch, which was engraved "*Adam at 6 A.M.*"

"Steve was a first-class individual, and we had some very deep and meaningful conversations in the six months I prepared for *Adam at 6 A.M.*," Purcell said. "My career started because Steve McQueen took the time to mentor me. He gave me a great pedigree by choosing me to star in his film—a film that was a very big deal to him personally. He wouldn't have spent the time grooming me, mentoring me, and educating me about the film business and life if this was some throwaway film. The day I got the role of Jerri Jo Hopper was one of the happiest days of my life.

"When you were in a room with Steve McQueen, you were truly in a different universe. He was so incredibly kind and wonderful to me, and his life lessons still reverberate. He will always have a special place in my heart."

• • •

Before principal photography commenced on *Le Mans*, Steve revved up his racing skills with Solar's purchase of a Porsche 908 Spyder. His wanted to test his mettle by driving with the big boys and prove to the public he was quite capable of performing his own stunts. "In most Hollywood movies, the star is doubled, but I don't want any doubles for me at *Le Mans*. If I can't cut it in the 908, then there's no point in making the film," McQueen said.

Haig Altounian, a chief mechanic and Can-Am specialist who was hired by Solar, assembled a couple of test sessions and groomed McQueen for the movie. McQueen participated in several Sports Car Club of America circuit races in Holtville and Riverside, California; Phoenix, Arizona; and Sebring, Florida. In Florida, McQueen teamed up with cosmetics heir Peter Revson, a ranked Formula One racer. "Steve was feeling confident and talked the film company into underwriting the expense of entering the club races and Sebring. Let's face it, Steve was going to get as much of this for himself as he could. He was having a ball," Altounian said.

McQueen competed in the 12 Hours of Sebring race in March 1970 with a cast on his left foot, which he had broken a few weeks before in a motorcycle race in Elsinore, California.[6] He was allowed to drive only after race officials made him wear a special boot and fireproof socks. Steve glued sandpaper to the bottom of the cast to get traction on the foot that worked the clutch. After the race, the gauze had practically melted into a limp cloth.

McQueen and Revson alternated every 90 minutes, and by the 10th hour of the competition, they were leading the race. It was an amazing feat considering that their car with its three-litre engine was competing against Mario Andretti's car and its five-litre engine. "It was a unique situation, and you could feel the excitement of the crowd start to build," Altounian said. "A movie star winning a real race would be history in the making." Solar associate Jack Reddish stated to everyone in the pits that he wanted McQueen in the car at the end of the race.

---

6 After McQueen's bike crashed into a dry wash, he broke his foot in six places. In an amazing display of steely grit and determination, he got back on the bike and finished the race, placing in the top 10.

Reddish may have had authority on a movie set, but the Porsche team felt he overstepped his authority. While McQueen was resting, Altounian approached him.

"You know Steve, we have a real shot at winning this thing," Altounian said. "Do you know how incredible that would be with a three-liter engine?"

"What will it take?" McQueen asked. Altounian took a deep breath and suggested Revson finish the race. McQueen nodded his head in the affirmative. Revson stayed but did not end up taking the checkered flag. Although the McQueen/Revson team did come in first in its class, Andretti, who was in his prime, ran the race of his career and surpassed Revson, beating him by a scant 23.8 seconds for the top prize. But judging by the crowd's reaction, McQueen and Revson were the real winners.[7] "You would have thought we had just won the Indy 500," Altounian said. "The crowd mobbed us, and it was mayhem. They started ripping pieces off the cars. We became concerned about Steve's welfare, and we grouped around him as well as we could. Then he stunned me as he stood on top of the car and gave the peace sign. It was like Moses parting the Red Sea, and there was now quiet and a semblance of order."

McQueen was still feeling the heady rush of Sebring when he flew to France for the 24 Hours of Le Mans, which took place on April 13–14, 1970. McQueen had gone there with the full intention of driving a Porsche 917 and racing with world champion Jackie Stewart as his codriver. But once the insurance company and film backers learned of his plans, they said he was too valuable to the production and put the kibosh on the idea. He had to settle for staged sequences after the actual race.

When he returned stateside, McQueen visited Neile and the kids at the Castle. As Neile settled into the back of the garden, he proposed the idea of a one-sided open marriage. "Look baby, I'm having a terrible time functioning. I can't breathe! You feel like a chain around my neck," Neile recalled him saying. "Christ baby, half my life is over, and I wanna fly!" Steve continued. "I wanna go!" Neile asked if he wanted a divorce, and he replied forcefully "no." The more she pressed him, the more agitated he grew. It appeared to her as if Steve wanted a free pass to fool around but didn't have the *cojones* to come out and say so. It was not as if he had ever felt he needed permission before.

For years, their marriage was Steve's religion, and the idea of divorce had never entered his mind. It's not really surprising that he never thought about divorce. He had it all—the palatial home, the cars, unimaginable wealth and fame,

---

7   For his gutsy display, McQueen was given the race's Hayden Williams Memorial Sportsmanship
    Award.

a devoted wife, and a tight family unit. McQueen would not divorce for several reasons. Divorce would mean defeat, and he never went down without a fight. No one would walk out on him; he would do the walking. Also, he never said he was out of love; he just wanted to make love to as many beautiful women as possible. He felt he had to live up to his star status. McQueen's upbringing and the love of his children also influenced him. He had come from a broken home and had suffered because of it. He was not willing to inflict that turmoil upon his own children.

Discretion had always been a hallmark of McQueen's extracurricular activities, and he had once tossed out Jay Sebring for bringing a floozy to one of his parties. "Not in front of my old lady," McQueen told the famed hairdresser before showing him the door. Now he no longer cared about such appearances. "In his flower-child era, he was sleeping around like crazy, flaunting his prowess, and it humiliated me. He had pushed me too far," Neile said. "I'd gone that extra mile, and now I just could not. It is such a lonely situation, and you can only share so much, even with your best friends."

The sexy superstar was taking Hollywood like Grant took Richmond. He cut a wide swath through the female population of actresses, groupies, professional party dolls, housewives, hitchhikers, waitresses, and fans; all of them were fair game. Steve and Neile left things unresolved, but the situation would come to a climactic head in Europe.

McQueen and the Solar Production staff and movie crew arrived in the town of Le Mans, France, in late May 1970. Neile, Chad, and Terry took a cruise from New York to Le Havre, France, and joined Steve in the latter part of June. His decade-long dream had come true, and it included all the perks: a state-of-the-art motor home, a composition of prefabricated structures and tents known as Solar Village, and a 15th-century 30-room castle called Chateau de Launay that served as McQueen's home while in France. This was in addition to all the hardware at his disposal—a Porsche 908, 911, and 917; Ferrari 512; Lola T70; Alpha Romeo 33; Mantra 650; Ford GT40; and the services of approximately 45 world-class drivers to play with, which included the likes of Derek Bell, Jacky Ickx, Masten Gregory, Jo Siffert, Jonathan Williams, Vic Elford, Richard Atwood, and David Piper.

Derek Bell said McQueen was on his best behavior when it came to his relationship with the sports car pilots. "It was apparent he would have happily been a race driver. He enjoyed mixing with us on our 'driver level,' and I think the fact that I had no ambition to be an actor relaxed him considerably," Bell recalled in 2009. "He was evidently used to avoiding aspiring actors who would try to upstage him, whereas we were very relaxed about the whole thing and he was in our world.

"Steve's passion for speed was obvious. He wanted to drive flat-out all the time, and the filming was almost a secondary reason for being there…which is probably why we got on so well and us pros were completely comfortable having him driving with us at 200 mph."

They might not have felt that way had they learned of a crash McQueen was involved in shortly after production commenced. While in France, McQueen wasted no time getting involved with another actress. This time it was costar Louise Edlind, a Swedish soap-opera star who had a small part in the movie. Edlind had been flitting in and out of McQueen's trailer on the set and was staying with him at the chateau at night. Solar gofer Mario Iscovich was with McQueen and Edlind when another crew member and Iscovich needed a lift back to their hotel near the circuit. Iscovich noticed that McQueen's eyes were dilated and that he was especially chatty. Even though Iscovich was barely 20 years old, he knew the signs—McQueen had been on an all-night coke binge and was about to get behind the wheel of a Peugeot. Iscovich and the other crew member tried to talk McQueen out of his keys, but it was fruitless.

It was 2:00 AM and raining, and Iscovich begged his employer to slow it down. "Cool it, Mario. We're gonna have us a great time! Oooowee!"

No sooner had McQueen muttered those words than he took a winding curve too fast and the car slipped out of his control. He crashed through a cement bunker and the car went airborne, heading for a grove of trees. When the car finally crashed, McQueen and Edlind went sailing through the windshield and onto the hood of the car. Iscovich's arm snapped, while the other crew member cracked two ribs. No one stirred for a few moments, and the only noise Iscovich heard was the steam sifting out of the engine block. Steve finally came to, but Edlind was still unconscious. McQueen panicked when he realized what had happened.

"Oooh shit! Oh, fuck man! I've had it! I've really done it this time. Fuck! What're we gonna do, man? I'll lose everything now. For sure. Oh, fuck! Mario, do you think she's dead?" Steve asked frantically.

Edlind finally stirred, and the battered group of four walked back into town around 2:00 AM. Steve had called agent Stan Kamen in California, who magically appeared the next day to clean up the mess. Iscovich later learned he was the fall guy for McQueen, but he kept his mouth shut. A few days later when he saw McQueen back to his old ways—picking up young women—Iscovich called out his boss, asking him, "Why are you carrying on like this? You have a wonderful wife, wonderful kids, and you're going to blow it." Steve, whose eyes were glazed, could only offer, "Hey, man, look at me. I'm the world's biggest movie star. The No. 1 sex symbol. All those women out there wanna fuck me, man. I want it all!"

Soon after the accident, Iscovich incurred McQueen's wrath when McQueen felt Iscovich was coming on to one of his groupies, which was absurd. Iscovich had enough and announced he was leaving. McQueen told him he'd never work in the business again if he left. Iscovich had one foot out the door when McQueen tried a different approach. "Mario, I don't want you to go," Steve said. Iscovich looked back and saw something in Steve's eyes—a wounded egomaniac with an inferiority complex; a man given to quixotic mood swings; a lost man-child who was out of control and drove everyone around him crazy. Mario slammed the door to the trailer and walked out of Steve's life.

McQueen showed the same lack of respect to John Sturges; he slighted the director in the press when he announced that, for Le Mans, he was the driver, actor, and filmmaker. "I'm wearing three hats. Sometimes I bump into myself," McQueen said jokingly.[8] But if Steve was the man in charge, where exactly did that leave Sturges, one of the greatest action directors of his time? Basically shooting racing footage and stewing in his chair while waiting for a suitable script that could be agreed upon. Solar flew in Petitclerc, Harry Kleiner, and sportswriter Ken Purdy, who worked on separate scripts in three different trailers. McQueen wasn't enthusiastic about any of them and summoned script doctor John Kelly to France. At one point in the production, six writers were working furiously to please McQueen, to no avail. "It became a competition as opposed to a team effort," said visual designer Nikita Knatz. "They would each be given the same problem. That's no way to make a movie."

While McQueen was trying to earn the respect of the racing community, the film team camaraderie ebbed as disharmony arose between McQueen and Sturges.

"Where's the human story?" the director kept asking, who wanted a personality-driven story with a romantic subplot set with the high-stakes world of auto racing as a backdrop. McQueen held firm on making Le Mans a personal love letter to racing and the men who commanded the machines. McQueen wanted total artistic control of the project, while Sturges eventually discovered there was no room for his own creative vision. The relationship between the two men was strained, and Sturges was about to bubble over. "When Steve wasn't a star, he listened to me and took direction," Sturges said. "But when he got so big and had

---

8   When McQueen discovered a Belgian driver had told a reporter he was doubling for the star, he was promptly fired.

to do it his way, it went right back in his face. On *Le Mans*, I wasn't in a position to tell Steve what to do. When he did *The Magnificent Seven* and *The Great Escape*, he did what I told him to do. For *Le Mans*, he was in a position of power, so if he didn't like a line, he didn't read it. If he didn't want to say anything, he didn't. And you could argue with him and he would say, 'Oh, I can get through by not saying anything.' It happens over and over with stars. Lots of stars get into producing and then get lost." For the first 37 minutes of *Le Mans*, there is no audible dialogue from any of the characters, including McQueen. Critics charged that McQueen had pushed his laconic act too far.

McQueen's relationship with Relyea was put to the test as well, and his paranoia surfaced when he heard a rumor that Relyea had hired a stunt double for Steve's driving sequences. "Steve was always paranoid, but on *Le Mans* it reached a psychotic state," Relyea said.

"[The drivers] are going to think I'm a candy ass. I know somewhere out there you've got a camera and someone else is doubling me," McQueen said in an accusatory tone.

"What the hell are you talking about?" Relyea said. "I don't have time to hide a double for you, Steve." Nothing Relyea said could dissuade McQueen from believing otherwise. Their relationship was showing cracks.

In addition to an unsuitable shooting script, *Le Mans* went through several weeks of production without a leading lady. Twiggy (too skinny), Diana Rigg (too tall), and Maude Adams (way too tall) were all considered at one time or another, but McQueen chose German-born Elga Andersen, a seductive blonde actress and singer who starred in several European films.[9] Not that it was much of a role. Andersen had about a dozen lines of dialogue, which was about equal to the amount of dialogue McQueen spoke.

While Sturges railed about the human story, the machines began to turn on the cast and crew. Several accidents and near misses occurred on the set. Six cars were purposely crashed at a cost of $45,000 per car, but other mishaps were unplanned. McQueen mistimed his shifting and blew out an engine at a cost of $43,000; a radio-controlled Ferrari 512 took an unscheduled U-turn and made a beeline for the crew, although no one was hurt; Derek Bell suffered burns to his face when his Ferrari caught fire and burned to the ground; McQueen almost met his maker when a misguided utility truck took a wrong turn into his path, but luckily it got out of the way.

---

9   Anderson sang the title song for 1961's *Guns of Navarrone*.

However, fortune didn't smile on racer David Piper, whose Porsche 917 hit a dime-sized oil spot on the track and cartwheeled the length of a football field, totaling the car's fiberglass body. After Piper was extricated from the mangled wreckage, it was discovered his right leg had suffered a triple compound fracture. When doctors realized the bones would not heal properly, they amputated below the knee. The film was dedicated to him out of respect.

Despite all the problems, there were some lighter moments, especially when Steve's mischievous spirit got the better of him. "McQueen was really a gutsy sort of guy," Derek Bell remembered. "I recall one sequence where he had to come through the old White House S-Bend, which we took at about 160 mph in the race, and of course we were trying to make the speeds look as realistic as possible. Jo Siffert and Steve were in Porsche 917s, and I was in a Ferrari 512. I was leading, McQueen was in second, and Siffert third. We all set off, about three feet apart, and I didn't back off. Neither did Siffert. So poor Steve, trapped between us, had to run flat out at 160 mph through the White House because he had no choice. When we got up to the end of the shoot, Steve was as white as a ghost. He climbed out trembling but with a smile. 'What the hell were you bastards doing to me out there?' he said. Everybody was laughing hysterically, including Steve, but he waggled his finger at me and told me he'd get even with us all.

"One day we both went out on a couple of small trail bikes. Anyway, we were leaping about on the sand dunes just before the Le Mans pits when Steve disappeared over the top of a slope for a few minutes. Then he came back and said, 'Hey, this is okay. You can really gun it up here.' So I took him at his word and hurtled over the brow, took off…and looked down to see that I was mid-air right over the top of a rubbish dump. It seemed like 100 feet at the time, but it was probably only 10. I came crashing down in the middle of this garbage tip, and Steve just stood there at the top of this hill shaking with laughter. He had paid me back good and proper."

McQueen remained recklessly committed to *Le Mans* and just as ready as ever to live life on the edge, recalled Bell. "There was another sequence with me leading Siffert…he was right on my gearbox, and as I eased to the right of the road, I saw something that made me do a double take. On the white line, in the center of the track, was not only a camera but a body lying behind it. When we finished, I said, "There's some nutcase lying on the ground in the middle of the corner out there." So Sturges immediately called up on his radio and said, 'Steve, get back up here quickly.' I'll never forget the sight as McQueen came roaring up on the bike, hair flowing in the wind, and Sturges said, 'Steve, who the bloody hell did you put in the middle of the road with that camera?' So Steve just grinned and said, 'Oh, that was me.' Bold as brass, lying in the middle of the circuit in order to get a better shot as we both went by at 160 mph within a couple of feet of his nose. It's something I'll never forget for the rest of my life."

Unfortunately, the good times on *Le Mans* were always short-lived, and the carnage spread to his marriage when Neile arrived with Terry and Chad in the latter part of June. Steve wasted no time breaking down the sleeping arrangements for her. A lot of women were going to be visiting him from around the world, and she should be prepared. "My heart started to pound, and I felt like my head was in a vice," Neile said. "I ran looking for a place to hide. I found a car, and I just sobbed my little heart out. I was exhausted."

Later that night, as Steve crawled into bed, he apologized for his behavior to Neile, although he did add the caveat: "But I gotta do what I gotta do." Neile had ingested a sleeping pill to blot out her misery. Sensing her melancholy, Steve offered her a bump of coke, which she took to appease him. Moments later, she was giddy... so giddy, in fact, that when Steve had asked her if she ever had an affair, her response cut to the quick: "Honey bunny, yours is not the only golden cock in the west, you know."

A year earlier, Neile was on a cross-country flight and was seated next to actor Maximilian Schell, who was known as one of Hollywood's premiere pickup artists. He turned on the charm, and soon the two arranged to meet up at a Beverly Hills hotel. It was payback for Steve's countless affairs, one-night stands, and secret trysts.

What Steve did next, Neile claimed, was to pull a gun on her and put it next to her temple. He demanded to know the name of the actor. She was in a state of shock and unable to say anything until he cocked the hammer of the gun. This act genuinely frightened Neile, and she instantly gave up the name.[10]

Years later, Neile said, "He had pushed me too far, and I felt downtrodden, so awful because here is the man you love and he's just carrying on. He started to flaunt it. It was becoming common knowledge."

The two decided it was in their best interest to separate, but Neile said even that was on Steve's terms. He issued a press release to the media on June 5, 1970, regarding their marital status, and then made sure Neile didn't leave his side. "I couldn't leave that place," she said. "It was a strange separation because I had to be in the bedroom in that bed."

---

10 McQueen and Schell did finally meet up in 1972 when the ink on Steve and Neile's divorce was drying. According to Neile, the two men tussled, after McQueen, who was having lunch with Genevieve Bujold, spotted Schell in the lobby of the Beverly Hills Hotel. Actor Jack Nicholson heard about the scuffle and called Neile. He asked, "Is your old man okay?"

If McQueen's behavior was strange, it was because his decade-long fantasy of an idealized marriage had suddenly gone up in flames and he had no coping skills, according to psychologist Peter O. Whitmer. "He had no sense of how to cope with the reality; he had never been required to do so before, and he had no template with which he could create any coping style," Whitmer said. "This marriage was all he knew."

Whitmer said that what brought to the surface McQueen's 180-degree emotional turnabout, needing Neile more than ever, was a sense of self-destructiveness and self-loathing. "He realized, at some level of awareness, that it wasn't all about Neile. He vented his rage over his own wanton, ceaseless philandering and then directed it at his wife's one sexual misstep. He was actually punishing himself for a decade of indiscretions," Whitmer said. "His anger directed at himself had been noted before when he mentioned suicide to Neile, as well as his bike and car driving episodes that repeatedly nearly killed him.

"Further, this act of putting a loaded gun to Neile's head was a drug-exaggerated episode of ill judgment that, after the fact, seemed even to McQueen so abnormal and inhuman that it was only natural for him to feel a guilt swing.

"An even greater power behind this thuggish scene, acted out in an on-and-off manner for months until their divorce, was the core issue to McQueen of 'trust.' This was the foundation of his psyche and the launching platform for all interpersonal relationships. Neile had been the primary recipient of the greatest trusting bond with McQueen, and trust was a strange emotion to him. It was always a huge source of ambivalence; he always questioned if trust was an absolute. And now, with her gun-forced confession, he had created a self-fulfilling prophecy, thus confirming his childhood's most searing emotional reality—that trust is not an absolute. It endorsed his most basic and dire view of humanity.

"Afterward, he would continue to vent; he would increase his self-medicating, and after an occasional guilt swing that would bring Neile back close to him, the atavistic spiral would begin anew."

All of McQueen's relationships suffered on *Le Mans*. On the 24th day of filming, Robert Relyea remembers walking out of the trailer, watching McQueen give instructions to the cameraman while Sturges sat in the director's chair, silently chain-smoking another cigarette. And then the director blew his stack.

'This is bullshit!' he said to himself as he marched back into his office. He picked up the nearest object, a lamp, and sent it sailing across the room where it crashed into a wall.

"This damn picture is out of control!" he exploded. At that very moment, Relyea spotted Cinema Center executive Bob Rosen peering up from a magazine in the corner. Rosen excused himself and placed a call to Cinema Center in the States. The picture was officially in peril.

Gordon Stulberg and a cadre of Cinema Center executives descended on *Le Mans* a few days later to have a showdown with McQueen's team of representatives, including Abe Lastfogel, Roger Davis, and Stan Kamen of the William Morris Agency. McQueen personally greeted Stulberg and gave him a ride to Solar Village. It turned out to be the ride of Stulberg's life. McQueen revved up his Porsche to speeds in excess of 100 mph and raced up and down the countryside. "Gordon's eyes were as big as saucers," said Bob Rosen, laughing. "Yeah, sure, it was Steve's way of intimidating him. Steve was that mischievous child both on and off the camera. But even then, it was endearing."

It wasn't much of a showdown. Cinema Center dictated the terms—either they were going to shut down the picture entirely, or McQueen would have to forfeit his $750,000 salary, plus any points he had in the picture.[11] It was a take-it-or-leave-it deal. There was nothing the William Morris executives could do for their client, and they acquiesced.

Bob Rosen was part of the brutal meeting sessions and said McQueen was a "basket case" who had mentally checked out. "Every part of his life was falling apart at the same time. He told me years later he wasn't the same person. He was under a lot of stress. He didn't help his case any when he told the Cinema Center executives, 'The script's in my head.' He would say and react to things that didn't help his cause." These were the sort of words that put a chill in the heart of the money men, confirming the film was more out of control than a high-speed Porsche without brakes.

Up to this point in his career, McQueen had achieved it all. He had gone from the stage to television and not looked back as he became a Hollywood legend. However, the stretch from film star to filmmaker proved to be a bridge too far. McQueen had dreamed of making the one movie that he could truly call his own and that he hoped would best represent his passions and personality. However, despite all of McQueen's power and influence, it was taken away from him. As a struggling actor, he had pushed and fought successfully to get his way. Now his lucky streak was over. Ironically, his star status was powerless to help him. Losing his power and control was like stripping McQueen of his manhood. Unfortunately, he would lose even more.

---

11 The studio even called Robert Redford to check on his availability in case negotiations with McQueen went south.

26

SNAKE EYES

STEVE MCQUEEN HAD GAMBLED EVERYTHING on *Le Mans* and rolled snake eyes. He wasn't used to losing and did not prove to be gracious in defeat.

Within minutes of Cinema Center's announcement that the film would be shut down for a period of two weeks, a mob of livid French extras, who had been told they'd have steady employment, blocked the entrance to Solar Village with their cars. McQueen was no longer communicating with Robert Relyea, who McQueen felt had blown the whistle on him. Relyea recalled that shortly after the meeting they went for a walk along the road that led to McQueen's chateau.

"Bob, you betrayed me," McQueen said. "You and I will never talk again."

Relyea said the tenor of their relationship had irrevocably changed. "He talked about his feelings and I talked about my feelings, which left us in the same hostile position. That was the last time we discussed anything. The rest of the picture was done very businesslike with a minimum amount of personal remarks to each other. We both just did our jobs," Relyea said.

The William Morris Agency was also in McQueen's sights. He viewed them as powerless when Cinema Center marched in and took over. When everyone left the chateau, Steve told Neile, "I'm going to let Stan [Kamen] go. I need a barracuda, and he can't hack it. He's too nice. Shit! They're all too goddamned nice." A few days later, Kamen received a cable from McQueen. It was direct and to the point:

> *Dear Stan,*
> *You're fired. Letter follows.*
> *Steve McQueen*

McQueen showed the same lack of respect to John Sturges, the director who had nurtured McQueen's acting talent early in his career. Sturges expected he and

McQueen would use the two weeks off to retool the script and finally make a movie. McQueen told him no, that he and Neile were off to Morocco for a much-needed vacation. Sturges felt that McQueen's highly unprofessional behavior put everyone in this predicament and that McQueen was allowing others to clean up the mess. Sturges wasn't in the mood for mop-up duty.

"I'm too old and too rich for this shit," Sturges declared, and then he told McQueen that he was done.

Relyea was on the phone after Sturges and McQueen had words. "I'll be off in just a second," Relyea told Sturges. "No, don't bother," Sturges said. "I just wanted to tell you I'm going home." Relyea thought he meant back to his hotel, but Sturges meant he was headed to Los Angeles. Sturges took the next available flight out of Paris. A week later, he was shooting *Joe Kidd* with Clint Eastwood.

While McQueen was in Morocco, Relyea and Jack Reddish frantically searched for another director. They found an unlikely candidate in Lee Katzin, who had just finished shooting a television movie for Cinema Center. Would he like to go to France to shoot a picture with Steve McQueen?

Katzin, a noted television director (*Mission: Impossible*), wasn't an unknown commodity. He had accompanied Relyea a few years earlier on a scouting trip to Berlin for *The Cold War Swap* and was being considered as the director. The two men happened to be in Czechoslovakia when the Russians invaded the country and were forced to return to America. The film was put on the back burner, but Katzin was now front and center.

The new director started work on August 3, 1970, just three days after he arrived. He read five different versions of the script on the plane, and he noted each one had its own set of problems. But the biggest problem Katzin had wasn't in the script. It was the film's male lead, who was still acting like a tyrant, when in reality he was captain of a sinking ship. "He was aware of who he was. He was a star," Katzin said.

Katzin, a Harvard graduate, was privately ridiculed by some of the crew for retaining his Ivy League shirt, tie, suit, and vest, and Relyea thought Katzin's Phi Beta Kappa key was a fake. Many of the crew, who were Sturges loyalists, didn't care for their new director. "It was a big chance for Lee," Haig Altounian said. "He was a good TV director, but this fact was kind of a joke among the crew. 'We've got a TV director now. Let's see what he can do!' was the gist of the comments I heard."

The drivers all knew and respected Sturges, who was a racing enthusiast, and were disappointed and frustrated when they learned of Sturges' fate. It also meant they had to go over the same ground with Katzin, who admittedly didn't know the first thing about racing. "I'd seen a couple of races when I was young, at state fairs in Michigan, but to say I came in cold was an understatement," Katzin said. "This is not to say I didn't have a flair for action sequences, many of which I'd done previously."

For all of his worldly education, Katzin's pedigree didn't come with instructions on how to deal with a major movie star. He was given a memorable welcome by McQueen when he made the unfortunate mistake of commenting on his slight stature for his first shot. The scene was an interaction between McQueen and Elga Anderson outside the racetrack. Katzin said, without a trace of emotion, "Steve, we're going to do this setup, and if you'll notice, I've had a hole dug for Elga to stand in so she'll be shorter than you." The crew winced, for they knew what was coming. McQueen lifted up Katzin by the tie and yanked him inches from his face.

"It's Mr. McQueen to you, and don't you ever forget it!" McQueen said, then marched into his trailer where he sulked for the rest of the day.

Katzin remembered, "Steve would have a blowup and would leave, and we'd have to shoot without him until he came back. It was a difficult set of circumstances for the first six weeks."

The director also failed to hit it off with the film's leading lady, Elga Andersen. In an attempt to establish some sort of rapport, Katzin invited himself to dinner at Andersen's rented home, which she shared with her personal hairdresser. Rumors circulated among the cast and crew that Katzin proposed a ménage à trois but got a double beating instead. "We found him in the gutter! Those two ladies just beat the shit out of him," Relyea said, laughing at the memory more than four decades later. "I don't even wanna know the details on that one." French police were called to the scene, and the two women admitted to the cops that they beat Katzin to a pulp, but Katzin refused to press charges.

McQueen never resorted to violence, but he could plead guilty to indifference. Some mornings McQueen would show; other days he would not. Katzin cleverly scheduled calls for both the Porsche and Ferrari pits. If McQueen didn't show, he sent the Porsche folks home and shot Ferrari or vice versa.

Driver Peter Samuelson said McQueen's behavior was disruptive but understandable given his background. "I thought he was an excellent example of someone who'd grown up without parents, with no role model to look up to and see how a person is supposed to behave," Samuelson said. "He was like an overgrown child…not unintelligent but uncouth. Very concerned and thin-skinned about whether he was getting enough respect.

"We'd be in the pits all set up and ready to go, waiting sometimes for him to show up for two hours. When he did, he'd arrive on his Husky, doing a wheelie down the pit lane, and say, 'So, what are we waiting for?' It was all very juvenile."

With the snap of a finger, McQueen changed his attitude and decided to end his feud with Katzin. Early one morning, Katzin was up before everyone else, trying to figure out a camera angle. McQueen, with a cup of coffee in his hand, opened the door to his trailer and spotted Katzin. He wandered over to Katzin and said, "Lee, I am no longer going to be against you. I see what you're trying to do, and I'm going to be working for you and not against you." It was as if a light switch had gone off in McQueen, and Katzin was stunned. "I had no idea where this was coming from," Katzin said. "From that time on, we hit it off. I was as surprised as anyone."

Steve's relationship with Neile, however, was on the decline. She was in her husband's crosshairs, and every move she made while in France was subject to interrogation. What did she do that day? Who did she talk to? Who approached whom? What were the other person's intentions? McQueen also rifled through her closet, rummaged through her drawers, and carefully inspected her mail. He also subjected her to his daily torments. "Tell me, why did you do it? Why another actor? Why somebody in my industry? Why? You fucking bitch! You see what you've done?" He couldn't seem to shake off her one and only infidelity, and he threw it in her face whenever he was consumed with rage.[1]

Neile was forbidden to step foot outside the chateau alone, and her presence was required at the set every day. She timed her visits to coincide at the end of the lunch break so that her appearance was duly noted by her husband. She hung in there for Terry and Chad, who loved spending time with their father. Chad remembered entering his first race in the two-hour Mini Le Mans kart track event. "I was following the fastest kid, who was in a white GT-40, and we came around a corner and I just kind of bumped him and he kind of went off and hit the hay bales," Chad said. "I got first place. To this day, I have that trophy. I remember my dad was really happy that I won."

The children may have enjoyed their time in France, but they had no idea about the private hell Neile was forced to endure. She grew depressed, punishing herself for the pain she'd inflicted on Steve, even forgetting that he had inflicted the same pain on her over the years. She hoped and prayed the nightmare would end, but matters got worse. Two weeks after Neile and Steve returned from

---

1   According to Neile, Steve even inquired into Maximilian Schell's availability just so that he could "beat the shit out of him."

Morocco, she discovered she was pregnant again. It took her three weeks to summon up the courage to tell Steve. The news did not go down well.

"Whose is it, woman?" he demanded to know. "Are you going to tell me, or are you gonna sit there and lie?"

Neile cried as each word had the effect of a sharp dagger. She had deteriorated to a point where she could barely function and spent many lonely days in bed, contemplating her current existence, her future with her husband and children, and the fate of their unborn child. Neile said that Steve practically made the decision for them when she asked if she should make the proper arrangements. He unhesitatingly approved.

After learning abortion was not legal in France, Neile went to London, accompanied by set designer Phil Abramson, where she had dinner at a Soho restaurant before the procedure the next day. It was a traumatic experience, but Neile was strong. She flew back to France, scooped up the kids to get them registered for school in California, and stayed with them a few weeks before heading back to France to pick up the pieces of their shattered lives. "The strain was enormous," Robert Relyea said. "[Le Mans] just wasn't a motion picture. It had to do with Steve's credibility with the racing world. I certainly didn't anticipate when we were shooting the film it would wreak so much havoc with everything. You can't be obsessed with something without it affecting the rest of your life. It had to have rubbed off on the marriage."

Le Mans was scheduled to end in September but ran into several delays and problems, most notably David Piper's unfortunate accident. Chad said his father took him to view the wreckage as a reminder that racing was indeed dangerous. "There were some rumblings about a big accident with a Porsche, and I thought maybe my dad got hurt or something," Chad recalled. "Some time went by, and my dad came by on his Triumph motorcycle and picked me up and said, 'I want you to see something.' I said, 'Okay,' and I hopped on the back of the motorcycle and held on. We went through Solar Village and down one of the roads. I remember seeing a 917 literally disintegrated. It was David Piper's. I asked, 'Why am I here?' My dad said, 'This is what can happen in racing.' I'll never forget that."

Steve and Neile visited Piper at the National Orthopedic Hospital in England, where they found him in surprisingly good spirits despite his injuries. Piper had not even contemplated litigation and simply accepted his fate. McQueen dashed off an October 22, 1970, letter to Sid Ganis, Cinema Center's Studio Publicity Director, imploring him to help Piper financially.

Dear Sid:

I talked to David Piper on the phone and he is as he says "a bit weak." He has had numerous operations and, of course, there is his mental state knowing that there is a good chance he will lose his leg.

I don't think the man is financially fit, and he is certainly through with racing one way or another. So many times before in the history of motion pictures, brave men have lost their lives and limbs and people have forgotten about it. If David loses his leg, I don't think we should forget about this one. I feel very strongly that we should dedicate the premiere to David Piper and give all the proceeds to him and his family.

Would you please pass this on to the higher ups, and I do think we owe this to racing for what they gave this film.

My best,

   Steve McQueen

Delays also posed another monumental problem. Porsche had agreed to loan the race cars to the production for only three months; now the company needed them back. One driver likened the situation to a kid having his toys taken away. Director of photography Robert Hauser said the situation triggered a desperate response when Robert Rosen told him, "Shoot until you run out of light, because we really have to finish the film." Hauser objected on the grounds that he could no longer see the drivers. "I'll tell you when you can't see them," Rosen tersely replied.

The film slogged through another two months when production finally wrapped on November 7, 1970, after five miserable months. The project also went $1.5 million over budget. The movie had no wrap party, no toasts, and no grand farewells; everyone quietly sauntered off. There was enough bad blood between them to fill a river. The film was a disaster financially in terms of budget, and there would be tensions as to whether the cost of the overruns could be recouped at the box office. However, the cost went far beyond just dollars. The true cost was immeasurable—friends were lost, drivers had been horribly injured, friendships and professional relationships has been severed forever, and a once-strong marriage was teetering on the edge. At the center of it all was Steve McQueen.

Katzin brought back 450,000 feet of film, featuring 90,000 on the race itself. He spent six months scoring, editing, dubbing, and piecing the film together. The project included 55 soundtracks—including one for each racing car—in addition to Michel LeGrand's score. Unfortunately, none of John Sturges' footage made it into the final cut.

Cinema Center had also banned McQueen from the postproduction process, leaving it all for Katzin and the editors to sort out. It was the first time McQueen had been barred by a studio. Sturges said it was just as well. "*Le Mans* never had a story. Nobody could tell anything that was going on except a lot of racing. In its final release, I challenge anyone to tell you the story of *Le Mans*." Relyea also said *Le Mans* was a big disappointment. "The movie was nothing. It certainly wasn't Steve's dream, and it certainly wasn't what I had desired," Relyea said. "We ended up making a film that fulfilled nobody's vision." Mechanic Haig Altounian said, "A lot of the good stuff that was filmed ended up on the cutting room floor. It was like [that] was because there was no script, so they cut a script into it. With what they had to work with, it probably couldn't have been any better."

Katzin believed there was potential for a storyline between McQueen and Elga Andersen, but it was never fully developed or explored. "We knew how the story was going to start. We knew how it was going to end. What we didn't know was what was the relationship between this woman whose husband had died in the race the year before and Michael Delaney [McQueen], if in fact that was going to be the story, if in fact he was going to meet this woman, and if they were going to have a relationship."

Robert Relyea and Jack Reddish, the two men perhaps most loyal to McQueen, knew there was going to be no personal relationship with him after the film wrapped. The Cinema Center deal was kaput after it took over the film, which halted any future Solar projects, including *Yucatan*. McQueen, on the advice of business consultant and financial troubleshooter Bill Maher, shut down Solar Productions, Solar Plastics and Engineering, and Solar Automotive for good in 1971. The three companies had drained all of his profits from *Bullitt*, and McQueen lost millions before he could turn off the tap. Maher discovered McQueen was financially insolvent, and the Solar dynasty was finished. Relyea said McQueen changed when Cinema Center wrestled *Le Mans* away from him. "The loss of control meant complete defeat to Steve," Relyea said. "It was something he couldn't live with, and it left a bad taste in his mouth." McQueen was fearful during his whole career of losing all he had built. Now he was the one who had put himself at risk. The fear of being back in that cold-water flat for $19 a month from his early days in New York must have eaten away at him. He was staring into the abyss.

McQueen couldn't entirely wash his hands of *Le Mans*. Cinema Center reps were anxious for his reaction to the final cut because they needed him to sell the picture to the media. "It was a frightening experience putting the film together," said Cinema Center executive Bob Rosen. "McQueen had nothing to do with the postproduction, and when we showed him the final version, he liked it. I was dumbstruck."[2] So was Katzin when McQueen called him to thank him for his efforts. "I wouldn't be surprised if Steve and I worked together again soon," Katzin bragged to Dan Knapp of the *Los Angeles Times*. "The last time we spoke, he asked me to read a script he was interested in." That offer never materialized, and after Katzin's next film, *The Salzburg Connection*, flopped, he was relegated to television for the rest of his career.

McQueen's next phone call was placed to John Sturges. Steve conceded the movie needed a story and that his ego had spun out of control. "He did back off on *Le Mans* and admitted to me he was a jerk. This was before it was released," Sturges said. "You didn't have to know before it was released that it wasn't going to be anything."

But Cinema Center wasn't going down without a fight. Promotion-wise, they pulled out all the stops for *Le Mans* and spent close to $2 million for prints and advertising. They also produced a 22-page press book for the media and a 48-page souvenir booklet that was available to moviegoers for the low cost of $1. The poster campaign was full scale, featuring posters and billboards of all sizes plastered at cinemas. The studio also handed out a free four-page tabloid-size newspaper called the *Le Mans Herald* for those who couldn't afford the booklet. Michel LeGrand's musical score, a jazz-tinged orchestration coupled with racing images and the roar of engines passing by, was distributed by Columbia Records, and complimentary copies were dispatched to radio stations nationwide. Not to be outdone, Gulf Oil printed approximately eight million copies of a free giveaway poster for 30,000 gas stations, who passed the gift on to loyal customers, putting images of McQueen on thousands of bedroom and garage walls.

Le Mans was everywhere, but McQueen was nowhere to be found. Despite a splashy world premiere in Indianapolis, Indiana—the racing capital of the United States—in June 1971, McQueen was a no-show. Even if McQueen had been there to charm the media, their opinions no doubt would have been the same—*Le Mans* was simply a bore. It was summarily blasted by critics for its weak storyline, lack of dialogue, and fetishistic orgy of racing shots. *New York Times* reviewer Howard Thompson wrote, "Racing buffs will probably flip over it, but mostly, it's a bore. McQueen's exchange of monosyllabic utterances and long, meaningful stares with other drivers simply added up to tepid, monotonous drama." Kathleen Carroll of the *New York Daily News* lamented, "There was no

---

2   Relyea disputed this claim and said McQueen hated Katzin's cut of the picture.

attempt at characterization. *Le Mans* is an excuse for Steve McQueen to indulge his passion for auto racing…Even a 24-hour endurance test like *Le Mans* does not make a movie in itself…a script is needed." Jay Cocks of *Time* wryly noted, "McQueen is potentially a good movie actor, but he needs someone to loosen him up, make him play a part, not pose for it. *Le Mans* may be the most famous auto race in the world, but from a theater seat, it just looks like a big drag." Charles Champlin of the *Los Angeles Times*, who was a champion of McQueen, found it hard to muster a positive review. He wrote, "Under the circumstances, it is surprising that *Le Mans* is anything but a total mishmash. It isn't though, although it is a little schizophrenic and remains bright, detached, and impersonal, as if it hadn't really had time to get acquainted with anybody."

Perhaps the most stinging review came from McQueen's personal racing hero, Stirling Moss. When asked for his assessment of *Le Mans*, Moss said, "To me, it was a great letdown. I'm surprised it ever got past him. Absolutely abortive. It had neither passion nor emotion. Utterly unrealistic. A very bad film in my opinion. One takes part in the sport because of the passion and humor. Racing drivers are a special lot—great fun. But none of this comes across in the film at all."

Cinema Center executive Bob Rosen said the film remains one of his greatest regrets and disappointments. "*Le Mans* had so much hype before the picture was released that when it came out, it was a major disappointment. The film made money, but it should have been one of the greatest movies of all time. If I went over my résumé of films and I saw *Le Mans*, I would say to myself, 'Now there was a picture that should have been great!'"

The box-office take for *Le Mans* was $22 million[3] worldwide, partly due to the American market's low recognition of the foreign race. In Europe, Japan, and other parts of the world, the film was heralded as a masterpiece. "A key difference between the Japanese and Americans lies in the question of who can understand *Le Mans*," said Ryuken Tokuda, a Japanese pop-culture observer. "McQueen put his heart and soul into the movie. 'Boring, not enough dialogue' and 'too many racing scenes' are what is said to have killed it in the United States. That's what made it a smash to the Japanese. 'Silence is beauty' and 'action without words' are adages of the Japanese culture that cherish such behavior as being honorable and wise. Few words, few gestures. That is why we Japanese are moved by the

---

3 According to industry calculations, *Le Mans'* break-even point was around $15 million after prints and advertising and financing costs. McQueen didn't see a dime because he gave up his salary and points after the takeover.

sense of reality and excitement that is portrayed in *Le Mans*. Steve McQueen's character, Michael Delaney, who had about a dozen lines in the movie, said all that needed to be said."

Racing enthusiasts have also held the same belief, and *Le Mans* finally found its vindication decades later. Motor heads have proclaimed *Le Mans* to be the most historically realistic representation in the history of the race, citing that the picture does not rely on an overdependency of stunt doubles or drivers to tell the story. "Technically Steve got the movie right," Robert Relyea conceded. "If you ask drivers, mechanics, team members, and race fans, yes, they'll tell you it's the only racing picture that is the most accurate. But man, it is a boring film."

It is also implicitly understood by the racing community how much McQueen sacrificed to make the picture and that the toll was enormous. He practically lost his marriage to Neile, and he did lose his production company. He severed ties with Sturges, Relyea, and Reddish. And his status as the world's biggest box-office champ was over, thanks to the one picture he dreamed of making for more than a decade.

The film may have been a painful saga in its making, but it has left an indelible legacy. In 2009, on the 40th anniversary of the Monaco watch, which McQueen wore in *Le Mans*, Tag Heuer created an entertaining commercial that used footage from *Le Mans* to create a mini-movie called "The Duel" that pitted McQueen as Michael Delaney against modern racing star Lewis Hamilton. The ad is heavy on great close-ups of the Porsche and McQueen, paying fitting homage to both. The ad is testament to the lasting impact of the film and its place in popular culture.

Unfortunately for McQueen, he never saw such praise in his lifetime despite all his efforts, and *Le Mans* continued to be an albatross around his neck. Two years after *Le Mans* was released, McQueen sued four Japanese firms for $1.6 million on April 5, 1973. The suit stated the companies—Dentsu, Matsushita Industrial Co., Towa Co., and Yakult—used still photographs from the movie to advertise their products without McQueen's consent. Almost five years later on April 24, 1978, McQueen showed up in a Tokyo courtroom in a suit and tie to testify. The four defendants delayed the case for another few years, and a final judgment was rendered on November 10, 1980, three days after his death. The judge found in favor of the four Japanese firms. No explanation for the ruling was offered.

• • •

Back in California, the McQueens spent the 1970 Christmas holiday in Palm Springs with *Le Mans* actor Siegfried Rauch and his wife Karen, along with

Taking a phone call inside "the Castle," McQueen's three-and-a-half-acre country-style stone mansion in the exclusive neighborhood of Brentwood, California, in 1964. The five-bedroom home included an imposing front gate, a winding stone driveway, an Olympic-sized swimming pool, a courtyard the size of a football field, a tennis court–sized den, a custom pool table in the sunken living room, an outdoor playhouse for the two kids, and a panoramic view of the Pacific Ocean. After years of living on the margin, McQueen had finally arrived. (*Courtesy of Karen Bruno Hornbaker*)

McQueen's expert handling of weapons is evident in many of his films. His cache of weapons greatly increased when close friends Sharon Tate and Jay Sebring were killed in a grisly massacre in August 1969. McQueen's arsenal included pistols, shotguns and semiautomatic rifles. In this photo he is standing below a mounted rifle and holding a collectible dueling pistol. (*Courtesy of Donna Redden*)

Steve McQueen's visit to Paris, France, in September 1964 caused the usually reserved French to lose their cool and continually mobbed him outside of his hotel. This visit was such a triumphant success that he was obliged to don a disguise in the form of a mustache and goatee to walk the streets during the daytime. (*Courtesy of Donna Redden*)

Relieving tension on a dirt bike in the California desert in the 1960s. McQueen and his machines are inextricably linked because they were his emotional outlet. He needed to have something on standby to allow him to escape to his own world. A car, a motorbike, a young starlet—all of these would provide ways for him to disconnect from Hollywood when he had to. He was never truly at ease as an actor, and riding helped him keep hold of the reality he had created for himself. *(Courtesy of Donna Redden)*

Proudly sporting an American jacket as a representative of the 1964 International Six Days Trials in East Germany. McQueen did well in the race until he was sideswiped by a spectator who suddenly rode his motorcycle out on the track. The actor was sent airborne and landed brutally, his face smashing against a rock and the skin torn from his kneecaps. *(Courtesy of Donna Redden)*

The Cincinnati Kid was the first of his five back-to-back worldwide hits and earned McQueen a slot as a top-10 box-office champ for the next decade. McQueen was justifiably nervous that costar and movie legend Edward G. Robinson, left, would end up stealing the film. However, the two actors interfaced well with each other, especially in the classic stud poker showdown at the end of the picture. (*Courtesy of Photofest*)

In *Nevada Smith*, McQueen's character, Max Sand, brought a unique cool to the cowboy way and helped establish McQueen as the modern-day American hero. (*Courtesy of Donna Redden*)

Playing against type in *The Thomas Crown Affair*, McQueen pulled off the role of a lifetime by playing a Boston banker who robbed banks for kicks. He also had plenty of on-screen chemistry with costar Faye Dunaway and dubbed her "the Great Lady." (*Courtesy of Photofest*)

Lord Richard Attenborough and Steve McQueen on the set of *The Sand Pebbles*. Despite their obvious personality differences, the two forged a lifelong friendship. *(Courtesy of Photofest)*

Smoking a cigarette on board the USS *San Pablo* in Taiwan during a break in *The Sand Pebbles*. The epic film was the most problematic of McQueen's career, but he was bestowed an Academy Award nomination for his role as Jake Holman. *(Courtesy of Karen Bruno Hornbaker)*

Shown here deep in conversation with *Bullitt* director Peter Yates on location in San Francisco, California, McQueen made Lieutenant Frank Bullitt the coolest movie detective of the 1960s, and was the defining role of his acting career. *(Courtesy of Photofest)*

This rare image of McQueen in *Bullitt* shows that he could make a pair of fruity pajamas look good. Today he is a silent pitchman, a fashion icon, an enduring mythical figure of alpha-male coolness, and his image and likeness are omnipresent. *(Courtesy of Kandee Nelson)*

A star arrives. Steve and Neile McQueen just moments before he immortalizes his hands and feet in cement at Grauman's Chinese Theatre in Hollywood, March 21, 1967. *(Courtesy of Donna Redden)*

As race car driver Michael Delaney in *Le Mans.* The racing picture clashed mightily with McQueen's midlife crisis, racking up several casualties along the way. The film would cost him dearly on both a financial and personal level. In one fell swoop, he lost his wife, agent, production company, and personal fortune. *(Courtesy of Donna Redden)*

McQueen's enthusiasm for motorcycle racing, as evidenced in 1971's *On Any Sunday*, made the 96-minute documentary a worldwide smash. The picture also helped spur the explosive growth of motorcycling in the United States, and made the 1970 Husqvarna 400 Cross a motoring icon. *(Courtesy of Kandee Nelson)*

Movie stars turned moguls and the partners of First Artists Productions (left to right) McQueen, Paul Newman, Barbra Streisand, and Sidney Poitier. (Dustin Hoffman later joined the group.) First Artists was a bold experiment designed to free superstars of the corporate shackles of big studios. At the time of its formation, the industry was slipping into a recession and the venture was a way to keep costs low for studios while rewarding stars on the back end for their risk. *(Courtesy of Donna Redden)*

Junior Bonner, about an over-the-hill rodeo rider who returns to his hometown and sees how his family is trapped in a changing West, was a departure for McQueen. Despite the fact the film did not do well financially, it won the hearts of critics and would eventually become one of his favorite movies. *(Courtesy of Donna Redden)*

By the start of 1971, when this picture was taken, Steve McQueen had experienced the "Star Trip" of booze, drugs, indiscriminate sex, and an impending divorce. He had been booted around by a merciless film industry after years of sticking it to producers and studios, and he was due for a karmic kickback. *(Courtesy of Donna Redden)*

With costar Ali MacGraw on the set of *The Getaway*, where the two fell in love almost immediately. McQueen and MacGraw's hot romance created a stampede at the box office and a windfall of free publicity. Their love affair read like a fairy tale, but their marriage was a mix of passion and poison. *(Courtesy of Donna Redden)*

A bearded James Garner, Steve McQueen and director Sam Peckinpah taking a break during *The Getaway*. Garner was McQueen's Brentwood neighbor and sometime film rival. He drove a orange Volkswagen Beetle in the 1972 film, and was paid $25 for his services. *(Courtesy of Andrew Antoniades)*

In *The Getaway*, McQueen used his perfectly honed skills in portraying Doc McCoy, a silent tough guy whose actions speak louder than words ever could. At no other time had he been able to play a character who goes though such a believable and truthful journey and one that would ultimately mirror his personal life. *(Courtesy of Donna Redden)*

McQueen and *Papillon* costar Dustin Hoffman got along just fine until McQueen kicked Hoffman's relatives off the set. The two used an emissary to communicate for the rest of filming. Despite this, McQueen gave an acting tour de force in the picture. *(Courtesy of Photofest)*

Preparing for the blast in *The Towering Inferno*'s grand finale, McQueen brought an authenticity to the role of fire captain Michael O'Hallorhan. The 1974 blockbuster was then the highest grossing film of all time and punched McQueen's popularity into the stratosphere. He also collected a hefty $14.5 million paycheck, making him the world's highest paid movie star. *(Courtesy of Donna Redden)*

The highly innovative movie poster for *The Towering Inferno* ended an 18-year footrace between McQueen and his perceived movie rival, Paul Newman. McQueen's name appeared on the left-hand side, which appeared first but was slightly lower, while Newman took the name on the right-hand side, which was slightly above but appeared second. McQueen made the correct choice and came across as the star to to the public. *(Courtesy of Photofest)*

The world's biggest box-office star took a few years off from the industry, grew his hair long, sprouted a beard and was barely recognizeable after *The Towering Inferno* blazed its way to the top. McQueen, left, with longtime friend Bud Ekins in the California desert on the set of *Dixie Dynamite*, a little-known B-film in which McQueen performed a few motorcycle stunts. *(Courtesy of Bonham's Auctioneers)*

A rare photo of McQueen taken circa 1976, during his hiatus from filmmaking. The public did not see him on screen for a period of nearly five years. *(Courtesy of Academy of Motion Picture Arts and Sciences)*

A bespectacled and bushy McQueen on the set of *An Enemy of the People*, filmed in 1976. McQueen spent the previous two decades perfecting his image of the rebel, the hunk, the hero behind a wheel, the handsome leading man, and the public was used to seeing him perform amazing stunts and bold acts of courage on the screen. This new role as Dr. Thomas Stockmann, who was a volatile, idealistic intellectual, was simply too much of a contrast and totally against type and audience expectations. Warner Brothers shelved the film for almost three decades and finally released it on DVD in 2009. *(Courtesy of Bonham's Auctioneers)*

McQueen enjoys an iced beer on the set of *Tom Horn*. The western was based on Will Henry's biographical story of the controversial desperado and took three years to get from inception to the silver screen. Counting McQueen, *Tom Horn* went through five directors. *(Photo by Barbara Minty McQueen)*

Dave Friedman's gentle picture of Barbara and Steve McQueen on the set of *The Hunter*. This photo, taken in the fall of 1979, captures the warmth and tenderness between the two, who share a quiet moment together. *(Courtesy of Dave Friedman)*

Ready for take-off at the Santa Paula Airport, spring 1979. McQueen loved the aviation lifestyle and was hands-on about every aspect of flying. *(Photo by Barbara Minty McQueen)*

In one of her favorite pictures, Barbara McQueen said that Steve reminded her of a World War II aviator. *(Photo by Barbara Minty McQueen)*

McQueen often described only daughter Terry as "the apple of my eye." In this candid 1967 photo, a pipe-smoking McQueen is watching his daughter fish in the wilds of Wyoming shortly after the filming of *The Sand Pebbles*. *(Courtesy of Academy of Motion Picture Arts and Sciences)*

Steve and son, Chad, on the set of *Tom Horn*, early 1979. Friends, family, and intimates say that McQueen was an exceptional father and his children loved him unconditionally. *(Photo by Barbara Minty McQueen)*

Sailing on the deck of the *Pacific Princess*, also known as television's *The Love Boat*, May 1980. Barbara McQueen's camera caught all the character in her husband's face: deep lines, age spots, mustache, and beard. (*Photo by Barbara Minty McQueen*)

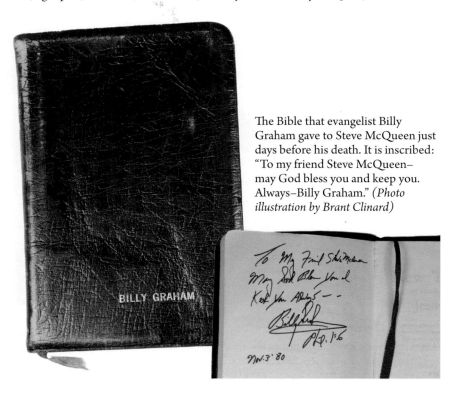

The Bible that evangelist Billy Graham gave to Steve McQueen just days before his death. It is inscribed: "To my friend Steve McQueen— may God bless you and keep you. Always–Billy Graham." (*Photo illustration by Brant Clinard*)

Barbara McQueen's photo captures an intimate moment of her husband drinking coffee and reading the paper by an open fire in the backyard of their Santa Paula home. This June 1980 picture was the last she ever snapped before he became seriously ill and sought an alternative cancer treatment in Mexico. In the 30 years since his death, she has yet to pick up a camera again. *(Photo by Barbara Minty McQueen)*

producer George Schlatter, his wife Jolene, and their daughter Maria. Neile didn't feel safe with Steve alone, and their presence was a welcome distraction.

It was in Palm Springs that David Foster witnessed a meltdown between the two and caused him to run back to Los Angeles after what he deemed one of the most horrible nights of his life. After a great day riding motorcycles in the sun, Steve, Neile, and Foster enjoyed a hearty dinner of Mexican food washed down with a few beers. Except McQueen ended up having a few more than the others. "He loads up on beer this particular night," remembered Foster, "'and then he starts in. Oh God, what a horrible night." Slurring his words, McQueen asked Foster while shooting Neile a dirty look, "Do you know what this bitch did? She had an affair with Maximilian Schell."

Neile sat there in stony silence while her inebriated husband berated her in front of their friend. When the three arrived back at the McQueen's Southgate home, Foster quietly excused himself and called it an early night. He waited a half hour before he packed his things and left in the middle of the night. "I was not about to go through that the next day. That was probably the most depressing emotional experience I've ever had in my life. It was just horrific, just horrific," Foster said. The sad truth is that as hard as that was for Foster to witness, it was just a glimpse. It was a million times harder for Neile, who was living this scenario on a daily basis.

The McQueens tried to salvage their relationship through marriage counseling, although the therapist didn't hold out much hope. The wealthy and the famous may listen intently to advice, but once outside the office doors, their egos get fed by handlers, business associates, and adoring fans, mostly of the female persuasion. McQueen was sure that would never happen to him, as he once told a reporter: "You take guys, put 'em in the limelight until then they're bitchin', but before long, all day long they're surrounded by people giving them love and attention. They're happy. They should be. They're the center and focus. And they get it all for nothing more than a hello or good-bye, whereas at home, you've got to work for the love you get. Earn it. The hero suddenly feels why should he work for this love and respect when he can get it from outside for free? And the next thing you know, he's off with a chorus girl from the Sands. Well, that's not going to happen to me."

If McQueen wanted to repair the marriage, he had a peculiar way of going about it. Everyone around him knew that if he wanted the marriage to work, Neile would have gone the distance. Longtime friend Hilly Elkins said, "His fooling around wasn't exactly a military secret. Neile tried to look the other way, but it was impossible to go anywhere and not bump into him with another woman. It was obvious enough so that the word would get back in two or three passes in an irreparable manner. That can poison after a while."

Bud Ekins could also sense the marriage wasn't going well, and he attributes the breakup to McQueen's womanizing. "He was with a different broad every night. It was kind of like, how long was Neile going to put up with it? The older he got, the worse he got. She was Mrs. McQueen and that's who she wanted to be, and she tried to keep being Mrs. McQueen as long as she could with him fucking around, making a fool out of her. She put up with it for years. It didn't matter what Steve did as long as he came home. Christ, he'd walk into a grocery store and walk out with some housewife and get laid that afternoon. Women were always chasing him. He didn't need to chase them; they did the chasing. Good lookers, too."

In the days preceding their divorce, Steve was linked publicly with several high-profile women. They included Barbra Streisand, Yvette Mimieux, Lauren Hutton, Raquel Welch, Jennifer O'Neal, and a well-known *Playboy* bunny. He also embarked on a passionate affair with singer Mary Wilson of the Supremes. "We met at a Hollywood party," Wilson said in 2008. "It was one of those moments where your eyes meet across a crowded room, and there's an immediate thunderbolt…I've had a few of those! Neither of us were in love, but we had some fun."

Fun isn't a word Neile would use to describe her husband when he returned from France. His cocaine habit continued to escalate along with his abusive behavior. At the suggestion of both of their psychiatrists, the two separated. Steve moved into a small guesthouse in the Pacific Palisades, where the two began the strange but necessary ritual of dating each other. The daily phone calls and their thrice-weekly dates brought them closer. Often they ended up at each other's place for the night, but Steve could never quite get a handle on Neile's infidelity. His anger had subsided until a producer asked to drop by a script for Steve to read. He readily agreed. There was just one catch—the producer had Maximilian Schell in the car and it would save him from doubling back to his hotel. Would Steve mind if he brought Schell by the house?

This was the boiling point. McQueen had never been one to forget an insult or attack, and he had let Neile's infidelity eat away at him for months. Now it was thrust in his face and was more tangible than ever. He became unhinged and growled for Neile when he hung up the phone. She immediately ran to meet him at the steps, thinking one of the children had been in an accident. She recalled in her memoir, "The man I met on the landing was not a normal man. His face was red, and his veins were sticking out of his neck, and his eyes revealed my deepest fear. He had lost control of himself, and for whatever reason, I was alone with him." Neile recounted that the producer, thankfully, never showed up with Schell, but she was the recipient of a manic outburst. She took refuge at a friend's home for three hours, and then returned to the Castle, where Steve gently greeted her and pulled her into his arms. Unfortunately, the worst was yet to come. Steve was a force of nature, and this moment of calm was just the stillness at the eye of the hurricane.

On Memorial Day in 1971, Neile greeted Steve at their Oakmont Drive home with the idea that they would get back together for good when he returned from Prescott, Arizona, where he was about to film his next picture, *Junior Bonner.* It was a happy occasion, and McQueen had already commenced the festivities. Neile noticed he was already high on grass, and after he kissed Terry and Chad good night, the coke came out after he started up the car. With the first snort, his personality switched from mellow to aggressive. He began the battery of questions, badgering Neile, grabbing her by the hair, and slapping her upside the head as the car wound down the driveway.

The fight escalated, and the car rolled to a stop. Neile jumped out of the car, and he caught up with her in the courtyard. He wanted to know why she had betrayed him, demanding an answer he was never going to get. His arm was cocked back and his fist was clenched and ready to strike when a housekeeper, who watched the fracas unfold, broke a radio against the wall to snap Steve out of his hypnotic state of aggression. It worked, and Steve rallied to attention. When he collected himself, Steve collapsed. His guilt immediately kicked in, and he profusely apologized. He realized that he didn't just destroy their union, he'd blown up all the bridges. He ushered his badly traumatized wife to bed and kissed her goodnight. They looked at each other through the tears and knew in their hearts it was finally over.

"I love you, and I will always love you," Steve said. "Remember that, will you?"

"Good-bye, my husband. I love you," Neile replied. "Take care of yourself."

The following day—June 1, 1971—Neile Adams McQueen filed for legal separation in the Superior Court of California, County of Los Angeles, from her husband of 15 years. The volcano had finally erupted, and the fallout had left nothing unscathed. McQueen had not just closed a door on one of the most important chapters of his life—he had slammed it tight. The woman who had been his kindred spirit, lover, mentor, confidante, wife, and mother of his children was now apart from him. The cause of this lay solely at his feet. One of his deepest fears and anxieties was crystallized—just as his mother had walked out on him, now his wife was gone, too. Only this time he had to shoulder the blame, whether he realized it or not. McQueen was a master of severing ties, often to his own detriment. However, he was also on the verge on starting new ones.

27

BACK IN THE SADDLE

TURNING 40 HAD NOT BEEN AN EASY MILESTONE for Steve McQueen. When he looked in the mirror, he saw a middle-aged man staring back. His "Live Now, Pay Later" attitude had finally caught up with him, and he was reeling.

By the start of 1971, Steve McQueen had experienced the "star trip" of booze, drugs, indiscriminate sex, and an impending divorce. He had been booted around by a merciless film industry after years of sticking it to producers and studios, and he was due for a karmic kickback. *Le Mans* took away all of his box-office heat, and the film was a vivid reminder that McQueen wasn't omnipotent and all powerful. In one fell swoop, he lost his wife, agent, production company, and his personal fortune. McQueen, who had never lost a game of cards, lost with uncommon stakes, not unlike his character Eric Stoner in the finale of *The Cincinnati Kid*. Cut adrift were old friends, business associates, and anything or anyone connected to his past glory. It was out with the old and in with the new.

McQueen had taken everything he could, but now Hollywood had bitten back.

He returned to a simpler life. He dissolved the three Solar companies and the lawyers, the accountants, the managers, and the public relations people. The suits and ties that he so proudly wore to the office went back into the closet and were mothballed. He painfully recalled, "I put up a suite of offices, a lot of secretaries, accountants, lots of people on the payroll. I was producing my own movies. Just terrific. But I wasn't making any money, I was working 16 hours a day, and I was the president of three corporations. And I was not very happy." Nor was he very rich.

At the end of *Le Mans*, McQueen was presented with a $2 million bill by the Internal Revenue Service for back taxes. It couldn't have come at a worse time. He had worked endlessly for years to have financial security. Now his worst fears were being realized; he could be broke again and on the street with an empty stomach.

Luckily his name still carried some significant currency. Agent Freddie Fields wasted no time brokering movie deals for his client, and in early 1971 McQueen had already been officially linked to three pictures: *Junior Bonner*, *The Getaway*, and *Papillon*, a film adaptation of a worldwide bestseller by Henri Charrière.

Fields said McQueen was different than all of his other celebrity clients. "Becoming a big star was not enough to take him out of that problem [his past]. It was not enough to cure the damage," Fields said. "He was so concerned about what he might lose that he was not really able to focus on what he had."

Fields had McQueen join First Artists Production Co. Ltd., a company he formed with David Begelman in 1969. Much like United Artists five decades before them, it was a bold experiment designed to free superstars of the corporate shackles of big studios. At the time of First Artists' formation, the industry was slipping into a recession, and it was a way to keep costs low for studios while rewarding stars on the back end for their risk.

In addition to McQueen, the list of box-office dynamos included Paul Newman, Barbra Streisand, Sidney Poitier, and later, Dustin Hoffman. Steve admitted, "I just had to take my lumps and move in a new direction. I could no longer depend on Solar alone. I needed more production muscle behind me."

Each star was committed to three films in exchange for creative control over their pictures and agreeing to forgo their customary seven-figure contracts for an off-the-top percentage[1] of the movie. However, they had to keep the budget of the picture less than $3 million. Warner Brothers agreed to put up two-thirds of the money, while First Artists ponied up the rest. By all appearances, it seemed to be a bold and innovative step for filmmaking and the makings of a gold mine. But somehow the formula got altered, and ultimately it turned out to be an albatross for a commitment-phobe like McQueen. After all, he had never worked well when forced to do something. On *Wanted: Dead or Alive*, he quickly tired of the daily grind and tried to get out of his contract. When Solar was tied up with Warner Brothers, it put him under immense pressure, and he wanted out. First Artists would be the same. He was under pressure to deliver, but this time he was essentially benchmarked against his other rival stars. Toward the end of his life, McQueen remarked that he felt as though this deal had triggered the beginning of the end for his career and body.

---

1   Industry reports vary as to the actual percentage. Most said it was 10 percent, but some reported it as high as 15 percent.

On Any Sunday was the first bright spot for McQueen that year and brought much-needed relief to the *Le Mans* debacle. The motorcycle documentary, which has often been credited as the best one ever made on the subject, was a surprise hit when it was released in July 1971. The 96-minute movie raked in $24 million worldwide[2] and helped spur the explosive growth of the sport during the 1970s. Brown's movie conveyed the fun and enjoyment that motorcycling added to people's lives. It also documented the 1970 season of AMA Grand National racing by following defending champion Mert Lawwill. "Most bike flicks in the past concentrated on the outlaw crap," McQueen said. "Hell's Angels and all of that stuff, which is about as far away from the real world of motorcycle racing as I am from Lionel Barrymore."

It also garnered McQueen a *Sports Illustrated* cover—a rare feat for an actor—which established his racing credentials, immortalized his racing pseudonym Harvey Mushman, and espoused his love of the two-wheeled machine, which dated back to the '50s when he bought a 1946 Indian Chief. "I remember how proud I was of it—I right away went over to see this girl I was dating to show it to her. When she saw it, she said, 'You don't expect me to ride around with you on *that*?' Well, I sure enough did. The girl went, but the bike stayed."

Unlike most of McQueen's pictures, which involved lots of drama or a troubled production, *On Any Sunday* was nothing but pure joy, reconnecting him to people outside the pampered world of the film industry. It was the breath of fresh air that McQueen sorely needed.

Rider Mert Lawwill said McQueen was in good spirits when he spent the night at director Bruce Brown's Dana Point home to film the first sequence. "We were going to shoot the beach scene at Camp Pendleton Marine Corps Base on the sand dunes the next day, and we had to get up early. We found ourselves relegated to Bruce's kids' bunk bed. It was funny because Steve looks around and all he saw were pictures of me and Dick Mann, the national-winning motorcycle rider, and a few photos of races. There were no pictures of him in sight. Steve said, 'Hey, don't you guys go to the movies?' It provoked a few laughs."

Brown recalled he had problems securing the Camp Pendleton location until McQueen, a former Marine, got on the phone and worked his magic. "I figured there would be no way to get approval to film on the Marine base," Brown recalled. "Steve McQueen said he'd see what he could find out. The next day he called and

---

2   Director Bruce Brown said the distributor purchased *On Any Sunday* halfway through filming and McQueen recouped his investment before the picture was released.

told me to contact some general, and the next thing you know we are shooting the beach sequences. It was pretty amazing the doors he was able to open."

Brown and Lawwill found McQueen a delightful, easygoing person who was genuine and never gave off a whiff of the movie-star vibe. In fact, McQueen stated that he was in awe of Lawwill, who was the American Motorcyclist Grand Champion of 1969. "One time he told me, 'You know Mert, you're No. 1 and you've earned that. In my job, I'm just an actor playing somebody else for a day and that's all.' It was amazing to me how insecure Steve felt about his place in society," Lawwill said.

He also found McQueen caring and generous; Steve came to his aid when Mert was seriously injured. Lawwill was involved in a riding accident in Castle Rock, Washington, shortly after the release of *On Any Sunday*. His hand was completely mangled, and the prognosis was not good. The doctor at the hospital told Lawwill he'd have to fuse his knuckles together and it would leave him with a club hand. When asked if there was an alternative, the doctor shook his head no and told Lawwill to get used to the idea. McQueen didn't accept the idea and arranged for Dr. Robert Stark, a specialist in Los Angeles, to give a second opinion.

Stark repaired the hand over a period of five operations, inserting seven pins in Lawwill's hand. He was able to race again, thanks to McQueen, and Lawwill never received a doctor's bill.

"I've always held Steve McQueen in high esteem, not just because my hand is relatively free of disability as a result of his generosity," Lawwill said.

On Any Sunday garnered warm critical reviews. *Variety* hailed it as "an exciting documentary of one of the most dangerous of all sports. McQueen's prowess as a racer is demonstrated time and again, and his name should spark interest in a film that alone stands as a spectacular piece of filmmaking." *The Washington Post* stated, "The last time an actor's athletic feat thrilled audiences for a sustained length of time was probably McQueen's motorcycle ride in *The Great Escape*." Roger Ebert concluded, "[*On Any Sunday*] does for motorcycle racing what *Endless Summer* did for surfing."

The documentary struck a particular chord with youngsters, who would hide in movie-theater bathrooms between showings so they could watch the film two or three times in one day. Thousands of kids across the country started saving money from their paper routes and summer jobs to buy a minibike after being inspired by the movie.

"I think many people changed their minds about motorcyclists after watching the movie," Brown said.

In addition to introducing motorcycling to the masses, getting youth revved up, and making studio chiefs take notice of its box-office intake, *On Any Sunday* was nominated for an Academy Award for Documentary Feature Film at the end of the year. However, it did not win. Regardless, it was a sweet ride for everyone involved. It is no wonder McQueen relished and enjoyed the experience. The pressure was off, and he would not have to take the fall too badly no matter how the film fared. He could ride bikes all day and outrun his financial and marital problems at 100 mph. For once, the weight of everyone's expectations and his own internal pressure to succeed was lifted from his shoulders. For a short while, he was free again.

· · ·

McQueen was taking a back-to-basics approach in his personal and professional life. "I've cut everything down," he said of his new philosophy. "Now I think of Laurence Olivier when he goes to work. He's got a little black bag with a couple of fake noses, his wig, or whatever he's got in there. And that's all I need—a pencil, a script, and a briefcase." Metaphorically speaking, he had been bucked off his high horse and landed hard in the dirt. After he got back on his feet and dusted himself off, he was ready to climb back in the saddle.

His film comeback was in direct contrast to *Le Mans*; he wanted a quiet picture and a character-oriented role where he wasn't required to do all the dramatic heavy lifting. "I'm tired of being the chief. I just want to be an Indian. I'm going to concentrate for a while on being an actor," McQueen said. The decision paid off handsomely, for McQueen turned in one of the most poignant and wistful performances of his career.

Junior Bonner, about an over-the-hill rodeo rider who returns to his hometown and sees how his family is trapped in a changing West, was a departure for McQueen. It would eventually become one of his favorite movies.

The concept for the film and the ultimate packaging came together at a fast clip. Writer Jeb Rosebrook drummed up the idea for *Junior Bonner* when he attended the Prescott Frontier Days rodeo in July 1970 in Prescott, Arizona. The professional rodeo was formed when a group of Prescott merchants and professional businessmen organized the first formalized "cowboy tournament" on July 4, 1888. Now the event is billed as the World's Oldest Rodeo. His 1970 visit was Rosebrook's first to the city in about 15 years, and the transformation was apparent. "I saw this old western town turn into a real estate boom and how it was paving the way for the future," Rosebrook said. "It was a contemporary western using rodeo as a metaphor."

Rosebrook's agent, Mike Wise of Creative Management Associates, called on the eve of Labor Day weekend to tell him that Robert Redford was looking for a "rodeo film" and did he have one? Rosebrook replied no, but the inquiry and the idea of Robert Redford starring in one of his vehicles got Rosebrook's creative juices going. That weekend he wrote a four-page outline based on his trip to Prescott called *Bonner*. Wise never heard back from Redford, but within days he received a reply from producer Joe Wizan (*Jeremiah Johnson*), who thought it was the perfect vehicle for Steve McQueen.[3]

Rosebrook started the first draft on Thanksgiving 1970, and he wrote 10 to 20 pages per day. He sent them to Wizan, who was on location in Utah for *Jeremiah Johnson*. Wizan suggested revisions here and there and had a finished draft in March 1971.

McQueen loved how the script tapped into the symbiotic relationship between the passing of the old and new West. He nicknamed Rosebrook "Shakespeare" because of McQueen's preference for less dialogue. But, according to Rosebrook, "[McQueen] related to that character. Both men's home lives were erratic. Both men never had a real relationship with their fathers. In fact, Steve insisted that [Bonner] call his father 'Ace' instead of 'Dad.'" Rosebrook met with McQueen at the Castle in April to go over his input on the script. McQueen asked Rosebrook, "Why am I called Junior?" The question took Rosebrook completely by surprise, who answered honestly, "I don't know." The two men laughed at the discovery, and it ended up on film when actress Barbara Leigh asks him the same question inside a telephone booth in The Palace Bar. Rosebrook said McQueen's other major contribution to the script is when Joe Don Baker confronts Steve at the bar and they have a punch-out, followed by a drink.

After McQueen signed with ABC Pictures Corp. in April 1971, *Junior Bonner* picked up speed. Director Sam Peckinpah was tapped to direct the following month, and everyone predicted fireworks, including McQueen. "Sam Peckinpah, boy, will he and I be some combination," McQueen said. "ABC has bought a lot of aspirin." Behind the scenes, McQueen wasn't so coy. He enlisted business manager Bill Maher to find out if he and Peckinpah would get along. He sent Maher as an emissary to meet with Bobby Visciglia, who had worked as a prop master for several of Peckinpah's films. The two met for lunch, and Visciglia broke the ice. "Bob, let's cut the bullshit. What is your concern?" Maher, on behalf of McQueen, wanted to know how Peckinpah felt about working with McQueen again after Peckinpah was fired from *The Cincinnati Kid*. Peckinpah

---

3   Wizan was a former agent at the William Morris Agency, where he knew McQueen.

felt McQueen could have done more to save his job, and McQueen sensed this. Visciglia, on behalf of Peckinpah, said there were no more hard feelings and that the two could work together and make the film. "Steve was very respectful to Sam during the making of *Junior Bonner*. He called him, 'Mr. Peckinpah.' Somehow, though, I always felt there was a shield throughout the movie between the two."

Peckinpah and McQueen cast the movie together in early June with the idea that cameras would roll on June 30 to capture the Frontier Rodeo Days parade, which is a vital part of the story. The McQueen-Peckinpah marquee and the film's story lured three extremely talented actors—Robert Preston, Ida Lupino, and Ben Johnson—who added great value to the picture.[4] "That was Marty Baum's doing," said Jeb Rosebrook, giving credit to the ABC Pictures executive who later cofounded the Creative Artists Agency. "He always felt that a good film had a great cast. He wanted to surround McQueen with a cast that would make him stretch his character, and he achieved that."

The other key roles—McQueen's brother Curly Bonner and his love interest, Charmagne—were also integral to the picture and had yet to be cast. Gene Hackman's name was suggested for Curly, but McQueen dismissed the idea rather quickly during a script meeting. "I think Gene Hackman's a good actor, there's no question about that. He'd be good, but he sure wants a lot of money." It is an ironic remark because McQueen was never shy about asking for the moon. For *Junior Bonner*, he collected an $850,000 paycheck and a percentage of the profits. McQueen then remembered Joe Don Baker, who shone so brightly in Solar Productions' *Adam at 6 A.M.*

Barbara Leigh, a stunning world-class model and actress whose looks embodied the naturalistic '70s, auditioned for the role of Charmagne in early June at Joe Wizan's Studio City office. As she walked in, actress Tiffany Bolling strolled out. The two smiled at each other and kept walking. Leigh, who thought she was reading for Peckinpah, was stunned when Steve McQueen was present as well. "The first thing I noticed about the two men was that they were short, with Sam being the shorter of the two. Steve stood about 5'10", but he slouched and had a very wiry frame, which made him seem smaller than he really was. When you grow up watching an actor you admire on the big screen, he becomes larger than life. His diminutive stature made him seem more human to me."

She read her lines with McQueen a couple of times, with Peckinpah giving some direction. After approximately 20 minutes, Peckinpah abruptly stood up

---

4   Lupino hadn't appeared in a movie since 1955's *The Big Knife*, while Preston had taken a seven-year hiatus from the film industry.

and thanked her for coming in. Leigh got the sinking feeling Peckinpah didn't want her for the role. She walked out of Wizan's office and was almost to her car, with keys in hand, when she heard someone calling her name. She turned and it was McQueen, who was running to catch up to her. She was somewhat bewildered. "I don't think the part's going to work out, but I'd like to take you to dinner," McQueen said shyly. Leigh admired his honesty and the fact that he didn't bullshit her by saying the part was hers or lead her on in any way, shape, or form.

"He let me know right up front, before our relationship went any further, that the part of Charmagne was not mine," Leigh says, "and I respected him immensely for that."

The two met for dinner and drinks at a quaint Malibu restaurant on Sunset Boulevard near the Pacific Coast Highway. Leigh says he was quite the gentleman, ordering her a drink and pushing out her bar stool for her. As they talked, they discovered they had similar backgrounds. Both were raised by people other than their biological parents—McQueen by his great-uncle while Leigh was a product of the foster-care system. Both had been deserted by their fathers at an early age and had mothers who were free spirits and not financially equipped to raise children. The subject of his current marital status also came up. "He spoke of his marriage to Neile and how it was nearing the end. He spoke of her with respect, which I found admirable. I think he needed to spread his wings and wanted to be free to take the next step in his life," Leigh recalled. "The romantic part of his marriage was over, and he wanted excitement. Sadly, Steve and Neile still loved each other deeply, but Steve, from what I knew and read, couldn't be faithful to her. He seemed a little lost and confused as to what he wanted in life."

Leigh's relationship status was not a topic they broached much. She had been dating MGM President Jim Aubrey[5] for more than a year and seeing Elvis Presley on the side. Leigh had a feminist's view of the situation. "Looking back, I think the fact that the three men in my life knew about each other made me more appealing—maybe more of a challenge to each of them. Who wouldn't have done the same thing in my place? It was fun," Leigh said.

McQueen and Leigh were instantly at ease with each other and became intimate in the weeks leading up to the filming of *Junior Bonner*. McQueen made her promise to visit him in Prescott, to which she agreed. But on July 1, 1971,

---

5   James Aubrey was the former head of CBS Television and was named by Kirk Kerkorian to head up MGM's film division. Aubrey, nicknamed "The Smiling Cobra" for his soulless business tactics, was the inspiration for Jacqueline Susan's *The Love Machine*.

three days before principal photography commenced, Steve called Barbara with life-changing news. Tiffany Bolling had to bow out, and they needed someone to fill her shoes. Was she available? "I was at a loss for words—I mean, I was absolutely dumbfounded," Leigh recalled. "Just like that, out of the clear blue. That was the single greatest thing to happen in my acting career, starring in a Steve McQueen movie directed by the great Sam Peckinpah. But that's Hollywood for you; overnight, anything can happen."

"Anything can happen" was indeed the tone set forth by Peckinpah, who ran a tight ship with his crew but a loose set with the actors. William Pierce, who was the chairman of Prescott's Rodeo Fair Association and served on Arizona's Picture Development Commission, got a taste of Peckinpah's controlled chaos when the director visited Prescott with ABC Pictures executive Jim Pratt weeks before they started shooting. Peckinpah was holed up at the Prescottonian Hotel with Pratt and a couple of other minions when Pierce met him for the first time. Peckinpah and Pratt still hadn't decided on a location[6] despite the fact the script was based on the Frontier Days Rodeo. Pierce remembered, "I knocked on the hotel door and Jim answered. He stepped outside and said, 'Okay, come on in. We're waiting around for Sam.' Jim was very hesitant in his manner, and it sounded strange coming out of his mouth, but in hindsight I think he was trying to warn me. I get in the room, and everybody is standing around while Sam is lying in bed. On the nightstand in between the bed was a bottle of Martel Brandy and a water glass. Nobody introduced me; nobody spoke; nobody said anything. Everybody acted as if he was the king and we were to say nothing until he spoke."

Pierce kept glancing at his watch as the minutes passed, which seemed to him like forever. Finally he had reached his boiling point and blew his stack. "You know, Jim," he said in an irritated tone, "I've got better things to do than this. I don't know what your routine is. I'm just a local guy, but I'm a busy man. I think you should make your movie here in Prescott—it's a good community; we've got great people and the best rodeo in the United States. Your rodeo film would be bogus if you didn't make it here."

His words had the effect of a record needle that scratched across a vinyl record, and everyone froze, except for Peckinpah. The words got his attention, and he leaped out of bed and stood next to Pierce. The director pronounced, "I'm going with him, and the rest of you sonofabitches can follow!"

Four days later, Pierce received word that Peckinpah had decided on Prescott and was bringing an all-star cast of Steve McQueen, Robert Preston, Ida Lupino,

---

6   Ruidoso, New Mexico, was the other location that was being contemplated by Peckinpah.

and Ben Johnson to stay for 10 weeks. It was as if a tidal wave had struck the small town, and they drowned in delight.

It was also a delight for everyone in the production. According to Barbara Leigh, everyone stayed at the Prescottonian, where it was a nonstop party. "It was a riot. Ida Lupino and Robert Preston were old friends and often left their doors open to welcome cast members and to have a drink with them. When you finished partying with Robert, you floated over to Ida's for more of the same. There was a lot of partying going on throughout the filming of *Junior Bonner*."

The Palace Bar was also a gathering place for locals and cowboys, who drank, danced, shot pool, and listened to honky-tonk music. For McQueen, it was a place to unwind, relax, have a beer, and shoot pool. John Allen was driving past Prescott that weekend when the transmission in his truck broke down. While he waited for his truck to be fixed, he checked into a hotel, then walked through the saloon doors of The Palace Bar and ordered a Seven and Seven. When he turned around to watch the house band, he felt as if he'd just entered a Fellini picture. "Steve happened to be standing in the front of the bar in a red sleeveless shirt and a beautiful brunette [Barbara Leigh] on his arm. He was hard to miss," Allen said.

Allen's former wife Gloria had grown up in Slater and was a childhood playmate of Steve's. When he saw McQueen standing at the bar, he approached the movie star. "I walked up behind him and said, 'Slater, Missouri.' Steve turned around to face me. 'How do you know about that?' he asked with a puzzled look on his face. I told him that Gloria was my wife and they had played together as kids. He remembered Gloria, and it was as if her name was a secret passcode into his world. He invited me for a drink."

Before too long, the two were carrying on like long-lost friends. Not only were they from Missouri, but both also served in the Marines and enjoyed racing. They even knew some of the same people in the entertainment industry. Before Allen switched vocations, he had managed country singer Johnny Duncan and befriended singer/songwriter Jerry Wallace. McQueen knew them both.

The two men were knocking them down pretty well, to the point where Allen felt comfortable enough to ask McQueen to write Gloria a note to say hello. An inebriated McQueen wrote:

> *Dear Gloria,*
>   *I'm a little drunk, and your Husband is trying to fight with me. He is good—so I hope all is good with you.*
>   *Steve McQueen*

Barbara Leigh says the film's big fight scene was fueled by alcohol, with Peckinpah taking over for the bartender. "Before the scene, Sam had the bar lined with drinks. All the main actors were positioned, and then the extras arrived. Everyone had a drink to loosen up, then the scene began. Everyone was literally smashed by the end. Sam made sure the booze in the glasses was real, not the customary iced tea used in movies. Only in a Sam Peckinpah movie could that have happened!"

William Pierce said that drinking on the job might have been Peckinpah's modus operandi, but not for McQueen. "Once Steve stepped in front of the cameras, he became a different person—intense, focused, and all business," Pierce said, who was lucky enough to share a scene with McQueen at the beginning of the movie. "We ad-libbed our lines and nailed the shot in three takes. Steve was surprised that I had never acted before and just about floored me when he told me I was a natural. He also admitted that even he had first-day jitters but I had helped him through it."

Actress Ida Lupino was from the old school of acting and didn't appreciate it when McQueen ad-libbed his lines with her, recalled Jeb Rosebrook. "Steve was always changing his lines the night before filming, and on this particular night before his scene with Ida in the kitchen, eating pie, there wasn't anybody around to consult with on the script, so he didn't learn his lines," Rosebrook said. "That next day, McQueen began to ad-lib the scene, throwing off Ida because he was saying things that weren't in the script. Ida blew up and told him, 'Tomorrow you either learn your lines or you're going to be eating a helluva lot of apple pie!'"

Barbara Leigh said McQueen may have been distracted during that sequence. The house next door to Lupino's had a robust vegetable garden, which included huge stalks of marijuana plants. "The stalks were pulled up and carted away by the local police, but not before Steve reacted with catlike reflexes and grabbed one for himself," Leigh laughs. "Steve smoked marijuana daily when I was with him. He especially loved the homegrown stuff."

McQueen redeemed himself with Robert Preston in the emotional scene at Prescott's railroad depot. Preston portrayed Ace Bonner, Junior's father. The scene is the first reconciliation between the two men, who haven't seen each other in close to five years. Rosebrook said Peckinpah described to him the evening before filming the scene how he would shoot it. "When Junior reveals he's broke and cannot finance his father's dream trip to Australia, Ace in frustration will cuff Junior's hat off because when Peckinpah was a boy this is what his father did to him," Rosebrook said. "It worked out beautifully on screen."

The scene also proved to be one of McQueen's finest cinematic moments because it was as close to crying as McQueen ever came to in a film. "Steve found it difficult to do a sensitive scene with another man. That's why he was so good in the film. He was breaking new ground," said Katy Haber, who worked as an assistant to producer Joe Wizan.

Barbara Leigh said watching McQueen work was a study in film acting, a master who was in top form. "Watching him perform was a trip," Leigh said. "Steve's approach to acting was different than most, and that's what separated him from most movie stars. He was a reactor instead of an actor. He didn't initiate action; he reacted with his facial expressions and body language. Most actors fight for lines; Steve fought for the shot. Where he placed himself was more important to him than what he had to say. He didn't appear to be acting at all, but that was his gift."

In time, Leigh moved in with McQueen at his private rental home perched on the side of a hill with a gorgeous view of the Prescott mountains. She says he was mostly relaxed during the shoot and often went over his lines with her during breakfast. The only drama that arose was when Elvis Presley called Leigh, asking her to join him in Las Vegas. She said she was committed to the film until August 15 and couldn't break away.

"I know," Presley said. "I'll come to Prescott. I've always wanted to see a real cowboy town. I wanna see my baby, and if I have to come there, then so be it."

It took Leigh a few seconds to muster the courage to confess that she was seeing McQueen. The voice on the other end of the line was silent, and Presley quickly got off the phone.

Leigh said it was obvious that McQueen and Presley were jealous of each other. "The funny thing was whenever Elvis inquired about Steve, he'd ask, 'How's that motorcycle hick?' while Steve asked, 'How's that guitar hick?' Both men came from humble beginnings, but it was funny they called each other hicks."

While he was by no means a hick, McQueen was keen to show he could still get down and dirty and wanted to show off his Midwestern roots by performing all of his own stunts. But Peckinpah wasn't having any of it. The director relegated McQueen to horses and a mechanical bull, later made famous on *Urban Cowboy*. McQueen felt emasculated, but Peckinpah stood his ground. He left the bulls to the pros. "It embarrassed [McQueen] to no end that he had to ride a machine instead of a real bull," Leigh said. "He hated to be thought of as a 'candy-ass' actor, but for insurance purposes the production company wouldn't let him ride a bull, even though he wanted to. When it came time for him to ride the mechanical bull, he allowed only a skeleton crew to film him. He let me on the set, but I had to watch it with a straight face—which was difficult. At the very least, he made the scenes look real."

Frank Kelly was a former Professional Rodeo Cowboys Association bull rider who was hired by Casey Tibbs to double McQueen. He was sitting on a bull, ironically named Sunshine, when McQueen walked up to him and caught him at a bad time. "I was sitting on the meanest bull west of the Mississippi with a silly blond wig on my head when Steve made the unfortunate mistake of telling me that he was concerned I might not be the right double for him. He said I had too many scars on my face and wasn't quite what he was looking for," Kelly said.

Kelly viewed his scars as a badge of honor, and each one was earned. Something about the remark set off Kelly, and he blew his stack. He told McQueen where he and his movie-star looks and attitude could go, and poked him in the chest to emphasize his point. McQueen was taken aback by this aggressive approach and took a step back when the gate opened. Kelly stayed on the bull for the full eight seconds, which was the grand finale of the movie, and McQueen came over to apologize after Peckinpah yelled "cut."

"Frank, I think you took my comment the wrong way," McQueen said, holding out his hand. "I'm sorry if I offended you." Kelly detected only sincerity in McQueen and reached out to shake his hand. According to Kelly, McQueen was nothing but a pure joy from that moment on. "Over time, Steve came to enjoy the company of cowboys. He liked the fact that we didn't request autographs, ask him to pose for pictures, or fail to put him in his place when he took on a bit of a Hollywood attitude."

The closest McQueen ever got to a bull was one called Docile Sunshine, who was fun, playful, and even kid-friendly. McQueen was not allowed to get near Evil Sunshine, who was the meanest, craziest bull in existence.

McQueen was able to successfully tweak the nose of Docile Sunshine but used Evil Sunshine to stub Peckinpah's nose. While Peckinpah was setting up another shot in the center of the ring with the sound and camera crew, McQueen thought it would be funny to release Evil Sunshine from the bull pen and into the ring. The bull wreaked holy havoc, recalled Katy Haber. "You've never seen so many people scatter so fast," Haber said. "I had grown men climb over me to get out of the way." The bucking bull demolished an expensive 35 mm camera. Peckinpah didn't think that was too funny. When the bull was finally contained and the crew gathered again for the first time, Haber was moved to ask aloud, "Whatever happened to women and children first?"

"Steve was basically a child at heart, a kid from the orphanage who was reliving his youth now that he was a movie star," Haber said.

McQueen pulled another stunt in the last scene of the picture, only this time his victim was prop master Bobby Visciglia. In the movie, Junior won first prize and was able to purchase a first-class ticket for Ace to Australia. The scene involved an exchange of real money, and when Peckinpah yelled cut, McQueen handed the bills back to Visciglia. In a re-creation of his days as a carnie, McQueen stashed a few bills for himself. Visciglia counted up the cash and realized he was out a few hundred bucks.

"Damn McQueen," Viscigila thought, "That son of a bitch shorted me!"

Rosebrook said McQueen was nondiscriminating when it came to shorting those financially less fortunate. But Rosebrook said he didn't mind. Steve was still the sharp hustler who had learned his craft on the streets. Even as a rich and famous star, he still retained his edge. "On the final day of filming, we ended up in the old mining town of Jerome, Arizona. Steve, as usual, carried no money. He needed a beer, so I bought it. He said it was a loan. For me, like that summer, it was a gift."[7]

McQueen didn't short movie-going audiences and turned in one of the more spectacular performances of his career. The film is a favorite for many fans, and it is not hard to see why. McQueen plays Bonner with an honesty and integrity that only he can do. His handling of the bulls, his horse, and his attire all appear completely natural. He does not just act the cowboy—he actually becomes one. This portrayal was so effective that the Stuntmen's Association of Motion Pictures made him an honorary member a few years later. But what really sets this performance apart? One has to think it must be the portrayal of the father-son dynamic between McQueen and Robert Preston. McQueen never had a relationship with his father, and those scenes in the film offer an insight into his feelings and sensitivities that he would never admit even to himself. In a rare moment, McQueen let down his guard and won over his fans yet again.

Critics seemed to be in agreement that McQueen was in peak form. "Steve McQueen is explosive and forceful in one of his finest performances," boasted the *Los Angeles Times*. "A nice, loose, easygoing rodeo picture. McQueen has met with a role that fits him like a glove," wrote Kathleen Carroll of the *New*

---

7   In 1972, Rosebrook wrote another screenplay intended for McQueen and Peckinpah called *Jack Ballard*. Set against the backdrop of the 1880s, Ballard (McQueen) is a lone gunfighter who rides into town and helps a wily widow fight off a group of heavies. According to Rosebrook, producer Joe Wizan gave the finished screenplay to McQueen and Peckinpah. Wizan never got a reply from either man. The script has now been retitled *No Man's Land*.

York Daily News. The *Sarasota Herald-Tribune* proclaimed, "This movie is strictly McQueen's."

Released in August 1972, *Junior Bonner* was part of a small wave of rodeo movies (*J.W. Coop, The Honkers,* and *When The Legends Die*) released within a three-month time frame. McQueen felt that ABC Pictures botched the marketing strategy, which doomed the picture from the start. "In distributing the picture, I was dealing with a man named Joe Sugar, who wanted to release it big—Grauman's Chinese and the whole bit," McQueen said. "I told him that it should be released as an art picture, starting in more select smaller theaters and letting the picture catch on. He continued to disagree and, of course, the picture was released his way and fell flat. But I think it's a picture that'll do well over the long haul. Not today, not tomorrow. But give it time, and people will recognize it for what it's worth." McQueen was correct in that *Junior Bonner* has been proven a succès d'estime. The film has undeniably aged well. This is due to many things. In particular, it is a gentle film, especially in contrast to other films directed by Peckinpah. It has a basic charm to it and is highly character-driven, not relying on fast cars and guns. Instead, it is the tour de force acting and nuanced performances that captivate and drive the story forward. It is this legacy that fans still connect with today.

Junior Bonner didn't do much to enhance McQueen's stature at the box office, however. The film went $1 million over its $2.5 million budget[8] and grossed $2.6 million in its first year of release. That amount doubled to $4.6 million in 1977 but was still $3.5 million in the red according to the studio bookkeepers.[9] McQueen reflected on his feelings about the movie's lack of box-office prowess: "I liked *Junior Bonner* very much. It was the first time I'd worked with Sam, and we got it together. I thought the script was tremendous—one of the best properties I've come across. But I think the film is a failure, at least financially, and in this business, that's what counts."

McQueen needed *Junior Bonner* to be a success. Mentally he needed it to restore his power and put him back on track. The film certainly did that, allowing him to enjoy himself and find new and pleasurable challenges. However, the same old problems and fears would surface, and he would not be able to

---

8 The $1 million overrun was due to the lack of preproduction time, high labor and equipment costs of maintaining up to nine camera crews for *Junior Bonner*'s rodeo sequences, a laborious editing process and a busted 35 mm camera courtesy of Evil Sunshine.

9 Movie studios are notorious for their "creative bookkeeping." Nearly 40 years later and several generations of VHS, DVD, and boxed sets of both, as well as thousands of screenings on network television and cable, *Junior Bonner* has surely generated a profit by now.

enjoy the artistic freedom and happiness of the film. Good times and personal fulfillment were not enough. Financially, McQueen needed every penny. When he got back to California, he came crashing back to reality. Neile presented him with divorce papers on September 10, 1971. The bill attached was a $1 million settlement, division of assets, and $500,000 per year alimony and child support for the next decade.

28

NEW VIBRATION

NOVELIST F. SCOTT FITZGERALD ONCE FAMOUSLY DECLARED, "There are no second acts in American lives." But the writer didn't live long enough to see Steve McQueen prove him wrong.

McQueen's life had changed immeasurably in the previous few years. He had taken a serious blow to his career with poor box-office receipts, and he had suffered a crisis in his personal life. His leading-man status was on the brink of fading. However, McQueen was never one to take anything lying down, and above all, he worked best when facing a challenge. Things could never stay the same for such a force of nature, and he would find new passions and repair his personal life. Over the next few years, McQueen not only recovered but also reached new heights and became the highest-paid star again, standing head and shoulders above the rest of Hollywood. But he would again have to fight to get back to the top. He was looking for a new vibration.

By the end of 1971, Steve McQueen was in need of two things—a quick infusion of cash and a box-office hit. The trifecta of Solar's collapse, $2 million in back taxes owed to the IRS, and his impending divorce to Neile had left the superstar cash poor.

The first portion of his dilemma was remedied when agent Freddie Fields turned to the Far East for help. "He needed money, and Steve wasn't a singer or dancer, so I couldn't make a deal for him in Las Vegas," Fields said. "So I tried Japan, and I hit pay dirt with Honda."

Fields secured a record-breaking fee of $1 million for a Honda commercial with the provision that it be shown only in Japan. That way, McQueen's movie-star image back in the United States wouldn't be tarnished. Sporting an orange long-sleeved T-shirt while on a motorcycle romp in the hills of Southern California, McQueen endorsed the Honda CR 250m Elsinore and put a particular emphasis on motorcycle safety in the 30-second spot. "This is what I do to relax. I ride fast. I ride fast in the dirt with the right safety equipment. When you're riding in the street, be safety-minded. Please don't ride too fast."[1]

McQueen did hit an emotional brick wall when faced with the reality that his marriage was finally over. "He was stunned when I filed for divorce," Neile said. "He couldn't understand that I needed to have an orderly life...be my own person. I had children to care for. He was furious when I filed." That was because Steve was in major denial, according to psychologist Peter O. Whitmer. "More than mere denial, when it came to being emotionally insightful, Steve McQueen could be severely blinded," he noted. "He saw himself first, foremost, and sometimes exclusively the legacy of having to be a lifelong survivor. His inability to react empathetically toward Neile goes back to his primitive sense of trust having been broken and feeling that this scarred him and not anyone else. And the depth of hurt that he experienced—the self-fulfilling prophecy—would stay with him and paint his next marriage with the same brush."

Terry and Chad had been placed in Neile's custody, but that was a mere technicality. There was an implicit understanding that Steve was going to continue to be a major part of their lives. To their credit, both Steve and Neile acted with maturity in the face of divorce, with neither one saying negative things in front of the children or in the press. "It took four years for us to become friends again," Neile said. "We were in touch, of course, even under the strain. It's an incredible agony you go through with divorce: more traumatic than death because you do it to yourself. The wounds were still raw, but we talked about the kids. He was in and out of the house checking on us, though we both had someone else."

For McQueen, that someone else was Barbara Leigh, his *Junior Bonner* costar. Leigh continued dating James Aubrey and visited with Elvis Presley while he was on tour. When McQueen called shortly after they returned from Prescott for a relaxing weekend in Palm Springs, she thought it sounded like fun. "We stayed in bed for what seemed like hours, making love, laughing, cuddling, settling back with a joint and a beer," Leigh recalled. "Later, Steve took my hand and led me... to the pool. We jumped in. We were happy and in a playful mood. The water felt great in the heat. I truly enjoyed Steve's company and didn't have a care in the world while I was with him."

---

1   McQueen's Japan-only provision was a quarter-century ahead of its time. By the late '90s Japanese businesses were routinely hiring Western movie stars to pitch their products. Arnold Schwarzenegger hawked elixir, Brad Pitt modeled jeans, Leonardo DiCaprio endorsed cars, Harrison Ford pushed beer, and Bruce Willis peddled coffee.

The two rode motorcycles, feasted on Mexican food and beer, traded industry gossip, swam, and soaked up the desert sun. McQueen hinted about the possibility of them moving in together when they got back to Los Angeles, but Leigh wasn't ready to give up the two other men in her life. "In some ways Steve could have been my brother, we were so much alike. We were both affectionately known as P.W.T.—poor white trash," Leigh said. "I knew if I decided to live with Steve, that there could be no other men in my life. But the question that bothered me was could Steve give up everyone else for me? I seriously doubted it. I didn't say no, but I didn't say yes, either. He was a hard man to turn down, especially because he was so used to getting his way."

Even though she adored McQueen, Leigh said there were a few things about him that bothered her. He could be crude, boorish, and coarse. He often ate with his feet on the table, burped aloud, and cussed like a sailor when the mood hit him. He was nowhere near as refined as Aubrey or as sweet and polite as Presley, Leigh said.

Leigh seemed to think that McQueen was searching for diversion rather than love, which proved to be true when he was seen nuzzling in public with Natalie Wood that same month. Wood's divorce from second husband Richard Gregson coincided with Steve's separation from Neile. Wood was enjoying the dating merry-go-round, which included the likes of Frank Sinatra, politician Jerry Brown, writer Tommy Thompson, and choreographer Harold Jeffreys. Wood told journalist Carol Welles that her *Love with the Proper Stranger* costar called her out of the blue. "I have known Steve for a long time but, naturally, never had anything to do with him romantically," Wood said. "He called me for a date one night, and I said, 'Yes.' That's how it all started."

The two were spotted at the Bistro, a posh Beverly Hills restaurant; the Old World on Hollywood's Sunset Strip; and a secluded eatery in the San Fernando Valley. Her pronouncements to Welles seemed somewhat premature. "We are just having too much fun together to really care whether anyone sees us or not," Wood said. "I don't see why people are surprised when a girl falls for Steve. After all, he's a terribly attractive man in more ways than one. And there aren't many around like him anymore in this effete town.

"Maybe it's love, after all. Who knows?"

Whatever emotions McQueen felt for Wood, it wasn't open for discussion. When Welles called him for his comment on their burgeoning romance, McQueen replied, "None of your damn business." That ended the query as well as his short-lived relationship with Wood. Neile McQueen said their pairing was not destined to last. "It was not a serious thing. I think they dated for about

10 days, something like that. Natalie was a child of Hollywood, and she really represented everything that Steve didn't like about Hollywood. When he first began, everything was new—the premieres, the parties, and all of that—but by the time he and I divorced, that was old. But Natalie still loved doing that. She always loved doing that."

When McQueen moved into a rental home on Mulholland Drive, he was feeling sad and alone. He began calling Leigh again but started to show his irritation when his phone calls weren't returned promptly. Even though he knew she was dating others, he was getting fed up with being worked into rotation, and he let Leigh know it. When they finally got together in late October 1971, he gave her an ultimatum—him or James Aubrey. "Steve knew that it would be difficult for me to leave James, but he had enough confidence in himself that he would be able to talk me into it, and he was right," Leigh said. "I said yes. My answer made him happy—for the moment. He hated to be alone. I spent the rest of the night in his arms, cuddling and feeling very needed and wanted."

But the feeling didn't last. The next morning, she skipped their usual morning tea and went home, where she became violently ill. At first she thought it was the idea of having to break it off with Aubrey. When the nausea became an almost daily occurrence, she decided it was time to see her doctor. On November 2, it was confirmed she was pregnant. In her heart, she wanted it to be Aubrey's, who already had two grown children. The thought of it being McQueen's baby never entered her mind. When she finally informed Aubrey over dinner that she was pregnant, he asked who was the father. Leigh was crushed by the remark, thinking Aubrey was cruel and insensitive. Finally he reached over and took her hands. "No, it's not mine," he said sweetly. "As much as I'd like to make you happy, I can't. You see, many, many years ago, I had a vasectomy."

The child was McQueen's.

Leigh weighed her options and instinctively knew that Aubrey wasn't going to help her raise the kid, nor did she want to upset or confuse McQueen, considering the personal turmoil in his life. Instead, she would tell him she was carrying Aubrey's child and make their breakup easier for both of them. "In hindsight, not telling Steve was a rotten thing to do," Leigh said. "He had every right to know I was carrying his child. I'll regret forever my choice not to tell him. I should have given him the opportunity to have a voice in my decision."

Over dinner, she told him she was pregnant, and before he could respond, she told him it was Aubrey's. She recalled his face tensed and almost looked melancholy. She told him she was going to terminate the pregnancy that weekend. "My problem wasn't what he expected to be the topic of conversation over dinner," Leigh said. "To hear the woman you're having an affair with is carrying another man's child is a little shocking, to say the least. I don't believe he ever thought for a moment that it might be his child. I was convincing. He trusted me, I'm sad to say."

Moments before Leigh checked into Cedars-Sinai Medical Center on November 6, 1971, she received a phone call from McQueen, wishing her well. Aubrey did not call, and his thoughtlessness made her feel horrible and alone. There were complications during the procedure, which meant Leigh had to stay a few extra days in the hospital. McQueen visited her twice in the hospital, both times at night so no one could see him, bringing a burger and a milkshake each time. His visits lifted her spirits momentarily but ultimately made her cry because of the secret she harbored. Steve's presence and Aubrey's absence left her emotionally devastated. Leigh says to this day she still contemplates her decision. "Through the years, I've often wondered what my child would have been like and the differences he or she might have made in my life. It's a decision I've thought about many times during the last four decades. If there is a spirit world beyond this Earth, I pray that the child's spirit I aborted and Steve's spirit are together again, and I'm forgiven."

• • •

For years, McQueen had encouraged publicist David Foster to become a producer. Foster was smart and knew the business, plus he had the connections and the right temperament to deal with major stars. Hell, if he could deal with McQueen, he could deal with anyone. Foster's first attempt at finding a project for McQueen was *Butch Cassidy and the Sundance Kid*, but he and a partner were outbid by 20th Century Fox, who paid a then-record $400,000 for the rights. He pursued another western called *McCabe and Mrs. Miller*, which eventually starred Warren Beatty and Julie Christie. Foster says McQueen was offended. "Oh, so you think Warren Beatty's a fucking better actor than me?" McQueen asked.

While McQueen was in France filming *Le Mans*, Foster acquired the rights to Jim Thompson's gritty crime novel *The Getaway* about a husband and wife bank-robbing team out for one last score. Thompson was a brilliant pulp-fiction writer whose literary stature grew in the late '80s and early '90s. In 1970, he was a 60-something, debt-laden alcoholic and living in virtual obscurity. "He was a really lonely guy," said actor/producer Tony Bill, who befriended Thompson in 1969. "I might have been the only friend he had. He was a major alcoholic and didn't drive, so I'd take him around town. Frankly, he didn't seem to want to go home at night. So he'd come over to my house."

Thompson found in Bill a champion of his work and gave him a mimeographed copy of *The Getaway* (it had been out of print for years) to shop around Hollywood. Bill was convinced the hard-boiled crime novel would make for a great film and turned it over to his agent, Mike Medavoy at International Famous. Medavoy knew the project needed a star attached to it, and he found a willing taker via Foster. "I knew Steve had always wanted to play a real Bogart character—a loveable crook—and when I saw *The Getaway*, I said, 'Wow. This is it!' Foster recalled. On August 5, 1970, Foster sent McQueen a photocopy of the novel and a week later was sent back a telegram urging him to "Lock it up."

Thompson's writing suited McQueen well. The role of Doc McCoy stands among McQueen's best for two reasons—it represents the familiar and yet the new. The character is a brooding force who starts the story confined in prison and silently getting angrier and angrier. This was perfect for McQueen, who never coped well with confinement and always needed to be free. Moreover, he could use his perfectly honed skills in portraying the silent tough guy whose actions speak a thousand times louder than words ever could.

However, the role offered something new because it was so multilayered. The scenes where Doc McCoy slaps his wife are challenging, but at the same time the character evokes sympathy because he finds it difficult to interpret and handle his emotions. This afforded McQueen the chance to play from the heart, as he often found it hard to reconcile his emotions with his outward actions in his own life. This conflict would allow both the character and McQueen to seek redemption by the end of the story when he confronts his demons and settles on a new life with his wife, putting the past behind him. At no other time had McQueen been able to play a character that goes though such a believable and truthful journey and one that would ultimately mirror his personal life.

"It's going to be difficult for me," McQueen predicted. "I usually play the Peter Perfect man." If the role was difficult, McQueen sure made it look easy. He tailored much of his character after Humphrey Bogart in *High Sierra*.

It was the first time Foster got an up-close look at McQueen as he prepared for a role, and he was amazed by McQueen's attention to detail. "He had such a strong fix on that character. He would sit in script meetings and say, 'I want my cuffs to be tattered at the bottom, because this guy doesn't have a tailor.' He was a nut for realism, which was really smart of him."

Foster and McQueen were lobbied by agent Jeff Berg to hire his client Peter Bogdanovich to direct *The Getaway*. Bogdanovich's *The Last Picture Show* garnered two Oscars and instantly made him Hollywood's next golden boy. According to Foster, McQueen "flipped" after a private screening and requested a meeting with Bogdanovich. Some time had passed before the men could meet, but during the interim, Bogdanovich had also been approached by Warner Brothers to direct *What's Up, Doc?* starring Barbra Streisand and Ryan O'Neal. Both were tempting offers, neither of which Bogdanovich was willing to relinquish so easily. As a result, Foster and McQueen ultimately lined up a far more appropriate choice for such an action-laden picture: Sam Peckinpah.

Regardless of how many times their egos clashed on *Junior Bonner*, McQueen enjoyed working with the maverick director. The question was, would he commit? "I went to Peckinpah on the idea with my heart in my throat, prepared to hype him 'til kingdom come, if necessary," Foster said. "Right away, he said, 'I know the story cold, for Christ's sake. I'll do it.'" Foster thought Peckinpah was putting him on because the book had been out of print for years. As it later unfolded, Peckinpah had contacted Jim Thompson to discuss a film version of his novel, but it was a bleak period in the director's career when mishaps with *Major Dundee* and *The Cincinnati Kid* had crippled his reputation for a few years. Peckinpah didn't have the juice to get it off the ground, but he knew the story front and back.

Peckinpah had such reverence for Thompson that he asked the author to pen the script in order to be letter-faithful to the original work. Thompson labored on the adaptation for four months and submitted a 95-page first draft to Foster and McQueen. His work included alternate scenes and episodes, plus a grisly ending where Doc and Carol McCoy suffer the claustrophobic interment of a coffin-sized cave in which they have to wait out a manhunt for two days, which leaves Carol close to losing her mind. Later they are hidden by a farmer in crawlspace disguised as a dung heap. Finally they make it into Mexico and spend most of their take from the robbery buying sanctuary at El Rey,[2] a place known as hell on earth. It is there where, as their funds run low and their relationship fragments, they start wondering how best to bump each other off. It was a conclusion that was faithful to the book but one that McQueen knew wouldn't work with movie audiences. Furthermore, McQueen found the script too dark and talky, and it didn't focus enough on the action.

Peckinpah reluctantly fired Thompson and replaced him with rookie screenwriter Walter Hill, who updated the story from the '40s to the modern day and injected some wickedly funny subplots. Seeking to preserve his $25,000 screen credit bonus, Thompson petitioned the Screen Writers Guild on July 11, 1972.

---

2   The concept of El Rey did not offend writer/director Quentin Tarantino, who was an avid Thompson fan. He used the literary Mexican criminal hideaway for himself in 1996's *From Dusk Till Dawn.*

Thompson stated Walter Hill's work was good but that the basis of the story and scenes were his own creation. The Guild ultimately ruled against Thompson, and *The Getaway* no longer belonged to him.[3]

The production slowly rolled along, and the search was on for a starring actress. Peckinpah had made a pitch for Stella Stevens, whom he had guided to a near-perfect performance in *The Ballad of Cable Hogue*. Angie Dickinson, Dyan Cannon, Farrah Fawcett, and Mariette Hartley were also on his short list. Foster came up with a left-field idea—what about Ali MacGraw? He could see the marquee in his head: McQueen and MacGraw. Surprisingly, McQueen felt MacGraw was not right for the part and was pushing for Tuesday Weld or Katherine Ross. But he had to concede that MacGraw's name had real heat.

MacGraw wasn't just a hot actress in 1971; she was a cultural phenomenon, a style icon, and America's newest sweetheart. Her role as Jennifer Cavilleri in *Love Story* saved Paramount Studios from the brink of financial ruin,[4] brought her overnight success, garnered an Academy Award nomination, and gave her instant box-office heat. "The 10 top box-office names of 1971 were nine men and one woman, and that woman was Ali," noted her agent Sue Mengers. "I can't think of another movie star who became as big as she became overnight."

The movie also had paired her with future husband Robert Evans, Paramount's head of production, who married her in July 1969. Six months later, she was pregnant with their son, Joshua. She gave up her tiny apartment in New York's Upper West Side and moved into Evans' luxurious Beverly Hills estate called Woodland, which once belonged to screen legend Greta Garbo. It certainly seemed like McGraw's reality had turned into a fairy tale. She was the metaphorical beautiful swan, but when Steve McQueen came along, she claimed she turned into a sitting duck.

David Foster brought *The Getaway* package to Evans, who saw great potential in the package of McQueen and his wife. In fact, he and McQueen almost did business twice. The first time was in the late '60s when Solar tried to make

---

3   Jim Thompson and his wife, Alberta, did attend an advance screening of *The Getaway* in late 1972 with McQueen, Ali MacGraw, and David Foster present. Thompson liked the final product— the movie made him a lot of money and brought the book back into print. Thompson died in April 1977 nearly broke and largely forgotten, with barely a handful of family and friends at the funeral. Posthumously he has attracted an international cult following, and most of his books have been optioned for movies, most notably *The Grifters, After Dark, My Sweet,* and *This World, Then the Fireworks.*

4   *Love Story* was the most financially successful film of 1971. Made for the bargain-basement price of $2.2 million, the picture grossed $136.4 million worldwide and shattered all previous box-office records for Paramount.

The Cold War Swap. Robert Relyea said Evans had been interested, but only if McQueen starred. McQueen declined. The second attempt was a controversial project called *Atlanta*. Model and actress Beverly Johnson recalled, "Way back in the '70s, Bob wanted me to star in an interracial love story. He wanted Steve McQueen to costar, but Steve didn't want to play opposite me, and no one wanted to make the movie."

Evans felt MacGraw's first two screen roles were similar college preppy types, and he wanted her to expand to adult parts. But the idea of playing a gangster's moll didn't appeal to MacGraw at all, nor did she believe she could pull it off. She had been holding out for the lead role of Daisy Buchanan in a movie adaptation of F. Scott Fitzgerald's *The Great Gatsby*, which Evans was setting up at Paramount. (MacGraw secretly hoped that McQueen would play Jay Gatsby.) It was a large-scale production and a good year away. Evans was smart enough to know that *The Getaway* had all of the elements of a smash and would only build her box-office credibility. MacGraw disliked the script and wanted nothing to do with McQueen or Peckinpah, said David Foster, neither did she want to be separated from Joshua, who was a year old at the time. "She was terrified of both of those guys," Foster said. "They were wild, two-fisted, beer-guzzlers. Sam would give himself shots of B-12 complex in the butt, right in front of you. These were the two guys he was pushing her to work with?"

When McQueen, Peckinpah, and Foster walked into the Evans mansion, MacGraw and McQueen experienced a thunderbolt of electricity. As soon as they locked eyes, the sparks began to fly. McQueen told friend Pat Johnson that as he drank her in, he thought, "She had the nicest ass I've ever seen on a woman." MacGraw said she was equally transfixed. "I remember sitting in the projection room and seeing Steve on the other side of the swimming pool, and you could see those eyes—the most extraordinary blue. I was just electrified. That's scary. It's very visceral. The brain isn't involved at that moment." When McQueen left the house, she dialed her old boss and mentor, fashion photographer Melvin Sokolsky, in panicked desperation.

"Mr. Melvin, I'm in trouble," MacGraw whispered into the receiver. The wheels of a real life love story were already in motion.

MacGraw finally committed to *The Getaway* on January 18, 1972, but under much duress from her husband and agent Sue Mengers, who spent close to a half-hour explaining why she needed to do the film. When Evans picked up on the vibe that Mengers was getting nowhere in convincing her, he ripped the receiver from MacGraw's hand and told Mengers, "Sue, she's doing *The Getaway*. That's it. Let's hear the deal, and it better be good."

The deal was very good. MacGraw's signature carried a $300,000 fee,[5] but it came at a steep price for Evans. He wrote in his autobiography, *The Kid Stays in the Picture*, that as soon as MacGraw signed the contract, Freddie Fields pulled a fast one. "With premeditated complicity, [Fields] loopholed Paramount's control of the now-hot McQueen/MacGraw *Getaway*, sliding it into his own First Artists Company, which he personally controlled. Nice guy, huh?"

Evans' bosses, Charles Bludhorn and Frank Yablans, were furious at him, and the *LA Times'* Joyce Haber rubbed salt in the wound when she wrote in her column, "Paramount had the property, and let it get away. Paramount's top brass is annoyed. Every top executive of every major studio is chuckling over the story."

With cameras set to roll, MacGraw was still reluctant and did her best to try and talk Evans into not going to Texas. Her underlying reason had yet to come out. "The real reason I had hesitated was that I knew I was going to get in some serious trouble with Steve. There would be no avoiding it. He was recently separated and free, and I was scared of my overwhelming attraction to him," she said.

When everyone arrived in Texas in early February 1972, they were in for a grueling six-city, 62-day schedule, working six days per week. For some, like Steve McQueen and Ali MacGraw, it was more than just a film; it was a seminal event in both of their lives.

Shooting began on February 7, 1972, at the Texas State Penitentiary in Huntsville, Texas, where the company spent a memorable three days. Peckinpah decided to use no extras and wanted real prisoners for several scenes. Fifty-two convicts signed releases, with only one holdout because he was still wanted in another state.

McQueen worked details with the white-clad convicts—in the textile mill, the shop (making license plates), and in the fields, where he hoed the ground in a long straight line, guarded by armed guards on horseback and a pack of snarling dogs. When Peckinpah yelled "cut," McQueen stepped out of line to walk toward his dressing room. He had been forewarned before the scene that the dogs were trained to attack anything in a white uniform that had strayed from the line, but he forgot when the action was over. Recalled Katy Haber, "[The dogs] followed Steve like a flash of lightning, teeth bared. Only the quick action of the guards prevented our star from turning into dog meat."

Another scene shot at the prison where his character is taking a shower with a group of prisoners also dismayed McQueen. Real prisoners were used, but

---

5   McQueen would receive no upfront salary for *The Getaway* but collected 22.5 percent of the film's
    net profit plus a 10 percent share of First Artists' gross.

McQueen later discovered it was the homosexual unit. "He became unglued," laughed prop master Bobby Visciglia. "It bruised his ego to think that he couldn't handle himself with the real hard-core convicts, but they would have loved to get their hands on Steve McQueen and possibly use him as a hostage. Sam wasn't going to let that happen."

A convict who had murdered two people told McQueen he once had a problem but solved it. McQueen asked what was the problem.

"The two people I killed," came the reply.

Ali MacGraw arrived the day after the prison sequence and describes an *Alice in Wonderland* scenario in her stirring memoir, *Moving Pictures*. "When I arrived in Texas for that first day of location work, I was met by Steve and Sam Peckinpah and driven back to the rented condominiums where the crew would stay. What a drive! Steve was showing off, and the first thing this ex–Formula One car driver did was to spin the rented car in a dizzying loop across the four lanes of the freeway. It was a prophetic start to our relationship."

As feared by MacGraw, their relationship instantly became physical, and MacGraw said she became obsessed with McQueen. "I was so attracted to my invention of Steve McQueen that I thought I could go off with him and be real again. I didn't think about my family life back in Beverly Hills. Selfishly, I just went on my way, rationalizing that I was saving my own life. It was as though I was operating outside of my own sanity and consciousness. I didn't feel complete unless I had a partner. Being in love was like a drug high."

Katy Haber felt the odd pairing was a classic case of opposites attract. "Steve was the ultimate male. He was a stunning-looking guy. He was Superman, and women fell prey to the movie-star allure," Haber said. "Ali, on the other hand, has a mind that needs to be constantly working. Steve preferred the company of simple folk rather than intellectuals, but Ali excited him."

Psychologist Peter O. Whitmer said more was at play than meets the eye— the two were the product of adult alcoholics, and in a room of 100 people, Steve and Ali would have inevitably discovered one another. "In social settings, there is a dance performed by many individuals who share a psychological history of trauma, especially of alcoholism among their parents," Whitmer said. "While it differs between individuals, there are common denominators that allow each to recognize the other—across a crowded room.

"This shock of recognition is as subtle in its beginning steps as it is destructive in its culmination. Somehow, there is contact made—a look, a glance, perhaps something fortuitous. From then on, it is all in the style and content of speech and body language and the dynamic of commonality that rises quickly to the surface.

"For example, the woman may have a strong need to 'mother'—this is her constant, often repeated yet never successful attempt to re-create a scene similar to those of her own troubled childhood where tension and discomfort and abuse wracked her development and formed her view of how to deal with others. This, she thinks, is the chance to get it right for once and for all.

"Many women report seeing this opportunity in a male counterpart who displays a sense of vulnerability that borders on being explosive or out of control, like an alcoholic, abusive father. Or perhaps there is a sign or signal she picks up that indicates that there is something immature or in need of nurturing. Focusing on that creates the opportunity to play out the 'mothering' role, to restructure the relationship so that all pathology—and all memories of it—disappear, and perfection reigns.

"The male counterpart, sharing a similar background, wants very much to be perfect yet doesn't really know what perfect is; adult children of alcoholic parents are driven by needs for approval and affirmation yet ironically they do not know themselves what 'good' and 'right' are. However, were another person—especially an attractive person of the opposite sex—to tell them their perception in him of mastery, strength, and perfection—well, here is an argument that is hard to deny. After all, isn't this what you have been searching for all your life?

"Further, as he is strong and mature, and has been affirmed, he can then nurture her! And 'nurturing' can easily grow into 'control.' To set up this dynamic is to dance like Fred [Astaire] and Ginger [Rogers]. But it takes only a few steps and each will know whether or not it will work."

Producer David Foster said it took him a few weeks to find out the two lovebirds were nesting right under his nose. "I'm not a naive guy. They could have gone to bed that first night for all I know. I wasn't aware of it until three weeks after we began shooting. I would see them snuggling. They got to be hot and heavy." After it finally sank in, it dawned on Foster that their breezy affair could cause a shitstorm. "I was thinking, 'How is this going to impact my picture? Is Bob Evans going to come down here with a shotgun? Is it going to become a scandal and the picture won't be taken seriously? Are the press going to descend here like they did with Richard Burton and Elizabeth Taylor on *Cleopatra*? If you have half a brain, this goes through your mind as a producer."

Foster had talks with both McQueen and MacGraw but gave it to McQueen with both guns blazing. "You're crazy! You'd better screw your head back on right!" McQueen tried to soothe Foster by telling him, "Everything's cool."

MacGraw told Foster that she was tired of the fairytale existence in the Evans household—the mansion, the 13 phones, the butler, the cook, the driver—and that she was bored. "If I wanted to make some scrambled eggs for myself," MacGraw said, "Bob would say, 'No, no, no. The cook does that.' If I wanted something out of the refrigerator, I couldn't. There was always somebody there. It wasn't real. It drove me crazy."

Life with McQueen was exciting, and every day brought new adventure. Costar Ben Johnson recalled the two nearly drowned when McQueen purposely drove a rental car into a spring. "Steve was a bit of a wild character," Johnson said. "He rented a station wagon, and he and Ali were in the parking lot driving around. All of a sudden he drives right off this parking lot and into this big hole of water, this big spring. It submerged all but the back end. Here we are, starting the movie, and he's pulling this stunt. I ran down there to help them, and they're both sticking their faces out the back window to breathe. I got down there and helped them out. I'll never know why he did that. Maybe he was drinking or something."

McQueen pulled other stunts as well. One night when the two attended a small party, McQueen ended up, according to MacGraw, "getting loaded." He flagrantly flirted with two young ladies in front of MacGraw, who stormed out of the party. It got worse. "Later that night Steve returned, and I could hear him in his apartment next door with the two girls. It was excruciating," MacGraw recalled. "The next morning he sauntered out onto his front door step and casually asked if I wanted to come and make him breakfast. And the amazing thing is, I went in and cooked it."

Psychologist Peter O. Whitmer said there was good reason why she mysteriously obeyed McQueen. "The normal dance of courtship was quickly and thoroughly turned on its head when Steve McQueen committed this hurtful act," Whitmer said. "The ending is a perfect capstone for a destructive relationship, where his outrageous demands were met with the slavelike response of a classic enabler, someone who blinds themselves to their need to live their own life and instead supports and condones and perpetuates the other's pathology. Ali cooking his breakfast proved this."

Steve also attempted to lure Neile back into bed when she called him on March 14, 1972, the day their divorce became final. The two were stunned that they were no longer married and Steve, without giving it much thought, invited Neile to El Paso.

"My God, do you realize what you're saying?" Neile asked.

"No, I'm not sure, but I'll sort it out later," McQueen said. "Anyway, come on down."

Neile decided to stay put in California. He was wreaking enough havoc in the Lone Star state, and reports of the affair with MacGraw had filtered back to Hollywood, which became fodder for gossip and movie magazines. Surprisingly, Robert Evans paid no mind. He was too consumed with his work to take notice and was shackled to *The Godfather*. The epic picture was a hellish shoot and had an even more complicated postproduction. His career was on the line if the movie flopped. Failure was not an option, and he had a bed moved into the studio so he could watch the dailies. On March 14 at a gala dinner at Manhattan's St. Regis Roof to celebrate the premiere of *The Godfather*, MacGraw was photographed slow dancing with her husband, gazing into his eyes, sharing in his triumph. "My ego was so enormous that I never picked up the slightest vibe that her head and heart were thousands of miles away. Worse, I was the last to find out," Evans said. "That memorable evening, to me and the thousands surrounding us, no two people looked more in love."

Even that picture, splashed across newspapers around the country, wasn't enough to quell the rumors of her affair with McQueen. Norma Mayo, who was the sales manager at the El Paso Holiday Inn Downtown, said she fended off daily calls from gossip columnists and reporters. "I told them that I hadn't had the vaguest idea. Everyone on the set knew they were having a fling."

Mayo said McQueen was a bundle of contradictions. He was a two-fisted drinker who got up at the crack of dawn to start work; a caring and loving father who had a good rapport with his children; a kind but temperamental man who changed his hotel room no fewer than eight times. "Finally, I had to put my foot down and say, 'Now, Steve, make up your mind.'"

While in El Paso, friend Katy Haber secured front-row tickets for an Elton John concert at University Football Stadium on April 20, 1972. Haber said McQueen and MacGraw escorted Chad and Terry to the concert, which turned out to be a short night. "Elton opened the show with either 'Tiny Dancer' or 'Levon' from the *Madman Across the Water* album, at which point, everyone sitting at the back of the field rushed forward to be close to the stage," Haber recalled. "Steve, thinking that the audience was surging to be near him, grabbed Ali and the kids and left the arena, missing the concert completely. I wasn't about to leave."[6]

The time to leave Texas was rapidly approaching, and Robert Evans was coming to El Paso to escort his wife back to California. He had kept his commitment

---

6 The Elton John Band did manage to squeeze in a visit to the set of *The Getaway*, where a suntanned and shirtless McQueen introduced Terry and Chad to "Captain Fantastic" and shared a beer with the musicians. Drummer Nigel Olsson said of McQueen years later, "What a cool guy!"

to Peckinpah to stay away and not disrupt the set, but that only served to allow the relationship between McQueen and MacGraw to flourish. They sheepishly approached Foster with an outrageous proposition. "I was sitting in Steve's hotel suite in El Paso, and he and Ali are both saying, 'Our lives are such a mess now.' She's married to Evans but loves McQueen, and she's not feeling very good about anything. So Ali, Steve, and I are sitting in his suite, and suddenly he says aloud, 'Okay, here's the game plan.' He takes over, right? He points to me and says, 'Foster, Ali and I are going to drive back to L.A. It's going to take me about three days to get there, and we can unwind and take it easy.' He then asks me, 'You're going to fly back tonight, right?' I say, 'Right.' He says, 'When you get back, I want you to have a meeting with Bob Evans and tell him that Ali is going to marry me.' I'm sitting there listening to this, and I say, 'Are you crazy?' How can a person think like that? Can you imagine?"

Foster told McQueen outright, "I've got news for you. I'm not going to do your dirty work for you. No way!" McQueen suddenly realized how idiotic he sounded, and the three burst into a long laughing jag. Soon enough, the situation grew serious again.

Evans was in Rome for the Italian dubbing of *The Godfather* when it finally hit him his wife was being unfaithful.

"You're with McQueen, aren't you?" Evans asked.

"Yes."

"I'm leaving for El Paso."

"Forget it! You missed the plane months ago."

Evans showed up in El Paso but was rebuffed. MacGraw begged him to let her finish the picture in peace, which was going to wrap in early May. Evans was concerned that his wife was on the verge of a nervous breakdown and made arrangements for a two-week stay at a spa in Murrieta Hot Springs near Riverside, California. Evans was hoping the pampering and solitude would help MacGraw sort herself out.

Peckinpah assigned Bobby Viscigila to escort MacGraw back to Los Angeles, where a limousine would pick her up and shuttle her to Murrieta for two weeks to collect her thoughts. Peckinpah had only one demand: "Steve McQueen is not to be on that plane. You got it?"

Twenty minutes into the flight, Visciglia and MacGraw were sipping wine in first class when he felt a tap on his shoulder. A stranger donning a hat and sunglasses told him his services were no longer needed. It was McQueen. "He found out what flight Ali was on and bought a coach ticket in disguise so that he could sit with Ali." Evans figured that might be the case and had an associate staked out at the airport, who spotted McQueen with no difficulty. Evans instructed him to ram the limo if they both got in it at the same time. Luckily, it didn't come to that. McQueen got into a car and headed into the city while MacGraw made a beeline to Murrietta Hot Springs.

The drama on the set and in their personal lives was rivaling the drama on screen in *The Getaway*. This publicity was putting the film, and above all McQueen's face, back on the front cover of every magazine again. He now had a choice to make—was this a fling or something more? Would he pursue MacGraw out of love, or would he make a getaway of his own? The McQueen Machine was rolling again.

29
PUNCH IT, BABY!

STEVE MCQUEEN WAS UNDOUBTEDLY A HIT with the opposite sex. He once proudly proclaimed, "Man, I had chicks coming out of the woodwork." This brazen ego was fueled by his need to succeed and conquer everything. His love affair with Ali MacGraw turned his life into chaos. He was used to being chased, but now it was he who was having to fight for her. MacGraw represented forbidden fruit, which is oftentimes the sweetest. She in turn was caught between two men—the Hollywood mogul Robert Evans and the superstar McQueen. This tug of war would leave everyone with rope burns.

Prescribed lots of rest at Murrietta Springs, MacGraw received little of it between the attention she was getting from the press, Evans, and McQueen. Joyce Haber of the *Los Angeles Times* documented MacGraw's stay at the spa in a May 17 column and was told by Evans' butler, "She's very thin." Haber cynically observed, "I have a great sympathy with exhaustion but not with skinniness."

In actuality, MacGraw was emotionally depleted, according to her memoir, *Moving Pictures*. "I went, guilty about one relationship, infatuated in another, and utterly exhausted from the drama. I saw the time alone as a possible stay of execution. But alas, it was not that simple," MacGraw wrote. "I knew that I had stepped over the edge with my now-too-public affair and that I had never bothered to examine the destruction I was causing in my own family. Besides the hurt and embarrassment I was causing Bob, there was the all-important issue of my son. My strongest memory of that time at the spa is of a numbness, a desire to have some decision made for me that would involve no one getting hurt. It was a very passive attitude, a wish impossible to accomplish."

McQueen could never be accused of being passive, especially when it came to matters of the heart. He sweet-talked an attendant into bringing the phone to MacGraw while she was receiving a massage. McQueen told MacGraw that he missed her so much that he wanted to drive by the spa to say hello. A guard posted at the front gate with an allegiance to Evans spotted McQueen's dark gray Porsche 911. He quickly phoned the spa's telephone operator, who relayed the message to Evans that McQueen was lurking.

MacGraw was in extreme conflict and ultimately decided that going back to her family was the right thing to do. "Come and get me, Evans," she said. "I'm ready to come home." Once safely ensconced back in Woodland, Evans planned a cure-all trip to Antibes, France, to try and rekindle the flame. They stayed at the Hotel du Cap, an elegant old-world luxury hotel on the water where they had spent many romantic getaways in the past. He also took her to Venice, Italy, MacGraw's favorite city in the world. The trip didn't do much for MacGraw, who made stealthy phone calls to McQueen back in the States, followed by passionate love letters and poems.

On Memorial Day weekend, the Evanses and Sue Mengers and her husband, Jean-Claude, vacationed in Palm Springs. The studio mogul must not have done his homework, for he should have known McQueen owned a home in the village. Feeling vulnerable and heartbroken, McQueen invited friend Katy Haber for the weekend. She recalled, "Both Steve and Ali were in Palm Springs, and yet Steve couldn't get a hold of her. They were so close yet so far. Steve was such a solitary figure. He had very few friends he could talk to. He never knew what it was like to be so passionate; he was so overcome with Ali. He said he was never in so much pain and that his neck was swollen like a deer."[1] It was the first time McQueen ever vowed celibacy or talked of spending the rest of his life with someone else. McQueen had Haber, who pretended to be in the neighborhood when she dropped by to see MacGraw, relay a message. When Evans was out of earshot, Haber whispered, "Steve wants you to call him." That weekend, McQueen swapped cars with Haber. She now held the keys to his Porsche 911 while he chugged along in her rented blue Pinto, which shielded him from being detected when he went into town for trysts with MacGraw. Evans suspected something was going on but was afraid to ask—he might be given an answer he wasn't prepared to hear.

MacGraw emotionally bounced back and forth between her loyalty to Evans and her undeniable attraction to McQueen. Evans made one last-ditch attempt to salvage their marriage by taking MacGraw and Joshua on a family trip to New York on June 27, 1972. That same day, approximately 4,400 miles away, Steve McQueen was in Anchorage, Alaska, flashing a peace sign while getting his mug shot taken by local police.

---

1   It is said that the neck of a male deer gets swollen when he is aroused.

Filmmaker Bruce Brown noticed McQueen had not been himself as of late and thought he'd extend an invitation to McQueen for a guys-only trip to Alaska. "He was feeling a little down and needed a change of scenery," Brown said. "I was friends with Ron Hayes, a hunting and fishing guide in Anchorage, and asked Steve if he wanted to join me and a few others on a rafting trip. His mood lightened considerably, and he said yes."

They rented a cabin for about a week and were having a ball. On the last day of their trip, McQueen and his group of friends shared a couple of bottles of wine over dinner at The Crow's Nest, a restaurant inside the Westward Hotel. Hayes owned an Oldsmobile Toronado, which was one of the first cars with front-wheel drive. It also sported a new pair of Firestone tires and a slogan as famous as its passenger: "You can't break loose from their grip."

Hayes raced around downtown Anchorage, where they blew through stop-lights, squealed around corners, and were about as conspicuous as bugs splattered on a windshield. McQueen was anxious to show off what he could do. The macho superstar looked at Hayes and said, "You want to see these tires get broke loose? Move over." Hayes complied, and McQueen buckled himself into the driver's seat. Bruce Brown, who was in the backseat, recalled the joyride. "He was driving fast, then slow, and a little crazy at times. Of course, we all had a little too much to drink. Next thing we knew, an Alaskan State Trooper was on our tail and flashing the blue lights. One of my friends was egging Steve on. 'Steve, you're a race car driver. You can ditch them.' Whatever he had in mind, I had a hint it might not be looked upon favorably by law enforcement."

Adopting a huge grin, McQueen floored the gas pedal and blew through a series of red lights, stop signs, and intersections before heading in the wrong direction down a back alley. He spun the car around and parked it perfectly at the entrance of the Westward Hotel. Eventually, the police came and arrested them. McQueen, said one bystander, was in rare form when he was finally apprehended.

"Hi, I'm Steve McQueen, and I'm having fun in your little two-bit town."

"Hi, I'm a policeman, and you're under arrest," came the reply.

Bruce Brown said McQueen thought Anchorage police would recognize his face and cut him a break. "He didn't know the Anchorage police. They grabbed him, tossed him on the hood of the car, and handcuffed him in one fell swoop," Brown said. "Steve was funny and asked them, 'Hey man, haven't you ever seen *The Blob*?' They didn't react. Then he said, 'What about *Never Love a Stranger*'? Then he started listing all his B-movies. '*Hell is for Heroes*? *The War Lover*'? The cops finally caught the joke, but they hauled us off to jail anyway."

Still in good humor, McQueen smiled at the police photographer, flashed a two-fingered peace sign, then pleaded innocent to charges of reckless driving. With the help of defense attorney Burton Biss, he posted a $250 bail. Throughout the years, McQueen has incorrectly been attributed to driving while under the influence of alcohol, which was most likely true. However, reckless driving was the official charge against him.

The Anchorage Daily News carried a front-page photograph of McQueen and Hayes (misidentified as actor James Arness) walking through the tarmac at the airport the following morning. The caption read, "The Great Escape?"

Biss decided that McQueen couldn't have a fair trial in Anchorage due to the media attention and asked the judge for a change of venue. It was granted, and the case was moved to Fairbanks, with attorney and later Alaskan governor Ron Cooper defending McQueen and Hayes against a charge of reckless driving.

Cooper was all set to defend McQueen as a licensed and certified race car and stunt driver, and he planned on showing clips of *Bullitt* and *Le Mans* to the court and jury to prove that McQueen could handle himself behind the wheel of a car. However, before the case reached Fairbanks, McQueen forfeited bail and the case was dismissed. Alaskan police weren't about to try and extradite a heavy-duty movie star on a traffic violation.

McQueen's 1972 arrest and iconic mug shot are part of Alaskan folklore that is often rehashed among the natives. The public saw what it wanted to see—the big star being arrogant and thinking he was above the law. What they didn't see was that this stunt was just one cathartic attempt by McQueen to try to conceal his pain for not seeing MacGraw. Despite the superstar facade, he was hurting on the inside.

Alcohol consumption also crept into MacGraw's life. She was drunk when a family friend, who also happened to be a lawyer, told the actress over a few cocktails that her conduct as of late was reprehensible. Something inside MacGraw snapped; she excused herself to another room where she called McQueen. It was the last straw. She was finally leaving Evans for good.

On August 3, 1972, MacGraw made good on her promise when she walked into the Santa Monica Superior Court and filed for divorce from Robert Evans, her husband of close to three years. Among the entries she made in her journals during her courtship with Evans, she ominously wrote, "To marry a second time represents the triumph of hope over experience." The McQueen experience would be even more turbulent.

With Evans on the ropes, McQueen decided to go for broke and called the producer to inform him he was going to change Joshua's last name to McQueen.

Evans recalls the not-so-nice exchange in his 1994 memoir, *The Kid Stays in the Picture*. "Your surroundings, the way you live, is not the environment that's right for Joshua. We're a family unit. For Joshua's sake, I intend to change his last name to McQueen … have full control … see that he's brought up properly," McQueen said.

"Are you finished?" Evans replied.

"Not quite. Bill Thompson is preparing custody papers."

"Good. Take your best shot, motherfucker. One of us, pal—only one of us—is going to come out in one piece."

There was nothing Evans could do about McQueen taking his wife, but attempting to take his kid's name turned this gentleman's quarrel into an alley fight. In an industry where powerful men cannot afford to look foolish or weak, Evans was desperate. He placed a call to his godfather, Sidney Korshak, a reputed mafia attorney and one of Hollywood's most feared and fabled "fixers." Korshak's vast network of connections included labor leaders, politicians, and Hollywood and Vegas moguls, and he brilliantly used them to his advantage. Korshak enlisted Arthur Crowley, one of Hollywood's top criminal defense attorneys, a man who was not afraid to use leverage to his advantage.

Crowley made national headlines and sent reverberations through Hollywood when he defended gossip magazine *Confidential* in a highly publicized trial in August 1957. Crowley's connection to *Confidential* and a then-corrupt Los Angeles Police Department gave him unprecedented access to many celebrities, and when Evans needed leverage against McQueen in two weeks' time, Crowley was able to deliver a 12-inch-thick dossier on the actor's past. It set Evans back about $150,000, but it contained professional kryptonite.

Evans' butler escorted McQueen and his custody attorney, Bill Thompson, into Evans' home, and Crowley quickly whispered, "You're holding four aces, kid. Sit back, relax, and watch the show."

Crowley's casualness put the two men on guard, and when Evans asked them if they'd like a drink, both shook their heads dismissively. They wanted this showdown over as quickly as possible. Crowley asked Thompson if he could have a word outside, where he would show him the explosive dossier. That left Evans and McQueen alone for the first time since their initial meeting for *The Getaway*. Evans, knowing he held a major trump card, was most hospitable to his guest and offered McQueen a beer. Evans said McQueen did a triple take.

Moments later, Thompson and Crowley walked in, and Evans noticed McQueen's attorney was as white as a sheet. He asked his client to step outside.

McQueen was told by Thompson that what Evans had would be career-ending information on him, and the proceedings were stopped cold.

As for the secret dossier he had on McQueen, Evans has remained mum on the subject for almost four decades. Adept at keeping secrets, Evans once said cryptically, "Silence is the only way to guarantee your next breath."

• • •

Maybe it was paranoia, maybe it was to keep in shape, or maybe it was another way to connect to his son, but in the summer of 1972, Steve and Chad McQueen walked into Chuck Norris' Sherman Oaks karate studio after Chad had gotten into a fight at school. The two had been taking lessons from Bruce Lee, who left the United States for Hong Kong to embark on a film career. Lee told McQueen, "If you ever want to take karate lessons, Norris is the best." Just a year before, Norris had caught *On Any Sunday* and marveled at McQueen on the big screen, racing competitively and not caring if he smashed his million-dollar mug. He remembered thinking, "If there's any actor in the world I'd like to meet, it would be him." Their destinies seemed almost fated, but the true reward for both McQueens was their enduring and intense friendship with Norris' best instructor, Pat E. Johnson, who became McQueen's instructor by proxy when Norris' film career started taking off.

"In order to retain [McQueen's] respect, you had to distance yourself from him socially," Johnson observed. "I never tried to ask questions of him because I never wanted him to think I was prying. I kind of had a feeling where he was coming from. I came from the same place."

Their upbringings were remarkably similar. They were both deserted by their fathers as small children, grew up in poverty, and learned at a young age to live by their own devices. "When one grows up in the streets, one learns to put on a false front and a lot of protective walls," Johnson said. "We both felt that everyone was potentially a con man, and you had to ensure you were never 'had.' You never fully trusted anybody, and you never showed any weakness. If you show weakness in the streets, you're dead. The less a person knew about you, the safer you were.

"On the streets is where you perfected your con. If you wanted something from somebody, you acted a certain way. You learned how to adjust, how to adapt, and playing different roles was how you survived. This I can tell you: Steve McQueen was an actor long before he ever came to Hollywood.

"Since Steve and I came from the same place, we understood each other, and there was no need for any false fronts. He could be honest with me and tell me his true feelings without me seeing it as a weakness. He often came to me for advice—certainly not in his career, he was the master of that—but for personal things. I could do the same with him. And as I trusted his advice, he trusted mine."

The two men sparred, kicked, and punched each other for three months, with McQueen being pushed to his physical abilities. With a week to go until Norris came back, Johnson let him know he was going to relinquish his training duties back to his boss.

"I'd rather keep training with you," McQueen said, to Johnson's astonishment. Their relationship would blossom into a friendship that would remain throughout McQueen's lifetime. Other than Ali MacGraw and his last wife, Barbara Minty, no one saw Steve more in his last decade of life than Johnson. He became a mentor, father figure, confidante, and a trusted and loyal friend—a role he continues to this day with Steve's son, Chad, and his three children.

• • •

McQueen and MacGraw chose not to live with each other until the custody issue was settled, but they did the next best thing—they rented separate homes in Coldwater Canyon within walking distance of each other; only a large field separated their living quarters. Their relationship was tempestuous, according to MacGraw. "Many were the nights that we would have some terrible row over nothing, and one of us would go out of the house to go home," MacGraw wrote in her memoir. "A half hour later, we would find each other, inching across the field, each of us checking up on the other. It wouldn't be long before we would be laughing at the melodrama of it all."

They were a glamorous couple filled with passion. There were fights but also reconciliations. MacGraw said at the time, "He's impossible... absolutely flat-out, 100 percent impossible... and terrific! We are both born Aries, so should I say we clash a lot of times, consistently about a couple of things. But we also understand each other. After the fact, of course. Being an Aries, I'm a fairly opinionated lady, which is not generally the kind Steve likes or is too thrilled to be around. He has very strong male attitudes. And I don't buy them all. If Steve and I ever lock horns, it's because I've said no when he wants me to automatically say yes. I find it funny. He doesn't like the women in his family to have balls."

When their lives reached some sense of normalcy, McQueen found himself testing the usefulness of First Artists regarding postproduction work on *The Getaway*. His contract with the production company gave him the final cut of the film, an almost unheard-of demand in its day. It was also the cause of numerous clashes with Sam Peckinpah. McQueen inserted numerous close-up shots of himself, cleaned up the sound effects, and later replaced Jerry Fielding's finished score with one by Quincy Jones.[2] Up until now, McQueen's desire to exert authority over the films he worked on was mainly driven by his desire to prove himself, to show he was powerful and by extension was therefore a success. This time, however, it was a different matter. McQueen had clawed his way to stardom in the '50s and '60s and needed *The Getaway* to be a success, because his star was at risk after *The Reivers*, *Le Mans*, and *Junior Bonner* failed to live up to the studio's expectations. He urgently needed to reassert himself at the top. He was no longer simply fighting for ego—he was fighting for his status and title.

Peckinpah praised McQueen for some of his suggestions and implored him not to go through with others in an October 13, 1972, letter to McQueen:

> *Dear Steve:*
>
> *Have gone over your suggested changes both in editing and dubbing and found three excellent ideas, such as added kiss at the end of the kitchen scene; drop the line "Christ, Carol—I saw him"; and include Carol's line in the car, "In God I Trust," and lengthening the walk out of the dump; and also dropping the license plate factory. I strongly suggest you not re-cut the swimming sequence and even more strongly suggest you leave the scene in Ali's apartment bedroom as is. Also, I like (it was one of my notes) that the credit roll-up be started later.*
>
> *I disagree completely—I like the idea of seeing the brief cut out of the doctor hanging. The entire point of the shot is lost if we don't see Rudy on the pot. Carol throwing her clothes out of the shower to Doc—I have cut out because I found it to be "cutesy." I suggest your taking a long look before you make your decision. Your suggestion of cutting the high-walled room I found doubtful at best.*
>
> *I would like to make clear to you and all concerned that replacing Fielding is an extraordinarily bad judgment. I think he did an excellent job with the time and monies provided and could have provided any other sweetenings necessary.*
>
> *As far as re-dub notes, I think you will find that the lines picked will, in general, play better than the original track. The rest of the dubbing notes, most of which I already had listed, I agree with. But I do hope you will take a long look and listen carefully before you fuck up the swimming scene and the scene in Carol's apartment.*
>
> *Sincerely,*
>
> *Sam Peckinpah*

McQueen was not about to a risk another box-office failure and he called Peckinpah the following morning and told him, "The music was shit," and "The

---

2   McQueen told Peckinpah he felt the Fielding score was "a little light for the show." In 2006, *Music for The Getaway: Jerry Fielding's Original Score* was issued as a limited-edition audio CD.

"But, Sam, it's not five o'clock."

Peckinpah drew a deep breath and thought for a moment. He looked at his watch and asked Gonzalez, "What time is it in New York?"

"Five-thirty."

"Then bring me a goddamned drink!"

The Getaway was proof that the public didn't always read reviews, and moviegoers flocked to the theaters when it opened for the Christmas season of 1972. *The New Yorker*'s Pauline Kael wrote, "The picture's bewildering con is that it makes the pair such lovely, decent gangsters that they can stroll off into the sunset with their satchel stuffed with money as if they'd just met over a malt at the corner drugstore. As for McQueen and MacGraw, they strike no sparks on the screen. (They don't even look right together; her head is bigger than his.) His low-key professionalism is turning into minimal acting, and it's indistinguishable from the blahs, while she is certainly the primmest, smuggest gangster's moll of all time. Last time I saw Candice Bergen, I thought she was a worse actress than MacGraw; now I think I slandered Bergen."

Kathleen Carroll of the *New York Daily News* felt *The Getaway* was, "Too vulgar and violent. At one point in their travels, McQueen and MacGraw wind up in a garbage dump, the very place for this film."

Jay Cocks of *Time* wrote, "If *The Getaway* had just rolled off the studio assembly line, the work of a competent craftsman, it could have easily been passed over and forgotten. It is, however, the work of a major American film artist. Peckinpah is pushing his privileges too far."

The Chicago Tribune's Rex Reed was the only major critic to defend the picture. "Because of the well-publicized MacGraw-McQueen romance on screen and off, *The Getaway* was destined to take its lumps, but the harshness of the criticism it has received seems grossly unfair to me," Reed wrote. "Its detractors object to two things: [1] The crooks get away and live happily ever after, and [2] Ali MacGraw can't act...Movies make strange heroes. Some people fancy godfathers, but I'll stick with Steve and Ali any day. They are never boring."

McQueen needn't have worried—Peckinpah was still in top form where it concerned his art. *The Getaway* is a stylish genre thriller and a solidly crafted piece of entertainment. It mixes various genres to superb effect. It had a top cast with everyone playing their roles to perfection. Action and tension is offset by moments of comedy and lightheartedness that only heighten the drama through their juxtaposition. The film also manages to provide a gripping study of love and betrayal. In terms of acting, Al Letteri as Rudy captures the right mix of off-balance humor with deep menace, and MacGraw as Doc's wife, Carol, is compelling as the woman in love willing to do what it takes for her man. McQueen pulls in another classic performance, from the opening scenes with hardly any dialogue while he festers in prison, confined like a caged animal, to the later explosive action scenes. He even valiantly plays a hurt husband, conflicted by his desire for his wife against his feelings of discomfort with intimacy after having been locked away for so long. The action set pieces are superb, with trademark Peckinpah slow-motion shots and lots of guns.

McQueen and MacGraw's hot romance created a stampede at the box office and a windfall of free publicity. First Artists lined up close to $7 million in guarantees from exhibitors around the world, who booked the film sight unseen. All they needed to see was the movie's film poster, which features their passport pictures, a gun, and .45 bullets. The stencil-font poster keeps the message short and sweet: "McQueen/MacGraw... *The Getaway*."

The Getaway recorded a then-whopping $36 million in worldwide receipts, [3]making it the seventh-largest grossing film of 1972. Although, in a stroke of poetic justice for Robert Evans, Paramount's *The Godfather*, the film that he had risked his health to get to the silver screen and ultimately led to the loss of his wife to McQueen, took top honors that year in terms of accolades, awards, and box-office grosses. The epic gangster film yielded $144 million worldwide, quadrupling *The Getaway* in earnings.[4] McQueen's take, 22.5 percent of the net profit and 10 percent of the gross, earned him a tidy sum, somewhere between $3.5 and $6 million, depending on the break-even point of the picture.

The Getaway had paid off literally for McQueen. It put him back at the top, gave him a certifiable smash, and made him plenty of money. All of his financial difficulties went away, and he treated himself to a Malibu beach house in a private community with a secluded beach, somewhere where he could have his own personal space and enjoy his life with MacGraw. McQueen was well and truly back in the hot seat of Hollywood and had taken back his crown. He had the power again and was prepared to go full throttle.

"Punch it, baby!"

---

3   Equivalent to $242 million in 2010 dollars.

4   If the truth be told, the X-rated *Deep Throat* was 1972's box-office champ, raking in an unheard of $600 million at the time of its release.

30
RUMBLE IN THE JUNGLE

FOR YEARS, STEVE MCQUEEN HAD HINTED that he was growing tired of the movie industry and had subtly threatened to pack it all in. After *The Getaway*, he told a reporter, "I sometimes hate to go back to work. I want my life as simple as possible. I'm at an age where I'm not as ambitious as I used to be. I've been surrounded by a whirl of activity for a long time. I just want to be happy. I don't really care that much. If I feel a film will have something to say, I'll do it. But now, it seems so fruitless to keep banging away." Despite his misgivings, by February 1973, McQueen was back on the acting merry-go-round when he reported to work in Spain and Jamaica for *Papillon*. It was the most ambitious role he had ever tackled.

The timing of the production placed a strain on his relationship with Ali MacGraw, who had divided loyalties between her son and McQueen. Robert Evans let it be known she was not to take their son, Joshua, out of the country, but her instincts told her not to leave McQueen alone for a few weeks at a time. When McQueen made proclamations such as, "If you're going to work 12 hours a day in the jungle, there'd better be a *Playboy* Club next door," it gave her ample reason to worry, and tensions simmered. MacGraw had the arduous task of making a new home, tending to a toddler, and shuttling back and forth to Spain and Jamaica to please her man. It was wearing her out. She told a reporter she was worn to the bone. "Everything inside of me is run down, my blood, my hormones, my emotions."

"I was no good to anyone, and Steve did not help," she later wrote in her memoir. "I felt guilty and sad when I left Joshua, and when I got to Jamaica it was always several days before Steve would warm up and trust me. It was his way of keeping intact the brittle survival shell that kept him from ever again being hurt by a woman. And the shell would be on again a few days before I left, to ensure he was prepared to survive the next two weeks without me." Psychologist Peter O. Whitmer said this was a "coping mechanism worked out over the years to allow the historically painful ebb and flow of the emotions of separation and reunion to pass with less pain. He created his own rules for beginning and leaving an intimate relationship.

"Indeed, McQueen had played this out full circle on the screen. At the end of *The Thomas Crown Affair*, around a bonfire on Cape Cod with Faye Dunaway, McQueen tells her about the next day's bank robbery and says, 'We are a pair, remember?' Then, in the very last scene, having scammed her and [having] left with no notice, he sips a drink, alone in first class of an airliner, smiles and... fades out."

MacGraw thought a romantic trip to Paris might be a relaxing prelude to the hectic four-month shoot planned for *Papillon*. The always-thrifty McQueen managed to finagle out of National General (the distributor for First Artists) an all-expenses-paid trip to Paris for the French premiere of *The Getaway*. Paris was one of Ali MacGraw's favorite cities, and she had visions of bistro dinners, romantic strolls along the Champs-Elysees, and kissing along the Seine. McQueen wasn't so keen on the trip but complied to make MacGraw happy. He arrived in France in a foul mood, according to Leonard Morpurgo, the publicity executive in France for *The Getaway*.

Morpurgo greeted McQueen and MacGraw at Orly Airport in France as soon as they stepped foot off the plane, but he was quickly brushed aside. "I'll find my own way to my hotel, and don't you try to follow me," McQueen said brusquely. "I was really in a difficult situation," Morpurgo recalled. "I indirectly represented First Artists, and he was one of the partners in the company. National General Pictures paid for their trip and expected me to set up some major media interviews. He and I had to talk." When Morpurgo showed up at McQueen's hotel, he got more of the same treatment.

"What the hell are you doing here, and how did you find out where I was staying?" McQueen demanded. "My hotel was supposed to be a secret." Morpurgo had dealt with some difficult stars before but none of his ilk. He thought he was dealing with a madman, especially when McQueen told him he was not doing any interviews. "He checked in at the hotel desk, leaving me nonplussed. From the other side of the lobby, he beckoned me imperiously. I accepted his summons and crossed the lobby," Morpurgo recalled. "It seemed he had changed his mind. 'If we're going to work together, you will never wear that coat in my presence again. You will take it home and burn it. You should wear a leather jacket and turtleneck sweaters. Do I make myself clear?'"

Morpurgo nodded because he did not know what to say to this bombastic assault. Morpurgo was happy to leave his long lambs-wool coat at home if he could get some interviews for his client.

"I will do one interview only," McQueen said. "One interview! And if there's any argument, I won't do that." Morpurgo quickly made a silent run through of the possible press. If he had just one shot, he wanted it to be *Paris Match*, France's top-selling weekly magazine. To his relief, McQueen agreed to do the photo shoot. "But it will have to be at Le Mans in two days. I'm taking Ali there to show her where I made the movie [*Le Mans*]." McQueen then gave Morpurgo the name of the hotel where they would be staying, vowing him to silence. The hotel doorman interrupted to tell McQueen that the self-drive Mercedes he had rented was waiting outside. A photographer was also waiting. McQueen's fury erupted again.

"How the hell did he find out I was here?" McQueen looked at the publicist accusingly, who shrugged his shoulders and suggested he had probably been tipped off by one of the hotel staff. "I'll take care of him," McQueen said, stalking out of the hotel followed by MacGraw and Morpurgo. The waiting photographer raised his camera, and McQueen brushed him aside. "I'll smash your damn camera in your face if you try to take a picture," he said. "Come on, Ali. Get in the car," McQueen said, gunning the engine. Morpurgo recalled, "The cameraman tried to get in his exclusive shot. Steve drove the Mercedes right at him. The photographer leaped out of the way but didn't quite make it. He was hit by the right fender and thrown to the ground. Steve screeched to a halt. He climbed out of the car, apparently realizing that he'd gone too far."

McQueen stopped the car to ask the photographer if he was okay. The man felt himself all over, stretched his bruised body, and looked at his miraculously undamaged camera. "I think so." Sensing that the actor might be more amenable after the accident, the man asked if he could get just one shot. The request revved up McQueen all over again, who began screaming at the photographer. Morpurgo had finally lost his patience. "Steve, get in the fucking car and get out of here. Don't make matters worse. I'll take care of the photographer. That's my job. Now go!"

Morpurgo said McQueen's reaction was priceless. "His mouth dropped open. He started to say something, then changed his mind. Without another word he drove off, going west and out of town. I don't think he was used to anyone talking to him that way."

Back in his office, Morpurgo called *Paris Match* and sold them an exclusive story on the condition that McQueen would get the cover. Two days later,

Morpurgo and the *Paris Match* photographer arrived at McQueen's hotel in Le Mans. Ali MacGraw was the first downstairs. Morpurgo said she looked pale and stressed out. He asked her if everything was okay.

"Leonard, I think what Steve told you about your coat and telling you to burn it was terrible, but don't feel too badly. He did the same thing to me today," MacGraw revealed. "We had a huge fight this morning, and he blamed it on my top coat. He said that every time I wore it, we fought. So he picked up the coat and threw it in the trash. There's going to be one happy chambermaid here today. That coat cost me $300."

MacGraw started to walk away, then turned back and said quietly to Morpurgo, "You probably wonder why I stay with this man."

"The thought had crossed my mind."

"I stay because I love him. I know what he is, but I can't help myself."

According to Morpurgo, "Ali MacGraw was as sweet as McQueen was mean. It was a strange match."

A few minutes later, McQueen joined them downstairs and was surprisingly affable. They drove to the nearby racetrack for the photo shoot. As the photographer made preparations, McQueen said casually, "By the way, I will only let you shoot in black and white."

"But why?" Morpurgo asked.

"Because that is what I want."

Morpurgo informed McQueen that all *Paris Match* covers were in color, and he was going to blow the whole deal. And what difference did it make to him if the pictures were in color or black and white?

"Take it or leave it. Black and white." The photographer shrugged. He wasn't about to get into an argument with McQueen. He was getting paid either way. He popped a roll of black-and-white film into his camera and took a series of shots of McQueen and MacGraw strolling along the racetrack. *Paris Match* used just one photo in the following week's issue—a picture of the two strolling next to a white guardrail. MacGraw's back is to the camera while McQueen is looking back at the photographer with a wide smile. It was tucked away deep inside the issue, a single column, 2 inches, and in black-and-white. And there was no cover.

• • •

Papillon is the film version of the sensational best seller—17 million copies sold worldwide and five million in the U.S. alone—based on the life of Henri Charrière, a safe cracker sentenced to life imprisonment but who could not be contained within prison walls. Nicknamed "Papillon" because of the butterfly tattooed on his chest, he is revealed as a self-disciplined leader of men, a loyal friend, and an ingenious enemy. But most of all, his is an indomitable spirit with an insatiable desire for freedom.

The movie was originally intended for Jean-Paul Belmondo, the star of Jean Luc Godard's ballyhooed debut, *Breathless*, but to finance a $13 million epic, the producers required an international star. The film then went through several years of development, with Warren Beatty and Roman Polanski packaged as its initial star and director. The project ultimately caved in because of a lack of funding. Producer Robert Dorfman rounded up a consortium of Franco-American bankers and placed it in the hands of Allied Artists, bringing the picture back to life after three years of dormancy... but only if one star put his name on the dotted line. For the privilege of securing Steve McQueen, they paid him $2 million plus incentives.[1]

Money wasn't McQueen's only motivation to do the part. He genuinely felt a connection to the story. "I kept being driven by this restless feeling. I seemed always to be looking for something—never knowing what it was—but always there was the sense that I couldn't be confined. And that's exactly what I felt in common when I read Charrière's *Papillon*," McQueen said. "This man who had been restless and moving suddenly found himself imprisoned, and his natural and involuntary reaction was, 'I must get out of this damned place.' Of course, the kind of inhuman, brutalizing treatment practiced in the French penal colonies in those days added to his desire to be free. My name could easily have been Papillon, too."

A major stipulation backers insisted on was that *Papillon* had to be delivered for a December 1973 release to capitalize on the holiday season. With a late February start date, that meant *Papillon* had to be filmed, scored, and edited in less than 10 months, a risky proposition for an epic. Compounding the problem was that only 60 pages of Dalton Trumbo's script was finished. "That, on the surface of it, would appear to be madness," said director Franklin Schaffner (*Patton*). "But either we proceeded or the financing would be jeopardized. Morale among the crew was hitting a questionable plateau, and after all the months I had been on the project, it seemed the wisest course of action was to sink or swim."

---

1 A July 18, 1972, contract for *Papillon* shows, in addition to McQueen's $2 million salary, he received 10 percent of the gross receipts derived in the United States and Canada in excess of $15 million, 5 percent of the gross receipts in excess of $30 million until gross receipts have totaled $40 million, and a deferred sum of $250,000 out of 50 percent of the first monies constituting net profits. All totaled, McQueen received a minimum of $6.7 million for *Papillon* and possibly more.

Trumbo, one of the Hollywood Ten who was blacklisted during the McCarthy hearings in the 1950s, was kept on location throughout the production. Only 10 pages ahead of schedule, *Papillon* was shot in sequence like a play. Franklin Schaffner explained, "When we began shooting, we didn't have a complete script. So with a few exceptions, we decided to shoot the entire film in sequence. The other factor in that decision was that the story covers 12 long, hard years, and the main characters clearly show the erosive effects. We felt that we could avoid many problems of makeup detail by filming in sequence."

Costar Dustin Hoffman, who portrays counterfeiter Louis Dega and eventually becomes Papillon's accomplice in escape, thought it was a definite advantage to the actors. "We acted out the scenes in approximately the same order the audience will see them," Hoffman said. "So when we first went to work, McQueen and I were getting to know each other. Any time you can use real-life parallels in your acting, you use 'em."

However, McQueen and Hoffman were almost polar opposites. They were two very different men playing very different characters. On screen, McQueen is the paragon of reckless masculinity and a man of few words, while Hoffman is the urbane but idiosyncratic intellectual. Off-screen, each man represented what the other wanted—McQueen sought the kind of respect Hoffman was afforded for his acting, while Hoffman in turn had always wanted to be a fabulously good-looking and financially well-compensated superstar like McQueen. Despite those fundamental differences, both seemed to understand much was at stake in this huge endeavor. "Both of us were suspicious; both of us wanted to come out of this multimillion-dollar film as career survivors," Hoffman said. "Both of us realized we needed each other's help and support. I can't really speak for him, but I believe he was thinking the same thing. In the movie, one character is saying, 'You've got to help me or die; neither of us can do it alone.' And for us as the actors, the meaning is, 'We'd better help each other, or we could die with this movie.'"

If they helped each other, it certainly wasn't noticeable to others on the set. McQueen was as suspicious and untrusting of his costars as ever. In Hoffman he saw a young upstart who would try to upstage him at a moment's notice. McQueen knew of Hoffman's reputation as an excellent actor and was not about to play second fiddle to him. Hoffman's method of acting seemed to play to these anxieties, especially when he showed up with ludicrously large wire-rimmed glasses and discolored teeth. However, McQueen still had the same tricks up his sleeve that had served him well early in his career when he was the hungry star desperately trying to break through. Recalling the gold tooth Eli Wallach wore in *The Magnificent Seven*, McQueen mentally filed the scene-stealing prop until he needed ammunition. The prop enhanced a torture scene where prison guards brutalize Papillion to the point where he screams aloud and exposes the gold tooth. This rivalry would ultimately reap dividends on the big screen as both actors pushed themselves to the limit, each one raising his game to produce performances and a real sense of an on-screen bond.

Director Franklin Schaffner said he had to strike a delicate balance when handling his two stars. "Obviously, Steve McQueen was the superstar in films. Dustin Hoffman was a star as an actor, if I can make that distinction. And they both looked forward to working with one another.

"I would always shoot on McQueen first to make him commit and then turn around and shoot on Hoffman. It seemed to work better that way because if I covered Hoffman first, Steve would become restless about what he was doing. The quicker you got him comfortable, the better the scene would play. Hoffman, on the other hand, is a totally electric performer. He comes in with 99 different ideas of how to approach a scene."

Though Hoffman may have been the more critically acclaimed actor, he didn't have McQueen's confidence or film experience and couldn't get a fix on one of the scenes. McQueen offered him some simple advice, "Less, Dusty. Do less. Just throw that out; you don't need it. Keep it simple." Hoffman confided the exchange to actor Charles Durning on the set of *Tootsie* almost a decade later. Durning asked Hoffman how he reacted to McQueen.

"I listened to him," Hoffman replied.

Actor Don Gordon, who had a small part in *Papillon*, said Hoffman's presence also lit a fire in McQueen. "Steve worked very hard on *Papillon*. He worked very hard as an actor," Gordon said. "A lot of people think he didn't, but he did. He was a working actor. Plus the fact that Dustin Hoffman kept McQueen on his toes, kept him honest. One day Dustin showed up with his teeth all colored and wearing Coke-bottle glasses. McQueen had to be aware; he had to work even harder than he normally did. He really came to maturation on *Papillon*."

Interestingly, one of McQueen's best on-screen moments wasn't with Hoffman but with character actor Anthony Zerbe, a classically trained actor from the theater world. Zerbe said McQueen impressed him because he was willing to dig deep for the part. "He was the perfect actor for the time, although he was not the warmest person in the world," Zerbe said. "He viewed all actors as competition, especially Dustin Hoffman and me. McQueen was charismatic and had tremendous presence in all his films, but I felt that he pushed himself in *Papillon*.

"In our scene together, I played a leper in a French colony who could help Papillon escape to freedom. As a test, I offered him a cigar that had already been smoked, and McQueen's character did not know whether I was infectious or not. The cool thing was, I had been chewing on that cigar all day, and I handed him this wet, drooled on, soggy stogie. This was intentional, because I wanted to see what that fucker was made of. It was obviously a challenge. McQueen, the actor, didn't have to take the cigar. He could have asked for a replacement during a cut but didn't. McQueen just put it in his mouth and continued with the scene. He delivered one of the most amazing reactions I have ever seen on the silver screen. Once the scene was over, I looked at him and said, 'Oh McQueen, you're something else.' He just looked at me and smiled. I thought it was an incredible thing to do and showed how far he was willing to go to bring respect to the part.

"When I think of McQueen as an actor, I'm reminded of a star who embodied a certain mythology and brought it to life."

Costumer Kent James said McQueen's work ethic was questionable when compared to his costar. While Hoffman subsisted on a coconut a day (he was applying the Method), McQueen downed lots of Red Stripe beer, smoked ganja, and feasted on native food specially prepared by a chef in his large oceanside villa. "He really had a weight problem on that film. He actually had quite a gut on him, and it kept getting bigger," James said. "I had to find bigger and baggier clothes to give McQueen an emaciated look."

James said McQueen's increasing girth almost made an alligator very happy when they visited a friend's home for dinner. "We were going to have dinner one night with Ross Kananga, a stuntman who owned a crocodile farm in Kingston, Jamaica," James said. "Steve and I arrived early and hit the buzzer at the entrance gate. No one answered, and Steve became a little antsy. He left the car and announced that he was going to climb over the six-foot wall that surrounded the property and knock on the front door. This was in spite of the fact there was a sign posted on the gate that read, 'Beware of Crocodiles.'

"Steve, don't go over that wall," James warned. "Those crocodiles can burst up to 30 mph on land." McQueen had climbed halfway up the wall when Ross drove up and confirmed that Steve would have been crocodile meat had he gone any further.

The next day, McQueen decided to have some fun at James' expense when he and Hoffman were required to tackle a crocodile during cleanup detail at the prison camp. For the scene, the animal was heavily drugged and had its mouth wired shut. James estimates the reptile was about 20 feet long, hissing at everyone, and it was by no means under control. McQueen could tell the razor-toothed reptile spooked James and asked if he would bring him a towel to wipe mud from his face. "I knew he was messing with me," James said, laughing. "I told him, 'I'm not going down there while that alligator is still alive.'"

"James, you're a big candy ass," Steve said.

"Yeah McQueen, you got that right!"

James said McQueen also had a soft side to him and was good to those who were less fortunate. "While on a beach in Jamaica, we asked a local to come to the set and cut up coconuts for the cast and crew. He was using a machete but accidentally sliced right through the coconut and almost severed his fingers. They folded all the way back, held together by skin. He went off to the local hospital, but Steve insisted this man have the best possible treatment. He arranged for him to fly to Miami where a top surgeon repaired his hand. Steve picked up the entire tab."

McQueen had an inherent goodness and desired to help people when they needed it most, said stuntman Stan Barrett, who had a deep discussion with the superstar about Christianity. The two men were friends with motorcycle rider J.N. Roberts, who had recently declared his faith. McQueen felt Roberts was "way out there" and had gone a little overboard. Barrett tried to explain the transformation in Roberts' life. "I said to Steve, 'This is a new experience in J.N.'s life, and he's pretty excited about it.' Steve said, 'Well, I'm religious.' I asked, 'But are you a Christian? Do you have a personal relationship with Jesus Christ? Just because you go into a barn doesn't mean you're a cow any more than you are a Christian.' It was a very intense conversation, and I hit him pretty hard. I didn't let him off the hook, either. Usually people don't like to be questioned like that, but Steve was open to it. We were inside the compound filming, and we took a walk along the hillside. At the end of our half-hour conversation, I promised to leave him a couple of books—*Mere Christianity* by C.S. Lewis and *Basic Christianity* by John Stott—which I did. Looking back, it was very unusual to have that conversation with Steve, but I'm glad I did. Obviously this had been a running theme throughout his life for many, many years."

But McQueen raised holy hell when he discovered the producers were running short of money and taking it out of the cast and crew. "From what I understand," Don Gordon said, "the producer would take a couple of reels of film, get on an airplane, go back to France, show them reels of film, get on an airplane, and bring it back on a lease." Things got so tight that once during filming a decision was made to cut out everyone's per diem living allowances. When McQueen found out, he went on strike until everyone else was paid, according to Gordon. "We weren't getting our per diems. McQueen wasn't getting his. Hoffman wasn't getting his. McQueen already had his salary up front, but he went to the producer and said, 'If the crew isn't paid, I don't work.'" McQueen was true to his word, and the production shut down for five days until everyone got paid.[2]

His generosity didn't extend to Hoffman, who had invited some relatives to the set about halfway though filming. They had the misfortune of bringing cameras to the set, and when McQueen spotted them, he had them tossed out. Kent James remembered, "Steve didn't like to have anybody on the set who wasn't supposed to be there. Dustin's relatives showed up, unbeknownst to Steve, and he had them kicked off. It really pissed Dustin off, and that was the end of their friendship. They didn't talk to each other for the rest of the picture. Any conversation that went on between them, I'd have to act as the go-between. I'd go to Dustin and say, 'Steve would like this,' and then Steve would ask, 'What did Dusty have to say?' Well, they weren't but 10 feet apart from each other, but they weren't budging." Almost 15 years later, Hoffman and James worked with each other again on *Rain Man*, and Hoffman shook his head in disbelief when they spoke of McQueen. "That son of a bitch! Can you believe he threw my guests off *Papillon*?"

Rumors of their famous rift drifted to the United States, and *Washington Post* reporter Tom Donnelly received a strange rebuttal from Hoffman when asked of his row with McQueen. "I always play it cool," Hoffman replied. "I never get involved with anybody while I'm making a movie or doing a play. And I mean anybody.

"There's no question that you're bound to lose out if there are emotional commitments; people saying, 'Oh, let's do it this way, let's do it his way.' People can use friendship as a lever to get you to alter what you believe in. So when I'm making a movie, I don't socialize with the cast. I don't go to dinner with them. After the day's work is done, I go home. I never met Steve McQueen before we made the movie, and I haven't seen him since." Hoffman has never commented on their relationship since that 1973 interview.

McQueen was poised to eject another visitor who came without warning or an invitation. Paparazzi photographer Ron Galella flew to Montego Bay, Jamaica, on April 18, 1973, on a calculated risk that he'd score a photo op with McQueen and MacGraw. There he encountered a hostile and scruffily bearded superstar, who had a distaste for the paparazzi. McQueen and MacGraw took great pains not to be photographed together since it was unknown if Robert Evans might seek sole custody of son Joshua. While in Spain, a paparazzo had waited for them in the hotel foyer and caught them holding hands as they came out of the elevator

---

2   Allied Artists' hasty decision turned into a $250,000 overrun, which could have been easily avoided.

lift. His photo exposed a very worried MacGraw and an intense McQueen, who made a beeline for the shutterbug.

"I'd like to buy that film," McQueen said forcefully.

"I'm not selling," said the frightened photographer, who beat a hasty retreat to the closest exit. He was thankful McQueen didn't give chase.

Galella was a different case. He didn't run away from anyone, including Marlon Brando, who once smashed him in the mouth and broke five of Galella's teeth.

The famed photographer was also friendly with Ali MacGraw, with whom he had numerous and pleasant encounters in New York City. He thought she would be his ticket to get onto the closed set in Jamaica. "I go to the studio, knock on the door, and give them a letter addressed to Ali MacGraw. It was simple and to the point: I wanted a picture of her with McQueen," Galella said in 2010. "The response was immediate—Steve came out of an office and said, 'No, no pictures with us together.' Then he said, 'I want you out of here. I'll send my black friends after you if you don't leave right away and get on the next plane.' You know how I replied? This is a good quote. I said, 'I'm from New York. I live with black people.' I flew a long way, and I wasn't going to take no for an answer."

Galella asked for 10 minutes of McQueen's time to take a few photos, and then he would leave. McQueen agreed to the terms and made Galella sign an affidavit. Galella said McQueen's word was as good as gold, and Galella snapped about a dozen pictures of McQueen in a dark blue T-shirt, cut-off blue jeans, walking toward the camera, holding a coffee cup and scratching his head. Over the years, Galella has made a small fortune on the photo session. "He was actually pretty nice to me when I started taking my pictures," Galella said. "He said, 'You really fucked up with Jackie Onassis,'[3] and we both laughed, and then I was done."

Another interesting visitor was Henri Charrière, the real life Papillon. He found the set to be almost identical to the actual prison where he was incarcerated 35 years before. He also saw the Devil's Island location, which he thought was absolutely perfect in its reality, and he watched the filming at the Colombian village location, which was an exact replica of the tiny village where he was sheltered and found romance during one of his many escapes. Everyone remembered Charrière as an open and charismatic figure who even managed to pull

---

3 Onassis claimed that Galella had stalked her, jumping out of a bush to take her photo. She took him to court in 1972 and the 26-day trial garnered media coverage around the world. The judge ordered Galella to stay 75 feet away from Onassis at all times.

the spotlight away from McQueen.[4] Charrière regaled the cast and crew with prison tales, brutality, and floating away from Devil's Island[5] on a bed of coconuts in shark-infested waters. *Time* magazine and *Paris Match*[6] took Charrière to task, who later admitted about 75 percent of his book was true. "He was a very open and gregarious fellow—although I suspect he also was something of a con artist," Shaffner told a *Los Angeles Times* reporter. "But it really doesn't matter whether the book is true...it's more a question of the man's spirit, which I think we capture." Schaffner continued, "Steve's performance in *Papillon* is the best he had given in his life."

Papillon is the natural successor to Hilts from *The Great Escape*. McQueen gives a performance that captures the essence of needing to be free despite the costs. His character experiences many torments and hardships to achieve his goal. But unlike Hilts, Papillon actually escapes at the end. The maturity that McQueen brings to this piece of work is impressive as he shows great valor but is also unafraid to be shown at his worst, especially in the scenes where he has been in solitary confinement and in an appalling state. McQueen had the skill and security in himself to play a character that by the end was ravaged of his good looks. He was now confident enough as an actor to stand aside from his image and let his acting do the talking. It is little wonder that *Papillon* remains a fan favorite.

In an uncanny repeat of *The Getaway*, critics savaged *Papillon* while audiences ate it up. Film critic Andrew Sarris wrote, "Schaffner has really made an exhilarating movie of the most dangerously depressing material." Pauline Kael observed that *Papillon* was "a monument to the eternal desire of moviemakers to impress people and win awards. To put McQueen in a role that requires intense audience identification with the hero's humanity is madness. If there was ever a wrong actor for a man of great spirit, it's McQueen."

Audiences seemed to disagree with Kael, who voted with their dollars. *Papillon* scored big at the box office and grossed $56.2 million domestically[7] and more than $100 million worldwide. It was also Allied Artists' most success-

---

4   Henri Charrière died on July 29, 1973, a few months after he visited the set. He never did see the film version of his life. Modern researchers believe that Charrière got much of the story from another inmate and view his autobiography as fiction. As of 2005, a Paris man, Charles Brunnier, who was in prison at the same time, is now thought to be the real life Papillon.

5   Today Devil's Island attracts close to 30,000 visitors a year, including a number of former prisoners' children and grandchildren as well as fans of the book and movie.

6   Reporter George Menanger wrote a story for *Paris Match* in the early '70s and hints that Charrière had a fertile imagination. His portrait of the man is that of a pimp and police informer, not a "pure thief" as Charrière painted himself.

7   Only *The Exorcist*, *American Graffiti*, and *The Sting* financially outperformed *Papillon* in 1973.

ful film ever. After his career slide with the failure of *The Reivers*, *Le Mans*, and *Junior Bonner*, McQueen had refortified himself, cementing what he had achieved with *The Getaway*. His star was brighter than ever, and the money was pouring in. Like his character in *Papillon*, McQueen had reminded everyone, "Hey you bastards, I'm still here." And he was right. McQueen was on top of the world again. However, his next role would quite literally place him even higher.

31
MAN ON FIRE

BLINDED BY THE GLARE OF THE SPOTLIGHT, the constant paparazzi frenzy, and lots of negative tabloid ink, Steve McQueen and Ali MacGraw retreated to a modest beachfront home in Trancas, just north of Malibu in late May 1973.

MacGraw said instinctively she knew their lifestyle would need to shift away from the limelight. "There was not even a dialogue about the subject.... We knew how private it would have to be," MacGraw said. "Otherwise, it would have become a circus every minute."

The actress whose once sunny disposition lit up entire rooms had turned inward. Critics had taken potshots at her performance in *The Getaway*, columnists had questioned her sanity after leaving Robert Evans, and a pair of protesters had waged a very public demonstration against MacGraw's selection as the 158th celebrity to have her hands and feet enshrined at Hollywood's world-famous Grauman's Chinese Theatre. A handful of demonstrators attended the ceremony, holding up a placard that read, "Let Us Give Credit Where Credit Is Due. Ali MacGraw, Who Are You?" Protester Don McGovern, a character actor who worked in Hollywood and New York, said, "When you think of all the great actors who are enshrined at Grauman's, and you think of having Ali MacGraw's next to them... it's an absolute outrage. What dues has she paid in this business?"[1]

She had become Hollywood's newest "sock-it-to-me" girl and was quite aware that she had fallen out of favor with the public. She admitted to a *New York Times* reporter the assaults and brickbats smarted. "I'm the scarlet lady. It's the opposite of the Golden Girl syndrome, and I was the Golden Girl for a time," MacGraw said. "I'm hurt by it."

---

1   McGovern and a fellow actor made a brazen attempt to cement over MacGraw's footprints and handprints before they were caught by a theater usher. The prank was chronicled by a movie magazine, which caught all the action on film.

It also cost McQueen. His guarded, angry, skeptical hostility resulted in his exploitation of those around him, including professional peers, other men's wives, directors, and producers—in a very small town. He was throwing his weight around and displaying almost complete disregard for anyone but Ali and those who were within his inner circle. The defensive instincts that he used to make it to the top were now being employed to safeguard himself and his relationship with Ali. The price was high for his behavior and was perhaps measurable in golden statuettes—some people in the Hollywood community felt it cost McQueen the Academy Award for *Papillon*.[2]

However, the sacrifice may have been worth it because peace and tranquility defined their early lives in Trancas. There was something magical and relaxing about the fresh salty air, powdery sand dunes, and miles of shoreline. Their neighbors included the likes of Jack Lemmon, Joe Cocker, Donald Sutherland, Sam Elliot, Katherine Ross, Carroll O'Connor, Don Felder (guitarist for The Eagles), and Keith Moon, who kept a pair of binoculars handy for when MacGraw sunbathed topless.

The McQueen home included Joshua Evans (2½ years) and Chad McQueen (12), with sister Terry (14) visiting on most weekends. Chad recalled of that time, "We had a strong bond. When my folks split up in the early '70s, I lived with my mom for a while but soon ended up with Dad. We moved around for about a year—including a stint in Texas while he shot *The Getaway*, where I watched him steal Ali MacGraw away from Robert Evans—but we finally ended up in Malibu, where I still have a home. Now everybody lives here—[Steven] Spielberg, [Sylvester] Stallone—but when we first moved here, Malibu was just a funky little beach town with auto mechanics."

Their family also included Junior, a feisty mutt that Steve had found in the desert and named after his character in *Junior Bonner*. Part shepherd and part collie, Junior was extremely loyal to Steve and the immediate family, but he was an indiscriminate biter. Chad recalled the time Junior penetrated Governor Ronald Reagan's security team and put the bite on the Old Gipper. "[Reagan] used to walk the beach with all these security guys. I was a surf rat, and whenever I'd go out in the water, my dog Junior would sit on the beach. One day I looked up and saw Junior biting Reagan on the ass. The security guys went berserk," Chad said.

---

2   Pat Johnson claimed that McQueen had been chosen by the Golden Globe committee for Best Actor category for his work in *Papillon*. He said the award came with a stipulation—McQueen had to be present for the award. He offered to issue a statement to the press but adamantly refused to appear in person. The committee's next phone call was to Al Pacino, who accepted the award on January 28, 1974, for *Serpico*.

Their days were filled with egg hunts on Easter, barbecues on the the Fourth of July, potluck dinners with neighbors, walks along the beach, tuna fish sandwiches, surfboards, bicycles, and a core of tight-knit friends. "Our life revolved around family and small town," MacGraw recalled. "I think we were both exhausted by the tremendous amount of tabloid attention we had received, separately and together; it was relief to spend time alone and with the children, on the beach or on long rides in the canyon. We stayed to ourselves, which started the rumor that we had both become hermits."

William Pierce, who spent 10 weeks with McQueen on *Junior Bonner*, said he sensed their new life in Malibu was therapeutic. Pierce had yet to meet MacGraw, but he recalled that their first encounter was more than just memorable. "I ring the bell and the door opens, and there's this lady without a stitch of clothing on, and she says, 'Hi, you must be Bill?' I said, 'Yes.' She said very casually, 'Hi, I'm Ali.'

"Now, I'm just a good ol' boy from Arizona and was married at the time and had a few kids, but I had never experienced anything like that before. I now know why Steve never wanted to leave the house," Pierce said, laughing.

Pierce said the two men sat out on the deck, drank beer, looked out at the ocean, and caught up with each other's lives. During *Junior Bonner*, the men bonded over their simultaneous separations from their wives and rode motor-cycles almost every day after filming. McQueen told Pierce how he fell in love with MacGraw on *The Getaway* and how she made him happy. "We had a nice visit, and it was the last time I ever saw him," Pierce said.

On June 7, 1973, Ali MacGraw was granted an interlocutory divorce decree from Robert Evans. There was no community property to be divided, and she refused alimony. She retained custody of Joshua, while Evans was granted visita-tion rights. MacGraw had given up a lot to be with McQueen—a marriage, her dream role in *The Great Gatsby* (Paramount brass saw to it that she would not get the role), and a white-hot career. Yet it appeared McQueen gave up nothing in return. They had talked of marriage for the children's sake, but MacGraw said the talk was only sporadic.

Scripts continued to flood in with roles for both of them as well as individual parts in separate movies.[3] McQueen acted as if he were looking for a project they could do together, but he ultimately discouraged anyone who offered her

3   Some of the offers included *The Johnson County War* (the title was changed to *Heaven's Gate*); *Convoy* (a movie MacGraw made a few years later); *Roy Brightwood*; *The Monkey Wrench Gang*; *The Long Good-bye*; *The Betsy*; *The Man Who Loved Cat Dancing*; *Gable and Lombard*; and an unnamed slightly erotic western. It was also reported that MacGraw wanted to costar with friend Candice Bergen in a TV movie production of *The Beautiful and the Damned*.

employment. "I was really angry at her," said MacGraw's agent, Sue Mengers. "The audiences loved her! It made me crazy! [Steve] was always very rude when I called because it was a sign that I might have a job for her."

In McQueen's eyes, MacGraw's job was to be at his side, having dinner on the table at 6:00 PM sharp, fetching beer, rearing the kids, riding pillion on his motorcycle with the Hells Angels, and making love to him at the end of the day. While Robert Evans pampered Ali, McQueen put her to work. Much like Uncle Claude, McQueen had no use for slackers.

Ali said she played the role of homemaker in a bid to please Steve. "It was complicated," she explained. "But it had to do with a child I take seriously and wanted to be a mother to and with a man I wanted to be with away from the public. I was brought up to wash, make beds, cook, and clean. It's natural to me. I feel okay about that life even if it doesn't make sense to someone else."

For a while, they were happy and it seemed to work. But their volatile relationship never gave Ali much security, especially after one of their knock-down, drag-out fights. She said one of those fights jarred a strange marriage proposal out of him. MacGraw remembered, "One night we had a terrific fight. After we calmed down, Steve said, 'Okay, baby—if you want to get married, it's tomorrow or never. That's it.' Not exactly moonlight and roses but pretty much in character."

What was also in character was McQueen's paranoia. He sprang the idea of a prenuptial agreement on MacGraw just before they made the trip to the altar. He had bitterly complained that his divorce to Neile had almost financially wiped him out, never mentioning that she gave up her career for him.

MacGraw reluctantly signed the four-page "Ante-Nuptial Agreement" on July 10, 1973, which was prepared by McQueen's representative, power attorney Kenneth Ziffren. MacGraw also had legal representation from Howard Kaufman from the Beverly Hills law firm of Pain, Lavine, Kaufman & Young. Years later, MacGraw said she feared McQueen's disapproval and wrath at the time, and she regretted her hasty decision. "I no longer feel, as I did when I was married to Steve, that the full-time job of housework and child rearing should go unrewarded financially if the marriage collapses," MacGraw said. "In my case, I gave up my film career at its peak, not just in popularity but in financial potential, as well."

Psychologist Peter O. Whitmer believes the proposal was an attempt by McQueen to do damage control on their relationship and to keep it intact. "It seems as if something had broken loose during their fight," Whitmer said. "To feel integrated, Steve needed to put it back in place, and put it back permanently, legally, albeit with a prenup. This also represents reconstruction for McQueen of a previous emotional peak. Steve thought marriage would maintain this. He saw marriage as something embodied in a Hallmark card or a Hollywood movie, but unfortunately, he never had a role model for what marriage is like."

With the prenuptial agreement signed, dated, and notarized, Steve, Ali, Chad, Terry, and Joshua headed to Cheyenne, Wyoming (McQueen thought the name sounded "cowboy-romantic") and rolled into town in a rented blue Cadillac. They checked into a tacky Holiday Inn, where Steve and Chad shared a bed while Ali and Terry shared the other; Joshua was placed in a rented crib underneath a coat rack. The next day—July 12, 1973—Steve and Ali were married by Justice of the Peace Arthur Garfield, who was playing a round of golf when he was interrupted by an urgent phone call from his secretary, Mimi Kreuzer. He was told the couple wanted to get hitched in the city's Holiday Park.

McQueen took painstaking measures to avoid publicity, even forsaking hiring an official wedding photographer. Instead, he stopped en route to the park and bought a Kodak camera. The judge cheerfully obliged when asked to take pictures. They were a funky bunch—McQueen was dressed in a short-sleeved cowboy shirt with snap buttons, while Ali and Terry wore matching white shirts and plaid shorts; Chad sported long hair and a '70s-style striped shirt, while young Joshua, who was thigh-high, wore overalls and tennis shoes. They were the very picture of the nuclear family, and they were about to embark on a new life together.

• • •

Eight days after his marriage to Ali MacGraw, Steve McQueen received the stunning news that his former karate instructor, Bruce Lee, had collapsed and died under mysterious circumstances in the Hong Kong apartment of actress Betty Ting Pei. It was ruled "death by misadventure."

Among the many celebrities that Lee counted as his pupils and friends—James Coburn, James Garner, Lee Marvin, Kareem Abdul-Jabbar, Jay Sebring—none were bigger or brighter than McQueen. Both were highly competitive men with massive egos. When Bruce Lee's star began to rise, it caused notable tension between the two and almost destroyed their friendship. By the end of 1972, Lee was a major movie star in Asia and was side-kicking all box-office records in the Orient. When he got back to Hollywood, the clean-living athlete went on a star trip, adopting Western designer duds, engaging in extramarital affairs, and surprisingly, smoking dope.[4] Lee also confided to Dr. Peter Wu, a Hong Kong

---

4 Lee's autopsy showed an inordinate amount of hashish in his system. Though most sources cite that Lee died of acute cerebral edema, his Hong Kong physician, Dr. Donald Langford, believes otherwise. He said Lee died from hypersensitivity to chemicals in cannabis or a cannabis byproduct.

neurosurgeon who treated him for a cerebral edema a month before his death, that McQueen turned him on to hash. "He said that it was harmless," Wu is quoted in Davis Miller's *The Tao of Bruce Lee*. "He said that Steve McQueen had introduced him to it and Steve McQueen would not take it if there was anything bad about it. I asked him if Steve McQueen was a medical authority, but he didn't get my joke."

Lee began bragging to friends that he was about to eclipse the King of Cool with his first major Hollywood project, *Enter the Dragon*, for which he was paid $3 million. James Coburn recalled Lee said, "I did it! I made more money than McQueen!"

Filled with a mixture of pride and resentment, Lee sent McQueen a barbed letter in which Lee essentially gloated that he was now more popular to a wider audience than McQueen. After that, McQueen felt it was time to take Lee down a notch, so McQueen sent Lee an autographed 8-by-10. It was signed, "To Bruce, my biggest fan."

The two did share one last bonding experience when Lee purchased his first Porsche after the money came rolling in. McQueen insisted Lee let him drive it to see how the car handled. But this was not just any driver, and this wouldn't be a quiet ride in the country.

The famous actor took Lee on a hair-raising tour through Mulholland Drive, one of the most winding thoroughfares in Los Angeles, and he gunned the sports car up to nearly 100 mph. Lee, who was a control freak, was a white-knuckled passenger.

"Now watch how I can slide it through these tight curves," McQueen said nonchalantly while Lee cringed, keeping one eye on the road and the other shut tight. "Now watch how this baby can do a 180 in the middle of the road," McQueen said as he downshifted and slammed on the brakes, spinning the car halfway around and heading back the opposite direction at full speed. Lee, who was naturally wound tight, exploded.

"McQueen! You crazy muddafucker! I kill you!" Lee screamed in his broken English. McQueen laughed aloud, but his smile vanished when he saw Lee was livid with anger. He began to accelerate the car again, attempting to gain control of the situation.

"Bruce, I'm going to drive the car as fast as I can until you calm down," McQueen said. Lee put his hands up and conceded. "Okay, okay. I'm calm, Steve."

McQueen had literally taken his friend Lee on the ride of his life. Unfortunately, however, Lee's life came to an abrupt end just as he became a global star. He was a physically perfect specimen, yet he dropped dead on July 20,

1973, at age 32. McQueen, along with James Coburn and Chuck Norris, flew to Seattle to serve as pallbearers at Lee's funeral at the request of his widow, Linda. (Lee also had a funeral in Hong Kong.) Coburn delivered a beautiful eulogy, and everyone who attended was in tears—that is, everyone but Steve McQueen. "We were all saddened by his death," Coburn said. "I think that I felt more saddened than Steve. Steve didn't feel that much because he wasn't that emotional of a guy. He wasn't sentimental about anything. He would hold it all inside."

• • •

McQueen was slowly detaching himself from the movie business and public life. A run-in with model Morganna Welch at that time confirmed as much for her. She briefly met McQueen in the driveway of Elmer Valentine's Palm Springs home in late summer 1973. She said he was already suffering from signs of burnout. "Me, Elmer, and the girl he was dating at the time were getting out of the car, and this guy drives up," Welch said. "He's scruffy, hasn't shaven, is dirty looking, and he looked like he was four-wheel driving for a week or camping. He came to retrieve his Jeep, and once he came up, I knew who it was. He was very unattractive, very dirty…I don't know. He was very distant and gave off a vibe as if he wasn't really interested in meeting anybody.

"So here was another actor I thought a lot of, and you could tell he was just burned out of the whole scene. I don't know if he was drunk or what, but you could tell that this guy was not only unkempt but probably doing a lot of drugs.

"I imagine for him it was keeping up the pretense of his image. There's a certain image you have to portray, and it's hard to let your guard down. That's the vibe I got from Steve McQueen that day. For some reason, I felt very sad and sorry for him."

With his home life fairly situated, McQueen was ready to go back after a yearlong break. He had just two provisions for agent Freddie Fields on his next film project: no out-of-state locales and a fat percentage on the back end. Fields delivered on a package that turned out to be the biggest commercial venture of McQueen's career and a personal financial bonanza that set him up for years. For agreeing to star in *The Towering Inferno*, the story of a fire inside the world's tallest skyscraper, McQueen was paid $1 million up front and 10 percent of the gross profits. It was a deal that ultimately yielded him an unheard-of sum of $14.5 million. And best of all, McQueen finally got top billing over his long-time professional rival Paul Newman.

The genesis of *The Towering Inferno* was unusual, even by Hollywood's standards. The movie was a coproduction between 20ᵗʰ Century Fox and Warner Brothers, a situation that was sparked when the two studios bought similar novels (*The Tower* by Richard Martin Stern and *The Glass Inferno* by Frank Robinson and Tom Scortia) for six-figure sums and wisely decided not to compete.[5] But they did not compromise when it came to hiring the man who could turn the $14 million production into a worldwide blockbuster—superstar producer Irwin Allen.

The Towering Inferno would be the biggest, grandest, and best disaster movie of them all, with approximately 100 stuntmen, 57 sets (of which only eight remained standing when filming ended), five locations, and four different camera crews.

Allen was meticulous in his work. Like John Sturges, Allen storyboarded his scripts and supplemented *The Towering Inferno* with 2,600 paintings to detail the action. "All the work is done in advance. I want no hysteria on the set," Allen said. "I believe in doing it visually, not with words. Words conjure up different things in different people's minds. Pictures are graphic and more precise for what I need." It was a vision that fell perfectly in line with McQueen's philosophy of filmmaking.

According to director John Guillermin, the role of the fire chief (known as Mario Infantino in the first script) was considerably smaller and originally offered to Ernest Borgnine, with McQueen intended to play the architect. "The fire chief had 10 pages in the first draft, but Steve had tremendous instinct for the heart of the picture," Guillermin said. "He felt the role of the architect was pasted together. Steve said, 'If someone of my caliber can play the architect, I'll play the fire chief.'" It was a shrewd move because the fireman is essentially a hero putting out the fire and saving lives. Although the architect character has awkward flashes of heroism, he is ultimately a party to the failure of the skyscraper.

McQueen admitted he once had visions of becoming a fireman. "I think there's not a kid in the world who hasn't at some time been interested in the fire department," McQueen said. "When I was a kid, I always looked up to firemen with their shiny red trucks and coats and helmets. It's kind of typical I think to have a hero thing for firemen as you grow up, and then it disappears." For McQueen, his "hero thing" reemerged in the form of movie magic, and his keen instincts served him well.

Producers chased down Paul Newman to play the role of building architect Doug Roberts, and they offered to reward Newman handsomely. While McQueen

---

5   The two studios agreed to split the production costs right down the middle. Fox kept the U.S. box-office receipts while Warner Brothers collected from the rest of the world.

never looked back, Newman later regretted his decision and felt he prostituted his talent for a big payday. As a result, Newman let down his guard and allowed McQueen the opportunity to eclipse him on film—a rare lapse in judgment for one of cinema's most distinguished careers. Essentially, McQueen stole the picture both in a monetary sense but also in terms of star performance.

The question of billing arose once again as it had on *Butch Cassidy and the Sundance Kid* five years before. McQueen and Newman were rivals. Newman may not have seen it this way, but McQueen certainly did. Virtually two decades before, McQueen had been trying to break into movies while Newman was riding in limos, collecting big paychecks, and nabbing choice roles, always one step ahead of McQueen. In McQueen's eyes, beating Newman was confirmation among McQueen's peers that he was numero uno once and for all. Both actors had blue eyes and were pinups for a generation. But in many ways, McQueen and Newman were polar opposites. McQueen had come from a hard beginning and was the rugged tough-guy actor wielding the gun. Newman had a more privileged upbringing and did not court controversy in the tabloids. Newman was the good, wholesome blue-eyed boy, while McQueen was still the edgier, more dangerous force of nature. The public was split in its loyalties in the same way one was either a Beatles or a Rolling Stones fan, a coffee drinker or a tea drinker. McQueen felt the winner in this arena would settle the score for good.

This time around, the billing was handled using the same method proposed for *Butch Cassidy and the Sundance Kid*. McQueen got over his paranoia and took the name on the left-hand side, which appeared first but was slightly lower, while Newman took the name on the right-hand side, which was slightly above but appeared second. McQueen was given the choice and opted for being billed first and slightly lower on the basis that people read left to right. The angle worked, and McQueen came across as the star. The stage was set for a cinematic showdown, and McQueen already had the drop.

Fox and Warner Brothers surrounded their twin superstars with an all-star cast that included William Holden, Faye Dunaway,[6] Fred Astaire, Robert Wagner, Susan Blakely, Richard Chamberlain, Jennifer Jones, Robert Vaughn, and O.J. Simpson.

With Newman on board, McQueen went into full bunker mentality and systematically dismantled the script. Adaptor Stirling Silliphant had taken seven main figures from each of the original novels purchased by the two studios

---

6   Dunaway's role was originally offered to Natalie Wood, who turned it down because she felt the script was "mediocre."

and incorporated them into the screenplay. McQueen counted the lines of the fire chief and architect, and he noticed that Newman had a dozen more lines. McQueen, who was never one to fight for dialogue, insisted that Silliphant give both characters the same amount of lines. In one of the greatest displays of Hollywood hubris, McQueen badgered a Fox executive to call Silliphant, who was on a deep-sea fishing expedition, to come back to shore and fix the problem. "McQueen insisted that Silliphant come back to shore that afternoon and write the 12 lines," said the Fox executive. "So he did, which satisfied Steve. But I can tell you, Silliphant wasn't too happy about having his trip ruined."

Silliphant didn't realize he was dealing with a man on a 18-year mission—a man on fire. "Steve would not tell me what he didn't like about certain parts of the dialogue," Silliphant said. "He just said, 'I don't like that shit.' I kept confronting him about it. I said, 'That's not shit. It happens to be very brilliant. Tell me what you don't like.' Finally, he took me out in the hall and said, 'Look, I'm not an educated guy. I was a street kid. I did time. Okay, I can't say certain things…certain words I can't say. I have trouble with Zs and Ss…Honestly, the dialogue is okay. I just can't say it." One tongue-twister Silliphant changed was the line, "There are Ping-Pong balls in the back room that are combustible." Silliphant offered years later, "Steve has the nagging instinct of what is right for him based on his ability. He doesn't like long speeches. He likes them to be terse, sharp, almost proverbial."

Together with Silliphant, McQueen changed the character's name from Mario Infantino to Michael O'Hallorhan and created a feisty but inspirational fire battalion chief who, like McQueen, as one writer stated, "emerges as the outsider, existing within his own set of principles and beliefs."

The beauty of the role is manifold, and the character and the performance are inspired. McQueen does not appear until 43 minutes into the film, when the fire is already raging and tensions are high. All the characters so far are either partly to blame for the fire or have side-story agenda. The stage is set for a hero, and that's McQueen. In his opening scene, McQueen marches in with absolute authority and tramples over everyone who enters into his sphere, especially Newman. Also, the ploy of ensuring that the fire chief and his character have the same amount of lines means that because Newman's character is around from the start, he has used up most of his lines by the halfway point. When McQueen appears on screen, it is virtually him all the way. His character is not hampered by a cumbersome and padded backstory like all the others. O'Hallorhan's story is simple—he is the courageous one who saves lives.

There is no doubt that McQueen had the right instincts in choosing the fire chief; he is every inch the hero. Instead of a knight on horseback in shining armor, he arrives in a patrol car in a shimmering fire helmet with an axe instead of a sword. It may have been an epic picture with an elite cast, but one star was shining brighter than all the others.

McQueen was also willing to put his body on the line, and he explained his philosophy when approaching the role: "I try not to take myself too seriously. But at the same time, they pay me an awful lot of money to do my job, and I do everything I can to see that it's done right," McQueen said. "I believe that today's audiences are smart and that you have the responsibility to articulate a part accurately. I mean, I don't look at it as play-acting. If I'm going to play a fireman, then for the period of that film—I am a fireman. For three months, or whatever, they own me, and I have a responsibility as a professional to do the best I can."

McQueen wasn't just blathering. "When Steve McQueen decided to become an actor, we lost a helluva firefighter," said Richard Baker, a captain on the Los Angeles Fire Department who, along with Battalion Chief Pete Lucarelli, served as technical advisers on the film. Baker said McQueen had the courage, physical tools, and mentality of a firefighter. He proved this a week before principal photography when a flash fire touched off the million-dollar blaze at two soundstages at Samuel Goldwyn Studios in West Hollywood on May 6, 1974.

McQueen had been training on another lot[7] with Peter Lucarelli and Richard Baker when the two men sped off to the real fire. Richard Baker recalled, "We were talking about the movie and Steve had just finished telling us, 'Ground floor fires only for this firefighter.' He freely admitted he was afraid of heights," Baker said. "Then the call came in over the radio and Pete looked at Steve and said, 'You want to see a real fire up close? This is as close as you're gonna get.' Steve said he was game and nodded his head yes." Luckily, for McQueen, it was a single-story fire.

Donning a fire hat, boots, and heavy jacket, McQueen joined 250 other firefighters and battled the blaze.[8] As Lucarelli, Baker, and McQueen entered the building, they grabbed on to a hose and started dousing a fire. One alert fireman caught sight of McQueen and did a double take. "Holy shit! Steve McQueen! My wife will never believe this." Without missing a beat, McQueen replied, "Neither will mine."

The incident made the national news wires around the country, including *Time* magazine. Reporters jockeyed to get an interview with the superstar, but he

---

7   A portion of *The Towering Inferno* was shot on the 10-acre Goldwyn lot when the actual fire erupted.

8   An investigation later showed the fire started when a studio light short circuited and sparks fell on top of a polyfoam cave used in the children's TV show *Sigmund and the Sea Monsters*.

granted only one—to Richard Baker, who was editor of the *Fireman's Grapevine*, an industry trade newsletter for firefighters. McQueen said the Goldwyn fire opened his eyes and gave him a real-world education. "I'm ashamed to admit, I was naïve about it all until Chief Lucarelli had me lose my virginity at the Goldwyn fire. One thing I did know was that the firemen seemed to be steady people, ready to help one another. It wasn't until the Goldwyn fire, though, where I had an opportunity to see them in action, that I realized how they had to work together and that their lives depended on the buddy system."

The only thing the public cared about was how the two superstars would get along and mesh on screen. Privately, McQueen and Newman got on famously, according to costar Robert Vaughn, who observed that the two men acted like old college buddies. They shared beers, swapped war stories, and ribbed each other. McQueen called Newman "Ol' Blue Eyes," joked about the value of their autographs ("You know, two Paul Newman autographs will get you one Steve McQueen autograph"), and ragged on Newman's wife, actress Joanne Woodward, for making Paul sell his motorcycle. ("Paul fell off his bike, and now he can't play anymore.") Professionally was another story.

Silliphant said trying to please both men was an arduous task. "Paul Newman and Steve McQueen, while good friends, had a natural, shall we say...jealousy might be too strong a word, but they had competitive instincts," Silliphant said. "Paul would come in and say, 'Why does Steve always have the last line in each of our scenes?' Then I'd make an adjustment. Then Steve would come in and say, 'Why are you changing this scene? I like it the way it is. You've ruined the whole thing.' I said, 'Where have I changed it?' He said, 'Well, you've added a line of dialogue for Newman.' And I couldn't say to Steve, 'Paul wanted it.' I had to take the blame. So I'd put McQueen's line in and Newman would come back and say, 'What's going on?' They never confronted each other. They never said to each other, 'Don't mess with my scene, baby.'"

Composer-songwriter Al Kasha, who cowrote *The Towering Inferno*'s theme song, "We May Never Love Like This Again," with his partner Joel Hirschhorn, visited the set to get a feel for the movie. What he got was an up-close look at a simmering rivalry that was palpable, even to a newcomer on the set. "I sensed that competition, yes, and they were both competitive with each other behind each other's backs. More McQueen than Newman," Kasha said. "Newman was more cooperative than McQueen in general. I felt that Newman put up with it okay, but McQueen was tough about it. He was a tough guy. I remember him looking at the playback monitor, and he would go through everything line by line, scene by scene, and he would ask to make changes if he didn't like the take. I think

McQueen felt that Newman got better roles than he did and felt secondary to Newman. He was a competitive guy, and he struggled to make it. And when he made it, he let you know he had made it."

One day Kasha walked into the middle of a conversation between producer Irwin Allen and agent Freddie Fields, who were arguing over the film's poster. "Freddie thought the movie poster should just read, 'McQueen/Newman,' while Irwin wanted a shot of a burning building and the film's title. Freddie even threatened to pull the two stars from the movie, which was too much to believe, because they were in the middle of filming. Freddie then turned to me and asked, 'Al, what do you think?' I said, 'Listen, I just wrote the song. I don't want to get involved.'"

Kasha sensed that McQueen was much more motivated than Newman and was like a prizefighter closing in on his opponent, ready to deliver the knockout punch. "Steve knew this was his big shot, and I admired that he was very ambitious. I felt Steve was much better cast than Newman and got the better role," Kasha said. "He read his lines very naturally and felt he came off much better in the picture than Newman. He was clearly motivated."

Newman's longtime friend A.E. Hotchner revealed that Newman was uninspired and angry when Hotchner visited him in his dressing room. "For the first time, I fell for the goddamn numbers," Newman told Hotchner. "I did this turkey for a million and 10 percent of the gross, but it's the first and last time, I swear."

Hotchner also said Newman was fed up with McQueen's dogged pursuit and his need to prove himself as the movie's big star. "You want to know what chickenshit goes on? McQueen actually made a count of our lines of dialogue, and when he found out I had 20 more lines than he did, he made the producer fatten up his part so he had the same number as me." One way to view this is that at least McQueen had the desire to make the demands needed to establish himself as highly as he possibly could. You could view them as petty acts—or the actions of a motivated and hungry individual.

Richard Baker explained another possibility as to why Newman didn't have his eyes on the prize. "Newman seemed to be pretty heavily occupied with the script girl, and he'd disappear in the dressing room periodically," Baker said. "God bless Joanne Woodward, but when you're operating on that level in that business with the charisma and the attractiveness of the people involved, you know, it's not surprising."

Baker said McQueen, on the other hand, was enamored with Ali MacGraw and enjoying married life. "She had just left Robert Evans and boy, you couldn't separate them with a climbing fork," Baker said. "They were very much in love."

MacGraw recalled a special dinner for *The Towering Inferno* where their chemistry was off the charts. "I came back to my room in the motel, and there were daisies and white roses everywhere," MacGraw said. "He loved daises; there were hundreds and hundreds of them."

Sadly, they experienced a low on the set as well. MacGraw happened to be sitting with McQueen on the 20th Century Fox lot when she looked down and saw a pool of blood. She'd had a miscarriage. She hadn't even known she was pregnant, but it was particularly upsetting to Steve. "He always felt that if we had a child, we could save our marriage," MacGraw said years later.

Somehow McQueen powered through that emotional loss and got back to the business at hand—taking Newman to task. The two insisted on performing their own stunts, which required them to battle both water and fire. But it was McQueen who sucked all the oxygen out of the room when he and Newman appeared together on screen. In those three scenes, never has McQueen dominated the silver screen with such ease.

McQueen still had one trick up his sleeve, and it was an ace. McQueen ensured that in the final exchange between their characters at the end of the film that he got the last word:

"You know, they'll keep building them higher and higher. And I'll keep eatin' smoke until one of you guys asks us how to build 'em," McQueen said in the film.

"Okay, I'm asking," Newman replied.

"You know where to find me. So long, architect."

McQueen bagged the glory of having the last word. Instead of bullets, McQueen was firing something far more effective than any shootout from *The Getaway* or *The Magnificent Seven*.

Although the blockbuster has not aged well, the movie is entertaining, randomly bewildering (O.J. Simpson pitched as the next big action hero), and has a cheesy '70s aesthetic. However, *The Towering Inferno* was a technical marvel in its day and was the most authentic fire-related movie up to that point. It also had the aura of a true Hollywood spectacle, dazzling critics and audiences alike.[9]

It also caught fire at the box office, setting records around the globe and becoming the highest-grossing picture of 1974. It raked in $116 million in the United States alone and almost doubled that figure worldwide.[10]

Though McQueen stood at street level amid the smoldering ruins at the end of the movie, in reality he was more like Godzilla dominating Hollywood beneath

---

9   Hollywood also rewarded the movie with three Academy Awards, two Golden Globes, and two BAFTAs.

10 Adjusted for inflation, *The Towering Inferno*'s domestic take in 2010 would be equivalent to approximately $670 million.

him as he virtually stood taller than the 138-story skyscraper he had just battled in the epic film. His popularity punched through the stratosphere. He had the box-office receipts and the paychecks to back him up, and he had the column inches, fan letters, and domination over his old rivals to placate even his ego. In every single respect, McQueen was now the undisputed King of Hollywood.

What he did next took everyone by surprise: McQueen doused his flaming-hot career by jumping into the abyss and waving good-bye to the public for the next five years.

32

ADRIFT

WHILE *THE TOWERING INFERNO* SET BOX-OFFICE RECORDS around the world, tucked away inside the movie's press kit was an ominous statement by Steve McQueen that seemed more like a farewell speech to the public rather than an innocuous quote to bolster the film. "Actors have a certain peak life span. There's maybe 10 years when they can do no wrong," McQueen said. "After that, their careers level off to a share of hits and misses.

"I don't consider acting a great achievement. I've really made very few films altogether. I only come back and make a movie when I need the bread.

"Pretty soon I'm going to go up to the mountains and disappear. I want to sit and watch a guy change a tire on a motorbike or watch an Angus cow eat. I want to lead a slower and more leisurely life.

"There's very little to say anymore."

There had been no leveling out for McQueen since the '50s. He had scaled the heights of superstardom and had remained in the public eye for almost 15 years. With each passing year, his popularity grew. His film comeback after *Le Mans* had been nothing short of miraculous. The worldwide receipts on *The Getaway*, *Papillon*, and *The Towering Inferno*—his last three films—had totaled close to half a billion in worldwide revenue. The last of these three all-star blockbuster films not only padded his bank account to the tune of $14.5 million but also finally gave him the financial independence most actors can only dream of. It's called "fuck you" money.

Instead of pursuing the brass ring, McQueen thumbed his nose at Hollywood. After 24 films in 15 years, he was emotionally spent and in desperate need of a break.

He sequestered himself with Ali MacGraw, and the two dropped out. Trancas Beach, California, had become a cocoon of self-banishment. First wife

Neile observed, "After *The Towering Inferno*, it was as if the effort to catch Paul Newman had tired him out."

Psychologist Peter O. Whitmer said Neile was right on the mark. "After *The Towering Inferno*, Steve McQueen had finally conquered his eternal, external enemy. He'd done this by the change in roles in the movie; by the change in the number of spoken lines; and in the placement of 'blurbage' on the ad, etc. He had conquered Paul Newman and thus lost a big chunk of his motivation.

"So if you find yourself in such a situation, what do you do? One, you drop out. Two, you do not dare do another movie, as making a movie is always a career risk, and why risk being knocked off the very top of that pinnacle? That next movie might just be a turkey that will bring crashing down your life's creation, the tower of success."

McQueen had even bequeathed his box-office crown to cinema's next big thing—movie star Burt Reynolds. While getting fitted for his wardrobe at Western Costume Company in Hollywood, Reynolds recalled that McQueen walked into the dressing room and said, "It's all yours, kid." Reynolds was baffled.

"What?"

"Number one, kid. It's yours," McQueen said. "I'm stepping down."[1]

McQueen grew a shaggy beard, let his trademark blond locks grow long, wore grungy clothes, and put on a few extra pounds.[2] McQueen systematically became unrecognizable and reveled in his newfound anonymity. The King of Cool was in his element, living on the edge of peace with no agenda or long-term plans.

After *The Towering Inferno* wrapped, it was time to relax. McQueen and MacGraw took a motorcycle jaunt to southern Idaho to witness Evel Knievel's ill-fated rocket ride over the 1,500-foot-wide Snake Canyon on September 8, 1974. McQueen also scored front-row tickets to a professional boxing match where they were sprayed by blood and sweat; MacGraw in turn took him to the ballet. "Baryshnikov and Gelsey Kirkland—I said, 'You can't not go!' It blew his mind," MacGraw recalled in 2010. "Mary Tyler Moore was sitting in front of us. She said, 'How amazing to see you here!' I wanted to smack her—what a comment! I think she was being flirtatious."

---

1   McQueen's instincts were uncanny. Burt Reynolds became the world's biggest box-office star from 1976 to 1980.

2   Despite a *National Enquirer* story that McQueen's weight ballooned to 240 pounds, his weight was at the most 185 pounds, said friend and karate instructor Pat Johnson. "I should know," Johnson said. "Steve was my biggest client, and it would have ruined my reputation if he'd gotten out of shape."

The McQueens skipped the gala opening for *The Towering Inferno*, but they did get dressed up for the American Film Institute's Salute to James Cagney on March 13, 1974. They hobnobbed with the likes of Paul Newman and Joanne Woodward, Frank Sinatra, John Lennon, Elton John, and Ronald and Nancy Reagan, and they sat with rocker Mick Jagger.[3] Later that month, Steve and Ali attended a fund-raiser for actor James Stacy (*Lancer*), who had been sideswiped on his motorcycle by a drunken driver in late 1973. The accident left Stacy a multiple-amputee and instantly killed his girlfriend. "After the accident, Steve McQueen and Ali MacGraw visited me in the hospital," Stacy said. "I told Steve what I planned to do when I was able to get out of there. I was going to tackle every sport I could, one-armed and one-legged. Steve listened, and when they turned to leave, he said to me, 'You ought to film it.'"[4]

What was supposed to be a fund-raiser for Stacy turned out to be an homage to McQueen, said friend Pat Johnson, who attended with his wife, Sue, and his boss at the time, Chuck Norris. "This was right after *The Towering Inferno* came out, and the cream of the crop from Hollywood came over to Steve to shake his hand," Johnson recalled. "Clint Eastwood, John Lennon, Burt Reynolds, and Carol Burnett all came over to the table. It was like they were paying homage to him. They were all in awe of him. He was not in awe of anybody."

James Stacy said McQueen and Ali MacGraw came by his table at the end of the night to pay their respects. Stacy said he asked McQueen if he would take him on the ocean for the first time since the accident. McQueen obliged. "I mean, who was I to ask Steve McQueen to do a favor for me, right? He was so above me in terms of our careers," Stacy recalled in 2010. "He had me over his house in Malibu and took me outside in the ocean and taught me how to body surf. It was the first time in a long time I felt good. I just loved that guy."

Stacy's fund-raiser was virtually McQueen's last public appearance for the next six years, and McQueen faded into the background as a means of self-preservation. "I think stardom is always an entrapment for people," said *Los Angeles Times* film critic Charles Champlin, who befriended McQueen. "They lose their mobility, and Steve lost that mobility. You almost have to go into hiding if you're

---

3 Jagger had penned "Star, Star" on 1973's *Goat's Head Soup*. The song was an ode to rock groupies with a naughty nod to McQueen, who gave the singer legal permission to use his name in the song.

4 The money from the benefit, "An Evening with the Friends of Jim Stacy" financed a documentary that showed the actor's new life after the motorcycle accident. Stacy was later awarded $1.9 million by a jury who deemed the bar continued to serve the intoxicated driver who ran into Stacy's motorcycle.

a certain kind of star. I think it galled Steve more than any other star. He was not comfortable as a public figure. He was a very private man."

McQueen said as much, too. "Being an actor is a gas; being a movie star is a pain in the ass. When that happens, you stop your personal growth. A movie star has a very strange situation going today. To have your identification and your obscurity is the ultimate. But if you have heat on you all the time…people constantly wanting me to live up to the stuff they see on the screen all the time… I'll die."

Having made himself unrecognizable, McQueen could move about as he pleased. Friend Gene Lesser said McQueen sporadically came by his Sunset Strip office wearing a construction helmet and tool belt, telling the secretary he was a telephone repairman. "He'd stop by and lie on my leather couch in my office, and we'd just bullshit about the old days," Lesser said. "That's the kind of fame he had, even in a town that dealt with celebrities. It was as if he just wanted to get away from everything and everybody."

McQueen also had a freestanding job as a bartender at the Old Place, a funky restaurant and bar nestled in the Agoura Hills on Mulholland Drive. The Old Place catered to an eclectic mix of bikers, actors, beach bums, cowboys, and local characters who made the establishment their own. McQueen often worked behind the bar, pouring beer and wine and serving patrons. Bartender Florence Esposito, who spent many evenings with McQueen, said it was therapeutic for the movie star. "Nothing made Steve happier than pouring drinks to unsuspecting customers," Esposito said. "When you work in such proximity to someone, you come to know who they are and where their heart is, and Steve had a big one. When he loved you, he loved you. When he cared about you, you could genuinely see it in his eyes. And he had the best eyes. Kind eyes you never forget."

His kindness was tempered with volatility and unpredictability. Something deep within was festering, but he didn't verbalize his feelings and no one around him understood what he was experiencing. McQueen's mission in his personal life had always been crystal clear—that is until the devil offered his confections. McQueen spent most of his days drinking beer, eating whatever he felt like, smoking pot, and riding aimlessly on his motorcycle. MacGraw, whose father was an alcoholic, grew increasingly alarmed. "He had this mood-swing thing that I suppose reminded me of my father. I mean, 'Who are you today? What time is it now? You're tender and bright and sensitive and loving.' Then boom! Nothing I could do was good enough."

Escapism was a lifelong ideal for McQueen. He had tried it with motorcycles, cars, women, and booze, but he could not find it now. He underwent a near metamorphosis to hide his identity to paradoxically allow him to truly be himself away from the public eye. Living the dream of freedom and shunning the trappings of stardom sounded ideal to him. However, the fact was he had been striving to be the biggest star on the planet for nearly the last quarter of a decade, so it was all he knew and it had become virtually his sole focus. Without this goal and with so much free time left to contemplate and slow down, he was struggling. McQueen never did anything by halves, but this was the equivalent of going cold turkey. His identity was somewhat in crisis—was he a movie star, racer, average guy, sex symbol, humanitarian, or rebel? He wanted to be all of these, but he did not want to be defined by any of them, and it was taking its toll on him and those around him. He was a caterpillar with a chrysalis forming around him. The question was, what would emerge from the shell? A butterfly, a more refined and elegant human being, or something else?

Until that time, however, McQueen was adrift. His relationship with Ali MacGraw began to unravel as a result of his midlife demons. Theirs was a war of wills, a war of words, and a war of silence. They told friends they were both born under the sign of Aries, which was why they butted heads frequently. Their fights were becoming more commonplace, and the toxic vapors of their relationship had consumed the house. Ali was known to throw dishes, glasses, and anything she could get her hands on. Steve was known to get physical as well. Chad recalled an incident when he and Terry were watching television at their Palm Springs home when a fight erupted. "Ali, you need to cool off, damn it!" they heard Steve yell. As they looked toward the window, they saw a large object fall from above and splash into the pool below. Both McQueen kids looked at each other in amazement.

"What was that?" Chad asked.

"I think it was Ali," Terry said. "Dad just threw her off the terrace."

MacGraw wrote years later that McQueen had hit her only once—a backhand that left a cut above her eyebrow as a result of a terrible blowout. MacGraw said McQueen was immediately remorseful and checked her into a hotel that night for a cooling-off period. "Getting married is very romantic; being married is not quite as romantic," Terry McQueen wryly noted. "Ali really wanted to work. She was a megastar at that point. Now he wants her to stay home, be there to make breakfast in the morning, cook dinner at night."

Their spats sometimes spilled over in public. The same publications that wrote of their steamy affair a few years before now gleefully reported there was trouble in paradise. *The Chicago Tribune's* Aaron Gold wrote of a meltdown at a Malibu bar and restaurant in February 1975. "Reports out of Hollywood for

the last year have had Steve McQueen and Ali MacGraw on the verge of breaking up," Gold wrote. "But the lovebirds say it isn't so, despite the recent *Who's
Afraid of Virginia Woolf* screaming match (that scared the waitresses) at the Crazy
Horse Saloon in Malibu." They also engaged in a fiery screaming match in the
lobby of the Los Angeles Dorothy Chandler Pavilion Theater that drew a score
of spectators. McQueen eventually stormed away, leaving his wife to watch the
second half of the show alone. She was escorted home by Robert Wagner and
Natalie Wood.

McQueen possessed a legendary stubbornness, while Ali had an ever-present
independent streak. She loved art, ballet, classical music, and theater, while his
interests remained bikes, beer, and his new hobby, collecting old trucks. Steve
expected his "old lady" to be there every night with meat and potatoes on the
table. "There were certain kinds of independent lady behaviors that I showed that
really threatened him on a profound level," MacGraw said in retrospect. "Not on
the level that the press likes to call 'Steve McQueen wouldn't let Ali MacGraw
work.' That's a total distortion. It was a much more profound thing. It was a deep,
deep sense of being abandoned, like a child."

Psychologist Peter O. Whitmer said he couldn't agree more. "Steve's relationship with both Neile and Ali involved close and strong emotions. I think he cared
deeply for Ali, but his 15 years with Neile had altered some of his attitudes toward
marriage," Whitmer said. "First, he had actually gotten his Norman Rockwell
'idealized' marriage to work—until the incident while making *Le Mans*. That
erased trust down to a nubbin. Consequently, with Ali, now he had to resort to
extremes to impose controls over her, thus protecting himself. Also, it was his
competitiveness and fear of a strong leading lady that caused him to pass on
making *Play Misty For Me*. And Ali was feisty, if not strong.

"Perhaps he had concerns that she might have eclipsed him professionally.
He had a taste of being known as 'Mr. Adams' and playing second fiddle when
married to Neile before he hit the big time, and he had no intention of ever being
back in that position. He was the superstar, no one else."

MacGraw's frustration over her marriage and dormant career boiled over. She
began seeing a Beverly Hills psychiatrist four times a week to save her marriage
and what little bit of sanity she had left. McQueen also went to see an analyst
but made MacGraw take a vow of silence. "Don't ever tell anyone I am seeing a
shrink," he warned. "I don't want anyone to think I am weak." However, he missed
so many scheduled appointments it was obvious he wasn't ready to deal with "his
stuff." Years later, MacGraw said Steve was "very damaged, and I don't mean that

at all in a nasty way. He was a combination of incredible darkness and anger and mystery and almost childlike vulnerability. His mood swings were incredible."

She also shouldered some of the blame by stating she was inauthentic at the beginning of their relationship. "I didn't state my case: 'You know, even though I told you I'd rather be on a motorcycle opening a can of beer, the truth is I'd rather go to Paris,'" MacGraw said. "If you don't say who you are up front, then you don't get to wake up two years later and say, 'Oh man, am I sick of doing this!'"

Steve made little digs at his wife's physical appearance—the crooked teeth, the knobby knees, lack of bosom—that eroded her confidence. It also sent her to the gym, where she engaged in rigorous daily workouts to keep her body lean and taut. MacGraw said it was "to make myself desirable, because he was the most desirable man on the planet, and I would think, I can't possibly be desirable enough for this creature. Every woman in the restaurant is looking at him!"

Conversely, McQueen was equally intimidated by MacGraw, whom he affectionately nicknamed his "New York intellectual." Friend Katy Haber said, "That was one of the conflicting issues in their relationship—her intellect, her consciousness, her creativity, and him always trying to rise to her ability. At the same time, he suppressed it in order for him to be the all-powerful one."

McQueen tried to sabotage a 1975 photo shoot when MacGraw was asked by fashion photographer Francesco Scavullo to appear in his book *Scavullo on Beauty*. MacGraw, who hadn't felt glamorous in many moons, immediately snapped up the photographer's invitation to fly to New York. Convinced Ali was carrying on a secret affair, McQueen made a cross-country flight to the East Coast and prevailed upon his wife the night before the shoot. Stunned and disheartened by his lack of faith, she slept in the bathtub while he took the apartment's only bed. Makeup artist Way Bandy had to Pan-Cake the dark circles under her eyes the following morning.

Steve also ruined Ali's 37th birthday a few months later when she dined at The Bistro, a trendy Beverly Hills eatery on Canon Drive, with a few close friends. The sound of McQueen's revving motorcycle engine shattered the evening's solitude. He then burst through the doors, weaving in and out of tables, holding a birthday cake with a shit-eating grin on his face. Motorcycle buddy Ty Ritter said MacGraw insisted McQueen make an appearance, and so he complied. "Steve set it all up with the owner beforehand," Ritter said. "He said he had to go in and pay tribute to Ali, but a group of us followed and watched through the window. He popped a wheelie, went over the curb and through the door, and everyone scattered but Ali. She just sat there with her jaw clinched tight. Let's just say she wasn't amused.

Before Steve exited out the back, he handed the owner this envelope stuffed with cash and then left. It was quite a scene."

Shunning most public appearances, industry parties, and private get-togethers, McQueen steeled himself for the rare ones he did attend. MacGraw said McQueen's anxiety almost paralyzed him from attending a Sue Mengers party in honor of England's Princess Margaret, Countess of Snowdon. She recalled, "He got high on coke. He knew it was bad for him. He got these catastrophic depressions, I mean the scariest. I said, 'Why in the world do you do this? The level of misery you set yourself up for!' He said, 'I'm so upset.' He had to be with his pack or he was terrified. It was heartbreaking."

McQueen was weighed down in emotional baggage. He could not move forward, and it appeared as if his life was stuck in reverse. In a fit of rage, he removed the mailbox from his home and tossed it into the ocean. He arranged for the mail to be delivered to the local gas station, where Chad was often dispatched to pick it up. McQueen also requested $50,000 to simply read a script. His new agent, Marvin Josephson, told him no one would pay it.

"Great. Then I won't have to read any more lousy screenplays," McQueen said testily.

Some people he couldn't turn away, like the formidable Katharine Hepburn. She showed up at Trancas hoping to recruit McQueen for a movie project called *Grace Quigley*. Hepburn wanted McQueen to play a hit man hired to off some of her friends in a nursing home. Ali MacGraw recalled the memorable meeting: "I was very excited and nervous. Just before she arrived, Steve said, 'I've got to go for a ride,' and he got on his motorcycle and drove off, leaving me to face the great Hepburn. She arrived, quite annoyed he wasn't there, and announced that she was hungry and would I make her lunch? The only thing I had was a salad, which she didn't want, and some canned soup. I made that, and when Steve came back, she was all charm with him—and he with her—and she complained I made bad soup."[5]

McQueen was indiscriminate to those whom he rebuffed, including *Getaway* producer David Foster, who came to him with a property written by A.J. Carothers called *Fancy Hardware*. Foster said the script's plot revolved around a womanizing salesman (to be played by McQueen) in the 1930s who meets and falls in love with a spinster (MacGraw). Foster said it was one of the best properties he had ever read. It was the perfect comeback vehicle for McQueen, and it would be a

---

5   Hepburn had to wait for another decade to make *Grace Quigley* and snared actor Nick Nolte in the role she had envisioned for McQueen.

triumphant return to the big screen for MacGraw in a role that would have suited her well. Not only did McQueen pull out at the 11th hour, but he turned over the script to his First Artists partner Barbra Streisand, who also wanted to produce the picture. McQueen didn't realize in optioning the property to Streisand, he gave up Foster's role as producer. Today Foster defends McQueen's actions but admitted it put a strain on their friendship. "I don't think Steve realized what he did. Yeah, I was really pissed back then, but I also realize Steve did a lot for me," Foster said. "He helped me build my public relations business. He would go around telling people, 'You gotta sign with Foster. He's the best publicity guy around.' He got me tons of clients, and I'm grateful for that. And *The Getaway* made me a lot of money, and I was still appreciative. But Steve's last act was a beauty; you just can't understand what that did to me.

"I think the bottom line was that he did not want Ali to work. He met her on our film and took her away from somebody. He was concerned the same thing might happen to him."

McQueen kept turning down plum movie offers, some that eventually became blockbusters, including *First Blood*, *One Flew Over the Cuckoo's Nest*, *The Gauntlet*, and *The Bodyguard*. And in November 1975, McQueen refused the lead in Francis Ford Coppola's *Apocalypse Now*.

Coppola met with McQueen and offered him $1.5 million to star in his epic Vietnam picture, but the idea of spending almost four months in the Philippines didn't exactly thrill McQueen. Taking a cue from Colonel Tom Parker, Elvis Presley's wily manager, he didn't say no but simply put his price out of reach.

"That's fine. I'll take the $1.5 million up front," McQueen paused, "and I'll take another $1.5 million deferred."

The director countered with a smaller role[6] that would take only three weeks to film. McQueen agreed but said his price still stood at $3 million. Coppola balked. "I thought about it for a very long time," Coppola recalled. "On the one hand, [McQueen] makes a valid point that his appearance in the picture has a solid commercial value regardless of the number of weeks he works. On the other hand, they all weigh how much other stars are getting per week. I began to see if this kept up, the industry would some day be paying $3 million for eight hours, plus overtime, and [you would] have to shoot at the actor's house. I can't blame him for asking."

McQueen was demanding by putting his price so high, but his instincts were probably very sound, because *Apocalypse Now* turned out to be one of the

---

6   The role of Colonel Kurtz was eventually played by Marlon Brando.

most lengthy and troubled productions in cinematic history. It was fraught with disaster, delays, extreme weather conditions, and health problems for the male lead due to stress (actor Martin Sheen suffered a heart attack). The movie nearly ruined everyone's careers. That was the kind of stress McQueen didn't need, and he dodged a bullet by turning it down. He may have lost his drive to make films, but he had lost none of his business acumen nor his sense of self-preservation.

He almost got his asking price from producer Joe Levine, who was willing to pay McQueen $2 million for a cameo appearance in Richard Attenborough's World War II epic, *A Bridge Too Far*. McQueen wanted $3 million for three weeks of work, which would have required him to fly to the Netherlands. But there was also a twist—McQueen wanted Levine to buy his $470,000 Palm Springs home and add a friend to the film's payroll at $50,000. Levine was outraged and secured the services of Robert Redford, who took the role for $2 million. Levine told a reporter, "We made a movie back in the old days [*Nevada Smith*]. He was a nice guy then, but money and fame can do funny things to a guy's head."

Director Mel Brooks said shortly after Levine's negotiation he received a surprise phone call from McQueen inquiring about a cameo role in his latest comedy, *Silent Movie*. "The day after we signed Paul Newman aboard, we got a call from Steve McQueen. Steve McQueen! A true recluse, calling me!" Brooks said in astonishment. "Here's a guy, McQueen. You leave a script for him at a gas station on the Malibu Highway, and along comes a guy in a German helmet, riding a motorcycle with a sidecar, to pick it up for McQueen. He calls, he wants to know if the wheelchair part is still available. This was the week after he turned down $3 million for three weeks of work."

When McQueen did go back to work, it was for a low-budget drive-in movie starring Warren Oates and Christopher George called *Dixie Dynamite*. Friend and motorcycle rider Gary Davis, who knew the actor from Bud Ekins' shop, said one afternoon in early 1976 he received a phone call from McQueen. "He asked me if I was up for a ride in the desert the next day. I told him I couldn't because I had a motorcycle sequence to do in a film called *Dixie Dynamite*. In fact, Bud Ekins was enlisted as a stunt rider and would be there too. Half kidding, I said, 'Well, you're welcome to play with the boys as well.'"

"You know what? That might be kinda fun," McQueen gamely replied.

The next day, McQueen and Ekins arrived on the set in Santa Ana, California, and reported to work as stunt riders. They were put on a Daily Scale Stunt Contract that netted them $172 a day. It was a far cry from the $14.5 million McQueen received on *The Towering Inferno*. One has to admire McQueen's sense of humor.

But McQueen wasn't laughing when he received a phone call from Phil Feldman, who was the new president, chief executive officer, and treasurer for First Artists Production Co. Ltd. The deal McQueen had made with the production company in 1971 had finally caught up to him. The company was in a dire situation, and McQueen still owed it two movies. Feldman was calling in his markers.

The stars who formed First Artists never held annual meetings to check on its status, and the output of production was slow—approximately 15 pictures in a decade. First Artists organizer-agent Freddie Fields opted out of the company and his agency business[7] to produce films full time. With no direction or prudent business management, the company was losing money[8] and credibility.

Feldman, formerly an executive at CBS and Warner Brothers, was brought in to reorganize First Artists and discipline its star shareholders, who made more pictures for other studios than for their own company. His first phone call was to Steve McQueen.

"He kept pressuring Steve, 'Hey, you owe me two pictures,'" said agent Marvin Josephson. "There were certain time frames, and he had a right to block Steve from doing other films until Steve had fulfilled his obligation. This kind of pressure drove Steve nuts."

To add insult to injury, there was no adjustment for inflation on all First Artists pictures, which remained at $3 million per film. The average cost of movie production in 1976 was about $5 million per picture. The idea that he was tied to a low-budget production galled McQueen.

Agent Marvin Josephson was asked by McQueen to abolish the First Artists deal, but the contract was ironclad. Feldman also threatened legal action. "[Feldman] was rigid," Josephson said. "From his point of view, he was the head of a public company. Steve's commitments were very valuable commitments. It became impossible to even talk to him about allowing Steve to do another film." Josephson said he fielded several movie offers with seven-figure paydays attached, including *Tara: The Continuation of Gone with the Wind*, *Raise the Titanic!*, *Raid on Entebbe*, *The Driver*, *The Towering Inferno II*, *Superman*, and *Close Encounters of the Third Kind*.

---

7 Fields ran Creative Management Artists with longtime partner David Begelman and merged with Marvin Josephson's International Famous Agency on November 4, 1974. Josephson later changed the name to International Creative Management and became Steve McQueen's third and final agent.

8 In 1975, First Artists lost $33,000 on sales of $9.3 million.

Backed into a corner, McQueen reflexively drew his knives. He announced he would do a movie but not the kind of action fare that had made him a household name. He chose a film adaptation of Henrik Ibsen's *An Enemy of the People*, a turn-of-the-century play about a doctor who stands up to municipal corruption in a Scandinavian resort town. Most intimates believe the move was done directly out of spite.

"He had to do a film for First Artists, he owed them that, and they kept saying, 'You've got to do a movie…You've got to do another movie for us,'" Neile said. "And one day, at Ali's and Steve's house, there were some books there, and he grabbed a book and he said, 'Okay, this one.' He opened the pages, and he said, 'I'm gonna do this one,' and it happened to be *An Enemy of the People*. It's as simple as that…It could have been any book."

Psychologist Peter O. Whitmer believes there was another more personal explanation for why McQueen chose *An Enemy of the People*. "McQueen's self-destructive beasts were off and roaring at this point in his life," Whitmer said. "He'd been in isolation for several years. One marriage went south, and his second was headed in that direction. Also, the intense sensitivity he always felt for not being educated said, 'Do Ibsen.'

"What's more, this was a book that he had picked up sort of randomly. Perhaps Ali had also read it, and he always referred to her as his 'New York intellectual sophisticate.' It seems to be a convenient confluence of an obscene gesture to Ali, and to Phil Feldman, all driven by his less than fully conscious attempts to cage the beasts of self-destruction."

But what started out as a slap in the face to Feldman turned into a labor of love for McQueen. When drawing up a list of directors, one name kept coming up—George Schaefer. The Emmy Award–winning director, who was known for his Hallmark Hall of Fame productions, said he was surprised when he received a phone call from the superstar in May 1976. "We met on a Sunday afternoon over at the Hamburger Hamlet in West Hollywood," Schaefer recalled. McQueen had just scored a couple of antique auto lamps at a Pasadena swap meet and proudly showed them to Schaefer. Baffled and intrigued, Schaefer wondered what the world's biggest box-office star wanted from him. When McQueen told him of his plan to bring *An Enemy of the People* to the silver screen, Schaefer didn't know quite what to think. What McQueen said next finally won him over. "I really wanna do this," McQueen said. "It's something I've got to get out of my system, and if we do it, I want you to hire the best cast in the world. I don't want you to protect me by getting people that I'm gonna not look so good against. It's my funeral if I can't act."

Schaefer said upon reflection years later, "I think Ibsen would have liked the idea. Ibsen was a very interesting man. He was an ornery cuss. He wrote *An Enemy of the People* because he was angry with the critics who criticized his play *Ghosts*. He dealt with subjects that were simply not done on the stage. Ibsen was a loner who didn't go along with the majority. He and Steve in another time would have hit it off."

The actor also hit it off with associate producer Phil Parslow, a former UCLA football player who had a fearless reputation for keeping tough actors in line. Parslow remembered that first meeting in Schaefer's Century City office in vivid detail: "I came in the room and saw him. I was surprised because he had this full beard, a T-shirt, and blue jeans on. He was a little chunky but not fat. I meet Steve, and he's staring at me. He then takes me in a corner and whispers, 'I'm crazy. I'm crazy. I think we'll get along great, but just remember what I'm telling you. I'm crazy.' He used the word 'vibe' a lot. That was one of his favorite words."

It took six months to ready the script (written by Alexander Jacobs and based on Arthur Miller's adaptation of the play), assemble the cast, build the sets, and prepare the $2.5 million production. Rehearsals were set for late September 1976. Everything went according to plan until actor Nicol Williamson, who was set to play opposite McQueen, failed to show on the first day of rehearsals at MGM studios. Schaefer received a call from an inebriated Williamson, who was phoning from Hawaii. McQueen had listened in on the other line and immediately gave him the heave-ho. Schaefer then called character actor Charles Durning and offered him the part of Mayor Peter Stockmann. It was a perfect fit. McQueen and Durning struck up an unlikely friendship. Durning recalled upon that first meeting, "People told me [McQueen] was short-tempered and had no regard for anyone. I found him to be the total opposite. I found him to be loyal to the people he worked with, even defending them."

Durning recalled an incident where one of the cast members unknowingly parked his car in a spot reserved for an MGM studio executive. An incensed guard entered the staging area and began berating the actor. McQueen immediately put a stop to the verbal assault and launched one of his own. "Do you know what you're doing to this man?" McQueen asked. "He's got to go inside and act. Do you know what an actor has to do to prepare himself for a role? All he brings to the table are his emotions, and you have just destroyed this man's potential to make a living today... If you ever talk that way to an actor again, I will see that you are walking the streets."

After years of delaying movie productions, upstaging costars, and making directors wait while he stewed in his trailer, Steve McQueen had finally become a team player. Maybe it was because he had already proven himself as a star, maybe it was because he'd played for his own one-man team for so long and seen the error of his ways—either way, McQueen had come full circle. He saw the wisdom of ensuring the whole team worked well for the mutual and enhanced benefit of all. McQueen had matured.

Before the first day of rehearsals, McQueen gathered the cast around him. He told them, "This is your world, not mine. I'm a little out of my depth here, but I can promise you I'll give the best I have in me. If I fail, I won't blame anybody. The fault will be mine." Everyone couldn't help but be endeared to him.

The 33-day shoot and the three-week rehearsal period coincided with the $50,000 remodeling of the McQueens' Trancas Beach home. McQueen took a suite at the Beverly Wilshire Hotel. During the week, he stayed to concentrate on the film and returned to Malibu on weekends. That sounded aboveboard to most, but it gave McQueen free rein to plunder through a parade of starlets, models, and professional party dolls while MacGraw remained at home. A familiar cycle of proving himself to the world was beginning again, both in terms of acting in his choice of film and as an alpha male capable of bedding every woman. The need for self-assurance and placating his ego were ever present.

MacGraw sensed what might be happening at the hotel, but the two devised a "don't ask, don't tell" policy. Years later, MacGraw said she regrets her inaction. "It was a place I never went, which was stupid. I should have gone in, opened the door, and kicked the shit out of whomever was in bed with him," she said. "He would have enjoyed it!"

McQueen was, however, faithful to his profession. He dedicated himself to the role of Dr. Thomas Stockmann. He not only tested himself by memorizing long chunks of dialogue, but he grew out his hair and beard and donned a pair of granny-style glasses to give himself a more scholarly look. He even wanted to add a pillow around his midsection to give the appearance of a spare tire, but the move was dissuaded by Schaefer. McQueen's desire to devote himself wholly to this endeavor was admirable; he even sacrificed his carefully crafted image in the name of his art.

By the time the three-week rehearsal period was finished, Schaefer said they could have taken the production to the stage had they so desired. It would seem as though McQueen could have conquered the stage and even laid to rest the specter of *A Hatful of Rain* and the trouble he had with that production all those years ago if he had wanted to.

McQueen was formidable when he was functioning, but his best takes were done in the morning. "Come the afternoon, though," Phil Parslow said, "[and] he couldn't remember his head." McQueen's pot smoking was a habit he couldn't or wouldn't give up. Schaefer said years later, "If I were ever to do a movie with Steve again, I would schedule another week to accommodate for Steve's work habits. I got irritated with him late in the day because he would smoke pot, which everybody knew, and then he would be on the telephone. Sam Peckinpah would be calling from Paris, and we'd be raring to work on the set and end up waiting 20 minutes for him. He would sneak in and never apologize, but what the hell—it was his own money and his own company."

Schaefer did explode at McQueen when he didn't learn his lines and it was obvious that McQueen was under the influence of grass. "Damn it, Steve, learn your lines!" Schaefer said aloud in front of the entire cast and crew. "Come pre-pared." No one had ever dared to talk like that to McQueen—not even the crusty Sam Peckinpah. The admonishment was enough motivation for McQueen to memorize the film's climactic speech, "I'm against the age-old lie that the major-ity is always right..." That was three pages of dialogue—the longest speech of McQueen's career.

But when he did show up for a scene, it was exhilarating, according to Charles Durning. "The better you were, the more he applauded you," Durning said. "He'd say, 'Give it more, Charlie. Give it more. Do more there, Charlie, go ahead.'" After one particular scene, Durning said McQueen pulled him aside and gave him the ultimate actor's compliment. "He said, 'I don't know when you're going to do it or how you're going to do it, but someday you're going to break through.'"

An Enemy of the People finished principal photography in November 1976, and Steve and Ali hosted a wrap party for the cast and crew in a posh Malibu restaurant. Producer Phil Parslow recalled a bittersweet moment during the meal when he was speaking to Ali MacGraw. McQueen, who was the only one who dressed down for the event, was sitting in between Parslow and MacGraw, who leaned back to talk to each other.

"Can you believe I gave up a mansion to ride on the back of a motorcycle with this guy?" MacGraw said.

"You must really love him, Ali," Parslow replied.

"Yeah, I do."

When postproduction was finished, the studio faced an even bigger chal-lenge—how to effectively market the film. Warner Brothers and First Artists spent nearly $400,000 on three different ad campaigns and test engagements in Minneapolis, Cincinnati, Denver, Seattle, San Diego, Santa Barbara, St. Louis, and Tyler, Texas. Nothing seemed to work. "People didn't know what to make of it," Parslow said. "Warner Brothers spent hours in campaign testing. How do you tell people that Steve McQueen is not in an action-adventure film?"

McQueen also invited Neile to a rough cut of the picture, but her reaction was not what he had hoped for. A few minutes into the film, Neile leaned over and whispered, 'Is that you?' He affirmed it was.

"I said this will never sell.... First of all, *An Enemy of the People* sounds like a western if you don't know anything about it at all," Neile said. "And second of all, they want to see a movie star, not some big fat slob with hair all over the place."

Neile was right. Warner Brothers didn't quite know how to market the movie and left McQueen to fend for himself in the press. "I'm not going to say anything," Phil Feldman said when cornered by a reporter to comment on the film. "I won't talk about *An Enemy of the People*." A Warner Brothers executive stated, "It's an embarrassment, a piece of junk. Who wants to see McQueen running around with a beard and weighing 210 pounds?" One famous screenwriter, who refused to be publicly identified, told the *New York Times*, "At first we thought it was a joke. It was as if John Barrymore, at the height of his career, had decided to play Tarzan."

The critics were also less than kind when the film received a limited release in March 1978 after having been in limbo for more than a year since shooting had wrapped. "Think of Clark Gable as the tragic Parnell or Gregory Peck playing Ahab as if he were Abraham Lincoln," wrote Michael Sragow of the *Los Angeles Herald-Examiner*. "Recall Elizabeth Taylor as the Cleopatra of Great Neck. Then add to this list of big-star follies the typically lean, tight-lipped action hero Steve McQueen. Here he's plump, bearded, and avuncular, a bit like Kris Kringle. For McQueen to play Ibsen's volatile, idealistic intellectual Dr. Stockmann is as unusual as it would be for Dr. Carl Sagan to try and play Darth Vader."

Arthur Knight of *The Hollywood Reporter* wrote, "It's a handsomely photographed, solid-looking movie, but it has no juice to it, no life to it at all. There's no way for that picture to make contact with a modern audience. McQueen has no understanding of the play, and it took me 20 minutes to recognize him under all those whiskers."

Actually, McQueen wasn't that bad. Actors of this period still had great limitations on what studios wanted them in, the roles they could play, and what the public wanted. Today it is a different story as actors jump from the big screen to the small screen to the stage, from comedy to serious productions all in great succession. Actors today arguably have much more freedom. Unfortunately, McQueen was almost certainly before his time in wanting to pursue any project he thought would stretch him against the accepted convention.

The truth was he had spent the last two decades perfecting his image of the rebel, the hunk, the hero behind a wheel, and the handsome leading man, and he had done his job well. The public was used to seeing him perform amazing stunts and bold acts of courage on the screen. This new role was just too much of a contrast and totally against type and audience expectations. No matter how good McQueen was in *Enemy*, he was doomed from the start, a victim of his own successful image.

Frightened by the harsh reviews, Warner Brothers decided no matter how they marketed the film, this was one sow's ear they couldn't turn into a silk purse, so why throw good money after bad? The studio refused to put up the distribution money for the movie, and *An Enemy of the People* sat on a shelf for the next three decades.[9]

McQueen was devastated by the film's failure. "I did *An Enemy of the People* because I wanted to do something pure," McQueen said. "I wanted to do this play about a little guy who was being dumped on but who still believed." Ironically, it was McQueen who was the one who got dumped on. He had taken another dramatic fall from grace in a straight drop from the dizzying heights of *The Towering Inferno* with this complete commercial failure. It was a long drop and a hard landing with nothing to break his fall. However, more failure was still to come, this time of a domestic nature, with even more pain to follow. Could the indomitable McQueen manage another comeback?

---

9   *An Enemy of the People* received another examination after McQueen's death in 1980 when it was released to select movie houses and aired on local cable stations in Los Angeles and Canada. The film eventually received a DVD release in 2009 as part of *Warner Brothers Archive*, an innovative print-on-demand program.

33

DIVIDED SOUL

STEVE MCQUEEN'S LIFE had never been straightforward or easy. Although there is no doubt that fate and circumstance dealt him some heavy blows while growing up, he was the master of his own destiny in his later years—if only he could work out which direction he would take.

McQueen was a mass of contradictions. His career embodies this. He wanted to maintain his status as the top-paid star and biggest name in Hollywood, but he made it difficult for himself to secure work, mainly by charging inflated fees just to read scripts. Warner Brothers offered him the lead in *Raid on Entebbe*, but McQueen put it out of reach by asking for $3 million and 15 percent of the gross. After *The Towering Inferno*, he was at the top of his career financially, but he starred in *An Enemy of the People*, a commercial failure that paid him nothing upfront. He had spent years creating his image as the ultimate rebel and tough guy, but he almost blew all his credibility behind a pair of spectacles and a shaggy beard. The young man who arrived in Hollywood desperate for the big time and financial security had worked hard "for the goodies" but was now risking it all and had seemingly lost his hunger.

The paradoxes of McQueen's career were matched only by those of his private life. He believed in the notion of the dutiful wife waiting at home and being faithful, yet he could not conform to his part in such a dynamic. While McQueen was married to Ali MacGraw and kept her in the role of the good wife, he still maintained a suite at the Beverly Wilshire Hotel. This gave him freedom and the chance to bed as many women as he pleased, including his ex-wife Neile, who found it thrilling to be the "other woman." This parallels another contradiction that McQueen struggled with—his sex-symbol status. He had been one of the most desirable men on the planet for nearly 20 years. But now his hard-living lifestyle was starting to catch up with him and a new generation of actors was on the scene. More than ever, he had to prove himself as the alpha male. This was essential for him in spite of his love for MacGraw and their bond.

As McQueen's status was in crisis, so was his persona. He wanted to live a simple life free from the pressures of stardom and the press, so he went out in a full beard and often in disguises. In spite of this, when his disguises worked too well and people would sometimes walk past him without noticing, he would get upset and his ego would kick in, questioning these people as to why they did not ask for his autograph. In many ways he was still the young child at heart who wanted everything his way and on his terms. His life was like a fractured mirror, splintered into so many pieces, and it was doubtful they could ever be reconciled. He was a divided soul.

• • •

McQueen's followup to *An Enemy of the People* appeared to be another attempt to sabotage Phil Feldman and First Artists—a film version of Samuel Beckett's *Waiting for Godot*. The 1952 tragicomedy follows the lives of a pair of men who divert themselves while they wait in vain for a man named Godot. But McQueen quickly ran into a roadblock when he discovered Beckett wasn't selling the rights because the play was his best source of royalties; furthermore, Beckett had never heard of Steve McQueen.

So McQueen continued looking at the stage and focused on a movie adaptation of Harold Pinter's 1971 play *Old Times*. McQueen wanted to star with Audrey Hepburn and Faye Dunaway in this three-person fugue with strong currents of sexual rivalry. He spent $50,000 to secure the rights, hoping First Artists would pony up $250,000 in production costs to green-light the project. Sensing another commercial failure on its hands, First Artists balked. In December 1976, McQueen promptly sued First Artists for breach of contract in the amount of $250,000, citing that he had met all of his legal obligations to advance the production money.

The two parties reached an out-of-court settlement on March 10, 1977. First Artists reimbursed McQueen $50,000 for costs associated with *Old Times* and gave him the right to make it with another studio if he dropped the lawsuit. In return, he agreed to star in a film version of *I, Tom Horn*, a western based on Will Henry's biographical story of the controversial desperado. "I've always wanted to do Horn's story; now it's just a matter of doing it a little sooner than I expected," he said.

McQueen prepared harder for *Tom Horn* than he did for any other role in his career, spending several years on research with writers, directors, historians, and costumers associated with the movie. He filled numerous journals and made many tape recordings with his ideas and observations, and he even visited the legendary cowboy's gravesite. Executive producer Phil Parslow said the similarities between McQueen and Tom Horn were uncanny. "Tom Horn was a hero. Time had passed him by. The Indians were gone; the West was gone. He was born on the cusp. He started young and had outlived his time. In my mind, there's a lot of Tom Horn–Steve McQueen similarities. They both even died at 50."

Much to his dismay, McQueen learned that *Tom Horn* wasn't going to be all happy trails. The movie, which was supposed to start principal photography in the summer of 1978, was pushed to the back burner by First Artists when it was announced that no fewer than three other *Horn* projects were in the pipeline. Universal Studios was planning on shooting a TV movie for NBC called *Tom Horn and the Apache Kid*, while rival network ABC and producer Steve Forrest declared they were making their version of the story. Longtime film rival Robert Redford was set to star in *Mr. Horn*, with Sydney Pollack directing a script penned by William Goldman. McQueen didn't care so much about the inferior television projects and boldly predicted that Redford wouldn't follow through. "Redford won't take me on," McQueen told Phil Parslow, who spent 18 months trying to prep the film. Quietly, as predicted, Redford dropped out in favor of a modern western, *The Electric Horseman.*

McQueen tried to recruit western novelist Louis L'Amour, his favorite author, as a consultant on the project. L'Amour declined but invited McQueen to research the life of Horn and the era of the Old West in his 17,000-volume home library in Los Angeles. "Steve wanted to take the books home, but Louis wouldn't let him. So he'd come out to our house every day and read," said L'Amour's widow, Kathy. "Louis and I would be working in his office while Steve was sitting over on the sofa studying and making notes. That went on for weeks.

"He was very nice," Kathy recalled. "Sometimes he and Louis would take a break and go to lunch together at the Bel-Air Hotel. They'd drive over in this old pickup truck, and the hotel would make them park around the back because they thought Louis L'Amour and Steve McQueen were delivery guys."

• • •

It was never publicly stated or declared, but Steve McQueen and Ali MacGraw had in all likelihood separated. It was either that or Steve had a very understanding wife. He continued to maintain a suite at the Beverly Wilshire Hotel well after *An Enemy of the People* had wrapped and had a small fleet of his antique cars in the hotel's garage.

As the scruffy-bearded "Fat Joe," McQueen privately held court in the El Padrino Room, a taproom inside the hotel, regaling patrons about his motorcycle adventures in the Australian outback and telling them that he ran a construction crew. "It's more fun here than at my neighborhood bar. I like to hear what the other half thinks," McQueen admitted to a reporter. "I get enough show business crap during the day. By pretending I'm a construction-crew boss, I can talk to people on a one-to-one basis—none of that 'star' stuff."

Psychologist Peter O. Whitmer said McQueen as "Fat Joe" had the best of both worlds. "I think he did this to see if he could get away with it—be an anonymous superstar right in web-center of superstardom," Whitmer said. "Could Marilyn Monroe have hung out at Hainano's and drunk beer, eaten cheeseburgers, and shot pool with no one hitting on her? I don't know if she would have wanted that, but this was Steve showing his sense of parsimony of life, of being a kid with no responsibilities other than menial chores back on the farm.

"What's more, he not only pulled it off but was still able to lure in the beauties and starlets and pecker-fodder. Still, at the time, it was Steve being Steve... and enjoying every iconoclastic minute of it."

The inordinate amount of time McQueen spent at the hotel did provoke questions from the press. "Everything between me and my wife is just fine," McQueen told a *People* magazine reporter, who noted that it had been four months since they had lived together as man and wife. He maintained the same stance with former Solar executive Robert Relyea, whom McQueen called out of the blue after several years of silence.

Relyea thought it was bizarre that McQueen wanted to "shoot the shit" after he had declared that Relyea betrayed him, vowed he would never speak to him, and dissolved their partnership after the *Le Mans* debacle. They met at an exclusive room in the back of the hotel's restaurant, where Relyea saw "a bear of a man" sitting alone and smoking a cigar. At first, Relyea didn't recognize McQueen, who had long, frizzy hair and sported an unruly beard. McQueen picked up on Relyea's initial shock and gave him a minute-long lecture about needing to "have an open mind" and "accepting people on face value."

They managed to have a civil dinner, reminiscing about the people they had worked with, the current state of the industry, and other related talk. But they never discussed Solar, *Le Mans*, or anything meaningful, according to Relyea. Dinner lasted three hours, and they spent another three hours walking around the block. Relyea couldn't quite place the tenor of the conversation other than it had a finality to it. Neither man wanted to say good-bye, but they knew the evening had to come to an end. Finally they shook hands, and Relyea drove away. They never spoke again.

McQueen also tried to rekindle his romance with *Junior Bonner* costar Barbara Leigh, whom he invited to have dinner in his room. Leigh said McQueen's appearance had changed dramatically in the five years since she had seen him. "Steve was one of the sexiest men alive when I knew him on *Junior Bonner*. Now I was looking at a man who was older, heavier, and sported long hair and a big, bushy beard. He reminded me of Heidi's grandfather," she said. They had their usuals—Leigh had wine, while McQueen nursed a beer. After some time had passed, Leigh's curiosity got the best of her, and she asked McQueen about the state of his marriage.

"Things aren't going too good with Ali, but I don't want to talk about her right now," McQueen said. "I want to know about you!" After a few libations, Leigh said some of the affection from their *Junior Bonner* days was starting to resurface.

"Who's the man in your life right now?" McQueen asked, testing the waters. Leigh told him that right now she was concentrating on her career. That was his cue to make a pass, and they began to kiss. No bells, whistles, or alarms went off for Leigh, and she decided to call it an early night. She said she had an early wake up call. McQueen smiled and said he had one, too.

"Are you sure you won't stay, babe?" McQueen smiled, nudging Leigh in a most gentle way.

"I'd better go, or else we might get into trouble," Leigh said, meeting his smile.

"I like trouble," McQueen said with a laugh.

Upon reflection, Leigh said, "Steve could be terribly charming, and for a split second I considered the idea of going back with him, but I knew it wouldn't work out in the long run. There was no going back in time for either of us. I kissed his cheek gently and bid him farewell. It was the last time I ever saw him alive."

McQueen tried his best to convince everyone that he was happy, but not everyone believed him. Phil Parslow, for one, wasn't buying whatever McQueen was selling. "We were going to talk about a possible project out at the pool. I go to the pool and there's this guy, pasty-looking, no suntan. His face was bearded, kind of grungy-looking. He looked like a bum," Parslow said. "He was sitting back, drinking an Old Milwaukee beer. He looked back and looked around, and he said to me, 'This is what it's all about, Phil. The suite, the pool, the Beverly Wilshire. This is what it's all about.' He said it, and I never saw him out there again. He was so out of place. He was all alone. It was bizarre. He didn't belong there. He didn't look right up there. He looked right on a motorcycle. He looked right in a pickup truck, but there he looked wrong."

When McQueen did go back to Trancas one weekend in early March 1977, he was faced with the news that Ali was ready to go back to work in a Sam Peckinpah film called *Convoy*. Based on the song of the same title by C.W. McCall, MacGraw was offered $400,000 to play a woman who becomes involved with a gang of truckers led by Kris Kristofferson. Ironically, the movie originally had been offered to her husband a few years before. MacGraw said she loathed the script and feared Steve's reaction, but her agent, Sue Mengers, had put everything into perspective for her, "Honey, your marriage is in trouble, you have no money, and you better take this job before it's too late. You haven't worked in five years, and you're lucky to get the offer."

When MacGraw finally summoned up the nerve to tell McQueen, who was sitting in a chair, nursing a beer, his reaction was as she had feared. "In that case, we are filing for divorce," McQueen said without a trace of emotion. MacGraw was steadfast and stoic; she told McQueen he had put her in a corner with the prenuptial agreement, and if they did get a divorce, she'd have nothing. McQueen had a ready-made remedy—he would pay her a large sum of money not to work. "I not only distrusted the offer, I also knew that part of me was dying from not working," MacGraw wrote in her autobiography. "I saw no way to win, and so with considerable misgivings about the project as well as the future of my marriage, I set off to New Mexico to begin one of the nightmare jobs of my career."

McQueen moved back into the Trancas beach house in late April 1977 to watch Joshua and Chad while Ali was 1,000 miles away on location in Albuquerque, New Mexico. The tables had been turned on McQueen, who didn't like having to play second fiddle to his wife. Ali defended McQueen to *Los Angeles Times* reporter David Lewin and played the heavy. "Whatever he was used to or not used to, Steve, when he married me, married a strong lady," MacGraw said. "I don't like the word tough—that's cheap. But I'm strong, and so is he. He has been terrific about this because he is very bright. I'm very vulnerable— but Steve is a street urchin. He knew who he married—a madwoman."

MacGraw later admitted the film was "a study in drugs, alcohol, and insanity, and I was certainly a manic participant. The cast and crew were pretty much divided between cocaine and tequila on one side and pot and beer on the other." MacGraw said her loyalties were with the former.

McQueen had suspected all was not well; industry reports had filtered back to him that Peckinpah's film was over budget, and the director's coke habit had spiraled out of control and into full-blown addiction. Steve also suspected Ali was having an affair. He placed many phone calls to her hotel room at all hours of the day and night. When she didn't answer, it raised his hackles. Decades later, MacGraw confirmed McQueen's suspicions weren't unfounded. "The truth was that I had a kind of druggy affair periodically during that movie [*Convoy*], but as it was now common knowledge that Steve had been living a flagrantly free life for some months, I thought that if I did not go into my escapade, the whole mess of our lives might blow over and offer us a fresh start," she wrote in her memoirs. For the sake of his marriage, McQueen swallowed his pride and flew with Joshua to visit Ali in New Mexico. When the two stepped off the plane, he greeted Ali with an empty beer can filled with daisies. She said she fell in love with him all over again.

In New Mexico, McQueen didn't know how to behave on a film in which he wasn't the star. "It was her show," said friend Pat Johnson. "She was the star and he felt funny, as if he were keeping an eye on her because of her alleged affair." Property master Bobby Viscigilia added, "Steve was completely in the background. He didn't appreciate the role he had to play."

Costumer Carole James said she genuinely felt sorry for McQueen, who spent most of his days lying by the hotel pool, dragging a Radio Flyer wagon filled with ice and Old Milwaukee beer. One day while Ali was filming, McQueen asked James to go for a walk. He specifically wanted to know how she and her husband Kent managed to juggle their professional and personal relationships as they worked together during the day and went home to each other at night. "Ali was a prisoner in that relationship and wanted to stretch. She wanted their marriage to work, but she also wanted to work," James said. "Steve was very old-fashioned. His ideal was for Ali to be barefoot and pregnant. He couldn't understand the concept that our marriage was based on a mutual respect for each other, that we were best friends as well as lovers. He couldn't grasp that idea."

When McQueen returned to Los Angeles, he called Pat Johnson and made a frantic visit to his Canoga Park home. He told Johnson that he didn't think his relationship with Ali was going to last, and for once, he was not in control. "I'm the most famous person in Hollywood, and I don't know what to do," Steve said. He mourned the failure of his five-year marriage, but he was perhaps even more upset for Joshua Evans, the stepson he had raised as his own. "The thought of deserting Joshua, and those were Steve's words, 'deserting Joshua,' was just too much," Johnson said. "He cried, literally bawled on my shoulder. I think he was reminded of his father abandoning him, and now he was abandoning Joshua."

Unfortunately, although McQueen and MacGraw were officially man and wife, the relationship had run its course. They were perhaps still in love with each other, but the fractures in their relationship had crystallized and widened beyond repair. It would never work on the terms they both wanted, and they had grown apart. A divorce was inevitable.

• • •

Fate had been equally cruel and generous to McQueen over the years. However, he would have one more crack at a love that could last and be unhindered by circumstance and irreconcilable personalities. This time, he would not wait for fate to intervene when he first laid eyes on international model Barbara Minty.

McQueen had spotted Minty in a Club Med advertisement and made arrangements with her agent, Nina Blanchard, to lure the 23-year-old model to Los Angeles and offer her a part as an Indian Princess in *Tom Horn*. Blanchard, who was always on the lookout for her clients, didn't seem to recall the part of an Indian princess in the script and thought it sounded suspiciously like a phony movie audition. She insisted on accompanying Minty to the meeting, which took place over the Fourth of July weekend at the Beverly Wilshire Hotel.

When Blanchard told Minty she was going to meet the star of *The Towering Inferno*, Minty thought it was Paul Newman. Instead she met the *other* star. "When Steve greeted us, he had long hair, sported a beard, and looked exactly like Dr. Thomas Stockmann, the character he portrayed in *An Enemy of the People*," Barbara Minty recalled. "Frankly, to me he looked more like a San Pedro beach bum than an international movie star." As a young girl, Minty had been a huge fan of *Wanted: Dead or Alive*, and Steve had been her first schoolgirl crush. But the man who sat across from her looked nothing like Josh Randall.

Blanchard and McQueen conversed for a good two hours while Minty sat in silence, drinking in every word of their conversation. She saw past the shaggy exterior and found something inside of him that was soft, tender, and kind—quite the opposite of the tough-guy persona he portrayed on the screen. After the meeting, Blanchard scolded her client.

"Can't you open your mouth and talk?" Blanchard said. "That was embarrassing." When Minty did speak, she couldn't believe the words that came tumbling out of her mouth. She said that one day she was going to marry Steve McQueen.

"It clicked for me right away. And I think it did for him, too," Barbara McQueen said more than three decades after that initial meeting. "He was the love of my life."

• • •

When *Convoy* wrapped on September 17, 1977, the McQueens' marriage was in tatters. McQueen's paranoia went into overdrive regarding MacGraw's on-location affair. His behavior became increasingly aggressive and more bizarre; every action, every move Ali made was heavily questioned and scrutinized. In a last-ditch attempt to salvage the wreckage of their past, the McQueens drove to Paradise Valley, Montana, to spend a few days at a lodge tucked away deep inside of Yellowstone Park. The drive, MacGraw said, was a shrill experience. "It was tense at first, with every conversation and every embrace accompanied by a question about my fidelity while I was away on location," MacGraw recounts in her autobiography. She compared McQueen's line of questioning to a "Nazi-esque grilling" that was painful and unrelenting. He had run her down emotionally, and she was hanging by a thread.

MacGraw quickly forgot the painful journey after they reached their destination. The daylong ride by horseback to the rustic lodge was therapeutic, and they spent a night in a small guest room. "I fell in love with him all over again," MacGraw said. On their return, they rode back to a quaint Montana restaurant where they shared a meal with their guide and a big-game hunter from South America. When MacGraw realized the hunter was conversant in several languages, she decided to pass the time by brushing up on her rusty Italian. She had no clue it would be the undoing of her marriage to McQueen, who "boringly talked camshafts and God only knows what" that evening with the guide. When they got back to their room that night, McQueen's distrust erupted. He accused Ali of making a fool of him by flirting in Italian with the game hunter, and he commenced a "sinister diatribe" that didn't let up the entire drive back to Malibu. "He kept at it and kept at it and kept at it," MacGraw said in 2010. "It was terrible and frightening and catastrophic." So catastrophic that she decided to move out of their Trancas home with young Joshua in tow. A few weeks later, she found a rental home a few hundred yards away from Steve so that Joshua could maintain a relationship with him. The night before Ali and Joshua moved in, she impulsively called Steve, telling him that she felt they had made a terrible mistake. His stoic reply wounded her heart: "I am not in love with you anymore," McQueen said. "I love you, but I am not in love."

McQueen filed for legal separation from Ali MacGraw on October 10, 1977. Almost a year later, they were officially divorced. McQueen's attorney's enforced the terms of the prenuptial agreement, and Ali MacGraw was left with nothing but the clothes on her back. As always, she put her best foot forward and kept a stiff upper lip. "I've never been happier," MacGraw said to a reporter at the time.

"I live in a crackerbox house at the beach filled with plants and canvas chairs. I've simplified my life down to the basics.

"During my life, I've lived in splendor and in difficult circumstances. Now I've surrounded myself with the things I want and need."

Thus ended one of the most publicized marriages in Hollywood.

Steve's son, Chad, said many years later that the divorce was not a big surprise to him or to those who had been around the couple. "That last year in the house, there was a lot of fighting going on," he said. "It was a drag, but I think that [divorce] was the only alternative to being completely miserable."

No matter how much pain, grief, and sorrow their relationship brought, MacGraw seemed to believe their relationship was fated, "It was very, very passionate and dramatic and hurtful and ecstatic. It was pretty much a wipeout for both of us. But I think it's safe to say it would have been impossible not to have fallen in love with Steve."

It is arguable that the pair proved the adage that opposites attract. He was a man of simple pleasures; she was sophisticated. He would rather repair a bike while she went to the opera. She spoke Italian; he spoke jive and street talk. They were undeniably attracted to each other, but with so many differences it is likely they were doomed from the start. Steve and Ali were dynamite together but could never keep their passions within a positive realm. They could never fully be what the other wanted in order to last a lifetime together.

What is for certain is that McQueen was changed forever in the aftermath. From this point onward, he would strip life back to the complete bare essentials. He would have another chance at love, but this time it would be with someone who could willingly and naturally be the type of person he needed instead of her having to be forcibly conformed to a role. McQueen had evolved in life. He was different from the young and power-hungry kid from the Midwest who came from humble origins, desperate to be a star, and who married Neile. He was past the period of being the established star at the top of Hollywood, the fully developed man who married Ali. With each chapter of his life, he was not simply putting these relationships aside; he had evolved and was a different, more mature McQueen. He had now come full circle and was ready for the final chapter of his personal life.

34
LAST CHANCE

For as macho as Steve McQueen's image was, his life can be defined by the women he ultimately chose as his domestic partners.

Neile McQueen represented Steve's struggle to get to the top and his halcyon years as a movie star. She was ambitious and highly talented, breaking into the world of entertainment just as Steve wanted to do. They were perfect partners in the sense that they were young, in love, and full of hopes and dreams. While he was reaching for stardom, they had only each other. However, McQueen would evolve beyond her after he had achieved his goals.

Ali MacGraw seemed to fill the gap in his life during the transition from established star to the start of middle age; she was America's sweetheart and the ideal other half of Hollywood's power couple. Her presence defined the final stretch of McQueen's domination of the film industry, the reconciliation of his alpha-male status with middle age, and his withdrawal from public life while they spent five reclusive years in Malibu. This too could not last, as he was undergoing another metamorphosis.

Finally, Barbara Minty represented a sense of peace and contentment. During this period, McQueen settled comfortably into middle age and was intent on finding peace—and himself—on his own terms.

McQueen did not simply get bored, tired, or incompatible with each wife. Each was his perfect partner but for only one part of Steve's life. His friend James Coburn often said that Steve had such passion that he managed to live several lifetimes in one. "It was like he bought a Harley-Davidson and rode it until it came to pieces," Coburn said. "He squeezed everything into his life. He shouldn't have been sad for one moment because he got everything out of it that was possible." He also managed to have three deep, meaningful relationships, each one worth a lifetime.

Friend Mike Dewey said McQueen told him of a life-changing moment during his stay at the Beverly Wilshire Hotel, which signaled the end of his midlife crisis. "He told me that he was standing out on the balcony of the hotel and saw this guy loading his motorcycle in a pickup truck," Dewey recalled. "He said it took this guy about a half hour to load it and tie it down, and Steve stood there watching the entire time, to the point where he watched him drive away. He said, 'Mike, that changed my life. I thought, *What the hell am I doing trapped up here when I can be out there on my bike doing my own thing? Why did I give up my freedom for a room in a fancy hotel? Why did I give up the one thing that made me the most happy? I need to get back to the simple things and the simple life.* So I packed my bags, checked out of the hotel, and started over again.'"

Barbara Minty seemed to be the right person at the right time for Steve McQueen. Despite the glamorous appearance of being an internationally known Ford model, Minty was refreshingly down-home and sweet. She was a spirited farm kid from Corvallis, Oregon, who told corny jokes, used salty language, and had an easy outlook on life. She preferred jeans, T-shirts, and flip-flops to dresses and high heels, and was ill at ease in the modeling world. She had graced the covers of *Cosmopolitan, Harper's Bazaar, Glamour,* and *Elle,* but she admitted she was in high fashion strictly for the money. Her ultimate goal was to earn enough to buy a ranch and stock it with horses, dogs, cats, and chickens. She had achieved most of her early life goals in her twenties and was semiretired from the industry when she met McQueen.

Despite the 25-year age gap, the two discovered they had much in common. They enjoyed the simple things—a cold beer, nature, or a quiet ride in one of McQueen's old trucks. "When Steve and I traveled, we stayed off the Interstate and preferred back roads and little-known routes to get to our destination, taking our sweet time," Minty said. "Often we'd pull out a road map and flip a coin to see what route to take. Time was not a concern, but our journey was—kind of like our relationship and how we lived our lives at the time."

McQueen came to trust Minty early in their relationship, for he allowed her unrestricted access to him with her 35 mm camera. Friend Pat Johnson said it was a milestone for McQueen. "The fact that he gave her free access to him with her camera almost blew me away," Johnson said. "It was that gesture that convinced me, more than any other single act, that he trusted her as he had no other person in his life."[1]

---

1   Minty's photo collection was eventually published as *Steve McQueen: The Last Mile* (Dalton Watson, 2006).

Sometimes, Minty said, it was quite obvious there was a generation gap between the two. Early in their relationship, he had taken her dancing at the Daisy, a members-only nightclub on Rodeo Drive. Times had changed, and the Daisy was no longer a hot spot. Disco now ruled the airwaves, and McQueen tried to show his new lady that he was still hip and relevant. "Steve wore this flowery silk shirt, white pants, and a gold chain around his neck, and he started dancing like Austin Powers," Minty laughed. "He did the Twist, the Shag, the Watusi, and the Clam, while everyone else danced to the pulsating beat of disco. I thought I was going to die of embarrassment."

She also claims his taste in music was suspect, and the Bee Gees' *Saturday Night Fever* got heavy rotation on his tape deck. Usually she ducked underneath the dashboard and tried to be as inconspicuous as possible, but once she let him have it.

"You're Steve fuckin' McQueen!" she screamed. "The Beatles or the Stones, yeah, I can understand cranking up the volume, but the Bee Gees?! Come on, honey. This ain't cutting it."

He made a vow to stop smoking and get back in "movie star" shape. To accomplish this goal, he enrolled under Pat Johnson's name in the world-famous Schick Centers for the Control of Smoking and Weight in Los Angeles. Under the five-week program, McQueen learned aversion techniques and counter-conditioning, which included being subjected to a mild electrical current from a 9-volt battery. In McQueen's case, it worked—he actually quit smoking cigarettes.[2] His other bad habits died hard though, Minty said. "He started out every morning in the same manner. He woke up around 8:30 or 9:00 AM, had a cup of coffee, and chased it down with a can of Old Milwaukee beer and a joint," Minty said. "And if there was any chocolate cake left over from the night before, he'd have a healthy slice of that, as well."

That's not to say McQueen was unhealthy. His body changed through a weight-lifting regimen and intense thrice-weekly karate workouts with Pat Johnson. Even though they still lived in remote Trancas Beach, McQueen became more social. Elliot Gould, Sam Peckinpah, and Peter and Becky Fonda came by for social visits, as did James Garner and Lee Majors. Minty, who was wearing short shorts and knee-high socks, recalled losing her composure when Garner stopped by Trancas.

---

2   McQueen did continue smoking cigars and chewing tobacco. And of course, smoking pot.

"Mr. Rockford, please come in," she said referring to Garner's famous TV character, who gave Minty a cheerful once over, thinking Steve was living out one of those high school cheerleader fantasies.

Actor Lee Majors, who came as often as he pleased, said he shared a special relationship with McQueen. "We both lived in Malibu, so we would spend time together. When I called, Steve would turn to his son, Chad, and say, 'Fill up the cooler; Lee's coming over,'" Majors recalled. "Off we'd go in his pickup truck with a cooler full of Old Milwaukee beer, heading to tiny, out-of-the-way antique stores up the coast.

"I don't know why he liked Old Milwaukee beer because it gave him gas—and he wasn't afraid to release it on our journey. When we were looking at junk and antique objects, we always outbid each other for the same pieces. For example, if a cast-iron car or truck was marked at $30 and he knew I intended to buy it, he'd offer the owner $35. I would say $40 and so on. The store owners loved to see us coming, and they would watch in amusement. Plus, they made a few extra bucks."

One person who was definitely barred from entering the McQueen household was rocker Keith Moon, who lived next door. The drummer for The Who added a little color to the neighborhood but over time became a nuisance. He spied on Ali MacGraw with his binoculars when she sunbathed topless, blared music at all hours of the night, and often dressed in a full Nazi uniform, complete with jodhpurs, knee-length boots, leather coat and cap, and a swastika armband. McQueen had actually saved Moon from drowning when he found him floating face down in the Pacific Ocean after an all-night drinking binge. McQueen pulled Moon by the scruff of the neck and dragged him through the sand and deposited him on his doorstep. However, the manic musician crossed the line when he tried to barge into the house while Steve was away and harass Chad. "He was loaded," Chad McQueen said. "He grabbed me by the neck and said, 'Make me a drink!' I said, 'You have five seconds to get out.' Then he tried to kick me. Well, I smacked him—bam!—and after he fell, I dragged him out, locked the door, and called Dad. When he heard what I'd done, he put down the phone and clapped."

When McQueen got back, he did more than just clap—he got the law involved. McQueen asked a friend who was a former FBI agent for his advice. The agent suggested a sit-down with Moon and his attorney, Mike Rosenfeld, in the office of the Malibu District Attorney's office, as a scare tactic. The idea, though sound, didn't go off as planned. Moon showed up in full Nazi regalia and he reeked of cognac.

"Is there any significance to your clothing?" the stunned district attorney asked.

"My client is shooting a commercial," said the fast-thinking Rosenfeld. His answer elicited a booming laugh from McQueen, who had seen Moon in this getup several times before.

Moon did come away from the meeting with the full understanding that he was not to encroach McQueen's property ever. In fact, during the next encounter they had, it was McQueen who broke the law, according to Minty. "Moon had a giant stained-glass window in his bathroom, and he kept the light on all the time. Unfortunately, it shone right into our bedroom," she recalled. "Steve called him over and over, politely asking him to turn off the lights."

One night McQueen had reached his limit. He grabbed a shotgun and marched to Moon's house. Moments later, Minty heard a shotgun blast and the sound of the stained-glass window breaking. "Steve calmly walked back in the house, put the shotgun away, and cracked open an ice-cold Old Milwaukee beer," she said. "'Chicken Little' here ducked underneath the bed and prayed the cops wouldn't come and haul us off to jail." Minty said McQueen slept like a baby, and Moon never said a word about the rather large hole in his stained-glass window.

When McQueen was not dealing with such things, their days consisted mostly of playing on the beach, taking relaxing drives up and down the Pacific Coast Highway, hanging out at motorcycle meets, or taking jaunts in one of his beat-up pickup trucks to Utah; Montana; and Ketchum, Idaho, where Minty maintained a 5-acre ranch. They also hung out with the Rolling Stones when they made a West Coast swing on their *Some Girls* tour in July 1978. McQueen scored tickets and a backstage pass, which thrilled Minty to no end. She thought she was going to witness some good old-fashioned rock 'n' roll debauchery, but she came away with an entirely different experience. "We arrived backstage and wandered around. Steve bumped into their bass player, Bill Wyman, and the two shared a beer and had a heartfelt conversation about kids," Minty said. "Here was this rugged, tough-guy actor and one of rock 'n' roll's greatest self-professed ladies' men, and they ended up talking about how much fatherhood meant to them. It was very dignified and proper—not at all what I expected."

McQueen's take on fatherhood was a mixed bag of discipline and non-traditional methods of child rearing.

Chad said Steve did not want to raise him in a sheltered Hollywood environment, and Steve stressed the need for Chad to work hard to get ahead. "I know a lot of people think that Hollywood kids don't know shit from Shinola about how to make a buck, but my dad was tight with his cash and taught me to be humble about things," Chad said. "If I asked to borrow $5, he'd say, 'Well, no.' If I wanted to go to Pizza Hut, I'd have to do my chores to pay for my slice. And when it got to the point where I needed real money, I had to earn it. He said, 'You want a car? Well, get a job, man.' I pumped gas for a year, and boy, the fucking ribbing I got there—shit like, 'What a cheap son of a bitch your dad is!'"

One of Steve's proudest moments was the time when an underage Chad stayed out all night at a Hollywood club but still reported for work on time. "I got home at 5:30 in the morning, and I had forgotten my key," Chad said. "Dad came to the door and shot me a look. I went to bed for a few hours, then went to the gas station."

A few hours later, Steve pulled up in one of his old pickup trucks and rolled down the window to give Chad a message. "I'm so fuckin' proud of you," Steve said. "You were out all night, and you still went to work."

Chad said, "That was his work ethic. He believed in 'work hard, play hard,' and as long as you took care of business, you could do what you wanted. I kept working and going out, and at the end of the year he found a restored 1949 Chevrolet pickup for me, and I paid him for it. I still have that truck."

• • •

Steve McQueen started his Hollywood exit in early 1978. That's when he plunked down $75,000 on a 5-acre parcel in Ketchum, Idaho. He planned on building a log cabin and was going to call it the Last Chance. He had also contemplated buying the North Fork Store, an emporium on Highway 93 that was featured in the Marilyn Monroe movie *Bus Stop*. "Steve wanted his own general store where locals could swap war stories and pour themselves a cup of coffee over an old-fashioned pot-bellied stove while an open fireplace kept everyone nice and toasty," Minty said. "It would also be a place to showcase all his antiques. For years he had toyed with the idea, and he even had a name picked out—Queenies."[3]

In late September 1978, McQueen purchased a 400-acre property in East Fork, Idaho, about a half-hour from Ketchum. He and Minty made plans to build a cabin, a guesthouse, and a private runway for his planes. They were going to call the ranch the Crazy M.

With each large purchase, McQueen came to the realization that it was time to get back to work. He instructed agent Marvin Josephson that his next movie deal, after his *Tom Horn* commitment was completed, needed to make major noise and money. "Let's make it really big," McQueen said. "It's really gotta knock their

---

3   Minty said local politicians prevented Steve from owning the landmark. "Idaho politics are difficult for outsiders to comprehend," she said.

socks off. I want a contract that will guarantee headlines." Josephson came through with flying colors, landing McQueen the biggest contract in Hollywood history.

Swiss producer Georges-Alain Vuille tendered an offer for McQueen to star in *Tai-Pan*, a $40 million two-part epic based on James Clavell's best-selling novel about adventurer Dick Straun, who dreams of establishing a trade empire in Hong Kong in the mid-1800s. McQueen received $1 million up front just for signing the contract, with deferred payments of $9 million plus 15 percent of the profits. In all, McQueen would receive a record-breaking $10 million minimum with a profit share taking this amount even higher.[4] Vuille said to the press, "McQueen is worth more than any actor in the world. We're delighted to have him as our star."

When Josephson brought the contract to McQueen for his signature, his star client threw him a curveball. "You do know that your commission for this picture is a million dollars?" McQueen asked. Josephson nodded yes, that was true, but he was the one who hustled the innovative deal and deserved to be rewarded. McQueen tried another approach: "Marvin, I thought you were my friend?" Josephson replied, "Steve, I do think we're friends. If you're defining friendship as I should take 5 percent, if that's your notion of friendship, I don't think one has to do with the other." McQueen was incensed and told Josephson that he would pay him his commission, but then he would no longer use his services. True to his word, he fired Josephson—for about three months. "I think he found out he wasn't going to read all those scripts that I was reading for him or field all of those phone calls," Josephson said. "If they sent it to him, then it could possibly sit for three months and they knew that Steve would eventually send it back to me." Ultimately, the *Tai-Pan* deal fell through when producer Georges-Alain Vuille was late with the second of 10 payments. McQueen's contract stated that if any payment was late, the contact was null and void. McQueen walked away from the deal and pocketed a cool $1 million.

First Artists and Warner Brothers had weathered the slew of *Tom Horn* projects, and in January 1979 they advanced the film. It was not the epic picture that McQueen had hoped for, which was a source of continual frustration for him and others who had worked hard to get it off the ground. "The pain and suffering that I went through on *Tom Horn* was the most I had ever gone through on a film," said Phil Parslow, who was the film's original producer. "We started thinking it

---

4 Josephson said that the terms of the *Tai-Pan* deal were far greater than what was reported in the press. He said McQueen was entitled to the film rights if the deal with Georges-Alain Vuille fell through, which it did. When the movie was released in 1986, Josephson said the rights belonged to the McQueen estate but neither he nor the estate pressed the issue.

was going to be a $10 million epic and then down to $6 million until it ended up being a $3 million TV movie. It went from an awesome concept to a so-so movie."

Parslow said he walked away from *Tom Horn* when McQueen wasn't going to fight the studio to sink more money into the budget. That meant the film could focus only on the last three years of Horn's life, not the glory years in which he captured the elusive and powerful Apache chief Geronimo. "At that point, Steve was too tired to fight any longer," Parslow said. "He wanted First Artists out of his life and was prepared to do anything, including compromising his power, something he had never done before."

McQueen had endured a fair amount of grief. In addition to his tug of war with First Artists and Phil Feldman, he parted ways with directors Don Siegel and Elliot Silverstein, two of the hottest directors at the time. Siegel, who had worked with McQueen in *Hell is for Heroes* in the early '60s, believed McQueen didn't have a clear vision for the movie. Silverstein also bowed out because he and McQueen communicated on different levels. "It was kind of difficult to tell what Steve wanted because he used to speak with a predicate or a direct object, but never both in the same sentence," Silverstein said. "His speech was like a rapid fire, almost like a Gatling gun, but it was difficult to tell what he meant. Even his closest people couldn't tell what he was saying."

If McQueen seemed to lack direction, it was most likely reflected by the fact the film had two different shooting scripts: a sweeping epic by Tom McGuane, which was twice the size of a normal screenplay, and a scaled-down version by Bud Shrake. "Steve McQueen gave me McGuane's screenplay and it was 300 and some odd pages long and they said, 'We need a two-hour movie out of this,'" Shrake said in 2005. "I thought, 'Boy, this is like stealing.' I thought McGuane was a really good writer, and all I've gotta do is take this screenplay and throw away half of it. But then when I got into doing it, I found that didn't work." Elements of both scripts were used in the final version of the movie. Cinematographer John Alonzo remembered, "Steve had both scripts in his hands when we were shooting. He would look at certain parts of both and decide which version we were going to shoot."

When McQueen did decide on a director, he baffled everyone by selecting James William Guercio, the former manager of the rock group Chicago. Guercio eventually became interested in motion picture production, and in 1973 he produced and directed the feature film, *Electra Glide in Blue* starring Robert Blake and featuring other members of Chicago in bit parts. Guercio took a salary of $1 in order to hire cinematographer Conrad Hall, who was rumored in Hollywood to be the real director of the film. *Tom Horn* producer Fred Weintraub said Guercio "did a number on Steve" and hung out on McQueen's front porch and sold him on the idea. Weintraub recalled, "I told Steve in front of Guercio, 'I'm completely against this man directing the film. He doesn't understand the movie business.' But Steve wanted it and I gotta say, Steve was the gorilla."

Weeks before principal photography, McQueen and Minty visited Horn's grave at the Old Pioneer Cemetery in Boulder, Colorado. "I just wanna see if I can pick up on Horn's vibration," McQueen said. The actor later told friends and associates that he felt Horn's presence and was asked by the legendary frontiersman to tell his story.

Minty said her antenna picked up a totally different vibe—an enraged and evil cowboy. "Horn's presence was definitely there at the grave," she said. "His ghost would later visit me during the making of the picture and left a lasting impression that haunts me to this day. 'Ha, ha, ha, you dumb little girl,' Horn's apparition taunted me. 'I killed the kid. I admit it. I did it.'

"I know Steve's portrayal of Horn in the movie was very sympathetic, but I can't say I feel the same way. I believe with all of my heart that Tom Horn was guilty as sin."

There were two things that McQueen had set his mind on—his on-screen character would wear a beard, and Tom Horn had to die at the end. Producer Fred Weintraub and screenwriter Bud Shrake tried to talk him out of both ideas. Weintraub pleaded, "Steve, you have a million-dollar face, and no one will know it's you." The two came to a temporary agreement—if McQueen would trim the beard, it could stay. Unfortunately, the trimmed beard did not look as good as Weintraub had hoped. However, fate intervened the day before cameras rolled when a fan walked up to stunt double Gary Combs, who was unshaven, and asked for his autograph in front of McQueen. Steve reported the next day for *Tom Horn* without whiskers.

Phil Parslow believed McQueen didn't want to shave off the beard for another reason—his age was starting to show.

Tom Horn was a western, but this film would not feature the sort of daring action sequences of McQueen's early westerns. He was a middle-aged man of 48, and time had finally caught up with him. The lines on his weather-beaten face were highly evident, and the years of partying and late nights were now showing. However, these items played to McQueen's advantage in two ways. First, he looked the part of Tom Horn, the aging cowboy. This was an ironic marked contrast to McQueen playing a teenage boy in *Nevada Smith* at the age of 35. Secondly, his good looks were not left to carry the film; McQueen was forced to rely on his acting, and it paid off.

Weintraub may have won the battle of the beard, but McQueen held firm when it came to Tom Horn's on-screen demise.

Principal photography for *Tom Horn* commenced January 15, 1979, in Nogales, Arizona, a few miles from the Mexican border. If *The Sand Pebbles* was the most problematic production McQueen endured, then *Tom Horn* was a close second. Several problems plagued the film throughout its various stages, and the first hitch occurred just three days into the shoot. McQueen realized Guercio wasn't cutting it as the director and fired him on the spot.

With Guercio gone, McQueen decided that he would simply take over as director. However, he learned that the Directors' Guild had a rule stipulating that an actor or anyone else previously involved in the picture could not assume the role of the director. Weintraub encouraged McQueen to fight the ruling, but it was possible that McQueen's actions could shut down the picture. Because this was McQueen's last film for First Artists, McQueen wanted it to be over with as soon as possible. First assistant director Cliff Coleman suggested that his friend, William Wiard (*The Rockford Files, M*A*S*H*), could act as the official director, while McQueen and Alonzo led the way. Susan Ekins, who was working on her first film, verified McQueen was the real director of *Tom Horn* and that Wiard basically sat quietly and collected a paycheck. "They were cordial to each other, but I wouldn't say that Steve held [Wiard] in the highest regard," Ekins said. "It was Steve's picture. It was his vision. It certainly has his trademark on it." If one counted McQueen, *Tom Horn* went through five directors.

McQueen's dedication couldn't be denied. In addition to living on the set in a Winnebago camper for three months, McQueen served as unofficial director, continually working on the script and going over his lines every night. His attention to detail was amazing, said costar Geoffrey Lewis. "Before we started shooting, Steve was running around and was in everybody's business. 'Put that light there…Was it there the last time?' But it was all to make the shot better. He knew how to come in and take charge of a situation and put himself on the line. That was in the movies, but you got the feeling that he could do it anyway. I just thought he had the most charisma and presence I had ever met, and that was in real life, too," Lewis said. "When they called for action, my back was to him, but when I turned around, I got the full force of Steve McQueen right in my face. He almost knocked me down. It was like a whack in the face. Those blue eyes… It was pretty intense."

Still photographer Dave Friedman said McQueen saw things that nobody else did and ensured the movie's authenticity. "I remember one time we were shooting on Mescal Street, and they had all of these horses saddled together. It was a wide shot with horses tied up on the railing in the background," Friedman said. "Well, McQueen walked down the street to make sure all the horses had period saddles on, and there's no way that you'd know if a horse down the street in this shot was even wearing a saddle. He was a stickler for that sort of thing, and God bless him, he truly cared about his craft."

McQueen also cared about his costars and took the time to ensure they gave the best performance possible. Linda Evans, whose beauty often overshadowed her performances, was McQueen's leading lady in *Tom Horn*. He told her on the first day they met, "You're absolutely wrong for this role." The remark elicited tears, but he smiled to let her know there was a silver lining. "You're still wrong for this role, but I'm going to make you right."

McQueen stripped away her makeup, placed her in a dowdy dress, and gave her a shiny gold tooth. "If you're going to be a real actress, you have to learn to live without props such as clothes and cosmetics," he said. "You'll start understanding yourself more and more—not the Linda you pretend to be, but the Linda who's just as beautiful without the props. Never be afraid to be yourself."

While it took some getting used to, Evans came to embrace McQueen's wisdom. She later credited her experience on *Tom Horn* as giving her the confidence that helped her eventually land the role of Krystle Carrington on TV's *Dynasty*.

The only time McQueen's confidence ebbed was near the film's finale when Tom Horn is led to the gallows and is hanged in a special Rube Goldberg contraption built by McQueen's stunt double, Gary Combs. The device consisted of a divided trapdoor, water containers, counterweights, ropes, and pulleys. The weight of the condemned, after being placed on the trapdoor, started the entire process so that, in effect, the convicted man would spring the trapdoor himself. Combs made the mistake of showing McQueen the device a few days before it was perfected. "I could see in his eyes that he had no desire to get in that rig and drop through that door," Combs said. Of all the death-defying stunts McQueen had performed in his career and personal life, this was the only one he respectfully declined.

Tom Horn was completed in March 1979, and the initial reviews when the movie was released a year later were a mirror reflection of the box-office take—a mere $12 million. One critic summed it up best: "*Tom Horn* suffered from public antipathy toward the genre. In an earlier decade, this lyrical, deeply felt little film would have been hailed as a classic."

Screenwriter Bud Shrake said McQueen once again sabotaged First Artists with the film's somber ending, which stunned audiences. "I thought it was a real good movie myself, except for the last 15 minutes. And that was all Steve McQueen's fault," Shrake said. "Warner Brothers was trying to talk him into letting Tom Horn live at the end. But McQueen wouldn't go for that; he wanted to get hanged onscreen. You couldn't hardly win an argument with him about anything. And the reason was because he had gone and slept on Tom Horn's grave for I don't know how many nights and communed with him. And Horn had told him everything. The producers kept saying, 'This is gonna cost us a fortune at the box office. People don't wanna see Steve McQueen die.' And they were right."

Jon Marlowe of the *Miami News* took McQueen and *Tom Horn* to task in his review of the film. "McQueen's Horn is a dull, plodding effort that requires the audience to first, stay awake; and second, fill in too many missing pieces. What's really upsetting is that any and all emotion is totally lacking.

"What makes *Tom Horn* a tragedy instead of just a miserable film is that too many moviegoers (including myself) have waited years and years for McQueen (once a stunning actor) to finally return to making films. And so this is what we're rewarded with, huh?"

Financially the studio may have predicted correctly, but in terms of acting and beauty, McQueen's performance was right on. A death scene is a big risk for an established star. After all, audiences had not wanted to see him die at the end of *The Sand Pebbles*. This could go either way as it risked either a downbeat ending to the detriment of the film, or it could be an emotionally charged climax full of pathos that grips the viewer. McQueen had the skill to ensure it got the latter reaction.

Despite the critics' initial reaction, McQueen's performance in *Tom Horn* marked a new level to his acting, a refinement of his craft. He had matured into a very fine and confident actor, not letting his good looks but his skills do the talking. Moreover, to McQueen's credit, he was perhaps taking himself less seriously and accepting his shortcomings with good grace. This is clear in the bar scene early in the film when a character mocks Horn's height, and McQueen, who is visibly shorter than the other actor, takes the insult well and with confidence. This was unimaginable a decade ago when height was virtually a taboo subject on set and being taller than McQueen would get a person fired.

The movie has gained respect and recognition in the years since it was released because in many ways the film and his performance were ahead of their time. Audiences were used to action-packed westerns with gunfights and brawls. McQueen offered them something different this time—a meditation on the West and a character study of one of America's best-known figures of the era.

"*Tom Horn*, I thought, was Steve's best movie," said actor James Coburn. "He was loose and free, and he wasn't guarded. Most of his films he was guarded. He had a form. If the film wasn't rigid enough, he was going to be good. I always felt Steve would really be a good actor if he ever grew up…I think he finally did on *Tom Horn*. That was him finding his adulthood."

The man who lived life at 200 mph was finally finding the comfort and happiness from a slower pace. Contentment and lasting peace were to be found in a small community about an hour north of Los Angeles in the hills of Santa Paula.

35

ON A WING AND A PRAYER

Parsimony was a continual theme in Steve McQueen's life. Plus the idea that he could take a midnight motorcycle ride or a cross-country trip at a moment's notice was a door that had to remain open. It did not matter whether he left his wife in the middle of the night or left a whole production team waiting hours to shoot a scene; he simply could not remain idle and had to have his freedom and liberty at all times. Was McQueen looking for something, or was he just in a continual state of flux, subject to his own whims and flights of fancy? The answer would not come yet. McQueen was looking for peace that he could find only later in his journey, through many more ups and downs, but he ultimately found it in Santa Paula, California.

"I'd rather wake up in the middle of nowhere than in any city on earth," McQueen famously said once. And it wasn't just a flippant remark made to a reporter; it was his life's philosophy.

Barbara Minty said McQueen once wanted to take a 700-mile road trip from Malibu to Salt Lake City just to see a rare Indian motorcycle and sidecar. "He said, 'Honey, pack a bag. We're going to Utah,'" Minty said. "I quickly grabbed a few essentials, some clothes, toiletries, my camera, and film. I was definitely what you would call a 'low-maintenance chick.' Soon we were on the road and on a new adventure. It was like that with Steve—you had to be ready at a moment's notice."

When *Tom Horn* wrapped in March 1979, McQueen and Barbara drove back from Arizona and retreated to the confines of their Trancas Beach home. McQueen usually spent each morning scouring the classified ads in his dime-store reading glasses, looking for the latest bargains. He spotted an excellent bargain for a bright yellow PT Stearman biplane in the pages of *Airplane Trader*. With a snap of his fingers, McQueen purchased the antique airplane for $35,000.

Many believe that McQueen wanted to fly planes because it was a way to reconnect with the father he never knew, a man McQueen believed was a barnstorming pilot. Some thought it was simply a way for McQueen to express his individuality and achieve that special freedom one attains when flying. Friend and fellow pilot Mike Dewey said, "I can only surmise that Steve became hooked on flying for the same reason every other pilot does—that sense of pure freedom and the feeling of accomplishment. Taking an aircraft off the ground and returning safely is one of life's greatest pleasures. Once airborne, it's just you and the sky and some of the most beautiful sights imaginable."

Psychologist Peter O. Whitmer said McQueen's interest in aviation came at the perfect time in his life. "It seems that two separate issues flowed together at the same time in Steve McQueen's interest in flying," Whitmer said. "It could be argued, given his early depiction of his father as an aviator when that profession was new and thrilling and dangerous and sexy—and the stuff of much cinema—that Steve McQueen had always harbored a yearning to learn how to fly. 'Is this what Dad did?'

"It just took the right timing—financial freedom, far fewer nagging controls of movie producers and their insurance companies—to actually create the time and do it. Furthermore, when he did, he entered into this new 'extreme sport' as viscerally and pointedly as he had with motorcycles or Ferraris. All or nothing; it was endorphin central, every flight a thrill, a death-defying event. It hit him, a rush, at his psychic core.

"Interesting, isn't it, that at about the same time in Steve McQueen's evolution, he found a new path in religion. Many stories have been told by astronauts of the spiritual impact on them of a space shot. So, too, of defying gravity and propelling yourself through one more dimension than is possible on a mere earthbound bike or car."

Whatever the case may be, learning to fly became McQueen's latest passion, and like everything else he did in life, he jumped into aviation with both feet.

Through some research, McQueen learned that Santa Paula, a small town about an hour north of Malibu, was the perfect place to indulge in his new hobby. Santa Paula was billed as the "Antique Capital of the World," so McQueen figured the place would be worth visiting if only for the relics and trinkets of yesteryear. But they might also have a few flight instructors who could teach him how to fly his World War II plane. With a little digging, McQueen discovered that pilot Sammy Mason was the best man for the job.

Mason was in his early sixties at the time and had more than four decades of flying experience, including a stint as an acrobatic flyer and test pilot for

Lockheed. His exploits were known throughout the aviation world, and he was once featured in *Life* magazine in the 1940s. But the former daredevil was semiretired and took a hard-line stance of not teaching novices. Then again, he had never taken on the likes of a stubborn movie star before. Mason recalled the evening in the spring of 1979 when he received a phone call from McQueen, asking him for lessons. McQueen, however, didn't reveal his true identity. "Somehow, during that conversation, I formed the idea he was either the attendant at the service station where I filled up my car or the butcher," Mason said. "I concluded that he must be the latter because he could afford to fly."

Mason steered McQueen toward his son Pete, who was an excellent teacher and was available. But McQueen was insistent that the elder Mason was the only person to teach him. Mason couldn't be bothered. McQueen peppered Mason with nightly calls and finally revealed his true identity. Sammy drew a blank and asked Pete if he knew of some actor named Steve McQueen. Rolling his eyes, Pete responded, "Dad, come on—*The Great Escape?*" As it turned out, the film was one of Sammy's favorites, but his answer was still no. Movie star or not, Mason simply didn't have the time to teach a novice. However, Mason agreed to meet McQueen to tell him if the Stearman he was about to purchase was mechanically sound and up to par.

Naturally, McQueen turned on the charm when they met and won over Mason, who eventually came up with a compromise—McQueen would take the first part of his instruction from Pete, then Sammy would train McQueen when he gained some experience. While Pete and McQueen became fast friends, Sammy turned out to be vastly important in McQueen's life. Sammy was the last father figure McQueen had and ultimately a person who piloted him to heights further than any plane could take him, discovering beliefs and a way of life that was both spiritual and transcendent.

Now armed with a plane and an instructor, McQueen decided to take the plunge and purchase a hangar to store his new toy. He sauntered into Screaming Eagle Productions, which was owned by Doug Dullenkopf and Mike Dewey, to see about leasing or even possibly buying a hangar. Dullenkopf said McQueen dropped a rolled-up $100 bill on the floor to test their honesty. When Dullenkopf picked up the currency and returned it to McQueen, he was ready to do business. This was an old carnie trick, demonstrating that he was still as mistrustful as ever. Getting into McQueen's private club was possible only for a privileged few. Even though he was worth millions, Dewey said McQueen flinched at the $300 per month rent on the 1,600-square-foot hangar.

McQueen's athletic ability and excellent hand-eye coordination from racing cars and bikes made him a natural aviator. He had a quiet determination to succeed and doubled up on his lessons, flying for hours at a time with both Sammy and Pete Mason. On May 1, 1979, he soloed his first flight and was supported by a small group of pilots and actor Lee Majors. It was one of his proudest accomplishments.

Later that month, Pete Mason attended the Watsonville Fly-In and Air Show, held on Memorial Day Weekend, with McQueen and a few of his pals, stuntman Chuck Bail, and World War II pilot Ted Petersen. It was there where Pete saw the less serious side of McQueen emerge. Pete Mason recalled, "We were at this hotel in Watsonville, and they were making this Hershey's fudge in the can with butter grease in the pan. McQueen stabbed into a pat of butter with his fork and flicked it on the ceiling and started throwing butter on the ceiling. Then the others joined in, and the entire ceiling was covered in pats of butter. It was wild. I was an 18-year-old kid who was raised in the church and had never seen anything like this before, nor had I ever seen grown men carry on this way."

A month later at an air show in Porterville, California, McQueen spied Chuck Bail furiously working on an original screenplay at the hotel pool called *The Last Ride*. The story was about a group of former Hells Angels, now approaching middle age, who get together for "one last ride." Bail had set up a deal with Sherry Lansing at Columbia, who loved the script.

The next day at the air show, Barbara Minty told Bail that Steve's feelings were hurt because Bail hadn't asked McQueen to read the script. Bail handed over his copy, and the next morning McQueen showed up at his motel doorstep at 6:00 AM with a cup of coffee in one hand, waving the screenplay in the other.

"This is the worst piece of shit I've ever read in my life," McQueen said.

Bail then shut the door in McQueen's face, not giving it another thought. McQueen called a month later, asking to have lunch. He told Bail he'd do *The Last Ride* if the studio would pay for someone to do a rewrite.

"I've already got the deal going," Bail said, slightly offended. "I don't need your muscle." McQueen was flabbergasted. He was the highest-paid actor in the world, and Bail was telling him he didn't need him. It didn't take long for Bail to correct his thinking. "What was I thinking? Steve was offering to do me a very, very big favor," Bail said. "I came to my senses and began to reconsider my position. Steve's name on the dotted line would change my status from a B-movie director to an A director."

The Columbia executives were delighted. Getting McQueen was like winning the lottery, and they pulled out all the stops, including tapping famed screenwriter

Walter Newman to do the rewrite. They also upped Bail's salary and changed his credit from director to director/producer. The studio sank several hundred thousand into preproduction costs with a possible start date in the spring of 1980. McQueen's professional and personal life was cruising at a comfortable altitude.

• • •

When he got a taste of the aviator's lifestyle, McQueen was in the market for a much larger hangar. In June 1979, he approached businessman Paul Lovemark to see if he might be willing to sell him his hangar, which was double the size of what McQueen was currently using. Lovemark had purchased his hangar in 1967 for $37,000, and his business, Helicopter Rebuild and Welding, was doing well. Lovemark told McQueen he wasn't interested in selling the hangar, nor did he want the aggravation of moving his entire operation. "McQueen was persistent to the point of being a pest," Lovemark said. "Finally, he asked, 'Well, what would it take for you to sell the place?' I threw out an outrageous figure—$180,000—and McQueen told me my price was ridiculous and left." An hour later McQueen came back. He told Lovemark that if he could vacate the premises within the month, he'd take it.

"I closed my toolbox and started packing," Lovemark said.

McQueen's aviation activities eventually led to the discovery of his last home, a place where he finally found inner peace and contentment.

Santa Paula, California, was a small rural town of 20,000 people and was a throwback to the California towns of the 1940s. It was a quaint agricultural town reminiscent of mainstream America but with a distinctive Mexican flavor.

Steve and Barbara's daily trips meant scenic drives through the orange, lemon, walnut, and avocado orchards of the Heritage Valley, the last great "citruscape" in California. The rustic, turn-of-the-century town itself had changed little over the decades and somewhat reminded Steve of his childhood home in Slater, Missouri.

People there weren't impressed with power, money, or Hollywood luminaries. Pilot Mike Dewey said, "Steve was looking for the right kind of town, the right kind of person to train him, the right kind of airplane to fit his personality at the time. It all came together when he got here."

After daily excursions to Santa Paula, Steve and Barbara decided to make the move after the purchase of the hangar was completed. The couple fell in love with the town and its people; McQueen felt he was returning to his roots. "This place is as close to home as I can find," he told Barbara. "I want to die here."

The two moved out of the Trancas Beach home and created a small living quarters in the 3,000-square-foot hangar until they found a suitable house. On July 8, 1979, they purchased a 15-acre ranch just a few miles from the airport. The four-bedroom Victorian home, built in 1892, was in dire need of repairs. They stayed in the hangar until renovations were completed and placed a king-sized mattress and box spring on the floor while a dining table and chairs sat nearby. A makeshift rod ran alongside the bed, which served as a wardrobe. A portable television sat at the end of the bed, which kept them entertained at night.

McQueen also moved in thousands of possessions—antique toys, jackknives, Kewpie dolls, old-fashioned cash registers and slot machines, scales, neon beer signs, airplane propellers, military hats and helmets, wall clocks, bicycles, framed movie posters, vintage gasoline pumps, jukeboxes, and more than 140 antique motorcycles. The hangar took on the look of a museum. It was McQueen's way of reclaiming a past that was lost to him as a result of his hardscrabble childhood, lack of parents, and relative poverty. Now he had it all within arm's reach. He hired Grady Ragsdale, a former helicopter pilot with a heart condition, to run his daily affairs and watch over his things. In time, Ragsdale became a trusted employee, confidant, and a loyal friend McQueen came to rely on.

Minty said life in the hangar was fun and never dull, and comprised her fondest memories of life in Santa Paula. She recalled getting stuck in the gut with a motorcycle handlebar a time or two and once whacking her head on the wing of the Stearman while getting up. Most days, she said, were golden.

"Every morning we'd wake, Steve would make coffee and bring it to me, open the hangar door, and we'd watch the world from our bed," Minty said. "Steve loved wearing the old-fashioned goggles, jumpsuits, and leather bomber jackets. He could hardly wait to get in his plane and taxi down the runway and fly around the sky free as a bird."

McQueen attended several air shows and embarked on jaunts to Santa Barbara, Porterville, Bakersfield, Delano, and Shafner Airports just to have pie and ice cream. He also loved the cuisine at the Santa Paula Airport, where he toiled away the morning hours eating breakfast, drinking coffee, reading the newspaper, and talking aviation with other pilots. "The people at the airport treated him no different from anyone else," said Bruce Dickinson, a longtime pilot and Santa Paula resident. "Steve didn't consider himself anything special. He didn't expect anything. He just wanted to be one of the locals and fly and do his own thing. He was probably the most down-home good ol' boy that I've come across."

At night Steve and Barbara watched television and hosted campfires outside of the hangar, sharing beers and swapping stories with the locals. They befriended many people at the airport and grew especially close to Larry and Crystal Endicott. The two were close in age, and their friendship was cemented when McQueen discovered Larry drank the same brand of beer—Old Milwaukee. "Every evening as the sun went down, he had people come by, as he had a fire going," Crystal Endicott remembered. "He always had to lie down on the concrete because his back hurt a lot. He would visit with people, just rest there and talk. He would talk about his past or the dreams he still had left."

The community embraced Steve and Barbara, and they became active neighbors. When Larry Endicott was diagnosed with cancer and Crystal couldn't find anyone to babysit their seven children—ranging in age from 2 to 12—so that she could tend to her husband at the hospital, McQueen stepped up to the plate.

"What do you mean no one will watch your kids?" McQueen asked incredulously. "You don't worry about it. I'll be there."

"And he was," Endicott said. "He brought my kids pizza. He stayed with them from Monday to Friday. Seven babies. He was a sweetheart. I couldn't ask for anybody nicer."

Something in McQueen had clicked, and he finally became the man he had always wanted to be. This period is arguably the most important in his life because it marked the full extent of McQueen's journey into someone genuinely special. To put it succinctly, McQueen was no longer the same person; he had changed unequivocally. Gone was the power-hungry star, gone was the selfish and ruthless actor, gone was the womanizer intent on proving his alpha-male status. He had changed into something more, something special. He was part of the community and no longer wanted to be the spoiled center of attention. Rather than using those around him to his advantage as the old McQueen would have done, he was now able to take pleasure from contributing to a community and being a pillar of it. He had realized that giving could be more fulfilling than simply taking. People looked up to him and respected him—not as McQueen the movie star but as McQueen the all-around good guy.

Finally comfortable in his own skin and letting his defenses drop, McQueen broke free from his old insecurities and the paranoia that had held him back his whole life. He discovered he had something within him that was more important than his star image. He had found happiness and was essentially reborn.

The seeds of Christianity had been sowing inside of him for decades, and his time in Santa Paula was a spiritual harvest. Despite McQueen's worldwide fame and that fact that financially he never wanted for anything, a certain calm had eluded McQueen most of his life. A solo trip he made to New York in the days following his divorce from Ali MacGraw to visit her brother, who was an artist, seemed to awaken the ghosts of the past and transform him. "At the time, Steve had a full beard and looked a bit wasted," said Bob Heller, who knew McQueen from the Actors Studio. "Why he was here and who he saw, I don't know, but not many people from his youth were still in New York. There were, however, a few stalwarts, like myself and photographer Roy Schatt,[1] who lived for years at the same street-level apartment on 33rd Street between Lexington and 3rd Avenues.

"Roy's darkroom window was on the street, and if the curtain was open, it meant he was not working. McQueen's face appeared through the window, and Roy didn't recognize him at first but invited him in. McQueen was looking for amiable company, and they spent much of the day together. Roy had once had rare access to take some great 35 mm shots of McQueen in his apprentice days, as well as famous shots of James Dean, Marilyn Monroe, Paul Newman, Grace Kelly, and other famous Actors Studio alumni. He was considered the Method photographer of his time.

"Steve was flipping through Roy's photos and started to get wistful about the old days. He admitted to being a user and a graceless bastard during his years in New York, and he asked Roy if he knew where certain people were so that he could apologize and make amends. I wasn't aware of any of this until years later when Roy and I put together his photo book on Jimmy Dean."[2]

There was no doubt about it—McQueen was a changed man able to see the mistakes of his past with maturity. He had developed to such an extent that he was now keen to put right any wrongdoing and make his amends. This strength of character marked an ongoing theme as he sought out those who had featured prominently in his life and deserved closure and the extension of peace.

Finding God was not a simple transition for McQueen, and it was by no means a cozy solution for how to direct his life. It was genuine, incremental, and above all, it was heartfelt. With his natural paranoia, McQueen never jumped into anything until he was absolutely sure there was no con involved. Stuntman Loren Janes remembers a couple of conversations he had with McQueen concerning God. "They were just brief chats," Janes said. "We'd start on the subject, and I'd just mention it and drop it and he'd drop it, too. But he was the one who always brought it up." McQueen knew that Pat Johnson was a strong man who was reared in the Catholic faith, but Johnson made it a point never to preach. "The quickest

---

1   Schatt took some of McQueen's best portrait photographs in a 1956 session, just days after James Dean's death, capturing some candid moments.

2   The 1982 book, *James Dean: a Portrait*, contains Schatt's familiar images known as the "torn sweater" series, depicting the actor's moody manner.

way to alienate Steve was to try and talk him into anything before he was ready to listen," Johnson said. "It had been years since he had been to Catholic Mass, and he accompanied me one Sunday. He found it was too 'showy' for him. I explained it was up to Steve to find his own connection to God but not to give up."

McQueen finally found the connection through his flying instructor, Sammy Mason. There was an inner confidence, a certain peace about Mason that McQueen could never quite grasp. After months of instruction, McQueen finally asked Mason what it was that made him different.

"That's because I'm a Christian, Steve," Mason humbly replied. Mason had stared death in the face many times as a test pilot for Lockheed and many other times as a stunt pilot. McQueen asked Mason about his faith in Christ. Mason gently answered McQueen's questions and made it a point to never argue with him if their opinion differed. Then one day out of the blue, McQueen asked Sammy if he and Barbara could attend church with Mason and his wife, Wanda. Sammy was thrilled.

The two couples occupied the balcony of the Ventura Missionary Church almost every Sunday, which was led by Pastor Leonard DeWitt. "Steve had always been one of my favorite actors," DeWitt said in 2008. "I didn't know much about him personally but liked the way he portrayed the characters in his films. When I heard that he was taking flying lessons from Sammy Mason, I chuckled because I knew that he had met his match. Sammy was not one of those people who pushed his religion down your throat. Rather, his faith was so much a part of his life that if you were around him for any length of time, it was going to rub off on you.

"This rugged actor liked the church. He asked to be treated the same as the rest of the congregation. People respected that and did not ask for autographs. Steve was coming to the house of God to seek the Lord and worship. Everyone wanted him to have the privacy he needed."

McQueen had been in attendance for about three months when he approached DeWitt one Sunday morning and asked if they could have lunch. They met at the Santa Paula Airport, where DeWitt said McQueen fired one question after another at him about the Christian faith for two solid hours. "Finally, Steve sat back and smiled, and said, 'Well, that about covers it for me,'" DeWitt recalled. "At that point I said, 'Steve, I have only one question to ask you.' [McQueen] was obviously anticipating this question and said, 'You want to know if I'm a born-again Christian?'"

McQueen had recalled for DeWitt a particular Sunday morning when he said the Holy Spirit had touched his heart.

"When you invited people to pray with you to receive Christ, I prayed," McQueen answered. "Yes, I'm a born-again Christian."[3]

Friends and family had noticed the subtle spiritual change, including motorcycle buddy Bud Ekins, the man most likely to have a salty conversation with McQueen. "He was just nicer, more considerate," Ekins said. "He wasn't going to preach to me. He knew better than that. He had those neat airplanes, which is what he wanted; a neat wife, which is who he wanted; those neat motorcycles, which is what he wanted. He was so happy in Santa Paula."

The summer of 1979 proved to be the happiest point in McQueen's life. Every Sunday after church, McQueen would throw open the hangar doors, as the sunlight would shine through, and announce out loud, "Welcome to another day in paradise."

And for an ephemeral moment in time, Steve McQueen was whole and fulfilled in body and soul.

• • •

It took three years for Steve McQueen's film swan song, *The Hunter*, to go from conception to the silver screen. McQueen had read the script in 1977 while he was ensconced at the Beverly Wilshire Hotel. Based on Christopher Keane's chronicle of modern-day bounty hunter Ralph "Papa" Thorson, the story was a throwback to an earlier, less complicated time when the lines between good and bad guys weren't so blurred. "I don't want to make ordinary movies at this stage of my life," McQueen said. "A script must really interest me, or I won't do it. Unfortunately, it's difficult finding suitable material these days. I was lucky to land *The Hunter*. [Thorson's] unusual, a man out of his time, and I guess that's what attracted me to him."

Producer Mort Engleberg, who had hoped for Lee Marvin or Gregory Peck, felt he had hit paydirt when McQueen called him at his Burbank office to tell him he was interested in the part. Throughout the meeting, McQueen continually asked about Thorson's life, and the two men eventually met for dinner at Thorson's North Hollywood home. Pat and Sue Johnson accompanied Steve and Barbara, who found Thorson an interesting man with numerous dichotomies. Aside from being a bounty hunter, he was a church bishop, bridge champion, astrologer, and a nutritionist, despite the fact he weighed around 300 pounds.

---

3 Though many cynics have claimed over the years that McQueen became a born-again Christian to "save his ass" because he knew he had cancer, an item from Liz Smith's June 1979 column disputes this. She was the first journalist to break the story, which was almost six months before he was officially diagnosed.

Thorson was a gentle-natured man, but his home was filled with knives, handguns, rifles, automatic weapons, and other various tools of the trade.

To soften Thorson's edges, McQueen incorporated into the script a random collection of quirky habits and attributes. He had not lost his eye for what made a character interesting, and he lifted them off the screen. His character likes classical music, particularly Tchaikovsky. He likes antique toys, gets around in an old Chevy convertible, and drives badly. He is even involved with a beautiful brunette almost half his age—reminiscent of McQueen's relationship with Barbara Minty.

After their meeting, McQueen agreed to do the picture, and Paramount Studios agreed to his asking price of $3 million and 15 percent of the gross, which added another $5.5 million to McQueen's pocket after the movie was released.

Author and screenwriter Christopher Keane said McQueen starring in the screen adaptation of his book was a surreal moment. "My introduction to the Hollywood we all dream about came on the day I met Steve McQueen," Keane said. "I rode the elevator to the 11th floor of the Beverly Wilshire Hotel, where some of the top movie stars kept their private suites when they were in town.

"It was a heady time. I was in my twenties, and Steve McQueen, the No. 1 box-office star and my childhood hero, had just announced that he was about to turn my book, *The Hunter*, into his next movie. I wasn't nervous. Not much."

Keane, Engleberg, and McQueen sat in the suite for five hours discussing how McQueen envisioned the book becoming the movie. Keane couldn't help but notice that in the next room sat a beautiful high-backed Victorian chair with a hole blown out of the back and the stuffing spread out all over the floor. He contemplated asking McQueen about the demise of the chair and finally mustered up the courage. Keane was told that director Peter Hyams was originally hired for the picture but turned out to be an insufferable bore with a gigantic ego, so McQueen wanted to teach him a lesson.

Hyams had been asked to sit in the chair. McQueen explained that he had made a huge mistake in hiring him and that Hyams was an imbecile who thought far too much of himself. McQueen said he was so mad that he wanted to shoot him. Instead, McQueen instructed Hyams to get up out of the chair and stand by the bar.

"When he did, I pulled this out," McQueen said to Keane, producing a .45-caliber hog-leg revolver. "I aimed it at the chair and pulled the trigger. I informed [Hyams] that I would have shot him if I could have gotten away with it, but just in case, I just killed the terrible aura he carried around and to get the hell out of my sight."

McQueen then laughed and said the most important thing in the film business was focus, and the reason he fired Hyams[4] was that all of his attention was on himself and not where it should have been—on the making of the movie.

"I learned that afternoon what focus was all about," Keane said. "Everything we discussed, whether it seemed important or not, Steve grabbed on to and fed into a greater power—the motion picture he was about to star in. Nothing else mattered. Not him, the bounty hunter, the book writer, or the producer. It was the story, and the script to follow, and not runaway egos that ensure pictures are made."

Hyams was out and, again, McQueen was going to direct until he realized that he was going to go up against the same Director's Guild ruling that he had faced on *Tom Horn*. Instead, he opted for Buzz Kulik, an old friend he had worked with in February 1958 on a live television episode of *Climax!* Kulik recalled McQueen at the time as "a little shit" who was on the verge of stardom. Kulik said that when he met up with the 49-year-old McQueen, the actor seemed "gentler, less driven. He settled on scenes a lot sooner than he did in the past. He knew he wasn't in good shape before the film, and he revealed that to me."

As he did on *An Enemy of the People* and *Tom Horn*, McQueen surrounded himself with a cast of actors who would contribute to the film rather than compete with him. They included veterans Eli Wallach, Ben Johnson, and Richard Venture, as well as newcomers LeVar Burton and Kathryn Harrold.

McQueen was particularly fond of Burton's Emmy Award–winning portrayal as Kunta Kinte in the groundbreaking miniseries *Roots*. McQueen not only pulled a few strings for Burton to get the job, but he also had the part of Tommy Price, a petty thief and bail jumper with redeeming qualities, rewritten for Burton.

McQueen was not as familiar with Kathryn Harrold's work, but he was enamored with her looks and felt she resembled a young Grace Kelly. Through a conversation, they discovered they were both graduates of the Neighborhood Playhouse in New York. Harrold said her training as a Method actress gave their film relationship an interesting dynamic. "There was something going on with him, like he was sort of laughing underneath it all," Harrold said. "I remember doing a scene without him, and he was on the sidelines, watching me, looking and shaking his head like, 'You Method actors.' I sort of liked that because it gave me something to play with. Our relationship was sort of combative in the film."

The normally difficult superstar who relished confrontations and dominating the film set for his scenes had turned over a new leaf when he arrived in Chicago

---

4   Hyams did retain his credit on the film as a co-screenwriter.

in early September 1979. McQueen's spiritual changes were not just on the inside—his newfound desire to achieve rather than obstruct was an exponent of his new work ethic. Producer Mort Engleberg reserved a plush suite for Steve and Barbara at the Drake Hotel in downtown Chicago, but McQueen refused when he discovered the crew was staying at a local Holiday Inn. "One of the things I found with McQueen was there was no real baggage with him," Engleberg said. "Any kind of special treatment, he seemed to go out of his way to avoid. There was no guile about him at all. What you saw was what you got with him. I had heard horror stories about him, but he was just a terrific person."

Barbara Minty said McQueen transformed on the set of *The Hunter*. She had always known him as a person with the capacity for great acts of generosity, but now he seemed more aware than ever that he had the power to initiate good works. McQueen had practically stopped giving autographs a decade before, yet he freely handed out more than 2,000 signed 8-by-10 glossies inscribed, "Steve McQueen, *The Hunter*" for fans. He also dispatched Pat Johnson to the local Catholic church to ask the priest if he had any immediate financial needs. When McQueen was given the amount, he pulled out his checkbook and wrote that amount. Before he handed over the check, he told Mort Engleberg, "This is what I'm giving to the church. I'd like you to match it."

When McQueen spotted local youth in the ghetto tossing around a football stuffed with rags, he shot stuntman Loren Janes a look. Without saying a word, Janes knew he was about to make a local sporting goods store owner very happy. "Steve later handed me a few hundred dollars in cash," Janes said. "I purchased 100 footballs, baseball bats, mitts, and baseballs. They were delivered to a dirt lot the next afternoon. Steve and I hid in a van and watched the kids rip open the boxes, screaming to their friends in excitement. I looked over at Steve, and his eyes were moist."

Despite McQueen's kind deeds, becoming a teenage girl's permanent guardian was something that took even Barbara Minty by surprise. Karen Wilson was a feisty 15-year-old tomboy who lived in a tenement slum where the movie was being filmed. She was hired as an extra, and she struck up a conversation with McQueen between takes. He wanted to know why she wasn't in school. Her response floored him.

"Because I need to make extra money," Wilson said. "My mom is very sick."

Steve and Barbara visited Wilson's mother, where they found the entire family living in squalor. The mother was dying of alcohol poisoning, and Steve and Barbara asked her if they could take Karen back to California and enroll her in a private school. Wilson's mother was slightly offended at first because she felt she wasn't doing such a bad job as a parent. But one look at her surroundings proved otherwise.

After *The Hunter* wrapped, they enrolled Wilson in a private boarding school in Ojai, California. On weekends they picked her up and brought her to Santa Paula to give her a sense of normalcy. They became her legal guardians when Wilson's mother passed away in June 1980. Steve and Barbara personally saw to it that she graduated high school. Today she works at an escrow company in Los Angeles, has been married for nearly 20 years, and has four children. She credits McQueen for saving her life. "He was a father to me, and I will never forget it," Wilson said, "and for this I will forever be grateful."

McQueen's warmth was offset by the blistering Chicago winter. He developed a persistent cough that stayed with him for weeks, and it remained when the crew moved back to Los Angeles in November. Director Buzz Kulik recalled a chilling moment when McQueen was required to chase down a suspect on the streets of Chicago and run up a couple of flights of stairs. After the take, Kulik said McQueen was "leaning against a brick wall, heaving very heavily." Something wasn't right.

Costar Kathryn Harrold recalled a particularly cold day during shooting when McQueen offered Harrold his jacket and the two struck up an odd conversation. "The night before I had a dream in which I had died. Well, Steve was dying of cancer but didn't know it then," Harrold said. "We hardly ever talked to each other, but for some reason we were standing together on the set, and I brought up this dream. I then asked, 'Are you afraid to die?' Steve's reply was firm.

"'No, I'm not,' McQueen said."

The Hunter was not a masterpiece. It did well financially but not superbly. McQueen had not had a big smash since 1974's *The Towering Inferno*. In large part, this was because he no longer wanted to make blockbusters—he wanted to make films that interested him. However, the shortcomings of the picture still stand out. The $8 million budget appears modest, and the film comes across as more of a television movie, not a big-budget spectacular. The story seems slightly confused, especially with a weak bad-guy protagonist who is neither believable nor menacing. The Michel Legrand soundtrack is a strange mixture of jazz and baroque, and it seems out of sync with what's happening on the screen.

McQueen's performance is good, but it heavily juxtaposes all of his action roles. He looks tired and out of breath in most of the action scenes. This is fair in the sense that his character is not exactly youthful. However, it is difficult for an audience to believe for two reasons. First, they are used to seeing their hero ride to victory on a motorbike and pursue crooks at high speed behind the wheel. Now, however, their hero looks to be struggling. Second, he was of course in difficult health in real life, short of breath and unfortunately short of time.

Perhaps the hardest thing of all, though, is the final scene. At the end of the film, Thorson goes to the hospital as his girlfriend is giving birth. The emotion of this act causes him to pass out cold on the hospital floor. What was meant to be a nice comedic touch is actually quite chilling. This was McQueen's last film appearance, and in retrospect it is difficult for many fans to watch knowing what happened to McQueen in real life just months later.

"God bless you," is an unscripted moment and McQueen's last cinematic line.

In spite of this, *The Hunter* has plenty of charm. Watching the film today offers a superb insight into McQueen himself. He put much of his own character into Papa Thorson, who makes a cameo in the film as a bartender. McQueen is genuinely having fun playing with the vintage cars and 1930s ephemera on the set. He is also able to poke fun at himself and his image during the hilarious scenes where he struggles to drive his character's car. This is a remarkable transition for someone who fired actors if they were taller than he was. McQueen was able to be comfortable with himself and was no longer concerned with self-promotion. The casting is also good, especially in the genuine friendship and rapport he has on screen with Ben Johnson, LeVar Burton, and old colleague Eli Wallach. These are certainly touching scenes. In essence, McQueen gains respect for allowing his character to grow old gracefully, no longer needing to impress anyone but himself.

The Hunter, as McQueen's final film, was certainly not the highlight of his career. In the context of the great films he had made and the timeless characters he created, it is not the one he will be remembered for. However, not many actors finish with their greatest cinematic triumph. What *The Hunter* does show in terms of McQueen's legacy is his power to have a film made; without McQueen, the film would not have happened. It emphasizes McQueen's star status given the colossal salary he received. It demonstrated that he was still a major force in Hollywood. Again, the poster campaign simply features McQueen in an action pose. The same message rang true as it had for the last 20 years—McQueen sold pictures. Also, it reinforced McQueen's desire to do the films he wanted to do. He liked the story and connected with it and made the film he wanted to make. As much as McQueen had changed and become a different man, some of the most impressive qualities he possessed still remained intact.

The film was met with a tepid response when it was released on July 28, 1980. *The Village Voice* pronounced McQueen a "tired daredevil," while the

Los Angeles Examiner thought McQueen was "way off stride... [his] once-crisp physical reflexes look shot."

Though it was a good earner for Paramount, especially in the television and VHS market, *The Hunter* took in about $16 million domestically and $37 million worldwide. It certainly wasn't the comeback vehicle McQueen had hoped for; in fact, it was a downbeat ending to a magical career.

However, McQueen's heart was no longer in the movie business, and this was not in a sad sense. He had beaten the best and achieved all of his film goals, so *The Hunter* was never meant to be the greatest blockbuster of all time. McQueen already had those accolades. The McQueen story had for years been played off of the film set, and his legacy had already grown from his actions and his life lived off-screen. McQueen's story had become one of personal fulfillment and making a positive impact in the community and on those around him. He found peace, and he had found God. His final chapter was looming, and he would be faced with the hardest battle he had ever faced. Soon he would be fighting for his life.

36

INDUSTRIAL DISEASE

STEVE MCQUEEN NEVER BELIEVED he was long for this earth. He once told Neile early in their marriage that he wasn't going to live long and that he intended to take a "big slice out of life." At the height of his career, when he was drowning in drink, drugs, adultery, and hubris, McQueen confessed to friend Von Dutch that he would never make it past the half-century mark. "Hey, my mother died when she was 50, my father died when he was 50, and I'm going to die when I'm 50," McQueen said. "That means I have 10 years to live it up."

McQueen, the man who had the world on a golden string, fulfilled his promise, always living life on his own terms, doing whatever he wished. In late 1979, the other shoe dropped, and he heard the thud loud and clear.

When Steve and Barbara returned from Chicago in early November, they finally moved into their restored Victorian farmhouse and built a 4,200-square-foot barn to store his motorcycles and antique cars. The cozy home came with horse stables and chicken coops. Joining the animal kingdom were a couple of dogs and more than a dozen cats. "Every time we had ever argued, he'd give me a kitten to make up," Barbara said. "We ended up with 13 by my last count."

They filled the house with old-fashioned toilets with high wall-mounted tanks and chain pulls, antique marble wash basins, brass fittings, period ceiling fans, Victorian multiglobe chandeliers, filigree light fixtures, wooden-crank telephones, and an old-fashioned stove and oven. One day when Barbara was in Los Angeles on a modeling assignment, Steve had a white picket fence erected to her delight. She felt their home and their life was perfect.

Among their first houseguests were Barbara's parents, Gene and Wilma Minty, and her grandmother Vica Minty. Gene was a no-nonsense man who was a little perturbed that his daughter had been "shacking up" with a Hollywood movie star for two years without an engagement ring. The dairy farmer was deeply concerned that McQueen was "not going to buy the cow when he kept getting the milk for free."

McQueen took Gene for a flight in his newly purchased ($65,000) Pitcairn PA-8 Mailwing. After a day of male bonding, the two returned to the house, and Gene decided it was time to have the talk. He asked McQueen to take a walk. When they returned, Barbara recalled her dad winked at her and McQueen was much nicer. "Steve pulled me aside and said, 'I told your father that we're definitely going to get married and that if anything ever happened to me, you would be well taken care of,'" Barbara said. "My dad had a slightly different version of their conversation and said, 'I told Steve that I'd kill him if he did anything to hurt you.'" Almost two months later, Steve and Barbara were married.

Their temporary bliss was interrupted when McQueen had difficulty breathing and began to experience night sweats. When Crystal and Larry Endicott dropped by for a casual visit one day, McQueen pulled Crystal aside. He specifically asked for the name of the doctor who examined Larry when he was diagnosed with melanoma. "Can he be trusted?" McQueen asked. Crystal assured him that the doctor was trustworthy.

On December 10, 1979, McQueen was examined by the Endicotts' doctor, and an X-ray revealed a spot on his right lung. The doctor urged McQueen to check into Cedars-Sinai Hospital in Los Angeles for further testing. On December 17 he checked in under the assumed name of Don Schoonover. A new set of X-rays revealed a massive tumor in his right lung. Exploratory surgery was called for on Saturday, December 22. He was diagnosed with mesothelioma, an incurable cancer of the lining of the lungs usually related to asbestos exposure. Surgery was ruled out because of the nature of the disease. Doctors implanted radioactive cobalt into his chest and experimented with chemotherapeutic drugs, which included interferon, a naturally occurring antiviral agent.

McQueen's prospects were grim.

The movie star spent his last Christmas in the hospital, and Barbara was accompanied by Grady Ragsdale and Sammy Mason. After a five-day stay and a battery of tests, McQueen was discharged on December 29. The news of McQueen's cancer diagnosis was met with mixed emotions, including grim determination, indignation, disbelief, and McQueen's signature sardonic sense of humor. Barbara recalled once when she was rolling him in a wheelchair down one of the hospital's long corridors and he was struck by a funny thought.

"Barbara, the long hall…Get it?" Steve said. The comment was a play on words and a private joke shared between the two of them. They had planned on publishing a photo book of their crazy lives together, using Minty's photos and McQueen providing the text. They were going to call it *The Long Haul*. She returned a polite smile, but the remark left Barbara hanging between a laugh and a tear.

• • •

Mesothelioma is an aggressive form of cancer primarily caused by the inhalation of dangerous asbestos fibers. The disease attacks the mesothelium, a protective two-layered membrane that covers the internal organs of the body, including the lungs, heart, and abdominal organs. The disease takes anywhere from 20 to 50 years to develop but is usually not diagnosed until it's in an advanced stage, often leaving victims with just months to live.

All types of industries began using asbestos in the early 20th century to insulate pipes, roofs, heavy machinery, car parts, and protective clothing. Asbestos use greatly increased during World War II as the United States and Great Britain prepared to do battle with Adolph Hitler's evil empire. The link between asbestos exposure and cancers of the lungs and abdomen wasn't really known until the 1960s when researchers found that the two were related and finally gave the disease its name. Only 24 cases of mesothelioma had been documented by 1980; all 24 victims had died.

The occupations most associated with mesothelioma were tradespeople, such as shipyard workers, electricians, plumbers, construction industry workers, pipe fitters, boilermakers, mine workers, and anyone subject to heavy exposure to dangerous asbestos and airborne asbestos fibers. Mesothelioma was mostly known as an industrial disease.

In McQueen's case, he had inhaled the tiny particles practically his entire adult life—at construction jobs and on soundstages. It resided in car brakes and in motorcycle helmets, gloves, and race suits. The race suits in particular were often lined with asbestos to make them more fireproof. McQueen would often roll the garments high up over his face, breathing through the fabric itself. He was exposed directly to asbestos while in the Marines when he served 41 days in the brig. Part of McQueen's penance was work detail in the ship's hold, where he and other men ripped out the asbestos-filled pipes. McQueen told a friend that the asbestos particles filled the air and that the men could barely breathe.

Crystal Endicott recalled her first conversation with McQueen when he returned from Cedars-Sinai Hospital. "I think he didn't tell anybody at first because he didn't believe it was real," Endicott said. "I think he felt, 'This isn't happening to me.' That's what goes through your mind when you're given a death sentence." Endicott's husband Larry had been diagnosed with cancer a few months before. She said Steve confided in Larry the most during those first few months. "They talked about it a lot because they were going through the same thing together," Endicott said. "My husband would come home and say, 'Steve felt bad today.' They could share this together."[1]

McQueen kept the diagnosis a secret from everyone, including his closest friends, and he didn't tell his son and daughter until months later. Several tabloids, including *The National Enquirer* and *The Star*, had reported McQueen's stay in the hospital revealed a rare lung infection but had shown nothing serious. McQueen's ranch hand, Grady Ragsdale, commented on the legitimacy of the accounts to his employer. "This stuff isn't true," Ragsdale said.

"Yes, it is," McQueen replied. "It's true as far as the public is concerned. I don't want anyone to know I have cancer."

Ragsdale also broached the subject of McQueen's movie career, which was still white-hot. Offers kept pouring in, including roles in such films as *Quigley Down Under, Dogs of War, Hang Tough,* and *Hand-Carved Coffins.* McQueen also received an offer for *The Manhattan Project.* McQueen turned down an offer for a firm $4 million offer from producer Carlo Ponti, who had wanted McQueen to costar with Ponti's wife, Sophia Loren. According to some, McQueen's new asking price of $5 million up front plus 15 percent of the box office gross was a way to hold producers at bay until McQueen figured out a cure for his cancer.

"My agent wants me to do another picture. I told him to put it on the back burner for a while and I'd think about it," McQueen told Ragsdale. "I don't think he'll be suspicious. I've gone a few years between pictures before. It's not like I'm bustin' to work all the time." Ragsdale replied that if his agent had a good script, why not read it?

"Let's face it, pal. I'm out of the picture business. I've done my last film," McQueen said. "It's time for me to move over and make room for somebody else."

With that proclamation, McQueen called friend Chuck Bail a few days later and requested they meet right away. "Can you keep a secret?" McQueen asked. Bail had already heard industry rumors about McQueen's health and suspected the worst. "Don't tell me," Bail replied. "I'm the biggest blabbermouth on the planet."

"Chuck, I can't do the film," McQueen blurted out. "I'm sick."

Morally, Bail was in a dilemma. If he told Columbia executives, the word would get out about McQueen's condition, which his friend wanted to keep quiet. Bail stalled the studio as long as he could, but a few months later it was

---

1 Larry Endicott died approximately a year after McQueen.

revealed in the tabloids that McQueen had cancer. *The Last Ride* was put on a shelf, where it has remained ever since. The decision not to tell the studio was simple for Bail. "I kept my promise to Steve not to tell, which is exactly what he would have done for me," he said.

Producer Phil Parslow said the cat was already out of the bag when he received a phone call from noted Hollywood agent Phil Gersh, who had hosted a bash to display his world-famous art collection. "McQueen is very sick," said Gersh, who had obtained the information from a doctor who attended the party. "How do you know?" Parslow asked. Gersh asked the doctor, "You mean, as in mortally ill?" Gersh said the doctor bowed his head and didn't respond.

• • •

McQueen forged ahead, making big plans, dreaming big, and valiantly living his life. He had seldom looked back during his life, and now, with the clock ticking, the only way was forward. On January 16, 1980, Steve McQueen and Barbara Minty became man and wife in the living room of their ranch home in Santa Paula. True to his nature, McQueen didn't get down on bended knee to propose or slip an engagement ring into a champagne flute for a surprise toast.

"Here, are you satisfied?" he asked with a sheepish smile, slipping the ring on to Barbara's finger after he had it sized a few days before. He then headed to the refrigerator and cracked open a beer.

The two were married by Reverend Leslie Miller, who was the associate pastor at the Ventura Missionary Church. The wedding attire was as casual as McQueen's proposal—McQueen wore a white button-down shirt, gray down jacket, and blue jeans held up by a turquoise belt buckle, while Minty donned a white pants suit and a small wreath of baby's breath. She held a bouquet of daisies, while McQueen wore a boutonniere pinned to the right side of his shirt pocket. McQueen's flight instructor Sammy Mason and his wife, Wanda, served as the witnesses. The ceremony was brief and to the point; it lasted all of 10 minutes. McQueen called stuntman Loren Janes, who had implored McQueen in Chicago to marry Barbara, telling him, "This is the greatest thing to happen to me."

Three days later, Neile also took a trip down the altar with Alvin Toffel, who was president of the Norton Simon Foundation. The two had met at a luncheon for Princess Grace of Monaco, who was in town for a 20th Century Fox board meeting in April 1979. Rupert Allan, McQueen's former publicist, remained friendly with Neile and had invited her to the luncheon. Allan also invited the recently divorced Toffel at the last minute, and Toffel was seated next to Neile. The two struck up a conversation and hit it off. Nine months later, they were married on Saturday, January 19, 1980. Toffel was a true gentlemen who was an impressive man in his own right. He was prepared to offer the stability and undivided attention that Neile deserved and that McQueen could never have given her. It is highly probable that McQueen himself would have been happy that Neile had found love and happiness and would be cared for in this next chapter of her life.

• • •

In February 1980, McQueen returned to Cedars-Sinai for more tests and examinations. New X-rays revealed that the cancer was spreading. The cancer was found in the lining of his stomach, and nodules the size of golf balls were discovered at the base of his neck and on his chest, making it impossible to operate. There was more bad news, too—he had a 5 percent chance of living through the end of the year. The clock was ticking, but McQueen stubbornly rejected the news that the end was near. "I can't believe it's over. I won't believe it," he said. "There is so much I want to do, have to do!"

Terry McQueen recalled in a 1991 interview that it was a life-changing moment for everyone in her father's life. "I remember going out with him, hand in hand, out of the Cedars-Sinai Hospital in Los Angeles. He had just learned the diagnosis," she said. "Outside, the weather was good. People laughed. For us, it was the beginning of a nightmare. For the first time, Dad needed me, and I as a child needed him. The disease had suddenly brought us even closer."

Radiation treatments were recommended for McQueen in the hope that they might slow the cancer, but McQueen cut short his first session when a nurse told him he needed to sit still. "I don't want to get this on your skin because it will burn and blister," she told him. His eyes narrowed, and his body shot upright. "What?" McQueen asked. The nurse repeated that the medicine would burn and blister if it got on his skin. "If it does that to the outside of my body, what will it do to the inside of my body?" McQueen asked rhetorically. His question was met with silence.

"Forget it," he said, and he walked out of the hospital.

Friend and karate instructor Pat Johnson said he returned to California on March 1, 1980, after a long film shoot in San Antonio. He, too, had heard rumors of McQueen's ill health but figured if McQueen had something to tell him, he would have picked up the phone. Johnson had been back only a day when he received the call from McQueen—they needed to talk. "There was no indication in his voice that anything was amiss," Johnson recalled. "It seemed important but certainly nothing really bad." Johnson agreed to drive to Santa Paula, where they met at McQueen's ranch. As soon as Johnson walked in the door, he sensed McQueen's somber mood. "Let's go for a walk," McQueen said.

Johnson remembered the sounds, sights, and smells of the oil wells pumping in the distance along South Mountain Road, the main thoroughfare that led to the ranch. After much silence, McQueen finally spoke. "Pat, they found something on my lung. They're not sure what it is. It could be potentially life-threatening. I thought you should know," McQueen said. "I don't know what the future holds, but whatever it is, I'm going to fight it all the way." Johnson said tears came streaming down his face, and his gut told him something was wrong.

"This can't be happening," Johnson said to himself.

Almost three weeks later, on March 11, 1980, McQueen's medical condition became public knowledge when the *National Enquirer* broke the news with a cover story and a declarative headline: "Steve McQueen's Heroic Battle Against Cancer." The article read:

> Frantic last-ditch efforts by doctors have failed to halt a vicious and inoperable lung cancer that is killing Steve McQueen.
>
> The end could come within two months, believes one of his doctors. But the steely-eyed screen hero is battling back bravely.
>
> In a desperate bid to shrink the cancer, doctors implanted radioactive cobalt, which kills cancer cells, in his chest—right on the malignancy. They sewed him up, leaving the cobalt inside.
>
> They removed the cobalt—and found that it had failed miserably.
>
> In fact, a doctor disclosed that one of McQueen's physicians personally told him that "there was only a 5 percent chance that McQueen would live for a year. He has terminal lung cancer."
>
> A Cedars-Sinai surgeon who was present at the operation to implant the cobalt confided to a close friend in January. "There is nothing we can do for him."

Some of the facts were incorrect—the article listed the diagnosis as lung cancer as opposed to mesothelioma—but many elements of the story were indeed true, such as the inoperable nature of the cancer, the failed cobalt treatment, and the dire prognosis.

The Florida-based tabloid, which sold about 5 million copies per week, ushered in a new era of tabloid journalism that allowed the public to peek into a celebrity's private heartbreak. In 1974 the tabloid hired newspaperman Iain Calder as its new editor, who honed his craft in the cutthroat journalism of the lowest common denominator of London, England, and his native Scotland. In the span of a few years, Calder turned the gross-out rag into a supermarket best seller and household name, helping to shape today's modern American media. To the surprise of scornful critics, Calder actually established more stringent policies in the newsroom, with an insistence on journalistic integrity and discipline. In particular, stories on celebrities had to be confirmed by at least two sources and satisfy the newspaper's legal advisers.

Calder's reporters were trained to do anything to get the story, including hopping fences, hiding in bushes, sneaking into VIP and red-carpet events, dressing in costume, bribing anyone with information, using unnamed sources in their stories, and giving handsome payouts for story tips. This audacious attitude pioneered a new kind of journalism in America, which now placed celebrities inside the 24-hour fishbowl of surveillance seen today. He pushed his reporters to new heights and extreme lows. In its history, the *National Enquirer* has bribed Elvis Presley's cousin Bobby Mann with $18,000 to sneak in a miniature Arco-Flex spy camera to take a postmortem photo of the King lying in an open casket; coaxed a confession from John Belushi's drug dealer that led to her conviction; discovered crucial clues in the O.J. Simpson case that police had overlooked; and dogged presidential candidate John Edwards into confessing paternity of an out-of-wedlock child after two years, which led to a federal investigation of misused campaign funds (and a much-publicized Pulitzer Prize nomination).

In the case of Steve McQueen, the *National Enquirer* assigned reporters Tony Brenna and Donna Rosenthal to Cedars-Sinai to get the scoop on McQueen's medical status. They also sent a young-looking newsman who posed as a college student in an attempt to infiltrate McQueen's surroundings in Santa Paula. The first place he strolled into was the Santa Paula Airport café, where he positioned himself near McQueen as he ate breakfast. McQueen had a weak spot for young kids and old people alike, and the young man ingratiated himself to the star. McQueen was on his own turf and was not on guard. After finishing his meal, McQueen invited him to the hangar to see his planes and motorcycle collection. When the two arrived, they were greeted by Barbara. The stranger marveled at the collection, pulled out a camera and started taking pictures. Alarmed but not threatened, McQueen stepped forward and casually asked, "What's the camera for?" The young man already had an alibi worked out. "Oh, in my art class in college, we're taking photos of anything that would make a fascinating picture, but if you would like me to stop taking pictures, I will." Touched by his sincerity, McQueen backed off. "No, go ahead," McQueen said. "It makes no big never mind to me." Now with McQueen's blessing, the photo enthusiast clicked away to his heart's content. The move was callous one, taking advantage of the star who defended his privacy to the utmost. When the story finally broke, it was accompanied by the surreptitiously obtained photos. They offered an unsanctioned glimpse into McQueen's private world and showed him in poor health. It was a tabloid dream come true but a nightmare for such a private and guarded person.

Perhaps more troubling was how the information was obtained and how the *National Enquirer* was able to gain access to McQueen's confidential records, which raises all sort of privacy issues. It was later discovered that two individuals who worked at the hospital had shopped McQueen's story to the press.[2] They found a more-than-willing buyer in the *National Enquirer*. The publication took a lot of flak for breaking the story, but Haydon Cameron, senior editor, was unapologetic when asked for an explanation. Humanity and respect were out of the window; it was all about circulation and sales. "The man is news," Cameron said, "and we are in the news-presentation business." He also charged that McQueen made a lot of money from the public, and therefore the public had a right to know of his medical condition.

A slew of tabloid coverage ensued after the *Enquirer* story. The same publications that adored McQueen's bad-boy ways had turned on him and dogged his every move. His life became a public circus, and the rumors had placed McQueen's professional career in jeopardy. Insurance companies don't bond ill stars who can't complete the work they are hired to do. It wreaked havoc on his personal life, upsetting many of McQueen's family members and friends. Friend Bud Ekins took the direct approach by marching into McQueen's backyard one Sunday after church with a copy of the *National Enquirer* clutched in his hand.

"What's this cancer stuff?" Ekins asked.

"Oh, those assholes are so full of shit," McQueen said. "I don't know why they write stuff like that." McQueen then took off his shirt and pointed out there were no surgical scars or any indication his body had been probed.

"The article said that the doctors had cut him open and found cancer and had sewed him back up and told him to forget it," Ekins said. "So I'm standing there, looking for where they've opened him up, and I don't see any scars where they've cut him. So I believed him." McQueen's incision was under his armpit, which he held down while Ekins looked him over, thus hiding the scar and shielding Ekins from the truth. McQueen later said he denied the story to protect his family and friends from the media. Ekins was one of his oldest friends, a man who had been beside McQueen during his absolute prime and his wingman on

---

2   The same incident happened to actress Farrah Fawcett in 2008, when a UCLA Medical Center staffer shopped the actress' medical file to the highest bidder. That also turned out to be the *National Enquirer*.

many adventures. Sharing the brutal truth with Ekins was undoubtedly too much for McQueen to cope with at that moment, but McQueen would go on to tell people incrementally in his own way.

The *National Enquirer* story also caused a ripple effect in the media and posed a dilemma of sorts. Should the mainstream press cover the story or continue allowing the tabloid press to scoop them? The answer to that question remedied itself in a few months when McQueen issued a press release confirming his condition while attempting to stick it to the *Enquirer*.

The Hollywood Reporter, a widely read trade publication in the entertainment industry, shortly followed suit and reported McQueen's second hospitalization at Cedars-Sinai. Agent Marvin Josephson did not deny McQueen's first trip to the hospital and claimed it was "a bronchial ailment." He dismissed the second hospitalization and said "that item was an error, and anyone can call the hospital himself to check the records." Of course, McQueen hadn't checked in under his own name and could plausibly deny the story.

McQueen called on mega-attorney Ken Ziffren to quell the story and issue angry denials. Ziffren immediately went after the *Enquirer* and wrote a short but stern note that the story was "untrue, damaging, and actionable." He threatened litigation if it didn't retract the story. When the *Enquirer* didn't back down, McQueen waged his own publicity campaign to combat the rumors by hiring high-powered publicist Warren Cowan. Cowan's first act was to issue a denial through syndicated columnist Liz Smith in her March 23, 1980, column. McQueen was quoted as saying, "I don't have terminal cancer, just terminal fury." McQueen also told Smith he would join fellow celebrities Carol Burnett, Shirley Jones, Rory Calhoun, Paul Lynde, Phil Silvers, and Ed McMahon in suing the tabloid, but McQueen never followed through.

Cowan also put the public-relations machine into overdrive by strategically placing McQueen in industry hotspots to show that he was alive and kicking. McQueen dined at Ma Maison in late March 1980, a West Hollywood restaurant that caters largely to the film industry. Cowan leaked to several reporters that the media-shy McQueen would be enjoying lunch at the eatery with his wife if the reporters wanted to engage McQueen. Columnists Army Archerd, Robin Leach, and Bill Boyce took Cowan up on the generous offer and were seated next to McQueen. The plan worked beautifully. All three wrote glowing bits that McQueen was back. Boyce, who had a syndicated column with Knight News Service, was especially effusive in his column:

> McQueen looked very thin, very tanned, and very happy. Clad in blue jeans and a western shirt, the actor was so light in mood that he didn't seem to

mind at all when I asked him what his reaction was to all the printed reports of his supposedly terminal illness.

It's a bunch of garbage," McQueen cracked. "Don't give it a thought. Don't worry about it. We're not." And for a man who is alleged to be suffering from the ravages of cancer, McQueen looked the picture of contentment as he smoked a big cigar all through his visit to the restaurant.

Hilly Elkins, who dined with McQueen that afternoon, was familiar with how the Hollywood machinery worked and instinctively knew it was a setup. He and McQueen had stayed in touch over the years, but it had been a couple of years since they had spoken. The last time was when McQueen solicited Elkins for a critique of *An Enemy of the People.* "It has a lot of words," Ekins said, getting right to the point. Elkins, too, had heard the industry rumors about McQueen's dire condition. When his old client suggested they dine at Ma Maison, Elkins immediately grew suspicious. "When someone who usually asks you to meet him at the back room of a Denny's asks you to meet at Ma Maison, you get worried," Elkins said. "It was so out of character that I literally pulled the phone away from my ear to look at the receiver because I couldn't believe it."

Actress and friend Suzanne Pleshette was also present that day with her husband, Tom Gallagher. Pleshette, who sat across the room from Steve and Barbara, stole a private moment with McQueen. The two, who had been friends since the '50s, caught each other's eye. "How are you?" McQueen mouthed out silently. Pleshette gave him a thumbs-up sign. She returned the question, "How are you?" He replied with a toothy smile and shot back two thumbs up. Years later she marveled, "He was worried about me, even though he was dying. I don't think he rested until I married Tommy. That was the only guy he approved of. I loved Steve then, and I will always love him."

Barbara McQueen said the luncheon was not only a way to quash the rumors but was also McQueen's Hollywood farewell. "He didn't want them to remember him as a weakened cancer victim," she said. "Steve wanted to be remembered as the man he once was, and that day, he acted the part beautifully."

The premiere of *Tom Horn* was also an effective tool in getting out the word that Steve McQueen was just fine. Once again, Cowan tipped off reporters that McQueen would be present at a press preview in Oxnard on March 28, 1980. The media and paparazzi showed up in full force. Barbara McQueen said in 2010, "Steve wasn't feeling well and wasn't looking forward to it at all," she said. "He wanted to get in and get out, and so that's what we did."

A few minutes before the 8:00 PM showing, Steve and Barbara drove up in his pickup truck, and a flurry of flashbulbs began popping as they made their way into the theater. A crush of reporters descended on the couple, and one of them asked, "Do you really have lung cancer?" McQueen replied with a sheepish grin, "I don't know where you get your information." As the McQueens pushed forward, the questioning became more intense. "Whatever you've heard is ridiculous, just rumors," McQueen said. "Do I look like I have lung cancer?" McQueen, who was sporting a beard, blue jeans, and a sharp-looking leather jacket, looked the epitome of health for a man who had just turned 50 that month. The statement seemed to placate the media, which allowed him and Barbara to enter the theater without having to take any more questions.

Just before the closing credits rolled, Steve and Barbara made a hasty retreat for the exit. Almost two hours after he first appeared, the media and hundreds of fans were still milling around, hoping to catch a glimpse of the superstar. Seeing the crowd converge on them, Steve and Barbara made it safely inside their truck before photographers started snapping the last public images of McQueen. He accelerated the truck forward, nearly running over an aggressive photographer.

The *Tom Horn* premiere left McQueen emotionally and physically exhausted, and when he returned to Santa Paula, he didn't leave his ranch house for an entire week. The effort involved in maintaining a smokescreen of health and fighting the invasive journalism must have been draining.

He could not keep up the current cycle of random and ineffective hospital treatments, followed by tabloid reports and the herculean efforts necessary to dispel the reports by appearing at events and releasing statements. All of this was taking its toll on McQueen mentally as much as physically. He knew he was on borrowed time and had no intention on wasting it with such futility. McQueen had played his own game his whole life and would do so again. He decided on a new strategy. Whether he realized it or not, the last battle was upon him, and he had drawn up his final plan of attack.

37

THE LAST MILE

While McQueen bid farewell to the public at Ma Maison, in private he was telling his other close friends good-bye, as well.

McQueen made a mental list of friends, associates, and people he cared about. This was a good-bye list, and he ensured he met each associate, friend, and even those he felt he had wronged over the years. It was an incredibly brave sentiment. With each person, McQueen would either tell them of his condition and its severity, subtly hint at it, or simply just use the opportunity for a final moment of bonding. Each meeting must have almost broken his heart inside, going through the shock of each person's reaction each time. He was a private person, but he recognized the impact he had on the lives around him and felt each person deserved his own personal contact with him. It was closure in a sense but also a poetic and valorous thing to do in the face of his condition. With so little time left, he was thinking about others and one by one said his farewells.

Lord Richard Attenborough, who costars with McQueen in *The Great Escape* and *The Sand Pebbles* and had developed a deep affinity for McQueen, said their last meeting was bittersweet. "Steve was never one of our great correspondents. He would never write, but he would call," Attenborough said. The two agreed to meet at the Brown Derby, a Hollywood landmark. Because Attenborough's flight from England had been delayed, he expected McQueen to greet him. As he was about to sit down, he caught sight of an old man staring at him from one of the bar stools. "A shiver ran through me—the old man was Steve."

Attenborough knew the purpose of the visit, but the two never broached the subject of McQueen's illness and kept the banter lighthearted. Attenborough recalled, "We ribbed each other about the day he scared the shit out of me on his motorbike. He reminded me about the time I dragged him to a football match at Stamford Bridge.

"He didn't mention that he had cancer and had only six months to live. When we hugged outside, neither of us said good-bye. I valued his friendship profoundly and miss him more than I can say."

Stuntman Loren Janes said McQueen flew his airplane to the Sand Canyon Airport to have lunch under the wing of his plane, where the two reminisced about their lives, careers, family, and friends. Janes said McQueen did discuss his cancer and wasn't afraid to try a radical treatment, nor was he afraid to die. He figured it was a win-win situation. "If I die sooner, it's less painful, and maybe if I try some things and they use me as a guinea pig and I die but they learn from it, maybe it can help someone else," McQueen offered.

Their last meal came to an end as the sun was slowly setting. The star and his stuntman of 22 years hugged farewell, and then McQueen flew off into the California sky.

Friend Steve Ferry, who gave McQueen shelter when he first arrived in California in the late '50s, also got a phone call from out of the blue. The two had been out of touch for almost a decade, and Ferry had since remarried. McQueen thought it would be a hoot if the men and their two young wives got together. The Ferrys traveled to Santa Paula, enjoyed a good meal, and had a few laughs.

Friend Don Gordon was also invited to Santa Paula, where the two men visited McQueen's hangar after a delicious meal. Gordon was preparing to fly to England for a film role, and McQueen promised they'd go flying once he returned. Gordon, who had no idea McQueen was sick, was surprised when McQueen hugged him.

"Now I realize in retrospect he was saying good-bye to me," Gordon said.

Sometime in April 1980, Bud Ekins said McQueen paid him a visit at his motorcycle shop. In his pocket was a stack of pictures of an antique motorcycle collection in Boston. He wanted Ekins to go with him to appraise the bikes. Ekins said yes, with the stipulation that McQueen purchase first-class tickets.

"Oh, he moaned about that one," Ekins laughed when he recollected the story in the early '90s. "I just did it to jab him a bit."

When they arrived in Boston, McQueen purchased the entire collection. On the flight back, Ekins noticed that his old friend was melancholy, drifting in and out of conversations, looking out the window for extended periods of time. Ekins said, "Out of the blue, Steve blurted out, 'If anything ever happens to me, I want you to have all my bikes.' I looked at him as if he were nuts. Steve said, 'Well, wouldn't you do the same for me?' I said, 'Hell no, I wouldn't leave you my bikes. I would want the money to go to my children.' Steve thought about it for a second and said, 'Tell you what—if anything ever happens to me, I want you to pick the best two bikes in my collection, and that's my final word on the matter.'"

The two men agreed and shook hands on the deal.

Ekins said in retrospect, "This was Steve's way of telling me he was going to die. He had already been diagnosed."

McQueen had one last loose end to tie up and a chance to make amends to someone he had hurt deeply during the making of *Le Mans*. A decade had passed since McQueen had run off Solar gofer Mario Iscovich with his wildly erratic and drug-induced behavior. Iscovich wasn't hard to track down. He had become quite successful in the film industry as a location scout, manager, and production executive, and he was working on a project for director Stanley Kramer when McQueen invited him to the Santa Paula ranch. The two caught up with each other, with McQueen beaming like a proud father over Iscovich's impressive list of accomplishments. After lunch, the two men relaxed in the living room to chat.

"Mario, I don't think I'm going to make it," McQueen said without warning. The comment momentarily took Iscovich by surprise, but he certainly knew what McQueen was talking about. He had heard the industry gossip, read the trade papers, and kept in touch with Neile, who had apprised him of Steve's situation.

"Is everything all right between you and me?" McQueen asked gingerly. "You're not sore at me anymore, are ya, kid?" Iscovich was gracious, and no matter what McQueen did in the past, he still loved the man.

"No, Steve. I was mad only for a little bit," Iscovich said. "I put it all aside many years ago." They embraced for the final time, with a tear running down Iscovich's face as they parted company.

Iscovich said of that final meeting, "You could see that Steve was not well. Just one look at him and I could see that he was not all right."

• • •

Faced with the grim prospect he most likely would not live through 1980, Steve McQueen turned to his new bride and discussed their future. "When Steve was told his cancer was inoperable, he looked at me and said, 'Honey, what do you want to do? Do you want to get in the truck and go to the desert and drink beer, shoot guns, and have fun? Or do you want me to fight this?'" Barbara McQueen said. "I was a young bride and wanted a life with my new husband, so for me there really was no choice. I said, 'Let's fight this thing.' Looking back, it may not have been the best idea because his quality of life really suffered in the end and it was a painful ordeal, but I was so in love with this man that I wanted to do everything humanly possible to help him get well."

Part of getting well meant fiercely protecting his privacy. On April 7, 1980, McQueen filed for a gun permit with the city of Santa Paula to carry two Colt automatic .45s—one for him and one for Barbara. The reason for the permit was listed as "business protection." McQueen was on the last stretch of his life, and he was pulling up the drawbridge. He wanted to be able to defend himself and guard the privacy he sorely wanted. Only the select few who were close to McQueen were allowed through. The final stand had begun.

• • •

By rejecting a traditional method to treat his cancer, McQueen's only other option was to traverse the strange and uncharted waters of alternative cancer therapy, which includes lots of empty promises, backroom treatments, snake-oil salesmen, and miracle peddlers. The first such doctor McQueen contacted told him that several weeks of intravenous feeding, large doses of minerals, vitamins, antioxidants, and a new diet could possibly reverse the cancer.

McQueen's vanity precluded him from receiving treatment in a hospital or clinical setting for fear that other patients, visitors, and staff could stare at him, so he rented a fully equipped RV and parked it outside the doctor's San Fernando Valley office. It was a painful ordeal, which required McQueen to lay flat on his back six hours a day, five days a week for seven weeks while the medication marinated in his circulatory system. His solitary thoughts must have been a dark place.

The injections were administered by Barbara McQueen since legally the doctor could not perform the treatments on the premises or on the patient. However, a nurse oversaw the process and taught Barbara how to tap a vein and inject the needle into Steve's arm. "The whole thing was way illegal, but I must say I became a pretty good shot," Barbara McQueen said. "Steve's eyes were as big as saucers the first time I administered a shot. Steve was desperate to find a cure, and that led us down a desperate path." When McQueen returned to Cedars-Sinai to check if the treatments had reversed the cancer, he was told "No." He dumped the doctor soon after.

McQueen pored through medical journals and articles on alternative cancer treatments, and a feature article on Dr. William T. Kelley in the *Journal of Health Science* caught his eye. Kelley, who advocated "pure living" and exercise, claimed that 86 percent of all cancer could be cured through dietary control.

Kelley's treatment sought to build the body's immune system and overall health through diet, exercise, and positive mental exercises so it could resist cancer. The three main elements of his "nonspecific metabolic therapy"[1] focused on nutrition, detoxification, and supplements of pancreatic enzymes. "The American Medical Association has always taught to treat the symptom. The Kelley method treats the individual's immune system," said a survivor of the Kelley cancer cure, who died in 1994 but asked for anonymity in her lifetime. "Modern medicine has been a generation of process. The practiced doctors have been trained to be disease fighters, but they are not health builders."

As was his nature, McQueen employed a detective to do a thorough background check on Kelley before he attempted to contact him. McQueen discovered in short order that the former dentist turned alternative cancer researcher was a strange man, to say the least. Kelley claimed that at the age of three, a vision of Jesus approached him as he was playing in a sandpile. Kelley said the Messiah picked him up into his arms and instructed him to become a medical missionary.

When Kelley turned 37 in 1964, he claimed a physician had discovered malignant lumps on his liver and pancreas and he would have only weeks to live.[2] His internist recommended surgery, but the surgeon felt Kelley wouldn't survive the operation. Kelley, who held a doctorate of dental surgery (D.D.S.) from Baylor University in Dallas, called upon his mother in Kansas to rescue him. She literally cleaned house, tossing out the junk food and meat, and instructed him to only eat fresh fruits, vegetables, nuts, grains, and seeds. After a few months, Kelley said he showed a marked improvement.

Regenerated, Kelley claimed to have experimented with large quantities of nutritional liver and pancreatic enzymes. He had also employed coffee enemas to cleanse and detoxify his body. As he gradually recovered, he began to tell other people who had cancer how he had healed himself.

In 1967, Kelley authored *One Answer to Cancer*, a do-it-yourself booklet on curing cancer through his metabolic method. More than 150,000 copies were sold, and the book soared in popularity. But two years later, the

---

1 The exact origin of the term "metabolic therapy" has never clearly been identified. Most attribute the concept to German doctor Max Gerson, who developed a treatment in the 1920s based on bowel cleaning and dietary changes. Gerson brought his treatment to America in 1938, where he practiced until his death in 1959.

2 Kelley claimed doctors were so certain of his death that they felt there was no reason to take a biopsy of his tumor, an omission that hounded his credibility for years. Kelley curiously never offered up his medical records to reporters, either.

Texas medical and legal officials launched an investigation of its author. Undercover officials posed as patients, and a year later the Texas Board of Medical Examiners issued a restraining order prohibiting Kelley from practicing medicine and publishing his pamphlet in the state. Kelley fought the injunction and appealed the decision to the United States Supreme Court, arguing that the restraining order was a flagrant violation of his First Amendment rights. The court felt otherwise and declined to hear his arguments. In 1971, the American Cancer Society put Kelley's therapy on its "Unproven Methods" blacklist, where it remains to this day.

It was in Grapevine, Texas, where Kelley established the International Health Institute of Dallas, but the name sounded a lot more impressive than the small brick building where Kelley worked and resided. It was here where Kelley is said to have cured thousands of people. Kelley gave thousands of recommendations to patients in the 1960s and 1970s, becoming the nation's leading authority on nontoxic cancer therapy. He had an endless supply of patients and a longer list of thankful cancer survivors who were ready to share their testimonials with the world if they were asked.

Kelley also had his fair share of detractors, and one Texas businessman said the practitioner wasn't taken very seriously in the Lone Star state. "He was the laughingstock of town for a while," said Dr. Jerry Burgess, a Grapevine dentist who knew Kelley. "People used to joke that he cured cancer with green onions." However, McQueen's background check also revealed that Kelley had been investigated by more than 15 government agencies, including the Internal Revenue Service, the Federal Bureau of Investigation, the American Medical Association, and the Food and Drug Administration. And Kelley wore each investigation like a badge of honor. "I'm so unorthodox I stink," Kelley quipped.

Unorthodox or not, there was a bill attached to Kelley's services. He sold supplemental vitamins at an exorbitant cost, and in April 1980, he contracted with Plaza Santa Maria, a health spa in Rosarito, Mexico, where patients paid up to $10,000 per month to follow Kelley's program.

McQueen decided to forge ahead. "When you're in my shoes, you'll grab at anything that works," he said.

A meeting between McQueen and Kelley was set up at Kelley's organic farm in Winthrop, Washington, a few hours northwest of Seattle. Steve and Barbara drove up the coast of Washington in a VW pickup and checked into the honeymoon suite of Spokane's Davenport Hotel on April 16, 1980. A day later, they checked out when a research assistant at the *Spokesman-Review* spotted McQueen and called in the tip to the newsroom. Reporter Larry Young was dispatched to the hotel and found Barbara in the lobby. "We're here on our honeymoon," Barbara said. "[Steve] likes the Northwest." Barbara also hinted they were there for privacy and got the feeling she wasn't going to get any. Young requested an interview with her husband, and Barbara told the scribe she'd pass along the message but was 99 percent sure it wasn't going to happen.

They hadn't planned to stay long at the Davenport Hotel because it was simply a ruse to cover their visit to Winthrop. When the two reached their final destination, they met Dr. Kelley and his wife, Suzi, who gasped when she first saw McQueen—"and not from being star struck!" He had grown noticeably thinner, his breathing had become difficult, his skin had a gray pallor, and the sparkle in his eyes had diminished. He looked gaunt and frail and had become increasingly self-conscious about his appearance.

Kelley explained his regimen in its entirety, which started with a "body-cleansing diet" of vitamins, coffee enemas, body massages, organic foods and vegetables, protein drinks, and natural foods high in fiber. He encouraged McQueen to check himself into the Plaza Santa Maria to work his regimen if he was serious about licking cancer.

Psychologist Peter O. Whitmer said it was no surprise that McQueen had connected with Kelley. "It appears that McQueen was somewhat of a 'doctor phobic,' mistrusting them. He did not go for regular physical checkups. He had no close friends who were physicians. He had no real knowledge of 'medicine' and little interest—he was too hedonistic for that.

"Kelley was, oddly, built out of a similar mold as Steve. First off, he was not a 'physician'; he was a dentist. Second, his entire theory and practice had been built on personal experience—the experience of going counter to culture. What Kelley claimed had 'cured' him was a theory and a regimen that the traditional medical world rejected.

"Regardless, Kelley seems to have been someone possessed with down-home charm, 'ordinary guy' speech and values, and the general presence of a person on Steve's level.

"He was just another guy, like Bud Ekins and [McQueen's] racing friends and his pilot friends...people who were salt of the earth ordinary and yet able to deliver at a higher level when called upon. In this capacity, McQueen could connect with and trust him."

Barbara McQueen said Kelley failed to impress her, and for three decades she kept mum about her true feelings. "I thought Kelley was kind of a weirdo, a little off. Naturopathic medicine wasn't as mainstream as it is today, and the whole thing had an underground feel to it. I didn't particularly care for Kelley, but this was Steve's choice and I was there to support him. How I felt about the man didn't matter in the grand scheme of things. I just wanted Steve to get well."

Everyone involved could be said to have had an agenda—Barbara wanted her husband well; McQueen wanted to be cured; and Kelley had perhaps a lot to gain...or lose. Treating and curing such a high-profile patient like McQueen would surely have made Kelley's career; by the same token, it could destroy it. It is arguable that Kelley needed McQueen almost as much as McQueen needed a cure.

Kelley described his program in great detail and told McQueen it was quite possible that he could heal himself if he adhered strictly to his diet regimen. They arrived in Santa Paula with boxes of plastic containers filled with vitamins, minerals, enzymes, proteins, and other diet supplements. McQueen had been instructed to take massive dose of the supplements, and he followed the regimen to a T.

With renovations to the ranch house under control, McQueen felt it was time to give his new bride a proper honeymoon a few weeks after their trip to Washington. McQueen booked a cruise to Acapulco, Mexico, where he and Barbara would stay at the famed Las Brisas Hotel. On April 29, 1980, the two were chauffeured in a Cadillac limousine to the Long Beach harbor where they boarded the *Pacific Princess* (the inspiration for TV's *The Love Boat* and incidentally one of Steve's and Barbara's favorite shows) for a seven-day cruise. A tabloid spotted the heavily bearded McQueen, who was photographed donning sunglasses and sporting Bermuda shorts, matching shirt, white shoes, a tacky straw hat and clutching a hardbound copy of Henry Kissinger's *The White House Years*.

Three days later, they were in Acapulco and checked into the cliff-top hotel. In the lobby, they were greeted with pink cocktails and then driven in a pink-and-white Jeep to their marble-and-mahogany casita, which overlooked the Acapulco bay. The newlyweds enjoyed a romantic candlelit dinner on the patio and feasted on beer and rich Mexican food. The following morning they had a relaxing breakfast by the pool. They were so relaxed, in fact, that they forgot the golden rule—don't drink the water. Montezuma's Revenge and nausea had struck them both at the same time. Barbara smiled at the memory of their unfortunate mishap. "We rushed into the bathroom, and it was a fight to see who got the toilet and who got the sink. All that was missing from our *Love Boat* episode was a laugh track." The two decided to cut their honeymoon short and hurried home from Acapulco by plane. After a few days of rest and good home cooking from their housekeeper, Wilma Peele, Steve and Barbara were back on their feet.

Later that month, McQueen's health took a steep decline, and he needed assistance breathing. A May 23, 1980, invoice from Barbara McQueen's records shows her husband ordered several tanks of oxygen from Hopper, Inc. in Bakersfield, California. "That poor man, he went through so much," Barbara said. "If I could give up a few extra years of my life in order for him to have more time, I'd do it in a heartbeat."

By June, McQueen stopped taking visitors. He no longer attended church and was rarely seen at the airport. Pilot Mike Dewey recalled, "He was embarrassed about it in a manly sort of way. His stomach started to swell. When he physically started to deteriorate, he stopped coming around to the airport. I think the fact that he didn't look good had as much to do with his not feeling good, either."

Flight instructor Sammy Mason got a call from McQueen later that month, asking him to take him up in the plane one last time. McQueen no longer had the physical strength to take it up alone and asked Mason to accompany him. Mason arrived at the hangar, but his pupil never showed. "He just didn't have the strength," Mason said.

Frightened of his worsening condition, McQueen called Kelley in desperation. "What can you do for me if I go all the way with your program?" McQueen asked. Kelley made no promises but told McQueen every second was precious.

On July 28, 1980, *The Hunter* was released to a mostly indifferent movie-going public. McQueen, dogged by cancer rumors and the subject of tabloid speculation, hounded by the paparazzi and legitimate press at almost every turn, was nowhere to be found. McQueen's lack of promotion most likely hurt the film's performance, and his absence left many wondering if the rumors were true. The public wondered where one of Hollywood's best-loved stars had gone.

Former Solar Vice President Robert Relyea happened to be setting up a film preview at a Westwood movie theater when he caught a matinee showing of *The Hunter*. Relyea looked hard at the screen, studying his old partner, and he felt McQueen was way off stride. The movement, the sparkle, the mesmerizing nature of McQueen's performance were not quite there. Then the lightbulb went off in his head. "There's a thing where it's not a limp, but if you know somebody well and they're moving tentatively, you can recognize it. I thought it was that strange. It looked like he was hurting. Very tough to articulate. I had heard no rumors up to that point. I just thought he looked strange, like he was hurting when he walked. It must have been a month later when somebody said, in typical Hollywood fashion, 'I hear that…' And then it turned out the rumor was true."

Two days after *The Hunter* premiered, McQueen checked into Cedars-Sinai hospital on July 30 for another diagnosis. While he was sedated, the doctors pulled Barbara McQueen aside and told her that Steve's cancer was progressing at an advanced rate and that she should prepare for the inevitable. "They pretty much told me right then and there he was going to die," Barbara said. "It was suggested that I keep him sedated all the time, and when the pain got to be unbearable, bring him back and they'd make him comfortable until he died in his sleep. That's something a young bride should never have to hear."

When Steve awoke, Barbara delivered the gloomy message from the doctors. The news pitched an already depressed, beleaguered man over the edge. He said defiantly, "I'm a fighter. I don't believe that bullshit. I believe I can make it."

What McQueen did next took everyone by surprise—McQueen called ranch hand Grady Ragsdale from his bedside phone and asked him to fuel up his silver Ford pickup truck. McQueen wasn't out of gas yet. His body may have been failing, but his spirit was strong and he was doing everything to galvanize himself. He was going to Mexico.

38
99 DAYS TO GOD

Mexican border clinics began treating international cancer patients and the terminally ill in the early '60s. Most of them were established by American citizens in response to increased regulation of nonstandard therapies in the United States, particularly after the Kefauver-Harris Amendments to the Food, Drug, and Cosmetics Act in 1962. The act triggered the start of the alternative health care movement in Tijuana, long known for its tequila bars, sex shows, betting shops, bullfighting, curio sales, and prostitution. Thus began a long and embittered war between practitioners of traditional and nontraditional medicine.

Laetrile[1] treatment had became a cause célèbre for alternative practitioners as the new cure for cancer and was the driving force behind a proliferation of Tijuana clinics in the 1970s.

Although the Plaza Santa Maria did use laetrile in its treatment of patients, including Steve McQueen, it did not bill itself as a "laetrile" or "cancer" clinic. It was a "metabolic therapy program" that included a strict diet, nutrients, tissue concentrates, enzymes, detoxification procedures, structural therapies, and psychological counseling.

So why would Steve McQueen, who had access to one of the greatest health-care systems in the world, check into a controversial Mexican clinic with no lab, X-ray equipment, or medical facilities and that was run by an eccentric Texas dentist with no medical degree? The answer was hope. Established medicine had written him off, essentially giving him a countdown and not much else. McQueen had a deep suspicion of the establishment and things he did not understand.

---

1   Laetrile is the chemical amygdalin, a substance derived of apricot pits. Several government agencies and cancer prevention organizations, including the U.S. Food and Drug Administration, the National Cancer Institute and the American Cancer Society, have never found any evidence to substantiate the use of laetrile in the treatment or prevention of cancer.

Modern clinical medicine embodied all the things that he mistrusted—doctors treating him as a patient and not a person, medicines he did not understand, medical jargon that was lost on him, alien hospital surroundings, and people he could not connect with. He simply did not trust this form of setup. Dr. William Kelley, on the other hand, was probably more easy to identify with. Kelley was more down to earth, he was consultative with Steve rather than prescriptive, and he offered a less conventional approach and setting to his treatment. When everyone was saying "no" to McQueen finding a cure, Kelley was saying "quite possibly." This was hope not just for McQueen but for those around him who wanted him to fight and wanted him to live on, and it offered him a chance to give them hope, too.

"It makes sense. Think of all the companies pushing drugs on cancer victims and all the doctors doing needless drugs or operations," McQueen said to employee Grady Ragsdale before his secret departure to Rosarito Beach, Mexico. "Then this guy comes along who says he has a cure without drugs or operations. If he's right, and he seems to know what he's talking about, the people who call themselves experts could be made to look real funny.

"I figure I've got to try Dr. Kelley's approach. And if he can help me down there, and I survive this, I'm going to help him all I can. What I mean is, I'm going to help Dr. Kelley out of the woods...stand up for him and tell the world, 'If a goner can make it, anyone can.' That should shut a lot of people up."

Barbara McQueen said the Plaza Santa Maria seemed like a viable alternative at the time, but her youth and Steve's desperation played a vital part in his decision to seek treatment in Mexico. "I was 26 years old at the time. Steve was 50. I thought Steve would live forever," Barbara said. "I never delved into Dr. Kelley's background. We'd heard that Dr. Kelley had cured cancer in a few patients, and he was something of a rebel. What he said seemed to make sense, but most importantly he gave Steve hope. I think, looking back, as anyone with cancer knows, you reach a point of desperation and start grasping for whatever sounds best. Dr. Kelley tested Steve's blood to determine what nutrients and vitamins he needed. His theory sounded good—detoxing the body and boosting the immune system to fight the tumors naturally. It made sense when nothing else at the time did."

The American Cancer Society argued that metabolic therapies such as Kelley's lacked reasonable scientific rationale or logic, and that few of the practitioners, including Kelley, had been specifically trained in oncology. Furthermore, they asserted that Kelley's program was an "unproven method of cancer management" and barely fell short of calling it quackery.

• • •

Steve drove himself and Barbara from Los Angeles to the Plaza Santa Maria in Rosarito Beach, Mexico, on July 31, 1980, where he registered under the alias of Don Schoonover.

The facility was located 20 miles south of Tijuana and had been an oceanside resort just 18 months prior. Now it was a last stop for cancer patients and victims of degenerative diseases.

Situated high on a sloping cliff overlooking the Pacific Ocean, the Plaza Santa Maria was a self-contained world isolated from the usual rural Mexican lack of American necessities. The one- and two-story cottages were fanned out like a rural American subdivision with detailed cobblestone streets, manicured lawns, and splashing patches of bright flowers. The grounds included a community swimming pool, sauna, open-air amphitheater, and Aztec decor and statues intermingled with Christian religious sculptures.

When Steve and Barbara drove up to the main entry of the Plaza Santa Maria, they were stopped by two uniformed guards, who vigilantly stood watch behind the arched iron gates. Dr. Kelley, Dr. Dwight McKee, hospital director Bill Evans, and Teena Valentino, who was assigned as McQueen's "metabolic technician" greeted Steve and Barbara when safely inside the compound. Valentino, who eventually formed an almost maternal-like bond with McQueen, was a former ship entertainer along with her husband, Jack. Teena Valentino's job was to educate McQueen about the principles of healing via the Kelley Program; she also obtained supplies, assisted with detoxification, and served as liaison between the patient and his doctors. She remembered upon their initial meeting that the cancer-stricken star's cheeks were sunken and his abdomen swollen, but the muscle tone in his arms was firm, although he had obviously lost a lot of weight.

McQueen, she said, was walking slowly and was gulping down tablets of codeine for his back pain. Valentino said McQueen was somewhat embarrassed by his appearance and sensed Valentino was staring at him.

"I don't look much like Steve McQueen," he said shyly. "You probably can't even recognize me."

"You look fine, Steve," Valentino replied. She stared at him all right, but not because of his appearance. It was because he had the audacity to walk into a cancer clinic with a lit Veracruz cigar in his mouth.

"They're my reward. No more than one a day," McQueen said. "I've got to have something to look forward to."

Valentino recalled McQueen's large, piercing blue eyes showed no trace of fear or uncertainty. He had a presence about him; he radiated an unusual combination of qualities: confidence, consideration, independence, and gentleness. She sensed he was a most unusual man in spite of the fact he was a movie star.

That day Valentino started an intimate, often cringe-inducing chronicle of McQueen's 99-day stay at the Plaza Santa Maria, which details his regimen, response to treatment, physical aches and pains, hopes, fears, and his emotional state of mind as he bravely battled cancer. She titled the 800-page diary *99 Days to God*.

After the McQueens checked into Cabana 2005, Steve was given a full checkup by McKee. In addition to tumors on his lungs, abdomen, and neck, McQueen complained of shortness of breath (it was later discovered that one lung had collapsed), a lack of appetite, nausea, swelled ankles, bleeding hemorrhoids, chronic headaches, and plugged and ringing ears.[2] In addition, he suffered from neck and back pain and was given shots of Demerol to ease his discomfort.

A review of his medical records revealed that in August 1978, McQueen was admitted to Cedars-Sinai for a chest condition, which was initially diagnosed as "viral pneumonia." At the time, the right middle lobe of his lung had collapsed. McQueen was given both a bronchoscopy and a bronchial biopsy, which were negative. There was no determination for the middle lobe collapse, neither was there any treatment involved.

After the examination, McQueen was given a 2,500-item questionnaire to determine his daily regimen. Kelley's computer diagnosed him as a Type IV metabolizer. Accordingly, he was placed on a diet of fish, chicken, beef two times a week, and large quantities of raw vegetables. In addition, he was given more than 50 pills, vitamins, minerals, and supplements a day to "restore his body balance."

Dr. Rodrigo Rodriguez, who had previously worked in a Tijuana laetrile clinic, told *People* magazine, "I have seen cases of complete remission of meso-thelioma at the Plaza Santa Maria and other hospitals in Mexico." Rodriguez, however, failed to produce names or medical files to bolster his claim.

After his check-up McQueen stuffed himself with shrimp and said he felt bloated. He found relief that evening by talking with Teena Valentino.

"Are you a Christian, Teena?" McQueen asked. The question was unexpected.

"Yes, Steve," she answered, feeling slightly uncomfortable and under the spotlight.

---

2   McQueen was diagnosed with temporal mandibular joint, which caused a list of symptoms such as headaches, ringing in the ears, muscle spasms, and reduced energy. A mandibular equilibration appliance or "dental splint," eventually corrected the problem.

"Do you read the Bible?" he asked.

"At times," she replied. Valentino realized that McQueen's directness, although unnerving, was actually refreshing.

"I try to read the Bible every day," he volunteered, his intensity relaxing. "I've made my peace with the Lord. Someday when I'm feeling better, I'll tell you how I found the Lord."

"I'd like that."

Several days after he checked in, McQueen wasn't feeling any better. It was discovered on August 5 that his lungs and abdominal cavity were filled with serosanguineous fluid. "When I lie down, I fill up with phlegm. I can't get air. I feel like I'm suffocating at times," McQueen complained to Valentino. A tap was arranged to relieve the discomfort, and a large hollow needle was inserted through McQueen's abdominal wall, removing 1,100 cc of reddish-amber fluid.

The daily regimen was monotonous for an impulsive creature like McQueen, and he quickly grew tired of the metabolic food he put into his system. Through Santa Paula pilots Pete Mason and Art Rink, McQueen arranged for weekly food shipments to be dropped off at Brown's Field near the California-Mexico border. From there, employee Grady Ragsdale would bring items such as pie, cake, ice cream, and soda through customs and past the Plaza Santa Maria guards. Pat Johnson said it was hard to say no to McQueen when he requested Johnson's wife's specialties—pork chops and blueberry pie. "When my wife, Sue, made these super-thin breaded pork chops, Steve made sure he was invited over," Johnson said. "When the meal was over, he took home the leftovers. They were delicious cold, and he, Chad, and his dog Junior would fight over them the next day. We spoke before I left for Mexico, and he made sure I brought my wife's pork chops and blueberry pie."

Valentino acknowledged it wasn't such a good idea to allow McQueen to stray from his diet, but he was a hard man to turn down. "He told me, 'I have very few pleasures in life right now; food is one of the few I have left.' He would have all of the sweets brought in and he would take one bite from each of the foods to get it out of his system. Eventually the taste didn't satisfy him any longer."

Sleep was also hard to come by, and he suffered from night sweats. While he shivered and shook, Barbara McQueen was there by his side, clinging tightly to him. "He needed my energy. When I was hugging his back at night and saying my prayers, I could feel something leaving me and going into him," she said.

After witnessing a week of interaction, Valentino said Steve and Barbara's marriage was a near perfect union. "I saw a marriage that was innocent and natural. They had childlike trust of each other. If Steve behaved disagreeably, he expected Barbara to understand and react impeccably. She did. To them, life and love were one inseparable act.

"Barbara worshipped Steve and bathed him constantly in her free-flowing energy. Steve was her breath of air, her motion in life, her purpose."

McQueen told Valentino on August 7 he had changed his T-shirt four times and that his body ached with sharp pains that felt like gas. He did manage to sleep a few hours that night and had a rare dream about his great-uncle Claude Thomson.

"I was going back to a location where there was redwood and pine. I had done a film there," McQueen said. "I saw the redwood and pine and decided I wanted to go back there to live. Then I saw my grandfather. I went to him. I was going to talk to him, but he went to sleep, so I couldn't. I was wishing again that I could have known him more as a child. He had introduced me to trees and fishing and stuff. Then I woke up. But I knew that if I could just live there, I would get better."

"That's a good dream, Steve," Valentino replied.

"Oh yeah? How?"

"You're wanting to return to natural things, to nature's peace and healing."

"But I couldn't talk to my grandfather. He went to sleep."

"Is he dead, Steve?"

"Yeah."

"Maybe that's why you couldn't quite reach him. He's dead, and it isn't your time yet."

• • •

McQueen's Plaza adventure had been highlighted with a new and painful therapy every three to six days. He allowed himself to be poked, prodded, pricked, and examined on a daily basis, and he subjected himself to colonics, enemas, liver and vinegar flushes, Epsom salt drinks, IV drips filled with castor oil, Magnatherm heat treatments, mustard foot baths, phosphorus drops, eucalyptus breathing treatments, Bach Flower treatments, and every homespun remedy Kelley's wild imagination dreamt up. With Teena Valentino's gentle guidance and caring hand, McQueen began to follow the Kelley Program to the letter. He also surrendered his ego and put all of his faith in God.

"Teena, I love the Lord, and I just can't figure out why He let me get cancer," McQueen said. "I took the Lord Jesus Christ as my Savior over two years ago. That was before I got sick … I just don't understand. But I tell Him I'm willing to do whatever He wants. My life is His … If He wants me to die, I'll die. I won't fight it."

Valentino, who was kneeling beside McQueen on the floor, remembered him staring into the unknown as he spoke those words. The look on his face wasn't asking for answers; he was simply sharing. She remained silent.

"But if He wants me to die, why did He lead me to Kelley? Why am I down here?"

That was the question millions of people appeared to be asking, as well. One of the world's most famous faces had vanished from sight. Fans wanted to know where their hero was and if he was well. They wanted their blue-eyed star back. The media demanded to know the story, and as always, they were as relentless as bloodhounds. The more they struggled to learn the truth, the hungrier they got and the more desperate for a scoop they became. They wanted to know if McQueen's blue eyes had lost their sparkle. Once again, the *National Enquirer* had the jump on the competition and felt obligated to lead the pack. Their reporters had been lurking in the shadows of the hospital perimeter, asking questions, putting out feelers, and papering the small sea town with money. The barbarians were at the gate.

Part of the fascination with McQueen was that he was contradictory to the point of confusion. He was willing to leave his native country for unorthodox medical treatment south of the border, but he made it clear he did not want to die in Mexico. In essence he was willing to go to any extreme to give himself any chance he could, but at heart he wanted to return to the quiet peace of rural America. This country was a symbol of tranquillity for him, and it reflected his desire for dignity.

While at the Plaza Santa Maria, McQueen was gripped by a recurring nightmare that he shared with Dr. Dwight McKee upon an August 12 examination. "I don't want to die here and have my body hauled out in a beat-up old green Mexican ambulance," McQueen said. He had an uncanny ability to sometimes predict his own destiny, and his fear was tangible. He had said before that he thought he would not make it past 50, and this was not the only prediction that came true.

· · ·

Mentally, McQueen dealt with his cancer valiantly for the first month of treatment, but he had two more months of scheduled therapy and was beginning to show signs of battle fatigue. Life at Plaza Santa Maria was a study in ritual and monotony. Emotionally McQueen lived in the present but was constantly having to choose and form his own reality. He perked up, however, when ranch hand Grady Ragsdale showed up on September 14 with food, supplies, a flying helmet, goggles, binoculars, and photos of McQueen's planes and Santa Paula ranch. After Ragsdale finished unloading, he delivered the best news McQueen had heard since he checked in. Evangelist Billy Graham had agreed to meet with McQueen in Burbank, California, on October 31, 1980. Graham was a longtime friend of Pastor Leonard DeWitt, who apprised the famed evangelist of McQueen's condition.

"Oh, I've got to see him," McQueen said desperately. "Promise you'll call him. Ask him if he'll come down here, and if he will, make all the arrangements. Rent a plane and come with him. Bring him to see me."

A few days later, flying instructor Sammy Mason and Pastor DeWitt visited with McQueen. They shared a private communion behind locked doors, and before they departed, McQueen asked Mason if he could set up a Bible study program for him. True to his word, Mason sent scripture-reading guidelines every week. After Mason left, McQueen told Valentino how aviation brought him closer to God.

"Sammy and me would fly, Teena, and he'd tell me about the Lord," McQueen said. "Flying and the Lord... He told me about the Bible. I'd listen and fly. It made sense. It made me feel good."

On September 18, McQueen was asked to read another kind of scripture—the gospel according to Dr. William Kelley. Kelley had sent Bill Evans as an emissary to feel out McQueen regarding a press release announcing his treatment at the Plaza. Surprisingly, McQueen didn't resist.

"If Kelley is ready to do publicity, tell him we'll have Warren Cowan come down to talk about doing it correctly," McQueen said. "Warren Cowan is my publicity agent."

The following day, September 19, McQueen was in a serious funk, according to Valentino's diary. She said his demeanor was colorless, as though the living force had been drained from his body. She recalled him as a sad figure, lying on the couch, wrapped in a towel, staring into the abyss.

"I'm so depressed, Teena," he said. "I feel like throwing in the towel." Valentino was alarmed because she had never heard defeat in McQueen's voice. His depression surfaced again when business manager Bill Maher visited McQueen a few hours later. Valentino and Barbara sat in the living room while Steve and Maher visited. Maher was there to discuss his one last act for McQueen—his last will and testament. But somewhere in the middle of the men's 45-minute conversation, both women overheard McQueen crying.

"Is that Steve?" Barbara asked.

"I think so," Valentino replied.

"That is so heartbreaking," Barbara said, her eyes brimming with tears. "I've never heard Steve cry."

On September 20, Dr. Kelley, Bill Evans, and Dwight McKee appeared at McQueen's cabana, and Barbara intercepted the men while Steve finished his IV drip. Inside Kelley's light brown briefcase was a prepared press release for McQueen to sign, but Barbara valiantly protested on her husband's behalf.

"Warren Cowan advised against doing anything. He said that Steve shouldn't sign anything," Barbara said. "And Steve wants Dr. Kelley to explain the program to Warren." The three men were deflated, and Kelley, with a trembling hand, placed the press release back into in his briefcase. Hours later they returned to tell Steve and Barbara they could no longer live in Santa Paula. McQueen's ranch, they explained, was in the middle of orange grove country and would continually be exposed to pesticides and poisonous sprays.

"But everything is there—my museum, my cars, my airplanes," McQueen pleaded.

"Our horses," Barbara added, who suggested they could move to the 400-acre property they purchased together in 1978.

"You all could come to Winthrop, to my place," Kelley offered.

"Barbara and I will talk it over," McQueen replied dismissively, hinting it was time for them to leave.

Everything had slowly been stripped away—first his health, then his dignity, and now his home. McQueen's spirits must have fallen to an all-time low. He had tried his hardest, adhered as best he could to Kelley's programs, and tried to do the right things, but now even little mercies were denied to him. He was struggling to find the reasons to carry on. It was a test of his resolve and inner strength. He still had his family and friends, but even these relationships could not be enjoyed in his current state. It was time for him to dig deep again and see what he had left in him.

Four days later, on September 24, McQueen's demeanor changed largely due to a spiritual lift he received from "Lydia," a blonde Christian faith healer from the Chicago area. After McQueen's morning therapy, Lydia strolled into Steve's bedroom and placed her hands on his abdomen and chest.

"I'm discerning the disease with my hands, Steve," she proclaimed while Barbara and Valentino looked on. "The Lord lets me see what's inside of you… You are full of it. But through the Lord Jesus Christ, you can be healed, Steve."

McQueen gazed at her, his eyes full of trust. She had his full attention.

"Steve," she began again, "Do you accept the Lord Jesus Christ in your heart?"

"Yes I do. I've already done it," McQueen said.

"Good. Now repeat after me," Lydia continued. "I love the Lord with all my heart and mind."

"I love the Lord with all my heart and mind," he repeated while Lydia uncapped a bottle of holy water and applied it to McQueen's forehead.

"I walk in the light of the Lord," she continued melodiously.

"I walk in the light of the Lord."

"The Lord is my strength."

"The Lord is my strength."

"I am healthy. I am strong. I am happy."

"I am healthy. I am strong. I am happy."

"The Lord heals me!" rejoiced the zealous woman.

"The Lord heals me!" McQueen echoed.

"Now repeat: Holy! Holy! Holy!"

"Holy! Holy! Holy!"

"The Holy spirit fills you," Lydia commanded. "It rebukes disease and replaces it with health. Out disease! Out cancer! Out! The Holy Spirit abides in you now and forever more. You are cleansed, you are healed. Praise the Lord!"

"Praise the Lord!" McQueen sighed.

Valentino recalled both McQueen and Lydia fell silent while the room tingled. The blonde minister smiled at the renewed man, who was momentarily beyond words. He was spiritually and emotionally depleted but smiling.

"Whew! That was really something…Did you feel anything? The power, the electricity—whatever it was?" McQueen asked to everyone in the room.

"The Holy Spirit," Lydia said, smiling. "Now Steve, the Lord has healed you. You must show your faith and walk."

Without the use of a cane, Lydia took McQueen by the hand, where he walked barefoot over grass and cobblestones to the community swimming pool. McQueen jumped into the aqua-blue water and splashed around, smiling, laughing, and grinning.

"He jumped in," Lydia laughed. "The Lord filled him with so much energy and joy that he went for a swim."

Word started spreading throughout the Plaza Santa Maria that a miracle had taken place: Steve McQueen had been cured from cancer. McQueen had always been at the center of speculation and gossip—that was part of his personality and megastar status. Even now, he was still the center of attention. Cancer could not take that way from him. The faith healer's power was undoubtedly questionable, and eventually it was revealed that no miracle had taken place. What actually

happened to McQueen did occur inside him. Unfortunately, it was not a physical transformation; it was spiritual. He was inspired and trying to find peace. He
was finding new depths and inner strength that were compensating for his failing
body. His soul was becoming whole.

39

BAD MEDICINE

AN HOUR AFTER STEVE MCQUEEN'S TRANSCENDENTAL EXPERIENCE, he was ready to tell the world he had been healed.

"Teena [Valentino], I'm ready to help [Dr. William] Kelley. I'll do everything," McQueen offered. "We'll bring the photographers down. We'll get coverage in all the magazines, showing me how I look now, and that I'm recovering due to the Lord and Dr. Kelley. You go call Kelley and tell him that I want another meeting down here with [Bill] Evans, Kelley, and [publicist] Warren Cowan." McQueen was also to attend, unannounced, one of Lydia's Chicago evangelistic meetings in a month, when he was strong enough to travel. He would testify for the Lord and financially contribute to the church and underwrite Lydia's various missions.

Valentino was hesitant to fulfill McQueen's request because it was an impulsive decision that could have many repercussions. She contemplated the impact of McQueen's endorsement of Kelley's program. Valentino concluded that Kelley would be torn from his quiet sanctuary and tossed into the fangs of the media. She offered no protestation because of McQueen's legendary stubbornness but dutifully nodded and headed out to find Kelley while Steve solicited wife Barbara's advice about which photographers to use.

Luckily for McQueen, first wife Neile arrived the following day with his children, Chad and Terry. When McQueen revealed that he was going to hold a press conference, she was horrified.

"My God, Steve, please. I beg of you. Don't let anyone con you into holding a press conference now," Neile pleaded. "Wait until you get well. Then hold all the press conferences you want and parade around as much as you want. And above all, don't let anyone photograph you now. If you get well, you'll regret those pictures, and if you don't, why not leave the world and your fans with the memory of the Steve McQueen they know? Don't you think that'll be kinder to everyone, including the children?"

McQueen had always benefited from Neile's sage wisdom, and he weighed her words heavily. He said, after much contemplation, "Yeah, maybe you're right."

Just as he made amends to those he wronged in the past, McQueen realized it was also time to extend an apology to Neile for his years of philandering and emotional abuse. For the best part of two decades, she had been an essential part of McQueen's life. Neile was more than just a wife and now ex-wife. She was mother to his children and his confidante. When he was a nobody, she was a somebody, and she gave it all up to enhance his career. Neile helped him every way she could, including emotionally. She understood his psyche and had a deep connection not least of all because they shared troubled childhoods. McQueen owed much of his success to her. After all, she had pushed him to read scripts and go for some of the most important films of his career. Throughout their marriage, there had been ups and downs with more downs toward the end. He had caused her a lot of pain and hurt with his jealous rages, egomania, and infidelity. McQueen had taken her love for granted, and now that they had been apart for nearly a decade, he could see clearly that he had to put things right. She deserved it. Their relationship was long and deep, but his apology was, in typical McQueen fashion, short and to the point.

"I'm sorry I couldn't keep my pecker in my pants, baby," his raspy voice said. "I never loved anyone more than I loved you. And that's the truth."

• • •

Sensing the end was near, McQueen summoned business manager Bill Maher and attorney Kenneth Ziffren to the Plaza Santa Maria to help draw up his last will and testament. The two men arrived around 11:00 AM on Saturday, September 27, 1980, with two cakes prepared by Neile. Before they got down to business, McQueen gulped down a piece of chocolate cake and chased it with a fresh glass of milk. The three men spent approximately two hours going over McQueen's multimillion-dollar fortune and how he would like to divide the assets.

After Maher and Ziffren left, Dr. Kelley came back to McQueen's cabana to once more ask for his endorsement. He showed McQueen two press releases— one prepared by him and one by Warren Cowan—as well as McQueen's personal statement. Valentino said Kelley drifted nervously back and forth between McQueen's bedroom and the living room, anxiously awaiting the go-ahead. McQueen put him off once more, stating he wasn't ready to pull the trigger.

The following day, McQueen had changed his mind. He was not only going to endorse Kelley but also favored his press release over Warren Cowan's, stating, "Warren's was too vague and dry." The two-page release, on Plaza Santa Maria letterhead, read:

Superstar Steve McQueen, diagnosed as terminally ill several months ago at the Cedars-Sinai Hospital in Los Angeles, has recently shown signs of possible recovery, according to his current doctors.

McQueen, suffering from mesothelioma, a rare form of lung cancer regarded as incurable, has improved in condition, say his doctors, during the last two weeks. He is a patient at Plaza Santa Maria General Hospital, a degenerative disease treatment center on the Baja, California, peninsula of Mexico.

"Mr. McQueen has exhibited shrinkage of tumor, partial cessation of discomfort, weight gain, and significant improvement in appetite since he became a patient here approximately two months ago," said a hospital spokesman.

McQueen's doctors at Cedars-Sinai Hospital, unavailable for comment, told the actor several months ago, and again several weeks ago, that the most common treatment for cancer, including chemotherapy, radiation, and surgery, could not cure this form of lung cancer.

Mesothelioma is generally associated with inhalation of asbestos particles approximately 20 to 30 years prior to onset of clinical symptoms of malignancy.

When McQueen became a patient at the Plaza Santa Maria General Hospital, which features several doctors who specialize in stimulating the body's own immune response to disease, the actor's cancer had spread to his neck, abdomen, and chest; he was having difficulty breathing; his abdominal cavity was swollen; and he had lost considerable weight.

Prior to becoming a patient at the hospital, McQueen had been consulting for two months with Dallas, Texas, metabolic researcher Dr. William Donald Kelley, whose programs directed at stimulating the immune response form the basis of the therapies at the Plaza. "We have been able to help prolong the patient's life," said Dr. Kelley. "But he really needed the intensive programs and therapies available at the Plaza Santa Maria General Hospital." Dr. Kelley is a consultant to the hospital.

Dr. Kelley agreed with the doctors at Cedars-Sinai Hospital that chemotherapy, surgery, and radiotherapy could not reverse the actor's condition. "However," said Dr. Kelley, who has worked with several thousand cancer patients over the past 20 years, "even this form of cancer will sometimes respond quite well to a concerted program of applied metabiology and immunology."

Dr. Rodrigo Rodriguez, medical director of Plaza Santa Maria General Hospital, said that McQueen's neck and chest tumors, since he became a patient at the Plaza, "have greatly diminished in size," that his breathing has improved, that swelling in his abdomen has decreased considerably, that he now experiences markedly less pain, that his appetite has improved, that he has gained weight, and that his emotional outlook has improved.

"We are not able to ascertain at this point if his disease has caused irreparable damage or will be able to be totally reversed," said Dr. Rodriguez, "But we are optimistic that he will recover completely."

McQueen, in a letter released this week, praised doctors at the hospital and lauded Dr. Kelley's approach to cancer and degenerative diseases. McQueen noted that the therapies he is currently undergoing have given him extraordinarily improved quality of life, some extension of life, and hope for eventual recovery.

The actor has starred in many films, including *The Great Escape*, *Papillon*, *Soldier in the Rain*, and *The Getaway*, as well as the television series *Wanted: Dead or Alive*, and is currently appearing in the film *The Hunter*. He lives in Los Angeles and is married to model Barbara Minty. McQueen, who has often been characterized as being iconoclastic and private, is said by acquaintances to be comfortable and in good spirits.

Valentino noticed that Kelley wasn't 100 percent satisfied with McQueen's approval of the press release—he also wanted McQueen to sign a personal statement that his daughter Kim had prepared so she could keep it as a personal souvenir. But McQueen brushed off the request, saying he would send Kim autographed pictures. "She'll like them better anyway," McQueen said.

When the press release reached the desk of Warren Cowan in Beverly Hills on September 29, the normally reserved publicist lost his cool. Valentino, who delivered the document to Cowan, recalled, "Warren looked this over and declared, 'We can't release this. That's why I wrote my release so carefully, offending no one but respecting Steve's wishes and doing Kelley a good turn.'"

The truth was that any press release of this nature was going to be inherently flawed and would fail to satisfy all parties. McQueen did not want to openly endorse Kelley, but he wanted the truth told. The drafted press release pleased no one; all it did was imply that McQueen was potentially stabilizing, with an emphasis of "potentially." It stated the facts of his condition and that Cedars-Sinai could not treat him. This last point was very delicate because it implied that Cedars-Sinai was ill-equipped to help him and wrote him off. This was dangerous territory in legal terms but also in terms of the message it would carry to the public regarding treatment. Therefore, this release served no party's best interest except Kelley, who would be the implied symbol of hope.

The reality was McQueen was still a very ill man, yet everyone appeared to feel the need to make proclamations one way or another that were simply inappropriate and inconclusive at this stage. Only McQueen could stand to lose from this kind of press release, and he had lost too much already.

Cowan called McQueen later that day and was forceful in his approach. There was no way they could release Dr. Kelley's statement without the good possibility of a lawsuit. McQueen got the message loud and clear, but Kelley continued to gently push when he visited McQueen for an examination the following afternoon.

"Need a drop of blood, Stevie," Kelley said, poking his head into McQueen's bedroom. One quick stab into his finger, one drop of blood between two pieces of glass, and Kelley had his sample. "Sure you don't want to sign that statement, Steve?"

"No," McQueen said simply, quietly, firmly. McQueen left no room for interpretation.

"Okay," Kelley laughed, turning to the door. "You all be good now." Before Kelley left, he placed five copies of the statement with Valentino, just in case McQueen changed his mind. Valentino said she felt as if she was trapped in the middle.

"I was beginning to get the picture," Valentino said. "The papers were very important to Kelley. Now that Warren had vetoed the other paper that explained successfully what was happening with Steve, substituting a more conservative, vague release, Kelley felt helpless to proceed in any forceful manner."

A few days later, it wouldn't matter. Peering through his blinds, McQueen spotted a few reporters from the *National Enquirer*. He was determined not to let them break the story, said Dale Olsen, who worked with Warren Cowan. Olson recalled, "A couple of carloads of people from the *National Enquirer* descended on Plaza Santa Maria and sniffed around. McQueen saw the trucks, and he instructed us to write and release the story. He told me, 'I don't want them to break it first.'"

McQueen shifted into high gear and requested the use of Rodolfo Alvarez's cabana, the proprietor and owner of the Plaza Santa Maria. McQueen felt the cabana was more secure than his bungalow and would make him less of a target. Alvarez visited with McQueen to discuss the move.

"You want to move into my cabana?" Alvarez asked.

"Yes, amigo," McQueen replied.

"Why didn't you ask me?" Alvarez said with a hurt tone. "Anything of mine is yours."

"I'll pay you extra," McQueen offered.

"I don't want any money," Alvarez said, slightly offended. "The cabana is yours."

McQueen, who was streetwise and savvy, would learn that no good deed goes unpunished.

When the McQueens were safely ensconced in Alvarez's cabana, McQueen pulled the trigger on Warren Cowan's October 2 statement to the press. This was a statement much more becoming of McQueen; it was blunt, honest, and protective. It read:

> The reason why I denied I had cancer was to save my family and friends from personal hurt and to retain my sense of dignity, as for sure, I thought I was going to die.
>
> The new treatment has given me an extraordinary improved quality of life. Hopefully, the cheap scandal sheets will try not to seek me out so I can continue my treatment.
>
> I say to all of my fans and all of my friends, keep your fingers crossed and keep the good thoughts coming. All my love and God bless you.

The following day, October 3, Steve McQueen's cancer condition was headline news across the country and the world. His request for privacy was ignored. News crews and services from around the world descended on the Plaza Santa Maria; reporters waved a microphone in the face of anyone who might have information, and photographers retreated to the nearby foothills, hoping to snap a picture of the reclusive star. A bounty of the poorest taste had been established—$50,000 for a photo of an ailing, cancer-ridden Steve McQueen.

Thus the death watch began the final countdown.

• • •

Steve McQueen was on the front page of almost every daily newspaper. Jack Valentino knocked on the McQueens' cabana door and dropped a stack of newspapers on the coffee table. Barbara grabbed the top copy, the *San Francisco Chronicle*, and was pleasantly surprised that the media ran Warren Cowan's entire statement. When Barbara asked if Steve wanted to read any of them, he turned his head in disgust.

"Take them away," he ordered. "I don't want to hear. I've been in this business a long time. You just have to ignore them, and they finally leave you alone."

But they didn't. McQueen's deathwatch endured supercharged coverage. This was a unique point in the history of celebrity news, marking the increased prominence and power of the tabloids aligned with the public's celebrity fever at its highest. In the past, the media had some degree of respect and good taste. If a star wanted some peace, he could pose for a few photos and then respectfully be left alone. However, the tabloids had taken the lead role in the media, and their style was to get the story no matter the cost, and the rest of the media had to try to keep up. This was to be McQueen's fate. He was hounded relentlessly. It was no secret that he was an extremely guarded and private individual; in fact, he made no bones about it. But the tabloids became frenzied. Every day was a battle for the journalists and photographers to get a photo and an exclusive; every day, editors of various news outlets awaited McQueen's death. Each wanted to be the first; each would have a potential headline ready to roll when the moment came. The more McQueen secluded himself, the more they pushed.

The media circus saw only the story and the next headline in the race to sell papers and magazines. What is most saddening about this landmark in celebrity hounding is that all of the magazines and publications forgot that this was just a man, a human being with a family who was going through the worst moment of their lives.

The Plaza Santa Maria was teeming with reporters and news media. One in particular, Televisa Mexico, had reached proprietor Rodolfo Alvarez. Sensing a once-in-a-lifetime opportunity to promote his hospital, Alvarez pulled aside Jack Valentino and asked for a favor.

"These people here with the TV equipment, they are from Mexico City, the largest TV station in Mexico," Alvarez said. "I would like you to find out if Steve would be willing to make a statement—no questions, no interview, no cameras, just a microphone. Thirty seconds, one minute, two minutes, five minutes— whatever he likes. Could you arrange for me to speak with Teena?"

It didn't take long for Alvarez to cash in on his favor. McQueen was stuck. When Alvarez had told him to take charge of his cabana because, "What's mine is yours, Steve," he must have forgotten to add, "And what's yours is mine." McQueen asked Alvarez respectfully for the use of his cabana and did so without expecting to have to do something in return. In fairness, McQueen had inadvertently done Alvarez the biggest of favors by going there. To Alvarez, McQueen was not a patient going through a trauma but a great opportunity to promote himself. It was Alvarez who owed McQueen, but Alvarez could only see the publicity angle and sold out the ailing actor.

A large gray van rolled up the street followed closely by another car driven by Alvarez, who parked behind McQueen's Mercedes. Three members of the media—one woman and two men—piled out of the large vehicle, opened the side doors, and rolled out tripods, TV video cameras, recorders, and microphones. Valentino met them at the door while Steve and Barbara went over his statement. A smiling Alvarez was handed the live microphone, who in turn handed it over to Valentino. She noted as soon as she received the microphone that the television camera started to roll tape. Valentino walked into the cabana with Alvarez a few steps behind. When she reached McQueen's bedroom door and handed over the microphone, Barbara peeped outside.

"There are cameras out there!" Barbara screamed. "They're taking pictures!"

McQueen was startled and jumped a few inches off his bed, looked angrily at Valentino, and threw the microphone to the ground. Valentino picked it up and marched outside to find out what was going on. She eventually discovered the crew was filming only the exterior of the cabana, not McQueen. Valentino relayed the information to Steve and Barbara, who had both calmed down a bit.

"I don't want to do the damned thing," McQueen said.

"You don't have to do it, but no cameras are coming into this house," Valentino assured. "It's okay."

"If you don't want to make the recording, you shouldn't do it," Alvarez said, trying to save face. "You're not obligated." McQueen stared at Alvarez and Valentino for a moment, and then broke his silence.

"All right. Bring me the mike."

The audiotaped message from McQueen that day said:

> To the President of Mexico and to the people of Mexico. Congratulations to your wonderful country on the magnificent work that the Mexican doctors, assisted by the American doctors, are doing at the Plaza Santa Maria hospital in helping in my recovery from cancer. Mexico is showing the world this new way of fighting cancer through nonspecific metabolic therapy. Again, congratulations—and thank you for saving my life. God bless you all...Steve McQueen.

McQueen handed the microphone to Valentino and swung his arm around to Alvarez, who bent down to take McQueen's hand. McQueen gave Alvarez a light handshake, then swiftly reached up to tousle his hair playfully.

"My friend," McQueen smiled, "just for you."

Alvarez took the microphone back to the reporters, who were sitting in their van listening to the playback and crying. Those tears reverberated around the world, nowhere more so than in America.

Former wife Ali MacGraw, who heard the broadcast while driving in her car on Pacific Coast Highway, said it devastated her. "The voice was raspy, but I recognized it as Steve's," she wrote in her memoir, *Moving Pictures.* "Evidently he was doing some kind of public relations favor for the controversial clinic and, at the same time, telling his fans around the world he was grateful for their prayers and support. Hearing that strange voice made me pull over to the side of the road and cry."

After McQueen broke his silence, Kelley, along with Dr. Rodrigo Rodriguez, held a press conference at the Greater Los Angeles Press Club on October 9. They started the conference by reading a statement prepared by Barbara McQueen:

> Steve's great wish is that the United States would allow the medical treatment he is undergoing in this country so we could go home and Steve could continue his program among the people and surroundings he loves. He has asked me to tell you, "My body may be broken, but my heart and spirit are not." He wants to thank the thousands of people who have sent their good thoughts and prayers and hopes they will keep them coming.

Reporters, who wanted to learn about McQueen's condition, were not permitted to ask questions during the 40-minute presentation, which espoused the merits of the Kelley Program.

"We have developed a new paradigm that will alter the course of medicine for the next 200 years," Kelley boasted. But the cynical press wasn't buying whatever Kelley was trying to peddle, prompting one newsman to say, "You gentlemen have come here to do a commercial for your hospital."

"How much of this are we going to have to go through?" another groaned angrily.

Kelley also appeared on Tom Snyder's *Tomorrow* show and in *People* magazine. He told reporters Sharon Watson and Kathy Mackay, "It took Winston Churchill to popularize antibiotic medicine. Steve McQueen will do the same for metabolic therapy."

Kelley was quick to see that the press could be used as a tool to promote his craft and his beliefs. However, it was duplicitous, unafraid to bite the hand that fed it. The press soon realized that Kelley was capitalizing on his star patient. They did not care whether this was motivated by passion for his craft or whether it was just blatant opportunism. They turned on him, and it proved to be his undoing, as negative publicity would do him more harm than any medical theories ever could.

McQueen used Kelley's press junket as an excuse to take a weekend excursion to Tijuana on October 10. Steve, Barbara, nurse Annie Martell, and Teena and Jack Valentino all piled into McQueen's Mercedes while two Plaza employees followed closely behind. They checked into the Hotel Palacio Azteca under Steve's new alias, "Don Cortez." He quickly ordered room service, and the meal was surely not on the Kelley Program: a banana split, a strawberry sundae, six glazed donuts, a glass of milk, three cups of coffee, and a side of french fries.

"It's just a little snack to look at," McQueen explained. "I just want to taste them. It's my vacation. I deserve a break."

Beer, coffee, and snacks flowed in and out of Suite 609 and kept room service hopping. But an occasional nibble on a doughnut was McQueen's only actual deviation from his strict diet. Steve was having a ball. "I'm staying another night," McQueen said adamantly. "This is my vacation. I like it here."

On Sunday, October 12, McQueen and company left the Azteca and drove to the Rosarito Marketplace. It was eye candy to McQueen, who had been cooped up since late July. His eyes drank in the crowded streets, rocky hills, honking horns, and the carnival colors of the city. They drove through the marketplace, where Steve bartered with the streetside vendors for two birds and a cage. Finally, he decided to get out of the car to buy local produce. Steve donned his sombrero and grabbed his cane. Barbara and Teena watched him stroll away proudly to a fruit stall, where they watched him interact with the vendor, touching the produce and finding a price that would satisfy them both. Cancer may have ravaged McQueen, but his street-smart instincts were as strong as ever. It was a rare chance of anonymity and normalcy, even though it was fleeting. Here McQueen was happy, free, and not under the watchful eye of the media.

On their return to the Plaza, McQueen was in a wistful mood, and his eyes were glued to the passing scenes. "Everything seems cleaner, not so dirty," McQueen said. "Mexico was always so dirty."

"It's still dusty, Steve," Teena replied.

"Maybe it's me. I'm the one who's changed. It means more to me now."

• • •

McQueen's admission that he had cancer provoked not just media attention but an outpouring of public support. Letters, cards, books, literature, homeopathic drugs, anointed handkerchiefs, holy water, and gifts from well-wishers, old friends, ex-lovers, herbalists, religious zealots, ex-convicts, movie fans, and crackpots flooded the Plaza Santa Maria. Anything that was appropriate and positive was dutifully read aloud to McQueen by Teena and Barbara.

While the mail, well-wishes, and good tidings buoyed McQueen's spirits, there was one man who made him plumb the depths of his soul—spiritual doctor Brugh Joy.[1]

Joy was a former Mayo Clinic doctor and clinical professor at UCLA who had been diagnosed with cancer in 1974. He claimed to have healed himself in six weeks through visualization, a concept that centers on body energy fields and healing techniques using energy transferred through the hands. It also includes collective energy dynamics and consciousness interacting with intuition. Joy and his partner Carolyn Langer made the trek to Plaza Santa Maria at the request of Dr. Dwight McKee. Their hour-long session was tape-recorded by Joy and given to McQueen. He gave a copy to friend Pat Johnson for safekeeping. These are the last tape-recorded words of Steve McQueen:

> *Brugh Joy*: Okay, why don't we just dive in? What do you think of the circumstances that might have led to the disease itself? How do you perceive that now?
>
> *Steve McQueen*: Two ways. One is asbestos poisoning in my lungs, which is very rare. Two is I think there were times in my life when I was under pressure. I had a battle in my business with somebody [Phil Feldman] for about five years. I think I really wanted to let go of the pressure.
>
> *Joy*: I've often felt diseases reflect what we want at a deeper level and something inside of you wanted out. Regardless of some of the other thoughts inside your head, there's a sense of me that feels like that it got screwed up in certain ways. I know there were drugs involved at one time. Is that correct?
>
> *McQueen*: Yes. I think that, you know, you see, in my life, there was so much that, you know, I was into a lot of dope. I've done everything there is to do, and a lot of my life I've wasted. I've done things that I wish weren't in my life.
>
> *Joy*: Well, I'm not sure that you did waste your life. I want to look at it from the standpoint of what you learned about it. In other words, we don't grow as beings, rich mature beings, without exploring these things. Without risking,

---

1 Joy declined this author's request for interviews in 1993 and again in 2009, citing that his meeting with McQueen was confidential. Joy died of pancreatic cancer on December 23, 2009.

and sometimes we can go overboard, but something inside of you now has looked at that and knows that it didn't lead to where it might have.

McQueen: No.

Joy: And it leads to guilt, Steve. It's a matter of experience. I'm looking inside your psyche at what's keeping you going inside right now, and that is something deep inside of you knows that you can teach somebody about your life's experiences, that you can share, not only as an actor, but as a human being. A human being who's been through a lot.

McQueen: Okay, let me say something. I'm reiterating what you just said. You see, I cut myself short in the drug area in freaking out and everything, because I could have had relationships with people that were meaningful instead of having relationships that were based on drugs. That's one. Two is, and you mentioned it earlier about finding a cure in my life. Well, that cure was finding the Lord in my life. When that happens, I know better than to say, 'Okay, God, I'll make you a deal. You let me live, and I'll do this.' So this was all before I was ill, before I found out. I really believe I have something, I think I believe, I'm pretty sure I believe, that I have something to give to the world as far as my relationship with the Lord, something I can teach to other people, something about a message that I can give. I don't know exactly where, but I've thought a lot about it when I'm by myself. I think that I should be here to do that, if not, and I've been in excruciating pain, and I've always tried to say that I've had faith and I never gave up. I've thought of suicide. I got a .45 automatic. I've thought about taking my plane out and crashing it. Thought of it all, and I'd like to think that I'm a good Christian. I'm trying to be. It's not easy, but that cure was finding the Lord, I think, and that's where I think I've seriously shortchanged myself.

Joy: But you know Steve, you could have never brought through what you're saying right now so simply. You could not state as simply as you just did, and as deeply as you just did, and it may not sound like you got up and put a lot of energy behind what you just said, but it's honest, open, and genuine. You could not say that without the experience behind it. In other words, the wisdom of life. Sometimes we tend to look at the events of something we should be ashamed of rather than looking at the resources gathered, even though it took you time to see that, that led you to a deeper realization. I'm not sure, Steve, that you could touch that without that experience. You know what I mean?

McQueen: Yes, I do. Where I'm at now, and I have to cut you in on this, and this is not something we can discuss with anyone. See, I'm on this program now; you know about it. It's pretty tough. I have nothing to look forward to. Day in, day out, pain and anguish. I get terribly discouraged. So I went on a sweet binge in town. So that was one thing. If it did something to me, I don't know. The other thing is that they [the doctors] won't let me have anything to ease the pain.

Joy: I know, and I'm going to talk to the doctors about that.

McQueen: So what I did was have a friend smuggle in some Percodan. I haven't been taking a whole lot of it, but, like, I took three of them in one day. I can't stand the pain all the time.

Joy: Listen, if I had what you had, I would be taking it, too. I really would. I know what they feel, but I also know what it's like to be under the constant pain of this thing. You don't have to tell them.

McQueen: I won't, but...I can't. Am I sitting here doing myself in or is it something that I can't handle anymore and need some relief? That's what I think it is. This is very important to me. It's my little world.

Joy: I think that if we were honest, there's probably a little bit of both in it. There's a portion of you that's really tired. We talked about your retirement. You're tired, you've got nothing to look forward to, but I want to talk about another factor. There's a portion of your psyche that could not imagine you beyond if you once started to lose ground. If you ever started to deteriorate, if you ever started to lose control of that sense of youthful power, there's a deep thought within your psyche that says, 'I'm not going to stay around. I'm not just going to lie around. I don't want to be taken care of. I either have my abilities or I don't have my abilities.' I don't know if that came on recently. My feeling is that, and a lot of the things that you did when you were younger were almost like, 'Live now, because you never know what is down the road.' Am I getting off track?

McQueen: I don't know. I know now that I've changed a lot. I used to be more macho, and now my ass is gone, my body is gone, is broken, but my spirit isn't broken, and my heart isn't broken. I would like to think that I do have the determination to beat this thing, and they keep telling me they think I can, but there is a chance that I might not. Every day I go through this thing where my friends tell me I'm not dying, and they say I should take morphine and keep me happy because I get tired of the pain and I wish it would go away. Even with my broken body, I want to go to...Ketchum, where I own a place. Move everything. My planes, bikes, antiques, my wife, all my animals. To start living again. That's what I'd like and to try and be able to change some people's lives. To tell people that I know the Lord, what I have to offer, what's happened to me. The thing has gotten bigger, you know? You see, in my mind, I planned this thing, this choice. In Chicago, I knew I was sick, and that if the Lord would help me, I would do something to help, and I didn't want to mix the Lord up with that. I've thought a lot about it because when I started up, I didn't want to mix cocaine with Christianity. I needed to separate the two. I didn't know it would fall under the chain of medicine, but I did plan to quit. All of this would open up and give people and tell people what did happen to me, and take it up to the American Medical Association and turn their head around a little bit. And by George it is happening, by accident. I'm just a delivery boy. My Lord, I have suffered, but all of the mail and the cards and all. People know I'm into the Lord, so that means I'm doing good, so I think I'm meant to stay here.

Joy: Where do you think the disease is now?

McQueen: It's grown bigger, not leveled off.

Joy: That's right, I want to talk about one other area that we need to open up and have a look at. One time, Steve, power and control are very important to you. To lose control over something is hard on you. Do you know what I'm getting at?

McQueen: I was thinking of where you were getting at. I don't like losing control over my personal destiny.

Joy: What I'm really going after here is that sometimes the portions of our awareness start to worry about the physical form and if it is going to make it. It's like a big vacuum cleaner. It starts sucking all the energy. I'm sensing that there has been a lot of dishevelment. You know what I mean?

McQueen: Yeah, I've got a lot of shit going on.

Joy: Not only that, but it is reflecting in your body. One day it's the back, the next day the darn stomach, and then the breathing isn't right, and maybe it's the hemorrhoids. It's like if it isn't one thing, it's another.

Carolyn Langer: Another way of putting it is to say that even though you are in close touch with your Lord, and he has a great deal of meaning in your life, you still have a lot more to open to him and that you will understand the Lord even more when you are free mind from your body.

McQueen: I don't know how to do that. To separate…

Langer: And it's not negating your relationship and understanding of the Lord. What we are saying is that there is more. More for you to do. More for you to open to as far as that God force.

McQueen: Let me say that now, I don't know if I'm good enough to do the Lord's work.

Joy: There's a portion of you that's felt contaminated. Tainted, not worthy.

McQueen: That's right.

Joy: This is one of the great things that has motivated you .... It's not a matter of if you are good enough or bad enough; you happen to be an instrument or a channel for this process, and I don't think it would come through you if you didn't have the feeling, if you were ready for it.

McQueen: I know that now. I've already tried to make a change.... I'm starting to feel better about myself than I ever have before. It's very, very, simple. Okay, I've had three years of therapy, so I have some small perception of myself. When a kid doesn't have any love when he's small, he begins to wonder if he's good enough. My mother didn't love me, and I didn't have a father. I thought, 'Well, I must not be very good.' So then you go out and try to prove yourself, and I always did things that other people wouldn't do. Some dangerous things. I never thought of myself as a particularly courageous person. I was always kind of a coward until I had to prove it to myself. I think that's where that came from, most of it. Also, taking everything right to the limit. Just like I'm taking this right to the limit.

Joy: It's called brinksmanship. Brinksmanship.

McQueen: I hope not, although I think you're probably right. I don't know. These are my hours of thinking.

Joy: Let's get back to your past. In most psychotherapy, they pick up the theme of 'That's really too bad, Steve. You had a mother who didn't love you. You didn't have a father and therefore you feel inadequate.' But I view it from a very different perception. For instance, if you were from a totally loving family, you wouldn't be who you are today, and you begin to find out one of the most important words is forgiveness. You see what I'm saying?

McQueen: That's fantastic. So simple, so difficult.

Joy: There's an area we need to pick up before I forget, because it keeps coming in my mid. That is, at one time, Steve, you went into the occult. Is that right? Did you go into any sort of...

McQueen: I was on the ring of it. Jay Sebring was my best friend. Sharon Tate was a girlfriend of mine. I dated Sharon for a while. I was sure taken care of; my name never got drawn into that mess. He [Sebring] was having an affair with the girlfriend of a warlock. It may be for the worse, but I was always against it. I was one of the ones who felt that I was one of the good guys, but boy I tell you, they did a number on me. I'm against that whole thing.

Joy: I know you are. The whole impact of what it means to you and what it meant to you, even then. There's a subconscious area that was attracted into the circle.

McQueen: Oh sure.

Joy: And it comes out of the power element of it.

McQueen: Not for me. It was the women, and the dope, and the running around. That's all that was.

Langer: There's women, and dope, and running around in many circles. There was something that intrigued you.

McQueen: But I didn't know it was the occult. It's bullshit is what it is. No, I really didn't know what it was, and by the time I did, I had never gone to any of the meetings. Never knew anything about it and was always against it. It was never for me.

Joy: Some place in your unconscious, you were reaching for power. There's a quality about you, a radiance. You're really an old soul who has a great deal of wisdom inside of you. Something about you, including being in front of millions of people, that is preparation, not only for the work you're about to do now, no matter which way this thing goes. To me, your work is inspirational.

McQueen: I don't know how to grasp that yet. I'm trying. The only thing I've been able to do is to put myself in the Lord's hands.

Langer: What it really means is a total trust so that it doesn't matter if you live or die, you trust Him enough to make the right decision and there's a connection there.

McQueen: Well, I get that.

Joy: The other thing is your interest in planes. To me, that sends a message to the deep unconscious. I've talked to many pilots who have said that they feel much closer to God up there all alone, where it's peaceful and quiet.

McQueen: I've had that experience. I've had it. I've prayed up there and talked to the Lord. I've found that my big thing is daydreaming into things that I'm going to do. Planning. You know, like when you daydream and go to sleep? In my life, my daydreams came true, but I ran out. Now I'm doing more. I'm building in Idaho and planning projects for myself.

Joy: All of those things are important, but it will never be more important than your connection to that deeper portion.

McQueen: That's what I need to work on. I need to put myself in the Lord's hands. That's the way I figure it.

Joy: And relax. Just enjoy it. Trust it. You can't lose, no matter what.

McQueen: That's what my preacher said. "God's a winner, and you can't lose."

Langer: Dying isn't losing, either.

McQueen: That's what he said, too.

Joy: Nope, it isn't.

McQueen: It's not that I'm falling apart, but I'm running out of gas.

Joy: My feeling is that, Steve, if you don't feel or see any dramatic improvement to where you are quite strong, then I would pack up and go home and make myself comfortable. I really would. I would make my peace, deepen my relationship with whoever's around me, and I would find a place that I was totally happy in, an environment that would totally make me feel good. That is what I would do. That's always been in the back of my mind.

McQueen: Is that what you see? That it's my time?

Joy: That's what I see. That it is weighted that way. I also see this other factor, Steve…your ability to do some unusual things.

McQueen: I see that, too.

Joy: But you have to go deep and find that out for yourself.

McQueen: I don't know. (Tape ends)

Joy's departure left McQueen deeply unsettled and unsure about his future and about how much time he had left. His demeanor was noticeably different, according to Teena Valentino.

"Dwight said this guy can tell whether I want to live or die. [He] says I'm leaning toward death," McQueen said.

McQueen also told Valentino that he noticed the doctors at Plaza Santa Maria, notably Dwight McKee, stopped paying attention to him. "As soon as I give them their publicity, they don't need me anymore," McQueen said. "All [McKee] talked about was the wonderful master [Joy] he had met—and he was going to study under him. He didn't even ask how I was. Just talked about himself."

Everything came to a head on Thursday, October 23, when McQueen let it be known he wanted to leave. That caught the attention of hospital director Bill Evans, who insisted McQueen finish his treatment.

"You can't do that, Steve," Bill Evans said forcefully. "Goddammit, man. You haven't followed your program. You been eating junk." Valentino, who was with Barbara McQueen, said Evans slammed the bedroom door shut, and the two men engaged in a war of verbal assaults and epithets. Evans told McQueen that a new CAT scan revealed McQueen's intestines were wrapped in cancer and that he couldn't leave. The admission caught McQueen by surprise, who realized his time at the Plaza Santa Maria had been wasted.

In that moment, McQueen was confronted with some stark reality. The days, weeks, and months of intense pain, diets, treatments, sleepless nights, and press interference and interviews that only helped others and exploited him were all for absolutely nothing. It was all bad medicine. He was fundamentally a fast-paced person who knew what he wanted, and to have essentially wasted time and achieved nothing must have cut him to the bone. He was worse off than ever, and he had reached the limit of what he would take. A few minutes later, Evans marched angrily out of the cabana and lit up a cigarette. Barbara McQueen followed Evans to plead on her husband's behalf while Valentino went into McQueen's bedroom. Pleading was futile. McQueen had tried it their way, and now he was going to do what he did best. He was going to do things his way.

"Get packed," McQueen exploded. "We're leaving. Now!"

40
15 MINUTES TO 12

HE HAD OUTLIVED HIS DOCTORS' PROCLAMATIONS that he wouldn't last but a few months. Almost a year after his cancer diagnosis, Steve McQueen was alive through a combination of courage, willfulness, and steely determination. Every day offered new realms of pain, agony, and humiliation. "The media was hounding us, and we wanted our privacy. We wanted to go home," Barbara McQueen said. "I wrote a letter to Ronald Reagan [who was elected president approximately a month later]. I asked him to cut us some slack, let us take the treatments in Santa Paula. I didn't know why it should be illegal for Steve to take holistic medicines. I mean, come on, the doctors in Los Angeles wrote him off, told him he had two months to live. Rosarito was a beautiful, magical place, but we wanted to go home. I was angry. Steve was suffering. Seven days a week for a solid month, he was taking coffee enemas and the calf liver. He wanted to go home."

His health was one matter, but his mental and spiritual well-being were quite another. McQueen had spent much of his life as a wanderer—literally while growing up, and in spirit certainly when he was an established star with the need to take off on his bike without warning. However, McQueen had relatively recently planted himself and grown roots in Santa Paula, California. He had found a home. Life, the passage of time, and the realization that he was against the clock only made him appreciate it more. He needed to come back to what he knew before his mind and spirit, let alone his body, could find peace.

As the McQueens prepared to depart the Plaza Santa Maria on Friday, October 24, 1980, Rodolfo Alvarez asked Teena Valentino for a moment of her time. He looked anxious and sad, Valentino recalled.

"Teena, I am going to lose Plaza if I don't get more money," Alvarez said. "I have until the first of November to pay." She looked at him sympathetically but was stymied for words. "I will not work with Bill Evans anymore."

Valentino knew nothing of the financial arrangement between Alvarez and Evans, but she anticipated what was coming next.

"I want you to ask Steve if he would like to be a part of the Plaza," Evans said.

"You mean ask him for money?" Valentino replied.

"Yes. I need money. Bill Evans cheated me," Alvarez affirmed.

A month prior, McQueen sensed the hospital was in financial trouble and told Valentino as much. "It's in too deep—not a good financial investment," McQueen said. "Bad management. Bill needs to hire him a real smart man to run things, a man who's intelligent enough to give Bill the credit. Then it will succeed. That's what I always did."

Then Alvarez tried a different tactic on Valentino—he said McQueen couldn't leave. "If he leaves, he can't come back to the Plaza. The doctors advise against this trip and won't accept the responsibility if he dies," Alvarez said. In a strange afterthought, Alvarez graciously offered up his cabana again. Valentino was confused but tried to diffuse the situation with a positive response.

"I must go, Mr. Alvarez. I'll tell Steve what you've told me. He is your friend. I'm sure he'll think about your request," Valentino said.

As Valentino was prepping McQueen's Mercedes for the trip home, Bill Evans suddenly appeared at her side. "What did [Alvarez] want? Money?" Evans asked. "Don't you let Steve give him any money. I just gave him enough to make his payment."

Valentino remained silent. She had no idea who was telling the truth, but her gut told her the Plaza Santa Maria was a house of cards that was about to collapse.[1]

Against the doctors' orders, Steve and Barbara, along with Teena Valentino and nurse Annie Martell, began driving back to Santa Paula. McQueen asked his wife to pull over the car two hours into the drive, and the four checked into a roadside hotel for the night. The following day, October 25, they reached Santa Paula safely.

"It sure is good to be back home," McQueen said as the car pulled into the driveway.

Though McQueen left the Plaza Santa Maria under negative circumstances, he still maintained a relationship with Dr. William Kelley, who told the media that McQueen was "taking a break from his therapy." According to Grady Ragsdale, McQueen maintained he hadn't lost faith in Kelley or the program. "Hey, accord-

---

1   Adelle Williams, a former Plaza employee, told a UPI reporter in December 1980 that the American employees were not paid their final salaries. An internal investigation by new Plaza ownership showed $152,000 in missing funds, which was also investigated by Mexican authorities.

ing to the other doctors, I shouldn't even be here now," McQueen said. "Kelley's kept me going six times longer than anyone else said I ever would. But at the rate we're progressing, it'll take forever to get rid of this thing in my stomach. And it's really starting to get to me."

The tumor not only distended McQueen's belly but put excessive pressure on his back, making bed rest unbearable. He was pushing to have it removed.

That night McQueen and his guests feasted on chipped beef, mashed potatoes, tossed salad, assorted fruit slices and wedges, chocolate chip cookies, and a variety of juices. McQueen smiled as he surveyed the people at his dinner table—Barbara, Valentino, Martell, and Ruth, the McQueens' part-time cook.

"The whole family is here," McQueen said affectionately. "It's nice."

• • •

After a couple days of rest and visitations from Neile, Chad, and Terry, Steve met with doctors Kelley, Dwight McKee, and Rodrigo Rodriguez on October 29. They also introduced Dr. César Santos Vargas, Mexico's finest surgeon.

Vargas recalled in a 2005 interview the strange circumstances that led to his bedside meeting with McQueen. "I had received an urgent phone call from a doctor in L.A. He said that he had examined a patient who was very famous and wanted me to fly to L.A. to meet him. It was strange to fly to America for a patient and not even know his name, but I agreed, based on my relationship with the doctor. I was told that a private jet owned by an influential U.S. politician would come to Mexico to pick me up.

"I met Steve McQueen the day after I arrived. It was immediately obvious to me that he was at the terminal stage of the cancer. He was seated in a chair with an oxygen mask covering his nose and mouth, and [he was] clearly in pain. It was a miracle that he was still alive. We have a saying in Mexico when someone is at the end of their life, that they are '15 minutes to 12,' and this is what I told Steve when he asked me about his condition."

McQueen immediately sized up Vargas and asked to see his hands. Vargas held them out, palms up, feeling as if he were on trial. McQueen then grabbed his wrists and examined his hands to see if they shook. He stared at Vargas for an uncomfortable amount of time.

"I will trust you because you are honest," McQueen said. "I want to live, and I am counting on you. Would you please perform my operation, Doctor?"

It was a difficult situation for Vargas because he knew the operation had little chance of success and would tarnish his reputation. "I was under heavy pressure, but I did not regret my decision," Vargas said. "He was a sick man in need, and it was my duty as a doctor and as a person to help him. I could not do anything less than that. His honesty and courage would not let me."

Surgery was scheduled for Monday, November 3, 1980, in Juarez, Mexico. It didn't give McQueen much time to digest the information, and he was hesitant, Valentino recalled.

"I'm scared, Teena," McQueen said, his eyes very troubled. "I need time." McQueen confessed he didn't want to exist on pain and Demerol while his body detoxified, yet the operation frightened him.

"The precious man never did discuss the pros and cons of the surgery at any length with anyone but God, although now and then he would make a comment or ask a question," Valentino said. "Mercifully, he fell fast asleep that night and got some much-needed rest."

McQueen consulted with a doctor at Cedars-Sinai over the phone on October 30 but got no satisfactory reply. The doctor said he could not offer advice without first seeing the X-rays. The same day, Pat Boone sent a portfolio of Christian tapes for McQueen to listen to and meditate over. McQueen also received a touching letter from a nun he had met in Chicago a year before:

Dear Steve,

My prayers and thoughts have been with you. No doubt you have forgotten about even meeting me, for I am only one of the many millions you have met.

Just a year ago this last September, you came to our school to use the hall and neighborhood in filming The Hunter. *I was the little white-haired Senior Sister of Mercy that gave you a Sacred Heart Badge. Remember? You promised to keep it in your pocket. Now I am enclosing another one in case you lost it in your busy travels.*

Steve, we went to see The Hunter. *It was great! All I could think of was what joy and laughter you brought to so many of God's people. He will reward you for working so hard and sharing your talents. You are a real "Star" in the eyes of God.*

The sisters have always enjoyed watching your movies—especially the one with our own "backyard" scenery.

Now Steve, I know you are keeping close to our dear Lord. No one but our Heavenly Father knows all the right answers. He has given each of us a time to be born and a time to die. We all must go at His call, and death is just a change of life.

You may not be able to answer or even read this letter, but I do want you and your loved ones to know I am with you in prayer and spirit.

God Bless you, Steve.

Sister MEM, R.S.M.

The day got a little brighter when the owner of a local Chinese restaurant sent a meal to the McQueen house as a "welcome home, get well" gesture. However, Dwight McKee, who was staying at the ranch, wouldn't allow his client to indulge.

"Steve, it's probably okay, but we have to be careful," McKee said. "Someone might have slipped poison in it."

"My friends wouldn't do that!" McQueen said indignantly.

"I know your friends wouldn't, but maybe someone else was hanging around who would like to see you dead."

McQueen stared at McKee incredulously and asked, "Who would want to see me dead?"

"Well, maybe someone who wants to see the Kelley Program fail," McKee said. "Steve, it's just a possibility. We have to consider it. You can't eat anything here unless we fix it, or unless the place where it's purchased doesn't know it's for you."

McQueen shook his head in disbelief. "This is brand new to me," he said. McKee, Martell, and Ragsdale left the room, leaving McQueen and Valentino alone.

"Who would want to hurt me, Teena?" McQueen asked.

"Nobody, Steve," she answered, shaking her head, thinking this journey was getting stranger by the minute.

But McKee's paranoia was somewhat bolstered when a disheveled-looking man walked up to the front gate, demanding to see McQueen. He proclaimed he was there to "fix him for good" and was going to "heal" Steve. The trespasser refused to leave, and Barbara McQueen called the police, who arrested him. However, he came back the next day, insisting that he was going to perform the final healing of McQueen. Barbara's nerves were frayed, and she marched into the kitchen and pulled a loaded revolver out of the cupboard. Ragsdale persuaded her to put the gun back and had the man jailed once more. He was frisked and cuffed, and police found a small piece of rope in his possession. He didn't show up a third time.

The unwanted intruder, plus the swarming press, drove Barbara McQueen to hire a guard dog for security. She also asked a friend, who was armed with a shotgun, to sleep in a camper van at their front gate.

• • •

The ranch was bustling with activity on November 1, 1980, as McQueen received several visitors. McQueen's secretary Joyce brought Karen Wilson, the teenager he and Barbara had saved from the mean streets of Chicago, to see Steve one final time. Karen had been attending a boarding school in nearby Ojai and displayed some of her newly acquired riding skills. Joyce had also called Pat Johnson and told him, "Steve doesn't want anyone to know, but he's back at the ranch. He doesn't want anyone to see him, but I know if you could see him, he'd feel better."

Johnson raced to the ranch from his Canoga Park residence and knocked on the door. Annie Martell answered and diplomatically told him McQueen was not home. "Look, you go and tell Steve that Pat is here. I'm standing by this door, and I'm not leaving until I see him." Martell went back to confer with Steve, then she came back and told Johnson, "Steve wants to see you."

Johnson and McQueen's agent, Marvin Josephson, had visited McQueen at the Plaza Santa Maria in mid-October and were pleasantly surprised at how well he looked. But since those two weeks, McQueen had taken a turn for the worse. "He looked terrible," Johnson said. "His belly was all bloated. He lost weight, and he didn't have that much weight to lose in the first place. His voice was raspy. He told me about all the pain he was in." McQueen admitted to Johnson the pain was becoming unbearable. At that moment, Johnson had taken notice of the loaded .45 pistol on McQueen's nightstand. Johnson assessed, "Steve had an extremely high threshold for pain, but the pain was too much. He was like a boxer who went 20 straight rounds, and he was getting his ass kicked every round. The man was hurting. For him to contemplate suicide, the pain had to be incredible."

Johnson was in tears and pleaded with McQueen to remain strong and see this journey to the end. McQueen said he would try. "I kissed him, and as I walked away, in my heart, I knew it was the last time I was going to see Steve," Johnson said. When Johnson got home that night, he wrote in his diary, "I have the feeling that I'll never see Steve again."

Neile, Chad, and Terry dropped by on November 2 to check on Steve's condition. Terry and Chad went with Barbara on an excursion into town, while Neile snuck quietly into Steve's room. He was sleeping soundly but sensed her presence in the room. He stirred, and it took a moment for him to realize it was Neile. She recalls their brief exchange in her 1986 memoir:

"Is that you, Nellie?" he asked in a raspy, barely audible tone.

"Yes, it's me honey."

"I thought I'd never see you again," he said, smiling at his former wife, mother of his children, close friend, and the woman with whom he shared a million dreams.

"Oh, I'll always be around."

"God, I'm so tired."

"Go to sleep, honey. I'll see you later."

It was an especially heartbreaking exchange given the date—exactly 24 years to the day they had exchanged wedding vows and carved out a life together. Despite their highs and lows, they maintained a deep love and friendship for one another.

• • •

"I'll do it," McQueen said on November 2.

Valentino stared at him. "Do what?"

"I'll have the operation."

Valentino smiled softly at McQueen, then she excused herself to tell Dwight McKee, who was sleeping in a trailer on McQueen's property. Thus began the mad scramble to work out all the details for McQueen's operation. There were frantic phone calls between Kelley and Santos, hotel accommodations, plane flights, X-rays, and CAT scans. They also had to find a blood match for McQueen and stay one step ahead of the media. And it all had to be worked out in a matter of hours.

When the details were finalized, Valentino shared with McQueen the new plan of attack. Valentino, McQueen, and Martell would take a Lear jet from the Ventura County Airport in nearby Oxnard to El Paso, Texas, where they would drive across the border to check into the Santa Rosa Clinic in Juarez. The news jarred McQueen.

"Tomorrow?" McQueen said, his eyes flying open and his lips tightening.

"I thought you said you'd have the operation, didn't you?" Valentino asked slowly.

"Not so soon," McQueen said. "In a couple of weeks, maybe. Not tomorrow."

"No, no. You won't have the operation tomorrow. The operation will be Wednesday, [November 5]" Valentino informed him. "But Santos needs more X-rays." McQueen stared at Valentino, not saying a word. "All the arrangements have been made. You're scheduled."

McQueen closed his eyes and slowly opened them again.

"I need time," McQueen sighed.

A few hours later, he finally came to terms with himself. He was going through with the operation.

• • •

McQueen was surrounded by turmoil, such as the numerous phone calls to be answered, people arriving at the door, planes being booked, and last-minute tests being performed. This was matched only by his own hopes and fears for the success of the operation and his future. Fate would intervene for McQueen one last time. Out of the chaos, a new figure emerged and brought serenity with him.

As everyone was busily packing and preparing for the trip to Mexico, Grady Ragsdale received a phone call from the Reverend Billy Graham. "Does Steve still want to see me?" he asked. "As soon as possible," Ragsdale replied. When Ragsdale relayed the information to his boss, it was as if a great burden had been lifted. McQueen cried tears of joy.

Graham recalled that first meeting, which took place on November 3, 1980, at McQueen's bedside. "Though I had never met [McQueen] before, I recognized him immediately from his pictures, even though he had lost considerable weight. He sat up in bed and greeted me warmly.

"He told me of his spiritual experience. He said that about three months before he knew he was ill, he had accepted Christ as his savior and had started going to church, reading his Bible and praying. He said he had undergone a total transformation of his thinking and his life."

McQueen told Graham how Sammy Mason led him to the Lord and that his new faith in Christ became his resource for extra strength after he was diagnosed with cancer. McQueen admitted he was flying to an undisclosed location for an operation and had about a 50 percent chance of survival. Graham read McQueen a number of passages of Scripture, and Graham prayed with McQueen several times.

Graham accompanied McQueen to the Ventura County Airport, while McQueen peppered him with questions about the afterlife. When the time came for the two men to part ways, they said one last prayer. After "Amen," Graham instinctively handed over his Bible to McQueen, which became McQueen's proudest possession. Graham wrote on the front inside flap:

> To my friend Steve McQueen,
> May God bless you and keep you always.
> Billy Graham
> Philippians 1:6
> Nov. 3, 1980

As Graham turned to leave, McQueen proclaimed, "I'll see you in heaven!"

· · ·

Pilot Ken Haas and copilot Mike Jugan received a call to pick up "Sam Sheppard"[2] in Oxnard, California, on November 3, 1980. Haas, who owned Ken Haas Aviation, knew Sheppard was Steve McQueen and informed Jugan to keep quiet. Jugan's nerves lit up because McQueen was a hero of his, having watched *On Any Sunday* "about 50 times" as a youth.

Jugan recalled having to park the plane away from the terminal because the paparazzi was out in full force, waiting to snap a picture of McQueen. After sitting on the ramp for a few hours, Jugan wondered if McQueen was going to show. Then he heard a sharp knock.

"I hear this 'knock, knock, knock' on the side of the airplane, and I opened it," Jugan said.

"There was a gentleman standing there with a hat on his head and asked, 'Are you with the Sam Sheppard party?'" I said, 'Yes, we are.' He stuck out his hand and said, 'I'm the Reverend Billy Graham.' At this point, I realized something special was happening."

A few minutes later, a large truck with a camper pulled up to the plane and a canopy had been arranged over the forward part of the aircraft, allowing McQueen to board discreetly. Jugan recalled that McQueen was wearing blue jeans, a T-shirt, and a sombrero, and he held a soda in his hands.

"Howdy, fellas," McQueen greeted the two pilots.

"I'm standing there looking at my childhood hero and my heart went out to him," Jugan said. "You could see his belly was distended and swollen with the tumor, and he was hammered with the cancer. But the look in his eyes was just fierce. He had this indomitable spirit about him."

After McQueen, Valentino, and Martell were situated, Graham said a special prayer, blessing the airplane, the pilots, the flight path, and finally McQueen. "It was like being in the presence of God himself," Jugan said. "It was such an overwhelming moment. That was such an event that I'm not sure I can properly convey how incredible it was."

As the plane reached cruising altitude, Jugan left the control area and conversed with McQueen for about 20 minutes. "He was snacking on crackers and soda. I wanted to discuss motorcycles, but Steve was more interested in the plane and asked me what it was like to fly a Lear jet," Jugan said. "I told him we climbed

---

2   Sam Sheppard was the Cleveland, Ohio, physician accused of killing his pregnant wife in July 1954, and almost a decade later the verdict was overturned. His story was the inspiration for the TV series and movie *The Fugitive*.

out at 5,000 feet per minute, and we were cruising at 41,000 feet and about 600 mph. He said with a chuckle, 'That's better than my Stearman.'"

It was a life-changing moment for Jugan, who is a born-again Christian. "This wasn't a man who was flying to his death but a man who felt as if he was going to live," Jugan said. "He was very optimistic about the surgery and the faith in his doctors. I have often marveled at the chance I was given that day to witness Steve's strength, peace, and courage. He was obviously sick, but I could sense that he was bigger than all that—that he would be back on this jet after the surgery, return to Santa Paula, and life would go on. He had a strength and peace about him that I cannot fully describe."

Valentino, Martell, and McQueen also conversed on the subject of McQueen's time in El Paso, Texas, when filming *The Getaway* about eight years before.

"Didn't you do a movie there or something?" Martell asked.

"Yes, *The Getaway*," McQueen said.

"That's right, with Ali MacGraw."

"Lotta good memories in El Paso and Juarez," McQueen said. "I was in love."

After the plane landed safely, McQueen, Valentino, and Martell were whisked to the Eastwood Medical Center in El Paso, where McQueen submitted to a CAT scan. It revealed a large tumor on the right lung, and the disease had metastasized around the liver, pelvis, and diaphragm.

When the X-rays were complete, the three were driven to the Granada Hotel, where they were met by Jack and Dolly Valentino [Jack and Teena's daughter]. Steve drifted off to sleep around 10:30 PM.

The following morning, November 4, Barbara, Chad, Terry, and Grady Ragsdale arrived, as did Dr. Kelley and Dwight McKee. Steve didn't want to converse with anyone and kept to himself in his hotel room. By midafternoon, an escort arrived and drove them across the border into Juarez, where he checked into the Santa Rosa Clinic, a nondescript red brick building that resembled a garage or warehouse. An orderly wheeled McQueen into No. 13, a two-room minisuite. McQueen quickly climbed into his bed, requested an oxygen mask, and asked that the tank by the head of his bed be switched on "4." He also requested additional fans, distilled water, and Chinese food.

At 6:00 PM, he had a hearty meal of soup, rolls, potatoes, vegetables, fish, and coffee. Two hours later, Barbara, Terry, Chad, and Grady tiptoed in to say good night. Steve was happy to see them but had mental preparations to make. His surgery was scheduled for the next morning, and he needed time alone. They drove back to the Las Fuentes Motel, which was near the clinic.

On November 5, McQueen's blood levels were tested by Dr. Vargas, who had lined up 12 donors. Chad was also tested, who remembered, "We were the same blood type, so I started eating raw steaks and getting popped for blood twice a day. That was a hard thing, but I remember when he said, 'You're giving blood—does it hurt?' I said no. It was the first time I ever really felt like an adult, felt truly grown up. Dad must have known that, too, because the last thing he ever said to me, right before he went into surgery, was, 'You're gonna be all right, pal.'"

Vargas erred on the side of caution and deemed that the operation should be delayed a day. The decision left McQueen emotionally exhausted.

On the morning of November 6, Dr. Vargas was ready to perform the surgery. Grady and Barbara met for coffee before heading to the clinic. Barbara had expressed a desire to see Steve before the operation but arrived too late for her wish to be granted. Her disappointment was obvious to those in the clinic. McQueen was given an enema, then he was bathed and prepped for surgery. All of his IVs were in place, and his shots had been given. He was then placed on a gurney, and the big moment had come. Teena Valentino recalled, "We moved out of the room and started slowly down the hallway. Steve reached for my hand. I held firmly until the doctors stopped me at the operating door." The two had a ritual at the Plaza Santa Maria whenever he entered the hot tub where he would hand his watch to Valentino before he took a dip in the waters. Once again he told her, "Hold my Bible and my watch, Teena." To her, that meant business as usual. "Steve had no inclination to die," she said. "He had a powerful body, and his immune system was building. He had a quiet, heroic substance to him."

Before McQueen disappeared, Valentino saw him give doctors Vargas, Kelley, and McKee the thumbs-up sign. Barbara, Terry, and Chad arrived a few minutes later, while Ragsdale called Billy Graham, who in turn called Ronald and Nancy Reagan. They all prayed for McQueen.

Vargas told McQueen that he would perform the operation as quickly as he could. However, if he died, he would suspend the operation.

"I want to live," McQueen said. "I am counting on you, doctor."

Vargas admitted in a 2005 interview that he was nervous. "I was tense before the operation. If I had made a mistake when performing on this world-famous person, it would have spread all over the world. I was under heavy pressure. But I did not regret the operation. Steve trusted me and came to Mexico."

The surgeon started the operation around 8:00 AM and was startled by the amount of cancer in McQueen's body.

"Oh my God, there's so much," Vargas remembered saying to himself. "Where do I start?"

Vargas cut out areas from the pancreas to the pelvis, from the bladder to the kidneys, and from the lungs and arteries. But McQueen hung in tough. Vargas cut and snipped for approximately three hours, removing a five-pound tumor from the ailing actor's stomach and another cancerous tumor from his neck.[3] Vargas finished around 11:00 AM and collapsed with nervous exhaustion. He grabbed a few hours of sleep before checking on McQueen.

"It's successful!" Kelley said aloud to those in the waiting room when Vargas finished. "His heart is doing fine. He's fine!" Everyone hugged each other.

When McQueen awoke from the operation shortly around 2 PM, his first words were, "Is my stomach flat now?" The legendary McQueen vanity was still intact.

Vargas recalled conferring with McQueen when he woke up. McQueen was tired but also excited. "He raised his thumb and said, 'I did it,'" Vargas said. "I told him to sleep and get well."

McQueen was kept heavily sedated and slept intermittently throughout the day, and Barbara, Terry, Chad, Ragsdale, Valentino, and Martell crowded joyously around the bed. Steve was in good cheer when he was awake. The room was filled with relief and quiet laughter. He had bravely defeated cancer, and now there was optimism in the air.

At 5:45 PM, everyone left to take a dinner break except for Dr. McKee, Valentino, and Martell, who stayed behind to monitor McQueen. His pulse, respiration, and heart were steady. He was recovering so well, in fact, that a heart monitor was removed from the room. Two hours later, his temperature was 35.5°C (96°F), his blood pressure was 120/90, and his pulse was a fast 100. Barbara, Chad, and Terry returned to say good night.

"Honey, we're going to go the motel now," Barbara said. "We'll see you in the morning." Steve waved them out with a touch of impatience. His mind was focused on something else.

"Ice cubes. I want more ice cubes," he said to Valentino. She was alarmed that he had already consumed three quarts and was concerned about the cold chunks hitting his stomach. Valentino also recalled that many of the Plaza patients craved ice just before they died. Around 8:00 PM, she approached Dr. Vargas about her concerns. He came back with her to check on McQueen and examined all of his vital signs.

"He's all right," Vargas smiled.

---

3   Vargas told a reporter that McQueen's tumors were so large that it would have been only a matter of time before they would have choked him to death.

But Valentino sensed something wasn't right despite the round-the-clock watch from her, McKee, and Martell. Around 11:00 PM, McQueen's breathing became irregular because he had been choking on some mucus, though his heart was still strong and steady. Valentino said around midnight she heard McKee command to McQueen, "Breathe in... breathe out... good. Turn up the oxygen." Valentino had been up for several days with very little sleep, and her body seemed paralyzed with exhaustion. She dozed off for about three hours until she was suddenly jolted out of her sleep a little after 3:00 AM.

"Annie, is the crisis over?" Valentino asked, referring to McQueen's midnight bout with respiration, wondering if he had stabilized or if he was feeling worse. He had major surgery, and on the face of it he seemed to be recovering well. However, something was not quite right.

"Uh, no," ominously answered Martell, who had just dozed off but was awake 10 minutes before.

Everyone present contemplated McQueen's condition. All of a sudden, panic and fear hit the air as it was clear that something had just happened in that moment. "Dwight... Dwight!"

McKee sprang up, and all three were at McQueen's side at once.

"Steve, God damn you—no! Steve, come back! Steve!" shouted McKee, who instinctively performed CPR while Martell slipped a respirator over McQueen's nose and mouth. Everyone worked on him furiously for 20 minutes, taking over when the others got tired, using all their might to try and bring him back. McKee gave McQueen a shot of adrenaline to the heart, which elicited no response. Medically, there was nothing left to do. Steve McQueen had drifted off into another realm.

McQueen was pronounced dead at 3:54 AM on November 7, 1980. He was 50.

One by one they all trickled out of the room, except for Valentino, who stood silently by McQueen's bed. Months before she had made a vow to McQueen that she would never leave his side during his illness; it was a promise she fulfilled despite the hardships.

"I told you, Steve, I would never leave you," she said. "I didn't leave you. You left me."

41

ASHES TO ASHES

Minutes after Steve's death, Barbara McQueen was awakened out of a deep sleep by a jarring phone call.

"That's it," she said to herself. "He's gone."

When she picked up the receiver, Dwight McKee confirmed that her husband was dead. Barbara's pain was intensified by the fact that she had not been able to say good-bye, but she consoled herself with the thought that during the three and a half years she and Steve were together, they spent every moment that was possible with each other. "Neither of us had to be reminded that our time together was limited," Barbara said. "We both had said everything we needed to say with a lot of 'I love yous' peppered in between."

Terry cried and immediately called her mother, Neile, who was keeping silent vigil in Los Angeles.

"Mom...Dad's dead," Terry said.

Chad McQueen was defiant when he was given the grim news by Barbara, and he refused to believe his father was gone. He had Grady Ragsdale take him to the hospital around 6:00 AM on November 7, where Teena Valentino remained with Steve. "I remember I went back to the hotel after the surgery. Then I got a call at three in the morning telling me that he was dead," Chad recalled. "I went to the hospital and went into the room, and he was lying there with his eyes open. I remember touching him and he was cold in the face, but his chest was warm. I never thought this man could die."

Chad asked Valentino for his father's watch and straw cowboy hat, which she handed over immediately. Ragsdale had asked her for the Bible that the Reverend Billy Graham had given to Steve just days before. It now rested on his chest, his hands clutching the small brown testament, which had been opened to Steve's favorite verse, John 3:16: "For God so loved the world that he gave his only begotten Son, that whoever so believes in him shall not perish but have everlasting life."

Chad closed his father's eyes, bent down and kissed him on the forehead one last time.

"So long, Pop. I love you."

• • •

Steve McQueen was dead, but his ordeal in Mexico wasn't over.

With the help of business manager Bill Maher, McQueen had meticulously planned and executed his stay in Mexico. But for all of the Xs and Os, McQueen had no exit strategy—no clear plan what to do in case he didn't survive the operation. According to Teena Valentino's diary, McQueen brought $4,000 in cash with him to Mexico. After everyone got paid—the hospital in El Paso, hotels, rental cars, Vargas' fee, a breathing specialist, etc.—there was nothing left to pay the mortician, who threatened to hold Steve's body until he was rewarded handsomely. Steve McQueen, who was the medical pride of Mexico, was now being held for ransom. There was a risk of a morbid and wholly inappropriate debacle to follow. It would seem as though in the pursuit of media exposure and greed, the powers that be were about to lose sight of the fact that a man, a husband, a friend, and a father had passed away, affecting countless lives.

Attorney Bill Carter remembered getting a frantic phone call from Maher on November 7 at his Little Rock, Arkansas, law firm on the morning of McQueen's death. "I need your help, Bill," Carter recalled in his 2006 autobiography, *Get Carter*. "Steve died in Mexico last night, and the Mexican government is refusing to release the body. As you can imagine, the family is beside themselves with grief over the situation. Steve's attorneys out here have been trying everything since we got the word, but they can't move the federales. I don't care what it takes, but I want that body out, and I know you can do it."

If anyone could pull it off, it would be Carter, who specialized in civil and criminal law. Carter was a former Secret Service agent under President John F. Kennedy's administration. He was also a political activist and an established entertainment "fixer." He had threatened President Richard Nixon with a lawsuit on behalf of ex-Teamster president Jimmy Hoffa. He had also sweet-talked the State Department into allowing the Rolling Stones to tour America in 1975, and he kept guitarist Keith Richards from going to a Canadian prison after he was arrested for heroin trafficking in 1977.

Carter was well-acquainted with the tactics of the Mexican authorities—he had negotiated the release of several Ivy League college students during the 1970s who had spent their spring breaks across the border, blowing off a little steam, binge drinking, and smoking a little reefer. Those cases usually carried a $50,000 bounty, but Carter could usually get them sprung through a contact in Tucson, who would dutifully make the trek to Mexico to pay off the authorities at a greatly discounted price. "Blackmail was common practice in those days," Carter said in 2010. "It was all a scam. They thought they had a prize in Steve McQueen's body. But I tricked them into thinking this was going to be an international incident."

Carter believed a Mexican police major and the funeral home director were in cahoots when they claimed they were "holding McQueen's body for investigation." Carter knew a scam when he heard one.

He placed his first phone call to Alfonso Prado of the Funerales Santa Rosa in Juarez, Mexico. "Look, I want to know what it will take to get the authorities to release that body right now," Carter commanded. "How much will it take?"

Prado backpedaled, double-talked, and fumbled for words, not expecting to be confronted so directly, according to Carter. After much prodding, Prado tossed out a figure of $160,000. Carter asked him once again—if Carter could produce the cash, would Prado release the body? Prado confirmed that was indeed the case.

The attorney worked the phones for the next two hours, calling high-ranking officials in the nation's capitol to lean hard on immigration and customs officials at the Mexican border. He also called the Mexican police major in charge of the case. Carter remembered with vivid detail the tenor of that conversation. "When he answered, I spoke in my most intimidating voice: 'This is Bill Carter in the United States. I have spoken to the State Department, the Bureau of Customs, and the Immigration and Naturalization Service, and there is about to be a major international incident if you detain Steve McQueen's body any longer. I want that body released.'"

Carter was playing a high-stakes poker game, but he had learned from his Secret Service days how to take control of a tough situation through intimidation. "If you speak with authority, you can immediately wrest control of any situation and succeed, but you must maintain control of the situation at all costs," Carter said. "Well, I had control of this guy from the time he picked up the phone."

What Carter could not control was the media, which had caught wind that McQueen had died in Juarez. All of the major news outlets—including NBC, CBS, ABC, UPI, AP, Reuters, *National Enquirer*, *Los Angeles Times*, *New York Times*, *New York Post*, *Paris Match*, *People*, and the Mexican press—were all desperate to break the news. Journalist Carlos Rosales of the *El Paso Times*, a 22-year-old journalist, got the jump on everyone.

Rosales says that he received a tip from a source in Mexico that McQueen had died a few hours earlier in a Juarez clinic. "I found out McQueen was here in our town and apparently looking for a cure for his illness—the Big C—you know? It's like, wow, you don't know what to say," Rosales recalled in 2009. "I had heard he was at Clinica Santa Rosa, and all I did was look it up and I went down there. At that point, it was just a rumor. Back then, there was no concern about [going] over the border to Mexico like there is now. I managed to talk to somebody inside and they confirmed, 'Yeah, he is here. He passed away.'"

Rosales located the funeral home, where he approached Alfonso Prado and struck up a conversation. Through their discussion, it turned out that Prado knew Rosales' grandfather who had died years before. Rosales, who had a camera around his neck, asked Prado if he could take some pictures of McQueen. Prado allowed the young photographer unrestricted access for a long period of time. This impromptu and opportunistic photo shoot resulted in ghoulish images of McQueen that were understandably shocking to a world used to seeing their favorite star full of life and with his blue eyes ablaze.

"To not have taken pictures would have been to drop the ball on the biggest story of my career to date," said Rosales, who today is an assistant news director at a major Southwest television station. "You've got to understand, McQueen was the guy of our generation, the top dog. To this day, I still consider him the best ever. He was my movie hero. I can still see images of him bouncing the ball inside his cell in *The Great Escape*. Part of *The Getaway* was filmed in El Paso. But it's tough, and you've got to do it. It was surreal.

"Some people might say, 'If you liked or admired the guy, why did you do what you did?' I say to them, 'It was my job.' You know, if I had come back with no film … I guarantee you I would have been fired. That's just part of the job, and sometimes in this business you do things you don't want to do. Believe me, it wasn't one of my proudest moments."

Rosales, however, wasn't alone. He said after he was done taking pictures, about a half-dozen members of the Mexican media converged on the funeral home and were also allowed inside the autopsy room. "I was trying to take pictures, let's just say, that were not graphic," Rosales said. "Everybody in there, the Mexican media guys, was in there taking close-ups. I was shooting as wide as I could without being too gross."

But it was Rosales' pictures, under his contract with international photo agency Gamma Liaison[1], that ended up on the front page of *The New York Post* and inside the pages of the *National Enquirer* and *Paris Match*.

---

1   Gamma Liaison was the same agency who offered photos of Diana, Princess of Wales, dying in a demolished car, to several tabloids for $250,000.

The images upset Ali MacGraw so much that she publicly cried on *Entertainment Tonight,* begging the media to stop the hurtful coverage of her former husband. "The most important thing in his life was his personal privacy," MacGraw said. "He was too weak to combat the kind of invasion he was experiencing. It made all of us who loved him crazy. I still have an amazing amount of anger at a magazine that ran a picture of him after he died. I don't understand it. The hurt is monumental, to be raped that way."[2]

Journalist Felipa Solis, who worked for KTSM-TV in El Paso, confirmed it was a free-for-all at Funerales Santa Rosa. "A stringer from Mexico had called me around 3:30 PM that day and told me in Spanish that there was a movie star who was dead and sitting in a funeral home in Juarez. She added that people from the medical school who brought him there were going to bring him to El Paso International Airport, so if I wanted to go, I'd better leave right away.

"The interesting thing was, the medical school students knew who he was, but I'm not so sure the Mexican press did. They knew he was a movie star, but they didn't know exactly who he was. So I walked into this dinky little funeral home and there he was, just lying on a slab. I got one look at him—he had a beard and this reddish hair. The cancer just riddled his body. The only thing that covered him was a sheet, and my knees buckled when I saw who it was—Steve McQueen."

Solis and other members of the media watched McQueen's body as it was placed into a pine casket and loaded into Prado's aged Ford LTD station wagon, which was used as a makeshift hearse. The car had recently come back from the mechanic, and its front wheels still shook unevenly. While Solis and other journalists followed the vehicle to the airport, Rosales rode with Prado and an assistant mortician in the wagon. Their destination was Southwest Air Rangers terminal at the El Paso International Airport, where two Lear jets were sitting on the tarmac, awaiting to transport McQueen, family members, and his entourage back to California.

At Mexican customs, Prado proudly boasted he had McQueen's body in the back of his station wagon and presented his death certificate to an official. Rosales said he was amazed they were waved through so quickly. "Today they would X-ray

---

2   Barbara McQueen said she, too, saw the photos a few weeks later when an anonymous envelope appeared in her mailbox. She said she opened the contents and out spilled several 8 x 10 glossies of McQueen in the morgue. She recalled immediately dropping to her knees and crying. "I don't know why anybody would take photos like that and then send them to me," she said. "Some people are just plain cruel."

the casket, check the body for drugs. But they just looked at the certificate and off we went," Rosales said.

While Barbara, Terry, and Chad sat inside one of the jets, Grady Ragsdale, Dwight McKee, and Teena and Jack Valentino all stood around inside the airport, anxiously awaiting the arrival of Steve's body. They all watched the various entrances to the airport but didn't know when the "hearse" would arrive, what it looked like, and if they could outrun the reporters to the planes. "Steve's body is arriving in a station wagon," McKee whispered to Jack a few minutes later. "I don't know what color… at least it won't be a beat-up green Mexican ambulance."

In the meantime, Teena had spoken to a ticketing agent, who had control of a button that admitted outside vehicles onto the runway. When Teena received her signal, she told the agent to press the magic button when the time came. Moments later, the station wagon arrived, Teena waved at the ticket counter, and the gates opened. Ragsdale, McKee, and the Valentinos, along with pilots Mike Jugan and Ken Haas, loaded McQueen's coffin into one of the planes before the press caught wind. However, they didn't notice Rosales clicking away until a few minutes later.

"Who are you?" Teena asked loudly, trying to be heard above the jet roar.

"I came with the station wagon," Rosales answered.

"Are you taking pictures?"

"No."

McKee turned around and glanced down from the jet steps as Steve's casket was nearly in. "If Steve was still alive, he'd beat the hell outta you for this!" McKee shook his fist.

Teena glared at Rosales, then thrust out her hand. "Give me that film," she demanded.

"No."

"Take that camera off your neck or I'll yank it off!" Jack said as he jumped down from the steps of the plane, coming almost nose-to-nose with Rosales. The photographer removed the camera from his neck slowly.

"Now give me the film," Jack said, his hand reaching for the black box. Rosales hesitated, but Jack's size and demeanor indicated he wasn't playing around. "I'll bust your camera."

Rosales opened the camera and pulled out the film, placing it in Jack's palm.

"Get out of here," Jack gruffly ordered.

As everyone made their final ascent up the stairs, Rosales ran up to the plane, waving his arms for them to wait. The photographer had a crisis of conscience, and according to Teena, tears streamed down Rosales' face. "I am sorry. Please forgive me," Rosales begged. "I don't know what came over me."

Everyone nodded and understood, then Jack stepped out to hug Rosales. All was forgiven—until a few days later when Rosales' postmortem photos hit the papers.[3] The damage was done; the insult was already made. McQueen's last picture was sadly grotesque and undignified. Thankfully, it is not how he is remembered today. The photographs have largely faded from public consciousness, and only the myriad images of McQueen in his prime remain in the public consciousness.

As the plane pulled onto the runway and was readying for takeoff, Teena looked out of the window and saw a throng of photographers racing toward the plane, still taking pictures.

"It was a chaotic scene, but what I remember most is that it was just unbelievably sad," said pilot Mike Jugan. "Barbara was crying, Terry and Chad were crying, the doctors and nurses were crying, and it was a very sad event. One of the doctors was sobbing and said, 'We got the tumor, and we saved him. We saved him.' He was devastated, sobbing like a little girl. We all were. I remember thinking to myself that just a few days before, Steve was so positive about the whole trip. I mean, this wasn't supposed to happen. He wasn't supposed to die. Nobody's getting out of here alive anyway, but it wasn't time for him to die."

Soon after departing El Paso, Grady approached the cabin and asked Jugan and Haas if they could do a "low pass" when they reached the Santa Paula Airport. Both men smiled and said they'd be glad to fulfill the request. Jugan recalled, "I remember when we reduced speed, full flaps, gear down and were about 100 feet off the ground and made our low pass along runway 22, a crowd of about 50 people had gathered outside, waving good-bye to Steve. Over the Unicom frequency I heard a voice coming through the radio saying, 'God bless you, Steve.' Man, talk about goosebumps."

Minutes after the tribute, they landed at Ventura County Airport, where Steve's body was taken to a mortuary for cremation. The ordeal was finally over.

• • •

The following day Barbara spent the evening surrounded by friends and loved ones, including Dr. Dwight McKee, Annie Martell, Grady Ragsdale, and Jack and Teena Valentino. The six of them had spent the last several months trying to save Steve's life and were emotionally drained from the experience. Barbara recalled, "We all got drunk, cried our eyes out, and talked until we were totally spent. I

---

3 Rosales' postmortem photos of McQueen were taken on another roll of film and stashed safely in his pants pocket.

collapsed into bed a little after midnight and awoke out of a deep sleep around 4:00 AM, which was right around the time Steve had died the prior morning. It was a cold night, but all of a sudden the room turned hot. I pulled down the sheets only to feel Steve's arms wrapped around me.

"It's okay, honey," she heard Steve's voice say. "Don't worry. I'm fine. Nothing hurts. I'm young again, and I'm so happy. Be happy and go on with your life."

Barbara says Steve's spirit gave her one final hug good-bye, and he was gone. When she awoke later that morning, she was smiling from ear to ear and dancing around the kitchen. Everyone was somewhat stunned by her sunny disposition, except Annie, who asked, "So Steve visited you, too?"

"My honey came to see me," Barbara said. "He was the Steve I knew, the man I fell in love with. Everything's okay."

• • •

On Sunday, November 9, 1980, a private memorial service was held for Steve at the ranch, and it was hosted by Barbara McQueen. Earlier that day, Pastor Leonard DeWitt held three church services, and McQueen's seat in the balcony row had been marked with a bouquet of roses and a small American flag. Barbara read the 23rd Psalm. The congregation sang the national anthem in McQueen's honor, barely leaving a dry eye in the house.

The memorial service was a more down-home affair with a buffet in the barn. Food, potluck dishes, and iced-down beer were served on the tailgates of some of the trucks. Inside the cozy home, visitors could see the sunlight streaming through the skylight, shining on a bouquet of roses and carnations, as well as other floral tributes to McQueen.

Terry, 21, and Chad, 19, were present, as well as Neile McQueen-Toffel and Ali MacGraw. It was the first time all three of Steve's wives had been together. No doubt this notion would have elicited one of those trademark McQueen grins if he had still been alive. Barbara graciously led the women into the master bedroom to Steve's jewelry box so they could reclaim the pieces that each had either given Steve or received from him. For example, he had saved both of his wedding rings to Neile and Ali. And Terry reclaimed the Zippo lighter that once belonged to Steve's father, William McQueen. Despite the fact that Steve had once told Bud Ekins that he had "pitched it in the weeds," he had kept the lighter all these years. It was the only possession he had from his late father.

Approximately four dozen people attended the memorial, including nurses and doctors from Plaza Santa Maria, such as Teena and Jack Valentino, Annie

Martell, and Dwight McKee; friends Bud Ekins, Pat Johnson, Elmer Valentine, Chuck Bail, and Nikita Knatz; business associates and actors such as James Garner, George Peppard, Robert Culp, and LeVar Burton; as well as various members of the Santa Paula community, including Sammy and Wanda Mason.

They all laughed, cried, prayed, reminisced, and told stories about Steve; every human emotion was on display.

"Steve operated at one speed—as fast as he could go—and he never knew the word quit," Sammy Mason said. "He would always insist on flying as long as possible to total exhaustion. Yet he was always willing to take instruction…when it came to flying, I was the boss."

DeWitt made sure that everyone knew who McQueen's real boss was, and he "shared the word of God with [the mourners]…how to become a Christian, how to walk with God. Steve would have wanted that."

The pastor read Steve's favorite verse, and as DeWitt closed the prayer, the roar of engines could be heard in the distance. As the gatherers looked up, they could see in the sky a seven-man memorial cross in the missing man formation— the empty spot was reserved for Steve. Larry Endicott, at the head of the formation, dipped his plane's wings in final salute and headed toward the Pacific Ocean, where Steve's ashes were scattered. In an amazing and touching twist of fate, a small proportion of the ashes were blown back into the aircraft. It was as if Steve's spirit was still flying, his determination living on. Fifty years after his birth, Steve McQueen had finally returned back to this earth.

• • •

Steve McQueen's death provoked a flood of tributes from around the world. And like so many talents taken for granted during their own lifetimes, McQueen's place in cinema has proven to be irreplaceable. Despite the circus-like coverage of his death, the media response was one of genuine grief and sorrow.

The Washington Post wrote, "Hollywood made him look like a guy who courted trouble. *Bullitt* gave theatergoers, not to mention the San Francisco Police Department, near–heart attacks. So did *The Thomas Crown Affair*, in which he piloted a soarplane to a lilting theme that left millions breathless…McQueen also buttressed his reputation in real life. He owned motorcycles, which he raced in the desert, and he broke enough bones to be considered authentic. He also raced automobiles and won, so when he was cast in the movie *Le Mans*, his role reverberated with verisimilitude.

"He seemed steady, and trustworthy, and wised-up." •

Films in Review wrote of him, "McQueen left behind, on film, more of himself than most people, even most actors, are allowed to leave. It's a worthy legacy."

Film historian Phillip Bergson noted, "His shocking early death at 50 robbed the cinema of an exceptional personality."

The New York Times' Vince Canby aptly nailed the zeitgeist of McQueen's appeal with a touching tribute: "The death of Steve McQueen at 50 deprives American movies of a great national resource—one that, although recognized by producers for McQueen's clout at the box office, was more or less taken for granted by the rest of us, probably because his was a career of such consistent quality…McQueen didn't 'act in' a movie. He inhabited it. He wore it, as if it were an old, somewhat shabby, utterly comfortable jacket—without ostentation.

"Like Cooper and Gable, McQueen contributed, through his particular presence, far more to the films he was in than he ever received from them."

• • •

The kid from the streets who had only a ninth-grade education left the world a wealthy man, and the estate he left behind is hard to estimate, given his secretive nature. Some believe that, given McQueen's legendary tightness, he had slush funds and hidden accounts around the world. What is known is what he left to his loved ones in a public will, which was drawn up and then executed by Bill Maher and Kenneth Ziffren.

Steve left to Barbara McQueen $2 million; 480 acres of unimproved land in Blaine County, Idaho; three antique motorcycles; a 1978 Rolls Royce Corniche; a 1958 GMC pickup truck; and their various furniture and furnishings.

He also bequeathed $200,000 to Boys Republic,[4] $100,000 to Ventura Missionary Church,[5] a PA-8 Pitcairn plane to Sammy Mason, an MCMD Stearman plane to Chuck Bail, and a 1972 Mercedes 300 SEL 6.3 to Pat and Sue Johnson.

The bulk of his estate, worth millions, was left to Terry and Chad in a testamentary trust. Steve had accumulated so many possessions that he could have easily opened a museum in Ketchum, Idaho, where he and Barbara had once contemplated operating a general store. In addition to 210 restored and unfinished motorcycles, McQueen owned approximately 55 antique cars and trucks, plus thousands of other items he had collected, including jackknives, pistols, rifles,

---

4   Boys Republic used the funds to build a recreation center, which was dedicated to McQueen on
    April 21, 1983.

5   Ventura Missionary Church designated the money to their private school operations and funded
    several scholarships for underprivileged children.

jukeboxes, buffalo couches, potbellied stoves, toys, refrigerators, gas pumps, tin bread boxes, coffee grinders, cash registers, bicycles, advertisements, tools, wooden propellers, and telephones.

Unfortunately, these items needed to be itemized, insured, maintained, and looked after, which would take constant time, attention, and money that no one apart from Steve could have ever done justice to. Unable to reasonably cope with this logistically unfeasible responsibility, Terry and Chad decided to auction everything over a two-day period in November 1984. The sale brought in more than $2 million. Even hardened bike and car collectors admitted to paying much more than the normal rate to acquire anything that belonged to McQueen. Steve had departed this world, but everyone still wanted a material and tangible connection to him. One buyer summed up the feeling among the boisterous crowd of 1,400 people: "He was a hell of a guy, and he led the life we all wanted to lead."

• • •

Steve's death cast a large shadow over the lives of his family and friends, and the event still has an incredible effect on those who knew him best. First wife Neile McQueen-Toffel wrote a memoir in 1986 called *My Husband, My Friend*, in which she recounts their 15-year marriage with unflinching candor. Her tale of their union, which includes detailed accounts of his womanizing, drug-taking, and wife battering, raised a lot of eyebrows among McQueen's cult of loyal fans. It also irked their old friends and drove a stake between Neile and son Chad for years.

Neile has softened her opinion of her first husband over the years and defends McQueen in every retrospective, biography, and documentary where she's been interviewed. The former dancer/actress is a doting grandmother who is on the cusp of 80. She is, if nothing else, a survivor.

In March 1998, Neile endured another tragedy when her 38-year-old daughter Terry died from hemochromatosis, a genetic disorder of metabolism. Individuals with hemochromatosis absorb too much iron, resulting in toxic levels that attack the liver, heart, pancreas, lungs, and other organs. Steve and Neile were both carriers of the rare genetic disorder but didn't suffer from the disease.

Some say Terry never quite got over the death of her famous father, even developing an ulcer months after his passing. She stated in a November 7, 1991, interview, "Eleven years have passed since my father died at age 50. That day, the world lost a star, and I lost not only my father but my best friend.

"Dad never leaves me. Every time I have to make an important decision, I wonder what he would have decided … I feel like his breath is on me."

Terry, whom Steve had once described as "the apple of my eye," left behind 10-year-old daughter Molly. Neile and second husband Al Toffel adopted and raised her as their own. Today, Molly is in her mid-twenties and bears more than a striking resemblance to her beautiful mother.

After Terry's death, both Neile and Chad set up the Terry McQueen Testamentary Trust, a nonprofit funding source that benefits troubled youth.

Unfortunately, Al Toffel, the man Neile said was "the glue that holds me together," died of a massive heart attack while vacationing in March 2005. He and Neile had been celebrating their 25th anniversary in Las Vegas when he died.

Toffel's death drew Neile and son Chad closer together; they had been estranged for several years over a business deal involving the estate, but they were finally able to put it behind them.

Chad also put acting behind him after two decades in the business, but he had already adopted the McQueen need for speed and decided to give professional race car driving a spin. "I didn't find acting fun anymore, so I decided to give racing a total commitment."

Chad drove a Ford-powered Crawford sports car in the Grand American 400 km race at California Speedway in April 2005. He was in good company with Dominic Cicero II, an American who raced Formula Renaults in Europe. One of Chad's ambitions was to drive in the 24 Hours of Le Mans, which was the focus of his father's 1971 film of the same name. Chad had entered the race in 2003 but broke his left leg in a motocross race. Three years later, the broken bones started to pile up.

In January 2006, Chad was running in a practice session behind the wheel of the Tafel Racing Porsche GT3 at the Daytona International Speedway while practicing for the 24 Hours of Daytona race. Another car lost control and took Chad out of the race, causing him to crash into a wall. It took several hours to extricate him from the car, and he suffered a litany of injuries, including a severely shattered leg and several broken vertebrae. He was lucky to have survived.

The accident gave Chad reason to pause, and he gave up racing for good. Now closing in on 50, Chad is a devoted husband and father, often dispensing his father's sage and streetwise advice to his three children—Steven, Chase, and Madison. "[Steve] would often give me little life lessons," Chad said. "His favorite was, 'Life's not fair, pal.' A lot of them stick with me. In fact, I find myself saying a lot of the stuff to my son."

Chad collaborates with Corbis, and is in charge of the Steve McQueen estate. In January 2010, he started McQueen Racing, a company that partners with leaders in the motorcycle and custom car industries to create limited-edition high-performance motorcycles and automobiles. There seems to be no checkered flag in sight for Chad's ambitions, who seems to bend, break, and roll with life's punches, usually ending up on top.

"Wherever Dad is, I hope he's happy with me. I've missed his guidance over the years, but I'm sure he'd be glad to know that I've never had a DWI, never been arrested for drugs," Chad said. "Everything I am is based on Dad raising me, and it's been a pretty good ride."

. . .

In the years following Steve's death, Ali MacGraw's ride was bumpy and filled with emotional potholes. She suffered a personal and professional meltdown in the early 1980s and was forced to sort out the wreckage of her past, which included unresolved feelings for Steve. In 1991, MacGraw resurfaced as a spokesperson for a line of cosmetics and wrote a *New York Times* best seller called *Moving Pictures*. The painfully honest autobiography tells of the heart-breaking miscarriage she suffered while McQueen was filming *The Towering Inferno*, and she recounts her life as an alcoholic and male-dependent for years. Through an intense 12-step program and daily inventory, McGraw claims she was able to refocus her addictive nature to yoga, which she credits as a positive force in "centering her."

In 1994, she parlayed her passion into a successful video called *Yoga: Mind and Body*, which updates her philosophy of yoga and a healthy lifestyle.

MacGraw, now 70, seems to have found serenity in her life in recent years. That's mainly due to the fact that she moved to the outskirts of Santa Fe, New Mexico, after a Malibu fire destroyed her home in 1993 while she was attending a yoga class. Former husband and legendary producer Robert Evans took her in immediately. The two remain very close and are extremely dedicated to their son, Joshua, who has written, acted in, and directed several feature films.

Santa Fe has embraced MacGraw, who is fully occupied by her work as an animal rights and environmental activist, artist, and accessories designer, and she lends her name to several worthy causes. Recently MacGraw became part of the McQueen legacy at the Boys Republic by agreeing to serve as Honorary National Chairman of the 2009 Della Robbia Wreath Campaign. MacGraw has drawn praise from McQueen friends and fans alike for never saying an adverse word against him. While she knew his faults, she measured Steve in his good deeds and has spoken about him only passionately and in a positive light. She is now living the life she has always wanted to lead and is in a good place.

. . .

Third wife and widow Barbara McQueen moved back to Ketchum, Idaho, in the days following Steve's death, where he had built a log cabin called "Last Chance." She remained respectfully silent about his death until her 2006 photo book, *Steve McQueen: The Last Mile*, was released. She also toured the world with a photo exhibit of the same name, traveling from London to San Francisco, meeting fans, shaking hands, signing autographs, and enjoying a revival of former glories.

Her poignant pictures reveal a much different side than McQueen's go-go Hollywood years. Her book depicts a more down-to-earth superstar who loved simple things, such as old pickup trucks, spur-of-the-moment road trips, vintage toys, and antique planes. This period demonstrates the final period of a man who lived many lives in a single lifetime. It also lends proof to the fact that McQueen had finally achieved the peace that eluded him for so many years.

Barbara, who turned 57 in 2010, has often wondered—if Steve had not died, what would her life be like today? She knows for certain "we'd still be living on our ranch in Idaho, perhaps with three or four kids and lots of dogs, cats, cows, and horses." She also believes he'd be very proud of her.

"He was a great teacher. He taught me so much. I don't take shit from anyone. He made me a strong woman. He made me what I am."

• • •

Unfortunately, part of McQueen's legacy will forever be linked to his unorthodox cancer treatment and his strange journey to Mexico to seek a last-ditch cure. William D. Kelley, McQueen's controversial doctor and one of the most recognizable names in the history of alternative cancer treatment, died on January 30, 2005, at age 79 from congestive heart failure.

His career both peaked and faded when he began treating McQueen at the Plaza Santa Maria on July 31, 1980. McQueen's death was a blow to Kelley's already questionable credibility and his claims of curing approximately 33,000 patients in his lifetime.

In July 1981, Kelley met Nicholas Gonzalez, a Cornell University graduate student. Gonzalez was asked by Kelley to evaluate his controversial work for the academic medical world. However, that medical world never accepted Gonzalez's findings after a five-year case study, neither did it accept Kelley as a legitimate cancer doctor. Kelley eventually gave up on cancer research and patient care, and he lost control of his organization in 1986. His marriage to wife Suzi had crumbled, and the two soon divorced. His mental and physical health showed signs of erosion as well.

Kelley did find love again, this time with a former cardiologist named Carol Morrison, whom he claimed to have cured of cancer. The pair moved to a rural setting in Saxonburg, Pennsylvania, in the early 1990s. The two barely lived above the poverty line, and the couple often resorted to scavenging for food in dumpsters.

Dr. Ralph Moss, a former associate of Kelley's, once visited the couple in Pennsylvania and was mortified to find the two living in squalor. Moss said Kelley continued to perform daily coffee enemas on himself, but he had reverted to slamming huge bottles of Coke, which he claimed had "health-giving" properties. Moss said the cancer pioneer was a shell of himself and no longer seemed remotely interested in treating the body or mind. "It was hard to connect this bitter wreck of a man with the vibrant individual of earlier decades," Moss said.

Kelley and Morrison purchased a printing press and spewed out racist and anti-Semitic literature, espousing their venomous and hateful view of the world. Kelley also attempted a bit of revisionist history where it concerned McQueen. He now claimed that a government agent wearing a doctor's smock came into McQueen's room on November 7, 1980, and tainted his "patient's" IV with a blood-clotting medication, which caused the actor's death. When Morrison died, Kelley moved back to his mother's 80-acre farm in Winfield, Kansas, where he had been born almost seven decades before.

He moved one last time to Weatherford, Texas, just outside of Dallas, to be closer to his immediate family. When he died of congestive heart failure in 2005, three of his four children, two brothers, and his cancer understudy were the only ones in attendance at his funeral.

It was a strange ending for a toddler who was told by Christ to heal.

McQueen had passed away, and those who were dear and close to him have all lived eventful lives of their own. However, even though he has long left this mortal realm, Steve's legacy lives on stronger than ever. He has become a cultural icon around the world, and his values and way of life resonate with many. Stop people in the street and ask them what they think of Steve McQueen. More than likely you will hear, "Oh, you mean the King of Cool?" And the nickname will almost certainly be accompanied by knowing nods of approval for the man and the legend.

42

LEGACY

ONE STAR SHINES BRIGHTEST. Steve McQueen's peers simply do not enjoy this level of fame. Brando, Dean, Newman, Clift, Beatty…the list goes on, and McQueen is still the biggest. These names have arguably faded slightly with time, while McQueen goes from strength to strength. Why is this? There is no one definitive answer, only countless reasons, each one different for every fan and admirer. Like a phoenix rising from the ashes, McQueen has only grown stronger.

Somewhere a wide-eyed youngster pulls back, pulse quickening, as he watches an intense blond-haired, blue-eyed actor command the wheel of a 1968 Ford Mustang 390 GT in a chase against a black Dodge Charger through the rolling hills of San Francisco in *Bullitt*. Somewhere someone watches for the 20th time on DVD *The Magnificent Seven* exchange bullets, and he enjoys it as if it were his first viewing. This fan sits in front of the screen, glued and transfixed. Like a child, the viewer is enraptured by those eyes, that cocky grin. Somewhere a youth envisions himself as a World War II POW trying to crawl underneath a barbed-wire fence in the video game version of *The Great Escape*. Or perhaps the youth has seen a mesmerizing face on the cover of a fashion magazine or in a popular car commercial and murmured aloud, "This guy looks cool."

That guy is none other than Steve McQueen, whose life was claimed by cancer three decades ago.

McQueen has been reinvented since his 1980 death as much more than a movie star. In today's world, he is a silent pitchman, a fashion icon, an enduring mythical figure of alpha-male coolness, and his image and likeness are omnipresent.

The public can't seem to get enough of the rugged animal magnetism of the macho superstar. Thirty years after McQueen's death, Hollywood and Madison Avenue are awash in McQueen nostalgia. Much like Elvis Presley, Marilyn

Monroe, Audrey Hepburn, and John Lennon, McQueen's death has become big business.

Nostalgia continues to be a multimillion-dollar business in today's world. The Steve McQueen mystique, including his persona and image, inundates the airwaves and world of digital media, generating big bucks for the license to his name. His hell-bent-for-leather take on life and pitch-perfect performances have been the subject of many books, articles, and documentaries since his untimely death in 1980. He is arguably more popular in death than he ever was in life.

His likeness and name have been used by approximately 50 companies to endorse various products, including TAG Heuer, the Gap, Levi's, Absolut Vodka, Wrangler, and continual campaigns on behalf of Ford automobiles, particularly the Mustang. McQueen, who was one of the biggest stars of the 1960s and 1970s and who became the highest-paid actor in the world of his generation, has also generated millions in merchandise licenses as a pitchman, using his star power to attract consumers. Yet his image and likeness are hardly franchised out indiscriminately. His license is carefully guarded by his son, Chad, and the McQueen estate, and licenses are granted to those only with products or businesses that Steve himself would have liked and are in the spirit of McQueen. The truth is there is enough demand for 500 companies wanting to leverage the McQueen cool.

The McQueen mystique has been used to promote sunglasses, computer games, liquor, watches, jackets, T-shirts, key chains, Zippo lighters, 12-inch figurines, model cars, trading cards, soundtrack CDs, DVDs, magazine features on his cars and bikes, mouse pads, foreign postage stamps, and scores of other products. But no one seems to have gotten more mileage out of McQueen than the Ford Motor Company, who put the icon back in the driver's seat of a car he helped make famous in *Bullitt*—Ford's Mustang. The amazing thing is that McQueen is not synonymous with these things; they are synonymous with him. They would be nothing without him.

The Michigan-based automaker secured the rights to McQueen's image and likeness from the estate for an undisclosed six-figure sum to make a commercial using the famous superstar's mug to sell the sports car in 1997, 2005, and 2010. Whatever Ford paid, it got back tenfold. That kind of cool is available from only one man—McQueen.

The Mustang commercial, titled "Cornfield," was conceived by J. Walter Thompson and shot by international production company Believe Media. It took six weeks to digitally resurrect McQueen, whose likeness was created by combining footage from *Bullitt* with a body double. The effect is dramatic and uplifting as McQueen steps out of a cornfield, takes the keys from a farmer, and slips into a shiny silver automobile for a test drive.

The Mustang commercial floored American audiences and pleased son Chad, who runs the McQueen estate. "The first time I saw the Ford spot, I got goosebumps," Chad said. "I think it's brilliant because all of a sudden there he is in prime time again, and kids are going, 'Who's that guy?' There's no downside to that."

The licensing is not just about money. It achieves something more, and as such it is essential. It keeps McQueen's name in the forefront of everyone's consciousness and introduces new audiences to a legend. The automobile has introduced McQueen to a new generation of hipsters young enough to be his grandchildren. "When you tell younger buyers that something's cool, it's instantly not cool," said Ford Marketing spokesperson Miles Johnson. "These younger buyers are figuring out on their own who Steve McQueen is. They're deciding he's cool on their own.

"They like the idea of going to the Internet or Blockbuster to find out who this guy is. They'll see a great car chase in *Bullitt*, then check out more of his films. When they put it together, they'll say: 'Wow.'"

"Wow" is indeed the appropriate reaction to McQueen, who is synonymous with high-speed motors. His contribution to the car and motorbike industry is deep and long lasting. He and Bud Ekins have been credited for creating the antique-bike collecting hobby, and by extension, they created the cottage industry surrounding it. Type McQueen into any Internet search engine, and most of the results will show him behind handle bars or behind the wheel of a car. The respect is deserved, too. He counted racing legends Stirling Moss and Mario Andretti as professional rivals. He defied convention and raced not for the money but to be free and to prove himself among the best. Racing was the great equalizer, and he competed with broken limbs for what he believed in. Sebring, Baja, Elsinore, and the International Six Days Trials are all well known to racing fans, and McQueen gave these different places his best on a varying number of wheels. This also encapsulates the appeal of McQueen. There is something to admire about the man. If it's not for his style, then you have to admire his racing. If it's not for his attitude, then you have to admire his films. There is always something to respect.

His cars and bikes regularly surface for sale, which is not surprising given how many he owned. When they do get sold, a few simple words always prefix the publicity, and invariably the piece is labeled "the Ex–Steve McQueen." This guarantees that the buyer will need a deep wallet—because Steve owned it, it will cost at least five times the price than if he had not. It is a mark of quality and greatness. What better thing for an enthusiast to tell his friends, "You see this bike? This was once Steve McQueen's." This will usually be followed by the sound of jaws dropping in awe.

Now perhaps more than ever, people need to have a piece of McQueen. Recent auctions of his belongings in 2006 and 2008 from Bonhams auction house had feverish and frantic bidders from all over the world. Bidders were desperate to own something McQueen had touched. Motorbikes, sunglasses, and screen-worn costumes all fetched large prices. However, even the mundane things sold for amazing prices. His iconic pair of sunglasses from *The Thomas Crown Affair* fetched $70,000. A simple giveaway ballpoint pen from a gas station that he used sold for thousands, as did a wire basket he sometimes used to collect eggs on his ranch. In anyone else's hands, these items would be worth nothing. As McQueen's possessions, they are virtually priceless. What is it that makes people desperate to own something McQueen had touched? They feel that to own something of McQueen's brings them not only closer to the man they respect and admire, but it also gives them a sense of pride. But most importantly, it brings them that little bit closer to greatness.

As a multimillion-dollar cottage industry still going strong three decades after his death, the McQueen estate generates $5 to $10 million per year from image and licensing fees. In addition to those fees, every time a McQueen movie is shown on television or cable, his estate gets a piece of the action, because the actor was clever enough to have secured a partial stake in most of his films. When a McQueen DVD or boxed set is repackaged or sold, the estate can also count on receiving a royalty check. McQueen, who was a top Hollywood earner during his lifetime, is also a bankable icon in death. According to *Forbes*, he consistently ranks among the 10 most popular celebrity-image earners, just behind Michael Jackson, Elvis Presley, John Lennon, and Marilyn Monroe.

In addition to familiarity and mass appeal, deceased celebrities offer the marketing community something living entertainers do not—peace of mind.

"Albert Einstein isn't going to get busted for drunk driving, and Steve McQueen is not going to have an affair and be in the tabloids," said David Reeder, vice president of Corbis' GreenLight, which represents McQueen and many other dead celebrities. "Anything that's happened is behind them, making them a safe harbor for advertisers."

Hollywood has continued to find the McQueen name bankable and has cranked out several television and theatrical remakes of movies he helped make famous. They include *Wanted: Dead or Alive*, *The Blob* (twice remade with a third in the planning stages as of 2010), *The Great Escape*, *The Getaway*, and

The Thomas Crown Affair. Remakes of *Bullitt* and *Papillon* have been planned, and bringing the aborted *Yucatan* to the silver screen has also been fodder for the industry trades.

McQueen's image on posters and marketing materials once sold movies almost single-handedly, and the same is true today. One thing is clear—McQueen sells. This happened yesterday, it happens today, and it will continue to happen long past tomorrow.

Legions of McQueen fans have sprung up all over Tinseltown, including many well-known actors who would do anything to capture his on-screen magic. The likes of Brad Pitt, Daniel Craig, Christian Bale, Kevin Costner, Pierce Brosnan, Mickey Rourke, Bruce Willis, Alec Baldwin, Mark Wahlberg, David Boreanaz, Michael Madsen, Jason Statham, Andy Garcia, and Woody Harrelson are all card-carrying members of the Steve McQueen Appreciation Society. Even today, McQueen is still the barometer of fame. Every new and emerging actor in Hollywood with even a glimmer of a chance of being a major star is always benchmarked against him. The press asks, "Is he the new McQueen?" Unsurprisingly, the answer is eventually always, "No."

After all, not many people have that X-factor. Given McQueen's cultural impact then and now, he had the X, Y, and Z-factor. This is most clear in his oft-used moniker, the King of Cool. Most people never get to choose their nicknames. People bestow these names and phrases on you, depending upon what they think best suits you, and you have no choice in the matter. McQueen was crowned the King of Cool—essentially, men wanted to be him, and women wanted to be with him. The smallest gesture, the simplest garment, anything he touched turned to gold. A look or a glance could convey a thousand words and emotions without McQueen uttering a single sound.

Today many directors say they would practically give their left arm to work with a talent such as McQueen, knowing a star of his caliber would not only bring commitment and verve to a role but could open their picture to huge returns. One only has to imagine McQueen in a wickedly violent Tarantino picture. If he was in *Reservoir Dogs*, you can bet audiences would not remember any character but his. He would have had the biggest gun, the best scenes, and the best shots. He could do a *Magnificent Seven* number and dominate, acting everyone else off the screen. Audiences would be thrilled at McQueen in a Steven Spielberg blockbuster or taking charge of one of Tony Scott's slick and choppy exercises. "Even though Steve McQueen was a huge star in his day, my feeling is that he was underrated," said director Phillip Kaufman. "Now that Steve McQueen is gone, we miss him."

The critics in McQueen's lifetime, who intimated that he was just playing himself, have been replaced by a new generation of scribes who now laud his performances with hyperbole, superlatives, and adjectives once reserved for gods.

He was a megastar in his lifetime. But if it is at all possible, his acting has become even more important. It is arguable that he was underrated as an actor. Today, however, his style and talent are admired for how good he truly was. He could play any character. No one did action quite as convincing as McQueen, whether wielding a shotgun in *The Getaway* or putting out a fire in *The Towering Inferno*. He developed the archetypal role of the rebel in films such *Papillion*, *The Sand Pebbles*, *Hell is for Heroes*, and *The Cincinnati Kid*. But he could also be a dashing matinee idol and war hero in roles such as *The War Lover* and *The Great Escape*. He could play a cowboy and hero of the west in *The Magnificent Seven* and *Nevada Smith*. When everyone said he could only play tough guys and rebels, he proved them wrong in *The Thomas Crown Affair*. He broke the mold with the ice-cool cop in *Bullitt*, and all that have followed are just pretenders to the throne. He could even make people laugh on occasion in *The Honeymoon Machine* and *The Reivers*, or he could play the romantic lead in *Love with the Proper Stranger*. Most impressively, he even learned to grow old gracefully with maturity and depth in *Enemy of the People* and *Tom Horn*. This range and quality would simply not be possible without genuine ability and talent.

What is now appreciated is just how hard he worked to get there. His rise to superstardom did not come easy. He had to work at these characterizations, improving them and making them definitive. His initiative and labor are now admired and respected. The fact is that McQueen has left a impressive body of work that is more than the sum of its parts. It is the legacy of a hardworking and highly talented actor with an instinctive knack for what worked.

This is a film legacy that only a few will ever attain in motion picture history. Most actors are lucky to leave behind five memorable films before they shove off to the great big epic picture in the sky. McQueen's canon of work—26 feature films and three as an uncredited extra, three top-rated seasons of *Wanted: Dead or Alive*, and the seminal documentary *On Any Sunday*—though small by comparison to other actors, includes at least five classics: *The Magnificent Seven*, *The Great Escape*, *The Sand Pebbles*, *Bullitt*, and *Papillon*. Each one arguably tops their respective genres or is at least considered as one of the best.

Is there a better cop drama than *Bullitt*? Is there a more beloved war film than *The Great Escape*? Racing fans would argue that *Le Mans* should be included, while other film buffs would make a case for *The Cincinnati Kid*, *The Thomas Crown Affair*, and *The Getaway*.

What is it that inspires such passion for these roles? For each fan there are myriad reasons. But there is one common theme—McQueen put himself into these roles. These characters were people he knew because they were part of him. Today, rich and pampered film stars purposefully create situations to find inspiration for roles. McQueen did not need this kind of cozy artifice because he had already lived his roles in real life and they were not enjoyable. This provided a rich well from which he was able to draw, projecting his power onto the screen.

McQueen knew Nevada Smith's loneliness because he was virtually abandoned himself. He'd traveled a hard route through Boys Republic and the Marines by the time he reached young manhood. He felt this pain for real. McQueen is The Cincinnati Kid, desperate to prove himself, desperate to be No. 1. McQueen knew firsthand this desire to be somebody in real life, scratching out an existence in a cold-water flat before he was famous. He is Jake Holman enjoying his work with the ship's engine; he knew machines and respected them from his time in the Marines. Frank Bullitt was a cop, but he was also a character who was operating on the fringes of authority, challenging those around him and doing things on his own terms—and all with resolute confidence in himself. This mirrors McQueen's innate combination of integrity, uniqueness, and individualism. He is Papillon trying to escape; by the mid-'70s, McQueen was growing weary of stardom and needed to find a form of escape. He had the same burning desire for freedom as the character he played. Even Thomas Crown, on the surface the polar opposite of McQueen, still captures part of the man. Crown was the character McQueen aspired to be most of all. Crown was financially secure and respected, which of course McQueen eventually succeeded in achieving. In all of his roles, McQueen was taking his own experiences, passions, desires, hopes, and fears and laying them bare for audiences the world over, delivering a beautiful honesty.

The actor from the other side of the tracks who rose above his circumstances to achieve great fame and wealth is a beloved figure today. His life experiences, insolent charisma, smoldering sexuality, and definitive cool made him a superstar of cinema. His fear of failure gnawed at him, and the paranoia that his self-supposed lack of acting talent would be found out was the driving force behind every one of his performances.

On screen he radiated a soulfulness and vulnerability behind the tough exterior. McQueen's insecurities were always brimming underneath the surface of a false bravado, the result of a personal life that was filled with childhood rage, pain, and emotional scars that never quite healed. He lived his life looking in the rearview mirror, always on the run, yet he sucked the juice out of life. He was authentic and original, and his audience simply couldn't get enough of him.

"He was very insecure," said director Norman Jewison, who directed McQueen in *The Cincinnati Kid* and *The Thomas Crown Affair*. "But I think that added to his popularity. People detected that insecurity; they don't want people who are too secure."

Director Mark Rydell, who guided McQueen in his finest comedic performance in *The Reivers*, said the macho superstar was beyond insecure. "He was a remarkable, exciting personality. Very tortured, very tormented, borderline psychotic, I would say. But he was just magic on film. You can't take your eyes off him."

The source of his insecurities highlights something positive from McQueen's story. He literally came from nothing. He was virtually abandoned as a child by his absent father and his poor excuse for a mother. He went to reform school and then began to slowly climb. He had to fight his way up from his beginnings as a nobody to become somebody—and then he became one of the 20th century's most famous faces. If he could achieve all that, then surely anything is possible if one tries hard enough. Part of his legacy is hope.

McQueen is a reminder of another era. He was the alpha male of his generation, but his image has managed to transcend time. Hollywood has never been able to define "it"—that indefinable quality that spells magic on the silver screen. Even son Chad, who inherited many of his father's traits, is a bit mystified by his old man's enduring mystique. "Listen, if I knew what it was Dad had, I'd bottle and sell it," he said. "He couldn't walk across the street without being mobbed. Obviously, it was something nobody else had or now has. That's the reason for this resurgence of interest in him."

For a dead movie star who would have recently turned 80, it's apparent Steve McQueen has still got "it" in spades.

He has endured because he appeals to everyone. Steve McQueen was one of the most contradictory people in popular culture, a true divided soul, and yet he achieved the impossible. He has unified cinema fans, motor and aviation enthusiasts, men and women, young and old, and even members of the fashion world. The definitive rebel has unified all. To so many, McQueen still means so much. Even he would raise a smile at the irony.

Long live the King. Long live the King of Cool.

ACKNOWLEDGMENTS

MOST PEOPLE THINK OF WRITING A BOOK as a solitary undertaking, but it is not. It takes a team of dedicated individuals with a singular purpose and vision to assemble an epic biography on a major entertainment figure such as Steve McQueen.

My first thanks must go to my wife Zoe, who allows me to indulge in what I call my "expensive hobby." Zoe understands my need to write, the amount of hours it takes to conduct research, and the mood swings that come as a result of deadline pressures. She has spent many days and nights away from our home, dined alone or with friends, and sacrificed vacations so I could get this last book out of my system. When Zoe is home, she keeps me amused with her repertoire of corny jokes, Broadway songs, and uninspired monologues. She is a bad entertainer but a great wife!

Andrew Antoniades, the pride of Great Britain, was the developmental editor of this monster project and became my personal hero in the writing of this book. He magically appeared from the heavens one week before I started writing and fulfilled the only request I had of him—to have the courage to tell me when I was wrong or off base. Andrew is the perfect editor—witty, balanced, insightful, analytical, energetic, and forever encouraging. He also has a naughty sense of humor, and we got each other from the start. He was able to read my mind, complete my sentences, and give a more global perspective on McQueen. Andrew's age belies his wisdom, and whatever he does, he is bound for greatness. With the completion of this manuscript, I have lost an editor but gained a great mate.

Veronica Valdez, a real-life Nancy Drew, was the chief researcher for this book and went far above the call of duty. Veronica not only awakened the ghosts of the past but also made them dance, sing, and come alive to finally tell their story. This normally mild-mannered lady transformed into an aggressive, old-school gumshoe when it came to finding out the truth, especially where it concerned William Terrence McQueen and Steve McQueen's ancestors. Veronica spent numerous hours in the library, combing over old files and microfiche. She walked around not-so-nice neighborhoods, knocked on doors, and did her detective work the old-fashioned way, with amazing results. Veronica always pushed, prodded, and never allowed me to settle. I'll forever be in her debt.

Donna Redden is my Canadian neighbor and a most reliable friend. Donna did a crucial second-line edit, donated numerous photos, and lent her encyclopedia-like talents to this book, especially concerning *Wanted: Dead or Alive*. Donna is always willing to lend a helping hand without ever asking for anything in return. Her comments on my work are always funny, sometimes biting, and to the point. But I wouldn't have it any other way.

Psychologist Peter O. Whitmer, Ph.D., who wrote the foreword and contributed heavily to this text, is the most effervescent man I have had the pleasure to know. I read his magnificent book, *The Inner Elvis* (a psychological biography of Elvis Presley) in 1997 and secretly wished that I could tap his talents to one day analyze McQueen. Thanks to a serendipitous introduction by author Alanna Nash, my dream became a reality in 2010. Peter has effectively been able to sum up McQueen's past behaviors and life choices for readers, which remained a mystery to me and many others for so long. Peter, by the way, was the first drummer for the band The Turtles. He is also my rock star.

Barbara McQueen, Steve's third wife and widow, is perhaps the craziest friend I have. Barbara and I met in 2005 and we wrote a book, *Steve McQueen: The Last Mile*, the following year. We have traveled the world together, experienced many adventures, and shared a lot of laughs in the last five years. Barbara has allowed me to extensively interview her about her life with Steve, including the last year of his life, which is never a pleasant topic. She bravely read this manuscript as a favor to me, as painful as it might have been, for the sake of veracity. Barbara has always been good, kind, and loyal to me, and her friendship is truly treasured.

Pat and Sue Johnson (aka "Team Johnson") are unofficially "America's Sweethearts" and still sticky sweet after almost four decades of wedded bliss. Pat and Sue were among Steve's role models, and they remain mine, as well. I love to see them, tease them (especially Pat, because he knows deep down I can take him), and just plain adore them. Pat was Steve's karate instructor, best friend, and perhaps the most loyal man I know. His dedication to Steve's memory three decades after his death is touching and inspirational, and it's easy to understand why Steve loved him dearly.

Thanks also to Terri C. McQueen, Steve's long-lost half-sister. Terri was a hard woman to find, and it took the employment of Colorado Special Investigations to do it. She had planned to take her secret family history to the grave, but she trusted me to tell her story with dignity and respect, and I am indebted. In 2010, she came with me to Slater, Missouri, to pay homage to Steve and to somehow connect with William. Terri is such a delight as a person, and we are now regularly in contact. I hope it stays that way.

Jean Black is the editor and publisher of *The Slater Main Street News*. Jean, whom I have affectionately nicknamed "Lady Boss," opened her arms to me and asked the people of Slater to do the same. Jean is smart, funny, and sassy, and she works hard for her success, which is well deserved. She also makes killer peanut butter cookies, which her son must now share with me every holiday season.

A big thank you to Barbara Leigh, Bob Relyea, Sharon Farrell, Katy Haber, Hilly Elkins, Leonard DeWitt, Lee Purcell, Ty Hardin, Chuck Bail, Richard Martin, Jack Garfein, Loren Janes, and Sandi Love for their enduring friendships. Steve had so many great relationships, and these people are proof that he chose wisely.

Ali MacGraw, Steve's second wife, actress, fashion icon, and the epitome of class is not only a beautiful, talented, and loving mother—but she is also an animal rights and environmental advocate. More than any celebrity I've observed, she uses her fame for all the right reasons.

Tony Seidl, my longtime agent and friend, who immediately found a great publisher for this work must also be recognized.

Thanks to the Triumph Team of Tom Bast and Katy Sprinkel. Tom was the person who purchased this property, while Katy has been a champion from the start and has gone to the mat for me, kindly extending my deadline when I missed the first one. And thanks to Merry Dudley for her copyediting skills.

John Gilmore, Adrienne McQueen, Kandee Nelson, Michael Manning, Darren Wright, Mike Jugan, Will Smither, Hikari Takano, and Dan Viets were great assets thanks to their additional research contributions.

And last but not least, thanks to my parents, Mike and Carolyn Terrill, who were there for the first book and are here for the last. They not only gave me life but a loving childhood. Their overabundance of love provided a beautiful blueprint for marriage. They are exceptional people and a source of never-ending love, support, and encouragement.

CHRONOLOGY OF MAJOR STAGE, TELEVISION, AND FILM ROLES

STAGE

Still Life, 1951, Neighborhood Playhouse, New York City.

Truckline Café, 1951, Neighborhood Playhouse, New York City.

Peg O' My Heart, 1952, starring Margaret O' Brien, in East Rochester, New York.

Member of the Wedding, 1952, starring Ethel Waters, in Rochester, New York.

Time Out for Ginger, 1953-1954, starring Melvyn Douglas, national road company tour.

Two Fingers of Pride, 1955, starring Gary Merrill, summer stock production, in Ogunquit, Maine. Steve played Nino.

A Hatful of Rain, 1956. Steve replaced Ben Gazzara in the lead role of Johnny Pope in his only Broadway appearance. McQueen was fired in the fall of 1956 and later toured in a road company production in the summer of 1957.

TELEVISION

Goodyear Television Playhouse: "The Chivington Raid" (NBC) March 27, 1955.

U.S. Steel Hour: "Bring Me a Dream" (CBS) January 4, 1956.

The Goldbergs: "Rosie the Actress" (Guild Films) 1956.

Studio One: "The Defender" (CBS) February 25, 1957 and March 4, 1957 [two-part episode].

West Point: "Ambush" (CBS) March 8, 1957.

The 20th Century Fox Hour: "Deep Water" (CBS) May 1, 1957.

Climax!: "Four Hours in White" (CBS) February 6, 1958.

Tales of Wells Fargo: "Bill Longley" (NBC) February 10, 1958.

Trackdown: "The Bounty Hunter" (CBS) March 7, 1958, pilot for "Wanted: Dead or Alive."

Trackdown: "The Brothers" (CBS) May 16, 1958.

Wanted: Dead or Alive (CBS) This half-hour series debuted on September 7, 1958, and ended on March 29, 1961.

Alfred Hitchcock Presents: "Human Interest Story" (CBS) May 24, 1959.

Alfred Hitchcock Presents: "Man from the South" (CBS) January 3, 1960.

The Dick Powell Theater: "Thunder in a Forgotten Town" (NBC) March 5, 1963.

FILMS

Girl on the Run, Astor Pictures, 1953. Screenplay by Arthur J. Beckhard and Cedric Worth. Directed by Joseph Lee and Arthur J. Beckhard. Starring

Richard Coogan, Rosemary Pettit, Frank Albertson, Harry Bannister, and Steve McQueen (uncredited).

Somebody Up There Likes Me, MGM, 1956. Screenplay by Ernest Lehman, based on the autobiography of boxer Rocky Graziano. Directed by Robert Wise. Starring Paul Newman, Pier Angeli, Sal Mineo, Everett Sloan, and Steve McQueen (uncredited).

Never Love a Stranger, Allied Artists, 1958. Screenplay by Harold Robbins and Richard Day, based on a novel by Robbins. Directed by Robert Stevens. Starring John Drew Barrymore, Lita Milan, Robert Bray, and Steve McQueen (as Martin Cabell).

The Blob, Paramount, 1958. Screenplay by Theodore Simonson and Kay Linaker, based on a story by Irvine H. Milligate. Directed by Irvin S. Yeaworth Jr. Starring Steven McQueen (as Steve Andrews), Aneta Corseaut, Earl Rowe, Olin Howlin, and Steven Chase.

The Great St. Louis Bank Robbery, United Artists, 1959. Screenplay by Richard T. Heffron. Directed by Charles Guggenheim and John Stix. Starring Steve McQueen (as George Fowler), David Clarke, Graham Denton, Molly McCarthy, and James Dukas.

Never So Few, MGM, 1959. Screenplay by Millard Kaufman, based on a novel by Tom T. Chamales. Directed by John Sturges. Starring Frank Sinatra, Gina Lollobrigida, Peter Lawford, Charles Bronson, Dean Jones, and Steve McQueen (as Sergeant Bill Ringa).

The Magnificent Seven, United Artists, 1960. Screenplay by William Roberts, based on Akira Kurosawa's *The Seven Samurai.* Directed by John Sturges. Starring Yul Brynner, Horst Buchholz, Steve McQueen (as Vin), Eli Wallach, James Coburn, Charles Bronson, Robert Vaughn, and Brad Dexter.

The Honeymoon Machine, MGM, 1961. Screenplay by George Wells, based on Lorenzo Semple's play *The Golden Fleecing.* Directed by Richard Thorpe. Starring Steve McQueen (as Lieutenant Fergie Howard), Brigid Bazlen, Jim Hutton, Paula Prentiss, and Dean Jagger.

Hell is for Heroes, Paramount, 1962. Screenplay by Robert Pirosh and Richard Carr, based on a story by Pirosh. Directed by Don Siegel. Starring Steve McQueen (as Reese), Bobby Darin, Fess Parker, Bob Newhart, Nick Adams, Harry Guardino, and James Coburn.

The War Lover, Columbia, 1962. Screenplay by Howard Koch, based on the John Hersey novel. Directed by Philip Leacock. Starring Steve McQueen (as Captain Buzz Rickson), Robert Wagner, Shirley Anne Field, Gary Cockrell, and Michael Crawford.

The Great Escape, United Artists, 1963. Screenplay by James Clavell and W.R. Burnett, based on the book by Paul Brickhill. Directed by John Sturges. Starring Steve McQueen (as Captain Virgil Hilts), James Garner, Richard Attenborough, Charles Bronson, Donald Pleasance, James Donald, James Coburn, and David McCallum.

Soldier in the Rain, Allied Artists, 1963. Screenplay by Maurice Richlin and Blake Edwards, based on the William Goldman novel. Directed by Ralph Nelson. Starring Jackie Gleason, Steve McQueen (as Sergeant Eustis Clay), Tony Bill, Tuesday Weld, Tom Poston, Chris Noel, and Adam West.

Love with the Proper Stranger, Paramount, 1963. Screenplay by Arnold Schulman. Directed by Robert Mulligan. Starring Steve McQueen (as Rocky Papasano),

Natalie Wood, Edie Adams, Herschel Bernardi, Tom Bosley, Harvey Lembeck, and Vic Tayback.

Baby, the Rain Must Fall, Columbia, 1965. Screenplay by Horton Foote, based on his play *The Traveling Lady*. Directed by Robert Mulligan. Starring Steve McQueen (as Henry Thomas), Lee Remick, Don Murray, Paul Fix, Josephine Hutchinson, and Ruth White.

The Cincinnati Kid, MGM, 1965. Screenplay by Ring Lardner Jr. and Terry Southern, based on the Richard Jessup novel. Directed by Norman Jewison. Starring Steve McQueen (as Eric Stoner), Edward G. Robinson, Ann-Margret, Karl Malden, Tuesday Weld, and Rip Torn.

Nevada Smith, Paramount, 1966. Screenplay by John Michael Hayes. Directed by Henry Hathaway. Starring Steve McQueen (as Max Sand), Karl Malden, Brian Keith, Suzanne Pleshette, Arthur Kennedy, Janet Margolin, Martin Landau, and Raf Vallone.

The Sand Pebbles, 20th Century Fox, 1966. Screenplay by Richard Anderson, based on the Richard McKenna novel. Directed by Robert Wise. Starring Steve McQueen (as Jake Holman), Richard Crenna, Richard Attenborough, Candice Bergen, Marayat Andriane, Mako, Simon Oakland, and Gavin McLeod.

The Thomas Crown Affair, United Artists, 1968. Screenplay by Alan R. Trustman. Directed by Norman Jewison. Starring Steve McQueen (as Thomas Crown), Faye Dunaway, Paul Burke, Yaphett Kotto, Jack Weston, and Todd Martin.

Bullitt, Warner Brothers–Seven Arts, 1968. Screenplay by Alan R. Trustman and Harry Kleiner, based on the Robert L. Pike novel. Directed by Peter Yates. Starring Steve McQueen (as Lieutenant Frank Bullitt), Robert Vaughn, Jacqueline Bissett, Don Gordon, Simon Oakland, Norman Fell, and Robert Duvall.

The Reivers, National General, 1969. Screenplay by Irving Ravetch and Harriet Frank Jr., based on the William Faulkner novel. Directed by Mark Rydell. Starring Steve McQueen (as Boon Hogganbeck), Sharon Farrell, Rupert Crosse, Mitch Vogel, and Will Geer.

Le Mans, National General, 1971. Screenplay by Harry Kleiner, based on the book *Le Mans 24* by Denne Bart Petitclerc. Directed by Lee H. Katzin. Starring Steve McQueen (as Michael Delaney), Siegfried Rauch, Elga Andersen, Ronald Leigh-Hunt, and Fred Haltiner.

On Any Sunday, Cinema 5, 1971. Written and directed by Bruce Brown. Steve McQueen appears as himself in this seminal motorcycling documentary.

Junior Bonner, ABC-Cinerama, 1972. Screenplay by Jeb Rosebrook. Directed by Sam Peckinpah. Starring Steve McQueen (as Junior Bonner), Robert Preston, Ida Lupino, Barbara Leigh, Joe Don Baker, and Ben Johnson.

The Getaway, National General, 1972. Screenplay by Walter Hill, based on Jim Thompson's novel. Directed by Sam Peckinpah. Starring Steve McQueen (as Doc McCoy), Ali MacGraw, Ben Johnson, Sally Struthers, Al Lettieri, Slim Pickens, Bo Hopkins, and John Bryson.

Papillon, Allied Artists, 1973. Screenplay by Dalton Trumbo and Lorenzo Semple, based on the book by Henri Charriere. Directed by Franklin Schaffner. Starring Steve McQueen (as Papillon), Dustin Hoffman, Don Gordon, Victor Jory, Anthony Zerbe, Robert Deman, Bill Mumy, and George Coulouris.

The Towering Inferno, 20th Century Fox and Warner Brothers, 1974. Screenplay by Stirling Silliphant, based on the novels *The Tower* by Richard Martin Stern and

The Glass Inferno by Frank M. Robinson and Thomas Scortia. Starring Steve
McQueen (as Battalion Chief Michael O'Hallorhan), Paul Newman, William
Holden, Faye Dunaway, Fred Astaire, Robert Wagner, Susan Blakely, Richard
Chamberlain, Jennifer Jones, Robert Vaughn, and O.J. Simpson.

Dixie Dynamite, 1976. Screenplay by Wes Bishop and Lee Frost. Directed by Lee
Frost. Starring Warren Oates, Christopher George, Stanley Adams, and Steve
McQueen (stunts).

An Enemy of the People, Warner Brothers, 1978. Screenplay by Alexander Jacobs,
based on the Arthur Miller adaptation of Henrik Ibsen's play. Directed by
George Schaefer. Starring Steve McQueen (as Thomas Stockmann), Charles
Durning, Bibi Andersson, Michael Cristofer, and Richard Dysart.

Tom Horn, Warner Brothers, 1980. Screenplay by Thomas McGuane and Bud
Shrake, based on the book *Life of Tom Horn, Government Scout and Interpreter*
written by Horn. Directed by William Wiard. Starring Steve McQueen (as Tom
Horn), Linda Evans, Richard Farnsworth, Billy Green Bush, Slim Pickens, Roy
Jenson, and Mel Novak.

The Hunter, Paramount, 1980. Screenplay by Ted Leighton and Peter Hyams,
from the book by Christopher Keane. Directed by Buzz Kulik. Starring Steve
McQueen (as Ralph "Papa" Thorson), Eli Wallach, Kathryn Harrold, LeVar
Burton, Ben Johnson, and Richard Venture.

MISCELLANEOUS

Family Affair, 1952. Bell System 26-minute commercial film. McQueen appears as
a sailor.

The Ed Sullivan Show (CBS) 1958. Season preview of new shows, which included
Wanted: Dead or Alive.

Viceroy cigarette ads (CBS). Viceroy was the main sponsor for *Wanted: Dead or
Alive*, and McQueen taped at least two ads, which ran weekly throughout the
show's three-season run (1958–61).

Jukebox Jury (ABC) April 24, 1959. McQueen appears as a celebrity panelist.

Perry Como's Kraft Musical Hall Show (NBC) May 4, 1960. McQueen makes a
guest-starring appearance.

It Could Be You (NBC) August 4, 1960. Host Bill Leyden welcomes guest star
Steve McQueen.

Here's Hollywood, 1962. Interview program. McQueen appeared on a few episodes
with series host Jack Linkletter, who traveled to Germany in 1962 to interview
McQueen on the set of *The Great Escape*.

The Tonight Show starring Johnny Carson (NBC) 1964. Promotional appearance
for *The Great Escape*.

Christmas Seals ad, 1965. Presented in movie theaters throughout the nation.

What's My Line? (CBS) December 18, 1966. McQueen is the Mystery Guest on
this episode.

The Ed Sullivan Show (CBS) 1966. Promotional appearance on behalf of *The
Sand Pebbles*.

The Tonight Show starring Johnny Carson (NBC) 1966. Promotional appearance
for *The Sand Pebbles*.

"The Coming of the Roads" (CBS) September 17, 1967. McQueen narrates this
conservation documentary.

The Ed Sullivan Show (CBS) McQueen takes Sullivan out for a dune buggy ride in
a taped segment, which aired in October 1968.

Honda motorcycle ad, 1971. This 30-second ad was shown only in Japan.

UNSEEN McQUEEN

FOLLOWING IS A LIST OF MOVIES AND TELEVISION PROJECTS that were once offered to, rejected by, or somehow associated with Steve McQueen.

Blackboard Jungle—An MGM memo dated August 4, 1954, shows that McQueen tested for the part of West in what is known as the first film of the rock 'n' roll era. According to producer Pandro Berman, McQueen tested well but ultimately lost out to actor Vic Morrow.

Be Still My Heart—McQueen and Steve Fisher, a crime writer turned screenwriter, talked about turning this novel, about a columnist who writes a problem page for a local newspaper, into a film. However, the idea was dropped when McQueen was offered a lead role in *The Blob*.

The 4-D Man—Producer Jack Harris' contract with McQueen gave him the rights to use him in his next two films after *The Blob*. The first of these two films was *The 4-D Man*, a 1959 film about a scientist who develops an amplifier that can freely pass into another object. Harris chose not to exercise the option because McQueen was such a pain in the ass, and Irwin S. Yeaworth, who directed this B-film, most likely did not want to work with the temperamental star.

Dinosaurus!—This 1960 film was the second option under McQueen's contract with Jack Harris, who chose not to enforce the deal. Interestingly, the rerelease of *The Blob* was featured in a double bill with *Dinosaurus!* and piggybacked off of McQueen's image on the poster.

Terror at Webb's Landing—Producer Robert Webb tendered an offer to McQueen in April 1959 to play a kidnapper who ends up taking his victim to the Florida everglades. McQueen was tied to *Wanted: Dead or Alive* and could not do the film.

The Execution of Private Slovik—Frank Sinatra enjoyed McQueen's company so much on *Never So Few* that he wanted him to star in this Sinatra-directed story of the only soldier in U.S. history to be executed for desertion. McQueen was faced with a tough choice—did he want to be linked to Sinatra forever, or did he want to strike out on his own? The story was eventually brought to television in 1974, starring Martin Sheen.

Ocean's Eleven—This was another part Sinatra had in mind for McQueen, who was being primed as a Rat Pack candidate.

The Golden Man—In July 1960, McQueen asked Warner Brothers to loan him Angie Dickinson, who was under contract, to star in this sci-fi thriller by Frances and

Richard Lockridge, which he could produce under the Scuderia Condor Enterprises banner. In return for Dickinson's services, McQueen would have to make a film for Warner Brothers called *Savage Streets*. The deal was never consummated.

Pocketful of Miracles—Director Frank Capra sought McQueen for this role after Frank Sinatra had turned it down. The part was later awarded to Glenn Ford after the director could not convince United Artists to give the "ballsy young actor" a chance. United Artists, the studio that made McQueen a movie star, did not feel he was bankable at the time. Execs soon changed their minds after *The Magnificent Seven* and *The Great Escape*.

Breakfast at Tiffany's—Steve was offered the lead role before George Peppard. The series *Wanted: Dead or Alive* prevented him from starring in this classic film. Given that the film centers almost completely on Hepburn, it would have been interesting to see how the scene-stealing McQueen, fresh from the success of *The Magnificent Seven*, would have handled this role.

The Champagne Complex—MGM offered McQueen an opportunity to star alongside its flagship artist, Debbie Reynolds. This improbable plot would have cast McQueen as the youngest vice president in U.S. history, engaged to a woman (Reynolds), who has an uncontrollable desire to take her clothes off when she drinks champagne. McQueen opted for another MGM property, *The Honeymoon Machine*.

The Victors—McQueen contemplated making this Carl Foreman film or *The Great Escape* with John Sturges. This movie would have costarred Warren Beatty, Ava Gardner, and Simone Signoret. McQueen's loyalty was with Sturges.

Beauty and the Beast—While in England, McQueen caught an updated version of this classic, written by Alun Owen (*A Hard Day's Night*). McQueen wanted to bring a TV version to the United States starring Sophia Loren. McQueen spent many years trying to find a film project that would allow him to work with Loren on-screen.

The Kimono—McQueen told columnist Hedda Hopper he was considering this sensual love story by prolific English author H.E. Bates.

Smile for a Woman—McQueen would have played an artist who is asked to paint a phony copy of the Mona Lisa. The picture would have reteamed McQueen with *Honeymoon Machine* costar Brigid Bazlen, and Michael Gordon was slated to be the director.

I Love Louisa—McQueen was flush from the success of *The Great Escape*, and producer Walter Mirisch wanted McQueen to star opposite Shirley MacLaine in this black comedy in April 1963. MacLaine plays Louisa, a woman starving for affection but cursed when it comes to love. All four of her husbands, who are poor when she marries them, eventually die off after achieving great wealth. The movie was later retitled *What a Way to Go!* Paul Newman eventually ended up with the McQueen role, which is an extended cameo.

Vivacious Lady—This was another McQueen-Sturges project that was discussed. He passed on this remake of the 1938 RKO classic in favor of another romantic comedy, *Love with the Proper Stranger*.

Two for Texas—Director Robert Aldrich tried to reunite McQueen with his Palm Springs neighbor, Dean Martin, and his *Never So Few* costar Gina Lollobrigida for this 1962 western.

Marooned—Producer/director Frank Capra wanted McQueen for this space movie when he optioned the novel in 1964. The movie ran into several roadblocks and was eventually made five years later with Gregory Peck in the lead role.

Luis Miguel Dominguin—Agent Stan Kamen had set up a deal with McQueen to portray the famous bullfighter. "That's another one I'm glad I missed," McQueen said.
"Ol' Steve-o-reno woulda been out there in the bullring for sure, wavin' a cape over a
sharp pair of horns. Man, that's a real mean trip, bullfighting."

A Thousand Clowns—McQueen told columnist Hedda Hopper in March 1964 he
would star in this picture, along with actress Sandy Dennis, about a young boy
who lives with his eccentric uncle Murray and is forced to conform to society. But
soon McQueen had *Day of the Champion* and *The Sand Pebbles* on his plate, and *A
Thousand Clowns* was filmed with Jason Robards in 1965.

Gable and Lombard—Steve and Neile were offered a chance to work together in this
portrayal of Hollywood's most glamorous couple. McQueen said of this project,
"They asked us to do it, but we both thought it was a howl. Neile's no Lombard,
and I'm no Gable. That was one less turkey in my life!" The project was offered to
McQueen again in the '70s when he married Ali MacGraw.

King Rat—Paul Newman was first offered this film but turned it down. Producers
turned to McQueen, who also took a pass. George Segal ended up in the lead role
and gave it a good turn.

Return of the Seven—Yul Brynner asked McQueen, now a major movie star, if he
would reprise his role as Vin for a sequel to *The Magnificent Seven*. McQueen reportedly told him, "I'd sure like to, but I'm too busy." Privately, McQueen felt the plot
was too absurd and bowed out. To make good, McQueen promised Brynner that he
would costar in his next film.

The Ski Bum—Because of the successful box-office return on *Nevada Smith*, producer
Joe Levine offered McQueen the opportunity to star in this film. However, Robert
Wise's offer to star in *The Sand Pebbles* superseded all other projects.

The Kremlin Letter—John Huston had wanted to work with McQueen for years, except
that Huston at that point was in England. McQueen didn't want to do another
movie in England so soon after *The War Lover*.

Triple Cross—This was the film that McQueen promised to do for Brynner, but
McQueen bowed out once again. He sent a cable to Brynner, which read: "I'm truly
sorry that I can't be with you, but my horse refuses to swim the Atlantic." Finally,
Brynner got the message loud and clear.

In Cold Blood—This was the first of several projects that would have teamed Steve
McQueen and Paul Newman. The two men were filming respective projects, and
director Richard Brooks ended up casting Robert Blake and Scott Wilson.

Two for the Road—This screenplay was placed in the hands of McQueen's friend
Elmer Valentine by a producer who thought Valentine might have some pull. The
film eventually starred Albert Finney and Audrey Hepburn. When McQueen discovered Valentine had shooed the producer away, he was slightly irritated. Hepburn
was on McQueen's Top 10 list of actresses he'd most like to "nail."

Man on a Nylon String—Solar Productions bought the rights to this *Life* magazine
story about a man who dies on a mountain and is stuck there for the whole town
to see. George Roy Hill was set to direct McQueen in this thriller. "It's lucky that I
never got around to that one. Probably would have broken my neck. It was about
mountain climbing—and I would have been doing all the stunt work myself,"
McQueen said.

Ice Station Zebra—Producer Martin Ransohoff tried to enlist McQueen to star in this
John Sturges project, which turned out to be Howard Hughes' favorite film. By then,

McQueen had too many obligations at Solar. The movie was made in 1968 with Rock Hudson in the starring role.

The Cold War Swap—Hilly Elkins bought the rights to this novel for $50,000, with John Sturges set to direct. Solar was set to film the picture in Berlin, but Warner Brothers had cut off McQueen's six-picture deal after *Bullitt*.

Applegate's Gold—This was a western novel by Todhunter Ballard that was presented to Solar. McQueen passed because he didn't want to do another western so soon after *Nevada Smith*.

The Yards at Essendorf—This World War II film would have been directed by John Sturges. "Things didn't pan out," McQueen explained.

Suddenly Single—Solar had slated this comedy, about a middle-aged man who gets divorced and finds himself in the singles world again, right after *Bullitt*. McQueen opted for *The Reivers* instead.

Butch Cassidy and the Sundance Kid—McQueen couldn't come to terms with the billing, and the role of the Sundance Kid eventually went to Robert Redford, which made him an overnight star.

Dirty Harry—This project was offered to McQueen a few years before it wound up with Clint Eastwood (and after it was rejected by Elvis Presley). After *Bullitt*, McQueen wanted to do something other than a cop film.

Mind Like Water—This was a karate documentary that Solar was going to finance for *On Any Sunday* director Bruce Brown. When Solar collapsed, so did the project. An interesting footnote is that this film was going to be made in 3-D.

Play Misty For Me—One man's scraps are another man's treasure, and Clint Eastwood was once again the beneficiary. Solar Vice President Robert Relyea tried to champion this film, but McQueen would not budge because "the woman has the stronger role than the man." Jessica Walter proved this as the love-crazed fan who stalks a smooth-talking disc jockey. "It is probably the best debut film of any American director," Robert Relyea said. Clint Eastwood picked this one up at a later stage, and the end product is quite well regarded.

Yucatan—This was the great "lost" McQueen film and the one he regretted not being able to do. Screenwriter Harry Kleiner (*Bullitt, Le Mans*) wrote a treatment about an Indian well in Mexico filled with ancient jewelry. The project fell through when Solar collapsed. The movie became the subject of a 2006 *New York Times* article when Chad McQueen found approximately 1,700 pages and drawings in a chest, and the project was revived. Screenwriter Paul Schuering (*Prison Break*) and director McG were attached. In June 2010, actor Robert Downey Jr. vowed to resurrect the picture.

Atlanta—Supermodel Beverly Johnson claims that sometime in the early 1970s, Paramount producer Robert Evans wanted her to star with Steve McQueen in an interracial love story set in the Deep South. Johnson said the project didn't get much traction. This was most likely due to a number of factors, not least of which were the difficulties McQueen had before and after *Le Mans* and the subsequent debacle with Evans after McQueen had become involved with Evans' wife, Ali MacGraw.

American Flag—This Elmore Leornard novel, about a western mining town, was going to be the first picture made under the First Artists banner. It was dropped in favor of *Junior Bonner*.

The French Connection—The role that made Gene Hackman a leading man and household name was originally offered to McQueen, who eventually presented Hackman with the Academy Award for Best Actor for this role. Director William Friedkin, who was a dyed-in-the-wool McQueen man, originally wanted McQueen as Popeye Doyle. McQueen didn't want to get typecast as a cop so soon after *Bullitt*. The film tried to follow the lead of *Bullitt* with a high-octane but less realistic car chase centerpiece. It regularly polls highly, but below *Bullitt*, in the list of top film car chases of all time.

The Monkey Wrench Gang—This was a story about a group of revolutionaries who plan to blow up the Hoover Dam. Director Sam Peckinpah wanted McQueen to star, surprisingly making a pitch to Martin Ransohoff, the man who fired Peckinpah on *The Cincinnati Kid*, to produce. Ransohoff took a pass.

Roy Brightwood—An unlikely love story about an Arkansas redneck tamed by the good love of a Jewish social worker, this story was set during the Great Depression. McQueen decided *The Getaway* was a much better fit.

Jack Ballard—In 1972, *Junior Bonner* screenwriter Jeb Rosebrook wrote another screenplay intended for McQueen and Sam Peckinpah. Set against the backdrop of the 1880s, Ballard (McQueen) is a lone gunfighter who rides into town and helps a wily widow fight off a group of heavies. According to Rosebrook, producer Joe Wizan gave the finished screenplay to McQueen and Peckinpah but never got a reply from either man.

The Man Who Loved Cat Dancing—MGM offered this psychologically intriguing western to McQueen after *The Getaway*, but he was already committed to *Papillon*. The part eventually went to Burt Reynolds, an outlaw who kidnaps an aristocrat after she witnesses his gang pull a train robbery.

The Johnson County War—An epic western, this film eventually morphed into the infamous turkey known as *Heaven's Gate*. It was also the first of many McQueen/MacGraw packages.

The Long Good-bye—Director and Trancas neighbor Robert Altman wanted McQueen to play Detective Philip Marlow in this contemporary film noir adaptation of Raymond Chandler's 1953 novel of the same name. Altman said McQueen wanted too much money, so he turned to Elliot Gould to play the lead.

California Split—Another Robert Altman project offered to McQueen, this story was about two compulsive gamblers, Bill Denny and Charlie Waters. The movie eventually starred George Segal and Elliot Gould, respectively. Writer Joseph Walsh recalled in 2008 that McQueen was interested in Waters, a free-spirited friend who tags along for the ride. But Walsh said McQueen balked because he wanted to play a "hepper" role. "First of all, I didn't have the heart to tell him nobody said 'hep' for the last 20 years," Walsh said. "If he meant hip, well, to me, the Elliot Gould character is one of the hippest of all time because he's so real. He's a free soul. He says what he wants, he does what he wants. He's as genuine as it gets." Walsh said he knew the negotiations were doomed when McQueen abruptly marched out of their meeting, saying he had to go "buy alley hats." Later Walsh realized McQueen meant he was going to purchase some hats for his new wife, Ali MacGraw. The movie was released in August 1974 and is considered one of the best movies on gambling. Some may argue that McQueen had already done the gambling angle superbly with *The Cincinnati Kid*, but it would have been fun to see McQueen show a more comical side of his acting repertoire.

Running the Big Wild Red—This western involves the conquest of the Colorado River rapids. Paul Edward's screenplay was sold to Columbia and developed over a period of several years with McQueen in mind, as well as director Martin Ritt. The idea was revived in the early 1990s with Mel Gibson in the lead.

Fort Apache, The Bronx—McQueen was tendered this role about a beat cop on the mean streets of New York immediately following the success of *The Towering Inferno*. It was revived almost six years later in 1981 by Paul Newman. In a reversal of fortune, McQueen started his career going for roles that Newman often won. As McQueen's career hit its peak, the two men were jockeying for projects as costars. But by this point, McQueen was given first refusal on many projects before they were passed to Newman. This would have no doubt pleased McQueen, who was highly competitive against his cinema rival.

Tara: The Continuation of Gone With the Wind—Agent Marvin Josephson carried this script under his arm when meeting McQueen for the first time in late 1974. McQueen was flattered by the epic scope of the movie and the large paycheck, but he didn't think he could pull off the second coming of Rhett Butler.

Jaws—Author and co-screenwriter Peter Benchley envisioned the superstar trio of Robert Redford (Richard Dreyfuss), Paul Newman (Roy Scheider), and Steve McQueen (Robert Shaw) for his shark thriller, which had become a national best seller. Benchley's vision for the troika of megastars was rejected by Universal, who probably envisioned the three superstar salaries on top of a difficult sea-based shooting script as one headache too many.

Silent Movie—Mel Brooks said he received a mysterious phone call from McQueen during his self-imposed exile from films, asking to do a cameo in this 1976 comedy. McQueen wanted the role of a man in a motorized wheelchair who is chased by Mel Brooks, Dom DeLuise, and Marty Feldman. McQueen's timing was off, however, as Paul Newman had nabbed the part just a week before.

Deajum's Wife—This picture was to be the first film directed by McQueen, but for reasons unknown, he declined.

The Betsy—McQueen and Ali MacGraw were initially offered the lead roles that eventually went to Robert Duvall and Katherine Ross.

First Blood—This script had been floating around Hollywood since 1972, and McQueen, who loved the motorcycle chase sequence, felt he was too old to pull it off. (He was 45 at the time.) He regretfully had to say no. He was followed by John Travolta, Al Pacino, Paul Newman, and almost every other leading man of the era. Finally Sylvester Stallone gave the role some justice and made the film a classic in 1982.

Islands in the Stream—McQueen and director Franklin Schaffner worked well together on *Papillon* and felt this script about a famous painter (McQueen) who lives the live of a recluse in the Bahamas might be a good fit. McQueen was interested in playing a father figure but felt neither the story nor the role was right for him. Before bowing out, he told Schaffner, "I think you need a better actor than me." Schafner noted, "Steve was always a difficult man to trap into a project. I'm sorry he didn't make it. He would have been marvelously interesting." George C. Scott landed the role, and the film bombed when it was released in 1975.

One Flew Over The Cuckoo's Nest—This was one of the many properties that Marvin Josephson read for McQueen. However, McQueen's understated style of acting was the polar opposite of Nicholson's Academy Award–winning performance.

Raid on Entebbe—Another Franklin Schaffner film, this one would have had McQueen starring as an Israeli commando leader. McQueen, in his reclusive period and buoyed by his success and financial prowess from *The Towering Inferno*, asked for $3 million and 15 percent of the gross, which was a turnoff to the studio. When McQueen passed, a TV movie was made in 1977 with Peter Finch.

Waiting for Godot—Now in his classics period, McQueen was devouring books from another era that were not in sync with his action-hero persona. One of McQueen's girlfriends at the time, who was a *Playboy* bunny, told a reporter, "I guess it started with that Ibsen. But he's read every classic he can get his hands on, Shakespeare, Chekhov—I don't know all those names—but just everything!" McQueen had considered making Samuel Beckett's novel into a film, but Beckett wasn't selling. (The royalties were a major source of income for him.) And, more astounding, Beckett had never heard of McQueen.

Orphan Train—This one was based on an actual case in which more than 100,000 homeless children were gathered off the streets of New York between 1854 and 1929 and sent west for adoption. Ali MacGraw was asked to play a dedicated but untested social worker for the Children's Aid Society of New York, who organizes the first train trip. McQueen would have played a more secondary role as a photographer who helps arrange the trip, photographs the journey, and ends up getting involved with MacGraw. When their marriage fell apart, however, so did the movie. Producer Dorothea Petrie eventually bought back the rights and brought it to CBS, which aired a two-hour TV movie in December 1979.

Raise the Titanic!—Sir Lew Grade offered McQueen a flat $3 million to head up an all-star cast based on the best-selling book by Clive Cussler. McQueen felt the script was flat. His instincts were correct; it was released in 1980 with Jason Robards and sank quickly.

A Bridge Too Far—McQueen's old friend and former costar Lord Richard Attenborough's directorial debut would have rewarded McQueen handsomely for three weeks of work. McQueen wanted $3 million, he wanted producer Joe Levine to buy his Palm Springs home for $470,000, and he wanted Levine to hire one of McQueen's buddies for $50,000. McQueen went a demand too far; Levine felt McQueen was being extreme and hired Robert Redford for $2 million and no headaches.

Fancy Hardware—McQueen was close to making this film about a World War II pilot who earns a living selling plumbing fixtures. Ali MacGraw was set to star as McQueen's love interest in this movie, which would have been produced by David Foster. Foster said it was one of the best scripts to ever pass through his hands, and he optioned the rights again in 2010.

Grace Quigley—Katharine Hepburn visited Trancas to recruit McQueen as a hit man who kills off some of her friends in a nursing home. The film was finally made in 1985 with Nick Nolte.

The Missouri Breaks—Director Bob Rafelson wrote this western about a bounty hunter and an outlaw. Rafelson wanted McQueen and Marlon Brando in the lead roles. Instead, Brando costarred with Jack Nicholson, and the picture was a flop.

The Towering Inferno II—Producer Irwin Allen offered McQueen a firm $3 million to reprise his role as Michael O'Hallorhan. McQueen turned it down with no explanation offered, and the project never moved forward. There appears to be a general theme that McQueen would avoid not only sequels but also roles that were too similar to ones he had done previously (see *The Return of the Seven, Dirty Harry, The French Connection,* and the various other sequels listed in this appendix). No doubt this displays a foresight to avoid typecasting and inferior products as well as underscoring McQueen's need for freedom and new options rather than repeat the stale and the old.

The Inspector General—McQueen originally wanted to do this remake with director George Schaefer, who told him it wasn't a good idea. They both agreed on *An
  Enemy of the People* instead.
Old Times—McQueen invested $50,000 in preproduction costs on this Harold Pinter
  play, which he had hoped would star Audrey Hepburn and Faye Dunaway. Sensing
  that McQueen was trying to sabotage their deal, First Artists vetoed the idea. They
  eventually came to terms on *Tom Horn*.
Nothing in Common—Director Tony Bill was set to direct this story about a kidnapper
  (McQueen) who takes a child for ransom, then develops a bond with his hostage.
  Producer Phil Parslow remembered that McQueen was so excited by the idea that
  he bounced around the office. First Artists chairman Phil Feldman eventually killed
  the idea.
The Bodyguard—Lawrence Kasdan originally wrote this screenplay in 1977 with
  McQueen in mind (although the superstar didn't know it) as an ex–Secret Service
  agent assigned to guard a famous diva/singer. Diana Ross was originally slated to
  star, while Ryan O'Neal was at one point considered as the leading man. The project
  eventually fell apart but was revived 16 years later when Kevin Costner (a McQueen
  disciple) and Whitney Houston agreed to star in the popcorn movie. Their version
  brought in more than $122 million domestically and $400 million worldwide.
The Sorcerer—This was another ill-fated project with action director William Friedkin.
  McQueen nixed the idea when Friedkin wouldn't allow Ali MacGraw to go on
  the payroll as a consultant. Years later Friedkin regretted the decision. "I believe to
  this day that the same film, with Steve McQueen, would have been a masterpiece,"
  Friedkin said. "McQueen could carry a film about fate because you know that this
  guy wouldn't stop fighting."
Tiger Ten—John Frankenheimer wanted McQueen to star in this World War II tale
  of the Flying Tigers. McQueen had problems with the script, and the idea was cast
  aside.
The Gauntlet—This was a script perfectly tailored to the McQueen persona. It was
  originally written for Barbra Streisand and Marlon Brando, but Brando bowed out,
  and McQueen was offered the lead. Streisand didn't want McQueen and made a
  pitch for Clint Eastwood. Eventually Streisand lost interest, and Eastwood enlisted
  then-girlfriend Sondra Locke. The film grossed $50 million worldwide in December
  1977.
Close Encounters of the Third Kind—Director Steven Spielberg's first choice for the role
  was Steve McQueen. However, McQueen felt he did not have the depth it took for
  the role (and had not learned the art of crying on film) and declined the part. No
  doubt McQueen had already had his fill of science fiction with *The Blob*. The movie
  was one of the biggest hits of 1978 and grossed more than $132 million in domestic
  box-office receipts.
Apocalypse Now—Francis Ford Coppola asked McQueen to play the lead role of
  Willard in this jungle-based Vietnam War epic. McQueen declined, although he
  said he would take the smaller role of the enigmatic Colonel Kurtz, who had considerable less screen time and required less work, and demanded $3 million, which
  Coppola was unwilling to pay. McQueen was ultimately put off by the amount of
  time he would spend on location in near-tropical conditions, something he did not
  want to repeat after his experience on *The Sand Pebbles*.

The Chinese Bandit—English producer Michael Deeley sent McQueen this screenplay about an American marine in China who forms a relationship with a Chinese renegade.

The Driver—Walter Hill's film about a professional getaway driver for hire fit McQueen like a glove. Hill said by this point in his career, McQueen was fed up with vehicles and guns. Ryan O'Neal ended up in the lead role and gave one of the best performances of his career.

Convoy—C.B. Macall's hit song was the inspiration for this dopey 1978 movie, and the lead was first offered to McQueen. Eventually Kris Kristofferson took the part with Ali MacGraw as his female lead.

Tai-Pan—McQueen was offered $10 million in 1979 by Swiss producer Georges-Alain Vuille to star in this James Clavell epic adventure. The contract included a $1 million signing bonus, and the rest of the payments were to be doled out in installments. If any of the payments were late, McQueen got to keep the $1 million free and clear. Vuille was late with the first payment, and McQueen, according to agent Marvin Josephson, pulled out of the deal $1 million richer.

Quigley Down Under—*The Hunter* director Buzz Kulik discussed this project, about a western that takes place in Australia, with McQueen in Chicago. However, McQueen was diagnosed with cancer soon thereafter. Actor Tom Selleck revived the project, and the film was released in 1990.

Hand-Carved Coffins—This Truman Capote short story was the centerpiece of his 1980 *Music for Chameleons*. The famed American writer was almost positive that McQueen would star in this movie adaptation planned by Andy Warhol. However, it's highly unlikely McQueen would have done the picture.

Superman—Both McQueen and the Man of Steel are American icons, so why not merge the two? McQueen was at the top of the list, but his name got crossed off when producer David Salkind felt McQueen was a little too hefty. The role eventually went to a then-unknown actor by the name of Christopher Reeve.

Dogs of War—*Variety* magazine reported in 1979 that director/producer Norman Jewison tried to recruit McQueen to star in this tailor-made role about a mercenary hired to overthrow a corrupt dictator in the African nation of Zangoa. McQueen either didn't want to go to Africa to film the picture or was feeling the impact of his cancer. Christopher Walken, fresh from his Oscar-winning performance in *The Deer Hunter*, took the role, and the film was eventually released in 1981.

The Manhattan Project—In December 1979, McQueen had established a new asking price of $5 million per picture plus 15 percent of the gross. To prove his point, he turned down a firm offer of $4 million from producer Carlo Ponti to star with his wife, Sophia Loren, in this tale of nuclear terrorism.

Midnight Plus One—Author Gavin Lyall said McQueen purchased the film rights to this 1966 novel about a morally questionable adventurer hired to drive a millionaire across Europe. Lyall said the film was never made due to McQueen's untimely death.

Megaforce—Director Hal Needham said he offered McQueen this picture in late 1979 or early 1980, but the star declined. Needham later installed actor Barry Bostwick in the campy action flick.

Hang Tough—Producers Herb Jaffe and Jerry Beck snapped up the rights to Elmore Leonard's tale of a Detroit detective in pursuit of cold-blooded killers. Marvin Josephson had to turn down the offer because of McQueen's illness.

The Last Ride—Stuntman and director Chuck Bail (*The Gumball Rally*) had set up a deal at Columbia for this picture about an over-the-hill group of motorcycle riders who take one last ride. The project was killed when studio executives learned that McQueen had cancer.

Pale Blue Ribbon—Friend and stunt double Loren Janes bought the rights to this story about Vietnam's two highest-decorated soldiers. McQueen agreed to do the film if his health improved. It is only fitting that this is the last motion picture McQueen contemplated.

CHAPTER NOTES

THE FOLLOWING CHAPTER NOTES are designed to give a general view of the sources drawn upon while preparing *Steve McQueen: The Life and Legacy of a Hollywood Icon*.

Chapter 1

For this chapter, the author interviewed Loren Thomson, Helen Kettler, Joe Giger, Mike Barnhill, Jean Black, William Smither, Dan Viets, and Peter O. Whitmer. Also included is the research of Veronica Valdez.

BOOKS

Cowan, Robert G. *On The Rails of Los Angeles*, Historical Society of Southern California, 1971.

Griffith, Russell E. and Ron Monning. *The History of Slater, Missouri: Our Community and Family*, Walsworth Publishing Company Inc., 2003.

History of Saline County, Missouri. St. Louis Historical Company, 1881.

Paris, Barry. *Louise Brooks: A Biography*, University of Minnesota Press, 2000.

Simmons, K.H. *Spanish American War Veterans from Nebraska*, Willow Bend Books, 2000.

Spiegel, Penina. *McQueen: The Untold Story of a Bad Boy in Hollywood*, Doubleday Books, 1986.

ARTICLES

"Captain John Thomson Obituary," *Franklin Missouri Intelligencer*, September 24, 1822.

"Col. Pike M. Thomson Obituary," *The Slater Rustler*, August 8, 1902.

"John William Thomson Obituary," *The Slater Rustler*, October 19, 1916.

"Pike M. Thomson Dead," *The Weekly Democrat News*, May 8, 1919.

"A Shooting Affair Last Wednesday," *The Slater Rustler*, December 25, 1921.

"Mrs. Julia Thomson Died Thursday," *The Slater News*, March 4, 1930.

"Claude William Thomson Was the Man Who (Sort Of) Raised his Great-Nephew Terrence Steve McQueen aka Steve McQueen," *The Slater News Rustler*, November 28, 1957.

"Steve McQueen: Slater Honors its Famous Actor," *Missouri Life*, April 2008.

DOCUMENTS

    1798-1940 U.S. Marine Corps Muster Rolls.
    1866-1938 U.S. National Homes for Disabled Volunteer Soldiers.
    1880-1900 United States Federal Census.
    1907-1918 Gould's Directory.
    1907-1942 Los Angeles City Directory.
    1916 The Story of Technical High School, Indianapolis Public Schools.
    1923-1924 Indianapolis City Directories.
    1924-1946 Index to Register of Voters, Los Angeles City Precinct No. 796.
    1917-1918 World War I Draft Registration Cards.
    1920 United States Federal Census.
    1927-1934 Indianapolis City Directory.
    1928-1929 Kansas City Directory.
    Marion County Health Department Birth Certificate of Terrance Stephen
        McQueen.
    1930 United States Federal Census.
    1938-1946 U.S. World War II Army Enlistment Records.
    Nebraska State Historical Society, Spanish American War Service Records for
        Louis D. McQueen.
    Social Security Death Index.
    State of California Certificate of Death for Jeannie McQueen Totten.
    State of California Certificate of Death for Oren McQueen Totten.
    State of California Certificate of Death of Louis D. McQueen.
    State of Tennessee Birth Certificate of William Terrence McQueen.
    U.S. Public Records Index.

VIDEOS

    The King of Cool. Myriad Pictures and American Movie Classics, 1998.

WEBSITES

    www.ancestry.com
    www.spanamwar.com
    www.stelizabethacademy.org
    www.stfrancishospitals.org

Chapter 2

For this chapter, the author interviewed Peter O. Whitmer, Helen Kettler, Loren Thomson, Elizabeth Simmermon, Joe Giger, Harold Eddy, Mike Barnhill, William Kiso, Thomas Allen Ryan, Fred McBurney, Christine Seigler, and John Berlekamp. This chapter also includes the research of Veronica Valdez.

BOOKS

    Griffith, Russell and Ron Moning. *The History of Slater Missouri: Our Community
        and Family*, Walsworth Publishing Company Inc., 2003.
    Nolan, William. *McQueen*, Congdon & Weed, 1984.

ARTICLES

    "Municipal Group Holds Art Exhibit," *New York Times*, September 30, 1936.
    "20 Art Exhibitions Listed for Week," *New York Times*, November 28, 1938.
    "Art and Artists off Washington Square North," *New York's Left Bank*, 1900–1950.

"Cornelius D. Crawford" obituary, *San Diego Union*, April 8, 1952.
"Variety in Media Marks Art Week," *New York Times*, November 24, 1957.
"Steve McQueen Not Afraid to Seek Success in Films," *Newark Advocate*,
    February 15, 1960.
"Steve McQueen—Rough," *Toronto Star Weekly*, October 24, 1964.
"Steve McQueen: The Lean and Hungry Look Made Him a Star," *Parade*,
    March 23, 1969.
"Actor's Years in Slater Troubled," *Saline County Daily Newspaper*,
    November 22, 1980.

DOCUMENTS
1870 United States Federal Census.
1880 United States Federal Census.
1900 United States Federal Census.
1910 United States Federal Census.
1930 United States Federal Census.
1934-1939 Indianapolis City Directory.
1949-1951 Manhattan City Directory.
Marion County History, compiled by Beech Grove Library.
Missouri Department of Health and Senior Services, Bureau of Vital Records
    Birth Record of Julia Ann Crawford.
State of California Certificate of Death for Cornelius D. Crawford.

VIDEOS
The King of Cool. Myriad Pictures and American Movie Classics, 1998.

WEBSITES
www.gvshp.org
www.stfrancishospitals.org

Chapter 3

For this chapter the author interviewed Lowell Boardman, Peter O. Whitmer, Ted
Petersen, Chuck Bail, Helen Kettler, Joe Giger, Mike Barnhill, Janice Sutton, Dan Viets,
Bob Holt, Sam Jones, Elizabeth Simmermon, Fran Rupert Donnelly, Charles "C.H."
Hines, Loren Thomson, and Harold Eddy. This chapter also includes the research of
Veronica Valdez.

BOOKS
Cowan, Robert G. *A Backward Glance Los Angeles, 1901-1915*, California for the
    Historical Society of Southern California, 1969.
DeMarco, Gordon. *A Short History of Los Angeles*, Lexikos, 1998.
Nolan, William. *McQueen*, Congdon & Weed, 1984.
Pitt, Leonard and Dale Pitt. *A to Z: An Encyclopedia of the City and County*,
    University of California Press, 1997.
Pugsley, William. *Bunker Hill: Last of the Lofty Mansions*, Trans-Anglo
    Books, 1981.
Spiegel, Penina. *McQueen: The Untold Story of a Bad Boy in Hollywood*, Doubleday
    Books, 1986.

ARTICLES
"The Taming of Steve McQueen," *Modern Screen*, November 1959.
"Steve McQueen—Rough," *Toronto Star Weekly*, October 24, 1964.
"Steve McQueen: The Lean and Hungry Look Made Him a Star," *Parade*,
    March 23, 1969.
"It Is True What They Say About Steve McQueen," *National Police Gazette*,
    September 1971.

DOCUMENTS
Fashion Drawing by Tedi Berri.
Pacific Electric Railway Map.
Superior Court of California, County of Los Angeles Divorce Complaint: Tedi
    Berri vs. Harold Berri.

WEBSITES
www.erha.org
www.usc.edu

Chapter 4

For this chapter the author interviewed Robert McNamara, Arden Miller, Max Scott, Peter O. Whitmer, and Lowell Boardman. This chapter also includes the research of Veronica Valdez.

BOOKS
Marcotte, Jerry and Patrick McMahon. *The Formation of a New Republic: A
    Photographic History of Boys Republic*, Donning Company Publishers, 2007.
McCoy, Malachy. *Steve McQueen: The Unauthorized Biography*,
    Signet Books, 1975.
McQueen-Toffel, Neile. *My Husband, My Friend*, Atheneum Books, 1986.

ARTICLES
"George Washington Slept Here—Play Opens Tonight in Ojai," *Oxnard Press
    Courier*, April 15, 1949.
"Ojai Art Center Summer Theater to Present Three One-Act Plays," *Oxnard Press
    Courier*, July 23, 1949.
"Hal Berri Succumbs at Home in Ojai," *Ventura Community Star Free Press*,
    January 4, 1950.
"The Defiant One," *Silver Screen*, June 1960.
"TV's Angry Young Star," *Saturday Evening Post*, January 14, 1961.
"Steve McQueen," *Movie TV Secret*, January 1964.
"Steve McQueen—Rough," *Toronto Star Weekly*, October 24, 1964.
"Steve McQueen: The Lean and Hungry Look Made Him a Star," *Parade*,
    March 23, 1969.
"Steve McQueen: They Told Me I'd Be Dead By Now!" *TV Inside Movie*,
    November 1969.
"Mr. Mansmanship," *Look*, January 27, 1970.
"It is True What They Say about Steve McQueen," *National Police Gazette*,
    September 1971.
"Steve McQueen Superstud," *Movie Digest*, March 1972.

Documents

  1921-1922 University of California Catalogue of Officers and Students.
  1922 Berkeley Blue and Gold Student Directory.
  1923-1924 Berkeley City Directory.
  1940-1997 California Death Index.
  1943 Application for Social Security Number for Steven Berri.
  1946 Gillespie's Guide Index to Streets.
  State of California, County of San Bernadino Marriage License for Harold Teale.
  Julian Crawford Bern Social Security Application, 1942.
  Berry and Tedi Halliwell Strashum.
  State of California, County of Ventura Certificate of Death for Harold Teale Berri.
  Superior Court of California, County of Los Angeles Divorce Complaint: Julian
    Elizabeth Berri vs. Harold T. Berri.
  Superior Court of California, County of Los Angeles Divorce Complaint: Tedi
    Berri vs. Harold Berri.

Videos

  The King of Cool. Myriad Pictures and American Movie Classics, 1998.

Websites

  www.ancestry.com
  www.boysrepublic.org
  www.jondieges.com

Chapter 5

For this chapter the author interviewed Peter O. Whitmer, Bobby Joe Harris, and Cliff
Anderson. This chapter also includes the research of Veronica Valdez.

Books

  McQueen-Toffel, Neile. *My Husband, My Friend*, Atheneum Books, 1986.
  Nolan, William. *McQueen*, Congdon & Weed, 1984.

Articles

  "TV's Angry Young Star," *The Saturday Evening Post*, January 14, 1961.
  "The Cast Iron Coffin," *Battle Station*, November 1961.
  "Hollywood's High-Speed Hipster," *True*, July 1964.
  "Steve McQueen—Rough," *Toronto Star Weekly*, October 24, 1964.
  "Steve McQueen: The Lean and Hungry Look Made Him a Star," *Parade*,
    March 23, 1969.
  "It Is True What They Say About Steve McQueen," *National Police Gazette*,
    September 1971.
  "Steve McQueen Superstud," *Movie Digest*, March 1972.
  "The Cast Iron Coffin," *Leatherneck*, June 2009.
  "Final Salute," *Leatherneck*, August 2009.

Documents

  1949 Manhattan City Directory.
  1947-1950 U.S. Marine Corps File for Terrence Steven McQueen.

Chapter 6

For this chapter the author interviewed Gene Lesser, Anatole Anton, Linda Lukens, Henry Less, Richard Martin, Harold G. Baldridge, Wynn Handman, and David Hedison. This chapter also includes the research of Veronica Valdez.

BOOKS

Brooks, Tim and Earle Marsh. *The Complete Directory to Prime Time Network and Cable TV Shows 1946-Present*, Ballantine Books, 2003.

Gilmore, John. *Laid Bare*, Amok, 1997.

Malden, Karl. *Where Do I Start? A Memoir*, Simon & Schuster, 1997.

Meisner, Sanford and Dennis Long. *Sanford Meisner on Acting*, Vintage Books, 1987.

Satchell, Tim. *McQueen*, Sidgwick and Jackson Limited, 1981.

Spiegel, Penina. *McQueen: The Untold Story of a Bad Boy in Hollywood*, Doubleday Books, 1986.

ARTICLES

"Confessions of an Ex-Beatnik," *TV and Screen Life*, June 1959.

"An 'Old' Hand Tries a New Wheel," *New York Times*, March 2, 1960.

"To McQueen's Taste," *Tucson Daily Citizen*, October 1, 1960.

"Todd Drives Warwick-Buick to Victory in Grand Touring Race at Thompson," *New York Times*, July 15, 1962.

"Steve McQueen Hollywood's Far-Out Swinger," *True*, July 1964.

"Steve McQueen—Rough," *Toronto Star Weekly*, October 24, 1964.

"500 View Premiere of Film on New York," *New York Times*, June 4, 1968.

"Steve McQueen: The Lean and Hungry Look Made Him a Star," *Parade*, March 23, 1969.

"Victor Lukens," *Craft Horizons*, March 1970.

"It Is True What They Say About Steve McQueen," *National Police Gazette*, September 1971.

"Steve McQueen Superstud," *Movie Digest*, March 1972.

"The Life of Reilly," *Kansas City Star*, December 28, 2007.

DOCUMENTS

1955-1956 Manhattan Telephone Directory.

Raw interview between Hedda Hopper, Steve McQueen, and Neile Adams, June 5, 1959.

Raw interview between Hedda Hopper and Steve McQueen, March 19, 1962.

WEBSITES

www.imdb.com
www.mcqueenonline.com
www.neighborhoodplayhouse.org
www.newyorktimes.com
www.teamdan.com
www.theboiler.com
www.themoneytimes.com
www.wheelsofitaly.com

Chapter 7

For this chapter the author interviewed John Gilmore, Richard Martin, Letty Ferrer, Edward Morehouse, Mimi Freeman, Theodore Mann, Nancy Malone, Robert Heller, Cheryl Farley, and Jack Garfein.

BOOKS

> Brooks, Tim and Earle Marsh. *The Complete Directory to Prime Time Network and Cable TV Shows 1946-Present*, Ballantine Books, 2003.
> Gilmore, John. *Laid Bare*, Amok, 1997.
> Leachman, Cloris. *Cloris: My Autobiography*, Kensington Publishing Corporation, 2009.
> Spiegel, Penina. *McQueen: The Untold Story of a Bad Boy in Hollywood*, Doubleday, 1986.

ARTICLES

> "I'm So Proud of My Grandfather," *Mail on Sunday*, November 5, 2006.
> "Judge Orders Repairs to Steve McQueen's One-Time Apartment Building," *New York Daily News*, May 9, 2008.
> "Diving Into the Life of an Unlikely Jewish Hero," *The Wrap*, June 15, 2009.
> "Yoo Hoo Mrs. Goldberg," *Broward Palm Beach*, October 6, 2009.

DOCUMENTS

> Playbill for *Peg O' My Heart*, June 30–July 5, 1952.
> Playbill for *Time Out For Ginger*, April 1953.
> Interoffice communication from Pandro S. Berman to Richard Brooks regarding tests for *Blackboard Jungle*, August 4, 1954.
> Letter from Al Altman to Pandro Berman, October 21, 1954.
> Ogunquit Playhouse 1955 Season Program.

WEBSITES

> www.ogunquitplayhouse.org

Chapter 8

For this chapter the author interviewed Jack Garfein, Robert Loggia, Richard Martin, Janet Conway, David Foster, Peter O. Whitmer, Robert Wise, Michael Dante, and John Gilmore.

BOOKS

> Brooks, Tim and Earle Marsh. *The Complete Directory to Prime Time Network and Cable TV Shows 1946-Present*, Ballantine Books, 2003.
> Corsaro, Frank. *Maverick*, The Vanguard Press Inc., 1978.
> Garfield, David. *The Actors Studio: A Player's Place*, Macmillan, 1984.
> Gazzara, Ben. *In the Moment: My Life as an Actor*, Carroll & Graf Publishers, 2004.
> Hagen, Uta and Haskel Frankel. *Respect for Acting*, Macmillan, 1973.

PERIODICALS

> "The Follow-Up Comment," *Variety*, March 6, 1957.
> "The Day Steve McQueen Almost Died," *TV Radio and Mirror*, December 1960.
> "The Escape Artist," *Premiere*, September 1999.

Documents
"And All That Jazz" by Steve McQueen and Patricia Roe, Actors Studio
 Recordings, Wisconsin Historical Society, May 29, 1956.
Playbill for *A Hatful of Rain*, July 23, 1956.
"Steve McQueen Biography" by The Mirisch Company, 1960.
Martin Landau interview by Hikari Takano, 2007.

Chapter 9
For this chapter the author interviewed John Gilmore, Robert Culp, Richard Martin, Jack
Garfein, Hilly Elkins, and Peter O. Whitmer.

Books
Brooks, Tim and Earle Marsh. *The Complete Directory to Prime Time Network and
 Cable TV Shows 1946-Present*, Ballantine Books, 2003.
Hirsch, Foster. *A Method to Their Madness: The History of the Actors Studio*, Da
 Capo Press, 2001.
McQueen-Toffel, Neile. *My Husband, My Friend*, Atheneum Books, 1986.
Shatner, William and David Fisher. *Up Till Now: The Autobiography*, St. Martin's
 Griffin, 2009.

Articles
"No Time for Dates," *Philippines Herald*, February 18, 1956.
"'Defender' Skimpy Play; Dan Enright Gets Away!" *New York Daily News*,
 February 27, 1957.
"Studio One (Net)," *Billboard*, March 16, 1957.
"CBS Buys Series of TV Westerns," *New York Times*, March 5, 1958.
"CBS Buys 4-Star 'Wanted,'" *Hollywood Reporter*, April 9, 1958.
"And There Were Six," *TV Guide*, August 2, 1958.
"And Still They Come," *TV Guide*, September 20, 1958.
"New Adult Western Series Star Owes Maturity to Active and Varied Life," *Los
 Angeles Times*, September 21, 1958.
"New Western Boasts More Action, Less Talk," *Troy Record*, October 11, 1958.
"TV Hero is Farmboy Turned Intellectual," UPI, October 25, 1958.
"Sharp Shadow Again," *Los Angeles Mirror-News*, October 28, 1958.
"*Wanted: Dead or Alive* Review," *TV Guide*, November 15, 1958.
"The TV Scene," *Los Angeles Times*, December 15, 1958.
"He Remembers Cedar Rapids!" *Cedar Rapids Gazette*, January 25, 1959.
"Wanted: Dead or Alive," *TV Movie Western*, February 1959.
"Wanted—Very Much Alive," *TV Radio and Mirror*, April 1959.
"We Start With the Character," *TV Guide*, April 25, 1959.
"So He Got a Horse!" *TV Guide*, May 30, 1959.
"Steve McQueen, Star of *Wanted: Dead or Alive*," *Western Horseman*, June 1959.
"Steve McQueen: Storm Center," *Chicago Sunday Tribune Magazine*, June 28, 1959.
"Don't Talk to Me Till After Breakfast," *TV Picture Life*, February 1960.
"Steve McQueen ... Rugged, Tormented, Thrill-Happy," *Look*, October 11, 1960.
"TV's Angry Young Star," *Saturday Evening Post*, January 14, 1961.
"Steve McQueen," *Hollywood Diary*, September 1, 1961.
"What Men Did to Neile," *Modern Movies*, July 1969.

"Neile Adams: The Former Mrs. Steve McQueen Recalls Her Life on Stage, Screen, and TV," *Filmfax*, August/September 2001.
"Only in Hollywood: Steve McQueen's Manila-Born Wife on Her Life and Biopic," *Inquirer Entertainment*, August 23, 2007.

DOCUMENTS
Letter from Herbert Brodkin to Steve McQueen, March 5, 1957.
CBS-TV bio on Steve McQueen, September 1958.
"Steve McQueen, Star of *Wanted: Dead or Alive*, Has Had Life of Adventure" news release prepared by Ted Bates & Company Inc., September 1958.
Raw interview between Neile McQueen-Toffel and Jane Ardmore, November 11, 1985.
Neile McQueen-Toffel Reveals the Good Times and Bad Times with Steve McQueen, *My Husband, My Friend*, interview with Jane Ardmore, 1986.
FBI documents on Steve McQueen, courtesy of the Freedom of Information Act.

VIDEOS
Steve McQueen: Man on the Edge, Wombat Productions, MPI Home Video, 1991.

WEBSITES
www.mcqueenonline.com
www.westernclippings.com

Chapter 10

For this chapter the author interviewed Richard Bright, Jack H. Harris, Russell Doughten, Howie Fishlove, and Robert Fields.

BOOKS
McQueen-Toffel, Neile. *My Husband, My Friend*, Atheneum Books, 1986.

ARTICLES
"The 'Shotgun Wedding' of Ruby McQueen," *Sunday Mirror Magazine*, April 21, 1957.
"Movieland Events," *Los Angeles Times*, September 11, 1957.
"McQueen Signed," *Los Angeles Examiner*, September 17, 1957.
"Gazzara Successor Debates Deal," *Los Angeles Times*, December 11, 1957.
"Steve McQueen," *Photoplay*, November 1959.
"I Live in a Strictly Steve McQueen World," *Photoplay*, February 1964.
"My Life with Steve McQueen—By Ex-Wife He Loved Till the End," *Star*, February 4, 1986.
"I'm So Proud of My Grandfather," *Mail on Sunday*, November 5, 2006.
"Memories of 'The Blob' from Aneta Corseaut," *Cinema Retro*, July 18, 2007.
"BlobFest Goes With a Bang," *Phoenixville News*, July 14, 2008.
"'The Blob' Gets Smart," *Metro*, July 9, 2009.

DOCUMENTS
Raw interview between Hedda Hopper, Steve McQueen, and Neile Adams, June 5, 1959.
Raw interview between Hedda Hopper and Steve McQueen, March 19, 1962.

Raw interview between Neile McQueen-Toffel and Jane Ardmore,
   November 11, 1985.

Chapter 11
For this chapter the author interviewed Robert Heller, Melburn Stein, Hilly Elkins, Robert
Culp, Don Gordon, Peter O. Whitmer, and Loren Janes.

BOOKS
   McQueen-Toffel, Neile. *My Husband, My Friend*, Atheneum Books, 1986.
   Nolan, William. *McQueen*, Congdon & Weed, 1984.

ARTICLES
   "McQueen in *St.L. Robbery*," *Hollywood Reporter*, October 2, 1957.
   "Movieland Events," *Los Angeles Times*, October 2, 1957.
   "McQueen to Star in Robbery Film," *Los Angeles Examiner*, October 9, 1957.
   "Nina Foch Will Star in Warren's 'Shiloh,'" *Los Angeles Times*, December 24, 1957.
   "By Way of Report," *New York Times*, February 16, 1958.
   "Students Take Lessons from Class Act," *Texarkana Gazette*, October 22, 2006.
   "Bravery Never Gets Old," *St. Louis Post-Dispatch*, January 25, 2009.

DOCUMENTS
   Raw interview between Hedda Hopper, Steve McQueen, and Neile Adams,
      June 5, 1959.
   Raw interview between Hedda Hopper and Steve McQueen, March 19, 1962.

Chapter 12
For this chapter the author interviewed Gene Lesser, Mike Sedam, Terri C. McQueen,
Joan Totten Wright, Esther McBurney, Pat Johnson, and Peter O. Whitmer. This chapter
also includes the research of Veronica Valdez.

BOOKS
   FitzGerald, Edward. *Rubaiyat of Omar Khayyam*, University of Virginia
      Press, 1997.
   McCoy, Malachy. *Steve McQueen: The Unauthorized Biography*, Signet
      Books, 1975.

ARTICLES
   "Joy Rides End in 4 Arrests," *Indianapolis Star*, November 24, 1918.
   "Alert Bank Robbery Suspects to be Tried," *Indianapolis Star*, January 26, 1928.
   "Ninety Appeal for Higher Court Trial," *Indianapolis Star*, February 20, 1928.
   "Come In and See...Joe Kelly's Restaurant," *San Francisco Examiner*,
      December 4, 1944.
   "Woman, Son Hurt as Car Crashes Pole," *Oakland Tribune*, January 3, 1953.
   "I Searched and Searched for My Father," *Photoplay*, August 1964.
   Marnsett and Peek Mortuaries death notice for William Terrence McQueen,
      Independent Press-Telegram (Long Beach), November 16, 1958.

DOCUMENTS
   1905-1995 California Birth Index.
   1926-1954, California Voter Registrations.

1930-1932 Los Angeles City Directory.

1937-1939 Culver City Directory.

1937-1951 National Maritime Center file.

1939-1946 U.S. Customs List or Manifest of Aliens Employed on the Vessel as Members of Crew.

1940-1997 California Death Index.

1949 San Pedro and Wilmington City Directory.

1951-1959 Long Beach City Directory.

1958 Polk's Long Beach Directory of Householders, Occupants of Office Buildings and Other Business Places.

1966-1984 California Divorce Index.

Mary J. Wyckoff and Richard W. Wyckoff Dissolution of Marriage Petition and Final Judgment of Dissolution of Marriage.

Military Personnel Records of William Terrence McQueen.

Second Judicial District Court Bureau of Vital Statistics.

State of California Certificate of Death for Edwin W. Wilson.

State of California Certificate of Death for Paul Zollner Sedam.

State of California Certificate of Death for William Terrence McQueen.

State of Washington Certificate of Live Birth for Terri Carol McQueen.

Superior Court County of Los Angeles, State of California Probate in the Matter of the Estate of William T. McQueen.

Western Telegram from William Terrence McQueen to Terri Carol McQueen, July 2, 1940.

WEBSITES

www.ancestry.com
www.culvercity.org
www.sailors.org
www.sos.mo.gov

Chapter 13

For this chapter the author interviewed David Foster, Hilly Elkins, and Robert Relyea.

BOOKS

Relyea, Robert E. and Craig Relyea. *Not So Quiet On the Set: My Life in Movies During Hollywood's Macho Era*, iUniverse Inc., 2008.

ARTICLES

"McQueen Joins Cast of Sinatra Movie," *Los Angeles Times*, April 10, 1959.

"Bounty Hunter 'Don't Talk Too Good Period,'" *Hays Daily News*, August 26, 1959.

"Population Show to be on TV Again," *New York Times*, January 1, 1960.

"The Not-So-Wild One," *New York Herald Tribune*, June 12-18, 1960.

"McQueen, Angie Dickinson Team in Lockridge's 'Golden Man,'" *Los Angeles Times*, July 22, 1960.

"Steve McQueen Values His Marriage and Career Over Sports Car Racing," *Lubbock Avalanche-Journal*, September 25, 1960.

"Steve McQueen's Reforming; He's Hot as a Firecracker," *Los Angeles Mirror*, November 1, 1960.

"TV's Angry Young Star," *Saturday Evening Post*, January 14, 1961.
"Steve McQueen—Rough," *Toronto Star Weekly*, October 24, 1964.
"Mondo Hollywood: Bullitt-Proof," *Details*, March 1998.

Chapter 14

For this chapter the author interviewed Hilly Elkins, Wallace Cundiff, Fred Krone, James Coburn, Peter O. Whitmer, Bob Bondurant, Sir Stirling Moss, Hal Needham, Bud Ekins, Dave Ekins, John Sturges, James Coburn, and Joseph Ruskin.

BOOKS

Relyea, Robert E. and Craig Relyea. *Not So Quiet On the Set: My Life in Movies During Hollywood's Macho Era*, iUniverse Inc., 2008.
Vaughn, Robert. *A Fortunate Life*, Thomas Dunne Books, 2008.
Wallach, Eli. *The Good, the Bad, and Me: In My Anecdotage*, Houghton Mifflin Harcourt Publishing Company, 2005.

ARTICLES

"McQueen Would Star in Own Racing Film," *Los Angeles Times*, October 3, 1959.
"Steve McQueen Stays Busy in Strikesville," *Los Angeles Times*, May 22, 1960.
"Beatnik Daddy," *Screen Spotlight*, December 1960.
"TV's Angry Young Star," *Saturday Evening Post*, January 14, 1961.
"Robert Vaughn: The Long Ride from U.N.C.L.E. to Auntie," *London Telegraph*, March 6, 2009.

DOCUMENTS

Interview with Robert Vaughn by Hikaro Takano, 2007.

VIDEOS

The E! True Hollywood Story, E! Entertainment, 1998.

WEBSITES

www.filmforce.ign.com

Chapter 15

For this chapter the author interviewed Peter O. Whitmer, David Foster, Hilly Elkins, James Coburn, and Sonny West.

BOOKS

Newhart, Bob. *I Shouldn't Even Be Doing This!*, Hyperion, 2006.
Rubin, Steven Jay. *Combat Films*, McFarland, 1981.
West, Sonny and Marshall Terrill. *Elvis: Still Taking Care of Business*, Triumph Books, 2007.

ARTICLES

"McQueen is Happy to be Out of TV," *Los Angeles Mirror*, April 26, 1961.
"Hell Breaks Loose on Location," *TV Radio Mirror*, December 1961.

Chapter 16

For this chapter the author interviewed Elisabeth Osborn, Lord Richard Attenborough, Hilly Elknis, Sir Stirling Moss, and Mike Frankovich Jr.

BOOKS

Wagner, Robert and Scott Eyman. *Pieces of My Heart: A Life.* Harper Entertainment, 2008.

ARTICLES

"I Find the Man Who Met Brynner—and Beat Him to the Draw," *London Sunday Express,* September 17, 1961.

"It's Tough Being a War Lover," *Photoplay,* March 1962.

"Steve McQueen: He's Wanted All Right—Alive," *Los Angeles Times,* June 10, 1962.

"Dad Taught Steve McQueen How to Drive: John Cooper's Son on a Childhood as 'Mini Cooper,'" *Daily Mail,* November 28, 2009.

"Shirley Anne Field Remembers Steve McQueen," *Cinema Retro,* 2009.

DOCUMENTS

Letter from Steve McQueen to Hedda Hopper, October 17, 1961.

Letter from Steve McQueen to Hedda Hopper, December 5, 1961.

Letter from Steve McQueen to Sidney Skolsky, December 14, 1961.

Letter from Steve McQueen to Columbia, January 1962.

WEBSITES

www.mcqueenonline.com

Chapter 17

For this chapter the author interviewed Bud Ekins, John Sturges, Robert Relyea, James Coburn, Lord Richard Attenborough, Sir Stirling Moss, and Kent Twitchell.

BOOKS

Attenborough, Richard. *Entirely Up to You, Darling,* Hutchinson, 2008.

Relyea, Robert E. and Craig Relyea. *Not So Quiet On the Set: My Life in Movies During Hollywood's Macho Era,* iUniverse Inc., 2008.

Rubin, Steven Jay. *Combat Films,* McFarland & Company Inc., 1981.

ARTICLES

"Garner, McQueen in *Great Escape,*" *Los Angeles Times,* February 21, 1962.

"Actor McQueen Discovers Sebring Action 'Tougher,'" *Miami Herald,* March 24, 1962.

"Actor Steve McQueen Happiest When He's Racing Sports Cars," *Los Angeles Times,* April 18, 1962.

"*Great Escape* From Billing Bind; Stars Waive Rights," *Variety,* April, 12, 1963.

"Briefs," *Variety,* June 23, 1963.

"Show Business," *Time,* June 28, 1963.

"The Bad Boy's Breakout," *Life,* July 12, 1963.

"Steve McQueen Hollywood's Far-Out Swinger," *True,* July 1964.

DOCUMENTS

Letter from Stirling Moss to Steve McQueen, June 28, 1962.

Letter from Steve McQueen to Hedda Hopper, August 8, 1962.

Chapter 18

For this chapter the author interviewed Edd Byrnes, Tony Bill, Chris Noel, Adam West, Robert Loggia, Lee Remick, and Sonny West.

BOOKS

Byrnes, Edd and Marshall Terrill. *"Kookie" No More*, Barricade Books, 1996.
Claxton, William. *Steve McQueen*, Arena Editions, 2000.
Schwarz, Ted, and Mardi Rustam. *Candy Barr: The Small-Town Texas Runaway Who Became a Darling of the Mob and the Queen of Las Vegas Burlesque*, Taylor Trade, 2008.
West, Sonny and Marshall Terrill. *Elvis: Still Taking Care of Business*, Triumph Books, 2007.

ARTICLES

"Steve McQueen Doing 'Traveling' & 'Stranger' On Participation Deal," *Variety*, February 18, 1963.
"McQueen partnered in Three 1963 Projects," *Hollywood Reporter*, March 3, 1963.
"McQueen, Remick in *Lady*; Foote Scripting," *Hollywood Reporter*, April 10, 1963.
"McQueen Reports June 10," *Hollywood Reporter*, April 15, 1963.
"McQueen Will Star in 'I Love Louisa,'" *Los Angeles Times*, April 15, 1963.
"McQueen, Remick to 'Travel' Together," *Los Angeles Times*, June 28, 1963.
"Looking at Hollywood," *Los Angeles Times*, July 6, 1963.
"The Education of Tony Bill," *Chicago Tribune*, October 6, 1963.
"A Rage to Love, A Rage to Live," *Photoplay*, December 1963.
"*Soldier in the Rain* Mixes Comedy, Drama," *Los Angeles Times*, April 17, 1964.
"Actors Battle for Rural Life," *Palo Alto Times*, July 30, 1964.
"James Garner, Rundberg in Near Fight at Hearing," *Los Angeles Times*, July 30, 1964.
Love with the Proper Stranger, *Photoplay*, October 1964.
"Steve McQueen—Rough," *Toronto Star Weekly*, October 24, 1964.
"*Baby, Rain Must Fall* Dreary Tale of Drifter," *Los Angeles Times*, January 29, 1965.
"Candy Barr Bares All," *Los Angeles Times*, October 14, 1984.
"A Revival of the Hippest," *The Independent on Sunday*, April 17, 1994.

Chapter 19

For this chapter the author interviewed Mamie Van Doren, John Gilmore, Peter O. Whitmer, Bud Ekins, Max Scott, Dave Ekins, and David Foster.

BOOKS

Gilmore, John. *Laid Bare*, Amok, 1997.
Van Doren, Mamie. *Playing the Field*, Berkeley Books, 1987.

ARTICLES

"Actor McQueen, Rundberg Clash at Mountain Hearing," *Los Angeles Times*, July 29, 1964.
"Movies, Motorcycles, McQueen," *Modern Cycle*, October 1965.

DOCUMENTS
> Letter from President Lyndon B. Johnson to Steve McQueen,
> November 19, 1964.
> FBI documents on Steve McQueen, courtesy of the Freedom of Information Act.

Chapter 20

For this chapter the author interviewed Bud Ekins, Martin Ransohoff, Suzanne Pleshette, Loren Janes, Gary Combs, Bud Ekins, John Calley, and David Foster. This chapter also includes the research of Veronica Valdez.

BOOKS
> Jewison, Norman. *This Terrible Business Has Been Good to Me: An Autobiography*, Thomas Dunne Books, 2005.
> Malden, Karl. *Where Do I Start? A Memoir*, Simon & Schuster, 1997.
> Seydor, Paul. *Peckinpah: The Western Films*, University of Illinois Press, 1980.

ARTICLES
> "Steve McQueen's Mother Dies," *Los Angeles Times*, October 16, 1965.
> "Mrs. Julian Berri," *Oakland Tribune*, October 17, 1965.
> "Steve McQueen Goes Mobile," *Mobile Home Journal*, August 1965.
> "The Photography of *The Cincinnati Kid*," *American Cinematographer*, November 1965.
> "She Loved Me More Than I Loved Her," *Photoplay*, February 1966.

DOCUMENTS
> Letter from Spencer Tracy to Steve McQueen, October 24, 1964.
> *Nevada Smith* Pressbook, 1966.
> State of California Certificate of Death of Julian E. Berri.

VIDEOS
> *Steve McQueen: Man on the Edge*, Wombat Productions, MPI Home Video, 1991.

Chapter 21

For this chapter the author interviewed Robert Relyea, Robert Wise, Mako, Loren Janes, Kaori Turner, and David Foster.

BOOKS
> Relyea, Robert E. and Craig Relyea. *Not So Quiet On the Set: My Life in Movies During Hollywood's Macho Era*, iUniverse Inc., 2008.

ARTICLES
> "McQueen Will Star in Two Features," *Los Angeles Times*, March 23, 1964.
> "Steve McQueen Delves Deep Issues," *Citizen News*, May 5, 1966.
> "Gunboat to Fire Wise's Next Salvo," *Los Angeles Times*, June 14, 1966.
> "A Loser Makes It Big," *Post*, January 14, 1967.

DOCUMENTS
> Warner Brothers film stock inventory for *Day of the Champion*, May 17, 1966.
> Western Union Telegram from Richard Zanuck to Steve McQueen, February 20, 1967.

Letter from Robert Relyea to Charles Cannon regarding costs for *Day of the Champion*, April 25, 1967.

Chapter 22

For this chapter the author interviewed Robert Relyea, Jack Garfein, Alan Trustman, Barbara McQueen, Jack Good, Nikita Knatz, Haskell Wexler, and Ed Donovan.

BOOKS

Dunaway, Faye. *Looking for Gatsby: My Life*, Simon & Schuster Inc., 1995.

Jewison, Norman. *This Terrible Business Has Been Good to Me: An Autobiography*, Thomas Dunne Books, 2005.

Relyea, Robert E. and Craig Relyea. *Not So Quiet On the Set: My Life in Movies During Hollywood's Macho Era*, iUniverse Inc., 2008.

Trustman, Alan. *The Screenplay Sell: What Every Writer Should Know*, iUniverse Inc., 2003.

ARTICLES

"The Coming of the Roads," *Hollywood Reporter*, August 31, 1966.

"Blue Chip Stock," *New York Times*, December 4, 1966.

"Solar to Produce 'String,'" *Los Angeles Times*, March 16, 1967.

"Steve McQueen's Co. to Produce Minimum Five Pictures per Year," *Hollywood Reporter*, March 23, 1967.

"McQueen Meets the Press—Again & Again & Again," *Los Angeles Times*, June 30, 1968.

DOCUMENTS

FBI documents on Steve McQueen, courtesy of the Freedom of Information Act.

Chapter 23

For this chapter the author interviewed Robert Relyea, Robert Vaughn, Alan Trustman, Robert Yates, Don Gordon, Nikita Knatz, William Fraker, Carey Loftin, and Bud Ekins.

BOOKS

McQueen-Toffel, Neile. *My Husband, My Friend*, Atheneum Books, 1986.

Relyea, Robert E. and Craig Relyea. *Not So Quiet On the Set: My Life in Movies During Hollywood's Macho Era*, iUniverse Inc., 2008.

Trustman, Alan. *The Screenplay Sell: What Every Writer Should Know*, iUniverse Inc., 2003.

Vaughn, Robert. *A Fortunate Life*, Thomas Dunne Books, 2008.

ARTICLES

"Just for Army Archerd," *Variety*, April 23, 1968.

"From Now On, Baby, We'll Do It Steve's Way," *Chicago Tribune*, May 18, 1969.

"*Motor Trend* Interview: Steve McQueen," *Motor Trend*, November 1969.

"McQueen," *Los Angeles Times*, November 23, 1969.

"Lessons from William Fraker," *MovieMaker*, September 23, 2004.

"The Mori Interview," *Cinema Retro*, January 2005.

"Steve McQueen Was Mr. Cool Filming *Bullitt* in San Francisco," *San Francisco Chronicle*, August 12, 2007.

"Robert Vaughn: The Long Ride from U.N.C.L.E. to Auntie," *London Telegraph*, March 6, 2008.
"Classic Chase Scene Set the Standard," *San Bernadino County Sun*, July 18, 2008.
"Film Fest for McQueen," *New York Times*, May 21, 2009.

DOCUMENTS
Raw interview between Neile McQueen-Toffel and Jane Ardmore, November 11, 1985.

Chapter 24

For this chapter the author interviewed Robert Relyea, Nikita Knatz, Bruce Brown, Freddie Fields, Bob Rosen, Mitch Vogel, Sharon Farrell, Michael F. Eagan, and Richard Moore.

BOOKS
Relyea, Robert E. and Craig Relyea. *Not So Quiet On the Set: My Life in Movies During Hollywood's Macho Era*, iUniverse Inc., 2008.

ARTICLES
"'Conquerors' for Wolper," *Los Angeles Times*, February 8, 1968.
"Rydell to Direct *Reivers*," *Los Angeles Times*, June 6, 1968.
"Cinema By, But Not Necessarily For, Television," *Los Angeles Times*, July 28, 1968.
"Companies Sign for Films," *Los Angeles Times*, August 8, 1968.
"Another *Reivers* Role Set," *Los Angeles Times*, September 27, 1968.
"McQueen Bypasses Studios," *Variety*, January 27, 1969.
"Steve McQueen: Do You Know Where It's At?" *Coronet*, March 1969.
"Movie Call Sheet," *Los Angeles Times*, March 19, 1969.
"McQueen Observes *Reivers* Race," *Los Angeles Times*, May 25, 1969.
"Steve McQueen, Phi Beta Hubcap," *New York Times*, August 4, 1969.
"Mando on the Town," *Los Angeles Times*, August 15, 1969.
"McQueen: Racing His Role," *Los Angeles Times*, August 26, 1969.
"Film Star of Year Turns to Creative Extension," *Los Angeles Times*, September 21, 1969.
"Steve McQueen Going Deaf! Wants to Quit Films!" *Photoplay*, October 1969.
"Rydell Films Frame Human Condition," *Los Angeles Times*, January 1, 1970.
"Mr. Mansmanship," *Look*, January 27, 1970.
"Pretty Actress Even With Foot in Her Mouth," *Los Angeles Times*, February 15, 1970.
"Rydell Sitting on Top of the Cinema Sundae," *Los Angeles Times*, March 26, 1972.
"Interview with Mark Rydell," *American Film*, June 1982.
"Mark Rydell vs. The Eight-Hundred-Pound Gorillas," *Movieline*, December 1991.

DOCUMENTS
Cinema Center Films Press Book, 1969.

Chapter 25

For this chapter the author interviewed Larry Geller, Bud Ekins, Robert Relyea, Alan Trustman, John Sturges, Lee Purcell, Haig Altounian, Mario Iscovich, Peter O. Whitmer, and Bob Rosen.

BOOKS

Keyser, Michael and Jonathan Williams. *A French Kiss with Death: Steve McQueen and the Making of* Le Mans, Bentley Publishers, 2000.

McQueen-Toffel, Neile. *My Husband, My Friend*, Atheneum Books, 1986.

Relyea, Robert E. and Craig Relyea. *Not So Quiet On the Set: My Life in Movies During Hollywood's Macho Era*, iUniverse Inc., 2008.

Trustman, Alan. *The Screenplay Sell: What Every Writer Should Know*, iUniverse Inc., 2003.

ARTICLES

"Hair Stylist Pans the Unkindest Cut," *Los Angeles Times*, December 13, 1966.

"Sharon Tate, Four Others Murdered," *Los Angeles Times*, August 10, 1969.

"Drugs Found at Murder Site," *Los Angeles Times*, August 13, 1969.

"Police Have No Tate Murder Suspect After Questioning 300," *Los Angeles Times*, September 3, 1969.

"Steve McQueen Sings Praises of Promising New Actress," UPI, September 25, 1969.

"Susan Atkins' Story of 2 Nights of Murder," *Los Angeles Times*, December 14, 1969.

"Dick Smothers, McQueen Win," *Los Angeles Times*, February 8, 1970.

"McQueen Second Behind Andretti," *Los Angeles Times*, March 22, 1970.

"Dear God, Watch Over Steve," *Screen Stories*, April 1970.

"'Adam at 6 AM' Sneers at Mid-America," *New York Times*, September 1, 1970.

"Miss Atkins Admitted Murder, Witness Says," *Los Angeles Times*, October 10, 1970.

"McQueen Plans Southland Return," *Los Angeles Times*, December 10, 1970.

"The 24 Hours of Le Mans," *Playboy*, June 1971.

"Former Coast Newsman Sentenced for Contempt," *Los Angeles Times*, July 29, 1971.

"Bill Farr on His Imprisonment: 'I Followed the Code of Any Good Reporter,'" *Los Angeles Times*, January 30, 1973.

"My Life with Steve McQueen—By Ex-Wife He Loved Till the End," *Star*, February 4, 1986.

Chapter 26

For this chapter the author interviewed Robert Relyea, John Sturges, Lee Katzin, Bob Rosen, Ryuken Tokuda, David Foster, and Hilly Elkins.

BOOKS

Keyser, Michael and Jonathan Williams. *A French Kiss with Death: Steve McQueen and the Making of* Le Mans, Bentley Publishers, 2000.

McQueen-Toffel, Neile. *My Husband, My Friend*, Atheneum Books, 1986.

Relyea, Robert E. and Craig Relyea. *Not So Quiet On the Set: My Life in Movies During Hollywood's Macho Era*, iUniverse Inc., 2008.

ARTICLES

"Off-Duty Life Bores *Le Mans* Crew," *Los Angeles Times*, September 23, 1970.

"Steve McQueen's Latest an Epic to be Believed," *Los Angeles Times*, November 22, 1970.

"The 24 Hours of Le Mans," *Playboy*, June 1971.
"24-Hour Spin at 'Le Mans,'" *Los Angeles Times*, June 16, 1971.
"*Le Mans* Movie Review," *New York Times*, June 24, 1971.
"Katzin Vrooms to Top," *Los Angeles Times*, August 4, 1971.
"Racing McQueen's 'Other Woman'?" *Los Angeles Times*, September 14, 1971.
"My Life with Steve McQueen—By Ex-Wife He Loved Till the End," *Star*,
    February 4, 1986.
"A Casual Conversation with Racing Legend Derek Bell," *Sports Car Examiner*,
    August 31, 2008.
"It's a Le Mans World," *Vanity Fair*, October 2, 2009.

DOCUMENTS
Letter from Steve McQueen to Sid Ganis, October 22, 1970.

Chapter 27
For this chapter the author interviewed Freddie Fields, Mert Lawwill, Bruce Brown, Jeb
Rosebrook, Bobby Visciglia, Ben Johnson, Katy Haber, Barbara Leigh, William Pierce,
Buck Hart, John Allen, and Frank Kelly.

BOOKS
Finstad, Suzanne. *The Biography of Natalie Wood*, Three Rivers Press, 2002.
Leigh, Barbara and Marshall Terrill. *The King, McQueen and the Love Machine*,
    Xlibris Corporation, 2002.
McQueen-Toffel, Neile. *My Husband, My Friend*, Atheneum Books, 1986.
Simmons, Garner. *Peckinpah: A Portrait in Montage*, University of Texas
    Press, 1982.

ARTICLES
"It Was Like Having Another Baby," *Movie Mirror*, 1971.
"Movie Call Sheet," *Los Angeles Times*, February 19, 1971.
"Steve McQueen Fourth in Race," *Los Angeles Times*, February 21, 1971.
"McQueen in Production Company Pact," *Los Angeles Times*, March 1, 1971.
"Steve McQueen to Play 'Papillon,'" *Los Angeles Times*, March 11, 1971.
"Comeback for Ida Lupino," *Los Angeles Times*, June 23, 1971.
"Take-Me-or-Leave-Me Steve McQueen Makes Good," *Los Angeles Times*,
    July 11, 1971.
"New McQueen Film for a 15% Cut," *Los Angeles Times*, August 19, 1971.
"Harvey on the Lam," *Sports Illustrated*, August 23, 1971.
"McQueen Stars in *Getaway*," *Los Angeles Times*, December 4, 1971.
"Natalie Wood & Steve McQueen," *Photoplay*, February 1972.
"Peckinpah Gets Nonviolent (Off Screen)," *Los Angeles Times*, May 21, 1972.
"*Junior Bonner* Is a Rodeo Family Close-Up," *New York Times*, August 3, 1972.
"The Making of *Junior Bonner*," *Arizona Highways*, June 2001.
"I'm So Proud of My Grandfather," *Mail on Sunday*, November 5, 2006.
"*Junior Bonner* Movie Alumni Share Memories," *Prescott Daily Courier*,
    October 5, 2008.

DOCUMENTS
Letter from Steve McQueen to Gloria Allen, July 1971.

Neile Adams McQueen vs. Steven T. McQueen Interlocutory, Final Judgment of
Dissolution of Marriage and Property Settlement Agreement.

VIDEOS
The King of Cool, Myriad Pictures and American Movie Classics, 1998.

WEBSITES
www.youtube.com
www.contactmusic.com

Chapter 28

For this chapter the author interviewed Freddie Fields, Peter O. Whitmer, Barbara Leigh,
David Foster, Tony Bill, Pat Johnson, Bobby Visciglia, Katy Haber, and Ben Johnson.

BOOKS
Bach, Steven. *The Final Cut*, William Morrow, 1985.
Evans, Robert. *The Kid Stays in the Picture*, Hyperion, 1994.
Leigh, Barbara and Marshall Terrill. *The King, McQueen and the Love Machine*,
Xlibris Corporation, 2002.
MacGraw, Ali. *Moving Pictures*, Bantam Books, 1991.
Simmons, Garner. *Peckinpah: A Portrait in Montage*, University of Texas
Press, 1982.

ARTICLES
"Ali, Steve and the One That Got Away," *Los Angeles Times*, January 19, 1972.
"Glamour of Movies Put Down in Texas," *Los Angeles Times*, March 2, 1972.
"Steve McQueen: An Embarrassment of Paradoxes," *Cosmopolitan*,
December 1972.
"The Resurrection of Jim Thompson," *Los Angeles Times*, March 11, 1990.
"At Peace with Herself: Book Helps Ali MacGraw Get Over Her Fame,
Alcoholism...and Men," *Waterloo Record*, April 11, 1991.
"The Confessions of Ali," *People*, May 6, 1991.
"Were Roles Too Controversial?" *Sun Sentinel*, January 8, 1993.
"Once in Love with Ali," *Vanity Fair*, March 2010.

Chapter 29

For this chapter the author interviewed Katy Haber, Bruce Brown, Tom Biss, Ron Cooper,
Pat Johnson, David Foster, Richard Bright, Walter Hill, and Chalo Gonzalez.

BOOKS
Evans, Robert. *The Kid Stays in the Picture*, Hyperion, 1994.
Leigh, Barbara and Marshall Terrill. *The King, McQueen and the Love Machine*,
Xlibris Corporation, 2002.
MacGraw, Ali. *Moving Pictures*, Bantam Books, 1991.
Morpurgo, Leonard. *Of Kings and Queens and Movie Stars*, Global Book
Publishers, 2009.
Scott, Henry E. *Shocking True Story: The Rise and Fall of 'Confidential,' America's
Most Scandalous Scandal Magazine*, Pantheon Books, 2010.
Weddle, David. *If They Move... Kill 'Em! The Life and Times of Sam Peckinpah*,
Grove Press, 1994.

ARTICLES

"Stars Lured Into Traps, Confidential Trial Told," *Los Angeles Times*,
August 8, 1957.

"Steve, Ali Down in Dumps," *Los Angeles Times*, May 6, 1972.

"Newsmakers," *Los Angeles Times*, June 30, 1972.

"A Wild Bunch at Peckinpah Screening," *Los Angeles Times*, October 17, 1972.

"Steve McQueen: An Embarrassment of Paradoxes," *Cosmopolitan*,
December 1972.

"Defending *The Getaway*," *Chicago Tribune*, February 4, 1973.

"El Pasoans Remember McQueen On, Off the Set," *El Paso Times*,
November 8, 1980.

"Once in Love with Ali," *Vanity Fair*, March 2010.

DOCUMENTS

Letter from Sam Peckinpah to Steve McQueen, October 13, 1972.

Letter from Sam Peckinpah to Norman Garey, November 3, 1972.

Letter from Sam Peckinpah to Steve McQueen, November 10, 1972.

Chapter 30

For this chapter the author interviewed Leonard Morpurgo, Anthony Zerbe, Kent James, Stan Barrett, Don Gordon, and Ron Gallela.

BOOKS

Evans, Robert. *The Kid Stays in the Picture*, Hyperion, 1994.

Kim, Erwin. *Franklin J. Schaffner*, The Scarecrow Press, 1985.

MacGraw, Ali. *Moving Pictures*, Bantam Books, 1991.

Miller, Davis. *The Tao of Bruce Lee*, Random House, 2000.

Satchell, Tim. *McQueen*, Sidgwick and Jackson Limited, 1981.

ARTICLES

"Ali MacGraw Cuts Short Her R & R," *Los Angeles Times*, May 17, 1972.

"New York Trip May Stop Split Talk," *Los Angeles Times*, June 29, 1972.

"Ali MacGraw Plans to File for Divorce Today," *Los Angeles Times*, August 4, 1972.

"Ali Won't Play Daisy, Says Her Agent," *Los Angeles Times*, October 9, 1972.

"Burt Reynolds to Star in *Cat Dancing*," *Los Angeles Times*, November 7, 1972.

Papillon Press Book, 1973.

"Ali MacGraw—'I Was the Golden Girl,'" *New York Times*, March 11, 1973.

"What's Left of Peckinpah's Kid," *Los Angeles Times*, May 14, 1973.

"Love Story Ends," Associated Press, June 8, 1973.

"The Nation: Creating a New Who's Who," *Time*, July 9, 1973.

"Just Married," Associated Press, July 12, 1973.

"Steve McQueen Ali MacGraw Wed," *Los Angeles Times*, July 13, 1973.

"'Papillon' and 'Alfredo Alfredo,'" *Los Angeles Times*, December 19, 1973.

"Papillon," *Washington Post*, December 28, 1973.

"Schaffner Has His Fingers Crossed," *Los Angeles Times*, January 4, 1974.

"Off the Screen," *People*, July 24, 1978.

"Allied Artists Seeks Help Under Bankruptcy Act," *New York Times*, April 5, 1979.

"Papillon's Prison Finally Sheds its Shame," *Telegraph*, April 24, 2004.

"Once in Love with Ali," *Vanity Fair*, March 2010.

DOCUMENTS
Movie contract for *Papillon,* February 22, 1973.
Ante-Nuptial Agreement Between Steven T. McQueen and Ali MacGraw,
July 10, 1973.

Chapter 31

For this chapter the author interviewed William Pierce, Peter O. Whitmer, Pat Johnson,
James Coburn, Morganna Welch, John Guillermin, Richard Baker, and Al Kasha.

BOOKS
Hotchner, A.E. *Paul and Me: Fifty-Three Years of Adventures and Misadventures
with My Pal Paul Newman,* Nan A. Talese, 2010.
Litwak, Mark. *Reel Power,* William Morrow and Company Inc., 1986.
Welch, Morgana. *Hollywood Diaries,* Xlibris Corporation, 2007.

ARTICLES
"Major Films Will Produce Film Jointly," *Los Angeles Times,* October 10, 1973.
Irwin Allen's Production of The Towering Inferno Press Book, 1974.
"Crisis King Casts Another Peril," *Los Angeles Times,* July 21, 1974.
"An Interview with 'Fire Chief' Steve McQueen,' *Fireman's Grapevine,*
August 1974.
"Defies Death in Hollywood Fire!" *Photoplay,* August 1974.
"*Towering Inferno*: Campfire of the '70s?" *Chicago Tribune,* December 23, 1974.
"*Towering Inferno* Tops 'Choice for Oscars' Poll," *Los Angeles Times,* April 8, 1975.
"Mondo Hollywood: Bullitt-Proof," *Details,* March 1998.
"Once in Love with Ali," *Vanity Fair,* March 2010.

Chapter 32

For this chapter the author interviewed Peter O. Whitmer, James Stacey, Gene Lesser,
Florence Esposito, Katy Haber, Ty Ritter, David Foster, Gary Davis, John Plumlee, Marvin
Josephson, George Schaefer, Phil Parslow, and Charles Durning.

BOOKS
Reynolds, Burt. *My Life,* Hyperion, 1994.

ARTICLES
"Reagan Joins AFI Tribute to Cagney," *Los Angeles Times,* February 20, 1974.
"Warm Outpouring for James Stacey," *Los Angeles Times,* March 26, 1974.
"Tower Ticker," *Chicago Tribune,* February 18, 1975.
"No Sex Symbol, Says Yul Brynner," *Los Angeles Times,* April 1, 1975.
"Stacy's Inward Ordeal," *Los Angeles Times,* September 17, 1975.
"Tower Ticker," *Chicago Tribune,* November 11, 1975.
"Movie Call Sheet," *Los Angeles Times,* February 9, 1976.
"Tower Ticker," *Chicago Tribune,* February 9, 1976.
"Movie Call Sheet," *Los Angeles Times,* May 10, 1976.
"Stars Go Pel-Mel for *Silent Movie,*" *Chicago Tribune,* August 2, 1976.
"*Islands* a Film With Hemingway in Mind," *Los Angeles Times,* March 13, 1977.
"Steve McQueen Goes for Ibsen—But Hollywood Doesn't," *New York Times,*
April 15, 1979.

"McQueen Is Back in the Saddle After a Classic Dud," *Chicago Tribune*, June 17, 1979.
"Cable Befriends McQueen *Enemy*," *Los Angeles Herald Examiner*, July 15, 1980.
"We Saw the *Enemy* and It Isn't McQueen," *Los Angeles Herald Examiner*, August 3, 1980.
"McQueen in 1976 *Enemy of the People*," *New York Times*, August 11, 1981.
"*Enemy Of The People* a Memory of McQueen," *Los Angeles Times*, October 20, 1981.
"The Curious Evolution of John Rambo," *Los Angeles Times*, October 27, 1985.
"Mondo Hollywood: Bullitt-Proof," *Details*, March 1998.
"Once in Love with Ali," *Vanity Fair*, March 2010.

WEBSITES
www.michaelmanning.tv

Chapter 33

For this chapter the author interviewed Phil Parslow, Peter O. Whitmer, Robert Relyea, Barbara Leigh, Pat Johnson, Bobby Visciglia, Carole James, Nina Blanchard, and Barbara McQueen.

BOOKS
MacGraw, Ali. *Moving Pictures*, Bantam Books, 1991.
Weddle, David. *If They Move...Kill 'Em! The Life and Times of Sam Peckinpah*, Grove Press, 1994.
Leigh, Barbara, and Marshall Terrill. *The King, McQueen and the Love Machine*, Xlibris Corporation, 2002.

ARTICLES
"Feldman Named to Artists Post," *Los Angeles Times*, January 16, 1975.
"Film Clips," *Los Angeles Times*, August 14, 1976.
"Whatever Happened to Ali MacGraw," *Redbook*, February 1976.
"First Artists' Formula Altered," *Los Angeles Times*, October 18, 1976.
"McQueen Sues First Artists," *Los Angeles Times*, December 16, 1976.
"He'll Leave the Driving to Them," *Los Angeles Times*, March 9, 1977.
"Ali MacGraw Returns in *Convoy*," *Los Angeles Times*, March 26, 1977.
"Ali MacGraw: She Won't Live Lying Down," *Los Angeles Times*, June 12, 1977.
"Peckinpah Wrests *Convoy* From an 18-Wheel Wild Bunch," *New York Times*, August 9, 1977.
"Ali," *New York Times*, February 10, 1978.
"Now, the Ben Bradlee Show?" *Chicago Tribune*, March 12, 1978.
"Film Clips," *Los Angeles Times*, March 27, 1978.
"First Artists—Star-Crossed Child of the 1960s," *Los Angeles Times*, December 23, 1979.
"The Rebel in Miss Perfect: Ali MacGraw," *Independent*, June 30, 1991.
"In Step with Ali MacGraw," *Parade*, April 28, 1991.
"Mondo Hollywood: Bullitt-Proof," *Details*, March 1998.
"Cowboy Cool," *Cowboys & Indians*, October 2004.
"Once in Love with Ali," *Vanity Fair*, March 2010.

Chapter 34

For this chapter the author interviewed James Coburn, Mike Dewey, Barbara McQueen, Pat Johnson, Lee Majors, Marvin Josephson, Phil Parslow, Elliot Silverstein, Fred Weintraub, John Alonzo, Dave Friedman, and Gary Combs.

BOOKS

Fletcher, Tony. *Moon: The Life and Death of a Rock Legend*, William Morrow, 1999.

ARTICLES

"Beauty as a 4-Letter Blob," *Los Angeles Times*, January 4, 1979.
"Film Clips," *Los Angeles Times*, February 5, 1979.
"'Shogun' To Be Filmed in Japan," *Los Angeles Times*, May 2, 1979.
"An I'll-Do-Anything Graduate," *Los Angeles Times*, August 4, 1979.
"Linda Evans," *Marquee*, March 4, 1980.
"Film Review *Tom Horn*," *Variety*, March 28, 1980.
"Mondo Hollywood: Bullitt-Proof," *Details*, March 1998.
"A League of Their Own," *Austin Chronicle*, July 6, 2005.
"Once in Love with Ali," *Vanity Fair*, March 2010.

DOCUMENTS

Steven T. McQueen vs. Alice MacGraw McQueen Dissolution of Marriage Petition, Ante-Nuptial Agreement and Final Judgment of Dissolution of Marriage.

Chapter 35

For this chapter the author interviewed Barbara McQueen, Peter O. Whitmer, Sammy Mason, Pete Mason, Mike Dewey, Doug Dullenkopf, Chuck Bail, Lee Majors, Paul Lovemark, Crystal Endicott, Bob Heller, Pat Johnson, Leonard DeWitt, Bud Ekins, Christopher Keane, Mort Engleberg, Buzz Kulick, Kathryn Harrold, Loren Janes, and Karen Wilson.

ARTICLES

"Chicago Elevated Finally *Found* by Filmmakers," *Chicago Tribune*, July 30, 1979.
"Love and Religion End Torment of Steve McQueen Over His Loss of Ali MacGraw," *Star*, November 13, 1979.
"Neile McQueen Repeats Vows," *Los Angeles Times*, January 22, 1980.
"For New McQueen, Life Begins at Fifty," *Globe*, March 25, 1980.
"On: The Hunter," *On Location*, July 1980.
"Again, Steve's Way Off Stride," *Los Angeles Herald Examiner*, August 1, 1980.
"Drawing a Bead on *Hunter*," *Los Angeles Times*, August 1, 1980.
"Bounty Hunter is Tougher in Real Life Than in Hit Steve McQueen Movie," *Weekly World News*, September 9, 1980.
"Steve McQueen's Former Santa Paula Ranch Home Listed for $1.95 million," *Los Angeles Times*, September 15, 2009.

Chapter 36

For this chapter the author interviewed Barbara McQueen, Bud Ekins, Crystal Endicott, Chuck Bail, Phil Parslow, Leslie Miller, Sammy Mason, Loren Janes, Pat Johnson, Hilly Elkins, and Suzanne Pleshette.

BOOKS

Lerner, Barron H. *When Illness Goes Public*, The Johns Hopkins University Press, 2006.

ARTICLES

"How New Bride Created a New Steve McQueen," *Star*, February 12, 1980.
"Steve McQueen's Heroic Battle Against Terminal Cancer," *National Enquirer*, March 18, 1980.

Chapter 37

For this chapter the author interviewed Barbara McQueen, Lord Richard Attenborough, Loren Janes, Don Gordon, Bud Ekins, Mario Iscovich, Peter O. Whitmer, Mike Dewey, Sammy Mason, and Robert Relyea.

BOOKS

Lerner, Barron H. *When Illness Goes Public*, The Johns Hopkins University Press, 2006.
Ragsdale, Grady. *Steve McQueen: The Final Chapter*, Vision House Books, 1983.

ARTICLES

"Dr. William D. Kelley: Another Answer to Cancer," *Mother Earth News*, September/October 1979.
"One Man Alone: My Investigation of Dr. William Kelley," *Townsend Letter*, August/September 2009.

DOCUMENTS

State of California License to Carry Concealed Pistol, Revolver or Other Firearm Permit for Steve and Barbara McQueen, April 7, 1980.
Invoice for oxygen, Hopper Inc., April 30, 1980.

WEBSITES

www.documents.cancer.org

Chapter 38

For this chapter the author interviewed Barbara McQueen, Teena Valentino, Pete Mason, Pat Johnson, and Leonard DeWitt.

BOOKS

Lerner, Barron H. *When Illness Goes Public*, The Johns Hopkins University Press, 2006.
Ragsdale, Grady. *Steve McQueen: The Final Chapter*, Vision House Books, 1983.
Valentino, Teena. *99 Days to God: A Steve McQueen Story*, unpublished manuscript, 1982.

ARTICLES

"McQueen Winning Secret Fight Against Cancer," Associated Press, October 3, 1980.
"Steve McQueen Has Rare Form of Lung Cancer," *Los Angeles Times*, October 3, 1980.
"Steve McQueen at Mexico Clinic," *Los Angeles Times*, October 5, 1980.
"McQueen Medic: Joke or Genius?" *Los Angeles Times*, October 7, 1980.

"McQueen's Doctors Extol Treatment, Ignore Queries," *Los Angeles Times*, October 10, 1980.
"McQueen's Holistic Medicine Man Claims He Cured His Own Cancer with His Unorthodox Treatments," *People*, October 20, 1980.
"Steve McQueen, Stricken with Cancer, Seeks a Cure at a Controversial Mexican Clinic," *People*, October 20, 1980.
"McQueen's Legacy of Laetrile," *New York Times*, November 15, 2005.

Chapter 39

For this chapter the author interviewed Barbara McQueen and Teena Valentino.

BOOKS

Ragsdale, Grady. *Steve McQueen: The Final Chapter*, Vision House Books, 1983.
Valentino, Teena. *99 Days to God: A Steve McQueen Story*, unpublished manuscript, 1982.

DOCUMENTS

Audiotape interview between Steve McQueen, Brugh Joy, and Carolyn Langer, October 21, 1980.

Chapter 40

For this chapter the author interviewed Barbara McQueen, Teena Valentino, Pat Johnson, and Mike Jugan.

BOOKS

McQueen-Toffel, Neile. *My Husband, My Friend*, Atheneum Books, 1986.
Ragsdale, Grady. *Steve McQueen: The Final Chapter*, Vision House Books, 1983.
Valentino, Teena. *99 Days to God: A Steve McQueen Story*, unpublished manuscript, 1982.

ARTICLES

"Steve McQueen May Require Surgery On Neck When He Returns to Mexico Clinic," *Los Angeles Times*, November 2, 1980.
"Steve McQueen Dies in Juarez," *Los Angeles Times*, November 7, 1980.
"Actor's Death Turns Attention on El Paso, Juarez," *El Paso Times*, November 8, 1980.
"El Pasoans Remember McQueen On, Off the Set," *El Paso Times*, November 8, 1980.
"Heart Failure Kills Film Star McQueen at 50," UPI, November 8, 1980.
"McQueen's Doctor Receives Praise and Criticism," *El Paso Times*, November 9, 1980.
"Steve McQueen Dies in Juarez," *El Paso Times*, November 9, 1980.
"One McQueen Doctor Says He Advised Against Surgery," *Los Angeles Times*, November 10, 1980.

PERIODICALS

"Mondo Hollywood: Bullitt-Proof," *Details*, March 1998.

DOCUMENTS

Letter from Sister MEM to Steve McQueen, October 30, 1980.
Mike Jugan's flight log book, November 4, 1980.
Associated Press teletype announcing Steve McQueen's death, November 7, 1980.

Chapter 41

For this chapter the author interviewed Barbara McQueen, Teena Valentino, Bill Carter, Carlos Rosales, Mike Jugan, Leonard DeWitt, Sammy Mason, and Nikita Knatz.

BOOKS

Carter, Bill and Judi Turner. *Get Carter*, Fine's Creek Publishing, 2006.
Ragsdale, Grady. *Steve McQueen: The Final Chapter*, Vision House Books, 1983.
Valentino, Teena. *99 Days to God: A Steve McQueen Story*, unpublished manuscript, 1982.

ARTICLES

"Bidders Will Get a Shot at Steve McQueen's Cars," *Los Angeles Times*, October 7, 1984.
"1,500 Flock to Steve McQueen Estate Auction," *Los Angeles Times*, November 25, 1984.
"Mondo Hollywood: Bullitt-Proof," *Details*, March 1998.
"McQueen and I," *Sunday Times Magazine*, May 13, 2007.
"The Rise and Fall of the Cooperative Agency," *PhotoMedia*, February 16, 2009.
"Ali MacGraw is Della Robbia Wreath Campaign Chairperson," *Boys Republic Report*, Fall 2009.
"Death Photos for Sale: $250,000," *USA Today*, November 9, 2009.

DOCUMENTS

The Last Will and Testament of Steve McQueen, Ventura County, California, July 30, 1980.
Mike Jugan's Flight Log Book, November 7, 1980.
Mike Dewey's Flight Log Book, November 9, 1980.
Steve McQueen Estate Auction, November 24-25, 1984.

WEBSITES

www.documents.cancer.org
www.cancerdecisions.com
www.oneanswertocancer.org
www.stevemcqueenweb.free.fr

Chapter 42

ARTICLES

"Top 10 Highest Paid Dead Celebrities for 2008," *Forbes*, July 4, 2009.
"Hollywood Turns to British Actors like Jason Statham and Christian Bale for Action Men," *Telegraph*, August 31, 2009.
"Fashion Channels the Steve McQueen Mojo," *Wall Street Journal*, September 2, 2009.

WEBSITES

www.mcqueenracing.com

SELECTED BIBLIOGRAPHY

BOOKS

Attenborough, Richard. *Entirely Up to You, Darling*, Hutchinson, 2008.

Bach, Steven. *The Final Cut*, William Morrow, 1985.

Brooks, Tim and Earle Marsh. *The Complete Directory to Prime Time Network and Cable TV Shows 1946-Present*, Ballantine Books, 2003.

Carter, Bill and Judi Turner. *Get Carter*, Fine's Creek Publishing, 2006.

Clagett, Thomas D. *William Friedkin: Films of Aberration, Obsession and Reality*, McFarland, 1990.

Claxton, William. *Steve McQueen*, Arena Editions, 2000.

Corsaro, Frank. *Maverick*, The Vanguard Press Inc., 1978.

Dunaway, Faye. *Looking for Gatsby: My Life*, Simon & Schuster Inc., 1995.

Evans, Robert. *The Kid Stays in the Picture*, Hyperion, 1994.

Fletcher, Tony. *Moon: The Life and Death of a Rock Legend*, William Morrow, 1999.

Garfield, David. *The Actors Studio: A Player's Place*, Macmillan, 1984.

Gazzara, Ben. *In the Moment: My Life as an Actor*, Carroll & Graf Publishers, 2004.

Gilmore, John. *Laid Bare*, Amok, 1997.

Griffith, Russell and Ron Moning. *The History of Slater Missouri: Our Community and Family*, Walsworth Publishing Company Inc., 2003.

Hagen, Uta and Haskel Frankel. *Respect for Acting*, Macmillan, 1973.

Hirsch, Foster. *A Method to Their Madness: The History of the Actors Studio*, Da Capo Press, 2001.

Hotchner, A.E. *Paul and Me: Fifty-Three Years of Adventures and Misadventures with My Pal Paul Newman*, Nan A. Talese, 2010.

Jewison, Norman. *This Terrible Business Has Been Good to Me: An Autobiography*, Thomas Dunne Books, 2005.

Keyser, Michael and Jonathan Williams. *A French Kiss with Death: Steve McQueen and the Making of* Le Mans, Bentley Publishers, 2000.

Kim, Erwin. *Franklin J. Schaffner*, The Scarecrow Press, 1985.

Leachman, Cloris. *Cloris: My Autobiography*, Kensington Publishing Corporation, 2009.

Leigh, Barbara, and Marshall Terrill. *The King, McQueen and the Love Machine*, Xlibris Corporation, 2002.

Lerner, Barron H. *When Illness Goes Public*, The Johns Hopkins University Press, 2006.

Lovell, Glenn. *Escape Artist: The Life and Films of John Sturges*, University of Wisconsin Press, 2008.

MacGraw, Ali. *Moving Pictures*, Bantam Books, 1991.

Malden, Karl. *Where Do I Start? A Memoir*, Simon & Schuster, 1997.

Marcotte, Jerry and Patrick McMahon. *The Formation of a New Republic: A Photographic History of Boys Republic*, Donning Company Publishers, 2007.

McCoy, Malachy. *Steve McQueen: The Unauthorized Biography*, Signet Books, 1975.

McQueen, Barbara and Marshall Terrill. *Steve McQueen: The Last Mile*, Dalton Watson Fine Books, 2006.

McQueen Toffel, Neile. *My Husband, My Friend*, Atheneum Books, 1986.

Meisner, Sanford, and Dennis Long. *Sanford Meisner on Acting*, Vintage Books, 1987.

Miller, Davis. *The Tao of Bruce Lee*, Random House, 2000.

Morpurgo, Leonard. *Of Kings and Queens and Movie Stars*, Global Book Publishers, 2009.

Newhart, Bob. *I Shouldn't Even Be Doing This!*, Hyperion, 2006.

Nolan, William. *McQueen*, Congdon & Weed, 1984.

Ragsdale, Grady. *Steve McQueen: The Final Chapter*, Vision House Books, 1983.

Relyea, Robert E. and Craig Relyea. *Not So Quiet On the Set: My Life in Movies During Hollywood's Macho Era*, iUniverse Inc., 2008.

Reynolds, Burt. *My Life*, Hyperion, 1994.

Rubin, Steven Jay. *Combat Films*, McFarland, 1981.

Satchell, Tim. *McQueen*, Sidgwick and Jackson Limited, 1981.

Schwarz, Ted, and Mardi Rustam. *Candy Barr: The Small-Town Texas Runaway Who Became a Darling of the Mob and the Queen of Las Vegas Burlesque*, Taylor Trade, 2008.

Seydor, Paul. *Peckinpah: The Western Films*, University of Illinois Press, 1980.

Shatner, William and David Fisher. *Up Till Now: The Autobiography*, St. Martin's Griffin, 2009.

Simmons, Garner. *Peckinpah: A Portrait in Montage*, University of Texas Press, 1982.

Spiegel, Penina. *McQueen: The Untold Story of a Bad Boy in Hollywood*, Doubleday, 1986.

St. Charnez, Casey. *The Films of Steve McQueen*, Citadel Press, 1984.

Stone, Matt. *McQueen's Machines: The Cars and Bikes of a Hollywood Icon*, Motorbooks, 2007.

Terrill, Marshall. *Steve McQueen: Portrait of an American Rebel*, Donald I. Fine, 1993.

Terrill, Marshall. *Steve McQueen: A Tribute to the King of Cool*, Dalton Watson Fine Books, 2010.

Trustman, Alan. *The Screenplay Sell: What Every Writer Should Know*, iUniverse Inc., 2003.

Valentino, Teena. *99 Days to God: A Steve McQueen Story*, unpublished manuscript, 1982.

Van Doren, Mamie. *Playing the Field*, Berkeley Books, 1987.

Vaughn, Robert. *A Fortunate Life*, Thomas Dunne Books, 2008.

Wagner, Robert and Scott Eyman. *Pieces of My Heart: A Life*, Harper Entertainment, 2008.

Wallach, Eli. *The Good, the Bad, and Me: In My Anecdotage*, Houghton Mifflin Harcourt Publishing Company, 2005.

Weddle, David. *If They Move...Kill 'Em! The Life and Times of Sam Peckinpah*, Grove Press, 1994.

Welch, Morgana. *Hollywood Diaries*, Xlibris Corporation, 2007.

West, Sonny and Marshall Terrill. *Elvis: Still Taking Care of Business*, Triumph Books, 2007.

INDEX